Applying Quality of Life Research

Best Practices

Series editor
Helena Alves, Department of Business and Economic, University of Beira Interior, Covilhã, Portugal

This book series focuses on best practices in specialty areas of Quality of Life research, including among others potentially: community development, quality of work life, marketing, healthcare and public sector management.

In today's world, governments, organizations and individuals alike are paying increasingly more attention to how their activities impact on quality of life at the regional, national and global levels. Whether as a way to tackle global resource shortages, changing environmental circumstances, political conditions, competition, technology or otherwise, the far-reaching impact of decisions made in these and other areas can have a significant impact on populations regardless of their level of development. Many lessons have been learned; yet many are still to be realized. Across a number of volumes on diverse themes, this book series will address key issues that are of significant importance to decision makers and participants across all sectors. The series will be invaluable to anyone with an interest in applying quality of life knowledge in contemporary society.

More information about this series at http://www.springer.com/series/8364

Walter Wymer
Editor

Innovations in Social Marketing and Public Health Communication

Improving the Quality of Life for Individuals and Communities

Springer

Editor
Walter Wymer
Faculty of Management
University of Lethbridge
Lethbridge, AB, Canada

ISSN 2213-994X ISSN 2213-9958 (electronic)
Applying Quality of Life Research
ISBN 978-3-319-19868-2 ISBN 978-3-319-19869-9 (eBook)
DOI 10.1007/978-3-319-19869-9

Library of Congress Control Number: 2015952643

Springer Cham Heidelberg New York Dordrecht London

Printed on acid-free paper

Springer International Publishing AG Switzerland is part of Springer Science+Business Media (www.springer.com)

Contents

Part I
Theoretical Developments

Chapter 1
Formulating Effective Social Marketing and Public Health Communication Strategies

Walter Wymer

1 Introduction

Social marketing campaigns and public health campaigns are developed in order to improve the quality of life for their target audiences. For example, if a campaign is implemented which encourages community members to stop cigarette smoking then the quality of life of those community members improves. They are less likely to contract a smoking-related disease, become disabled, and die prematurely. Family members are less likely to contract disease from second-hand exposure to cigarette smoke, they will have greater disposable income since money will not be spent on tobacco, and they will not have a family member die prematurely (with all the negative associated consequences). The community benefits as well. Smokers that would have needed costly health care, or families that might have needed public assistance will no longer need these public benefits. Individuals who quit smoking, indeed, are likely to remain healthy, productive citizens longer than if they had remained smokers.

When social marketing campaigns and public health campaigns are made more effective, their contributions to the quality of life for individuals and for the community increases. The purpose of this chapter is to present a strategy for developing more effective social marketing and public health campaigns. Improving the quality of life for individuals and communities motivates the creation of social marketing and public health communications. Hence, improving the effectiveness of campaigns enhances the quality of life they target.

Effectiveness is defined as the extent to which a social marketing program achieves its intended purpose or function. For example, if an anti-obesity program wants to solve the obesity problem in a population, what level of obesity reduction

W. Wymer (✉)
Faculty of Management, University of Lethbridge, Lethbridge, AB, Canada
e-mail: Walter.wymer@uleth.ca

W. Wymer (ed.), *Innovations in Social Marketing and Public Health Communication*, Applying Quality of Life Research,
DOI 10.1007/978-3-319-19869-9_1

would a reasonable person accept as evidence of effectiveness? Is it reasonable to claim that a 1 % reduction in obesity is ineffective and a 70 % reduction is effective? Effectiveness is also relative. For example, if Program A reduces obesity by 20 % and Program B reduces obesity by only 5 %; one can claim that Program A is more effective than Program B.

One problem that has resulted in low effectiveness of social marketing and public health campaigns in the past has been a concomitant emphasis on individual behavior change and a failure to combat structural or environmental contributors to the social or public health problem. For example, public health campaigns target tobacco users with smoking cessation messages, products, and programs. Meanwhile, the tobacco industry, made up of large multinational corporations, continues its multigenerational marketing campaign to acquire new smokers. Meanwhile, public policy continues to allow tobacco marketing to citizens.

- A central point of this chapter is that effective public health and social marketing communication strategy requires addressing the primary causes of the problem.

Assume, for example, that a widely-used chemical has an associated risk of causing breast cancer. The chemical is present in trace amounts in the air and in most municipal water reservoirs. Traditional social marketing and public health communication strategies might attempt to educate women on the need to conduct regular self-exams as a means of early cancer detection. This strategy is typical because it focuses on individual behavior change and education, while ignoring non-individual causes of the problem (Wymer 2011). The typical strategy is relatively ineffective because it does not reduce the cause of the problem. Cancer rates are not reduced. If social marketers and public health officials want to reduce cancer rates, they should concentrate their efforts on removing the chemical from the environment. This circumstance, however, puts social marketers and public health practitioners into an awkward (politically sensitive) position. Social marketing and public health practitioners are accustomed to developing educational and behavioral change campaigns aimed at individuals. They are not used to advocating governmental changes in public policy. However, if a social or public health problem is best solved with a change in public policy, then the communication strategy should target the needed public policy change. The desired end, that is, effectively solving social and public health problems (thereby increasing the quality of life for individuals and communities), needs to dictate the means of its achievement. Unfortunately, some practitioners are only willing to apply a means with which they are accustomed (behavioral change campaigns targeting individuals), regardless of its effectiveness (Wymer 2010).

2 Social Marketing and Public Health Initiatives

Social marketing has most often been used to provide solutions in the public health area (Grier and Bryant 2005; Helmig and Thaler 2010). Public health officials sometimes use social marketing tactics to increase the effectiveness of their public health campaigns. Because of the interdependency between social marketing and public health communications, social marketers would do well to inform their social marketing planning by including concepts from the public health field rather than a strict adherence to commercial marketing concepts more appropriate for selling consumer goods than affecting social change. Primary prevention is an important sub-field of the public health discipline (Cohen et al. 2007; Gullotta and Bloom 2003). Primary prevention is defined as activities, programs, or policies designed to reduce the incidence or the number of new cases of a disease or problem (Wallack 1984).

Primary prevention tactics are categorized into three parts: health promotion, disease prevention, and health protection (Leddy 2006). Health promotion deals with educating and training healthy populations to lead healthy lifestyles (Wallack 1984). The emphasis is on educating individuals to make healthy choices in order to attain longer and healthier lives.

Health promotion campaigns are familiar to social marketers. Examples are campaigns that address tobacco consumption, alcohol consumption, diet, and exercise issues. These types of programs mesh easily with social marketers' customary practices.

Disease prevention programs provide preventive services to high risk populations. Examples include stress reduction classes, smoking cessation classes, clinical screenings, and counseling. Similar to health promotion tactics, disease prevention programs target individuals. Social marketers often view disease prevention programs as social marketing "products" (Novelli 1990; Solomon and Dejong 1986).

Health protection strategies are aimed at benefiting the entire population without requiring individuals to change their behaviors, make choices, or take actions. Health protection improves health and wellness for all by altering the environment surrounding the community. Health protection strategies have proven to be the most effective at improving public health. These strategies emphasize regulatory measures that place the preponderance of responsibility on producers rather than on individuals (Wallack 1984). Examples of health protection are reducing community exposure to radiation, carcinogens, and other toxins. Other examples are motorcycle helmet laws, seat belt laws, food safety laws, and worker safety laws.

Health promotion and disease prevention are consistent with the traditional social marketing framework because they are aimed at individuals – to inform, to change attitudes, and to change behaviors (Grier and Bryant 2005). Health protection strategies, however, diverge from traditional social marketing thinking. Health protection's emphasis is on the environment in which a community lives in order to reduce or eliminate harmful and unhealthful elements in the environment.

In the following section, a simple model is presented that informs the decision-making of social marketing and public health practitioners. The model is informed by the public health concepts discussed previously. The model is developed for the purpose of helping to develop strategies with increased effectiveness. The choice of strategy is derived from the context of the public health problem to be solved. The model encourages practitioners to clearly understand barriers to correcting a public health problem and then to remove those barriers. The model is holistic in that it includes both individual and environmental barriers.

3 Pyramid Model for Analyzing Contributors to Public Health Problem

Wymer (2011) presented a pyramid model to inform the identification and weighting of contributors of a social or public health problem. The model diverges from the tacit assumption (as evidenced by the social marketing and public health campaigns) that individuals are largely responsible for their own health quality. This can be true is some cases. For example, contracting a sexually transmitted disease is often within an individual's volition. Hence, public health campaigns that promote safe sex practices can be effective. (Even, here, however, there are cultural barriers that may have to be overcome.) The model is presented in Fig. 1.1.

- The assumption that is the foundation for the pyramid model shown in Fig. 1.1 is that health quality is an interaction between the individual and the larger social and physical environment.

The planning pyramid contains four categories. Each category represents a class of variables. The bottom two categories represent classes of environmental variables. The top two categories represent classes of individual variables. The analysis should begin at the bottom and work upwards, and this is how these categories will be described next. Once variables that contribute to the social health problem are identified, they then become barriers which need to be overcome in a public health or social marketing campaign.

3.1 *Pathogenic Agents*

Pathogenic agents refer to variables present in the environment that cause or contribute to an unhealthy condition. The potential list of pathogenic agents is large, but an example might be the presence of toxins in the ecological or biophysical

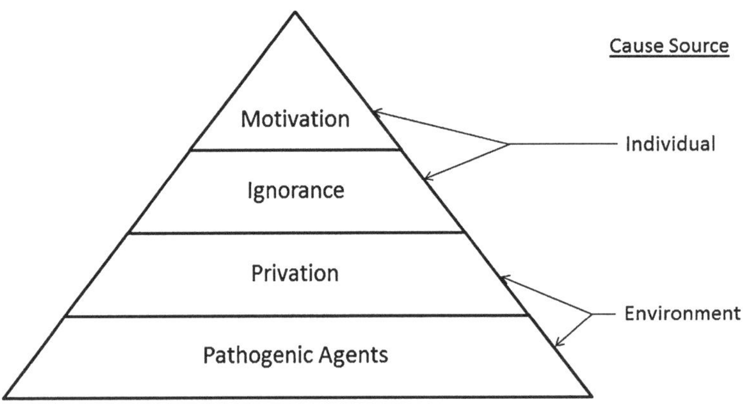

Fig. 1.1 Pyramid model

environments. Toxins in the soil, air, or water may create an unhealthy condition. For example, living close to a petrochemical plant has been shown to increase cancer risks (Belli et al. 2004). Regulations to reduce the carcinogenic waste of petrochemical facilities may be needed to improve the community's health and, therefore, quality of life.

Another example deals with childhood obesity, a social problem serious enough in America to be included in a presidential State-of-the-Union Address (Obama 2010). Obesity is a complex social problem, but research finds that food industry product offerings and marketing activities are a major contributing factor (Chopra and Darnton-Hill 2004; Kessler 2009; Nestle 2007). Regulations and laws may be needed to change food industry practices.

Achieving changes to public policies, regulations, or laws to deal with pathogenic agents may require lobbying and activism (Wymer 2010). Affected industries will most likely resist reform. This is especially the case in America, where corporations have the right to speak freely on political issues, lobby government, and to make unlimited, anonymous donations to the election campaigns of their patron political officials (Liptak 2010).

3.2 Privation

The presence of a privation barrier indicates that one or more variables are absent from the environment, variables that are required for people to live with good health and well-being. For example, what if the program's objective is to reduce infant mortality in a community in which mothers lack access to proper sanitation? Obviously, improper sanitation creates a pathway for disease. Removing privation barriers will usually requires intervention by government, nongovernmental, or private sector organizations.

3.3 Ignorance

In some cases, individuals may not know enough about an issue to take corrective measures to protect themselves. For example, when individuals consider buying a new home, how many check to see how close the home is to a high-traffic road, high-voltage electric lines, or cell phone towers, all of which are linked to increased cancer rates (Draper et al. 2005; Reynolds et al. 2004; Wolf and Wolf 2004)?

3.4 Motivation

Sometimes, individuals are insufficiently motivated to make a lifestyle or behavioral change that would improve their health and quality of life. In affluent countries, most people know that eating more vegetables, smoking less, drinking less, and exercising more would be good for them. Yet, they do not make these changes but instead retain their less healthy behaviors.

3.5 Using the Pyramid Model Holistically

Identifying the causality of social and public health problems is not always a simple process. There may be multiple causal influences. The causes may have different levels of influence. Hence, once the various causes are identified, they should then be weighted with respect to their proportion of influence to the social or public health problem.

3.5.1 Example 1: Ebola Epidemic

For example, at the time of this writing over 13,000 people have contracted Ebola during 2014. Obviously the root cause is the Ebola virus (a pathogenic agent). The spread of the current epidemic, which is concentrated in western Africa (primarily Sierra Leone, Liberia, and Guinea), is primarily a public health resource problem. That is, countries like Liberia tend to have too few public health resources (a privation barrier). There are too few health care workers with proper training and equipment, too few well-equipped hospitals, and too few medicines. The impoverished conditions of affected populations, especially in the rural areas (which have even less access to medical care) contribute to the epidemic (Fox 2014).

Because the disease has such serious consequences for its victims, people are highly motivated by fear and concern for family members to avoid contracting the disease. Whereas people may have been ignorant initially about how the disease spreads, it is common knowledge now that the disease is spread through exposure to bodily fluids of an infected person. People's inability to get sick family members into rapid isolation and intensive medical treatment continues to contribute to the epidemic (Anonymous 2014).

With respect to the Ebola epidemic, the major causes are environmental. The reason the Ebola pathogen has been successful is chiefly due to privation. The various privation variables are chiefly due to government failure. The governments of the affected West African nations have failed to alleviate their poor public health conditions. The governments of other nations have failed to assist affected West African nations.

An interesting but vital cause of the Ebola epidemic is the absence of a vaccine (privation). We have been aware of Ebola since the 1970s. However, because those people most likely to contract the disease are poor or live in poor communities, there was insufficient profit incentive for the corporate pharmaceutical industry to invest in developing a vaccine (Corsi 2014; Huff 2014).

Examining the problem holistically reveals substantial systemic environmental barriers to preventing epidemics like Ebola from occurring in the future. One remedy requires a reduction in government corruption, where it exists, that produces poverty and inadequate public health care. Greater international cooperation and resource sharing is needed. A change in government policies are required that transfer health care from the public sector to the private sector where priorities are determined by profitability rather than effectiveness and need.

3.5.2 Example 2: Tobacco Use

Tobacco companies have known for decades that smoking causes cancer. Yet they have continued to market cigarettes to acquire new customers. Smoking has caused millions of deaths (Kessler 2002).

According to the U.S. Centers for Disease Control and Prevention (CDC), smoking causes cancer, heart disease, stroke, lung diseases, and diabetes. Smoking causes more than 480,000 deaths in the U.S. each year (DHHS 2014). For every person who dies from a smoking-related disease, about 30 more people suffer with at least one serious illness from smoking. More than 16 million Americans suffer from a disease caused by smoking (CDC 2014).

Tobacco is the leading preventable cause of death. Globally, tobacco use causes five million deaths per year, an annual rate that is projected to climb to eight million by 2030 (WHO 2011).

Even though tobacco use is clearly harmful, the tobacco industry still exists. It continues to market its tobacco products. Cigarettes enjoy an interesting characteristic that distinguishes it from other consumer products. This characteristic is that cigarettes, when consumed in the manner intended by the manufacturer, harm consumers. The fact that the industry is permitted to market products that kill consumers is evidence of government failure and corruption.

The tobacco industry aggressively markets its products. It spent $8.4 billion (about $23 million each day) in 2011 on cigarette advertising and promotions in the U.S., resulting in the sale of over 273 billion cigarettes to U.S. consumers in 2011 (FTC 2013). In the U.S., more than 3200 persons under the age of 18 years smoke their first cigarette and about 2100 youth and young adults who had been occasional smokers become daily cigarette smokers (DHHS 2014).

The facts make clear that tobacco use in general and cigarette smoking in particular cause a major public health problem. It is difficult to imagine a consumer product that kills millions of people and is not considered to be a problem worth addressing by most elected government representatives. Yet, this is the case.

Table 1.1 First tobacco causality analysis

Priority order	Causal weighting	Potential success of action (%)	Utility of taking action
Pathogenic agent	1.0	5	0.05
Privation			
Ignorance			
Motivation			

Using the pyramid model, we will consider the public health problem caused by tobacco use. See Table 1.1. First note that the priority order begins at the bottom of the pyramid and works upward. This is the logical order to proceed in the causality analysis. (For brevity, we will combine cigarette smoking and other types of tobacco consumption.)

In our first causal analysis of the tobacco public health problem, notice that tobacco is viewed as a pathogenic agent. Its consumption causes harm. Hence, if tobacco were not marketed (made available and promoted) to consumers, the public health problem would not exist. Therefore, tobacco as a pathogenic agent is given a causal weighting of 1.0 in Table 1.1.

Removing tobacco from the marketplace would solve the public health problems caused by tobacco consumption. The government could ban tobacco cultivation, tobacco product manufacturing, tobacco marketing, and tobacco importation. Even though banning tobacco is the rational action to remove such a harmful consumer product from the marketplace, getting the government to protect the public health of its citizens by banning tobacco may be quite difficult. It appears that Bhutan is the only nation to have banned tobacco by making smoking in public and selling tobacco illegal (Weiner 2005). For a variety of reasons, governments do not want to ban tobacco (Debate.org 2014; Yahoo Answers 2006). Therefore, the potential for success of a public health communications campaign resulting in a government ban of tobacco is given a meager 5 % chance of success.

Even though banning tobacco would solve the public health problem, it would be very difficult to achieve this outcome (only a 5 % probability of success). Therefore, it would not be a wise course of action for social marketing and public health professionals to commit their time and resources to achieve a total tobacco ban. The causal weighting (1.0) multiplied by the potential success of action (0.05) results in a utility of taking action of 0.05 (5 %).

In the second causal analysis, we will examine the utility of taking action to overcome privation barriers to smoking cessation. This is presented in Table 1.2.

Privation causes to the public health problems caused by tobacco smoking suggest that if smoking cessation products and services were easier to acquire and use, those people who wanted to quit smoking would have greater assistance to help them quit. We have given privation a causal weighting of 0.10, which can be interpreted to mean that about 10 % of the public health problems caused by smoking are caused by the absence of products and services to help smokers quit. The potential

Table 1.2 Second tobacco causality analysis

Priority order	Causal weighting	Potential success of action (%)	Utility of taking action
Pathogenic agent	1.00	5	0.05
Privation	0.10	20	0.02
Ignorance			
Motivation			

Table 1.3 Third tobacco causality analysis

Priority order	Causal weighting	Potential success of action (%)	Utility of taking action
Pathogenic agent	1.00	5	0.05
Privation	0.10	20	0.02
Ignorance	0.01	70	0.01
Motivation			

success of taking action on removing privation barriers is given a 20 % probability. The utility of taking action means that if resources are devoted to overcoming privation barriers, the reduction in the public health problems caused by smoking is likely to be reduced by 2 %.

In the third analysis, we will examine the utility of taking action to remove ignorance barriers that contribute to the public health problems associated with tobacco consumption. This analysis is included in Table 1.3.

The third causal analysis presented Table 1.3 gives ignorance a causal weighting of 0.01. This means that about 1 % of the public problems caused by smoking are caused by ignorance among some members of society. The weighting is very low because it is commonly known that cigarette smoking is harmful. Most countries even make sure such a warning is printed on cigarette packaging. However, it is likely that some ignorance remains. For example, some people may not understand that smoking causes many other health problems besides an increased future probability of acquiring lung cancer.

In the U.S., in the 1960s, smoking rates were about 42 %. However, around 1965 public health officials became aware that smoking causes cancer. They advocated policies to educate citizens about the dangers of smoking. Over the years, public ignorance about the dangers of smoking has largely been removed. Currently, about 22 % of Americans are smokers. The decline of smoking rates in the U.S. has declined from 42 % to 22 % (Ashton and Streem 2014). Because public education has occurred during a period in which laws were passed (1) to restrict the age at which people could buy cigarettes, (2) to increase cigarette prices due to increase cigarette taxation, and (3) to place restrictions on cigarette marketing to children and on television; it is difficult to attribute a portion of smoking rate declines to reducing ignorance.

Table 1.4 Third tobacco causality analysis

Priority order	Causal weighting	Potential success of action (%)	Utility of taking action
Pathogenic agent	1.00	5	0.05
Privation	0.10	20	0.02
Ignorance	0.01	70	0.01
Motivation	0.89	15	0.14

The potential success in improving public health by overcoming ignorance barriers associated with smoking is assigned a probability success of action of 25 %. This means that a well-resourced and well-implement public health communication campaign has a 70 % chance of removing the ignorance still remaining in society about the public health problems caused by smoking. The utility of taking action (0.01) is the product of the causal weighting (0.01) and the potential success of action (0.70). This means that a successful public health communications campaign overcoming ignorance barriers would likely result in a 1 % decline in smoking.

In the fourth analysis, we will examine the utility of taking action to remove motivation barriers that contribute to smoking rates in our society. This analysis is included in Table 1.4.

The fourth causal analysis presented in Table 1.4 assigns motivation a causal weighting of 0.89. This is a very high assignment of the causality of the public health problem to individual motivation. Recall, however, that in our initial analysis we assigned all of the causality to cigarettes as a pathogenic agent. That is, if cigarettes did not exist, there would by definition not be a public health problem caused by cigarettes. However, because of the economic and political influence of the tobacco industry (an example of political corruption), we concluded that it would be virtually impossible to remove cigarettes and tobacco products from existence. Hence, we continued onward in our analysis to identify areas in which we could have a greater effect in addressing this public health problem.

Note that the weights assigned to privation, ignorance, and motivation barriers to resolve this public health problem total to 1.00. We have essentially disregarded eradicating cigarettes from consideration. The next logical greatest contributor to this public health problem is individual motivation. Individuals choose to smoke of their own volition. Hence, smokers are motivated to smoke and lack the motivation to quit smoking.

This is a simplistic conclusion, of course. We know that smokers may have some personality trait differences from nonsmokers. We know, for example, that some people are more sensitive to social influences than are other people. We also know that individuals are exposed to ubiquitous tobacco industry marketing from cradle to grave (a pathogenic agent).

Regular smoking is a reinforced behavior. For example, smoking is associated with drinking alcoholic beverages. When individuals go to clubs (bars and pubs) with friends, smoking may accompany drinking as a custom. Hence, smoking becomes associated with drinking, both of which are reinforced behaviors, potentially addictive, and difficult to discontinue once addiction in vulnerable people has been established (Anonymous 2007; Bien and Burge 1990).

As another example, nicotine, one of the more potent chemicals in tobacco, is thought to be addictive and produces a biological effect from its consumption. There are socio-psychological reinforcers from smoking as well as biological reinforcers. Regular smokers develop an identity as a smoker; it is who they are, part of their self-image. Smokers may be part of social networks of other smokers. Smoking is part of this type of social network's identity, one of its norms (Jarvis 2004; Pomerleau et al. 1993).

Motivating individuals sufficiently to quit smoking and to resist the various reinforcers long enough for them to become permanent nonsmokers is challenging. For people who smoke regularly, the benefits of smoking outweigh the costs. The skeptical reader may counter-argue this point, arguing that the potential for acquiring cancer and other health problems far outweighs any benefits from smoking. However, this is obviously not the case from the perspective of smokers. Otherwise, they would not smoke. A simple cost versus benefit analysis will clarify this point.

In Table 1.5, we see a simple listing of a smoker's perceived benefits and costs from smoking. A disinterested person who is a nonsmoker may look at Table 1.5 and notice that the costs related to the potential for health problems is so great that all other considerations become meaningless. (This attitude accounts for the promotion of "white knuckle abstinence".) Note that the costs and benefits are based on the perspective of the individual smoker. Also note that people are not always purely rational decision makers. (Otherwise, we would all be trim athletes who would never buy a sports car or a time-share condo.) People, in fact, are often emotional decision makers (Camerer et al. 2005; Loewenstein and Lerner 2003). From the perspective of a teenage smoker, feeling confident and attractive from smoking may feel quite valuable.

From the perspective of the smoker, quitting smoking would involve forgoing the benefits in order to avoid the costs listed in Table 1.5. It may further help the skeptical reader to realize that the perceived value of the costs and benefits are weighted with respect to time. That is, a benefit or cost that is experience immediately is weighted higher than if it were to be experienced in the future. Note that the benefits are generally experienced in the near term, whereas the health problems are experienced in the distant future (Wymer 2011). Even though smokers know there is link between smoking and cancer, they tend to minimize the health risk of smoking (Weinstein 1998). It is difficult to imagine an individual feeling sanguine about smoking if the

Table 1.5 Costs and benefits of smoking

Costs	Benefits
Price of cigarettes	Feeling of relaxation
Inconvenience of not being allowed to smoking in various locations	Confident, independent self-image
Bad breath	A shared common interest in friends
Stained teeth	Helps curb food appetite, keeping body weight down
Potential health problems	Gives something to do with hands, helps with nervous energy

Table 1.6 Costs and benefits of not smoking

Costs	Benefits
Weight gain	More money for other purchases
Withdrawal and nervousness	Better health
Social awkwardness or isolation	

odds of waking up the next morning with cancer were one in four. It would be similar to playing a game of Russian roulette. With respect to Russian roulette, because the odds of losing are strong and the consequences of losing are great (and experienced immediately), few are motivated to play. However, with smoking, individuals are able to lower their perception of the risk because the consequences of losing are experienced in the distant future. Hence, smokers continue to play.

It is important to realize that smoking cessation is a different behavioral routine than smoking. From the perspective of the smoker, not smoking is a changed behavior that has its own set of costs and benefits. We will illustrate this in Table 1.6.

To become a nonsmoker, an individual's benefits are essentially the avoidance of the costs associated with smoking. An individual's costs are essentially derived from resisting the various reinforcers of smoking (social, psychological, and biological). Given the principle that what is experienced in the near term has greater weight than what is experienced in the far term, note that the costs are experienced in the near term and the main benefit, better health (compared to contracting a smoking-related disease 20 years in the future) is experienced in the far term. Considering the costs and benefits of smoking and not smoking, with consideration given to the time weighting, it becomes easier to understand why smokers continue to smoke.

Now that we have discussed how social marketers and public health professionals can assess the causes of public health problems and, thus, barriers to their resolution; it is appropriate to discuss communication tactics for acting upon the causality analysis. The public health communication strategy utilized should be influenced by the category of cause that has been presented in the pyramid model.

4 Public Health Communication Strategies

It's all about the outcomes!

One of the key reasons that the field of social marketing has been lacking in providing effective campaigns to solve social problems is that the social marketing practitioners and scholars have tended to be more concerned about their tactics than their outcomes (Wymer 2011).

Early social marketing research applied commercial marketing concepts to the amelioration of social problems (Rothschild 1999). Unfortunately, there are marked differences between an economic phenomenon defined by a buyer-sell dyad and a public health phenomenon defined by citizens responding to the environment in which they live. Social marketers have been relatively ineffective because they have been misapplying one set of tactics to a variety of social problems in order to achieve their desired outcomes (Peattie and Peattie 2003). The main point is that the corrective tactics to achieve the desired outcomes should be derived from the causes of the public health problem. The tactics should be determined by the public health causal analysis. Traditionally, social marketing have had a fixed tactical model that they applied regardless of the nature or cause of the public health problems, often resulting in ineffectiveness (Wymer 2010).

- Tactics to solve public health problems should be derived from the causal analysis of the public health problem.

4.1 Communication Strategies for External Causes

Generally, if a primary cause of a public health problem is caused by a pathogenic agent or privation, government action is required. The reason for government action is that, often, large resource levels are needed or new laws and regulations (or meaningful enforcement of existing laws and regulations) are required to address the public health problem.

For a privation example, there may be impoverished communities that have high rates of infectious diseases because they lack resources to produce clean drinking water and effective public sewage removal systems. Government intervention may be required to provide the resources to build the necessary infrastructure and to ensure that proper health standards are maintained.

For a pathogenic agent, industry activities (production and marketing) often emit toxins into the physical environment or the industry markets unhealthy products (alcohol, cigarettes, unhealthy food and beverages). Government involvement is needed to protect public health. Government is often needed to restrict the actions of harmful industries. Unfortunately, governments are often hesitant to act in the public interest if the needed actions are opposed by business interests and their wealthy owners (Gilens and Page 2014; Wymer 2010).

To influence governmental change, public health communication strategies need to assume the perspective of activists or advocates. Many social marketers are quite reluctant to consider social movement marketing because it is markedly different from the traditional, commercially-oriented business paradigm. Nevertheless, if one is serious about solving externally-caused social problems there are often few alternatives. (Admittedly, for some contexts in which privation is the cause a social entrepreneurship paradigm may prove effective on a small scale.)

4.1.1 Changing Public Policy: Issue Marketing

The goal of issue marketing is to influence government or corporate policy indirectly by changing public attitudes, beliefs, or opinions about a cause. For example, an advocacy group may want a corporation to change its practices or a government to pass a law or regulation. The advocacy group may feel the best or only way to attain this goal is to influence public opinion, which will pressure the corporation or government to act. Issue marketers can face several hurdles in accomplishing their aims:

1. The public may not know about the issue.
2. The public may have forgotten about the issue.
3. Public opinion on the issue may have been influenced by the opponent's propaganda.
4. The public may believe the issue is unimportant.
5. The public may not know enough about the issue to have formed an opinion.
6. The public may disagree with the social marketer about the need to act on the issue.

The public level of knowledge and attitude about the issue will determine the appropriate marketing tactic.

For example, most of the world knew for many years that apartheid existed in South Africa. However, in the 1980s, human rights groups became more focused on bringing apartheid to the world's attention. Human rights organizations appealed to governments to oppose the apartheid government but were generally unsuccessful until the news media began to inform the public on a regular basis about what was happening in South Africa. Over time, public opinion began to turn against the white minority South African government. This development led to various advocacy groups' pressuring corporations to stop doing business with South Africa. Later, the governments of some nations issued trade sanctions against South Africa.

Because of South Africa's poor image in the world and the poor economic environment caused by the sanctions, social conditions in South Africa actually worsened for a time. In 1989, sanctions hurt the economy further, the national currency (the rand) collapsed, and reformist F. W. de Klerk came to power. Afterward, virtually all apartheid regulations were repealed, political prisoners were released, and negotiations about forming a new government began. Free elections in 1994 resulted in a victory for the African National Congress, and Nelson Mandela became president.

What would have happened if activists had not been successful in attracting media attention to the problems of South Africa? What would have happened if the public had shown little interest in the early news reports? This example of successful issue marketing was effective because conditions favored the development of a virtuous cycle, in which public concern was aroused about the issue, which in turn stimulated business and government to act. Our discussion will now focus on how the virtuous cycle was created. Figure 1.2 represents issue marketing communication patterns in an issue marketing campaign.

Issue marketers present their case to government officials (policy makers). In some instances, one or more officials champion the issue by encouraging a change in policy (legislative or administrative) and by communicating their support for the issue to the public through the media.

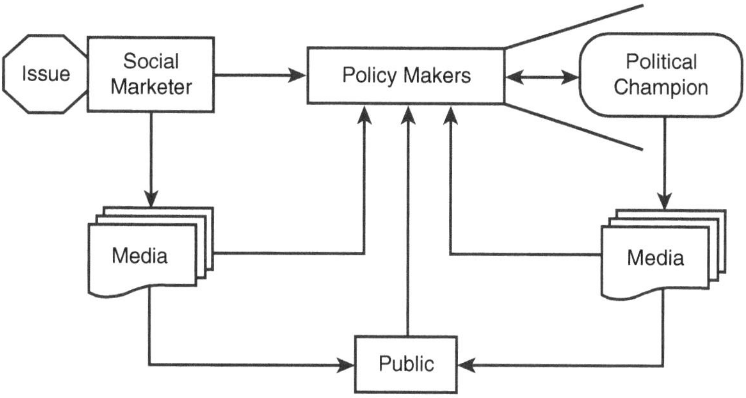

Fig. 1.2 Issue marketing communication patterns

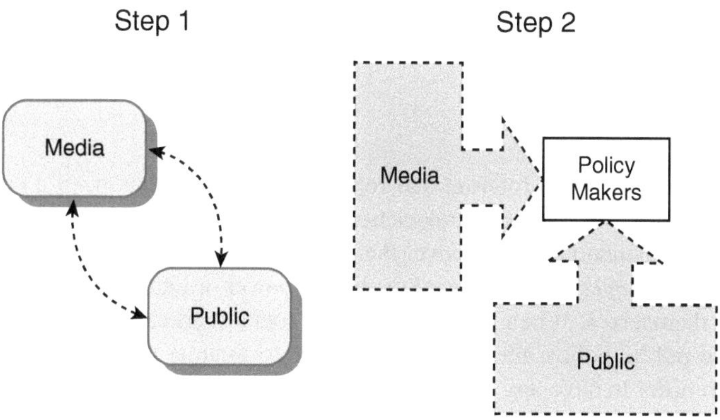

Fig. 1.3 Interrelationships between media, public, and policy markers

Issue marketers also try to build public awareness and support for the issue by presenting their case to the public through the media. This implies that the media find the issue marketers' case newsworthy. If the public supports the issue, that support can influence government officials to reform policy.

Although issue marketing could be affected by an appeal to a government official who immediately supports the issue and implements policy reform, it is generally the case that policy makers are influenced by public opinion. The success of issue marketers' efforts, therefore, depends on their ability to influence public opinion. For issue marketers to influence public opinion, a virtuous cycle must be created. As depicted in Fig. 1.3, if issue marketers can gain the attention of the media and if the media report the issue to the public and if the public shows interest in the issue, a virtuous cycle can begin.

In Step 1 in Fig. 1.3, the media report on the issue. Assuming the media's audience shows interest in more reporting on the issue, a positive feedback loop (virtuous cycle) can develop in which the media's reporting increases the public's interest, which increases the media's reporting on the issue, and so on. If Step 1 is successful, the media will add a new story to their reporting: the public's growing interest in the issue. As the media's reporting on the issue continues and their reporting on public interest in the issue grows, policy makers begin to focus on the issue as a growing concern (Step 2). Policy makers also perceive an increasing level of constituent support for the issue. If public support continues to grow, policy makers will eventually experience sufficient influence to support the issue.

Issue marketers are challenged to present an important and credible case to the media. If the issue experiences growing support, a faction of policy makers will probably oppose it. The opposition will develop a strategy to present its case to the public through the media, which may create a public debate about the merits of the issue.

Interest in issue marketing is growing among social marketers. In the following section, we will discuss more emerging issues in social marketing.

4.1.2 Online Advocacy

The development of the Internet and related technologies has been a catalyst for civic engagement in democratic societies. It used to be that organizations had to wait for a mainstream media to cover their causes in order to spread their messages. Internet technologies, such as social media, empower ordinary people to spread the message themselves. When public health and social marketing professionals want to change public policy, they must often have to assume the role of advocate or activist in order to have any meaningful effect. Therefore, our discussion will have the social marketing or public health professional assume the role of an activist trying to affect the desired change by promoting a social movement.

We will use the terms online activism and online advocacy interchangeably. When we use these terms, we are referring to online tactics individuals and organizations use to work towards social change or a change in public or government policy. These tactics are aimed at building grassroots support for a cause, media relations, and lobbying politicians.

The Internet offers several advantages. It's available to a good proportion of the population. It's convenient and easy to use. It allows for rapid, inexpensive communication. It allows for individuals to network for collaboration. Three technologies that are important tools for online activists are e-mail, websites, and e-newsletters.

For example, in the U.S. the volume of email Members of Congress receive has increased fourfold in the last 10 years to over 200 million messages a year. About 90 % of communications sent to Members of Congress is now in the form of e-mail. The proportion of Americans who are contacting Congress has increased 18 % since

2004, representing 44 % of the voting age population (approximately 100 million adults). Over 80 % of individuals sending their Congressional representatives e-mail were prompted to do so by an interest group.

Activists face challenges in furthering their causes. They must educate people, inspire them to take action, let them know what they can do to get active and give them the tools to make real, sustained change. Some examples of the tools they use are:

1. Send emails to Members of Congress or Members of Parliament
2. Print out flyers and other online materials and distribute locally
3. Provide resources for their members, such as having research available on issues and votes of legislators
4. Online forums and webchats
5. Encouraging members to use information to write articles, Op-Eds, Letters to Editor in their local newspapers

We will discuss some of the various tactics and online tools available to public health communication strategists. Because technologies and applications change regularly, we will avoid in-depth discussions of specific about specific applications like Twitter or RSS feeds. We will, however, discuss their appropriate use for online advocacy. The interested reader can readily find resources for using a specific application through simple Google, Yahoo, or MSN searches.

Activist groups will find that the most effective strategy is one that combines both the communication power of the Internet with the interpersonal power of face-to-face advocacy. For example, MoveOn.org has found that it is easy for politicians to ignore mass generate emails, but difficult to ignore a petition when presented in person. MoveOn.org has found that a holistic, integrated approach works best.

For advocacy to be effective, it must be done in an integrated manner. In the online format, this implies that tactics using e-mails, websites, and e-newsletters must work together using a focused message strategy. Integration also requires online tactics to reinforce offline tactics. Offline tactics include telephone calls to politicians, personal visits to their offices, editorials in newspapers, and so forth. The combined, integrated use of offline and online tactics has a greater effect than either could achieve alone.

Online activism should work in concert with real-life, on-the-ground activism. Facebook, Pinterest, Twitter, and Flickr are useful in building relationships, helping essential resources to be found, enabling news and ideas to be shared easily. It is important that these tools not detract from on-the-ground activism.

Changing public policy is the consequence of citizen action. Advocacy groups much gain support for their causes from a variety of constituencies to be effective. However, they typically have fewer financial resources than government and corporations, and often find it difficult to disseminate their messages (Waters and Lord 2009). Developing relationships with likeminded individuals is one of the most important determinants of advocacy success.

Online activism helps to give more citizens more power to work collaboratively in making social change. It allows for much easier communication among a large number of people. Simply being able to communicate, however, is insufficient. Online tools enhance activists' ability to develop stakeholder relationships through which it achieves its goals.

Activists rely on growing grassroots support from citizens. Individual citizens have little power, but working together, they can change their society. Online technologies allow citizens to exchange information easily and find other, likeminded individuals.

By communicating with the organization's members regularly, advocacy groups learn as much as possible about their motivations and interests. They use this knowledge to communicate to members in a meaningful and relevant manner, which increases participation and loyalty. One method of doing this is by collecting emails of website visitors (that is, building a list) in order to send them periodic updates on the organization's activities. Having an RSS feed that visitors can subscribe to is another effective way of staying in touch with supporters.

Successful advocacy campaigns are viral, meaning that the grassroots communicating is grown by member-to-member recruitment. The organization should encourage its members to send messages to their friends and make it easy for them to do so. Many activist organizations that effectively encourage their members to help recruit new members find that about 10 % of members taking action during a campaign are new members. New members are helpful in future campaigns, they help replace former members who have become inactive, and there are a resource for donations and volunteering (Bhagat 2005).

To become viral, an advocacy organization needs to successfully self-promote its cause. The first step in self-promotion is being a resource. The advocacy organization that has the best organized, most easily accessed and most complete source of information of the cause of interest will attract the vast majority of visitors interested in the issue. The website that becomes the definitive site for a specific issue will be linked to from other sites having links related to the cause.

Once the organization has rich and meaningful content on its website, it should submit its site to the major search engines, like Google, Yahoo, and MSN. Although the search engines will eventually scan the site to index its content, submitting it instead of waiting on the search engines' software to find the site will allow this to happen much quicker. It is also useful to submit pages on the website that related to specific issues. Finally, when making substantive updates on the organization's website, it is a good idea to submit it to the major search engines so that the website will be indexed with the new information.

In order to give visitors to the website an incentive to return, the content must be updated periodically to be current and dynamic. Developing podcasts and video segments are a good way to give visitors fresh content that can educate and that they can use. Be sure to let people know that the information on the site is being maintained. Highlight new material, perhaps by having a "What's New" section on the front page.

Experts who can write columns are useful in putting new content on the website. Online editions of major newspapers use this technique effectively by promoting their regular columnist and featuring their columns on regular days. For example, one columnist or a given topic should be featured every Monday.

Relationships with politicians are important in helping the activist group to further its cause. If a politician cares about a specific cause, she will want to have a relationship with the activist community. Politicians who care about the cause can be important champions who can bring attention to the cause.

Most politicians, whether or not they care about a cause, do care about their relationships with their own constituents. Where an activist organization can be most effective is in encouraging its members to communicate with their elected officials in support of the cause. Politicians may ignore communication from activist organizations or individuals who are not their constituents. However, they are less likely to ignore communication from individuals who are eligible to vote for them. This is especially true as the number of constituents supporting a cause increases.

Activist organizations can most effectively influence a politician by developing a grassroots movement within the politician's geographical constituency. Members in that area can send the politician messages that voice their advocacy of the cause. Some online activists create email messages which members forward to their government representatives. When politicians receive a large number of the same email (although from different people) they treat the messages as a single message. It is better to have members use their own words when communicating with their representatives, although the organization can suggest talking points. The effectiveness of sending email messages to political leaders is greatly improved by having members place phone calls with their government leaders, meeting with them in person, talking with them at events, or sending editorials to newspapers in the politicians' districts.

Activist organizations should use a variety of pathways for promoting its mission and attracting attention to its website. All communications from the organization should contain its URL (website address). Disseminating press releases helps get the organization's message out. The organization can send its press releases directly to journalists. Online press releases can be distributed through gateway sites, such as P.R. Newswire or PRWeb, which can be captured by news aggregating sites like Google News.

Journalists are bombarded with quantities of information. Therefore, it is important to write concisely, with facts. As mentioned previously, having the definitive website on a specific issue allows reporters a location for more detailed information. Chapter 4 discussed having a section of the website dedicated for journalists. On that section, press releases, fact sheets, and reports could be organized by topic and date. There should be easy to find links to advocacy issues. The section should allow journalists to add their email addresses to a list for future press releases. Because most busy journals use Blackberries and iPhones, they receive much of their email as text messages. Therefore, email messages should be brief to catch the reporter's interest. She can then go to the website for the full release if interested. Finally, contact information that reporters can use for follow-up questions should be available.

When representatives of the activist organization make speeches, they should be recorded as podcasts. If these speeches are properly sorted on the website, interested persons can find it easily. Links to recent speeches should be highlighted on the front page.

Media alerts are an excellent means of sending summary news releases to members of the media to allow them to efficiently determine if developing a story on your news release is of interest to their audience. A media alert is a memo-style announcement that provides basic information to the press about an event and its details. Media alerts are written so that reporters can promptly understand the essentials. The alert should begin by answering the "Who" question in bold font. Next, the alert should address the "What" question, that is, describe what will happen at the event. The alert should go on to answer the "When," "Where,", "Why," and "How" questions. Only essential information is included in the alert, which ends with contact details for the person with whom to communicate for further information (Bhagat 2005).

Collaborating with Other Organizations

Building coalitions with other advocacy groups concerned with the same issue can bring greater public attention to the cause and help motivate change (Sabatier 2007). The "Stop AETA" campaign is a recent example of how a lack of coalition building can impede the desired change. In October 2005 the U.S. Congress was considering the Animal Enterprise Terrorism Act (AETA). AETA was the result of successful industry lobbying attempting to prevent animal rights protestors from engaging in activism opposing industry. Opponents of the proposed law worried that legal, non-violent activism would be categorized as terrorism and be punished severely. More than 250 different organizations opposed the proposed law. Unfortunately, their efforts failed and the law was passed with overwhelming support in Congress. Professors Richard Waters and Meredith Lord analyzed the activities of these organizations and concluded their inability to stop this industry-protective law cloaked under the fear of terrorism was the result of the groups failing to work together in an effective coalition (Waters and Lord 2009).

Professors Waters and Lord recommend that activist organizations focus on building and maintaining relationships with other similar organizations for more effective collaboration and, ultimately, success. Based largely on the work of Grunig and Grunig (1991), Waters and Lord's relationship strategies include access, assurances, networking, openness, positivity, and sharing of tasks. Each strategy will be discussed below.

Access refers to ensuring that collaborating groups have the ability to quick contact key decision makers in each organization. Partners must be willing to engage in dialog regarding complaints or questions. Promptly responding to email messages or being easily reached for a telephone conversation enhances access among collaborating groups.

Assurances refers to building a culture among collaborating groups that communicates that each group's concerns are valid and that collaborating groups are committed to maintaining the collaborative relationship. Groups can allow members of theirs and partnering organizations to submit their concerns on their websites through feedback forms. Websites should inform visitors that the organizations will not sell or spam their email addresses.

For the efforts of collaborating activist groups to be productive, they must network effectively. Effective networking is established through the number and quality of contacts among members of the collaborating groups. Collaborating groups can feature their network on their websites by communicating that they are part of a network, working together for change, and featuring links of collaborating organizations.

Openness refers to collaborating organizations directly discussing their relationships, both the nature of the relationships and how to make them more productive. Openness also refers to the free disclosure of thoughts and feelings among members across the groups. Greater disclosure enhances trust.

Positivity refers to efforts of collaborating organizations to make their interactions pleasant for participants. This implies that the organizations are working towards making the relationships more enjoyable for collaborating partners. Organizations should aim for their interactions to be unconditionally constructive. One dimension of positivity is the ease of use of organizational websites. This can be achieved by ensuring that navigation is easy, inclusion of a sitemap, and the availability of a search engine. For more information on improving websites, please refer to Chaps. 3 and 4.

Sharing of tasks implies that when decisions are made that impact multiple organizations, responsibilities pertaining to those decisions are equally shared. Collaborating organizations jointly solve problems. Through the use of online technologies, collaborating organizations can encourage members to become involved in advancing their message.

Factoring in the Opposition

The anti-methamphetamine campaign in the state of Montana provides an example of an effective public health communications campaign. The *Montana Meth Project* is a nonprofit organization that was created to develop and implement a public health communication campaign to reduce youth and young adult drug use of methamphetamine (Montana Meth Project 2012).

The public health communication campaign featured a series of television, radio, and print advertisements (see http://www.montanameth.org/Our-Work/view-ads.php) aimed at youth that depicted very frightening consequences of Meth consumption. The campaign has been quite successful (Morales et al. 2012), perhaps because of the disgust-evoked fear appeals of the ads inoculated youth and young adults in Montana from social influences that encourage meth consumption.

In effect, the anti-meth campaign targeted individuals rather than the pathogenic agent, and was successful. Law enforcement tactics have failed to eradicate meth from society. In our earlier example with cigarettes, we concluded that we would be unable to eradicate cigarettes from society (although for political reasons). The anti-meth campaign was able to use an ad campaign (ads that were presented to the target audiences with sufficient frequency to have an effect). Anti-cigarette smoking campaigns, however, have been substantially less effective even though meth is far more addictive than cigarettes.

The key reason cigarettes have been resistant to public health communication campaigns is the opposition of the tobacco industry. The industry spends vast sums on advertising and marketing, sums that dwarf any possible resources available to a public health campaign. The industry markets its cigarettes over the long-term, year after year; whereas public health communication campaigns are comparatively short-lived. Hence, the tobacco industry is able to effectively nullify any substantive effects from the occasional anti-smoking campaigns that might emerge over time (Kessler 2002).

The main point is that if social marketers and public health professionals are faced with a major oppositional force such as an industry that wants to prevent a change in public policy, the ability of the public health professional to influence change will be impeded. This is why trying to solve some public health problems caused by the tobacco or alcohol industries have been so difficult. In these instances, it might be advisable to target the pathogenic agent rather than avoid it. Even though successful will be very difficult in the short-term, ultimately it may be the only way to solve the public health problem.

Now that we have presented some strategies for externally-caused public health problems, we will next discuss communication strategies for internally-caused public health problems.

4.2 Communication Strategies for Internal Causes

Referring to Fig. 1.1, we presented two categories of internal causes for public health problems: ignorance and motivation. The goal in for the public health or social marketing professional is to effect behavior change. In the case of ignorance, the public health communication campaign is developed to make sure individuals have accurate, relevant information pertaining to the focal public health problem. The assumption is that individuals will be motivated to make changes that are beneficial to themselves or their loved ones.

Public health education campaigns are made more effective by (1) good design of the communication media used, (2) ensuring that targeted audiences are reached by the communication messages, and (3) ensuring sufficient message exposure to facilitate audience learning. Media refers to communication channels used to transmit the message from the sender to the audience (e.g., television, radio, print media, internet, etc.).

Table 1.7 Effective media design resources

Media	Citation
Posters and flyers	http://www.who.int/about/history/publications/9789240560277/en/
	http://www.sswm.info/category/planning-process-tools/demand-creation/demand-creation-tools/awareness-raising-demand-cre-3
Radio	http://www.sswm.info/content/media-campaigns-radio-dc
Internet and Email	http://www.sswm.info/category/planning-process-tools/demand-creation/demand-creation-tools/awareness-raising-demand-cre-2
Video	http://www.sswm.info/category/planning-process-tools/demand-creation/demand-creation-tools/awareness-raising-demand-cre-5
Traditional versus social media	Newbold and Campos (2011)
Mass media	Wheeling Walks (2014)

With respect to effective media design, there are many resources available for guidance. Going into depth on the design of ads, posters, social media, and so forth is beyond the scope of this chapter. Some citations for further reading are presented in Table 1.7 for the interested reader.

Reach refers to the number of different people in the target audience who are presented with the public health message at least once. Frequency refers to the number of times audience members receive the public health message. The aim is to present the public health message to audience members a sufficient number of times that audience members understand and remember the message. Furthermore, a sufficient amount of reminder communications is needed to reduce forgetting among audience members.

Whether or not an education campaign is sufficient to motivate behavior change is dependent upon the degree to which the unhealthy behavior is reinforced. Generally, there are two categories of reinforcers: biological and psychological. Biological reinforcers refer to biologically-active components are experienced as a consequence of engaging in unhealthy behavior, usually the consumption of unhealthy products. A few examples are listed for illustrative purposes in Table 1.8.

A public health communication strategy with respect to dealing with biological reinforcers needs to determine if the reinforcers can be removed. Each of the examples listed in Table 1.8 contain chemicals that could be removed from the product. Removing the bio-active reinforcers from the products will decrease individuals' motivation to continue to consume unhealthy products. Imagine what might happen to smoking rates if nicotine were removed from cigarettes.

Biological reinforcers are treated as pathogenic agents, targets for removal. Public health communication strategies in these cases are directed at changing public policy as discussed in the previous section. The goal is to motivate the government to mandate the removal of biological reinforcers from consumer products. Manufacturers will oppose the passage of such laws. However, it may be far easier to get elected officials to agree to the removal of a product ingredient than to the product's removal from the marketplace. Business-friendly government officials

Table 1.8 Biological reinforcers

Unhealthy behavior or product	Bio-active reinforcer
Cigarette smoking	Nicotine
Alcoholic beverages	Alcohol
Energy drinks	Caffeine and sugar
Soft drinks	Caffeine and sugar
Processed snack foods	Sugar, fat, salt, flavorings, and additives

may not like restricting the activities of product manufacturers, but it is more difficult for a politician to oppose removing nicotine from cigarettes than it is to oppose banning the manufacturing of cigarettes.

Another public health communication strategy is to suggest in the campaign that audience members change their consumption to product versions that lack the bio-active reinforcer. If a regular beer drinker can switch to a non-alcoholic beer, then the original behavior is maintained without the negative effects of the bio-active reinforcer. If a regular soft drink consumer can switch to a caffeine-free version of the preferred soft drink brand, the gradual transition from a regular drinker to an occasional drinker is facilitated. Obviously, forgoing the bio-active reinforcers changes the experience for the individual. However, given that there may also be psychological reinforcers motivating the unhealthy behavior, the removal of the bio-active reinforcer from the individual's experience may ease the transition toward more healthy behaviors.

Psychological reinforcers refer to non-biological benefits individuals experience from the consumption of unhealthy products or engaging in unhealthy behaviors. We discussed previously how cigarette smoking may provide some individuals with self-image and social benefits. Certain individuals may find it thrilling to engage in potentially dangerous activities.

Public health communication professionals first need to fully understand the context within which individuals are motivated to maintain their unhealthy behaviors. Some issues to consider are…

- What are the psychological reinforcers?
- Are the psychological reinforcers experienced differently by individuals with certain personality traits or by certain demographic groups?
- How are the potential benefits of changing to healthy behaviors perceived by the various groups?

In formulating a public health message that will be effective in motivating individuals to discontinue an unhealthy behavior, a cost versus benefit assessment may be helpful. Discontinuing the unhealthy behavior requires individuals to sacrifice the benefits they experience from the psychological reinforcers. These will be perceived as costs to individuals. The costs will be experienced as soon as individuals discontinue the reinforced behaviors. If individuals continue their unhealthy behaviors, they will continue to receive the psychological benefits experienced from the unhealthy behaviors. In many cases, the negative consequences (costs) of the unhealthy behaviors are experienced in the future, sometime the distant future.

Table 1.9 Message development

	Unhealthy behavior	Healthy behavior
Benefits		
Costs		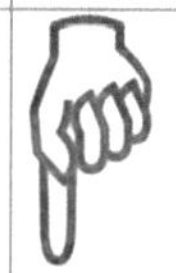

We discussed earlier that a cost experienced immediately is perceived to be greater than if that same cost wereexperienced in the distant future. This perceptual issue helps explain the apparent irrationality of cigarette smoking, for example. To the nonsmoker, cigarette smoking seems irrational. Why would someone risk acquiring lung cancer or another type of disease? The nonsmoker fails to appreciate the benefits cigarette smokers perceive. Young smokers particularly have limited experiences with people who have contracted lung cancer. Their peers do not have cancer. They understand that they may get cancer when they become much older, but acquiring cancer is not a certainty and people die from all kinds of causes. Meanwhile, young smokers receive an array of perceived socio-psychological benefits.

There are costs and benefits of the unhealthy behavior and the healthy behavior. As illustrated in Table 1.9, the public health communication message should try to (1) lower the perception of the benefits of the unhealthy behavior, (2) raise the perception of the costs associated with maintaining the unhealthy behavior, (3) increase the value of the benefits of adopting healthy behaviors, or (4) lower the perceived costs of changing to healthy behaviors.

Public health communication campaigns targeting cigarette smoking and alcohol consumption have often followed a strategy indicated in Table 1.9. Public health communication campaigns are often funded at insufficient levels. This reduces campaign effectiveness, particularly when the affected industry has been investing fortunes in advertisements that send their messages to target audiences. Industry advertisements emphasize the benefits of unhealthy behavior. Hence, a brilliantly conceived public health communications campaign can be effectively nullified by an economically powerful and politically influential industry.

4.3 *Strategic Pragmatism*

Perhaps there is a pragmatic approach to public health communication strategic development. When removing an unhealthy product from the marketplace is politically impossible and when short-lived public health campaigns are nullified by

Table 1.10 Pragmatism analysis for cigarette smoking reduction

Option	Potential political support (1 = very low; 10 = very high)
Removing cigarettes from marketplace	1
Removing nicotine from cigarettes	3
Banning cigarette advertising	5
Banning cigarette advertising directed at youth	8
Banning new flavors of cigarettes from market	7
Removing menthol flavored cigarettes from market	4
Increasing legal age of purchasing cigarettes	5
Increase cigarette taxes	6

enduring corporate advertising, perhaps incremental changes can be advocated that will gradually improve the health context in our environment.

There are a variety of reasons why a politician may refuse to the removal of a harmful product from society (like cigarettes). Reasons may range from concern about unhappy voters, to political ideology, to outright corruption. The public health strategist must find a pathway that offers the greatest public health benefits that can be achieved considering the political context. While banning a product may be politically impossible, more moderate reforms may be possible.

With respect to cigarette smoking, a variety of strategy options are presented in Table 1.10. Each potential option for having some effect on reducing cigarette smoking is listed along with an estimate on how substantially politicians would resist supporting the option. While the most effective public health option would be to ban cigarettes, the government will not support a ban. However, political officials are more flexible with respect to cigarette advertising. A ban or reduction in cigarette advertising and marketing will result in the public being exposed to fewer messages that emphasize benefits of smoking. Government officials are somewhat flexible on raising cigarette taxes. Hence, this is a way to increase the immediate cost of smoking which should have some effect on reducing cigarette smoking, especially for people with less money.

5 Conclusion

In this chapter, we have discussed an array of strategy considerations for informing the direction and development of public health communication campaigns. Conducting an analysis of the causal influences of the public health problem helps to inform strategy development. Failing to target pathogenic agents and instead targeting individual behavior change has resulted in a history of ineffective social marketing and public health campaigns. Similarly, campaigns that were underfunded in comparison with the onslaught of corporate advertising often trivialized social marketing campaigns or rendered them ineffective.

Effectiveness of the public health campaign must be the key concern. The reason for developing and implementing the public health campaign is to achieve an outcome. The outcome is typically to reduce the severity of the public health problem or even to eradicate the public health problem altogether. The campaign, then, is a means to a desired end. Campaign effectiveness reflects how successfully the desired end was achieved.

Social marketers and public health officials negate their own effectiveness when they cling to a methodology which is useful in a specific context, but which they unwisely apply across all contexts. To be effective, the public health professional must sometimes think like an educator, must sometimes think like a behavioral scientist, and must sometimes think like an activist. The nature of the public health problem and the environment in which the public health problem exists should determine the tactics.

References

Anonymous. (2007). Alcohol and tobacco. *Alcohol Alert, 71*, 1–6. http://pubs.niaaa.nih.gov/publications/AA71/AA71.pdf. Accessed 22 Nov 2014.

Anonymous. (2014). *"Wise people" help to fight Ebola in remote villages*. Report by World Health Organization. http://www.who.int/features/2014/ebola-in-villages/en/. Accessed 14 Nov 2014.

Ashton, K., & Streem, D. (2014). *Smoking cessation*. Report by Cleveland Clinic Center for Continuing Education. http://www.clevelandclinicmeded.com/medicalpubs/diseasemanagement/psychiatry-psychology/smoking-cessation/. Accessed 16 Nov 2014.

Belli, S., Benedetti, M., Comba, P., Lagravinese, D., Martucci, V., Martuzzi, M., Morleo, D., Trinca, S., & Viviano, G. (2004). Case–control study on cancer risk associated to residence in the neighbourhood of a petrochemical plant. *European Journal of Epidemiology, 19*, 49–54.

Bhagat, V. (2005). Online advocacy: How online constituent relationship management is transforming the way nonprofits reach, motivate, and retain supporters. In T. Hart, J. Greenfield, & J. Johnston (Eds.), *Nonprofit internet strategies: Best practices for marketing, communications, and fundraising*. Hoboken: Wiley.

Bien, T., & Burge, R. (1990). Smoking and drinking: A review of the literature. *Substance Use and Misuse, 25*(12), 1429–1454.

Camerer, C., Loewenstein, G., & Prelec, D. (2005). Neuroeconomics: How neuroscience can inform economics. *Journal of Economic Literature, 43*(1), 9–64.

CDC. (2014). *Smoking & tobacco use*. http://www.cdc.gov/tobacco/data_statistics/fact_sheets/fast_facts/. Accessed 15 Nov 2014.

Chopra, M., & Darnton-Hill, I. (2004). Tobacco and obesity epidemics: Not so different after all? *British Medical Journal, 328*, 1558–1560.

Cohen, L., Chavez, V., & Chehimi, S. (2007). *Prevention is primary: Strategies for community well-being*. San Francisco: Jossey-Bass.

Corsi, J. (2014). U.N. blames rich nations for Ebola outbreak. *WND Health*. http://www.wnd.com/2014/11/u-n-blames-rich-nations-for-ebola-outbreak/. Accessed 14 Nov 2014.

Debate.org. (2014). Should the government ban smoking? *Debate.org*. http://www.debate.org/opinions/should-the-government-ban-smoking. Accessed 16 Nov 2014.

DHHS. (2014). *The health consequences of smoking – 50 years of progress: A report of the surgeon general*. A report by the U.S. Department of Health and Human Services. http://www.surgeongeneral.gov/library/reports/50-years-of-progress/full-report.pdf. Accessed 15 Nov 2014.

Draper, G., Vincent, T., Kroll, M., & Swanson, J. (2005). Childhood cancer in relation to distance from high voltage power lines in England and Wales: A case-control study. *British Medical Journal, 330*(7503), 1290–1294.

Fox, M. (2014). Why it's not enough to just eradicate Ebola. *NBC News*. http://www.nbcnews.com/storyline/ebola-virus-outbreak/why-its-not-enough-just-eradicate-ebola-n243891. Accessed 14 Nov 2014.

FTC. (2013). *Federal Trade Commission cigarette report for 2011*. Federal Trade Commission. http://www.ftc.gov/sites/default/files/documents/reports/federal-trade-commission-cigarette-report-2011/130521cigarettereport.pdf. Accessed 15 Nov 2014.

Gilens, M., & Page, B. (2014). Testing theories of American politics: Elites, interest groups, and average citizens. *Perspectives on Politics, 12*(3), 564–591.

Grier, S., & Bryant, C. (2005). Social marketing in public health. *Public Health, 26*, 319–339.

Grunig, J., & Grunig, L. (1991). Conceptual differences in public relations and marketing: The case of health-care organizations. *Public Relations Review, 17*(3), 257–278.

Gullotta, T., & Bloom, M. (2003). *Encyclopedia of primary prevention and health promotion*. Norwell: Kluwer.

Helmig, B., & Thaler, J. (2010). On the effectiveness of social marketing – What do we really know? *Journal of Nonprofit and Public Sector Marketing, 22*(4), 264–287.

Huff, E. (2014). Ebola outbreak caused by Big Pharma greed, concludes UN. *Natural News*. http://www.naturalnews.com/047594_ebola_profits_big_pharma_world_health_organization.html. Accessed 14 Nov 2014.

Jarvis, M. (2004). Why people smoke. *British Medical Journal, 328*(7434), 277–279.

Kessler, D. (2002). *A question of intent: A great American battle with a deadly industry*. New York: Public Affairs.

Kessler, D. (2009). *The end of overeating: Taking control of the insatiable American appetite*. New York: Rodale.

Leddy, S. (2006). *Integrative health promotion: Conceptual bases for nursing practice*. Sudbury: Jones and Bartlett.

Liptak, A. (2010, January 22). Justices, 5–4, reject corporate spending limit. *The New York Times*, p. A1(L).

Loewenstein, G., & Lerner, J. (2003). The role of affect in decision making. In R. Davidson, K. Scherer, & H. Goldsmith (Eds.), *Handbook of affective sciences* (pp. 619–642). Oxford: Oxford University Press.

Montana Meth Project. (2012). Montana Meth project. *Wikipedia*. http://en.wikipedia.org/wiki/Montana_Meth_Project. Accessed 27 Nov 2014.

Morales, A., Wu, E., & Fitzsimons, G. (2012). How disgust enhances the effectiveness of fear appeals. *Journal of Marketing Research, 49*(3), 383–393.

Nestle, M. (2007). *Food politics: How the food industry influences nutrition and health*. Berkeley: University of California Press.

Newbold, K., & Campos, S. (2011). *Media and social media in public health messages: A systematic review*. Report by the McMaster Institute of Environment & Health. http://www.mcmaster.ca/mieh/documents/publications/Social%20Media%20Report.pdf. Accessed 28 Nov 2014.

Novelli, W. (1990). Applying social marketing to health promotion and disease prevention. In K. Glanz, F. M. Lewis, & B. K. Rimer (Eds.), *Health behavior and health education: Theory, research, and practice* (pp. 342–369). San Francisco: Jossey-Bass.

Obama, B. (2010). *State of the Union Address*. Washington, DC: The White House, Office of Press Secretary, 27 Jan. http://photos.state.gov/libraries/ukraine/164171/pdf/state_union10.pdf. Accessed 14 Nov 2014.

Peattie, S., & Peattie, K. (2003). Ready to fly solo? Reducing social marketing's dependence on commercial marketing theory. *Marketing Theory, 3*, 365–385.

Pomerleau, O., Collins, A., Shiffman, S., & Pomerleau, C. (1993). Why some people smoke and others do not: New perspectives. *Journal of Consulting and Clinical Psychology, 61*(5), 723–731.

Reynolds, P., Von Behren, J., Gunier, R., Goldberg, D., & Hertz, A. (2004). Residential exposure to traffic in California and childhood cancer. *Epidemiology, 15*(1), 6–12.
Rothschild, M. (1999). Carrots, sticks, and promises: A conceptual framework for the management of public health and social issue behaviors. *The Journal of Marketing, 63*, 24–37.
Sabatier, P. (2007). *Theories of the policy process*. Boulder: Westview Press.
Solomon, M., & Dejong, W. (1986). Recent sexually transmitted disease prevention efforts and their implications for AIDS health education. *Health Education and Behavior, 13*, 301–316.
Wallack, L. (1984). Social marketing as prevention: Uncovering some critical assumptions. *Advances in Consumer Research, 2*, 682–687.
Waters, R., & Lord, M. (2009). Examining how advocacy groups build relationships on the internet. *International Journal of Nonprofit and Voluntary Sector Marketing, 14*(3), 231–241.
Weiner, R. (2005). The first nonsmoking nation. *Slate*. http://www.slate.com/articles/news_and_politics/how_they_do_it/2005/01/the_first_nonsmoking_nation.html. Accessed 16 Nov 2014.
Weinstein, N. (1998). Accuracy of smokers' risk perceptions. *Annals of Behavioral Medicine, 20*(2), 135–140.
Wheeling Walks. (2014). *Mass media public health campaign*. http://www.wheelingwalks.org/WW_TrainingManual/chapter1/chapter1.asp. Accessed 28 Nov 2014.
WHO. (2011). *WHO report on the global tobacco epidemic, 2011*. World Health Organization. http://www.who.int/tobacco/global_report/2011/en/. Accessed 15 Nov 2014.
Wolf, R., & Wolf, D. (2004). Increased incidence of cancer near a cell-phone transmitter station. *International Journal of Cancer, 1*(2), 123–128.
Wymer, W. (2010). Rethinking the boundaries of social marketing: Activism or advertising? *Journal of Business Research, 63*(2), 99–103.
Wymer, W. (2011). Developing more effective social marketing strategies. *Journal of Social Marketing, 1*(1), 17–31.
Yahoo Answers. (2006). Why doesn't the government ban cigarettes as smoking being injurious to health? *Yahoo Answers*. https://in.answers.yahoo.com/question/index?qid=20070301081539AA0lFXb. Accessed 16 Nov 2014.

Chapter 2
Using Publicity to Enhance the Effectiveness of a Child Obesity Prevention Program

Simone Pettigrew, Lisa Weir, Mark Williams, and Sharyn Rundle-Thiele

1 Introduction

Fierce advertising of non-core foods has become a global issue (Story and French 2004). Food items are now the most advertised products on television in developed countries, including the USA, the UK, and Australia (Hurry et al. 2005; Lobstein and Dibb 2005). A key challenge faced by those advocating for public health relates to resourcing. Share of voice for messages promoting healthy eating is significantly outweighed by that of commercial marketing messages that are promoting products such as packaged non-core grocery products and fast food (Hastings and Angus 2011; Wymer 2010).

Within public health, social marketing is one approach that can target individuals, communities, and environments to support behavior change. Social marketing enlists a range of methods adopted from commercial marketing (Andreasen 2002), of which promotion tends to be the most widely used (Carins and Rundle-Thiele 2014). Advertising and publicity activities are key elements of the promotional mix that sit within the broader marketing mix. Advertising is a paid form of promotion, while publicity is unpaid and in the context of health promotion typically includes activities such as constructing and disseminating press releases and writing letters to media editors (Hastings and Haywood 1991; Thackeray et al. 2007). Both advertising and publicity are often used to remind the target market of a social brand and

S. Pettigrew (✉)
School of Psychology and Speech Pathology, Curtin University, Perth, WA, Australia
e-mail: simone.pettigrew@curtin.edu.au

L. Weir • M. Williams
SA Health, Government of South Australia, Adelaide, Australia

S. Rundle-Thiele
Social Marketing @ Griffith, Department of Marketing and Menzies Health Institute Queensland, Griffith University, Brisbane, QLD, Australia
e-mail: s.rundle-thiele@griffith.edu.au

W. Wymer (ed.), *Innovations in Social Marketing and Public Health Communication*, Applying Quality of Life Research,
DOI 10.1007/978-3-319-19869-9_2

to serve as a call to action (such as trialing or repeating a particular behavior). In an environment where the amounts expended by commercial competitors significantly outweigh social marketing budgets, publicity is a focal tool for social marketers because of its lower cost. Publicity serves all aspects of the downstream to upstream marketing continuum by achieving awareness raising and advocacy purposes simultaneously (Hoek and Jones 2011). This in turn may lead to change at individual, social, and environmental levels, all of which are needed to combat the obesity epidemic (Gortmaker et al. 2011; Wymer 2011).

The dominant consideration of social marketing evaluations is to understand the outcome(s) of programs, with a particular focus on attainment (or not) of behavioral change (Huang and Story 2010). However, it is also important to undertake process evaluations to understand how programs are implemented (Pettigrew et al. 2014), thereby providing deeper insight into the factors contributing to program success (or otherwise). For this reason, it is recommended that both process and outcome evaluations are undertaken wherever possible (Walsh et al. 1993). This chapter presents the results of a combined process and outcome evaluation of the publicity generated for OPAL, a child obesity prevention program operating in South Australia. This chapter outlines the quantity and type of publicity that was obtained and discusses how this form of promotion is likely to contribute to the broader OPAL Program outcomes (Weir and Williams 2013). The results provide insights of relevance to other public health programs using a social marketing approach that are constrained in their ability to use varying forms of promotion due to limited promotional budgets or because they are required to target specific communities. Advances in knowledge in this area have the potential to increase campaign effectiveness, thereby enhancing quality of life among the target population segments.

2 The Case of Child Obesity

Obesity is a substantial public health issue, with worldwide obesity rates doubling since 1980 and an estimated 3.4 million adults dying each year as a result of being overweight or obese (World Health Organization (WHO) 2014). In Australia, 63 % of adults and 25 % of children are now overweight or obese (Australian Bureau Statistics (ABS) 2013b). Recent projections suggest that these rates will continue to rise, with adult obesity rates exceeding 70 % by 2025 (Walls et al. 2012). It is important to address weight problems in childhood because overweight children are more likely than their normal weight peers to become overweight adults (Singh et al. 2008).

Overweight and obesity contribute to a range of diseases including diabetes, ischaemic heart disease, and some cancers (WHO 2014). Children who are overweight or obese can also suffer psycho-social stigma and a range of developmental issues, including impacts on friendships, body image, and educational outcomes (WHO 2000; French et al. 1995). There are therefore substantial quality of life implications for overweight children that may be averted with the implementation of effective obesity prevention programs.

While overweight and obesity can sometimes be viewed as simply an imbalance between energy consumed and energy expended, the causes are highly complex and involve the interplay between a wide range of individual, behavioral, social, environmental, and genetic factors (Gortmaker et al. 2011). This complexity means that a simple downstream approach will have little impact on obesity rates, and instead a whole systems approach is required to account for the multiple factors and their interactions (Rutter 2011). As a result, the reduction of overweight and obesity has become a focal point for public health planning and intervention internationally. Social marketing has been proposed as an approach that can assist in implementing these planning and intervention processes (Aschemann-Witzel et al. 2012; Gordon et al. 2006; Gracia-Marco et al. 2010). A comprehensive social marketing approach entails action to be taken at downstream, midstream, and upstream levels to facilitate a comprehensive approach to behavior change that does not solely rely on action by the individual (Andreasen 2002).

Publicity is an important element of this approach because it is capable of drawing the attention of the general public and policy makers to important health issues (Thackeray et al. 2007). Publicity can be effective in embedding a program into a local community by enhancing the profile of the program and increasing its legitimacy. High levels of public concern about child obesity have resulted in the issue receiving significant media attention, making publicity a valuable tool for obesity-prevention programs.

3 The OPAL Program

South Australia, the central, southern mainland State of Australia, is large at 983,482 km^2. This makes it nearly double the size of France (547,660 km^2). Unlike France, South Australia is sparsely populated with just 1.68 million inhabitants (ABS 2013a). Most South Australians (1.22 million) live in the city of Adelaide, with the remaining 460,000 spread across the rest of the State. Outside of Adelaide there are several regional centers with populations of up to 25,000, with other towns being smaller and wide spread. The climate is considered temperate (average temperature 12–22 °C), with hot dry summers and cool winters. Unemployment in South Australia is relatively low at 5.9 % (ABS 2014), although there are pockets of disadvantage throughout the State.

In 2008, State Government projections indicated that by 2032 the entire State budget would be required to meet health care costs as a consequence of an ageing population and lifestyle-related diseases (Department of Health 2011). Obesity, insufficient physical activity, and poor nutrition were identified as prime factors contributing to this outcome (National Obesity Taskforce 2003). The Minster for Health at the time called for the State's largest ever investment in child obesity prevention and announced that South Australia would adopt the successful French program EPODE (Ensemble Prévenons l'Obésité Des Enfants, translated as "Together we can prevent childhood obesity") (Romon et al. 2009).

The South Australian version of EPODE was named OPAL, which stands for Obesity Prevention and Lifestyle program. It commenced in 2009 and was supported by Federal, State, and Local Governments with a dedicated investment of AUD$40 million over 9 years. OPAL, like the French model, operates out of councils, which are local government institutions. Of the 68 South Australian Councils, 19 were selected based on their extent of need (assessed via index of disadvantage, level of overweight and obesity, number of children, and level of Aboriginal population) to house 20 OPAL sites. Of these, 11 are metropolitan sites and 9 are regional (www.opal.sa.gov.au). The populations of each OPAL community varied from 5800 to 68,000, with the intervention reaching approximately 400,000 South Australians since its inception. This represents a reach of around a quarter of the State's population.

The South Australian Health Department (SA Health) adapted the EPODE model to develop a locally relevant version (OPAL) that adhered to the key principles of the approach. Each of the 'four pillars' of EPODE was important across program development and implementation, with some coming to the fore at different times: (1) gaining political commitment, (2) securing resources to run the program, (3) using a sound evidence base and evaluating OPAL, and (4) delivering social marketing services for those supporting and implementing the program (Borys et al. 2012). The stated aim of OPAL is "To improve the eating and activity patterns of children, through families and communities in OPAL regions, thereby increasing the proportion of 0–18 year olds in the healthy weight range".

Within the framework of public health, three complementary philosophies were melded to provide the framework from which OPAL operates. The first, a socio-ecological approach, acknowledges the need to address the multiple tiers of society in which children are nested (Dahlberg and Krug 2002). The second, community development, recognizes the need to capitalize on the drive of the community to bring about lasting change through community participation, community capacity building, and community mobilization (Nutbeam and Harris 1998). Finally, social marketing was used to identify and implement effective strategies to stimulate behavior change (French and Blair-Stevens 2006).

OPAL acknowledges the complexity of dealing with overweight and obesity and consequently involves whole systems changes to influence individuals and the environments in which they live. This is achieved through OPAL's Seven Strategy approach that encompasses programs and services, partnerships, policies, environments, awareness, education, and evaluation (Weir and Williams 2013).

All initiatives undertaken as part of the OPAL program are linked by focusing on a defined target segment and a specific behavior. For example, to encourage children to drink more water (and fewer sugar-sweetened beverages), initiatives across the OPAL Seven Strategies were utilized. This included the development of tailored messages (awareness), supporting water-only policies in schools (policy), education material for a range of stakeholders (education), and modifying physical environments to include drinking water fountains (environments). Within the strategy of awareness, numerous initiatives were employed that included advertising (outdoor, print, and local radio), publicity (media releases and articles in council and library newsletters), direct marketing (brochures and electronic mail), public relations (displays and activities at community events), and sales promotions (supermarket displays, tastings, and samples).

From the outset, OPAL sought to raise awareness of both the program as a whole and specific healthy lifestyle messages. During the study period, regular themes provided focus around individual issues that can have a positive impact on healthy weight:

1. 'Introducing OPAL' positioned OPAL as a program that supports each community to eat well and be active. Implemented in the first 6 months of the program, it involved a needs analysis and auditing of the community prior to the implementation of interventions. Publicity was used to introduce the program to the community and invite input to the planning phase (see Fig. 2.1).
2. 'Water. The Original Cool Drink' promoted the benefits of water as the drink of first choice and targeted a reduction in the consumption of sugar-sweetened beverages. The associated publicity took two forms: promotion of new infrastructure (i.e., water coolers) and recognition of stakeholders (e.g., congratulating the council for the installation of a water drinking facility). Public recognition of stakeholders was critical for building capacity and support at the local level (see Fig. 2.2).

EFFORTS to combat obesity and help residents discover healthy lifestyles are being rolled out across the north.

Playford Council launched its OPAL Festival earlier this month to provide a range of low-cost or free activities that promote a healthy lifestyle to children and their families.

Fig. 2.1 Example of media coverage to introduce OPAL

Fig. 2.2 Example of media coverage for the theme 'Water. The Original Cool Drink'

3. 'Give the screen a rest, active play is best' promoted active play as an alternative to screen time and provided the community with a range of alternate activities. Local press coverage publicized the importance of children being active and away from screens.
4. 'Make it a Fresh Snack' focused on the replacement of energy-dense nutrient-poor snacks with foods from core food groups. Working upstream with retailers around the promotion of 'fresh snacks' was one strategy employed that proved to be effective in providing publicity opportunities for both the retailers and the theme.
5. 'Think Feet First – step, cycle, scoot to school' encouraged active travel to and from school. Interventions included safe walking routes to school, bike hire initiatives, and infrastructure to support bike parking at schools. These activities provided numerous opportunities for the media to report positive community stories.
6. 'A healthy brekky is easy as…Peel, Pour, Pop' addressed the nutritional quality of breakfast. This theme provided a range of education, program, awareness, and partnership opportunities, including a curriculum resource for schools, education sessions for parents, healthy eating policies in Out of School Care settings, and working with retailers on the promotion of healthy breakfast choices.

The multi-component OPAL evaluation incorporates a quasi-experimental design with 20 intervention and matched comparison sites. Given the nature of the matched comparison evaluation, it was critical to attempt to contain awareness of the program to those geographic regions identified as OPAL sites. As a result, most activities were conducted at the local level, with intentionally very limited statewide exposure. This meant the traditional reliance on mass media advertising was not available to the OPAL program, requiring a heightened emphasis on other promotional elements, especially publicity via local media. This was considered an appropriate approach because of the role of the media in forming and influencing attitudes and behaviors, broadening community knowledge, building credibility, contributing to the establishment of social norms, and gaining public recognition for key stakeholders. Publicity was actively sought by OPAL staff members who were trained in media skills, including media release writing, interview preparation, effective messaging, and relationship building with media outlets. Staff members were actively encouraged to write media releases to promote events and activities and to share positive achievements of the program.

4 Data Collection

Media monitoring data were captured by a media agency over the 4 years May 2009 to April 2013. Over this period, there were 20 active OPAL sites, 9 of which were regional and 11 were in the metropolitan area. Each OPAL story that appeared in the media was allocated to one or more pre-determined coding (sub)categories: *type of media*, *primary area of focus*, *target behaviors*, and *lead message*. Each of these categories is explained below. In addition, the proportion of favorable, neutral, and unfavorable coverage was recorded within each of the categories. The media agency used a standardized methodology involving multiple coders to assess the valence of each episode of coverage. Media mentions that were critical of individual elements of the OPAL program or the program in its entirety were classified as unfavorable, those that were clearly supportive were classified as favorable, and the remaining mentions were classified as neutral. Passing mentions of OPAL were not included in the evaluation – only stories that featured OPAL as a primary topic of interest in the article were captured and analyzed.

There were two categories of *media type* – press and broadcast. Press included local and state-wide print publications. Broadcast included reports appearing on radio and television. Although there were also efforts made by some councils to communicate via social media, these were not officially included in the OPAL promotion mix and hence were not monitored. *Areas of focus* in the media monitoring process included the two primary lifestyle behaviors of diet and physical activity and news items relating to the overall implementation and management of the program. The category of *target behaviors* included more specific forms of diet and exercise behaviors that were the topics of the various OPAL themes over the data collection period. Finally, the category of *lead message* related to more global mentions of the OPAL program and its effectiveness.

In addition to the media monitoring, a CATI (computer-aided telephone interview) survey was conducted over 6 weeks in mid-2013 (27 May–4 July 2013). The aim of the survey was to assess the extent to which the OPAL program was achieving its objectives, particularly in terms of program awareness and attitudinal and behavioral change. The survey was administered to 1082 parents in the intervention communities (councils where the OPAL Program was implemented) and 298 parents in the comparison (non-intervention) communities. Across the sample, three-quarters (73 %) were female and just over half (54 %) were based in the metropolitan area (46 % in regional areas). The age range with the greatest representation was 40–54 years (51 %), followed by 31–39 years (29 %). There was substantial variation within the sample in terms of income levels and occupational categories. The survey items assessed awareness of OPAL, recall of any media coverage of OPAL, and reported attitudinal and behavioral changes as a result of exposure to the program.

5 Results

Over the 4-year period, 377 media stories were identified that featured OPAL. Of these, 341 (90 %) were in the press media and the remainder were in the broadcast media. Of the press media stories, 91 % were in local media outlets and 9 % were in state-wide outlets. The percentage of state-wide media was intentionally low to limit exposure to OPAL in the control sites to avoid contaminating the evaluation. Nearly three-quarters (71 %) of the stories appeared in regional media outlets, with the remainder in metropolitan media outlets.

Table 2.1 shows the results of the data categorization process. Reflecting the alternate attention given to healthy eating and physical activity in the OPAL themes adopted as part of the social marketing program, approximately half of the media mentions that were coded to the focus areas and target behavior categories related to diet and half to physical activity. Relatively few media mentions related primarily to the organizational or administrative aspects of the program, with most attention being given to the health messages being disseminated.

Most of the media stories were assessed to be favorable (84 %). Of the remaining stories, 14 % were neutral and 2 % were unfavorable. Examples of media stories allocated to each of these valence categories are provided in Fig. 2.3. The few instances of unfavorable mentions were clustered into two main areas: dietary-related issues and perceived program effectiveness. However, even within these categories, the instances of unfavorable coverage were in the minority.

Among the CATI survey respondents in the intervention councils, 20 % demonstrated spontaneous awareness of the OPAL Program (i.e., they nominated OPAL when asked whether they were aware of any campaigns or programs that aim to support healthy eating or physical activity among children). This compared to only 1 % of those in the control communities. The spontaneous awareness rate in intervention communities was significantly higher among respondents residing in

Table 2.1 Publicity episodes by coding category and valence (n=377)

Category	Sub-category	Favorable n (%)	Neutral n (%)	Unfavorable n (%)	Total
Media type	Press	289 (85)	48 (14)	4 (1)	341
	Broadcast	29 (81)	4 (11)	3 (8)	36
Focus area	Healthy eating	93 (84)	14 (13)	4 (4)	111
	Physical activity	116 (83)	24 (17)	0 (0)	140
	Combined healthy eating and physical activity	63 (89)	7 (10)	1 (1)	71
	OPAL Program evaluation	11 (69)	3 (19)	2 (13)	16
	Council application for OPAL involvement	5 (71)	2 (29)	0 (0)	7
Target behavior	Improve home meals	115 (96)	5 (4)	0 (0)	120
	Increase fruit and veg as snacks and decrease junk food snacks	56 (100)	0 (0)	0 (0)	56
	Increase water consumption and decrease soft drink consumption	24 (96)	1 (4)	0 (0)	25
	Increase healthy breakfasts	6 (75)	1 (13)	1 (13)	8
	Increase active travel	87 (91)	9 (9)	0 (0)	96
	Increase active leisure	66 (88)	9 (12)	0 (0)	75
	Increase use of parks and places	16 (89)	2 (11)	0 (0)	18
	Decrease screen time and increase active play	13 (100)	0 (0)	0 (0)	13
Lead message	OPAL promotes positive health outcomes	245 (100)	n/a	0 (0)	245
	Government support for OPAL	61 (92)	n/a	5 (8)	66
	OPAL engages with the community	108 (100)	n/a	0 (0)	108
	Effectiveness of OPAL as a public health initiative	19 (68)	n/a	9 (32)	28

councils located in regional areas (30 %) compared to those in the metropolitan area (12 %; $p<0.001$). Total awareness (i.e., spontaneous and prompted awareness combined) was 41 % in the intervention communities. The equivalent figure for the control communities was 9 %. Once again, awareness levels in the intervention communities were significantly higher among respondents residing in the regional councils (54 %), compared to those residing in the metropolitan councils (29 %; $p<0.001$).

When asked where they had heard about OPAL, the primary category of responses related to campaign advertising in the form of brochures (76 %), posters (70 %), and signage (61 %). Publicity-related communications were the next most frequently mentioned category and included newspaper articles (40 %) and radio discussions (7 %).

Favourable

Amazing race for families

MUST VISIT FIVE PLAYGROUNDS

Ken McGregor

FAMILIES do not have to travel the world to be a part of *The Amazing Race* this summer – they just need to head to their playground.

The Obesity Prevention and Lifestyle Program (OPAL) has selected 20 Charles Sturt playgrounds as part of its own Amazing Race challenge which encourages families to get outside and enjoy their parks.

"It (the race) is a great idea because my kids are very active and I think they will love the challenge
- Natalie Phillipou

getting outdoors and would visit many of the playgrounds this summer.

"It (the race) is a great idea because my kids are very

Unfavourable

THE Opposition has criticised the $650,000 spent on a program develop company with junk-food industry links.

The Health Department is paying $653,070 in licensing fees over five years i the program, designed by French company Proteines.

It has been adapted for South Australia and introduced to schools and local c as the Obesity Prevention and Lifestyle (OPAL) program.

Neutral

HEALTH

Funds secured for prevention

A PROGRAM promoting healthy eating and physical activity will continue.

The Federal Government withdrew its $7 million funding of the Obesity Prevention and Lifestyle Program, which is run in partnership with local councils.

The State Budget did not outline if the shortfall would be covered, but the State Government last week committed $6.3 million over the next three years.

Fig. 2.3 Example of favorable, unfavorable, and neutral media

Attitudinal and behavioral change resulting from exposure to OPAL was also assessed. Forty-one percent of respondents reported that they felt they had a better understanding of "the benefits of eating well and being active" since exposure to the program, and 33 % indicated that they had "positively changed (their) attitudes towards eating well and being active". Almost one-third (30 %) reported that as a result of the program they had changed their dietary and exercise behaviors, and a further group of similar size (29 %) stated that they had "thought about changing (their) behavior towards eating well and being active but haven't changed yet".

6 Discussion

Social marketing is recognized as a comprehensive approach to social problems that includes consideration and inclusion of both downstream and upstream intervention measures (Andreasen 2002; Hoek and Jones 2011). The OPAL program described in this chapter incorporates a broad spectrum of upstream and downstream strategies to improve the quality of life of South Australians by encouraging healthy lifestyle behaviors, especially among children (Weir and Williams 2013). Part of the program implementation process involves attracting publicity across multiple media outlets to inform the public of the program, promote specific healthy behaviors, encourage the use of existing and new health-related infrastructure, and engender and maintain public support for the program to facilitate its continuation. Publicity is therefore used as a mechanism to achieve both upstream and downstream program outcomes because of its dual emphasis on individual behavior change and advocacy (Lefebvre 2011).

There are high levels of community interest in and concern about child obesity (Pettigrew et al. 2012; Thomas et al. 2014). This makes the issue newsworthy and therefore attractive to media outlets. Of the 377 media mentions that featured OPAL between 2009 and 2013, almost all were favorable (84 %) or neutral (14 %). In the absence of a traditional mass media campaign, this non-paid media coverage contributed to the outcome of 41 % of respondents in the intervention councils being aware of the program. The high level of favorable media coverage and the resulting contribution to community awareness are positive outcomes given the need for government-funded initiatives to receive community support to enhance the likelihood of their acceptance and ongoing sustainability.

There is always the risk of social marketing efforts resulting in unintended outcomes (Spotswood et al. 2012). In the case of publicity, this can occur in the form of unfavorable stories appearing in the media. In the small number of instances where unfavorable media coverage of OPAL was received over the 4-year study period, there was a tendency for diet-related issues, particularly concerns regarding body image, to attract more criticism than issues relating to physical activity. This outcome is consistent with the highly cultural and social nature of food (Douglas and Isherwood 1979; Kniazeva and Venkatesh 2007), which can make behavioral change in this area complex and contentious (Block et al. 2011). By comparison, behavioral recommendations in the domain of physical activity are relatively consistent and appear to have achieved a higher level of consensus and acceptance. This outcome may have implications for other public health programs using social marketing programs to achieve behavioral change across both diet- and exercise-related behaviors. By appreciating the increased likelihood of adverse publicity resulting from healthy eating messages, social marketers may be forewarned and therefore better able to anticipate, avoid, and deflect unfavorable coverage.

Effective social marketing requires a deep understanding of the role of communities (Lefebvre 2012). Communities are the context in which behaviors occur and where conversations relating to those behaviors take place, and as a result community-based initiatives are recognized as one of the most effective forms of social marketing application (Beall et al. 2012). As a community-based program that features intervention and control communities that are in close proximity to each other, OPAL relies on forms of communication that are capable of disseminating information at the community level. This situation is well-suited to print-based media outlets that reach specific geographical areas, and to a lesser extent radio stations that primarily service specific locations. This is reflected in the majority of publicity episodes occurring in the print media, most of which were in the form of local newspapers. The results also demonstrate that some communities may be more receptive than others to publicity relating to health programs. In this case, members of communities based in regional areas exhibited significantly and substantially higher levels of program awareness relative to those in the metropolitan area. This may reflect the differing characteristics of these communities, including greater prevalence of population and child obesity (ABS 2013c) and higher levels of social capital in regional/rural areas (Western et al. 2005). In addition, media outlets in regional areas often actively sought out OPAL stories to include in features about local events and activities. In combination, these factors may increase the exposure to and salience of OPAL messages in those in regional areas.

The study results have implications for other social marketing programs that do not involve traditional mass media communications due to the need to achieve differences in message exposure between adjacent intervention and control communities. In addition, few social marketing campaigns have generous budgets, making insights into the role and value of non-paid media potentially relevant to a wide range of social marketing applications. While the value of publicity as a commercial marketing tool is well understood (Berger et al. 2010), and many social marketing programs are likely to be already utilizing this tool to some degree, the study results indicate that publicity as a particular form of promotion may be worthy of increased attention and resourcing to capitalize on the potential for enhancing awareness of a program and its associated key communications messages.

This study has several limitations worthy of mention. In the first instance, records were not kept over the evaluation period of the number and type of media releases that were disseminated in aggregate or by individual councils. As a result, it is not possible to state the ratio of media releases generated to media coverage achieved. Second, although some councils were informally using social media to communicate with their community groups and other stakeholders, these activities were not monitored. This prevented any analysis of the extent to which they generated other forms of unpaid information dissemination relating to OPAL. Finally, a more comprehensive analysis would have included all forms of promotion utilized within OPAL to identify the relative contribution of publicity compared to other elements. However, this was beyond the scope of the present study.

To conclude, this analysis of the publicity generated for a comprehensive, community-based obesity-prevention program encompassing a social marketing approach indicates that publicity can play an important role in achieving program objectives to enhance the quality of life of target segments. This finding is important in the context of continuing concern about obesity rates and the recognized importance of social marketing programs to address this social problem (Beall et al. 2012). There are therefore likely to be many future programs of this kind, for which existing evidence-based guidance is lacking (Pettigrew et al. 2014). The results of the present study indicate that publicity can be used strategically to disseminate important information to target groups. This information can include both specific messages relating to health-related behaviors and more general messages relating to the purpose and effectiveness of the program.

Acknowledgements The authors acknowledge the contributions of the following organizations: Colmar Brunton for collecting and analyzing program-related data; iSentia for the analysis of the media articles; SA Health Media and Communications Branch for ongoing support of staff in their media work; and the Public Health Partnerships Branch of SA Health for their leadership in public health in South Australia.

References

Andreasen, A. (2002). Marketing social marketing in the social change marketplace. *Journal of Public Policy and Marketing, 21*(1), 3–13.

Aschemann-Witzel, J., Perez-Cueto, F. J., Niedzwiedzka, B., Verbeke, W., & Bech-Larsen, T. (2012). Lessons for public health campaigns from analysing commercial food marketing success factors: A case study. *BMC Public Health, 12*(1), 139–149.

Australian Bureau of Statistics. (2014). Labour force, Australia, Aug 2014. Catalogue no. 6202.0. Canberra: Australian Bureau of Statistics.

Australian Bureau of Statistics. (2013b). *Australian health survey: Updated results 2011–2012*. Catalouge no. 4364.0.55.003. Canberra: Australian Bureau of Statistics.

Australian Bureau of Statistics. (2013c). *Profiles of health, Australia, 2011–2013*. Catalogue no. 4338.0. Canberra: Australian Bureau of Statistics.

Australian Bureau of Statistics. (2014). *Labour force, Australia*. Catalogue no. 6202.0. Canberra: Australian Bureau of Statistics, Aug 2014.

Beall, T., Wayman, J., D'Agostino, H., Liang, A., & Perellis, C. (2012). Social marketing at a critical turning point. *Journal of Social Marketing, 2*(2), 103–117.

Berger, J., Sorensen, A. T., & Rasmussen, S. J. (2010). Positive effects of negative publicity: When negative reviews increase sales. *Marketing Science, 29*(5), 815–827.

Block, L., Grier, S. A., Davis, B., Ebert, J. E. J., Kumanyika, S., Laczniak, R. N., Machin, J. E., Motley, C. M., Peracchio, L., Pettigrew, S., Scott, M., & Ginkel Bieshaar, M. N. G. (2011). From nutrients to nurturance: A conceptual introduction to food well-being. *Journal of Public Policy and Marketing, 30*(1), 5–13.

Borys, J.-M., Le Bodo, Y., Jebb, S. A., Seidell, J. C., Summerbell, C., Richard, D., De Henauw, S., Moreno, L. A., Romon, M., Visscher, T. L. S., Raffin, S., & Swinburn, B. (2012). EPODE approach for childhood obesity prevention: Methods, progress and international development. *Obesity Reviews, 13*(4), 299–315.

Carins, J. E., & Rundle-Thiele, S. R. (2014). Eating for the better: A social marketing review (2000–2012). *Public Health Nutrition, 17*(07), 1628–1639.

Dahlberg, L. L., & Krug, E. G. (2002). Violence-a global public health problem. In E. Krug, L. L. Dahlberg, J. A. Mercy, A. B. Zwi, & R. Lozano (Eds.), *World report on violence and health* (pp. 1–56). Geneva: World Health Organization.

Department of Health. (2011). *Health in all policies: Background and practical guide* (p. 9). Version 2. Government of South Australia.

Douglas, M., & Isherwood, B. (1979). *The world of goods: Towards an anthropology of consumption*. London: Allen Lane.
French, J., & Blair-Stevens, C. (2006). From snake oil salesmen to trusted policy advisors: The development of a strategic approach to the application of social marketing in England. *Social Marketing Quarterly, 12*(3), 29–40.
French, S. A., Story, M., & Perry, C. L. (1995). Self-esteem and obesity in children and adolescents: A literature review. *Obesity Research, 3*, 479–90.
Gordon, R., McDermott, L., Stead, M., & Angus, K. (2006). The effectiveness of social marketing interventions for health improvement: What's the evidence? *Public Health, 120*(12), 1133–1139.
Gortmaker, S. L., Swinburn, B. A., Levy, D., Carter, R., Mabry, P. L., Finegood, D. T., Huang, T., Marsh, T., Marjory, L., & Moodie, M. L. (2011). Changing the future of obesity: Science, policy, and action. *Lancet, 378*, 838–847.
Gracia-Marco, L., Vicente-Rodríguez, G., Borys, J. M., Le Bodo, Y., Pettigrew, S., & Moreno, L. A. (2010). Contribution of social marketing strategies to community based obesity prevention programs in children. *International Journey of Obesity, 35*, 472–479.
Hastings, G., & Angus, K. (2011). When is social marketing not social marketing? *Journal of Social Marketing, 1*(1), 45–53.
Hastings, G., & Haywood, A. (1991). Social marketing and communication in health promotion. *Health Promotion International, 6*(2), 135–145.
Hoek, J., & Jones, S. C. (2011). Regulation, public health and social marketing: A behaviour change trinity. *Journal of Social Marketing, 1*(1), 32–44.
Huang, T., & Story, M. T. (2010). A journey just started: Renewing efforts to address childhood obesity. *Obesity, 18*(Suppl 1), S1–S3.
Hurry, J., Nunes, T., Bryant, P., Pretzlik, U., Parker, M., Curno, T., & Midgley, L. (2005). Transforming research on morphology into teacher practice. *Research Papers in Education, 20*(2), 187–206.
Kniazeva, M., & Venkatesh, A. (2007). Food for thought: a study of food consumption in postmodern US culture. *Journal of Consumer Behaviour, 6*(6), 419–435.
Lefebvre, R. C. (2011). An integrative model for social marketing. *Journal of Social Marketing, 1*(1), 54–72.
Lefebvre, R. C. (2012). Transformative social marketing: Co-creating the social marketing discipline and brand. *Journal of Social Marketing, 2*(2), 118–129.
Lobstein, T., & Dibb, S. (2005). Evidence of a possible link between obesogenic food advertising and child overweight. *Obesity Reviews, 6*(3), 203–208.
Nutbeam, D., & Harris, E. (1998). *Theory in a nutshell: A practitioner's guide to commonly used theories and models in health promotion*. Sydney: National Centre for Health Promotion.
Pettigrew, S., Pescud, M., Rosenberg, M., Ferguson, R., & Houghton, S. (2012). Public support for restrictions on food company sponsorship of community events. *Asia Pacific Journal of Clinical Nutrition, 21*(4), 609–617.
Pettigrew, S., Borys, J. M., Ruault du Plessis, H., Walter, L., Huang, T., Levi, J., & Vinck, J. (2014). Process evaluation outcomes from a global child obesity prevention intervention. *BMC Public Health*. doi:10.1186/1471-2458-14-757.
Romon, M., Lommez, A., Tafflet, M., Basdevant, A., Oppert, J. M., Bresson, J. L., Ducimetiere, P., Charles, M. A., & Borys, J. M. (2009). Downward trends in the prevalence of childhood overweight in the setting of 12-year school – and community-based programs. *Public Health Nutrition, 12*(10), 1735–1742.
Rutter, H. (2011). Where next for obesity? *Lancet, 378*(9793), 746–747.
Singh, A. S., Mulder, C., Twisk, J. W., van Mechelen, W., & Chinapaw, M. J. (2008). Tracking childhood overweight into adulthood: A systematic review of the literature. *Obesity Reviews, 9*(5), 474–488.
Spotswood, F., French, J., Tapp, A., & Stead, M. (2012). Some reasonable but uncomfortable questions about social marketing. *Journal of Social Marketing, 2*(3), 163–175.

Story, M., & French, S. (2004). Food advertising and marketing directed at children and adolescents in the US. *International Journal of Behavioral Nutrition and Physical Activity, 1*(1), 3–3.
Taskforce, N. O. (2003). *Healthy weight 2008 – Australia's future: The national action agenda for children and young people and their families*. Canberra: Commonwealth Department of Health and Ageing.
Thackeray, R., Neiger, B. L., & Hanson, C. L. (2007). Developing a promotional strategy: Important questions for social marketing. *Health Promotion Practice, 8*(4), 332–336.
Thomas, S. L., Olds, T., Pettigrew, S., Yeatman, H., Dragovic, C., & Hyde, J. (2014). Parent and child interactions with two contrasting anti-obesity advertising campaigns: A qualitative analysis. *BMC Public Health, 14*, 151–161.
Walls, H. L., Magliano, D. J., Stevenson, C. E., Backholer, K., Mannan, H. R., Shaw, J. E., & Peeters, A. (2012). Projected progression of prevalence of obesity in Australia. *Obesity, 20*(4), 872–878.
Walsh, D. C., Rudd, R. E., Moeykens, B. A., & Moloney, T. W. (1993). Social marketing for public health. *Health Affairs, 12*(2), 104–119.
Weir, L., & Williams, J. (2013). OPAL: Using a social marketing approach to reducing childhood obesity. In S. Rundle-Thiele & K. Kubacki (Eds.), *Contemporary issues in social marketing* (pp. 173–194). Newcastle upon Tyne: Cambridge Scholars.
Western, J., Stimson, R., Baum, S., & Van Gellecum, Y. (2005). Measuring community strength and social capital. *Regional Studies, 39*(8), 1095–1109.
World Health Organisation. (2000). *Obesity: Preventing and managing the global epidemic* (WHO technical report series). Geneva: World Health Organisation.
World Health Organization. (2014). *Overweight and obesity fact sheet no. 311*. Available http://www.who.int/mediacentre/factsheets/fs311/en/
Wymer, W. (2010). Rethinking the boundaries of social marketing: Activism or advertising? *Journal of Business Research, 63*(2), 99–103.
Wymer, W. (2011). Developing more effective social marketing strategies. *Journal of Social Marketing, 1*(1), 45–53.

Chapter 3
Digital Innovation in Social Marketing: A Systematic Literature of Interventions Using Digital Channels for Engagement

Krzysztof Kubacki, Sharyn Rundle-Thiele, Lisa Schuster, Carla Wessels, and Naomi Gruneklee

1 Introduction

Social marketing uses commercial marketing techniques to deliver interventions for social benefit in order to improve quality of life for individuals and communities. Behaviour change is the primary objective of social marketing interventions (Andreasen 2002). The aim of this systematic review is to provide insight into social marketing interventions and their evaluations published in peer-reviewed journals so as to identify the key elements of social marketing employed by these interventions as well as understand the use of digital channels for engagement. Social marketing provides a strategic planning framework combining consumer research, targeting and segmentation, behavioural focus and the marketing mix (MacFadyen et al. 2003).

The evidence synthesis on which this article was based was funded by Victorian Health Promotion Foundation (VicHealth). The funders played no role in study design, collection, analysis, interpretation of data, or in the decision to submit the paper for publication. They accept no responsibility for contents.

K. Kubacki (✉) • C. Wessels • N. Gruneklee
Social Marketing @ Griffith, Menzies Health Institute Queensland, Griffith University, Nathan, QLD 4111, Australia
e-mail: k.kubacki@griffith.edu.au

S. Rundle-Thiele
Social Marketing @ Griffith, Department of Marketing and Menzies Health Institute Queensland, Griffith University, Brisbane, QLD, Australia
e-mail: s.rundle-thiele@griffith.edu.au

L. Schuster
School of Advertising, Marketing and Public Relations, QUT Business School, Queensland University of Technology, Brisbane, QLD 4000, Australia
e-mail: lisa.schuster@qut.edu.au

W. Wymer (ed.), *Innovations in Social Marketing and Public Health Communication*, Applying Quality of Life Research,
DOI 10.1007/978-3-319-19869-9_3

Several planning frameworks have been developed by social marketers, including Levebvre and Flora (1988), French and Blair-Stevens (2006), and Robinson-Maynard, Meaton, and Lowry (2013). Some frameworks do not offer mutually exclusive criteria for categorisation purposes, for example, consumer orientation and insight are not easily distinguishable in the French and Blair-Stevens (2006) framework. Developed by Andreasen (2002), six social marketing benchmark criteria were proposed to distinguish social marketing from other public health approaches. The six benchmark criteria advocated by Andreasen (2002) include behavioural change, formative research, segmentation, the use of marketing mix, exchange and competition, and have been endorsed in the later frameworks (see French and Blair-Stevens 2006; Robinson-Maynard et al. 2013). See Andreasen (2002) and French and Blair-Stevens (2006) for detailed description of the six social marketing benchmark criteria.

Based on evidence demonstrating that when employed fully, the six social marketing benchmarks offer greater potential to change behaviours (Carins and Rundle-Thiele 2014), content analysis was undertaken to understand the extent to which the six benchmark social marketing criteria were employed in interventions using digital channels for engagement.

2 Methods

Following the systematic literature review procedures outlined in Carins and Rundle-Thiele (2014), a literature search was conducted to identify social marketing interventions using digital channels for engagement published between January 2000 and October 2013. Nine databases (see Table 3.1) were searched using the following terms: "digital*" OR "online*" OR "internet*" OR "mobile*" OR "social media*" AND "intervention*" or "Randomi#ed Controlled Trial" OR "evaluation" OR "trial" OR "campaign*" OR "program*" OR "intervention" or

Table 3.1 Databases and articles retrieved in initial search

Database	Number of articles retrieved by Researcher 1	Number of articles retrieved by Researcher 2
ProQuest All Databases	91	104
Web of Science	69	69
EBSCO All Databases	80	80
Medline (R; and InProcess) (Ovid)	116	116
PsycINFO (Ovid)	53	53
Taylor and Francis	8	9
INSPEC (Web of Knowledge)	12	22
Emerald	0	0
ScienceDirect	53	53
Total number of articles retrieved:	482	506

"interventions" AND "social marketing". Two independent researchers searched the nine databases shown in Table 3.1 in October 2013 using the same search procedures to ensure reliability. The search undertaken by Researcher 1 yielded 482 publications, and the search undertaken by Researcher 2 yielded 506 publications, which represents a greater than 95 % accuracy rate. The variance of records between databases can be attributed to the size and the specialisations of each database and how closely they relate to the search terms. ProQuest, for example, is made up of 20 databases.

All downloaded records were collated using Endnote, giving a total of 988 records. As multiple databases include the same journals, duplicate records had to be removed reducing the number of unique publications to 237. In the next stage, titles and abstracts of the remaining 237 publications were reviewed and classified. Publications were excluded on the following grounds: formative research, papers with no social marketing claim, review/conceptual papers, not journal articles and no digital component.

Following the application of the exclusion criteria, 32 articles comprising evaluations of social marketing interventions using digital channels remained. Backward and forward searching using authors' names and websites, intervention names, Google Scholar, "Publish or Perish" and reference lists was completed to identify a further 103 relevant publications from the corresponding time period and other publications providing additional information about the identified interventions, giving a total of 135 articles. In the next stage, the role of the digital component in each social marketing intervention was reviewed independently by two senior researchers. All interventions were discussed and classified into one of two groups:

- Major digital component: the interventions where the digital component played a significant role. Only the interventions where digital components formed a central role in influencing behaviour change in the intervention were included in this category.
- Minor digital component: the interventions where the digital component played an insignificant role, for example, in cases there was only a website describing the intervention, a contact email, intervention resources were placed online or a small amount of online advertising was used to recruit participants. Studies involving a minor digital component were excluded from the current study.

Both researchers were in agreement for all but one intervention, which was excluded following discussion between the researchers. Sixty-one articles outlining interventions involving a major digital component across 20 interventions were included in the final review presented in this paper. Figure 3.1 shows the literature search process. All interventions included in this paper self-identified as social marketing interventions.

All 61 included articles were analysed to identify evidence of each of Andreasen's (2002) six social marketing benchmark criteria. Further analysis was also completed to further explicate the digital channels used in the interventions. All identified relevant excerpts were reviewed by three social marketing researchers.

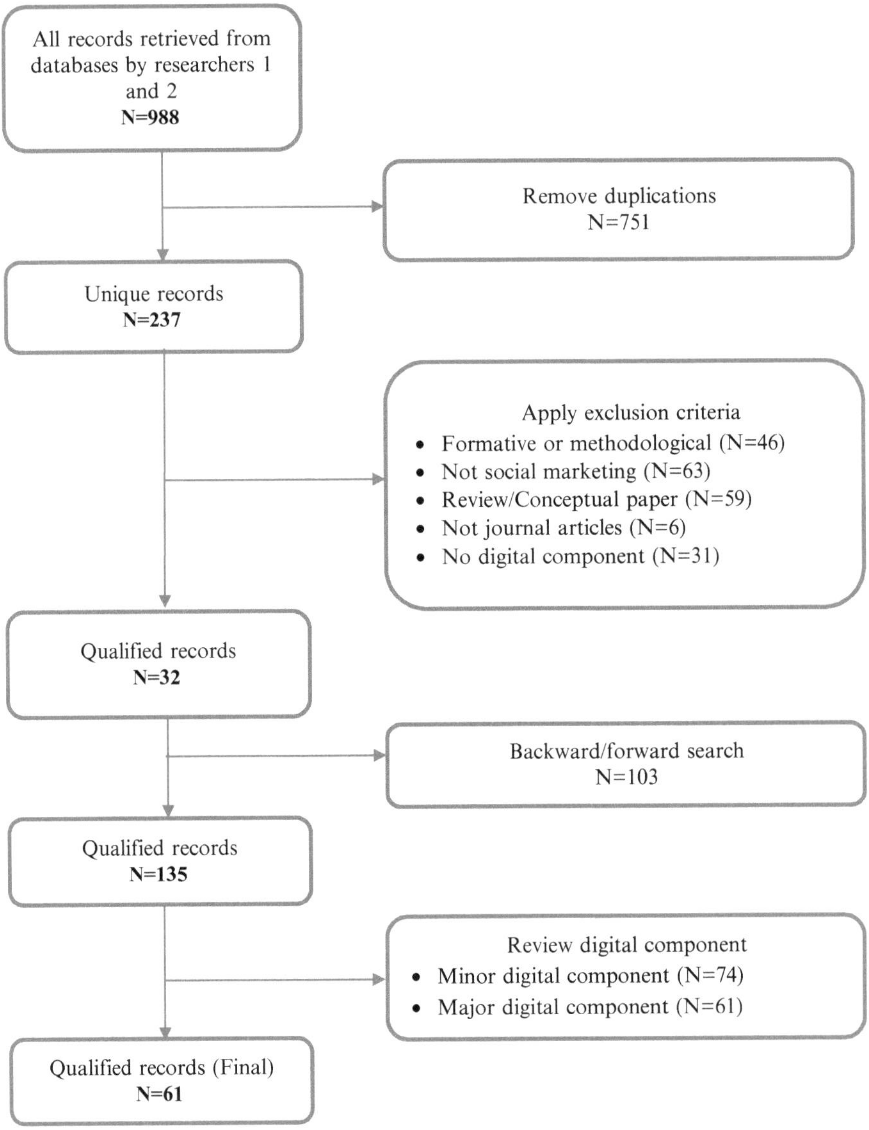

Fig. 3.1 Flowchart of the literature search process

3 Results and Discussion

3.1 Andreasen's (2002) Benchmark Criteria

Table 3.2 presents the assessment of each of the 20 social marketing interventions against Andreasen's (2002) benchmark criteria. Two of the interventions provided evidence indicating that they addressed all six social marketing benchmark criteria

Table 3.2 Assessment of the use of Andreasen's benchmark criteria in social marketing interventions

Intervention	Target audience	Behaviour	No. of SMBC	Behavioural objective	Segmentation	Formative research	Exchange	Marketing mix	Competition
Huhman et al. (2008)	Tweens	Physical activity	6	✓(+)[a]	✓	✓	✓	✓(3)[b]	✓
Purdy (2011)	Young professionals in Turkey	Sexual health	6	✓(+)	✓	✓	✓	✓(4)	✓
Short et al. (2006)	Community physicians	Intimate partner violence	5	✓(+)	✓	✘	✓	✓(3)	✓
Harris et al. (2009)	California physicians	Intimate partner violence	5	✓(+)	✓	✘	✓	✓(3)	✓
Buller et al. (2009)	18–65 year olds	Healthy eating	4	✓(=)	✘	✓	✘	✓(2)	✓
Justice-Gardiner et al. (2012)	Hispanic cancer survivors	Cancer support	4	✓(*)	✓	✘	✘	✓(3)	✓
Thompson et al. (2013)	Undergraduate students at a US university	Alcohol consumption	4	✓(+)	✘	✓	✓	✓(3)	✘
Ahrens et al. (2006)	Gay and bisexual men	Sexual health	3	✓(+)	✘	✓	✘	✓(4)	✘
Artz and Cooke (2007)	420 employees	Environmental behaviours	3	✓(+)	✘	✓	✘	✓(2)	✘
Atkinson et al. (2011)	Young alcohol drinkers, 18–24 years	Alcohol consumption	3	✓(*)	✘	✓	✘	✘	✓

(continued)

Table 3.2 (continued)

Intervention	Target audience	Behaviour	No. of SMBC	Behavioural objective	Segmentation	Formative research	Exchange	Marketing mix	Competition
Bryn (2011)	Tweens, 9–13 years and the adults in their lives	Bullying	3	✓(*)	✗	✓	✗	✓(3)	✗
Dixon-Gray et al. (2013)	Latinas, 18–29 years, born in the US	Sexual health	3	✗	✓	✓	✗	✗	✓
James et al. (2013)	Primary food preparer with children 10 and under	Food safety practices	3	✓(+)	✗	✓	✗	✓(3)	✗
Macario et al. (2013)	Older teens	Drug abuse	3	✗	✗	✓	✗	✓(2)	✓
McDonnell et al. (2010)	Korean Americans, 18 years or older, current smokers	Smoking	3	✓(=)	✗	✓	✗	✓(2)	✓
Plourde et al. (2008)	Floridians	Flu prevention	3	✓(+)	✓	✓	✗	✗	✓

Rotblatt et al. (2013)	African American, Latina females aged 12–25 years	Sexual health	3	✓(+)	✓	✘	✘	✓(4)	✘
Rundle-Thiele et al. (2013)	14–16 year old high school students	Alcohol consumption	3	✘	✘	✓	✘	✓(2)	✓
Vessey and O'Neill (2011)	9–14 year olds; with documented disability	Bullying	3	✘	✘	✓	✓	✓(3)	✘
Whittaker et al. (2008)	16 + years, current daily smokers, ready to quit	Smoking	3	✓(=)	✘	✓	✘	✓(3)	✘

[a]+ positive behavioural outcomes reported, = no behavioural change, * behavioural outcomes not reported
[b]The number of Ps reported in the intervention

(see Huhman et al. 2008; Purdy 2011). Consistent with previous literature reviews (Carins and Rundle-Thiele 2014), if the use of at least two of the marketing mix elements (product, place, price or promotion) was reported in an intervention, it was considered to have employed the marketing mix.

3.1.1 Behavioural Objective

Digital channels offer interactivity and anonymity to audiences that would not be accessible by, or willing to engage with, more traditional media. Private behaviours were most frequently the focus of interventions within the review (n = 8). Four interventions focused on sexual health behaviours including preconception health among young Latina females (Dixon-Gray et al. 2013), safe sex and condom use among young professionals and young married couples (Purdy 2011), syphilis testing among gay and bisexual men (Ahrens et al. 2006), and chlamydia and gonorrhoea testing among Latina females aged 12–25 years (Rotblatt et al. 2013). Two interventions promoted online continuing medical education for intimate partner violence to a target physician audience (Harris et al. 2009; Short et al. 2006) and another two focused on bullying among children (Bryn 2011; Vessey and O'Neill 2011).

According to Andreasen (1994), "the bottom line of social marketing is behaviour change" (p. 111). The interventions' behavioural aims were directed toward the target behaviour or adoption of the digital tools to promote behaviour change. Sixteen social marketing interventions aimed to change behaviours. Nine interventions aimed to change more than just behaviours, with eight interventions also aiming to change knowledge and/or awareness. The majority of interventions targeted very specific behaviours. For example, Plourde et al. (2008) aimed to reduce the spread of flu by targeting hand washing and other preventive behaviours, and Rotblatt et al. (2013) tried to encourage young women to screen routinely for sexually transmitted diseases. Ten of the interventions reported positive behavioural outcomes, and no negative outcomes were reported in any of the interventions.

It is interesting to note that three interventions had explicit engagement aims (Atkinson et al. 2011; Bryn 2011; Macario et al. 2013), and two of them reported positive outcomes (Bryn 2011; Macario et al. 2013). Atkinson et al. (2011) aimed to engage young adults by generating online peer-to-peer conversations about the negative consequences of binge drinking. The long-term objective of this intervention was to encourage behaviour change by delivering sensible drinking messages in a realistic and engaging manner. Macario et al. (2013) aimed to create a community of teens to provide them with a forum responding to current teen interests. In contrast to the previous two interventions' aims, which relate to encouraging the target audience to engage with the campaign, Bryn (2011) aimed to engage organisational partners in the campaign by developing and fostering relationships.

3.1.2 Segmentation

One of the key principles underpinning marketing thinking is an understanding that the allocation of scarce resources needs to be optimised to maximise the effectiveness of the intervention. Andreasen's (2002) third benchmark criterion states that careful segmentation of target audiences "ensures maximum efficiency and effectiveness in the use of scarce resources" (p. 104). Segmentation can employ one or more demographic, psychographic, geographic, behavioural and epidemiological factors, and is based on the understanding that populations are typically heterogeneous (Evers et al. 2013), but that groups with similar needs and wants can be identified. Although all of the social marketing interventions reviewed in this chapter had clearly defined target audiences, only eight exhibited evidence of segmentation.

Purdy's (2011) intervention provided two types of condoms, Fiesta and Kiss, with Fiesta condoms targeted at more affluent consumers at a higher price point and with more variants than Kiss condoms. The Short et al. (2006) and Harris et al. (2009) interventions developed separate sets of cases tailored to health professionals in different clinical areas, while specialised messages and media strategies were developed for Native American, African American, Asian American and Hispanic/Latino tweens through extensive formative and message-testing research in Huhman et al. (2008). The last four interventions adapted their materials into at least one other language: Spanish and English (Dixon-Gray et al. 2013; Justice-Gardiner et al. 2012; Rotblatt et al. 2013), and Spanish, Creole and English (Plourde et al. 2008). Six out of eight interventions employing the principles of segmentation reported positive behavioural outcomes.

3.1.3 Formative Research

Formative research was reported in 16 of the social marketing interventions included in the review. Formative research is essential to any social marketing intervention (Andreasen 2002) as it provides an opportunity for the social marketer to learn about the target audience and how to best design an intervention to meet their needs. A clear focus on interviews, secondary research and focus groups as formative research methods was observed. Focus groups were the most popular method used (11 interventions), followed by secondary research (seven interventions) and interviews (six interventions). The use of more than one formative research method was evident in 12 interventions, and only James et al. (2013), Atkinson et al. (2011), and Artz and Cooke (2007) relied solely on secondary research. Further, five interventions (Bryn 2011; Huhman et al. 2008; Thompson et al. 2013; Vessey and O'Neill 2011; Whittaker et al. 2008) used three or more different methods to investigate their target audience(s). Finally, two of the interventions in this review incorporated use of other methods in their formative research design. For example, Huhman et al. (2008) used additional ethnographic inquiries and audience research, while prototype review and card sorting activities were used in Buller et al. (2009).

3.1.4 Exchange

According to French and Blair-Stevens (2006), exchange in the context of social marketing describes something that a person has to give up in order to get the proposed benefit of the intervention. In this review, exchange was treated as *direct exchange*, meaning that the target audience is required to relinquish something tangible or intangible in order to receive a direct benefit. Over time, performing an exchange or multiple exchanges is expected to lead to the desired behaviour. Six interventions identified in this review included clear evidence of exchange, and five of them reported positive behavioural outcomes. In two interventions targeting students, participants were required to forego drinking alcohol as a condition of attending the alcohol-free events (Thompson et al. 2013). Participants were offered incentives including a celebratory party, a certificate of participation and a *Stop Bullying Now* t-shirt in exchange for participation in a support-group program in Vessey and O'Neill (2011). In another two interventions, health professionals were required to give up their time in order to complete the program in exchange for a continuing medical education credit (Short et al. 2006; Harris et al. 2009). In Huhman et al.'s study (2008), tweens could exchange the amount of physical activity they recorded for additional energy and tricks/moves for their 'ViRTs' or virtual sidekicks, and for entry into sweepstakes for prizes such as a scooter or bike. Finally, more traditional market exchange was offered by Purdy (2011), whose intervention provided condoms available for purchase by consumers.

3.1.5 Marketing Mix

Social marketing interventions involve the use of multiple strategies, including the 4Ps of the traditional marketing mix: product, price, place and promotion (Evers et al. 2013). Interventions which use a single element of the marketing mix are generally less effective than those interventions that use more than one (French 2009). Three interventions employed the entire marketing mix and reported positive behavioural outcomes (Ahrens et al. 2006; Purdy 2011; Rotblatt et al. 2013). In contrast, another three interventions solely relied on promotion (Atkinson et al. 2011; Dixon-Gray et al. 2013; Plourde et al. 2008), and only one of the interventions reported positive behavioural outcomes. They therefore represent examples of what Carins and Rundle-Thiele (2014) described as social advertising.

In the context of an intervention, major product elements include the benefits derived from an exchange by the target audience and any goods and services required to support the desired behaviour (Lee and Kotler 2011). Seventeen interventions included either a tangible good or intangible service designed to support or facilitate the desired behaviour(s). For example, six interventions provided educational programs and resources (Buller et al. 2009; Harris et al. 2009; McDonnell et al. 2010; Rundle-Thiele et al. 2013; Short et al. 2006; Thompson et al. 2013). In terms of tangible goods, Rotblatt et al. (2013) provided a home testing kit for chlamydia and gonorrhoea to encourage testing in young African American and Latina women. In Huhman et al.'s (2008) intervention, as another example, 500,000 yellow balls were distributed across the US, each with a unique code enabling tweens to register the ball and blog about what they did, before passing it on to another tween. In terms of intangible services, one intervention comprised support group sessions based on 12 webisodes to help students with disabilities manage bullying (Vessey and O'Neill 2011).

Promotional tools are used to communicate desired outcomes and inform, remind and persuade the target audience about the value of the product and behaviour change (Andreasen 2002). All of the social marketing interventions in this review used promotional tools to raise awareness of the intervention, enforce a particular message and/or to promote social marketing activities. A range of traditional offline and online media were employed. For example, Huhman et al. (2008) reported the use of paid advertising in targeted television (e.g. Cartoon Network), radio (e.g. Radio Disney) and print media (e.g. Teen People), which the intervention supplemented with an expanding digital presence including websites and interactive advertising on the floors of more than 80 malls and movie theatres (i.e. Reactrix). Further, 'street' teams were employed, consisting of five to eight college-aged men and women hired to engage tweens in being physically active at events and tween hangouts. Another intervention included advertising on television and radio as well as billboards, posters and stickers in English and Spanish, and incorporated using social networking (e.g. MySpace), video sharing websites (e.g. YouTube) and blogs to further engage people in flu prevention behaviours (Plourde et al. 2008). The intervention was integrated through its focus on 'Ben Mitchell', a fictional character played by an actor, shown to be continually breaking flu hygiene rules and highlighting the negative reactions of the people around him.

Price is the cost or sacrifice exchanged for the product. Costs in social marketing may be monetary or non-monetary in nature, including the time, effort and energy required to perform the behaviour, in addition to the perceived psychological risks and losses as well as physical discomforts that may be associated with the behaviour (Lee and Kotler 2011). This review focused only on the overt monetary costs associated with the social marketing intervention or with the desired behaviour(s). Seven interventions (Bryn 2011; Ahrens et al. 2006; Harris et al. 2009; Purdy 2011; Rotblatt et al. 2013; Short et al. 2006; Whittaker et al. 2008) provided their products at no, or a subsidised, monetary cost as is typical in social marketing.

Place, on the other hand, refers to where and when the target audience enters into an exchange. In this review, seven interventions considered place. For example, alternative syphilis testing sites were established (Ahrens et al. 2006) and alcohol-free activities were offered on a university campus (Thompson et al. 2013).

3.1.6 Competition

Andreasen's (2002) social marketing benchmark criteria require recognising and addressing the competition of the behaviour targeted by an intervention. The social marketer has to understand what other behaviours or ideas are competing for the chosen target audience's time and attention in order to develop strategies that minimise the impact of the competition (Andreasen 2002; Peattie and Peattie 2003). According to Hastings (2003), social marketing needs to offer "unique and meaningful benefits" (p. 8) that provide better value than the competition. Twelve of the reviewed interventions featured some evidence of considering competition. Seven of the interventions (Harris et al. 2009; Justice-Gardiner et al. 2012; McDonnell et al. 2010; Plourde et al. 2008; Purdy 2011; Rundle-Thiele et al. 2013; Short et al. 2006) considered other campaigns as direct competition, while three identified commercial messages in the media as a form of competition (Atkinson et al. 2011; Macario et al. 2013; Rundle-Thiele et al. 2013). Three interventions viewed other behaviours as competition, for example sedentary activities such as watching TV and playing computer games (Huhman et al. 2008), consumption of processed food (Dixon-Gray et al. 2013), and using less healthy recipes (Buller et al. 2009). Last, other commercial brands of condoms were mentioned by Purdy (2011).

3.2 Digital Components of the Interventions

Increasingly, social marketing interventions are employing digital channels, such as the Internet and mobile devices, due to their low cost and high reach. However, these new channels are not replacing traditional channels; rather, they are being added to the mix (Bernhardt et al. 2009). This augments the complexity of designing and implementing integrated interventions that achieve behaviour change. Nevertheless, there is growing evidence that social marketing interventions which employ digital technology have the capacity to change behaviour (Cugelman et al. 2011). Digital channels formed a major component of all the interventions included in this review. Seven interventions utilised four or more digital components (Huhman et al. 2008; James et al. 2013; Macario et al. 2013; Plourde et al. 2008; Purdy 2011; Rotblatt et al. 2013; Thompson et al. 2013). The most commonly used digital components were websites (n=13), social media (n=7) and online advertising (n=7), which were used as a means to deliver targeted information, videos and webisodes or to promote the intervention and its messages. These tools were also used to redirect users to websites, online programs and/or online games. Table 3.3 outlines the digital components of the 20 social marketing interventions in this review.

Sixteen of the interventions employed more than one digital channel. For instance, the *Sara Bellum Blog* (Macario et al. 2013) formed part of an integrated outreach program for teens that also included webisodes, online games, YouTube videos, a presence in virtual worlds (i.e. Whyville) and social media (i.e. Facebook and Twitter), a Virtual Information Centre database, a listserv and downloadable t-shirts.

Four of the 20 interventions used online programs in conjunction with one or more of the following: online advertising, websites and/or mobile phones. Online programs included testing programs (Ahrens et al. 2006; Rotblatt et al. 2013), an online teaching program (Harris et al. 2009) and an online self-help smoking

Table 3.3 Digital components of social marketing interventions

Intervention	Online program	Mobile phone	Video-sharing	Social media	Webisode (s)	Website(s)	Online game(s)	Online ad(s)	Blog(s)/ discussion board(s)	Email
Dixon-Gray et al. (2013)				✓		✓				
Thompson et al. (2013)			✓	✓		✓		✓		
James et al. (2013)		✓	✓	✓		✓				
Purdy (2011)			✓	✓		✓		✓	✓	✓
Plourde et al. (2008)			✓	✓		✓			✓	
Buller et al. (2009)						✓	✓			
Rundle-Thiele et al. (2013)							✓			
Ahrens et al. (2006)	✓							✓		
Atkinson et al. (2011)					✓	✓			✓	
Rotblatt et al. (2013)	✓	✓				✓				✓
Justice-Gardiner et al. (2012)		✓		✓		✓				
Short et al. (2006)	✓									
Harris et al. (2009)	✓					✓		✓		

(continued)

Table 3.3 (continued)

Intervention	Online program	Mobile phone	Video-sharing	Social media	Webisode (s)	Website(s)	Online game(s)	Online ad(s)	Blog(s)/ discussion board(s)	Email
McDonnell et al. (2010)	✓							✓		
Macario et al. (2013)			✓	✓	✓	✓	✓		✓	
Bryn (2011)					✓	✓	✓			
Whittaker et al. (2008)		✓						✓		
Artz and Cooke (2007)										✓
Vessey and O'Neill (2011)					✓					
Huhman et al. (2008)		✓				✓	✓	✓	✓	

cessation program (McDonnell et al. 2010). Another five interventions utilised mobile phones as a means to inform, notify and/or encourage target audience(s), for example, iPhone/iPad applications were developed to encourage safe food handling of leftovers (James et al. 2013). Text messages provided information (Justice-Gardiner et al. 2012; Whittaker et al. 2008), encouragement to perform the desired behaviour (Huhman et al. 2008), and were used to notify individuals of test results (Rotblatt et al. 2013).

Video-sharing involved posting videos on popular video sharing sites such as YouTube, Yahoo and Daily Motions, and five interventions used this digital strategy (James et al. 2013; Macario et al. 2013; Plourde et al. 2008; Purdy 2011; Thompson et al. 2013). These interventions, together with Dixon-Gray et al. (2013) and Justice-Gardiner et al. (2012), also used one or more social media sites (i.e. Facebook, MySpace and/or Twitter) to inform, educate, engage and/or raise awareness amongst target audiences. Several other interventions also used blogs and/or discussion boards (n=5), webisodes (n=4) and online games (n=5).

Online advertising (i.e. Google AdWords, Yahoo! Search Ads, banner advertisements and advertisements on other websites) was employed by seven interventions to promote and/or redirect users to the intervention websites. The majority of interventions used websites (n=13). Websites can serve multiple purposes and incorporate a variety of functions ranging from providing information, resources and support (Bryn 2011) to interactive components such as a Blood Alcohol Calculator (BAC) calculator and other activities/tips (Thompson et al. 2013). In Purdy's (2011) study, the intervention website promoted condom use and also included a section entitled "safe sex" where visitors could access educational materials. Another intervention posted information and episodes from a radionovela to the website weekly (Dixon-Gray et al. 2013), whilst women with positive results could receive guidance on the website in the Rotblatt et al. (2013) study.

4 Conclusions

This chapter sought to review interventions that self-identified as social marketing that reported major use of digital channels for engagement to identify the role and extent to which key elements of social marketing were employed in the interventions. Using commercial marketing techniques, social marketing delivers interventions for social benefit to improve quality of life for individuals and communities. The use of digital technologies is a highly innovative and rapidly growing area within social marketing. This review indicates that social marketers are following commercial marketing trends by adopting new, more interactive digital media to improve quality of life. Their relatively low cost per contact and significant creative opportunities to engage audiences in behaviour change offers important benefits to social marketers. However, this review indicates that only two of the 20 social marketing interventions applied social marketing to its fullest extent, and 13 interventions applied three of the social marketing benchmark criteria (Andreasen 2002).

While behavioural objectives, formative research and marketing mix clearly featured in the majority of the interventions, evidence of widespread use of segmentation and exchange was lacking. As the online environment creates many low-cost creative opportunities for segmentation, future research needs to focus on the effective use of market segmentation in social marketing online interventions.

This review adds to the growing evidence base supporting the use of digital technologies in social marketing. Previous research indicates that digital technology in social marketing can change behaviours (Cugelman et al. 2011). Many of the interventions targeted private behaviours (e.g. sexual health, intimate partner violence, bullying). The most commonly used digital channels included intervention websites, social media and online advertisements, and the majority of interventions used more than one channel to increase their effectiveness and engage audiences in behaviour change. It is evident that further opportunities exist in the use of online screening (e.g. webisodes), video-sharing, online games and mobile phones. Last, it is important to note that digital technologies is a relatively new and fast growing area of social marketing, and 13 of the studies reviewed in this chapter were published between 2010 and 2013.

References

Ahrens, K., Kent, C. K., Montoya, J. A., Rotblatt, H., Mccright, J., Kerndt, P., & Klausner, J. D. (2006). Healthy penis: San Francisco's social marketing campaign to increase syphilis testing among gay and bisexual men. *PLoS Medicine, 3*, 2199–2203. doi:10.1371/journal.pmed.0030474.

Andreasen, A. R. (1994). Social marketing: Its definition and domain. *Journal of Public Policy & Marketing, 13*(1), 108–114.

Andreasen, A. R. (2002). Marketing social marketing in the social change marketplace. *Journal of Public Policy and Marketing, 21*(1), 3–13. doi:10.1509/jppm.21.1.3.17602.

Artz, N., & Cooke, P. (2007). Using e-mail Listservs to promote environmentally sustainable behaviors. *Journal of Marketing Communications, 13*, 257–276. doi:10.1080/13527260701250828.

Atkinson, A. M., Sumnall, H., & Measham, F. (2011). Depictions of alcohol use in a UK Government partnered online social marketing campaign: Hollyoaks "The Morning after the night before". *Drugs: Education, Prevention, and Policy, 18*(6), 454–467. doi:10.3109/09687637.2010.534745.

Bernhardt, J. M., Mayes, D., Eroglu, D., & Daniel, K. L. (2009). New communication channels: Changing the nature of consumer engagement. *Social Marketing Quarterly, 15*(1), 7–15. doi:10.1080/15245000902960924.

Bryn, S. (2011). Stop bullying now! A federal campaign for bullying prevention and intervention. *Journal of School Violence, 10*, 213–219. doi:10.1080/15388220.2011.557313.

Buller, M. K., Kane, I. L., Dunn, A. L., Edwards, E. J., Buller, D. B., & Liu, X. (2009). Marketing fruit and vegetable intake with interactive games on the internet. *Social Marketing Quarterly, 15*(1), 136–154. doi:10.1080/15245000903038316.

Carins, J. E., & Rundle-Thiele, S. R. (2014). Eating for the better: A social marketing review (2000–2012). *Public Health Nutrition, 17*(7), 1–12. doi:10.1017/S1368980013001365.

Cugelman, B., Thelwall, M., & Dawes, P. (2011). Online interventions for social marketing health behavior change campaigns: A meta-analysis of psychological architectures and adherence factors. *Journal of Medical Internet Research, 13*(1), e17. doi:10.2196/jmir.1367.

Dixon-Gray, L. A., Mobley, A., McFarlane, J. M., & Rosenberg, K. D. (2013). Amor y Salud (Love and Health): A preconception health campaign for second-generation Latinas in Oregon. *American Journal of Health Promotion, 27*(3), S74–S76. doi:10.4278/ajhp.120113-ARB-29.

Evers, U., Jones, S. C., Caputi, P., & Iverson, D. (2013). Promoting asthma awareness to older adults: Formative research for a social marketing campaign. *Journal of Asthma and Allergy Educators, 4*(2), 77–84. doi:10.1177/2150129713481039.

French, J. (2009). The nature, development and contribution of social marketing to public health practice since 2004 in England. *Perspectives in Public Health, 129*(6), 262–267. doi:10.1177/1757913909347655.

French, J., & Blair-Stevens, C. (2006). *Social marketing National Benchmark Criteria*. London: UK National Social Marketing Centre. http://www.snh.org.uk/pdfs/sgp/A328466.pdf. Accessed 2 July 2014.

Harris, J. M., Jr., Novalis-Marine, C., Amend, R. W., & Surprenant, Z. J. (2009). Promoting free online CME for intimate partner violence: What works at what cost? *Journal of Continuing Education in the Health Professions, 29*(3), 135–141. doi:10.1002/chp.20025.

Hastings, G. (2003). Competition in social marketing. *Social Marketing Quarterly, 9*(3), 6–10. doi:10.1080/15245000309109.

Huhman, M., Bauman, A., & Bowles, H. R. (2008). Initial outcomes of the VERB campaign: Tweens' awareness and understanding of campaign messages. *American Journal of Preventive Medicine, 34*(6 Suppl), S241–S248. doi:10.1016/j.amepre.2008.03.006.

James, K. J., Albrecht, J. A., Litchfield, R. E., & Weishaar, C. A. (2013). A summative evaluation of a food safety social marketing campaign "4-Day Throw-Away" using traditional and social media. *Journal of Food Science Education, 12*(3), 48–55. doi:10.1111/1541-4329.12010.

Justice-Gardiner, H., Nutt, S., Rechis, R., Mcmillan, B., & Warf, R. (2012). Using new media to reach Hispanic/Latino cancer survivors. *Journal of Cancer Education, 27*(1), 100–104. doi:10.1007/s13187-011-0267-2.

Lee, N. R., & Kotler, P. (2011). *Social marketing: Influencing behaviors for good* (3rd ed.). Los Angeles: Sage.

Levebvre, R. C., & Flora, J. A. (1988). Social marketing and public health intervention. *Health Education Quarterly, 15*(3), 299–315. doi:10.1177/109019818801500305.

Macario, E., Krause, C., Katt, J. C., Caplan, S., Payes, R. S., & Bornkessel, A. (2013). NIDA engages teens through its blog: Lessons learned. *Journal of Social Marketing, 3*(1), 41–55. doi:10.1108/20426761311297225.

MacFadyen, L., Stead, M., & Hastings, G. (2003). *Social marketing: The marketing book* (5th ed.). Oxford: Butterworth Heinemann.

McDonnell, D. D., Lee, H., Kazinets, G., & Moskowitz, J. M. (2010). Online recruitment of targeted populations: Lessons learned from a smoking cessation study among Korean Americans. *Social Marketing Quarterly, 16*(3), 2–22. doi:10.1080/15245004.2010.500441.

Peattie, S., & Peattie, K. (2003). Ready to fly solo? Reducing social marketing's dependence on commercial marketing theory. *Marketing Theory, 3*(3), 365–385. doi:10.1177/147059310333006.

Plourde, C., Cook, L. C., Mitchell, P., & Jennings, C. (2008). Talk to the fifth guy: A lesson in social marketing. *Cases in Public Health Communication and Marketing, 2*, 11–38. www.casesjournal.org/volume2. Accessed 25 July 2014.

Purdy, C. H. (2011). Using the internet and social media to promote condom use in Turkey. *Reproductive Health Matters, 19*(37), 157–165. doi:10.1016/S0968-8080(11)37549-0.

Robinson-Maynard, A., Meaton, J., & Lowry, R. (2013). Identifying key criteria as predictors of success in social marketing: Establishing an evaluation template and grid. In S. Rundle-Thiele & K. Kubacki (Eds.), *Contemporary issues in social marketing* (pp. 41–58). Newcastle upon Tyne: Cambridge Scholars Publishing.

Rotblatt, H., Montoya, J. A., Plant, A., Guerry, S., & Kerndt, P. R. (2013). There's no place like home: First-year use of the "I Know" home testing program for chlamydia and gonorrhoea. *American Journal of Public Health, 103*(8), 1376–1380. doi:10.2105/AJPH.2012.301010.

Rundle-Thiele, S. R., Russell-Bennett, R., Leo, C., & Dietrich, T. (2013). Moderating teen drinking: Combining social marketing and education. *Health Education, 113*(5), 392–406. doi:10.1108/HE-07-2012-0041.

Short, L. M., Surprenant, Z. J., & Harris, J. M. (2006)). A community based trial of an online intimate partner violence CME program. *American Journal of Preventive Medicine, 30*(2), 181–185. doi:10.1016/j.amepre.2005.10.012.

Thompson, E. B., Heley, F., Oster-Aaland, L., Stastny, S. N., & Crawford, E. C. (2013). The impact of a student-driven social marketing campaign on college student alcohol-related beliefs and behaviors. *Social Marketing Quarterly, 19*(4), 52–64. doi:10.1177/1524500412472668.

Vessey, J. A., & O'Neill, K. M. (2011). Helping students with disabilities better address teasing and bullying situations: A MASNRN study. *Journal of School Nursing, 27*(2), 139–148. doi:10.1177/1059840510386490.

Whittaker, R., Maddison, R., Mcrobbie, H., Bullen, C., Denny, S., Dorey, E., & Rodgers, A. (2008). A multimedia mobile phone-based youth smoking cessation intervention: Findings from content development and piloting studies. *Journal of Medical Internet Research, 10*(5), e49. doi:10.2196/jmir.1007.

Chapter 4
Does Context Matter? Australian Consumers' Attitudes to the Use of Messages and Appeals in Commercial and Social Marketing Advertising

Sandra C. Jones and Katherine Eagleton

1 Introduction

There is considerable ongoing debate in Australia, as in other countries, about the ethicality of current advertising practices. In recent years there has been an increase in the public focus on offensive or unacceptable advertising – such as overt sex appeals, racial vilification, and promotion of unsafe use of consumer products – arguing that many of these advertisements are contrary to community standards. The industry, on the other hand, argues that it produces ads that are designed to appeal to target audiences and be consistent with community standards.

A 2004 Morgan poll reported that only 13 % of the Australian public rated the advertising industry as "high" or "very high" on ethics and honesty, with only three other professions (newspaper journalists, real estate agents and car salesman) receiving a lower ranking (Morgan Poll 2004). Brinkmann (2002, p. 160) expressed the view that "there is almost a suspicion that marketers' references to values and ideals are a marketing trick, an oxymoron." There is no comprehensive data on the nature of community standards in relation to advertising – both in terms of what is deemed to be (un)acceptable and the underlying philosophical viewpoints on which these decisions are based; the current study was designed to begin to address this gap.

S.C. Jones (✉)
Centre for Health and Social Research (CHaSR), Australian Catholic University, Melbourne, VIC, Australia
e-mail: Sandra.Jones@acu.edu.au

K. Eagleton
Medical School, Australian National University, Canberra, ACT, Australia
e-mail: katherine.eagleton@anu.edu.au

W. Wymer (ed.), *Innovations in Social Marketing and Public Health Communication*, Applying Quality of Life Research,
DOI 10.1007/978-3-319-19869-9_4

1.1 The Commercial Advertising Context

Commercial advertisers seek to develop advertisements that will maximise the appeal of their product to the target market, and the likelihood of purchase (while not breaching any legal or regulatory requirements, or offending other members of the community). This can require a trade-off on the part of the advertiser (e.g., the likelihood of selling a product to single adult males may be increased if you can persuade them that it increases their chances of sexual success, but such a message would be in breach of advertising regulations and would likely alienate female viewers).

Studies in the 1980s found that sexual images in advertising had become more overt over time (Soley and Kurzbard 1986), and that models were wearing more suggestive clothing (Soley and Reid 1988). This trend has continued into the 1990s and beyond, with eroticism and nudity in magazine advertising becoming more prevalent and increasingly blatant (e.g., Lambiase and Reichert 1999). The use of sexual appeals in advertising is an area that is constantly debated and is consistently the most common issue attracting complaints to the Australian Advertising Standards Board (ASB); for example, in 2009 40.5 % of complaints to the ASB were under Australian Association of National Advertisers (2012) Code of Ethics (AANA) clause 2.3 'sex, sexuality and nudity'.

1.2 The Social Marketing Advertising Context

Although social marketers (and health promoters) are rarely targeted in discussions of the ethics of advertising, it is important that social marketing messages are developed and conveyed in an ethical fashion. The purpose of *all* marketing communications – whether they be commercial- or government-originated – is to persuade people to adopt a new product, belief, or behaviour (e.g., Kotler 2003).

While it has long been said that one cannot *not* communicate (Watzlawick et al. 1967), as Witte (1994) argues, one cannot *not* manipulate when communicating about health and disease. That is, the very nature of health-related information means that a doctor's communication with his/her patient, or a social marketing campaigns' communication with the target audience, will change the way people understand, feel, or act in relation to the health issue concerned. Witte (1994) proposes that health communicators can begin to address this ethical dilemma by:

1. deciding in advance what their health-related goal is, and then constructing their messages to fit that goal;
2. promoting the "common good" (i.e., the world-wide ethical standard of "the greatest good for the greatest number of people"); and
3. ensuring that a community standard is used to determine the common good.

The third point is often overlooked in the development and dissemination of public health campaigns. Traditionally, the common good is defined by the social marketer. This has resulted in a large number of advertising campaigns which are designed to increase the "common good," by utilising messages and strategies which would be considered unethical if used to sell commercial products. Much of the debate around ethics in social marketing advertising has focused on fear appeals, and whether the use of high-fear messages can be justified based on the social good that would result from audiences making the recommended behaviour changes, such as safer driving or smoking cessation (e.g., Arthur and Quester 2003; Duke et al. 1993). Many campaigns utilise exaggerated claims to achieve socially beneficial outcomes – such as implying a greater degree of certainty in the occurrence of negative health effects than is actually the case – but this is generally seen as acceptable because it promotes the common good. For example, Viscusi (1992) has demonstrated that if Americans were provided with accurate information on the statistical likelihood of negative health effects from smoking, there would be a considerable increase in the proportion of smokers.

Witte (1994) argues that to truly address the community's health-related concerns and priorities, community representatives (representing different interest groups) should decide what the common good is for that community and, specifically, what health-related messages should be disseminated and how those messages should be presented.

1.3 The Regulatory Context: Deciding on Regulatory Standards

All advertisers (that is, both commercial and social advertisers) in Australia, as in the U.S. and the U.K., are bound by an industry-designed self-regulatory code of ethics which covers permissible advertising content. Theoretically, within a self-regulation market, compliance with Industry Codes results in greater social benefit and a reduced Government or regulator spend on penalties for non-compliance; however, it has been argued that this can only occur of a culture of zero tolerance, with strict and meaningful penalties for those who violate the Code (Parsons and Schumacher 2012).

Following the demise of the Advertising Standards Council in 1996, the major industry body, the Australian Association of National Advertisers (AANA), developed the Advertiser Code of Ethics (which applies to all forms of advertising), and established the Advertising Standards Board (ASB) and the Advertising Claims Board (ACB) to deal with complaints and breaches of this code. Under the new regulatory system, the ASB deals with complaints about taste and decency in advertising, and the ACB deals with rival advertiser complaints. The authority of the two boards rests on the willingness of advertisers to adhere voluntarily to ethical standards.

Harker (2003) reviewed 12 years of complaints to the now defunct Advertising Standards Council, which assessed complaints from both the public and rival advertisers, and found more than ten thousand complaints and two thousand breaches of the codes (i.e., approximately 20 % of complaints were upheld). In comparison, of the total of 31,192 decisions on complaints against advertisements that were reported by the ASB for the period 1998–2009, only 2,018 of the decisions (i.e., 6.5 %) were to uphold the complaint.[1]

Section 2 of the AANA Code (the section administered by the ASB) includes clauses about discrimination and vilification, violence, sexuality and nudity, obscene language, and health and safety (see Fig. 4.1).

Note that the code was revised in 2012; and the data reported in this chapter was collected prior to the implementation of the new code. The revisions included: changes to the numbering of clauses; the introduction of a new clause (clause 2.2 above); and the removal of the clauses regarding the FCAI Code and the Advertising to Children Code. The latter change reflects the introduction of new codes, and reorganisation of other codes which are now all administered under section 3 (AANA's Code of Advertising & Marketing Communications to Children; Federal Chamber of Automotive Industries Code of Practice; AANA Food & Beverages Advertising & Marketing Communications Code) as well as the AFGC Responsible Children's Marketing Initiative and the Quick Service Restaurant Children's Marketing Initiative. Table 4.1 outlines the differences between the two codes.

However, recent studies which have examined advertising against the additional Regulatory Codes – specifically those focusing on motor vehicles and advertising of food to children – suggest the introduction of these Codes has not had the proposed impact, and that commercial advertisements for motor vehicles and food advertisements targeting children continue to be non-compliant with the new and revised codes (Donovan et al. 2011 and King et al. 2012). Perhaps one thing that they do achieve is to reduce the apparent number of complaints lodged under each of (the clauses of) the existing codes.

2.1 Advertising or Marketing Communications shall not portray people or depict material in a way which discriminates against or vilifies a person or section of the community on account of race, ethnicity, nationality, gender, age, sexual preference, religion, disability or political belief.

2.2 Advertising or marketing communications should not employ sexual appeal in a manner which is exploitative and degrading of any individual or group of people.

2.3 Advertising or Marketing Communications shall not present or portray violence unless it is justifiable in the context of the product or service advertised.

2.4 Advertising or Marketing Communications shall treat sex, sexuality and nudity with sensitivity to the relevant audience.

2.5 Advertising or Marketing Communications shall only use language which is appropriate in the circumstances and strong or obscene language shall be avoided.

2.6 Advertising or Marketing Communications shall not depict material contrary to Prevailing Community Standards on health and safety.

Fig. 4.1 Section 2 of the 2012 AANA code of ethics

[1] Calculated from complaint statistics on the ASB website (http://www.adstandards.com.au/storage/55eb81b8b615d57e0ab73ce5b2f33ed8.Stats2009Graphs%20-%20finalx.pdf)

Table 4.1 The AANA code of ethics pre- and post-2012

Clause	Current code	Pre-2012 code
Discrimination or vilification	2.1	2.1
Exploitative or degrading	2.2	N/A
Violence	2.3	2.2
Sexuality and nudity	2.4	2.3
Language	2.5	2.5
Health and safety	2.6	2.6
Advertising to children	Section 3	2.4 (must comply with relevant code)
FCAI code	Section 3	2.7 (must comply with relevant code)

Table 4.2 Issues attracting complaint (%)

AANA section	2013	2012	2011	2010	2009	2008
2.1 Discrimination or vilification	18.1 %	28.5 %	20.7 %	19.6 %	16.3 %	22.8 %
2.2 Exploitative and degrading	8.3 %	14.0 %	N/A	N/A	N/A	N/A
2.3 Violence	16.1 %	5.9 %	11.8 %	9.6 %	7.9 %	17.7 %
2.4 Sex, sexuality and nudity	23.2 %	23.4 %	32.0 %	45.2 %	40.5 %	25.6 %
2.5 Language	7.1 %	12.2 %	6.1 %	4.8 %	5.3 %	7.2 %
2.6 Health and safety	15.6 %	9.5 %	13.6 %	9.6 %	8.4 %	6.0 %
2.7 FCAI code	4.4 %	1.9 %	3.5 %	1.1 %	1.2 %	3.1 %
Advertising to children code	NIL	NIL	1.3 %	2.3 %	0.6 %	0.5 %
Food and beverage code	1.7 %	1.0 %	6.3 %	3.1 %	2.5 %	1.3 %
AFCG[a] & QSR[b]		0.6 %	2.5 %	1.4 %	N/A	N/A
Other	≈5.5 %	≈2.5 %	2.1 %	3.1 %	17.2 %	15.8 %
	5.4	5.7	7.1	5.6	5.7	9.3

[a]AFGC Responsible Children's Marketing Initiative
[b]Quick Service Restaurant Children's Marketing Initiative
[c]Exact figure not stated in report, figure estimated from graph

Between 2008 and 2013, the most common issue attracting complaints was the portrayal of sex and nudity; clause 2.3 (sex, sexuality and nudity) of the pre-2012 code, and clauses 2.2 (exploitative and degrading) and 2.4 (sexuality and nudity) of the 2012 revised code (ASB 2009; 2010; 2011; 2012; 2013; 2014). This was followed by 'discrimination or vilification' (clause 2.1 in both codes) and 'violence (clause 2.2 in the previous and 2.3 in the current code). See Table 4.2 for the number of complaints lodged under each clause of the AANA Code. It is important to note that the definitions provided do not always relate directly to, or use the same terminology as, the clauses to which they are relevant.

While the majority of complaints to the ASB relate to commercial advertisements, in the period 2008–2013 at least 5 % of complaints each year, and as high as 9.3 % in 2008, were in the category 'community awareness' (ASB 2012, 2013), demonstrating that social advertisers are not immune to negative community reactions.

1.4 Determining Right and Wrong

This study utilises the distinction between the deontological ('means') and teleological ('ends') perspectives of the regulation of advertising (Agarwal and Malloy 2002; Malhotra and Miller 1998; Okleshen and Hoyt 1996). Deontologists believe that to be ethical we must use the right means regardless of the outcome (Emmanuel Kant's categorical imperative). Proponents of this view would argue, for example, that advertisers should not use overt sex appeals in cigarette advertising as this behaviour is frowned upon by society – regardless of whether doing so leads to harm. Teleologists (or utilitarianists), such as the pragmatist Jeremy Bentham, believe that it is the goodness or badness of the outcome that counts. Proponents of this view would argue, for example, that advertisers should not use characters in cigarette ads who have high appeal to young people as these characters may encourage children to smoke, which is a bad outcome. It is hypothesized that members of the general public may have differing views about the ethical requirements for the two broad types of advertisers. That is, it is possible that that commercial advertisers, who are seen to have self-serving end points (such as increased profits) are held to a more deontological evaluation; whereas social advertisers, such as NGOs who have community-serving end points, are held to a more teleological evaluation (e.g., "it's alright to use high-fear advertisements to stop people smoking but not to get them to take out an insurance policy").

The advertising industry, at least in Australia, appears to be doing a reasonable job of demonstrating to the public that it places a high value on teleological ethics. For example, when it was argued that portrayals of fast or unsafe driving in car ads leads to speeding and unsafe driving among the general public, the industry proposed a voluntary code to regulate such portrayals (now covered under section 2.7 of the AANA). When it was argued that junk food advertising causes children to become obese and inactive, the industry offered to develop an ad campaign to encourage healthy eating and exercise. However, the industry appears to be doing a poor job of demonstrating to the public that it places a high value on deontological ethics. Of the six clauses of the AANA Code of Ethics, at least four are based on a deontological perspective of right and wrong: (2.1) discrimination/vilification; (2.2) violence; (2.3) portrayal of sex/sexuality/nudity; and (2.5) language; but the large numbers of complaints to the ASB each year suggest that advertisers continue to use appeals that offend the community. While it could be argued that an ad should not be removed because it offends a very small minority of the population, there is no clear yardstick by which we can decide how many or what proportion of people must be offended by an ad before it is deemed unacceptable. A review of the complaints lodged with the ASB between 1999 and 2001 identified apparent inconsistencies in the application of the Code, resulting in decisions which did not appear to reflect the community standards it was established to protect (Jones 2003).

It appears that the ASB may share advertisers' teleological perspective; particularly in the context of social marketing (or 'community awareness') advertising. Only one of the 59 complaints in the ASB's 'community awareness' classification was upheld in the period 2003–2007 (Advertising Standards Bureau 2004, 2005, 2006, 2007, 2008); and decision records were issued with wording such as "The Board noted the important public health message underlying the images used in the advertisement and that such messages justify impactful advertising" (Case Report 63/10) and "The Board agreed that some members of the public who had experienced a premature baby or had been affected by SIDS may find the images distressing. However, the Board also noted that the images were used in the context of an important health message about the effects of smoking on babies and children" (Case report 146/09). To date, there is an absence of research into whether consumers share this perspective with those who develop, and adjudicate on, advertising.

1.5 Rationale for the Study

A review of industry responses to ethical dilemmas (Jones 2007) suggests that industry responses tend to be based on teleological rather than deontological ethics, with the primary motive being to avoid deleterious outcomes for the industry (such as government regulation of advertising) rather than for society as a whole. There is a need to investigate the community's views on the use of potentially controversial appeals in advertising – such as the portrayal of nudity, illegal behaviour and violence – and whether these views are consistent with those of advertisers and the complaints handling body (the ASB). Further, there is a need to examine whether these views, or standards, differ depending on the intent of the advertiser. We hypothesise that the community will use a different yardstick for commercial and social advertisers, with social marketing advertising allowed more latitude in the types of appeals and messages used due to the social good of their intended outcomes.

2 Method

A questionnaire was developed to assess consumer attitudes towards the use of specific appeals and images in advertising messages, in both a commercial and a social marketing context. As recommended by O'Donohoe (1995) the development of items for the questionnaire was informed by consumer-based exploratory research. That is, while it included items that matched the clauses in the current self-regulatory advertising code, it also included items that originated from prior qualitative studies that were designed to identify messages and imagery of concern to Australian consumers. In these previous studies a total of 20 focus groups were conducted to explore in depth consumer attitudes to advertising and perceptions of current advertising standards. In order to address the role of ethical perspectives in attitudes towards commercial and social marketing advertising, four items from the Ethics Position Questionnaire (EPQ; Forsyth 1980) were also included in the questionnaire.

The draft questionnaire was then critiqued by two focus groups of consumers, in which participants read through and discussed the questionnaire, identifying any questions or response items that were unclear, confusing, or potentially leading. This process resulted in minor changes to the wording of some items, and the inclusion of some definitions and clarifications in the instructions. The revised questionnaire was then pilot-tested on a convenience sample of 25 people, with respondents asked to complete the questionnaire and then (on the last page) to note any items that they had found confusing or difficult to answer. All 25 respondents completed all of the questionnaire items and no further modifications were suggested or made.

An electronic database of names and addresses in the Illawarra, New South Wales Local Government Area was purchased from a commercial research agency. This database consisted of 6097 addresses (after data cleaning), and 4,000 were randomly selected to receive the survey. The initial mail out resulted in the return of 656 completed surveys. Non-respondents were sent a reminder letter and a replacement, resulting in the return of an additional 216 completed surveys (i.e., a total of 872 surveys, representing a response rate of 21.8 %).

The final questionnaire included a series of questions about general attitudes towards advertising (reported elsewhere); 17 items on the acceptability of appeals and images in commercial advertising (defined as "advertising for commercial products such as cars, food, alcohol or clothing"); 15 items on the acceptability of appeals and images in social marketing advertising (defined as "social education and health promotion advertisements such as anti-speeding, safe drinking, anti-smoking or healthy eating")[2]; the four EPQ questions (EPQ items 3, 8, 13 and 20); and a demographic section.

For each of the acceptability items, responses were on a 5-point scale, where 1 represented "strongly disagree" and 5 represented "strongly agree". The focus of the current paper is responses to 11 paired items on perceived acceptability of different types of messages and appeals in commercial and social marketing advertising context. Chi-square tests were conducted to (a) determine differences in perceived acceptability of appeals and images in commercial and social marketing advertising; (b) determine demographic differences in perceived acceptability in each context; and (c) examine associations between moral perspectives and attitudes towards the use of appeals and images in commercial and social advertising.

[2]This terminology was used as both the survey pre-test and previous focus group research identified that the majority of consumers were unfamiliar with the term "social marketing".

3 Results

Of the 872 returned surveys, 39.8 % of respondents were male and 60.2 % female. All respondents were aged 18 and over, and the age distribution was similar to that of the underlying population (Australian Bureau of Statistics 2008), with 19.8 % aged under 35 years, 16.6 % aged 35–44, 20.9 % aged 45–54, 18.9 % aged 55–64, and 22.3 % aged 65 and over. Respondents self-identified as having a range of religious affiliations, which were categorised for the purpose of analysis into 'no religion' (23.7 %), 'Catholic' (23.4 %), 'Anglican' (20.5 %), 'other Christian' (21.5 %), and 'other' (10.9 %).

The majority of respondents (71.0 %) had some post-secondary education (including bachelors degree or higher, trade certificate, or other certificate or diploma). A further 7.3 % reported completing a Higher School Certificate or equivalent (i.e., 12 years of schooling); and the remaining 20.5 % completed some or no secondary education. Approximately 80 % of the sample (77.6 % of males and 81.6 % of females) stated they had children.

3.1 Differences in Acceptability of Appeals in a Commercial or Social Advertising Context

As shown in Table 4.3, there were significant differences in the perceived level of acceptability of the use of nine of the 11 appeals between commercial advertising and social marketing advertising.

3.2 Use of Coarse Language, Portrayal of Violence, Portrayal of Illegal and Unsafe Behaviours

The majority of respondents did not agree that "It is acceptable to use coarse language in an advertisement", with this view more widely held in the context of commercial than social marketing ($x^2=28.10$, $p<0.01$). Similarly, the majority of respondents did not agree that "It is acceptable to use violence or violent images in an advertisement", again more so in commercial than social marketing advertising ($x^2=198.06$, $p<0.001$).

In relation to the issue of whether "It is acceptable to show illegal behaviour in an advertisement", responses varied by advertising type. In this case, the majority disagreed with the portrayal of illegal behaviour in commercial advertising but less than half disagreed in the context of social marketing advertising ($x^2=257.16$, $p<0.001$). A similar effect was found for the portrayal of unsafe behaviour, with the majority disagreeing with the portrayal of unsafe behaviour in commercial advertising but less than half disagreeing in the context of social marketing advertising ($x^2=45.385$, $p<0.001$).

Table 4.3 Acceptability of appeals in a commercial vs social marketing context (questions phrased as "It is acceptable to....")

	Disagree		Neither		Agree	
	Comm	Social	Comm	Social	Comm	Social
Use coarse language	84.4	74.2	8.7	10.9	6.9	15.0
Use violence or violent images	84.3	53.1	8.2	11.5	7.5	35.5
Show illegal behaviour	79.1	44.5	12.7	13.7	8.2	41.8
Portray unsafe behaviour	80.2	45.7	9.5	11.1	10.3	43.2
Show nudity	77.1	65.6	14.3	16.8	8.6	17.7
Portray women as sex objects	80.3	76.3	12.0	14.2	7.7	9.5
Portray men as sex objects	78.8	75.2	12.6	14.4	8.6	10.4
Stereotype or make fun of people	81.1	75.0	11.1	11.5	7.9	13.6
Make fun of well known people	50.6	54.2	26.1	23.6	23.3	22.2
Directly target children	64.7	30.8	18.2	16.8	17.1	52.4
Distressing or frightening images	67.4	38.6	15.1	14.2	17.6	47.2

3.3 *The Portrayal of Nudity and Sexualisation of Males and Females*

The majority of respondents did not agree that "It is acceptable to show nudity in an advertisement", with this view more widely held in the context of commercial than social marketing advertising (77.1 % vs 65.6 %; $x^2=17.692$, $p<0.01$). Similarly, the majority did not agree that "It is acceptable to portray women as sex objects in an advertisement", again more so in the context of commercial than social marketing advertising ($x^2=1.73$, $p<0.05$); or that "It is acceptable to portray men as sex objects in an advertisement", in this case with no significant difference between advertising contexts.

3.4 *The Use of Stereotypical or Derogatory Portrayals (of Groups and Individuals)*

The majority of respondents did not agree that "It is acceptable to stereotype or make fun of particular groups of people in an advertisement", with this view more widely held in the context of commercial than social marketing advertising ($x^2=9.657$, $p=0.01$). Approximately half of respondents did not agree that "It is acceptable to make fun of well known people such as politicians or celebrities in an advertisement". Although not a statistically significant difference, this was the only item for which there was a *higher* level of disagreement for social marketing (54.3 %) than for commercial (50.6 %) advertising.

3.5 The Use of Messages That Impact on Children

The majority of respondents did not agree that "It is acceptable to directly target children in an advertisement". However, their responses varied by advertising type with the majority disagreeing with the targeting of children in commercial advertising but less than one-third disagreeing in the context of social marketing advertising ($x^2=251.30$, $p<0.001$). Similarly, while the majority of respondents did not agree that "It is acceptable to show images or messages that may be distressing or frightening in an advertisement", two-thirds disagreed with the use of distressing or frightening images in commercial advertising but less than half in the context of social marketing advertising ($x^2=206.26$, $p<0.001$).

3.6 The Role of Demographics

Those who were parents were less likely[3] to agree that it was acceptable to use coarse language in commercial advertising or social marketing advertising; to portray violence in commercial advertising or social marketing advertising; to portray illegal behaviour in commercial advertising; to portray unsafe behaviour in commercial advertising; to portray nudity in commercial advertising or social marketing advertising[a]; to portray women as sex objects in commercial advertising or social marketing advertising; and to portray men as sex objects in commercial advertising or social marketing advertising. Parents were also less likely than non-parents to agree that it was acceptable to utilise stereotypical or derogatory portrayals of groups of people in commercial advertising; to make fun of well-known people in commercial advertising or social marketing advertising[a]; to directly target children in commercial advertising or social marketing advertising; and to use distressing or frightening images in commercial advertising or social marketing advertising[a].

Females were less likely than males to agree that it was acceptable to use coarse language in commercial advertising; to portray violence in commercial advertising[a]; to portray unsafe behaviour in commercial advertising; to portray nudity in commercial advertising or social marketing advertising; to portray women as sex objects in commercial advertising; and to portray men as sex objects in commercial advertising. Females were also less likely than males to agree that it was acceptable to utilise stereotypical or derogatory portrayals of groups of people in commercial advertising[a]; to make fun of well-known people in commercial advertising or social marketing advertising; and to use distressing or frightening images in commercial advertising.

[3] For ease of reading, chi-square and p-values are not itemized, but all differences were significant at $p<0.01$ (or $p<0.05$ where marked[a]).

Those who did not have a university education were less likely to agree that it was acceptable to use coarse language in commercial advertising or social marketing advertising; to portray violence in social marketing advertising; to portray illegal behaviour in social marketing advertising; to portray unsafe behaviour in commercial advertising or social marketing advertising; and to portray nudity in commercial advertising or social marketing advertising. Those without a university education were also less likely to agree that it was acceptable to utilise stereotypical or derogatory portrayals of groups of people in social marketing advertising[a]; to make fun of well-known people in commercial advertising or social marketing advertising; to directly target children in commercial advertising or social marketing advertising; and to use distressing or frightening images in social marketing advertising.

Older respondents[4] were less likely to agree that it was acceptable to use coarse language in social marketing advertising; to portray violence in commercial advertising or social marketing advertising; to portray unsafe behaviour in commercial advertising; to portray illegal behaviour in commercial advertising or social marketing advertising; to portray women as sex objects in commercial advertising; to portray men as sex objects in commercial advertising. Older respondents were also less likely to agree that it was acceptable to utilise stereotypical or derogatory portrayals of groups of people in commercial advertising or social marketing advertising; make fun of well-known people in commercial advertising; directly target children in commercial advertising or social marketing advertising; and to use distressing or frightening images in social marketing advertising.

Those who identified as having a religious affiliation were less likely to agree that it was acceptable to use coarse language in commercial advertising or social marketing advertising; to portray violence in social marketing advertising; to portray illegal behaviour in social marketing advertising[a]; to portray nudity in commercial advertising or social marketing advertising[a]; to portray women as sex objects in commercial advertising; and to portray men as sex objects in commercial advertising[a]. Those who identified as having a religious affiliation were less likely to agree that it was acceptable to utilise stereotypical or derogatory portrayals of groups of people in commercial advertising[a] or social marketing advertising[a]; to make fun of well-known people in commercial advertising or social marketing advertising[a].

3.7 The Role of Moral Perspectives

Across the sample as a whole, 65.6 % agreed or strongly agreed that "the existence of potential harm to others is always wrong, irrespective of the benefits to be gained" (hereafter referred to as 'avoiding harm'); and 89.4 % that "the dignity and welfare

[4]The majority of differences in relation to commercial advertising were between those aged above and below 45 years, whereas the majority of differences in relation to social marketing advertising were between those aged above and below 65 years (full details can be provided on request to the authors)

Table 4.4 Responses to the four EPQ items

	SD (%)	D (%)	N (%)	A (%)	SA (%)
The existence of potential harm to others is always wrong, irrespective of the benefits to be gained [avoiding harm] (n=838)	3.5	13.6	17.3	37.8	27.8
Moral standards should be seen as individualistic [individualistic morals] (847)	6.6	20.5	9.4	48.6	14.8
The dignity and welfare of the people should be the most important concern in any society [protecting dignity] (851)	1.4	2.7	6.5	43.6	45.8
Whether a lie is judged to be moral or immoral depends upon the circumstances surrounding the action [circumstantial morals] (846)	12.9	25.9	17.1	35.6	8.5

of the people should be the most important concern in any society' (hereafter referred to as 'protecting dignity') (Table 4.4). Conversely, 63.4 % agreed that "moral standards should be seen as individualistic" (hereafter referred to as 'individualistic morals') and 44.1 % that "whether a lie is judged to be moral or immoral depends upon the circumstances surrounding the action" (hereafter referred to as 'circumstantial morals').

Women were somewhat more likely to agree with 'avoiding harm' ($p<0.04$), but there were no gender differences on the other items. Older respondents were more likely to agree with 'protecting dignity' ($p<0.001$); and less likely to agree with 'individualistic morals' ($p<0.005$) and 'circumstantial morals' ($p<0.001$). Those with a religious affiliation were more likely to agree with 'protecting dignity' ($p<0.05$); and less likely to agree with 'individualistic morals' ($p<0.001$) and 'circumstantial morals' ($p<0.001$). Those with a higher level of education were more likely to agree with 'protecting dignity' ($p<0.005$), and 'avoiding harm' ($p<0.05$).

Those who were parents were more likely to agree with 'avoiding harm' ($p<0.05$), and 'protecting dignity' ($p<0.05$); and less likely to agree with 'individualistic morals' ($p<0.001$) and 'circumstantial morals' ($p<0.001$)

There was a strong association between responses to the EPQ items and the responses to the advertising message items, in both the commercial and the social marketing context. The following section reports differences that were statistically significant (i.e., $p<0.05$).

Those who agreed that "moral standards should be seen as individualistic" were more likely to agree that it is acceptable in a commercial or a social marketing advertisement to use coarse language, show violence and (in a commercial advertisement only) to show illegal behaviour or unsafe behaviour in a commercial advertisement; that it is acceptable in a commercial or a social marketing advertisement to show nudity, show women as sex objects and show men as sex objects; that it is acceptable in a commercial or a social marketing advertisement to stereotype or make fun of people or to make fun of well known people.

Those who agreed that "whether a lie is judged to be moral or immoral depends upon the circumstances surrounding the action" were more likely to agree that it is acceptable in a commercial or a social marketing advertisement to use coarse language, show violence, show illegal behaviour or show unsafe behaviour; that it is acceptable in a commercial or a social marketing advertisement to show nudity, show women as sex objects and show men as sex objects; that it is acceptable in a commercial or a social marketing advertisement to stereotype or make fun of people and to make fun of well known people; and that it is acceptable in a commercial or a social marketing advertisement to directly target children.

Conversely, those who agreed that "The existence of potential harm to others is always wrong, irrespective of the benefits to be gained" were *less* likely to agree that it is acceptable in a commercial or a social marketing advertisement to show violence or show illegal behaviour; that it is acceptable in social marketing advertisement to use coarse language or show unsafe behaviour; that it is acceptable in a commercial or a social marketing advertisement to show women or men as sex objects or to show nudity; that it is acceptable in a commercial or a social marketing advertisement to stereotype or make fun of people and to make fun of *well known* people; that it is acceptable in a commercial or a social marketing advertisement to directly target children; and that it is acceptable in a social marketing advertisement to show distressing or frightening images.

Additionally, those who agreed that "The dignity and welfare of the people should be the most important concern in any society" were *less* likely to agree that it is acceptable in a commercial advertisement to show unsafe behaviour; that it is acceptable in a commercial or a social marketing advertisement to show women or men as sex objects or to show nudity; that it is acceptable in a commercial or a social marketing advertisement to make fun of well known people or in a commercial advertisement to stereotype or make fun of people; and in a commercial advertisement to directly target children or show distressing or frightening images.

4 Discussion

We surveyed 872 Australian adults to ascertain their views regarding the acceptability of appeals and images in advertising, with a specific focus on identifying any differences in attitudes between a commercial marketing and a social marketing context. That is, as argued by the advertising self-regulatory authority and some social marketing advertisers "does the end justify the means?" The answer appears to be "sometimes". We found, as anticipated, substantial differences in responses between the two contexts; with evidence of a level of agreement with the teleological approach taken by the Advertising Standards Board in assessing complaints about social marketing advertisements.

However, this does not mean that consumers are willing to accept all forms of messages and appeals from social marketing advertisers. Of the 11 items included in our survey, there were only two for which a greater proportion of respondents agreed with their use than disagreed – it is acceptable for social marketing advertisements to directly target children (52.4 % agreed, 30.8 % disagreed) and it is acceptable for social marketing advertisements to show distressing or frightening images (47.2 % agreed, 38.6 % disagreed). This latter finding is consistent a study on attitudes towards fear-based advertisements, which found that participants believed fear-based social marketing advertising could encourage the public to comply with rules and behavior deemed socially acceptable, but that if the imagery was too graphic and emotional, there was the risk of emotional trauma (Brennan and Binney 2010).

There were a further two items for which respondents were fairly evenly split – it is acceptable for social marketing advertisements to show unsafe behaviour (43.2 % vs 45.7 %) and it is acceptable for social marketing advertisements to show illegal behaviour (41.8 % vs 44.5 %). For the remaining seven items, the majority of respondents did not agree that their use was acceptable in social marketing advertising, ranging from just over half for 'show violence' and 'make fun of well known people' to three-quarters for 'show women as sex objects', 'show men as sex objects' and 'stereotype or make fun of people'.

Importantly, we found a number of significant differences in attitudes across demographic groups. These were most evident in relation to parental status (with a lower level of acceptability of most appeals and images in both contexts), age (particularly in relation to commercial advertising) and education (particularly in relation to social marketing advertising). We also found significant differences across most items as a function of ethical perspectives, as measured by a subset of items from the EPQ. However, it is important to note these statistical differences do not mean that these types of appeals were only seen as unacceptable by a small sub-set of the population, with high levels of agreement on most items across demographic groups. Indeed, the ASB acknowledged in a recent research report that "any complaint is an indicator that a substantial proportion of the community is likely to find an ad unacceptable" (ASB 2009).

4.1 Limitations

There are several limitations of the current study that should be acknowledged. First, the data was collected from adult consumers in one geographic region (Wollongong LGA, New South Wales), which means that the results may not be generalisable to the broader Australian population (although there is no concrete reason to suspect that this is the case). Further, the response rate (21.8 %), while not unusual for a study of this nature, means that our sample may under-represent some groups (such as those from CALD communities). However, comparison of the demographics of our sample to ABS data suggests that they did not differ from the underlying population on key variables. This does not, however, discount the possibility that our sample over-represents those who have a strong view about advertising standards and under-represents those who are ambivalent (as is often the case with studies with voluntary participation). An important limitation is that our respondents did not look at individual advertisements or images, but rather responded to written statements; thus, for example, we cannot comment on the *level* of nudity that would be considered unacceptable, or what specific words our respondents would consider to be 'coarse language'. Future research could expand on this study by examining consumer responses to advertisements containing increasing levels of the factors of interest (for example, women in different levels of undress).

4.2 Implications for Marketers

Our findings have important implications for both commercial and social marketers. It is clear that our respondents are less accepting of the use of a range of appeals and images in commercial compared to social marketing; with significant differences on nine of the 11 items, all in the expected direction. In a commercial advertising context, our respondents clearly disagreed with the use of all 11 of the message or image types included in the survey, with none of the items seen as acceptable by the majority of respondents, and only four acceptable to more than one in ten: make fun of well known people (23.3 %), show distressing or frightening images (17.6 %), directly target children (17.1 %), and show unsafe behaviour (10.3 %).

However, it is clear that consumers are also concerned about the use of 'controversial' images in social marketing advertising and while many may accept the 'need' for some confronting images (such as distressing images) they are strongly opposed to others. For example, more than two-thirds disagreed with the use of nudity, women or men as sex objects, coarse language, and stereotyping or making fun of people. Thus, it is likely that some recent approaches to social marketing advertisements are offending substantial proportions of consumers. For example, road safety campaigns have utilised coarse language (e.g., the Victorian TAC's "drink, drive, bloody idiot" message which has been widely utilised) and making fun of people (e.g., the NSW RTA's "Speeding. No one thinks big of you.").[5] We are not criticising these campaigns, but rather raising for consideration the potential for them to cause widespread offence, predominantly among people who are *not* the target audience. Related to this, we note that our respondents were less likely to agree that "It is acceptable to make fun of well known people such as politicians or celebrities" in a social marketing than a commercial advertisement. We suggest that this represents a view that social marketing advertising should hold to high moral standards and while there may be situations in which the use of other appeal types is deemed acceptable because of the over-riding aim of the message (such as showing illegal or unsafe behaviour in an anti-speeding advertisement or showing nudity

[5] The advertisements show young men speeding, with others (predominantly women) responding by wiggling their pinkie finger at another bystander, with the message being that the young man is not displaying virility by speeding but rather "overcompensating" for something (with the small finger intended to imply he has a small penis).

in a cancer screening advertisement) making fun of an individual is not seen as justifiable.

It is also important to note that, while in most cases there was a clear consensus on the acceptability of different messages/images, there were also statistically significant demographic differences. For example, parents expressed higher levels of disagreement than non-parents in relation to all of the items in a commercial advertising context and eight of the 11 items in a social marketing context; importantly, in both contexts, this included being less likely to agree that it was acceptable to directly target children and to show distressing or frightening images. Social marketers may need to be aware of the potential backlash from parents if they are perceived to be targeting children with such messages. Similarly, we found that level of education had a far greater impact on reaction to the items in a social marketing than a commercial marketing context, with those with lower levels of education considerably more opposed to social marketers showing violence, illegal behaviour, distressing images or stereotypes (differences which were not evident in the context of commercial advertising). Given that many social marketing programs target lower SES population groups (for example, smoking rates are higher and exercise levels lower among those without a university education), it is important to ensure that these messages are not interpreted by members of the target audience as denigrating or stigmatising them.

4.3 *Implications for Regulators*

Our findings also have important implications for those responsible for the regulation of advertising, and for adjudicating consumer complaints regarding advertising messages. While we focus on Australian complainants and the Australian self-regulatory system (as this was the context of our study), these implications are equally relevant for regulators in other countries. First, it is evident that there are a number of issues on which the community holds consistent views, such as the portrayal of women and men as sex objects. Thus, there is a role for industry bodies, and perhaps governments, to set clear guidelines on the use of sexual and sexist messages and images.

Second, it is clear that the demographic differences that do exist suggest that the current level of complaints to Australia's ASB under-represent the level of community concern. For example, we found that older respondents were more likely to state that many of the images and appeals were unacceptable than younger respondents, but only 15 % of the complaints received by the ASB were from people aged 55 and over (Advertising Standards Bureau 2010). Previous studies of complainants to the ASB have concluded that complainants tend to have a higher income and higher level of education (Volkov et al. 2005) and complainants may only be the 'tip of the social iceberg' (Volkov et al. 2002). Our finding that it is older people and those with a lower level of education who are more likely to disagree with the use of coarse language, violence, stereotypes and other controversial appeals supports the conclusions of these previous studies and suggests that regulators need to take steps to ensure that the views of these groups are incorporated in the development of advertising guidelines and the adjudication of complaints.

Finally, this data supports the ASB's teleological approach to the assessment of complaints against social marketing advertising (but not commercial advertising) by demonstrating that, while there are members of the community who are offended by the portrayal of distressing or frightening images, a substantial proportion of the community supports their use where there is a social benefit from bringing about behaviour change (this would include graphic images of road traffic accidents designed to reduce speeding and distressing portrayals of cancerous organs to encourage smoking cessation). However, our data suggests that there are limits to consumers' acceptance of controversial appeals even when the intended outcome is an important social good; for example, the use of coarse language or messages which stereotype or make fun of individuals or groups of people.

Our findings support calls for the direct involvement of broadly representative groups of consumers in the assessment of complaints about advertising, rather than a reliance on those who create the messages to self-regulate their content.

Acknowledgements This research was funded by a Discovery Grant from the Australian Research Council and the data reported herein was used, in part, for the second author's Masters by Research thesis.

References

Advertising Standards Bureau. (2004). Review of operations 2003. http://www.adstandards.com.au/publications/reviewofoperations

Advertising Standards Bureau. (2005). Review of operations 2004. http://www.adstandards.com.au/publications/reviewofoperations

Advertising Standards Bureau. (2006). Review of operations 2005. http://www.adstandards.com.au/publications/reviewofoperations

Advertising Standards Bureau. (2007). Review of operations 2006. http://www.adstandards.com.au/publications/reviewofoperations

Advertising Standards Bureau. (2008). Review of operations 2007. http://www.adstandards.com.au/publications/reviewofoperations

Advertising Standards Bureau. (2009). Review of operations 2008: http://www.adstandards.com.au/publications/reviewofoperations

Advertising Standards Bureau. (2010). Review of operations 2009: http://www.adstandards.com.au/publications/reviewofoperations

Advertising Standards Bureau. (2011). Review of operations 2010: http://www.adstandards.com.au/publications/reviewofoperations

Advertising Standards Bureau. (2012). Review of operations 2011: http://www.adstandards.com.au/publications/reviewofoperations

Advertising Standards Bureau. (2013). Review of operations 2012: http://www.adstandards.com.au/publications/reviewofoperations

Advertising Standards Bureau. (2014). Review of operations 2013: http://www.adstandards.com.au/publications/reviewofoperations

Agarwal, J., & Malloy, D. C. (2002). An integrated model of ethical decision-making: A proposed pedagogical framework for a marketing ethics curriculum. *Teaching Business Ethics, 6*, 245–268. doi:10.1023/A:1015225623047.

Arthur, D., & Quester, P. (2003). The ethicality of using fear for social advertising. *Australasian Marketing Journal, 11*, 12–27. doi:10.1016/S1441-3582(03)70115-3.

Australian Bureau of Statistics. (2008). *3101.0 – Australian Demographic Statistics*. Canberra: Australian Bureau of Statistics.

Australian Association of National Advertisers. (2012) *AANA code of ethics*. http://aana.com.au/self-regulation/codes/Australian Bureau of Statistics (2008). 3101.0 - Australian Demographic Statistics, Dec 2008. Canberra: Australian Bureau of Statistics.

Brennan, L., & Binney, W. (2010). Fear, guilt and shame appeals in social marketing. *Journal of Business Research, 63*, 140–146.

Brinkmann, J. (2002). Business and marketing ethics as professional ethics. Concepts, approaches and typologies. *Journal of Business Ethics, 41*, 159–177.

Donovan, R. J., Fielder, L. J., Ouschan, R., & Ewing, M. (2011). Self-regulation of motor vehicle advertising: Is it working in Australia? *Accident Analysis and Prevention, 43*, 631–363.

Duke, C. R., Pickett, G. M., Carlson, L., & Grove, S. J. (1993). A method for evaluating the ethics of fear appeals. *Journal of Public Policy and Marketing, 12*, 120–129.

Forsyth, D. R. (1980). A taxonomy of ethical ideologies. *Journal of Personality and Social Psychology, 39*, 175–184. doi:10.1037/0022-3514.39.1.175.

Harker, D. (2003). The importance of industry compliance in improving self-regulatory processes. *Journal of Public Affairs, 3*, 63–75. doi:10.1002/pa.134.

Jones, S. C. (2003). Sexism is in the eye of the beholder: Does the advertising standards board reflect "community standards"? In G. Guersen, R. Kennedy, & M. Tolo (Eds.), *Proceedings of the Australian and New Zealand marketing academy conference*, Adelaide, 1–3 December 2003.

Jones, S. C. (2007). Fast cars, fast food, and fast fixes: Industry responses to current ethical dilemmas for Australian advertisers. *Journal of Public Affairs, 7*, 148–163. doi:10.1002/pa.256.

King, L., Hebden, L., Grunseit, A., Kelly, B., & Chapman, K. (2012). Building the case for independent monitoring of food advertising on Australian television. *Public Health Nutrition, 16*(12), 2249–2254.

Kotler, P. (2003). *Marketing management*. Upper Saddle River: Prentice Hall.

Lambiase, J., & Reichert, T. (1999). Cheesecake and beefcake: No matter how you slice it, sexual explicitness in advertising continues to increase. *Journalism and Mass Communication Quarterly, 76*, 7–20.

Malhotra, N. K., & Miller, G. L. (1998). An integrated model for ethical decisions in marketing research. *Journal of Business Ethics, 17*, 263–280. doi:10.1023/A:1005711311426.

Morgan Poll. (2004). Finding No. 3701 – January 08 2004, http://www.roymorgan.com/news/polls/2004/3701/

O'Donohoe, S. (1995). Attitudes to advertising: A review of British and American research. *International Journal of Advertising, 14*, 245–261.

Okleshen, M., & Hoyt, R. (1996). A cross-cultural comparison of ethical perspectives and decision approaches of business students: United States of America versus New Zealand. *Journal of Business Ethics, 15*, 537–549. doi:10.1007/BF00381929.

Parsons, A. G., & Schumacher, C. (2012). Advertising regulation and market drivers. *European Journal of Marketing, 46*(11/12), 1539–1558.

Soley, L., & Kurzbard, G. (1986). Sex in advertising: A comparison of 1964 and 1984. *Journal of Advertising, 15*, 45–54.

Soley, L. C., & Reid, L. N. (1988). Taking it off: Are models in magazine ads wearing less? *Journalism Quarterly, 65*, 960–66.

Viscusi, W. K. (1992). *Smoking: Making the risky decision*. New York: Oxford University Press.

Volkov, M., Harker, D., & Harker, M. (2002). Opinions about advertising in Australia: A study of complainants. *Journal of Marketing Communications, 8*, 229–242. doi:10.1080/13527260210142329.

Volkov, M., Harker, D., & Harker, M. (2005). Who's complaining? Using MOSAIC to identify the profile of complainants. *Marketing Intelligence and Planning, 23*, 296–312. doi:10.1108/02634500510597328.

Watzlawick, P., Bavelas, J. B., & Jackson, D. D. (1967). *Pragmatics of human communication*. New York: Norton.

Witte, K. (1994). The manipulative nature of health communication research: Ethical issues and guidelines. *American Behavioral Scientist, 38*(2), 285–293.

Chapter 5
Internal Social Marketing, Servicescapes and Sustainability: A Behavioural Infrastructure Approach

Linda Brennan, Wayne Binney, and John Hall

1 Introduction

This ongoing research study aims to establish a benchmark for sustainability within an organisational context. A group of experts in the field of sustainability education have provided answers to how they implement sustainability within their organisations. This will present a picture of what are the barriers and facilitators for sustainable behaviours in an organisational context, where multiple behaviours are required for sustainable practice. Herremans and Reid (2002) suggest that for any action to be truly sustainable, it should also consider the social, environmental and financial dimensions. That is, without all three dimensions being traded off equally, one will take precedence over the other. For example, cheap recycling facilities and a market for the recycled product are a prerequisite to actual recycling occurring; for without this, financial sustainability will take precedence. For true sustainability, consideration must be given to the combination of the three dimensions of sustainability. Given the trade offs that need to be made, it is extremely difficult to determine the 'right' thing to do. In order to improve the quality of life for all stakeholders involved in fostering sustainability, it is important that organisations engage motivated individuals in creating systems of interactions. Such systems will enable people to participate in resolving social-structural problems such as sustainability.

L. Brennan (✉)
RMIT University, Melbourne, VIC, Australia
e-mail: linda.brennan@rmit.edu.au

W. Binney • J. Hall
Deakin University, Melbourne, VIC, Australia
e-mail: wayne.binney@deakin.edu.au; john.hall@deakin.edu.au

W. Wymer (ed.), *Innovations in Social Marketing and Public Health Communication*, Applying Quality of Life Research,
DOI 10.1007/978-3-319-19869-9_5

2 Sustainability and Higher Educational Institutions

Higher educational institutions (HEI) have a major role to play in tackling one of the world's most 'wicked' problems (Buchanan 1992; Rittel and Webber 1973); that of sustaining the biosphere (Hamann 2012; Howarth et al. 2013; Killeen 2012; McGregor 2012). HEIs are, firstly, responsible for educating those people who will lead the way in resolving the complexities that make up the problems (Shriberg and MacDonald 2013; Sylvestre 2013). Secondly, they are often responsible for researching and disseminating to the world the solutions to the problems that they see (Shephard 2010; Tilbury 2011; Waas et al. 2010). Thirdly, they can take the lead in declaring that the biosphere and our environment matter sufficiently to take action (Lozano et al. 2013; Sibbel 2009; Stephens et al. 2008). The transformative potential of universities in the sustainability space is a powerful one (Adomßent 2013).

Given this potential, one has to wonder what goes wrong when sustainability programs are designed, developed and implemented in HEIs; and why therefore, sustainability in HEIs remains an issue of such scale that there are entire UNESCO conferences devoted to it (Müller-Christ et al. 2014). In order to examine this phenomenon, a social marketing approach was used to understand the behavioural ecology of sustainability in HEIs (see Fig. 5.1).

The behavioural ecological model (BEM) (Hovell et al. 2002), suggests that people's behaviours can be seen as a series of bi-directional influences in a social system where the individual is at the end of a chain of influences, ranging from societal level (macro-system), through community and local levels (meso-systems)

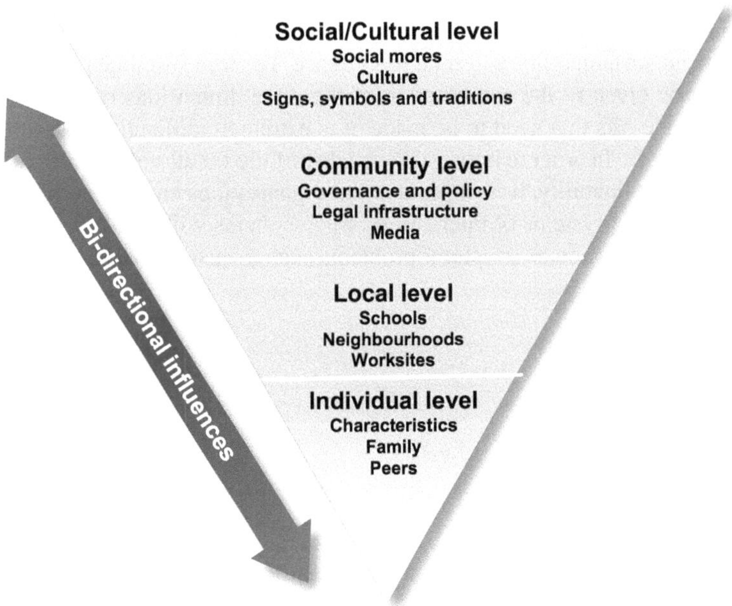

Fig. 5.1 The behavioural ecological model (Adapted from Hovell et al. (2002))

and to the individual in their micro-system. The interplay between these influences directs the outcomes that an individual, an organisation or a society can produce. In the case of HEIs, they operate at the meso-level social system, at the nexus between the community and local levels. However, as a result of their transformative power, they have a wider scope of influence than is normally the case for an organisation.

The first component of a BE approach is to understand the motivations and behaviours of people within their social system. How people behave within their social system, what they do in order to act on their motivations, take account of opportunities and adapt to the behavioural ecology is a relatively new field of research in social marketing settings. Much previous research has been focused on individual behaviour change (Brennan et al. 2014), this chapter suggests that a systems approach is needed for sustainable organizations.

One theoretical framework for understanding behavioural ecologies is that of services marketing. The framework has been used successfully to understand how people interact in the physical, social and procedural environment for women's health services (Zainuddin et al. 2011), government services and public health (Zainuddin et al. 2007, 2009), and the homeless (James and Skinner 2009). The services marketing literature is premised on the idea that servicescapes can be mapped and managed (Bitner 1992; Gronroos 1984). This mapping results in a behavioural environment that is designed so that people, processes and the physical environment interact and produce better service quality outcomes for the consumer (van Doorn et al. 2010). Servicescapes consist of the elements outlined in Fig. 5.2.

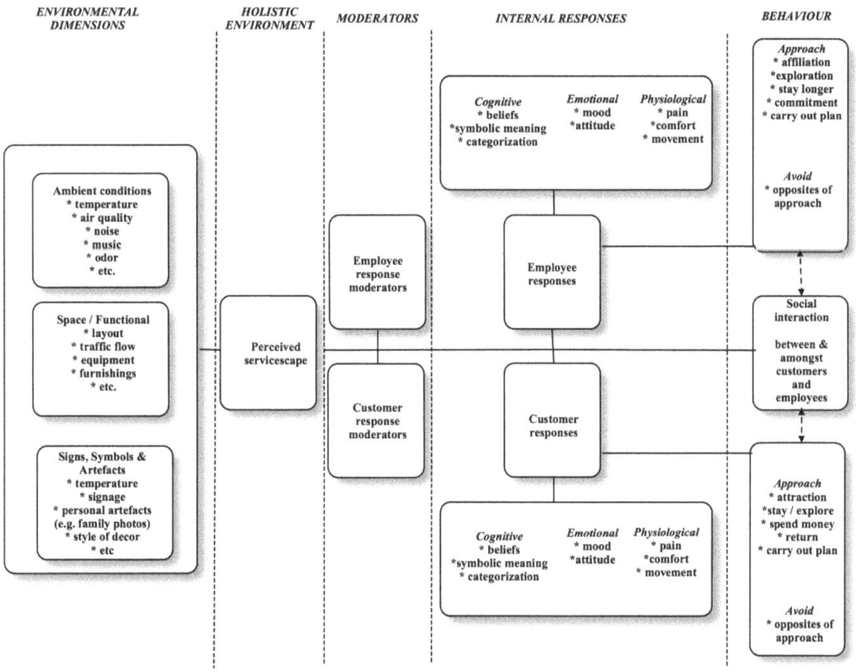

Fig. 5.2 The servicescape model (Adapted from Bitner (1992))

Services marketing is pertinent to the HEI domain because it is an intangible, people dominated 'industry'; where people's behaviours have to be aligned to produce quality outcomes for a variety of stakeholders, including students, employers, governments and society. People oriented services use tools and techniques such as internal marketing to improve outcomes and business performance (George 1990; Piercy and Morgan 1991). Internal marketing is a planned effort using a marketing approach to overcome resistance to change and to align, motivate and coordinate employee behaviours (Rafiq and Ahmed 2000). The desired behaviours will be aligned with corporate and functional strategies and designed to deliver improved outcomes for all stakeholders: internal and external. Internal marketing has been efficacious in the social marketing domain (Previte and Russell-Bennett 2013; Smith 2011) where there is a need to align the behaviours of multiple people in the servicescape to deliver higher quality outcomes. It is especially important where there is a need for co-creation of value (Russell-Bennett et al. 2013).

However, it appears that sustainability in the HEI sector has multiple foci and that there is no coherent effort to create a system wide solution to the sustainability efforts (Brennan and Binney 2011; Krizek et al. 2012). According to Krizek et al. (2012), there are four phases of development of sustainability programs in HEIs: (1) grassroots level; (2) executive acceptance of the business case for sustainability; (3) the visionary campus leader and (4) the fully integrated campus. These micro-meso level systems are commensurate with the 'people' aspect of the servicescape and do not take into account the physical environment or the processes, procedures or behavioural infrastructure that needs to exist in order for sustainability to be achieved. By focusing on only one component of the problem – the business case – the variety of stakeholders who *need* to be involved are not *able* to be engaged with the problem. For example, grass roots movements must prove their financial worth and sell the business case to the executive in order to make progress. This is problematic in university settings where the majority are not privy to the information they require to make a business case.

HEIs tackle sustainability in different ways, however they frequently rely on passionate individuals to make the case for change, such as Krizek et al.'s grassroots champions and visionary leaders. This focus on the individual often leads to surveys of attitudes, intentions and behaviours (see for example, Coy et al. 2013; Figueredo and Tsarenko 2013; Pfahl et al. 2014; Swaim et al. 2013). Further, a majority of this work is with students, who have very limited opportunity to change the campus infrastructure or the behavioural ecology in which they find themselves. Their attitudes may be important, but without the wherewithal in terms of power, they are unlikely to make changes at the university level. Motivated individuals require permission (Hobson 2003), as well as assistance for sustainability to be adopted (Leal Filho 2009). Using the servicescape metaphor, this is tantamount to asking the customers to design their own services. While this might be a goal of the co-creation model in the service dominant logic (Vargo 2011; Vargo and Lusch 2004), it is unlikely that students alone will be able to change campus wide sustainability matters. There is a need for a multi-stakeholder approach, in which the university community is wholly engaged in the process of making the campus sustainable.

Thus, the servicescape must be designed to empower and enable environmental action, in addition to educating people about sustainability and the environment.

3 Behavioural Infrastructure

The servicescape consists of people (students, faculty, professional staff, stakeholders and community), processes, and the physical environment. Any one of these factors can inhibit or enhance the likelihood of achieving a particular outcome. In looking at the people factor only, an opportunity to design an effective system is missed. For example, Binney et al. (2006) using Rothschild's (1999) Motivation-Opportunity-Ability (MOA) framework, found that no matter how motivated people are, they must also have the opportunity to behave in a sustainable manner, in addition to having the ability to make the change and behave sustainably. For the individual this means that opportunities to behave sustainably must be possible; that is, the barriers to the intended behaviour must be removed. Furthermore, there must be an enabling system that empowers people to behave sustainably; thus building their ability to participate in a sustainable way. This creates a dilemma for institutions; as if the costs of recycling are too high, the service will not be provided thereby decreasing the possibility of recycling. In another example, if the building is leased, as is the case for many institutions with central business district locations, it will be impossible to install the water saving, electricity saving or green office facilities without very high levels of cost and the landlord's permission. However, from a behavioural perspective, if motivation is sufficient, then the individual will endeavor to overcome opportunity deficits if they have enough ability (Amico et al. 2005; Berridge 2004). The integration of activities of communities, organisations and individuals can produce synergistic enhancements to quality of life for all.

Behavioural infrastructures are designed to make the behaviour possible (Christmas et al. 2009). At times, motivated and committed people are simply unable to initiate, establish or maintain desired behaviours. For example, when it comes to recycling, products must be manufactured with recycling in mind; recycling facilities have to be available; an endpoint lifecycle for the product being recycled must exist or be established; a procedure whereby people are able to participate must be developed and communicated to the recyclers; and so on throughout the entire life-cycle of the recycling process. As can be observed from this complexity, there are a number of levels and types of behaviour change that must be facilitated in order for a sustainable recycling system to work. Individuals must be able and willing but if they cannot overcome barriers that they have no control over then the recycling behaviour cannot occur. These distal barriers are disconnected from the behaviour and the individual may have no control or influence over them (Booth et al. 2001). Moreover, recycling is only one of many factors in campus sustainability and the chain of effects from individual to institutional sustainability might seem overwhelming for someone at the bottom of the behavioural ecology triangle (Tones and Tilford 2001). Alignment of the proximal-distal chain of effects is required before an individual can behave in a sustainable manner. That is, if too many factors are out of the control of the individual's primary behavioural 'space' they may give up rather than trying to change other components in the system. Behavioural infrastructure can be explicit or implicit. It is not always clear what barriers and facilitators to behaviour can be manipulated for improved environmental outcomes. Behavioural infrastructure is established at the organisational or meso-level of social marketing. That is, the individual (micro-level) may be powerless to change themselves given the macro, exo and meso circumstances that prevail (Gordon 2013). In an example of how behavioural infrastructure can be a barrier to behaviour, Brennan and Binney (2011) examined extant social systems in the Australian higher education system and found that sustaining the environment (biosphere) was espoused by only 7 of the 39 universities in Australia; thereby making it difficult, from an individual practice point of view, to be sustainable. They proposed a framework for organisational infrastructure that would embed sustainability within the social system (in this case the university). This is illustrated in Fig. 5.3.

The underlying premise is that all of these elements must be aligned for an individual to be persuaded to participate in saving the biosphere. There should be an overarching *philosophy*; a clear statement of *policy* – transparent and articulated in terms that the individual can engage with; a *process* by which sustainability can be managed; local *procedures* that consider the micro-level requirements of the individual within the behavioural setting; *promotion* of the issue (including related processes and procedures); advocacy and championship within the organisational context (*people*); there should be a system that provides for observations of

Fig. 5.3 The Nine Ps model of organizational sustainability

behaviours and alerts when 'breaches' occur so that there are social consequences associated with unsustainable behaviours (*policing*); then, as with all things behaviour change, following up (*phollow up*) and perseverance are required for maintained positive change. Behaviour change can sometimes be a matter of providing enough facilitators and benefits to outweigh the barriers and risks inherent to the change. What follows is the results of an examination for how behavioural infrastructure could be created within universities to enable, empower and motivate the participants in the system to co-create a sustainable university. In this study, the role of internal social marketing is to create the interactions between participants in the system that enable co-creation of sustainability to take place. The meso-level participants develop the behavioural infrastructure and create the opportunities for sustainability on each of the platforms: social, financial and environmental. In order to examine how this takes place within university settings we collected data from members of the Australian Campuses Towards Sustainability association (http://www.acts.asn.au/). Members responded to a survey on how sustainability was enacted within their institutions.

4 Methodology

A qualitative phase of research, comprising in-depth interviews and focus groups, was used to develop the quantitative instrument that was used for data collection. In-depth interviews were conducted with university staff who were involved in environmental sustainability. This involvement included teaching, researching and implementing changes in sustainability practices. Discussions were guided by the elements described in Table 5.1 (The Nine Ps framework for environmental action in universities). Using the principles of scale development suggested by De Vellis (2003), after a literature review, a pool of items was developed and discussed with an expert panel of people from four Australian universities. These people were senior members of staff responsible for sustainability operations and initiatives in their universities. Subsequently, a focus group of 10 university employees discussed the draft questionnaire; these participants were not involved in implementing sustainability and were therefore useful informants in terms of content validity, especially in relation to behavioural expectations and institutional performance. The participants were from different universities in order to ensure a range of views were available. The outcome of the focus group was a shorter and more semantically consistent set of items. Using the multi-trait-multi-method approach to validation (Algesheimer et al. 2012; Campbell and Fiske 1959), related items were grouped in sets of three items to ensure that variations could be identified and results triangulated.

The draft questionnaire was then pre-tested on a sample of 20 participants. Participants were involved in environmental sustainability change management across a range of universities. This confirmed that the instrument was ready for use. An ethics approval was prepared and after authorization the instrument was emailed to all members of ACTS in the 27 member universities.

Table 5.1 The Nine Ps of institutional behaviours with regard to the environment

Factors (Nine Ps) & Cronbach alpha	Items	Perf.[a]#	Imp.##	Gap ++
Philosophy 0.77	1.1 A statement of commitment to environmental issues in any planning or strategy documents	5.07	5.75	−0.68
	1.2 Indicative principles of behaviour in relation to the environment are readily available	3.80	5.80	−2.00
	1.3 A clear set of objectives in relation to environmental issues	4.70	6.11	−1.41
Policy 0.88	2.1 An easily understood and readily available policy	4.34	5.52	−1.18
	2.2 An environmental action plan	4.66	6.23	−1.57
	2.3 Both a Policy and a System	3.45	5.74	−2.29
Process 0.76	3.1 Demonstrated initiatives in relation to environmental issues	4.98	6.29	−1.31
	3.2 Measurement of effectiveness in relation to environmental issues	4.28	6.33	−2.05
	3.3 A distributed set of expected behaviours for individuals to do that relate to environmental issues (e.g. turning of lights, printing emails …)	3.50	5.98	−2.48
Procedures 0.83	4.1 An environmental management system (set of processes and procedures)	3.23	5.56	−2.33
	4.2 Environmental sustainability is included in new staff induction	3.09	6.23	−3.14
	4.3 A clear set of steps designed to achieve the various environmental policies	3.64	5.98	−2.34
Promotion 0.96	5.1 Regular internal communication about environment issues (e.g. emails, web updates, e-news)	4.24	6.00	−1.76
	5.2 Regular reporting of the outcome of environmental initiatives	4.26	6.05	−1.79
	5.3 Regular advertising of the successes in dealing with environmental issues (e.g. printed materials, posters placement, etc.)	3.77	6.02	−2.25
People 0.84	6.1 Appointment of environmental champions	3.74	5.81	−2.07
	6.2 Reward and recognition of environmental actions taken by individuals	3.02	5.62	−2.60
	6.3 Support for people undertaking environmental activities (e.g. empowering activism, time off, monetary reimbursement)	2.57	5.07	−2.50

(continued)

Table 5.1 (continued)

Factors (Nine Ps) & Cronbach alpha	Items	Perf.[a]#	Imp.##	Gap ++
Policing 0.73	7.1 Regular audits of environmental sustainability activities	3.72	5.77	−2.05
	7.2 Enforcement of breaches of the environmental policies of the organization	2.45	5.26	−2.81
	7.3 Protection from consequences for people who make complaints about environmental issues within the organization	2.90	5.64	−2.74
Phollow up 0.83	8.1 Closed loop reporting of environmental issues (e.g. issues are addressed and the outcomes are reported to senior management)	3.72	6.00	−2.28
	8.2 Future strategy development in relation to the outcomes of the measures	4.14	5.86	−1.72
	8.3 People are required to complete professional development in relation to environmental sustainability as well as other training (e.g. OH&S, Trade Practices Compliance, Privacy Act, etc.)	2.44	5.44	−3.00
Persevere 0.77	9.1 Long term (greater than 5 years) goals and strategies in relation to environmental issues	3.79	6.02	−2.23
	9.2 Any initiatives that are implemented are given a long term budget and lasting organisational support (greater than 12 months)	3.93	6.49	−2.56
	9.3 Investment in relation to environmental issues is indicated in strategic plans, departmental budget, staff deployment and secondment, etc.	3.86	6.43	−2.57

[a]All significantly lower performance (0.05 level)
performance, ## importance, ++ Gap = Perf-Imp

The questionnaires were checked for completeness and accuracy and the data were prepared for analysis. Frequencies were summated and analysis was undertaken to assess the relationships between 'importance' and 'performance' of the behaviours under investigation.

5 Importance Performance Analysis

This study has a focus on Importance Performance Analysis. Importance performance analysis (IPA) is used as a means of evaluating the implementation of sustainability practices in a university setting. IPA is based on the mean performance of

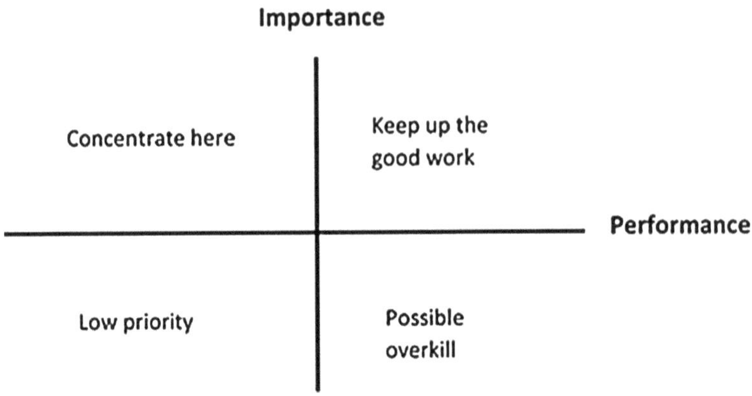

Fig. 5.4 Importance-performance plot (Source: Oh 2001)

and mean importance gained from surveyed respondents for a number of attributes or characteristics of a product or service. This was considered to be a suitable form of analysis for this study as the survey instrument used in this study, is comprised of a battery of 27 items aimed at assessing expectations and performance in regards to sustainability.

IPA is commonly presented on a two dimensional graph anchored by importance on the vertical axis and performance on the horizontal axis. The graph is divided into four quadrants by crosshairs, which are the vertical and horizontal lines. There remains some controversy over the method of crosshair placement, with the two most frequently used being the 'middle of the measurement scale' and using the mean result averaged over all attributes. For this research, the means were used to place the cross hairs where by the vertical axis, or y-axis of the graph illustrates the mean of the respondent's perceived importance of the various variables within the study. Similarly the horizontal axis, or x-axis shows the mean of the respondent's perceived performance in relation to the variables. This decision was based on the arguments presented by Taplin (2012b) (Fig. 5.4).

IPA is a popular, low-cost, easily understood way to arrange information about the attributes of a product or service and provide management strategies for a business to set priorities for potential change. Oh (2001) suggests that this method of analysis has gained popularity among researchers for its "simplicity and ease of application" (p. 617). IPA was used as a method of analyzing information about attributes of sustainability in this research due to its clear results and enabling various management decisions, including reallocation of resources.

Gap analysis is also a way of measuring satisfaction and is frequently used in tandem with IPA quadrant analysis. It is a type of benchmarking, with performance being measured against importance. The importance performance gap was produced by the importance score being subtracted from the performance score (Taplin 2012a). A test was then performed to identify if this difference varied significantly from zero. If the test did not vary significantly from zero then performance had matched importance, if it varied significantly with a positive gap then performance was greater than importance, if the gap is negative then performance is less than expectations.

6 Results

Table 5.1 shows the relative importance and performance analyses whereby results were collected on both perceived importance and whether or not the university undertook this type of activity in support of sustainability.

It should be noted that all of the performance variables score below the importance variables and all are significantly lower at the 0.05 level. Aspects that were seen as being of high importance and necessary for successful implementation of sustainability as evidenced by having a score of six or greater for importance are shown in Table 5.1. This shows that the important factors are having objectives (item 1.3), plans in place (item 2.2), having demonstrated initiatives (item 3.1), having measures of effectiveness (item 3.2), training in new staff induction (item 4.2), regular internal communication (item 5.1), regular reporting on initiatives (item 5.2), regular advertising of successes (item 5.3), closed loop reporting (item 9.1), budgeting and lasting organisational support (item 9.2) and investment in relation to environmental issues (item 9.3).

It should be noted that many items that were considered as being important for sustainability were not being practiced (as evidenced by the low performance levels). This seems somewhat surprising considering that the participant completing the survey was responsible for sustainability policy setting and sustainability activities within their university.

In addition, Table 5.1 shows that performance levels are highest for the initial stages of change such as philosophy, policy, process, and promotion. However, the lower levels for procedures, people, policing, phollowup and persevere indicate that these aspects were not being practiced at satisfactory levels at many universities. This is problematic when it comes creating a behavioural ecology conducive for the widespread adoption of environmental sustainability. The evident disconnect between policy and practice does not bode well for a sustainable organization.

7 Importance/Performance Ratings

The results of the Importance-Performance analysis is graphically depicted in Fig. 5.5. Tables 5.2, 5.3, 5.4, and 5.5 collate the items that appear in each quadrant.

Table two shows those activities that are deemed to be low priority (Table 5.2). These results indicate that there are gaps between performance on these activities but that these are seen as being of lesser importance in achieving organizational goals for sustainability.

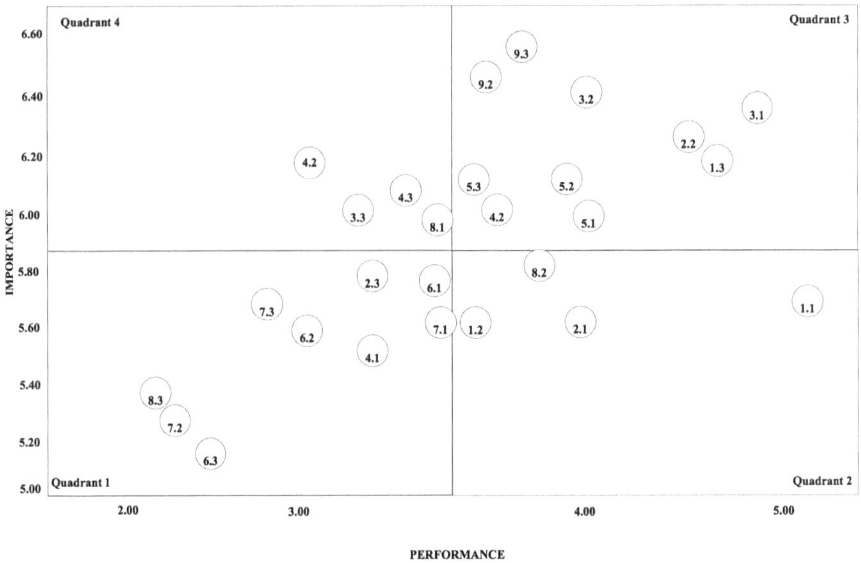

Fig. 5.5 Importance-performance plot for survey results

Table 5.2 Quadrant 1 "Low priority"

Item no.	Item	Gap
2.3	Both a policy and a system	2.29
4.1	An environmental management system (set of processes and procedures)	2.33
6.1	Appointment of environmental champions	2.07
6.2	Reward and recognition of environmental actions taken by individuals	2.60
6.3	Support for people undertaking environmental activities (e.g. empowering activism, time off, monetary reimbursement)	2.50
7.1	Regular audits of environmental sustainability activities	2.05
7.2	Enforcement of breaches of the environmental policies of the organization	2.81
7.3	Protection from consequences for people who make complaints about environmental issues within the organization	2.74
8.3	People are required to complete professional development in relation to environmental sustainability as well as other training (e.g. OH&S, Trade Practices Compliance, Privacy Act, etc.)	3.00

Table 5.3 Quadrant 2 "Possible overkill"

Item no.	Item	Gap
1.1	A statement of commitment to environmental issues in any planning or strategy documents	0.68
1.2	Indicative principles of behaviour in relation to the environment are readily available	2.0
2.1	An easily understood and readily available policy	1.18
8.2	Future strategy development in relation to the outcomes of the measures	1.72

Table 5.4 Quadrant 3 "Keep up the good work"

Item no.	Item	Gap
1.3	A clear set of objectives in relation to environmental issues	1.41
2.2	An environmental action plan	1.57
3.1	Demonstrated initiatives in relation to environmental issues	1.31
3.2	Measurement of effectiveness in relation to environmental issues	2.05
5.1	Regular internal communication about environment issues (e.g. emails, web updates, e-news)	1.76
5.2	Regular reporting of the outcome of environmental initiatives	1.79
5.3	Regular advertising of the successes in dealing with environmental issues (e.g. printed materials, posters placement, etc.)	2.25
9.1	Long term (greater than 5 years) goals and strategies in relation to environmental issues	2.23
9.2	Any initiatives that are implemented are given a long term budget and lasting organisational support (greater than 12 months)	2.56
9.3	Investment in relation to environmental issues is indicated in strategic plans, departmental budget, staff deployment and secondment, etc.	2.57

Table 5.5 Quadrant 4 "Concentrate here"

Item no.	Item	Gap
3.3	A distributed set of expected behaviours for individuals to do that relate to environmental issues (eg turning of lights, printing e-mails...)	2.48
4.2	Environmental sustainability is included in new staff induction	3.14
4.3	A clear set of steps designed to achieve the various environmental policies	2.34
8.1	Closed loop reporting of environmental issues (e.g. issues are addressed and the outcomes are reported to senior management)	2.28

Table 5.3 illustrates that there are activities taking place that may not be necessary – they are potentially 'overkill' and resources might be better invested elsewhere. Mostly these are policy and strategy, indicating perhaps that action is needed, activities that go beyond the written document might be needed.

Table 5.4 illustrates the items where HEIs can claim to be doing good work. Firstly the gaps between performance and importance are lower in this quadrant. Secondly, the reporting and communication elements of sustainability appear to be in hand, as is the alignment between strategies, plans and environmental issues.

Table 5.5 indicates the areas that require some focussed effort on behalf of HEIs if they want to take their environmental efforts to the next level. These items relate to the people aspect of the servicescape and show that working at the organisational (meso) level is required to produce individual level outcomes. For example, procedures that help people understand how to implement sustainability in the workplace start by being communicated in the induction process.

8 Discussion and Implications for Practice

There is a wide range of actions that institutions of higher education can implement to make the transition towards the university-wide adoption of sustainability. This study has identified a set of activities that have been identified as being 'important' and provided an estimate of the level of importance as judged by those responsible for implementing sustainability at a majority of Australian universities. In addition, the study has also provided an estimate of the 'performance' level of these activities across these institutions. Many of the behaviours that have been assessed as being important, have not apparently been implemented (performed). For an HEI to become sustainable, the servicescape must be addressed to ensure that all actors are able to perform sustainability in the work place. Knowing what to do and how to do it, starts with a sustainability philosophy and carries through the entire process from writing policies to ensuring that staff induction includes an introduction to sustainable behaviour.

The results suggest that, in general, it is likely that important sustainability practices are not being performed. These should be implemented as a matter of priority to optimize the overall level of sustainability adoption within the HEI.

Quadrant 1 (low importance/low performance) is referred to as the "Low priority" category. Here, the results show that management would probably obtain more benefit from concentrating on other activities. Examples of practices in this segment include, "support for people undertaking environmental activities" (item 6.3), "enforcement of breaches of the environmental policies of the organisation" (item 7.2) and "people are required to undertake professional development in relation to environmental sustainability..." (item 8.3). These activities are not seen as an implementation priority. Therefore the 'gap' between performance and importance for these practices should not be a concern for university management.

Quadrant 2 (low importance/high performance) is referred to as the "Possible overkill" category. Practices found in this quadrant should be examined as they may be using resources that could be better used in other areas. Practices such as "a statement of commitment to environmental issues is included in any planning or strategy documents" (item 1.1) and "indicative principles of behaviour in relation to the environment are available to all" (item 1.2) are included in this category. Participants are suggesting that as these practices are of low importance and should receive less attention by those involved in implementing organisational environmental sustainability.

In contrast, practices in ***Quadrant 3 (high importance/high performance)*** are already being practiced and this should be maintained. This quadrant is referred to as the "Keep up the good work" quadrant. Practices such as "an environmental action plan" (item 2.2) and "a clear set of objectives in relation to environmental issues" (item 1.3) are included in this category.

Finally, ***Quadrant 4 (high importance/low performance)*** is referred to as the "Concentrate here" category. The practices in this quadrant should be a high priority for implementation in order to improve the level of performance of sustainability overall. Current practices such as "a distributed set of expected behaviours...." (item 3.3), "environmental sustainability is included in the new staff induction" (item 4.2) and "a clear set of steps designed to achieve the various environmental policies" (item 4.3) and "closed loop reporting of environmental issues..." (item 8.1), are included in this category. Participants suggest that the performance of these practices should be improved in order to improve environmental sustainability.

9 Conclusion

Overall, this study has provided insight into management practices surrounding sustainability within HEIs. Using the foundation principle that people are both a contributor to the problem and contributors to any solutions that may arise, a servicescape model using a behavioural framework was established (Nine Ps). This framework argues for the alignment of activities ranging from philosophy, through people to perseverance in the face of continued issues in implementing sustainability within organizations. The servicescape model (Fig. 5.2) illustrates the relationship between the context (conditions, physical environment) and responses to the context. The cognitive, emotional and physiological, as well as behavioural responses to the servicescape influence outcome. For example, a cluttered and littered environment often leads to greater levels of littering as people feel overwhelmed and believe that their effort will not be worthwhile. The social interactions between people within the servicescape result in the outcome, for example, once someone starts cleaning up, others may join in and so on. The management of the servicescape is a process of managing the environment in which the behaviours occur. Internal social marketing is required in order to align activities with the goals of sustainability.

Important to the conceptualization of the servicescape is the element of co-creation of value; where individuals, organisations and the community of practice work together to create desired outcomes. The behavioural framework results show that people are at the nexus of sustainable organisations; the tipping point in the middle of the process. However, the framework might also be a useful diagnostic for ensuring that the behavioural infrastructure exists within the servicescape to enable people to act appropriately when it comes to sustainability within HEIs. In this instance, the role of internal social marketing is to foster and enable the internal communications and social networks required to shift the focus from creating policy to connecting people with the actions they need to take in order to enhance environmental sustainability.

This study identifies a series of activities that make up the behavioral ecological environment for sustainable HEIs. Further, we identify that there is insufficient perfusion of policy level decision making to the individual within their micro-level social setting with large gaps between importance and performance dimensions in this regard. In order for the organizational goals to be aligned with the principles of sustainability, employee responses and behaviours must also be aligned. Such alignment can be brought about by the use of internal social marketing. To create the desired behaviors within the servicescape there is also scope for adjustments to the behavioural infrastructure beyond communication of the issue. For example, our study identified that procedural and people related activities such as including sustainability issues in staff induction (item 4.2), and ensuring that people were clearly told about expectations of behavior how to behave (item 3.3) were important but underperforming opportunities for achieving positive change. Managing expectations is a fundamental platform of services marketing and the principles applied in that domain might be useful in the HEI sector when it comes to enhancing sustainable practice. Again, internal social marketing will be required to set and manage expectations and outcomes of the co-creation process.

Importantly, this study illustrates that the people factor is critical to sustainability and while processes and procedures are necessary, it is a focus on how humans behave in human settings that will enable sustainability to be achieved. HEIs have a role to play in building the behavioural ecology that allows staff, students and the communities they serve to practice sustainability on a very human level. The impact of community level activity can be felt in other levels of the behavioural ecology, for example, by influencing macro and exo level constituencies.

Additionally, using a servicescape mentality can enable operations to determine what changes in the environment are required to bring about desired changes in responses. Each of the elements identified in the behavioural framework has an interactive and cumulative effect on the outcome. Adjustments to policy documents are pointless if people are unable to act or if they cannot access the resources they need to behave responsibly (e.g. recycling). The results of this research show that perseverance and follow up are important components in a behavioural infrastructure system. Hence, there is a need to consider sustainability behaviour as a continuous process that does not end at one event or incident. Thus, the sustainability servicescape has a response loop back to previous dimensions of the model where co-creation of new outcomes can take shape.

From the perspective of co-creating a servicescape environment, our results show that it is important to get the processes and sub-processes right to maximize the cumulative value contributed by people when they engage in sustainability activities. The gaps indicated in Table 5.1 show that there is much to be done in helping people with processes and procedures that describe, permit and empower sustainability. Further, these processes must be underpinned by communication to the right people at the right time in order to generate the desired outcomes; policies on their own do not suffice when it comes to co-creating sustainability.

In using a behavioural framework to explore sustainability in HEIs this study aimed to contribute to emerging research on servicescapes in social marketing. In this case, the servicescape consists of more than a customer > organization dyad. The sustainability servicescape is multi-level (e.g. the actors in the behavioural ecological model are all contributors to the co-created value). It is also complex and multi-dimensional within the organization and the community. However, the Nine Ps framework allows for a relatively simple calculation of the various barriers and facilitators to sustainability practice within HEIs. As such, it offers potential for social marketers aiming to enhance quality of life factors in other domains.

References

Adomßent, M. (2013). Exploring universities' transformative potential for sustainability-bound learning in changing landscapes of knowledge communication. *Journal of Cleaner Production, 49*(June), 11–24.

Algesheimer, R., Bagozzi, R. P., & Dholakia, U. M. (2012). *Key informant models for measuring group-level variables in small groups*. Available at SSRN 1992439. http://dx.doi.org/10.2139/ssrn.1992439: Social Science Research Network.

Amico, K. R., Toro-Alfonso, J., & Fisher, J. D. (2005). An empirical test of the information, motivation and behavioral skills model of antiretroviral therapy adherence. *AIDS Care, 17*(6), 661–673.

Berridge, K. C. (2004). Motivation concepts in behavioural neuroscience. *Physiology and Behaviour, 81*(2), 179–209.

Binney, W., Hall, J., & Oppenheim, P. (2006). The nature and influence of motivation within the MOA framework: Implications for social marketing. *International Journal of Nonprofit and Voluntary Sector Marketing, 11*(4), 289–301.

Bitner, M. J. (1992). Servicescapes: The impact of physical surroundings on customers and employees. *Journal of Marketing, 56*(2), 57–71.

Booth, M. L., Wake, M., Armstrong, T., Chey, T., Hesketh, K., & Mathur, S. (2001). The epidemiology of overweight and obesity among Australian children and adolescents, 1995–97. *Australian and New Zealand Journal of Public Health, 25*(2), 162–169.

Brennan, L., & Binney, W. (2011, April 10–13). *Making sustainability a behaviour in the tertiary sector*. Paper presented at the 2nd World Social Marketing Conference, Dublin.

Brennan, L., Binney, W., Parker, L., Aleti Watne, T., & Nguyen, D. (2014). *Social marketing and behaviour change: Models, theories and applications*. Cheltenham: Edward Elgar.

Buchanan, R. (1992). Wicked problems in design thinking. *Design Issues, 8*(2), 5–21.

Campbell, D. T., & Fiske, D. W. (1959). Convergent and discriminant validation by the multitrait-multimethod matrix. *Psychological Bulletin, 56*(2), 81–105.

Christmas, S., Young, D., Skates, A., Millward, L., Duman, M., & Dawe, I. (2009). *Nine big questions about behaviour change*. http://webarchive.nationalarchives.gov.uk/20110504054311/http://www.dft.gov.uk/pgr/scienceresearch/social/behaviour-changes/pdf/questions.pdf

Coy, A. E., Farrell, A. K., Gilson, K. P., Davis, J. L., & Le, B. (2013). Commitment to the environment and student support for "green" campus initiatives. *Journal of Environmental Studies and Sciences, 3*(1), 49–55.

De Vellis, R. F. (2003). *Scale development: Theory and applications* (2nd ed., Vol. 26). Thousand Oaks: Sage Publications.

Figueredo, F. R., & Tsarenko, Y. (2013). Is "being green" a determinant of participation in university sustainability initiatives? *International Journal of Sustainability in Higher Education, 14*(3), 242–253.

George, W. R. (1990). Internal marketing and organizational behavior: A partnership in developing customer-conscious employees at every level. *Journal of Business Research, 20*(1), 63–70.

Gordon, R. (2013). New ideas–Fresh thinking: Towards a broadening of the social marketing concept? *Journal of Social Marketing, 3*(3), 1–1.

Gronroos, C. (1984). A service quality model and its marketing implications. *European Journal of Marketing, 18*(4), 36–44.

Hamann, R. (2012). The business of development: Revisiting strategies for a sustainable future. *Environment: Science and Policy for Sustainable Development, 54*(2), 18–29.

Herremans, I. M., & Reid, R. E. (2002). Developing awareness of the sustainability concept. *Journal of Environmental Education, 34*(1), 16–20.

Hobson, E. (2003). *Conservation and planning: Changing values in policy and practice*. London: Routledge.

Hovell, M. F., Wahlgren, D. R., & Gehrman, C. A. (2002). The behavioral ecological model. In R. J. DiClemente, R. A. Crosby, & M. C. Kegler (Eds.), *Emerging theories in health promotion practice and research. Strategies for improving public health* (pp. 347–385). San Francisco: Jossey Bass.

Howarth, L. M., Roberts, C. M., Thurstan, R. H., & Stewart, B. D. (2013). The unintended consequences of simplifying the sea: Making the case for complexity. *Fish and Fisheries, 15*(4), 690–711.

James, S., & Skinner, H. (2009). The shoreline project for street drinkers: Designing and running a supported housing project for the "Unhousable". *Social Marketing Quarterly, 15*(3), 49–66.

Killeen, T. (2012). Chapter 14: Global environmental sustainability: An "All-Hands on Deck" research imperative. In L. E. Weber & J. J. Duderstadt (Eds.), *Global sustainability and the responsibilities of universities* (pp. 167–178). Paris: Economica.

Krizek, K. J., Newport, D., White, J., & Townsend, A. R. (2012). Higher education's sustainability imperative: How to practically respond? *International Journal of Sustainability in Higher Education, 13*(1), 19–33.

Leal Filho, W. (2009). *Sustainability at universities: Opportunities, challenges and trends* (Vol. 31). Frankfurt am Main: Peter Lang.

Lozano, R., Lukman, R., Lozano, F. J., Huisingh, D., & Lambrechts, W. (2013). Declarations for sustainability in higher education: Becoming better leaders, through addressing the university system. *Journal of Cleaner Production, 48*(June), 10–19.

McGregor, S. L. (2012). Complexity economics, wicked problems and consumer education. *International Journal of Consumer Studies, 36*(1), 61–69.

Müller-Christ, G., Sterling, S., van Dam-Mieras, R., Adomßent, M., Fischer, D., & Rieckmann, M. (2014). The role of campus, curriculum, and community in higher education for sustainable development–A conference report. *Journal of Cleaner Production, 62*, 134–137.

Oh, H. (2001). Revisiting importance–Performance analysis. *Tourism Management, 22*(6), 617–627.

Pfahl, M., Casper, J., Trendafilova, S., McCullough, B. P., & Nguyen, S. N. (2014). Crossing boundaries: An examination of sustainability department and athletics department collaborationregardingenvironmentalissues.*CommunicationandSport*.doi:10.1177/2167479513519253, 2167479513519253.

Piercy, N., & Morgan, N. (1991). Internal marketing—The missing half of the marketing programme. *Long Range Planning, 24*(2), 82–93.

Previte, J., & Russell-Bennett, R. (2013). The need for internal social marketing (ISM): Extending the people focus to service employees. In G. Hastings & C. Domegan (Eds.), *Social marketing: From tunes to symphonies* (pp. 326–334). Milton Park: Routledge.

Rafiq, M., & Ahmed, P. K. (2000). Advances in the internal marketing concept: Definition, synthesis and extension. *Journal of Services Marketing, 14*(6), 449–462.

Rittel, H. W., & Webber, M. M. (1973). 2.3 planning problems are wicked. *Polity, 4*, 155–169.

Rothschild, M. L. (1999). Carrots, sticks, and promises: A conceptual framework for the management of public health and social issue behaviors. *Journal of Marketing, 63*(4), 24–37.

Russell-Bennett, R., Wood, M., & Previte, J. (2013). Fresh ideas: Services thinking for social marketing. *Journal of Social Marketing, 3*(3), 223–238.

Shephard, K. (2010). Higher education's role in 'education for sustainability'. *Australian Universities' Review, 52*(1), 13–22.

Shriberg, M., & MacDonald, L. (2013). Sustainability leadership programs: Emerging goals, methods & best practices. *Journal of Sustainability Education, 15*, 153–167. 10.1016/S0952-8733(02)00006-5.

Sibbel, A. (2009). Pathways towards sustainability through higher education. *International Journal of Sustainability in Higher Education, 10*(1), 68–82.

Smith, A. M. (2011). Chapter 20: Internal social marketing: lessons from the field of services marketing. In G. Hastings, K. Angus, & C. Bryant (Eds.), *The SAGE handbook of social marketing* (pp. 298–316). London: SAGE.

Stephens, J. C., Hernandez, M. E., Román, M., Graham, A. C., & Scholz, R. W. (2008). Higher education as a change agent for sustainability in different cultures and contexts. *International Journal of Sustainability in Higher Education, 9*(3), 317–338.

Swaim, J. A., Maloni, M. J., Napshin, S. A., & Henley, A. B. (2013). Influences on student intention and behavior toward environmental sustainability. *Journal of Business Ethics, 124*(3), 465–484.
Sylvestre, P. A. (2013). *Multiple visions of sustainability as an organizing principle for change in higher education: How faculty conceptualizations of sustainability in higher education suggest the need for pluralism.* Master of Environmental Studies, Dalhousie University, http://hdl.handle.net/10222/21924
Taplin, R. H. (2012a). Competitive importance-performance analysis of an Australian wildlife park. *Tourism Management, 33*(1), 29–37.
Taplin, R. H. (2012b). The value of self-stated attribute importance to overall satisfaction. *Tourism Management, 33*(2), 295–304.
Tilbury, D. (2011). Higher education for sustainability: A global overview of commitment and progress. *Higher Education in the World, 4*, 18–28. Retrieved from.
Tones, K., & Tilford, S. (2001). *Health promotion: Effectiveness, efficiency and equity.* Cheltenham: Nelson Thornes.
van Doorn, J., Lemon, K. N., Mittal, V., Nass, S., Pick, D., Pirner, P., & Verhoef, P. C. (2010). Customer engagement behavior: Theoretical foundations and research directions. *Journal of Service Research, 13*(3), 253–266. doi:10.1177/1094670510375599.
Vargo, S. L. (2011). Market systems, stakeholders and value propositions: Toward a service-dominant logic-based theory of the market. *European Journal of Marketing, 45*(1/2), 217–222.
Vargo, S. L., & Lusch, R. F. (2004). The four service marketing myths remnants of a goods-based, manufacturing model. *Journal of Service Research, 6*(4), 324–335.
Waas, T., Verbruggen, A., & Wright, T. (2010). University research for sustainable development: Definition and characteristics explored. *Journal of Cleaner Production, 18*(7), 629–636.
Zainuddin, N., Russell-Bennett, R., & Previte, J. A. (2007). Conceptualising a relational approach to value creation in a government service: Implications for social marketing. In G. Sullivan Mort & M. Hume (Eds.), *Social entrepreneurship, social change and sustainability: 2007 international nonprofit and social marketing conference*, Brisbane, 27–28 Sept 2007.
Zainuddin, N., Previte, J., & Russell-Bennett, R. (2009). *A qualitative investigation of sources of value in social marketing from the lens of a public health service.* Paper presented at the proceedings from Australian and New Zealand Marketing Academy conference 2009: Sustainable Management and Marketing.
Zainuddin, N., Previte, J., & Russell-Bennett, R. (2011). A social marketing approach to value creation in a well-women's health service. *Journal of Marketing Management, 27*(3–4), 361–385.

Chapter 6
Faces of Power, Ethical Decision Making and Moral Intensity. Reflections on the Need for Critical Social Marketing

Jan Brace-Govan

1 Introduction

Any 'mythunderstandings' of social marketing were tackled by Donovan (2011) where Rothschild's (1999) separation of marketing from law and education is roundly dismissed and the exchange process with a consumer orientation reaffirmed. Education, law, advocacy and environmental influences are all to be enlisted to achieve socially desirable goals. As Hastings moves from tunes to symphonies (Hastings and Domegan 2014), *Dove* is hailed as a commercial social marketing success (Anker and Kappel 2011) and many social marketers from the UK recognise the increasing impact of nudge and practice theory at government level. Recent commentary published in the *Journal of Social Marketing* recommends brokering new collaborations and extensions to social marketing's reach, most particularly through 'upstream' influence. However, social marketing's increasing influence is not without its critics. In a general marketing context, Crane and Desmond ask what happens when those who defend social interest fail to secure sufficient power to have marketers taken them seriously (2002, p. 558) and find that relying on the individual as the moral agent "veils the social context" and the imbalance of power relations (2002, p. 562). Critics posit that this is the case for social marketing as well (Tadajewski et al. 2014).

There is dearth of critical, published social marketing that reviews its own performance as a social actor and influencer of social norms with the intention of improving its contribution to our quality of life. Especially lacking is critically derived research that aims to support social marketing in avoiding inadvertent, uncalculated effects that result in reactance, counternormative uptake, stigma or

J. Brace-Govan (✉)
Department of Marketing, Monash Business School, Monash University,
Melbourne, VIC, Australia
e-mail: jan.brace-govan@monash.edu

W. Wymer (ed.), *Innovations in Social Marketing and Public Health Communication*, Applying Quality of Life Research,
DOI 10.1007/978-3-319-19869-9_6

discrimination. Recognising that this type of engagement relies on debates more active in other disciplines around social relations of power and ethical decision making, this chapter argues for the incorporation of critical theory. Two theoretical debates are drawn from other disciplines to show a way forward that embraces critical thinking and analysis. One theoretical debate from critical management studies is summarised to show how organisational power might be discussed and how thoughtfulness around the empowerment of organisational members is required in order that ethical decisions can be arrived at with the least compromise of virtuous action. The other, from macromarketing, highlights some key ideas for ethical decision making and is extended to take moral intensity into account. It is a contribution of this chapter to engage with conceptions of power that identify the role of organisations. This moves beyond the current over-individualised view of social marketers' responsibilities to recognise the separate and important responsibility of social marketing organisations, particularly when those are configured as collaborating consortia, and their ability to wield power under neoliberalism.

The chapter will proceed firstly with a brief history of social marketing to set the scene and recognise its beginnings in commercial marketing also identifying several promising directions that are emerging in response the challenges, particularly in the *Journal of Social Marketing*. After noting the comparative lack of critical debate and the depth of some critiques of social marketing, the role of critical marketing in addressing these shortcomings is asserted. The implications of moving 'upstream' are reviewed before frames of power, ethics and morality are considered as important, interlinked and indicative of a need for both education and evaluation.

2 From the Beginning and Setting the Scene

The history of social marketing is widely reported (see for example Dann 2010; Dibb 2014; Lefebvre 2011; McAuley 2014; McDermott et al. 2005; Moor 2011) and typically the initiation of social marketing is attributed to Kotler and Zaltman (1971) who first proposed a controversial approach to planned social change that incorporated the principles of marketing. Distinguishing social marketing from commercial marketing focussed on social marketing's commitment to behaviour change (Andreasen 1994, 1995, 2002), a distinction used to identify 'genuine' social marketing (McDermott et al. 2005; Lefebvre 2011; Luca and Suggs 2010). Definitions also incorporated the aim of behaviour change through social marketing as benefitting society and individuals (Andreasen 2006; Donovan and Henley 2010; French et al. 2006; Hastings 2007; Kotler and Lee 2008; Sargeant 2005). The increasing institutionalisation and consolidation of social marketing has led to international and local professional associations using fairly consistent definitions of social marketing. The International Social Marketing Association (iSM) (2014) offers this:

> Social Marketing seeks to develop and integrate marketing concepts with other approaches to influence behaviours that benefit individuals and communities for the greater social good. Social Marketing practice is guided by ethical principles. It seeks to integrate

research, best practice, theory, audience and partnership insight, to inform the delivery of competition sensitive and segmented social change programmes that are effective, efficient, equitable and sustainable

This flexible and broadly encompassing definition reflects some of the debates social marketers have engaged in over the years. An over association with communication (McAuley 2014; Luca and Suggs 2010), a fixation with the 4Ps (Peattie and Peattie 2003, 2009) and the complications of engaging with communities are some of the challenges debated by social marketers.

In response to the additional complexities of social marketing Sargeant (2005, p. 193) suggested extending the usual marketing mix of the 4 Ps (product, price, place, and promotion) by adding policy and partnerships to create 6Ps. These additions recognised that social marketing campaigns often bring together multiple different organisations focussed on changing the same behaviour through partnerships and, that influencing policy through persuasion or political lobbying upstream was often crucial to achieve enabling regulatory change (Donovan and Henley 2010; Hoek and Jones 2011). A good example are anti-smoking campaigns where upstream the regulations around tobacco packaging and smoking in buildings were altered by government, while downstream support for individuals who smoked was tailored to different segments of the population defined by variations in stages of quitting. A further extension to the complexity of social marketing, when compared to commercial marketing, resides in manipulating the concept of exchange. In commercial marketing this is perceived to be “the act of obtaining a desired object from someone by offering something in return” (Kotler et al. 2009, p. 882). Social marketing attempted to retain the concept of exchange but recognised that this varied considerably. It could demand significant personal change, such as quitting smoking, or it could be comparatively low as in littering, or of more immediate benefit to the community than the individual (Rangan et al. 1996). The emphasis on exchange and individual change utilised theories of behaviour change drawn from psychology and widely utilised by public health, such as health belief model, theory of reasoned action, and theory of planned behaviour (Spotswood and Tapp 2013, p. 277).

To address highly demanding interventions and improve uptake, suggestions were made to broaden social marketing through community based models. In addition to engaging with the complexity of changing people’s lifestyle, key to this strategy was recognition that communities have a significant role in shaping social norms. An early example is the Community Readiness Model (Kelly et al. 2003) based on the Stages of Change. In essence the market research, intervention and evaluation stages of a social marketing campaign extend the focus to incorporate the engagement of community leaders. This created socially relevant champions for the intervention who work with the campaign to actively integrate the intervention into multiple facets of community life. For example, a youth drug initiative could be centred on a school, be extended to public discussion forums, incorporate additional recreational facilities for young people and establish parent support groups (Kelly et al. 2003, p. 419). The community model embraced the broader social context, midstream, and has been used extensively in sustainability initiatives (McKenzie-Mohr 2000; McKenzie-Mohr and Schultz 2014). Thus the political, legal, demographic, economic, social, cultural, technological and political factors would be considered (Donovan and Henley 2010). While this acknowledges a multiplicity of inputs, it is less clear what their relation to each other is except that within that mix there is a target audience.

The interplay between individuals and their context is also addressed at the intersection of public health, health promotion and social marketing. While this relationship between the disciplines continues to evolve, and even though Andreasen (2002) called for social marketing to assert its dominance, nevertheless efforts to combine the forces of behaviour change are available. For example the *People and Places Framework* (Maibach et al. 2007) engages multiple levels of research and a range of approaches. Described as a framework for "public health action rather than a theory or theoretical framework for research purposes" (Maibach et al. 2007, p. 3), importantly, social marketing is argued to be a key skill for health promotion professionals. The model, shown below in Fig. 6.1, combines many attributes of either people or places (Maibach et al. 2007). This omnibus framework identifies attributes of people in the categories of individuals, social networks, community, and the attributes of place through the local level and population level.

The National Social Marketing Centre (NSMC) (undated) also embraced a diversity of elements, and developed criteria to define a social marketing approach, extending and refining Andreasen's original six benchmarks to eight. Also an omnibus model, the NSMC model lays out the key underlying tenets of social marketing drawn from its commercial cousin (marketing mix; segmentation; exchange; customer orientation; market/audience research). The relative openness of definitions leaves social marketers able to utilize multifarious and diverse resources for their toolkit (Dibb 2014), making this also a flexible, responsive model.

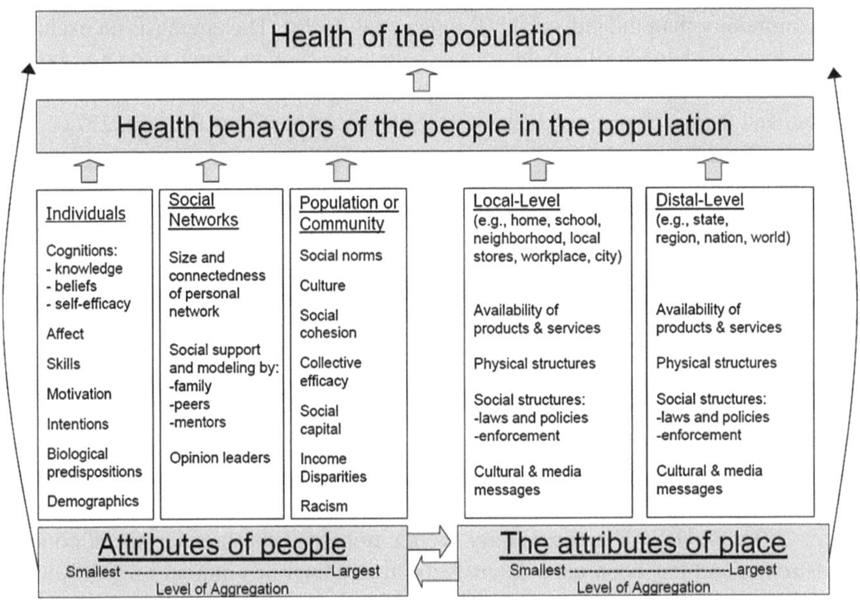

Fig. 6.1 A people and places framework for public health influence (Maibach et al. 2007)

Moving beyond reliance on commercial marketing's 4Ps was a challenge for social marketing with which Peattie and Peattie (2003, 2009, 2011) engaged. Noting the usefulness of social marketing to the wider social policy agenda, particularly in health, they proposed that social marketing could develop its own 'marketing mix' to better address its functionality (Peattie and Peattie 2003, 2009, 2011). In brief, they suggest propositions instead of products, accessibility instead of place, costs of involvement instead of price, and social communication instead of promotion, by which they intended a more interactive style where the focus was on building relationships (Peattie and Peattie 2009, pp. 263–264). Working through the key tenets of relationship marketing identified the value of collaboration and cooperation with the target audience, and also emphasised the importance of partnerships. Hastings (2003) was amongst the first to develop a relational approach that incorporated interaction, dialogue and value creation, arguing that such a framework was strategic and holistic (cf. Marques and Domegan 2011).

Recently, other approaches have been suggested for social marketing. For example, the burgeoning importance of service dominant logic (Vargo and Lusch 2004) has been taken up and a services approach to social marketing proposed (Russell-Bennet et al. 2013a, b). Drawing from the 7Ps of services marketing Russell-Bennett et al. (2013b) argue for the centrality of the service experience, the criticality of the service employee, the quality of the service and the customer as an active participant in the delivery of service. Others have also noted the applicability of value co-creation in developing social marketing interventions, although not without some reservations around the transfer of these commercial marketing developments into the social change arena (McHugh and Domegan 2013; Domegan et al. 2013). For example, noting that customer orientation could be a misnomer given that interventions are "designed and managed by experts" rather than by the targeted participants and communities, thus questioning the actual extent to which co-creation occurs (Domegan et al. 2013, p. 246). Nonetheless the interest in meaningful and productive engagement with communities and their quality of life continues to attract new approaches, such as Fry's (2104) consideration of communities of practice as a means to intervene and connect individuals in their efforts to change drinking habits.

Asserting the limitations of the 4Ps, Tapp and Spotswood have made two further propositions in this debate. One relies on sociological theory to draw attention to the need for cultural understanding through Bourdieu (Spotswood and Tapp's 2013), and the other offers a wheel model derived from a systematic review in public health (Tapp and Spotswood 2013). While Dibb (2014, p. 1165) notes the wheel could be conceived of as a competitor, the effort to integrate this into social marketing is a good example of the interrelationship with public health, particularly as this is presented as an alternative to the 4Ps. The Behaviour Change Wheel (Michie et al. 2011) was devised from a systematic review of frameworks for behaviour change that generated 19 different approaches to intervention for assessment and is shown in Fig. 6.2 below.

The inner circle of the figure (Michie et al. 2011) is derived from a combination of behavioural theorists and US criminal law assertions that in order to commit a crime, volitional behaviour relies on capability (means), opportunity and motivation

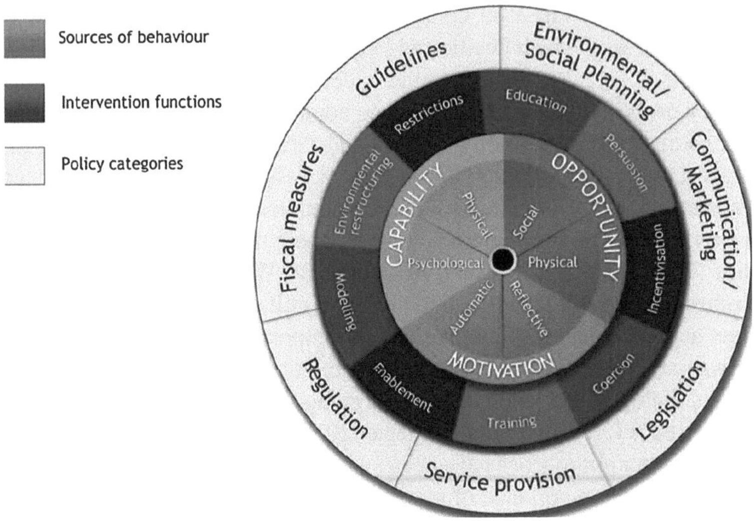

Fig. 6.2 The behaviour change wheel (Michie et al. 2011)

(Michie et al. 2011, p. 4). The definitional separation of interventions and policies identifies nine types of intervention aimed at behavioural change and seven types of policy where responsible authorities enable or support interventions, thus arguing that interventions lie between policies and behaviour (Michie et al. 2011, pp. 6–7). But, the atomistic, individualised decision focus at the centre of this model downplays the social context within which individuals must live, even though it is suggested that a strength of this "framework is that is *incorporates context very naturally*" (Michie et al. 2011, p. 8 {emphasis added}). While it is noted that "context is key to the effective design and implementation of interventions" they also remark that this "remains under-theorised and under-investigated" (Michie et al. 2011, p. 8). This latter comment echoes Spotswood and Tapp's (2013) concern where they identify the most significant role of culture (a more complex concept than context) in achieving successful and lasting behaviour change.

Absorbing social context into models has the potential to make spurious assumptions, particularly about motives and influences (cf Bourdieu in Spotswood and Tapp 2013) and the values that underpin perceptions of what is quality of life. The theorisation of cultural context is strong in disciplines such as geography or sociology, which have recently turned their focus to considering how to achieve social and behavioural change for the sustainability of the environment and to address issues of over-consumption. Indeed Shove (2010) initiated a heated debate over what she termed psychology's simplistic ABC of behaviour change. Challenging theorists to more fully engage with the habits, lived contexts and taken-for-granted social norms, as well as the role of artefacts and technology, Shove was scathing of the ability of individualist models that relied on rationality to address the significance of the change required. Behavioural economics has also investigated habits and their resistance to change (Thaler and Sustein 2008) noting that it often takes significant disruption, like moving house, to alter some ingrained habits (Verplanken and Wood 2006). These alternatives to social marketing have come to governments' attention and there are calls to broaden and deepen the field (Dibb 2014), as well as to extend upstream (Gordon 2013; Hoek and Jones 2011).

In sum then, social marketing emerged from commercial marketing. Initially reliant on the traditional marketing mix, social marketing began to expand its definition to better reflect its additional complexities and the valuable work it was undertaking both downstream and upstream. Lefebvre (2011) suggests that there were two streams of social marketing: one in developing countries where the exchange base of the 4Ps was appropriate for the tasks; and another in developed nations which required more varied approaches. Through HIV/AIDS and anti-tobacco campaigns social marketing's compatibility with public health extended its sphere of activities to encompass all manner of interventions to improve quality of life, including for example the renewed interest around sustainable living behaviours. However, with that expansion, particularly with the intention to engage at the group, community, midstream level came challenges that seemed to require adjustments to the underpinning approaches, models and rationales.

While this wider uptake has had the most positive effect of establishing social marketing internationally and professionally, it has also had paradoxical effects. Such as drawing social marketing closer to public health (Wymer 2010, 2011) thus increasing the need for professional collaboration while concurrently distinguishing the contribution of social marketing and, at the same time, exposing the shortcomings of the individualised rational exchange approaches. However, social marketing's increasing usefulness to the implementation of public policy has opened up some critique of its influence. Tadajewski et al. (2014, pp. 8–10) issue strong warnings and accuse social marketing of downplaying power relations, neglecting moral reflection, and institutional actors (organisations and governments) colluding in an ideology of pseudo-participation to manipulate people. A contribution of this chapter is to consider how social marketing can take such a damning critique on board and proactively adjust. It is suggested that, accusations that social power has been overlooked or misconstrued needs to be more closely examined from a perspective which clearly acknowledges interaction effects and avoids descending into relativism. To address this first we will turn to a brief history of reviews and critiques, following which a useful lens for continued self-review is offered by critical marketing, which concurrently can serve as a means to consider the impacts of wielding power in social arenas that affect quality of life.

3 Reviews, Critiques and Implications

In spite of close connections to public health and the prevalence of reviews in that discipline, published reviews that go beyond considering the definition of social marketing are limited, which could be attributed to reluctance on the part of editors, authors or funders. A review of social marketing for nutrition (McDermott et al. 2005) addressed the question of identifying "genuine" social marketing using Andreasen's (2002) six benchmarks. These benchmarks are: behaviour change; audience research; segmentation; exchange; marketing mix (4Ps); and competition. Interestingly, a systematic review of nine electronic databases requiring that only two out of six benchmarks for a social marketing study were met generated only 16 studies. Broadening the search beyond studies that self-described as social marketing but also requiring that all six benchmarks were met generated 27 studies. A more recent review of 15 databases across a broad range of interventions also used Andreasen's (2002) benchmarks and generated 17 interventions out of which the 'complete' marketing mix (6Ps) was found in only four interventions (Luca and Suggs 2010). The study found that Promotion (17 studies) was addressed most thoroughly, and that Product (17 studies), Place (17 studies), Partnerships (17 studies) and Price (13 studies) received good attention, but Policy was almost overlooked with only four studies discussing this facet out of the set of 17. Important to this discussion is the very small number of studies that either review found that met the stated criteria of social marketing. The implications are that either a great deal of high quality social marketing is conducted without being published, or that a significant number of studies are unable, for whatever reason, to cover all aspects of high quality social marketing in the published version, both of which are possible.

Moving beyond identifying studies that meet definitional criteria, a review by Pechmann and Slater (2005) pointed out how rare it was to find discussion of negative or unintended consequences of social marketing. Understated in most published work are concerns that social marketing campaigns have unintended consequences such as stimulating interest in, or weakening resistance to, targeted undesirable behaviour, like illicit drug use (Pechmann and Slater 2005, p. 185). Pechmann and Slater speculate that there is limited published evidence on the negative effects because adverse effects are rare or limited, or editors are unwilling to publish null effects, or research is not designed to capture such evidence (2005, p. 186). They suggest eight different negative effects including counternormative reactions and reactance. Counternormative reactions occur when a social marketing campaign describes an undesirable behaviour as prevalent and those who were not actually engaged in that behaviour start to perceive themselves as deviating from a norm and take up the undesirable behaviour (such as long showers or taking drugs). Reactance is when people feel so pressured to make a change that they are motivated to act in the opposite way, especially if it appears that their freedom is threatened (Pechmann and Slater 2005, pp. 193–195). Better quality messaging with high quality pretesting is given as the remedy (Pechmann and Slater 2005, p. 202). While the criticisms are well made, it is unclear how more of the same will transform the crucial interaction.

However, for an industry and academic discipline that shoulders the burden of adjusting social attitudes and norms with the clear intention of changing behaviour this is inadequate. The lack of research on the deleterious effects of social marketing is a seriously neglected area deserving of attention, especially as the intention of most programs is to alter peoples' ideas around social norms, thus making social marketing complicit in the creation of deviance and the negative labelling of those who do not comply (Gurrieri et al. 2013). Open and available self-review is a fundamental and crucial democratic obligation for any discipline that aims to direct human behaviour so that wider critical debate about the negative, unintended consequences of interventions is possible. Publishing in social marketing therefore needs to move beyond recording activities and the search for the perfect definition, to debate short-comings, inadvertent effects and the responsible, moral means of wielding significant social power, whether on their own behalf or on the behalf of funding partners. There are several implications here. One implication of this is that high quality evaluations need to be incorporated into social marketing campaigns and made available through publication. Clear professional ethical requirements would support social marketers in achieving this goal. Another implication is that a deeper debate around moral intention and ethics is required, which relies on and is deeply connected to the third implication that an overt discussion of power needs to be undertaken.

Fundamentally, the key overlooked dimension here is the unequal distribution of power in the social marketing process. In this social marketing follows the commonplace, agnostic approach to power exhibited through most commercially focussed micro marketing (Dholakia 2012). The underlying power and influence that is exerted through the 'exchange' mechanism was recognised by Brenkert (2002) who correctly identified that, unlike commercial marketing, there are more than two parties to this exchange process (if exchange can even be asserted to exist). Brenkert (2002) notes that behind the 'exchange' between the consumer and the social marketing intervention there is another usually unacknowledged and often powerful partner in the government or funding agency. Moreover, the intention to alter behaviour and this asymmetrical relationship creates a moral relation between social marketers and their target audiences (Brenkert 2002, p. 21, 2008, pp. 211–215).

Overall then, social marketing has evolved from its commercial cousin to encompass all manner of upstream, midstream and downstream strategies and tactics. There are ongoing discussions around the complexity of social marketing that focus on partnerships either through working with communities or with decision makers. Drawing from other disciplines is valuable, but less attention has been paid to the disciplines that clarify the relationship between elements, contexts and social impacts, such as sociology, politics or management. There is a distinct lack of focus on the effects of power, particularly that wielded by organisations, and a reluctance to examine the unintended consequences of shifting social norms. Despite the profound lack of discussion of the politics of social change, nonetheless the significance of this power is unconsciously acknowledged through considerations of the ever widening scope of social marketing. Thus upstream lobbying, the involvement of community are all discussed with the intention of increasing the chances of achieving the targeted behaviour. The unacknowledged facet here is the power that has to be grasped and wielded, albeit with good intentions, and this raises two important and connected questions: how will power be theorised and; how will this impact on the ethics of the social marketing organisation? A well-established interdisciplinary way into these discussions is through critical theory and the next section briefly considers critical marketing and critical social marketing before moving on to examine theories of power and the implications of upstream.

4 Critical Marketing's Connection to Social Marketing

Any critical contribution of social marketing needs to move beyond utilising a "degree of realism" achieved through experience (Hastings and Saren 2003, p. 315) and engage more deeply with social theory. In order to scrutinize the wider effects of social marketing adopting a critical stance has much to offer (Gordon 2013) and could challenge what Wymer (2011) calls the filters of mental models and tacit assumptions that bias social marketing towards individual behaviour. A key contribution is the ability of critical perspectives to adopt a panoramic view through engagement with macro-level studies where other disciplines can enhance theorisations (Dholakia 2012). Thus critical social marketing would need move well beyond simply studying the impact of commercial marketing with a view to influencing policy, as suggested by Gordon (2011, p. 92). Engaging with a critical discourse is not to be confused with using a critical theory to demystify an ideological position, question the nature of reality and knowledge, and through critique envision new possibilities (Burton 2001, p. 726). Critical theory is *not* a single definable entity and so pursing definitions is illusory (cf. Gordon 2011). Critical theory is not "a single unified theory", rather it comprises theories "about values and what ought to be" (Burton 2001, p. 726), and draws from a range of politicised viewpoints with the clear aim of emancipation. Such a perspective shifts critical social marketing closer to activism than advertising (cf. Wymer 2010).

Therefore critical marketing challenges the marketing concept (4Ps) and customer orientation as ideological and part of a normalising discourse (Ellis et al. 2011) that legitimates and legitimises marketing and marketers (Marion 2006). Fundamental to the carriage of the marketing discourse is the neoliberal commitment to the free market and lean government. Sociological analysis of the rise of neo-liberalism and its "vociferous attack" on welfarism is widely documented (Centeno and Cohen 2012, p. 325). Through the neo-liberal oeuvre, faith in market mechanisms has been profound (Centeno and Cohen 2012, p. 330) normalising market effects to the status of a "natural law of social life" whereby free markets became synonymous with democracy (Centeno and Cohen 2012, p. 329). Moreover the concept of 'individual choice' underpinned much of the persuasive rationale of governments, not least within the public sector where 'consumer choice' was touted as the means to generate competition and so achieve high quality service and lean financial management in services previously provided by government under the welfare model. Labelled the New Public Management (Laing 2003), this style of management was enabled through specific finance and quality processes and rested on the conceptualisation of individual choices as unconstrained. Beyond the management of government institutions, the citizen is hailed as a consumer and the responsibilities of government are shifted away from provision. Through critical discourse analysis social marketing was identified as a vehicle to bring market rationalities into the public sphere and thus change the relationship between government and citizens (Raftopoulou and Hogg 2010, p. 1210). In this study the complexity of framing, citizenship and surveillance are juxtaposed to reveal social marketing as a tool in restricting the political dialogue and promoting the incumbent government (Raftopoulou and Hogg 2010, p. 1219). Reliance on individualism largely ignores relevant and potentially defining social and economic contexts (cf. Bourdieu 1984; Moor 2011, p. 307; Wymer 2010, 2011). In addition, by locating the source of the problem in individual choice, the debate around *other* causes of social problems, and the means to address these, is suppressed (Centeno and Cohen 2012; Moor 2011, p. 312; Raftopoulou and Hogg 2010, p. 1211).

Moor's (2011) detailed critical analysis of social marketing identifies several implicit assumptions and oversights. For example, the assumption that people lack "motivation" and "information" individualises issues and turns a blind eye to the effect of social structures and institutions (Moor 2011, p. 303). The lack of a "robust social basis" for social marketing concepts (Moor 2011, p. 302) but the neat fit of these concepts with "prevailing political philosophies and modes of governance across a range of national contexts" (Moor 2011, p. 304) brings her to assert that social marketing is not "simply a body of knowledge *about* the world but also a form of action that is *constitutive* of the spheres in which it seeks to intervene" (Moor 2011, p. 306 {emphasis in original}). Thus as a source of expertise and a legitimated, institutionalised source of intervention social marketing is deeply implicated in reframing socio-moral issues as the responsibility of the individual and away from the rights of citizens to care and support (Moor 2011). A crucial part of the technologies of government, social marketing supported the emergence of the entrepreneurial self whose citizenship is manifest in personal fulfilment (Rose and Miller 1992).

A strong proponent of critical marketing is Tadajewski (2010, 2014), but in pointing to the lack of consideration of power relations, Tadajewski et al. (2014, p. 9) accuse social marketing of "pseudo-participation" and "thinly veiled socialisation" (2014, p. 10) to be avoided by the nascent transformative consumer research. Given the arguments that social marketing has been complicit in generating and maintaining the neoliberal discourse, engagement with a theoretically critical view could enhance understanding of inadvertent or uncalculated effects of social marketing and thus enhance its contribution to quality of life.

Although a separation between macro and critical marketing can be made (Tadajewski 2014), there is also a valuable overlap where the societal level of macromarketing can engage with the critical theories of social sciences (Dholakia 2012). Moreover, critical macromarketing's concern with questioning certain values that have flourished under neoliberalism is especially applicable here (cf. Kilbourne et al. 1997). Saren also surveys the critical marketing field for its usefulness to social marketing but, in contrast to the strong criticism above, he asserts that it is well-placed to utilize the opportunities more holistically than commercial marketing (2011, p. 96). Acknowledging the somewhat low profile of critical marketers within the discipline, Saren identifies a range of perspectives (feminism, radical ecology, literary criticism, and poststructuralism) that subscribe to "emancipatory aspirations" (2011, p. 98). Importantly then, while critiques from other disciplines can distil analyses and alert us to shortcomings, Saren directs us to the long standing, persistent critique that resides within the discipline itself, albeit with a comparatively quiet voice. Saren (2011, p. 103) draws our attention to the strong case for paradigmatic, and methodological pluralism made by Arndt (1985) and its value to our research. If social marketing is to broaden and deepen its engagement and thus extend its range, then it would behove us to consider these implications more carefully and critically. A first point of clarity would be to unpack what is intended by 'upstream' and then briefly consider the implications of a critical review with suggestions for the future.

5 Upstream to Power

Increasing social marketing's relevance to the ever broadening field of behaviour change through collaboration across other disciplines (Dibb 2014; Domegan et al. 2013; Gordon 2013; Spotswood and Tapp 2013; Tapp and Spotswood 2013), often recommends engaging more deeply with upstream. Calls to move upstream aim to achieve regulatory change for example to food labelling (so the consumer knows what they are buying), to increase the price of energy-dense foods (so that if the consumer remains ignorant they are pushed by price to avoid these calories), to reduce, even remove, junk food advertising, particularly from children (so that they are protected) (cf. Hoek 2011). The parallels to the campaign against tobacco can be seen here. Upstream is a broad umbrella term for all kinds of decision making, policy generating, and funding of interventions. However, the label belies the power that resides here. Gordon (2013) bemoans the lack of training and guidance for upstream targeting to alter the structural environment calling it a gap in the knowledge base. But no consideration of the wider effects of power relations are undertaken, the point being that this is not unusual in discussions of this kind. On the other hand, criticism of commercial marketing and its transgressions of power to capture, persuade and distort perception abound (cf. Hastings 2013). The argument here, as shown above (Moor 2001; Raftopoulou and Hogg 2010; Tadajewski et al. 2104), is that critiques of marketing's power cuts both ways. Social marketing needs to be explicit about the balance between power to generate changes, the socially constitutive role it plays (particularly under neoliberal governments) and the ethical responsibility that generates (Spotswood et al. 2012, p. 167). To properly engage with quality of life, social marketing needs to insightfully, critically and transparently review its role in social interventions, the effects, both intended and unintended, and the implications that entails. In short, social marketing needs to engage critically with the power that it wields at the levels of organisation and institution.

At this point, it is also important and pertinent to observe that the "right" kind of social marketing campaign was enlisted to support Gordon's argument. In this instance anti-tobacco lobbying which now has widespread support as a result, it should be noted, of high quality sustained social marketing that employed upstream, midstream and downstream interventions. However, tobacco is a unique product and an extreme example because it kills even when used as the manufacturer intends (Hastings and Saren 2003, p. 314). Had a less vivid intervention been selected, or an intervention that is not popular with its target audience, where accusations of social control, paternalism and insensitivity could be made, would the argument have been as cogent? This observation is not a criticism of Gordon perse as the process of enlisting the "best" example is commonplace. The relevance is that, along with the innocuousness of the term 'upstream', there is dampening of a crucial concept: moral intensity. The moral intensity of the example increases the impact of the argument and hails the legitimacy of social marketing in this context, but this cannot always be assumed. Therefore a clearer conceptualisation of 'impact' needs to be pulled into the discipline through a more detailed engagement with ethics, but this will be dealt with in due course. First, the low key characterisation the term 'upstream' conveys underplays entirely the highly significant and powerful social role sought under this label. Determining how we behave, how we think about all manner of actions, how our attitudes are calibrated in many kinds of situations and the concomitant effects that this has on our value judgements of other human beings, is heady stuff. Nor is the suggestion here that it is without social value for our quality of life. The focus here is on a topic that remains under-researched and under-discussed in social marketing but is more often the focus of critical marketing – power, relations of power and social power. Within the constraints of space, two intersecting theorisations will be brought together to posit a way forward: one will outline a facet of power that pertains to organisations; and the other will sketch the key components of ethical decision making.

6 Power *Through* Organisations

From here, for the sake of clarity, the practical context (who or what has power and over whom) will be separated from the moral context (the responsibilities of being able to wield power). Also it should be emphasised that neither power, nor the ability to wield power, is necessarily negative, although often viewed as deleterious due to associations with the removal of freedoms. Without denying the controlling facets of power, it can also be imagined as a capacity, or a capability, and so be productive and achieve positive outcomes. Importantly, the focus will narrow further still to note that power is not simply held by individuals but is often a feature of organisations. It is a contribution of this chapter to engage more directly with organisationally based conceptions of power thus moving beyond the individualised responsibility of professional conduct to invoke the responsibility of organisations and consortia of organisations that collaborate; this is the significant imbalance that Brenkert (2002, 2008) observed. An example that revealed the sources and devices of power that initiate and sustain change would be of value here.

Derived from historical analysis Humphreys (2010) teases out the synergies between organisations, government and the media in bringing about a profound change to the legitimacy of casino gambling in the USA. In brief, the connections and linkages amongst networks of powerful players, their enacted practices and frames of meaning created, maintained and evolved into a marketplace. Moreover, the enactment of systemic power (discussed further below) is shown to be a dialectical effect between organisations, government and the wider culture whereby the circulating flow of effects simultaneously reinforce and move practices along (Humphreys 2010). In theorising how a market was legitimised and created a new Humphreys (2010) drew out the circulations of power effects through the social, cultural and legal frameworks. Humphreys shows that "stakeholders use specific frames to shape the perceived legitimacy of an industry and that these frames are effective in negotiating the political environment" (2010, p. 3). Thus the reformulation of a disparaged market into a legitimate source of profit is shown to be an institutional and an informational process in which the activities of organisations interact with shifts in legislation and discussion in the media.

Locating sources of power in circuits of reproduction through critical analysis can also be future focussed, evaluative and, contain managerial intent. Power and power relations are deeply complex, have been debated for centuries, and are inflected in all aspects of social life. Therefore what is covered here can only be indicative and selective; several excellent sources offer more detailed accounts (Clegg and Haugaard 2009; Scott 2001). Given that social marketing campaigns are planned and contracted action that relies on expertise and is most often conducted as part of a partnership, the conceptualisation of agency needs to broaden beyond the individual. Rather the organisation or consortium is the social actor. There is a vast and complicated literature on power so, focusing on organisational power, a potted history locates a few key concepts, then a contemporary framework orders the field and situates a narrow focus on a specific facet of organisational power.

An early key contribution to debates about power was Bachrach and Baratz's (1962) *Two Faces of Power* where, in addition to a social actor being able to exercise power over another to achieve an intention (first face of power), they argued that organizations could mobilise bias over the choice of which issues were in range, and which were not. Thus an effect of power was to limit the choices available to others by removing options (second face of power). Lukes (1974) seminal, first work *Power: A Radical View* observed that latent power was exercised where practices, actions, ideas, were influenced indirectly by structural and cultural institutions (third face of power). This thesis was much debated, and Lukes offered a revision in 2005 that accommodated Morriss' (2002) critique that power was also a type of 'ableness', or capacity for action, that is not always exercised – the *power to*. Approaching power from quite a different position was Foucault whose contribution to understanding the performative and productive aspects of power has been profound (Foucault 1979). Binding knowledge and power together, Foucault's analyses examined the constitution of the subject through its subjectification (fourth face of power). This is a significant shift away from the agentically laden power of the first three dimensions offering insights into how the subject is constituted through their everyday understandings and performances (Foucault 1979).

Foucauldian theories of biopower and governmentality have been shown to be useful in explaining and identifying the effects of power over populations (Rose and Miller 1992), particularly under neoliberalism.

A review of the extant literature on organisations and power generated a useful framework (Fleming and Spicer 2014). Power is asserted to be "a resource to get things done" (Fleming and Spicer 2014, p. 239). Encapsulating the long running theoretical debate alluded to above, this focus on organisations is especially relevant here. Across their framework of the four faces and four sites of power Fleming and Spicer (2014) distinguish 16 different facets by combining the site where power is evident and the ways by which power is exercised. Several of the labels used in this framework appear quite loaded with meaning, however, these are the jargon used with this theoretical debate and will be retained here for clarity. The first distinction is between the direct exercise of power called *Episodic* and the influences of institutional structures labelled *Systemic*. Within episodic power there are two faces that shape the behaviour of others: *coercion* which directs others to act in a particular way (noted above as the first face of power) and *manipulation* which seeks to limit and direct the issues and boundaries (the second face of power). Under systemic power the face of *domination* develops Lukes' third dimension as organisational ideology where shared assumptions are an important facet of institutionalisation and legitimacy. In labelling the fourth face, also under systemic power, Fleming and Spicer (2014, pp. 244–245) draw in conceptualisations of *subjectification* where the very shaping of the subject is evident in their micro-practices and the discourses they enlist, clearly echoing Foucault.

Coupled with the four faces are the four sites of organisational power. *Power in* organisations focuses on the maintenance of, and resistance to, internal hierarchies. *Power against* organizations are efforts from outside the organization to alter its activities through activism for example. *Power over* organisations are struggles over the composition and direction of the organization and could be instigated by government through regulation or shareholder activism. Although all sites have potential value to a critical analysis, the focus here will be on the remaining site: Power *through* organizations "when an organization as a whole becomes a vehicle or agent to further certain political interests and goals" (Fleming and Spicer 2014, p. 246). Under this rubric *power through* organisations is a means to achieve objectives by utilising organisations and their resources. *Power through* organisations can be asserted through any one of the four faces: coercion, manipulation, domination or subjectification.

Analyses of coercive power *through* organisations reveals the importance of resources and the ameliorating potential of mediating factors such as social, or professional networks (Fleming and Spicer 2014, p. 252). Manipulation *through* organisations is identifiable in lobbying and asserted to be more effective than coercion in changing political views due to the "appearance of democratic deliberation" (Fleming and Spicer 2014, p. 256). This face of power also relies on what Nye (1990) termed "soft" power and draws its effectiveness from influence, particularly through the connections that exist amongst social elites or professional networks. Domination *through* organisations emphasises the ability of organisations to affect the civil society through ideological framing thus shaping social values and preferences, as shown in the gambling example above. Often not straight forward, shaping social norms was also noted as achieved through "informal bonds of trust and cooperation" (Fleming and Spicer 2014, p. 264) as might be found in professional networks. Subjectification *through* organisations is envisaged as bringing about changes in a broader organisational field by using the organisation as a focal point, or role model. Implications from this include a need for activism and protocols to avoid reversals in practices (Fleming and Spicer 2014, p. 270). Fleming and Spicer use the example of the rhetoric around professional multi-disciplinarity invoked for accounting/law partnerships and the role of expertise as a boundary shifting identity (2014, p. 271).

From this all too brief excursion into organisational power, it is evident that the push to move upstream seems a most effective means to achieve organisational goals. Moreover, given the appreciable institutionalisation and expansion of social marketing, the potential to utilise professional networks to achieve increased levels of influence is high, and in keeping with recommendations to collaborate more widely. However, the capacity to wield power carries with it responsibility (Lukes 1974, 2005). Even when intentions seem compliant with a utilitarian sense of the greatest good, relying on fear, guilt and shame can have negative effects (Brennan and Binney 2010). The effect of emancipating those who do not wish to be emancipated is that their autonomy is disrespected and disregarded (Benton 1981) and has the potential to generate reactance, or counternormative uptake, or unintended deviance and stigma. This point resonates with critical marketing's assertion that the individual consumer is rarely king (Ellis et al. 2011) and queries about whether community interventions run by experts can actually constitute co-creation (Domegan et al. 2013, p. 246). Furthermore, following up on the proposition to incorporate analyses of culture, Hayward (1998) famously identified that different social classes are schooled into different relationships to power on the basis of whether they can expect to be subject to power or wield power. In the first instance these comments draw our attention to the notion that, despite some social problems being wicked, or complex, facilitative or productive power needs to secure compliance and consensus without coercing those who need persuasion. It also needs to recognise its own strength and the deficits socialisation creates in specific populations. Clearly engagement with communities has been a potentially appropriate response but this review of *power through* organisations should alert us to the potential for professional networks to become sources of self-reinforcement, not necessarily critical insight. There is an implication here that a clear understanding of the moral and ethical landscape is needed to explicate and make transparent the machinations of power. Earlier the concept of moral intensity was raised, and we now turn to examine this notion, ethical codes of conduct and ethical decision-making.

7 Morality, Ethics, Codes and Dialogues

Ethical issues such as paternalism and moral imperialism are noted by leading social marketers (Donovan and Henley 2010; Hastings and Domegan 2014), although the medical adage of 'do no harm' in the first instance is the most common position.

Beyond the social marketer's own conscience and assessment of the intervention there is limited guidance or advice. Some have even asserted the neutrality of social marketing and its 'toolkit' (Dann 2007). Notwithstanding the positive quality of life outcomes of many social marketing interventions and the success of social marketing as an industry (McAuley 2014), others are more reflective of the impact that interventions have, and the accuracy of the depictions of their activities (Szmigin et al. 2011). At a practical level Hastings and Angus (2011) are critical of industry-funded social marketing campaigns and question the value of corporate social responsibility programmes undertaken by the perpetrator of harms. Indeed, about marketing in the hands of powerful corporations Hastings (2013) is quite adamant that the soft power, or influence, of marketing needs to be challenged, curbed, and reclaimed for 'our own good'. However, to claim that social marketing is without blemish was challenged by Gurreiri et al. (2013, 2014) who described and identified the inadvertent negative effects of social marketing in three cases that focussed on women. Usher goes further to assert that "ethics is immanent, *it is always already* in practices" (2006, p. 136 {emphasis in original}). In other words, ethics is already embedded in organisational practices, whether acknowledged or not.

The extent to which social marketing draws on commercial marketing for its practices and processes remains a concern, particularly given the agnostic approach micro (commercial) marketing takes towards issues of power (Dholakia 2012). Some have pointed to the need for a societal-based morality for any kind of marketing arguing that the marketing decision-making process tends to exclude, degrade and marginalize morality (Crane and Desmond 2002, p. 562). They draw on Etizoni to argue, counter-intuitively, that weaker corporate cultures allow better engagement with more nuanced moral decision making (Desmond and Crane 2004, p. 1227), because less rigid cultures are open to questioning, innovation, and contextually sensitive decision-making. This highlights the need for social marketing to focus less energy on finding a single, universal definition, and rather expend greater energy on self-review, critique and critical engagement with their interventions.

Laczniak and Murphy (2006) offer a way forward through normative perspectives for ethical and socially responsible marketing. They propose seven basic premises and offer a protocol for a strategic ethical evaluation (Laczniak and Murphy 2006, p. 169), see Figs. 6.3 and 6.4 below.

A book length version offers a worked example and several cases (Murphy et al. 2012). Interesting features include the assessment of marketing managers' ethical thinking that sorts different approaches into four hierarchical categories: egoistic or relativist; legalist; moral strivers and; principled managers. An overview of several different approaches to ethical thinking, including religious traditions, usefully moves beyond the usual comparison of deontology with teleology, as well as showing the advantages and disadvantages of each approach. Lastly, a process for moral reasoning is distilled into seven steps and stimulates moral imagination beyond adherence to simple protocols.

Ethical responsibility based on reflection and critique needs to recognise the singularity of the case at hand (Messner 2007). Moral and social issues are not 'one size fits all'. Rather, they are open to varying ethical perspectives (cf. Laczniak and

1. Ethical marketing puts people first
2. Ethical marketers must achieve a behavioural standard above the law
3. Marketers are responsible for whatever they intend as a means or end with a marketing action
4. Marketing organizations should cultivate better/higher moral imagination than their managers and employees
5. Marketers should articulate and embrace a core set of ethical principles
6. Adoption of a stakeholder orientation is essential to ethical marketing decisions
7. Marketing organizations ought to delineate an ethical decision making protocol

Fig. 6.3 Essential basic perspectives for evaluating and improving marketing ethics (Laczniak and Murphy 2006, p. 157; Murphy et al. 2012, p. 7)

Fig. 6.4 Protocol for ethical evaluation (Laczniak and Murphy 2006, p. 169; Murphy et al. 2012, p. 42)

1. Cultivate ethical awareness and sensitivity
2. Identify the ethical issues or questions
3. Articulate the stakeholders in the decision
4. Select an ethical theory or standards
5. Specify alternatives and ethical analysis
6. Make and justify a decision
7. Monitor the decision's outcomes

Murphy 2006), and varying moral imperatives. Recognising moral intensity is an important, additional component of any social marketing ethical decision-making process. Jones (1991) argues for the significance of moral intensity and extends Rests' (1986) four steps of moral decision making. The steps are, once a moral issue has been recognized, a moral judgement is made, moral intention is established and finally moral behaviour is engaged (Rest 1986, as cited in Jones 1991, p. 379), which matches well with the Laczniak and Murphy (2006) protocol (see Fig. 6.4 above). Moral intensity will affect each one of the steps in ethical decision-making. When moral issues are of high intensity they are more emotional, concrete, proximate and immediate (Jones 1991, p. 381). However, the vividness of moral intensity can be exaggerated through overly simple presentation (Jones 1991, p. 381), therefore care must be taken to represent the intensity of the issue at an appropriate level so as to avoid inadvertent over-engagement, such as stigmatisation or reactance.

Recalling our focus on the organisational level of power, organisational settings can create impediments to engaging with moral decision-making (Jones 1991, p. 390) and individuals often make complex moral choices in the context of organisations (Cohen 2006). With the rise of new public management came an increasing interest in installing organisational codes of ethics, particularly where contracted service agencies are involved (Muetzelfeldt 2006, p. 106). However, it cannot be assumed that organisational codes of ethics necessarily resonate at all with employees. Therefore, moral choice exists simultaneously at the level of the organisation and the individual (Cohen 2006). Nor do organizations always facilitate the best ethical behaviour (Jones 1991, p. 390). Codes of ethics can be experienced as a career risk in that noncompliance will threaten future employment (Muetzelfeldt 2006, p. 106). But, remembering the assertion that weaker organisational cultures allow more responsive thinking, it has also been asserted that without deviant behaviour corporations/organisations cannot grow and develop (Babeau 2007). Thus, while on the one hand organisational ethical codes are necessary, at the same time, sufficient institutional flexibility must be incorporated to allow open, responsive discussion that addresses the singularity of the social context and its culture, and the moral intensity of the issue.

Labelling formal codes of conduct monologic, Muetzelfeldt (2006) calls for dialogic ethical knowledge whereby critical, reflexive professional thinking is embraced. In a similar vein, Statler and Oppegaard (2007) posit *phronesis*, or virtue ethics which locates moral good in actions where the virtuosity is assessed through community held values (cf. Murphy et al. 2012, pp. 30–33). This has the advantage of being flexible and responsive to shifting community views. Consequently, should the target community of a social marketing campaign hold alternate views (cf. Szmigin et al. 2011) these may be disregarded as the *power through* the organisation is directed to *manipulate* a shift in views to align with those promulgated by the social marketing organisation or consortium. Importantly then we are returned to the discussion of social power and the interlinked nature power/ethics. "Power relations play an important role in the constitution of ethics" and "ethics takes shape through power relations that are played out between different actors" (Seemann et al. 2007, p. 204).

In sum, organisations need to be cognisant of the diverse sources of morals which can be converted into ethical codes of conduct. But, for social marketing organisations any formalisation and development of protocols should be approached with an innovative agenda because being overly formulaic can limit moral imagination and ethical action, especially in response to issues of moral intensity where social marketers are not in alignment with the target audience (cf. Szmigin et al. 2011). While the current focus on individualised ethical responsibilities reflects an awareness of this complexity, the collaborative organisation or consortium needs to be overtly and sensitively engaged due to the nexus of power and ethics. Fundamentally, and through deliberation, the intersection of power relations, ethics and moral action requires careful consideration by social marketers, and critical theories with their intention to emancipate have much to offer. However, relying heavily on professional reflection requires a further steps: intervention into the social marketers' education and active thorough evaluation of programs.

8 Education and Evaluation

The formal explicit knowledge garnered through educational curricula is not only an essential first step but also in need of diversification. One crucial extension is to move beyond marketing, and its helpmate psychology, and engage deeply with disciplines that examine society, community and social power such as sociology, anthropology, political science and cultural studies and are generally the source of critical theories. Curiously, in their 10 year review Fox and Kotler made such a suggestion for societal marketing (1980, p. 32). As much critical marketing with emancipatory ambitions shows, these disciplines have long traditions and highly developed theories that are essential for understanding the implications of wielding the power to alter social norms. Critical marketing has resources and a history of offering marketers a solid foundation in this arena (Ellis et al. 2011; Saren 2011), which could in turn be an essential facet of professional credentials. A key contribution to a critical social marketing curriculum would be a well-developed ethical decision-making education, such as that offered in Murphy Lacziniak and Prothero (2012).

A second, connected step, is to develop extended ethical dialogues and to ensure that social marketing is properly funded to undertake relevant and informative critical reviews of its social interventions. This kind of research, fully funded and published for wider review, offers a source of ongoing professional education and engagement that can fully examine issues of ethics and organisational power in social change arenas. It is also a sound means to avoid inadvertent negative outcomes, thus better enabling overall quality of interventions. Indeed there is scope here to conduct critically based evaluative research that fully acknowledges "power is everywhere" (Lukes 2005, p. 123). Such a research agenda could take up Fleming and Spicer's (2014, p. 285) comment that institutional theory has recently neglected the role of class and corporate power, thus overlooking the impact of elite groups. While it can be helpful to examine a range of practices and artefacts to identify their role in social contexts, it can also be depoliticising. In spite of the impact that many devices and habits may have, nonetheless some social agents have more power than others and furthermore the power to alter and affect the social context exists, whether or not it is recognised. A deeper engagement here could excavate and articulate social marketing's role, train high quality professionals, avoid extreme criticism and consider more carefully the impacts of upstream activism.

9 Conclusion

Opening with a brief overview of the evolution of social marketing, this chapter noted recent suggestions to broaden and deepen social marketing. Without denying social marketing's successes, and recognising the complexities with which social marketing must wrestle, critical theory was proposed as a means to better evaluate the implications of social marketing interventions, particularly recommendations to move upstream. Despite the potential of a critical lens for social marketing, others are less enthusiastic (Tadajewski 2014) suggesting that social marketing is too wedded to an agnosticism about its power and social effects and there were some indications that this is the case.

However, the argument here is that if social marketing was to fully engage with conceptualisations of power and processes of ethical decision-making, then much of this criticism could be neutralised. Introducing some frameworks of power is a contribution that offers a starting point to think through different kinds of circulations of power and the dynamics within the practices of deliberate change. Given the broader role of 'upstream' confluences identified through Humphreys (2010)) historical work, if intervention strategies that rely on coalitions of organisations are to undertake altering social norms, which can inadvertently create deviance, then a program of research that better understands the machinations of power and the professional practices that allow this to eventuate would be a valuable undertaking. Undoubtedly all faces and sites of power (Fleming and Spicer 2014) would be relevant to a critical analysis of the social marketing organisation. Important too is Lukes' (1974, 2005) insistence that power entails responsibility. It is argued here that responsibility has moral and ethical implications, and that a mature discipline can engage with its responsibilities through published critical debate.

A second, linked contribution is consideration of ethical-decision making within the context of complexity and as an organisation, rather than simply as individuals. Organizational practices, for either the social marketing firm or a collaborative consortium, should allow for nuanced, complex moral responsiveness. Or, to put this another way, if organisations adhere too closely to overly-defined formulaic protocols then individual social marketer's moral decision-making is inevitably constrained by the limits of the organisational culture. Acknowledging the significance of social marketers as individual moral agents points clearly to the importance of a critical education for novices and ongoing critical, evaluative research as informative for professionals. Future research would also benefit from a deeper consideration of the convergence of professional elites in the field of behaviour change and the power relations inherent in this endeavour to improve our quality of life.

References

Andreasen, A. (1994). Social marketing: Its definition and domain. *Journal of Public Policy & Marketing, 13*(1), 108–114.

Andreasen, A. (1995). *Marketing social change: Changing behavior to promote health, social development, and the environment*. San Francisco: Jossey-Bass.

Andreasen, A. (2002). Marketing social marketing in the social change market place. *Journal of Public Policy & Marketing, 21*(1), 3–13.

Andreasen, A. (2006). *Social marketing in the twenty-first century*. Thousand Oaks: Sage Publications.

Anker, T. B., & Kappel, K. (2011). Ethical challenges in commercial social marketing. In G. Hastings, K. Angus, & C. Bryant (Eds.), *The sage handbook of social marketing* (pp. 284–297). London: Sage Publications.

Arndt, J. (1985). On making marketing science more scientific: Role of orientations, paradigms, metaphors, and puzzle solving. *Journal of Marketing, 49*(Summer), 18–23.

Babeau, O. (2007). Granting disorder a place in ethics: Organization's deviant practices and ethics. In C. Carter, S. Clegg, M. Kornberger, S. Laske, & M. Messner (Eds.), *Business ethics as practice* (pp. 32–48). Cheltenham: Edward Elgar.

Bachrach, P., & Baratz, M. S. (1962). Two faces of power. *The American Political Science Review, 56*(4), 947–952.

Benton, T. (1981). "Objective" interests and the sociology of power. *Sociology, 15*, 161–184.

Bourdieu, P. (1984). *Distinction: A social critique of the judgement of taste*. London: Routledge.

Brenkert, G. G. (2002). Ethical challenges of social marketing. *Journal of Public Policy & Marketing, 21*(1), 14–36.

Brenkert, G. G. (2008). *Marketing ethics*. Malden: Blackwell.

Brennan, L., & Binney, W. (2010). Fear, guilt, and shame appeals in social marketing. *Journal of Business Research, 63*, 140–146.

Burton, D. (2001). Critical marketing theory: The blueprint? *European Journal of Marketing, 35*(5/6), 722–743.

Centeno, M. A., & Cohen, J. N. (2012). The arc of neoliberalism. *Annual Review of Sociology, 38*, 317–340.

Clegg, S., & Haugaard, M. (2009). *The Sage handbook of power*. Los Angeles: Sage Publications.

Cohen, S. (2006). Management ethics, accountability and responsibility. In S. R. Clegg & C. Rhodes (Eds.), *Management ethics. Contemporary contexts* (pp. 113–134). Abingdon: Routledge.

Crane, A., & Desmond, J. (2002). Societal marketing and morality. *European Journal of Marketing, 36*(5/6), 548–569.

Dann, S. (2007). Reaffirming the neutrality of the social marketing toolkit: Social marketing as a hammer and social marketers as hired guns. *Social Marketing Quarterly, 13*(1), 54–62.

Dann, S. (2010). Redefining social marketing with contemporary commercial marketing definitions. *Journal of Business Research, 63*, 147–153.

Desmond, J., & Crane, A. (2004). Morality and the consequences of marketing action. *Journal of Business Research, 57*, 1222–1230.

Dholakia, N. (2012). Being critical in marketing studies: The imperative of macro perspective. *Journal of Macromarketing, 32*(2), 220–225.

Dibb, S. (2014). Up, up and away: Social marketing breaks free. *Journal of Marketing Management, 30*(11/12), 1159–1185.

Domegan, C., Collins, K., Stead, M., McHugh, P., & Hughes, T. (2013). Value co-creation in social marketing: Functional or fanciful? *Journal of Social Marketing, 3*(3), 239–256.

Donovan, R. (2011). Social marketing's mythunderstandings. *Journal of Social Marketing, 1*(1), 8–16.

Donovan, R., & Henley, N. (2010). *Social marketing. Principles and practice*. Cambridge: Cambridge University Press.

Ellis, N., Fitchett, J., Higgins, M., Jack, G., Lim, M., Saren, M., & Tadajewski, M. (2011). *Marketing. A critical textbook*. London: Sage Publications.
Fleming, P., & Spicer, A. (2014). Power in management and organization. *The Academy of Management Annals, 8*(1), 237–298.
Foucault, M. (1979). *Discipline and punish: The birth of the prison*. Harmondsworth: Penguin.
Fox, F. A., & Kotler, P. (1980). The marketing of social causes: The first 10 years. *Journal of Marketing, 44*(Fall), 24–33.
French, J., & Blair-Stevens, C. (2006). *Improving lives together: Harnessing the best behavioural intervention and social marketing approaches*. London: Westminster City Council.
Fry, M.-L. (2104). Rethinking social marketing: Towards a sociality of consumption. *Journal of Social Marketing, 4*(3), 210–222. http://dx.doi.org/10.1108/JSOCM-02-2014-0011.
Gordon, R. (2011). Critical social marketing: Definition, application and domain. *Journal of Social Marketing, 1*(2), 82–99.
Gordon, R. (2013). Unlocking the potential of upstream social marketing. *European Journal of Marketing, 47*(9), 1525–1547.
Gurrieri, L., Brace-Govan, J., & Previte, J. (2014). Neoliberalism, and managed health: Fallacies, facades and inadvertent effects. *Journal of Macromarketing*. doi:10.1177/0276146714542953.
Gurrieri, L., Previte, J., & Brace-Govan, J. (2013). Women's bodies of sites of control: Inadvertent stigma and exclusion in social marketing. *Journal of Macromarketing, 33*(2), 128–143.
Hastings, G. (2003). Relational paradigms in social marketing. *Journal of Macromarketing, 23*(1), 6–15.
Hastings, G. (2007). *Social marketing: Why should devil have all the best tunes?* London: Butterworth-Heinemann.
Hastings, G. (2013). *The marketing matrix. How the corporations gets its power – And how we can reclaim it*. Abingdon: Routledge.
Hastings, G., & Angus, K. (2011). When is social marketing not social marketing? *Journal of Social Marketing, 1*(1), 45–53.
Hastings, G., & Domegan, C. (2014). *Social marketing: From tunes to symphonies*. Abingdon: Routledge.
Hastings, G., & Saren, M. (2003). The critical contribution of social marketing. *Marketing Theory, 3*(3), 305–322.
Hayward, C. R. (1998). De-facing power. *Polity, 31*(1), 1–22.
Hoek, J. (2011). Critical marketing: Applications. In G. Hastings, K. Angus, & C. Bryant (Eds.), *The Sage handbook of social marketing* (pp. 241–252). London: Sage Publications.
Hoek, J., & Jones, S. (2011). Regulation, public health and social marketing: A behaviour change trinity. *Journal of Social Marketing, 1*(1), 32–44.
Humphreys, A. (2010). Megamarketing: The creation of markets as a social process. *Journal of Marketing, 74*(March), 1–19.
International Social Marketing Association. (2014). Definition of social marketing. http://www.i--socialmarketing.org/about-us-ftr#.VD3plWPvFx0. Accessed 14 Oct 2014.
Jones, T. M. (1991). Ethical decision making by individuals in organizations: An issue-contingent model. *Academy of Management Review, 16*(2), 366–395.
Kelly, K. J., Edwards, R. W., Comello, M. L. G., Plested, B. A., Thurman, P. J., & Slater, M. D. (2003). The community readiness model: A complementary approach to social marketing. *Marketing Theory, 3*(4), 411–426.
Kilbourne, W., McDonagh, P., & Prothero, A. (1997). Sustainable consumption and the quality of life: A macromarketing challenge to the dominant social paradigm. *Journal of Macromarketing, 17*(4), 4–24.
Kotler, P., Brown, L., Adam, S., Burton, S., & Armstrong, G. (2009). *Marketing* (7th ed.). Australia: Pearson.
Kotler, P., & Lee, N. (2008). *Social marketing: Improving the quality of life*. Thousand Oaks: Sage Publications.
Kotler, P., & Zaltman, G. (1971). Social marketing: An approach to planned social change. *Journal of Marketing, 35*, 3–12.

Laczniak, G. R., & Murphy, P. E. (2006). Normative perspectives for ethical and socially responsible marketing. *Journal of Macromarketing, 26*(2), 154–177.
Laing, A. (2003). Marketing in the public sector: Towards a typology of public services. *Marketing Theory, 3*(4), 427–445.
Lefebvre, R. C. (2011). An integrative model for social marketing. *Journal of Social Marketing, 1*(1), 54–72.
Luca, N. R., & Suggs, L. S. (2010). Strategies for the social marketing mix: A systematic review. *Social Marketing Quarterly, 16*(4), 122–149.
Lukes, S. (1974). *Power: A radical view*. London: Macmillan.
Lukes, S. (2005). *Power: A radical view* (2nd ed.). Basingstoke: Palgrave Macmillan.
Maibach, E. W., Abroms, L. C., & Marosits, M. (2007). Communication and marketing as tools to cultivate the public's health: A proposed 'People and Places' framework. *BMC Public Health, 7*, 88. doi:10.1186/1471-2458-7-88http://www.biomedcentral.com/1471-2458/7/88
Marion, G. (2006). Marketing ideology and criticism: Legitimacy and legitimization. *Marketing Theory, 6*(4), 245–262.
Marques, S., & Domegan, C. (2011). Relationship marketing and social marketing. In G. Hastings, K. Angus, & C. Bryant (Eds.), *The sage handbook of social marketing* (pp. 44–60). London: Sage Publications.
McAuley, A. (2014). Reflections on a decade in social marketing. *Journal of Social Marketing, 4*(1), 77–86.
McDermott, L., Stead, M., & Hastings, G. (2005). What is and what is not social marketing: The challenge of reviewing the evidence. *Journal of Marketing Management, 21*, 545–553.
McHugh, P., & Domegan, C. (2013). From reductionism to holism: How social marketing captures the bigger picture through collaborative system indicators. In K. Kubacki & S. Rundle-Thiele (Eds.), *Contemporary issues in social marketing*. Cambridge Scholars: Newcastle-Upon-Tyne.
McKenzie-Mohr, D. (2000). New ways to promote proenvironmental behaviour: An introduction to community-based social marketing. *Journal of Social Issues, 56*(3), 543–554.
McKenzie-Mohr, D., & Schultz, P. W. (2014). Choosing effective behaviour change tools. *Social Marketing Quarterly, 20*(1), 35–46.
Messner, M. (2007). Being accountable and being responsible. In C. Carter, S. Clegg, M. Kornberger, S. Laske, & M. Messner (Eds.), *Business ethics as practice* (pp. 49–67). Cheltenham: Edward Elgar.
Michie, S., van Stralen, M. M., & West, R. (2011). The behaviour change wheel: A new method for characterising and designing behaviour change interventions. *Implementation Science, 6*, 42. doi:10.1186/1748-5908-6-42http://www.implementationscience.com/content/6/1/42
Moor, L. (2011). Neoliberal experiments: Social marketing and the governance of populations. In D. Zwick & J. Cayla (Eds.), *Inside marketing, practices, ideologies, devices* (pp. 299–319). Oxford: Oxford University Press.
Morriss, P. (2002). *Power: A philosophical analysis* (2nd ed.). Manchester: Manchester University Press.
Muetzelfeldt, M. (2006). Management ethics and public management. In S. R. Clegg & C. Rhodes (Eds.), *Management ethics. Contemporary contexts* (pp. 99–112). Abingdon: Routledge.
Murphy, P. E., Lacziniak, G. R., & Prothero, A. (2012). *Ethics in marketing. International cases and perspectives*. Abingdon: Routledge.
National Social Marketing Centre (NSMC). (undated). Social Marketing National Benchmark Criteria. www.snh.org.uk/pdfs/sgp/A328466.pdf. Accessed 30 Oct 2014.
Nye, J. S., Jr. (1990). Soft power. *Foreign Policy, 80*, 153–171.
Peattie, K., & Peattie, S. (2003). Ready to fly solo? Reducing social marketing's dependence on commercial marketing theory. *Marketing Theory, 3*(3), 365–386.
Peattie, K., & Peattie, S. (2009). Social marketing: A pathway to consumption reduction? *Journal of Business Research, 62*, 260–268.
Peattie, K., & Peattie, S. (2011). The social marketing mix – A critical review. In G. Hastings, K. Angus, & C. Bryant (Eds.), *The sage handbook of social marketing* (pp. 152–166). London: Sage Publications.

Pechmann, C., & Slater, M. D. (2005). Social marketing messages that may motivate irresponsible consumption behaviour. In W. Ratneshwar & D. G. Mick (Eds.), *Inside consumption* (pp. 185–207). Abingdon: Routledge.
Raftopoulou, E., & Hogg, M. K. (2010). The political role of government-sponsored social marketing campaigns. *European Journal of Marketing, 44*(7/8), 1206–1227.
Rangan, V. K., Karim, S., & Sandberg, S. K. (1996). Do better at doing good. *Harvard Business Review, 74*, 42–54.
Rose, N., & Miller, P. (1992). Political power beyond the state: Problematics of government. *The British Journal of Sociology, 43*(2), 173–205.
Rothschild, M. (1999). Carrots, sticks, and promises: A conceptual framework for the management of public health and social issue behaviors. *Journal of Marketing, 63*(October), 24–37.
Russell-Bennet, R., Previte, J., Gallegos, D., Hartel, C. E. J., Smith, G., & Hamilton, R. (2013a). A services approach to social marketing programs. In K. Kubacki & S. Rundle-Thiele (Eds.), *Contemporary issues in social marketing*. Newcastle-Upon-Tyne: Cambridge Scholars.
Russell-Bennett, R., Wood, M., & Previte, J. (2013b). Fresh ideas: Services thinking for social marketing. *Journal of Social Marketing, 3*(3), 223–238.
Saren, M. (2011). Critical marketing: Theoretical underpinnings. In G. Hastings, K. Angus, & C. Bryant (Eds.), *The Sage handbook of social marketing* (pp. 95–106). London: Sage Publications.
Sargeant, A. (2005). *Marketing management for nonprofit organizations*. Oxford: Oxford University Press.
Scott, J. (2001). *Power*. Cambridge: Polity Press.
Seemann, S., Laske, S., & Kornberger, M. (2007). The constitution of ethics: Discourse, practice and conflict in health-care center. In C. Carter, S. Clegg, M. Kornberger, S. Laske, & M. Messner (Eds.), *Business ethics as practice* (pp. 190–208). Cheltenham: Edward Elgar.
Shove, E. (2010). Beyond the ABC: Climate change policy and theories of social change. *Environment and Planning A, 42*, 1273–1285.
Spotswood, F., & Tapp, A. (2013). Beyond persuasion: A cultural perspective of behaviour. *Journal of Social Marketing, 3*(3), 275–294.
Spotswood, F., French, J., Tapp, A., & Stead, M. (2012). Some reasonable but uncomfortable questions about social marketing. *Journal of Social Marketing, 2*(3), 163–175.
Statler, M., & Oppegaard, K. (2007). Practical wisdom: Integrating ethics and effectiveness in organizations. In C. Carter, S. Clegg, M. Kornberger, S. Laske, & M. Messner (Eds.), *Business ethics as practice* (pp. 169–189). Cheltenham: Edward Elgar.
Szmigin, I., Bengry-Howell, A., Griffin, C., Hackley, C., & Mistral, W. (2011). Social marketing, individual responsibility and the "culture of intoxication". *European Journal of Marketing, 45*(5), 759–779.
Tadajewski, M. (2010). Towards a history of critical marketing studies. *Journal of Marketing Management, 26*(9–10), 773–824.
Tadajewski, M. (2014). What is critical marketing studies? Reading macro, social and critical marketing studies. In R. Varey & M. Pirson (Eds.), *Humanistic marketing*. Houndmills: Palgrave Macmillan.
Tadajewski, M., Chelekis, J., DeBerry-Spence, B., Figueiredo, B., Kravets, O., Nuttavuthisit, K., Penaloza, L., & Moisander, J. (2014). The discourses of marketing and development: Towards 'critical transformative marketing research'. *Journal of Marketing Management*. doi:10.1080/0267257X.2014.952660.
Tapp, A., & Spotswood, F. (2013). From the 4Ps to COM-SM: Reconfiguring the social marketing mix. *Journal of Social Marketing, 3*(3), 206–222.
Thaler, R., & Sustein, C. (2008). *Improving decisions about health, wealth and happiness*. New Haven/London: Yale University Press.
Usher, R. (2006). Management ethics and organizational networks. In S. R. Clegg & C. Rhodes (Eds.), *Management ethics. Contemporary contexts* (pp. 135–154). Abingdon: Routledge.

Vargo, S. L., & Lusch, R. F. (2004). Evolving to a new dominant logic for marketing. *Journal of Marketing, 68*(1), 1–17.
Verplanken, B., & Wood, W. (2006). Interventions to break and create consumer habits. *Journal of Public Policy & Marketing, 25*(1), 90–103.
Wymer, W. (2010). Rethinking the boundaries of social marketing: Activism or advertising? *Journal of Business Research, 63*, 99–103.
Wymer, W. (2011). Developing more effective social marketing strategies. *Journal of Social Marketing, 1*(1), 17–31.

Chapter 7
Social Influence and Blood Donation: Cultural Differences Between Scotland and Australia

Rebekah Russell-Bennett, Geoff Smith, Kathleen Chell, and Jennifer Goulden

1 Introduction

Social marketing is a strategy for facilitating voluntary change in the desired social product to improve individual and social welfare. Social marketers deal with a wide variety of social products within the social marketing mix ranging from behaviours of recycling to preventative health. One activity where social marketing has been used is blood donation with the ultimate aim of contributing to the health quality of life for the community. Given the beneficiary of the blood donation service is not the blood donor, rather the benefit is improving the quality of life of others and society, this type of behaviour is altruistic and can thus be classified as an altruistic social practice using the social product definitions of Kotler and Zaltman (1971) and

R. Russell-Bennett (✉)
Queensland University of Technology, Brisbane, QLD, Australia

University of Strathclyde, Glasgow, Scotland
e-mail: Rebekah.bennett@qut.edu.au

G. Smith
Australian Red Cross Blood Service, Melbourne, VIC, Australia
e-mail: geoff.smith.7.0@gmail.com

K. Chell
Queensland University of Technology, Brisbane, QLD, Australia

Australian Red Cross Blood Service, Melbourne, VIC, Australia
e-mail: kchell@redcrossblood.org.au

J. Goulden
University of Strathclyde, Glasgow, Scotland
e-mail: jennigoulden@hotmail.com

W. Wymer (ed.), *Innovations in Social Marketing and Public Health Communication*, Applying Quality of Life Research,
DOI 10.1007/978-3-319-19869-9_7

Kotler and Roberto (1989). The increasing use of blood products has led to enormous improvements in quality of life for people suffering from illnesses such as haemophilia, and has saved many lives of babies whose mothers are Rh-Negative (ARCBS 2014). Blood and blood products improve the general well-being of individuals and societies. Increasing and varying demand for blood products is a serious health issue challenging blood collection agencies worldwide. The retention of existing blood donors is therefore critical to the maintenance of a national blood supply (Germain et al. 2007; Reich et al. 2006).

Young adults represent the largest proportion of new and current blood donors but have the lowest retention and donation frequency rate compared to other demographic groups. This is problematic as this group is essential to the maintenance of a sufficient and sustainable donor base in the future. Recruitment and retention of younger donors poses a significant problem to blood donation organisations worldwide. One of the factors that is known to influence younger donors are the opinions and beliefs of others (social norms) therefore an understanding of social norms on donation is an important component of developing effective social marketing strategies aimed at encouraging donation. The impact of social influence on blood donor intentions and behaviour is well-documented with studies investigating how social norms facilitate or inhibit donation (Masser et al. 2008). Prior research in blood donation and the influence of social norms has largely relied on applications of the Theory of Planned Behaviour (Ajzen 1991), and extended models; focusing on a single type of social norm, subjective norms (what friends/peers think we should do), with limited research on descriptive norms (what people do) and no research on injunctive norms (what society thinks we should do). In addition there is no evidence of the impact of donor susceptibility to interpersonal influence. These three types of norms are likely to influence behaviour in different ways depending on overall cultural norms, and a 'one size fits all' understanding may not be sufficient.

Research has identified that social norms can vary between cultures that are deemed relatively similar resulting in intra-cultural variation (Au 2000). Given that marketing strategies to increase blood donation are often derived from successful examples in other countries, and some of these strategies relate to social influence, it seems appropriate to identify any differences that may occur in social influence between two countries of a similar cultural background. For this purpose we have selected Australia and Scotland, two countries that are described as 'close in character' based on evolved industrialisation, economic structure and continuing cultural connections (Richards 2010). In particular, both countries have been identified as being from the same cultural cluster (House et al. 2002) with a strong sense of national identity or patriotism and similar cultural values of being easy-going, providing friendly hospitality, work-ethic, commitment and belonging (Reicher et al. 2009; Rossiter 2007). However despite these similarities there are differences in consumption patterns and behaviours raising the question of whether there are intra-country variations within a cultural cluster.

Thus this chapter seeks to address two gaps in the literature the first being the lack of research investigating multiple types of social norms and susceptibility to interpersonal influence on blood donation behaviour (intentions) and the second being the lack of studies comparing the effects of social norms on donor behaviours between two seemingly similar countries. This leads to two research questions; RQ1: What is the role of social influence on intentions to donate blood and RQ2: Are there any differences in social influence on donor intentions between Scottish and Australian samples?

2 Literature Review

2.1 Social Norms

Given that individuals rarely make decisions in complete isolation, behaviour cannot be fully understood unless consideration is given to the social environment in which the behaviour is performed. The expectations and behaviour of others is often considered when deciding on an appropriate action. Social norms have consistently been seen as an important and often powerful determinant of an individual's attitude, values and behaviour (*see* Burchell et al. (2013) for a review of research on the social norm approach in social marketing). Positioned in the wider field of interpersonal (social) influence, norms are a social phenomenon of appropriate behavioural expectations for one's own behaviour, shaped and propagated by the direct and indirect actions of others (Lapinski and Rimal 2005). Varying in the source of behavioural expectations (Prentice 2007), distinct types of norms exist with distinct influences on behaviour (Deutsch and Gerard 1955). The variety of terms found in the literature (e.g. social norms, subjective norms, normative influence) reflects a lack of conceptual clarity and inconsistent use of terminology in social norm research (Kenny and Hastings 2011; Real and Rimal 2007). This chapter follows the categorisation of norms presented by Kenny and Hastings (2011) based on a distinction between what others do (descriptive norms) and what others approve of (prescriptive norms).

2.1.1 Descriptive Norms

Descriptive norms pertain to an individual's perception about the prevalence of an attitude or behaviour (Lapinski and Rimal 2005). The greater perceived prevalence, the greater the individual's propensity to engage in the behaviour because it is considered normative. Such perceptions of what the majority does are taken as a guide to appropriate behaviour (Pool and Schwegler 2007), particularly in novel or ambiguous contexts: "*if everyone is doing it, it must be a sensible thing to do*" (Cialdini et al. 1990, p. 1015). Descriptive norms obtain their power from social proof (Schultz et al. 2007). This process, or 'bandwagon' effect, is referred to as 'informational social influence', defined by Deutsch and Gerard (1955, p. 629) as accepting "*information obtained from another as evidence about reality*". Operating through the process of internalisation, information obtained may be sourced directly (e.g. an individual may search for information from knowledgeable others) or through inferences based on observations (Bearden et al. 1989).

2.1.2 Prescriptive Norms

In contrast to descriptive norms, which specify perceptions of what most people do, prescriptive norms specify perceptions of what people 'ought' to do (Cialdini and Goldstein 2004; Prentice 2007). Prescriptive norms pertain to perceived pressure to conform based on regulations, opinions and values that constitute approved or disapproved conduct, rather than the behaviour of the majority (Cialdini et al. 1990), and can be further classified as either injunctive or subjective (Kenny and Hastings 2011). *Injunctive norms* are based on perceptions of what is socially acceptable, or otherwise, by most people, and most closely relates to the 'ought to' connotation of prescriptive norms (Burchell et al. 2013). As articulated in the theory of planned behaviour, *subjective norms* are concerned with an individual's motivation to comply with the opinions of important referents regarding socially approved behaviour (Lapinski and Rimal 2005). Subjective norms are based on perceptions of whether important referents think they should or should not perform behaviour. The tendency to conform to expectations of others is a process referred to as 'normative social influence' (Burnkrant and Cousineau 1975), whereby individuals modify their attitudes and behaviour to emulate the socially sanctioned course of action (Prentice 2007).

Accordingly, it is important in social norm research to distinguish between descriptive and prescriptive norms, and their relative influence, because both types can exist simultaneously in a given social context with either congruent or contradictory implications on behaviour (Cialdini et al. 1990; Rimal and Real 2003). Often, descriptive and prescriptive norms are congruent. For example, individuals who use public transport may notice that, because others are silent and non-disruptive (descriptive norms), that is the socially sanctioned course of action and must act in a similar way (prescriptive norms). In fact, normative influence over behaviour is found to be strongest when descriptive and prescriptive norms are harmonious (Rimal and Real 2003; Smith et al. 2012). However, there are also situations when these two types of influence are incongruent, such as blood donation, where people approve of, but do not engage in, the behaviour.

2.2 *Social Norms and Blood Donation*

Research investigating the impact of social norms (or social influence) in blood donation has predominantly relied on applications of the Theory of Planned Behaviour (TPB) and extended models (France et al. 2014). In particular, the subjective norm component of the TPB model has received mixed support in its predictive capacity on blood donation. Subjective norm is often found to be either an insignificant predictor (Armitage and Conner 2001; Charng et al. 1988; Masser et al. 2012) or the weakest predictor (Holdershaw et al. 2011; Masser et al. 2008; McMahon and Byrne 2007; Veldhuizen et al. 2011) of blood donor intentions and behaviour. Within an extended TPB model, Godin et al. (2007) found both subjective and descriptive norms not to significantly predict blood donor intentions.

These findings, however, are contrary to the importance given to others' expectations (i.e. social influence) and external normative pressure in the wider blood donation literature. Bednall et al. (2013) found both subjective norm and descriptive norm to have a positive association with blood donation intentions (France et al. 2007; Lemmens et al. 2005). Beyond applications of TPB, Sarason et al. (1991) found that interventions utilising social learning principles (e.g. portraying blood donation as an accepted social norm) were much more successful in stimulating behaviour than either an educational (informational) approach alone or traditional interventions used by blood donor centres.

Further, there is limited research exploring injunctive norms despite being conceptually distinct from subjective and descriptive norms (Kenny and Hastings 2011). Injunctive and subjective norms are often viewed as equivalent (Rimal and Real 2005), given that in most situations (e.g. extreme violence) the injunctive norms of society at large are congruent with the subjective norms of important others. But in other situations, variation in norms can occur. For example, in the case of smoking, an individual's peers (subjective norm) may encourage smoking but the wider society communicates disproval of this behaviour. Similarly, it is more appropriate to view injunctive and subjective norms as distinct sources of influence in blood donation, given that whilst society as a whole (injunctive norms) may encourage participation in blood donation, an individual may not receive the same level of encouragement from peers (subjective norms). This research seeks to address this research gap by taking a holistic approach to the influence of social norms in blood donation by investigating the effect of descriptive, injunctive and subjective norms simultaneously on intentions to donate blood.

2.3 *Susceptibility to Social Influence*

Responding to the varied importance of social influence in prompting and maintaining blood donation behaviour, researchers have put forward a number of behavioural and individual characteristics that could be contributing. Lapinski and Rimal (2005) propose that the level of social influence varies according to attributes of the behaviour; in particular the degree of ambiguity (whether the appropriate course of action is unclear) and behavioural privacy (the extent to which a behaviour is performed in a private or public setting). This research provides an alternate explanation for the varied level of impact of social influence in blood donation; an individual's susceptibility to interpersonal (social) influence, that is, individuals are more likely to perform a behaviour when social pressure is perceived as influential (Armitage and Conner 2001). Bearden et al. (1989, p. 473) defines susceptibility to interpersonal influence as "*the need to identify with or enhance one's image in the opinion of significant others through the acquisition and use of products and brands, the willingness to conform to the expectations of others regarding purchase decision and/or the tendency to learn about products and services by observing others or seeking information from others*", Similar to the concept of 'influenceability' (McGuire 1968), susceptibility to interpersonal influence is centred on the notion that individuals vary in their response to the influence of others.

Such influence can manifest through informational or normative means. Informational social influence reflects a tendency to base judgements on the actions of others (Kuan et al. 2014), creating an informational decision shortcut when choosing how to behave in a given situation. While normative social influence reflects a tendency to base judgements on the perceived expectations of others (Bearden et al. 1989). Thus, susceptibility to social influence is the extent to which an individual accepts behavioural (informational) and attitudinal (normative) information obtained from others as a guide to appropriate behaviour (Kuan et al. 2014; Prentice 2007). In that respect, an individual's susceptibility to social influence will affect the impact of social norms on blood donation behaviour.

Moreover, susceptibility to interpersonal influence is considered a general trait that differs across individuals (Chang 2012; Mourali et al. 2005). In addition to personal characteristics such as age (Park and Lessig 1977; Rivis and Sheeran 2003), and public self-consciousness (Netemeyer et al. 1992), individual susceptibility to interpersonal influence is also influenced by cultural orientation (Mourali et al. 2005).

2.4 Intra-cultural Variation: Scotland vs Australia

Culture can be defined as "*shared motives, values, beliefs identities and interpretations or meanings of significant events that result from common experiences of members of collectives and are transmitted across age generations*" (House et al. 2002, p. 5). A common cultural construct used to distinguish cultural differences is the individualism-collectivism dimension (Hofstede 1980). Individualism and collectivism refers to an orientation towards relationships with others; collectivist cultures have stronger ties to the collective, such as family and country, than individualist cultures where behaviour is often guided by individual self-interest than the interest of the group (Triandis 1989). Not surprisingly, susceptibility to interpersonal influence is found to be more prevalent in collectivist than individualistic cultures (Kropp et al. 2005; Park and Levine 1999). Likewise at an individual level, Kongsompong et al. (2009) found individuals with a collectivist orientation to be more subject to social influence than those with an individualist orientation, regardless of nationality.

Whilst Australia and Scotland are both considered typically individualistic cultures (House et al. 2002), the strength of social norms can vary between cultures resulting in intra-cultural variation (Au 2000). Expanding on this, Gelfand and Nishii (2006) introduced a multi-level theory of cultural tightness-looseness;

grounded in earlier work by Boldt (1978) and Triandis (1989). Whether a culture is considered 'tight' or 'loose' is determined by the strength of social norms (i.e. how clear and prevalent norms are within a society) and the strength of sanctioning (i.e. the level of tolerance for deviance from norms within a society) (Gelfand and Nishii 2006). This research seeks to provide preliminary support for the presence of intra-cultural variation between Australia and Scotland in relation to the role of social influence on donor intentions.

3 Conceptual Framework

The development of a conceptual framework serves to identify key donor outcomes of social norms, susceptibility to interpersonal influence and intra-cultural variation in blood donation. The framework addresses two research gaps in the social marketing blood donation context as well as the broader social influence literature. These gaps are addressed through testing the proposed model (see Fig. 7.1). The following sections provide reasoning behind hypothesis development.

3.1 Donor Outcomes of Social Norms in Blood Donation

One dominant and enduring concept used to understand and evaluate blood donation behaviour is an individual's intention to donate blood (Masser et al. 2009). Several behavioural models specify that an individual's intention is the most proximal determinant of that behaviour (Ajzen 1991). The more one intends to engage in behaviour, the more likely is its actual performance. Previous research investigating

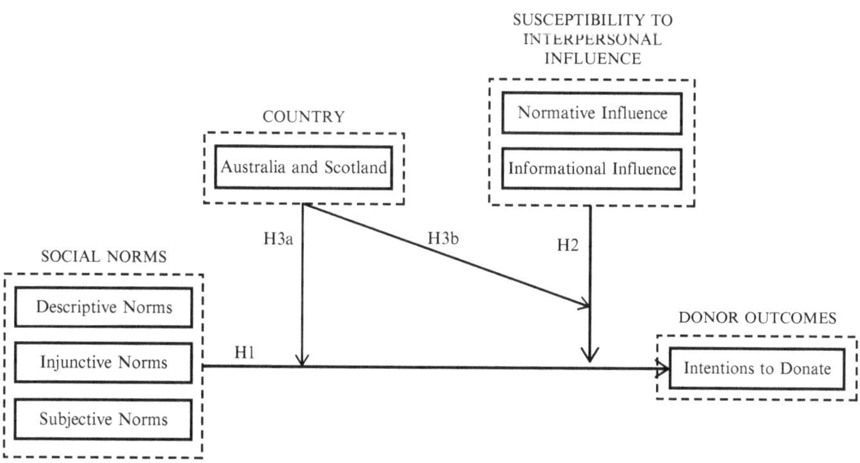

Fig. 7.1 Proposed model of social influence in blood donation

the role of social norms in blood donation has produced mixed results; found to be either a significant predictor (Bednall et al. 2013), weak predictor (Holdershaw et al. 2011) or insignificant predictor (Godin et al. 2007) of intentions to donate blood. However, such research has most often focused on a single type of social norms, rather than investigating the influence of descriptive, injunctive and subjective norms simultaneously. In line with the importance given to social pressures in the wider blood donation literature, we hypothesise:

H1: Social norms (descriptive, injunctive and subjective) around blood donation will be positively related to intentions to donate blood

3.2 The Role of Susceptibility to Interpersonal Influence

This research offers a new explanation for the varied importance of social norms in blood donation. Susceptibility to social influence is the extent to which an individual accepts information obtained from others as a guide to appropriate behaviour (Kuan et al. 2014; Prentice 2007). Therefore, the extent to which an individual accepts behavioural (descriptive norms) and attitudinal (prescriptive norms) information as indicative and influential to the performance of appropriate behaviour (e.g. donating blood) is dependent on their susceptibility to interpersonal influence. For instance, others' blood donation activity (descriptive norms) will only influence an individual's intention to donate blood to the extent that the individual accepts such information as a guide to appropriate behaviour. In that respect, an individual's susceptibility to social influence will affect the impact of social norms on blood donation behaviour. To this end, we hypothesise:

H2: Susceptibility to interpersonal influence (informational and normative) will moderate the relationships between social norms and intentions to donate blood

3.3 Intra-cultural Variation Between Australia and Scotland

Susceptibility to interpersonal influence has been found to vary dependent on cultural orientation (Mourali et al. 2005), specifically the cultural construct of individualism-collectivism (Kongsompong et al. 2009; Kropp et al. 2005; Park and Levine 1999). Although Australia and Scotland are considered fairly individualistic cultures (House et al. 2002), the theory of cultural tightness-looseness (Gelfand and Nishii 2006) argues for intra-cultural variation in relation to the strength of social norms between similar (in this case individualistic) cultures. In tight cultures, which are typically homogeneous with respect to particular attitudes and behaviour, norms are explicit (strong social norms) with low tolerance for non-conformity (strong sanctioning). Loose cultures, on the other hand, are typically more heterogeneous where norms are flexible (weak social norms) and more freely chosen (weak sanctioning). In a study by Gelfand et al. (2011), Australia scored a 4.4 tightness score whilst the United Kingdom scored 6.9, indicating that people within the United Kingdom have stronger social norms and lower tolerance for deviation from norms than Australians. On this basis, it is likely that cultural tightness-looseness can influence susceptibility to social influence and the impact of social norms on behaviour. Thus, in tighter cultures (e.g. Scotland), social norms appear to exert a more powerful impact on behaviour than more loose cultures (e.g. Australia). To this end, we hypothesise:

H3a: The relationships between social norms and intentions to donate blood will be stronger for Scottish participants than Australian

H3b: The moderation effect of susceptibility to interpersonal influence on the relationship between social norms and intentions to donate blood will be stronger for Scottish participants than Australian

4 Methodology

4.1 Sample and Procedure

This study employed a quantitative cross-sectional research design administering an online questionnaire survey. The speed and ease associated with online survey distribution allowed data to be collected from a geographically dispersed population (Sue and Ritter 2007); consistent with the study's aims of obtaining a sample from across the populations of two separate countries (Australia and Scotland). These countries were chosen in order to examine the prevalence of intra-cultural variation of social influence as a driving force of blood donation in key English-language markets often considered culturally similar (House et al. 2002). Australian participants were drawn from a random sample of Australians, sourced through the Australia Post Australian Lifestyle Survey consumer panel, who self-identified as a blood donor. Scottish participants were recruited through more convenient means, whereby the online survey was shared within networks available to the researchers.

4.2 Measures

All scale items for each construct were adapted from previous studies and measured on five-point Likert-type scales (anchored at 1-strongly disagree/very unlikely/ not at all important and five-strongly agree/very likely/extremely important). Following the approach by Staunton et al. (2014), single item measures for norm constructs have been used. This facilitated a shorter survey which was designed to attract respondents amongst online audiences. While the authors acknowledge that single-item measures and a smaller sample may raise questions, we believe that these limitations are not sufficient to prevent us from reporting the results for what they are; small-scale research designed to offer initial evidence of intra-cultural variation in the role of social influence on blood donation between two countries often considered culturally alike. In view of these limitations, however, any generalisations drawn from the research have to be treated tentatively.

Single item measures, adapted from Godin et al. (2007) and other sources, were used to measure descriptive, injunctive and subjective norms. In particular, injunctive norm research tends to use an experimental design, where injunctive norm is manipulated to be made salient or not. As a result there is no established measure of injunctive norms with various methods of measuring used. Asking the individual about their beliefs of whether a behaviour should or should not be performed as a way of determining injunctive norms has been used by Taylor and Sorenson (2004). Items to measure susceptibility to informational and normative interpersonal influence were adapted from Bearden et al. (1989). Intentions to donate blood were measured using a single item scale adapted from Godin et al. (2007). The operationalisation of measures used in this study is outlined in Table 7.1.

5 Analysis

As all independent and dependent variables were measured on a five-point Likert-type scale, systematic measurement error caused by common method bias was assessed using the single factor test (Podsakoff et al. 2003). With 35.31 % of the variance explained by one factor, which is below the maximum threshold of 50 % (Podsakoff and Organ 1986), common method bias did not impact the validity of this study. Tests for normality revealed that most variables were not normally distributed. Acknowledging that normally distributed variables are difficult to find in social research and given the nature of the sample and variables examined, non-normally distributed data would be expected in this population. The normal probability plot (P-P) of the regression standardised residual supports the decision to leave the items unaltered, since the points lie reasonably straight in a diagonal line, indicating no major deviations from normality in the dependent variables. Multicollinearity did not pose a threat to the analyses as inter-correlations between the constructs did not exceed the threshold of ±0.85 and higher.

5.1 Sample Characteristics

A total of 218 respondents participated in the study, with more respondents from Scotland ($n=131$) than Australia ($n=87$). Hair et al. (2010) contend that a ratio of 15–20 respondents to each independent variable is the desired sample size for regression analysis. Given that there are six or fewer independent variables in each multiple regression and moderated multiple regression test, the sample size is

Table 7.1 Construct operationalization

Descriptive norms (DES_NORM)	
Definition: perceptions of what most people do (what people believe is normal)	
Scale items adapted from: Godin et al. (2007)	
Validated scales (α=0.54)	**Items used in survey**
A lot of the people I know give blood Among the five people you know best, how many of them do you believe give blood more than once per year? *(0 person/5 people)*	A lot of people I know donate blood
Injunctive norms (INJ_NORM)	
Definition: perceptions of what people should do (what people believe should be normal)	
Scale items adapted from: Godin et al. (2007) *and* Taylor and Sorenson (2004)	
Validated scales (α=0.74)	**Items used in survey**
I think that it is all right for a person of my age to give blood again … my sex to give blood again I believe it is appropriate for a person in my state of health to give blood again	Do you believe people your age should donate blood?
Subjective norms (SUB_NORM)	
Definition: perceptions of whether important others think they should perform a behaviour (what people believe their friends' think should be normal)	
Scale items adapted from: Lemmens et al. (2005), Holdershaw et al. (2011) and Godin et al. (2007)	
Validated scales (α=0.86)	**Items used in survey**
Most of the people important to me would recommend I give blood again … think I should give blood again If I were to give blood again, most of the people who are important to me would approve/disapprove	Would your friends encourage you to donate blood?
Susceptibility to 'Informational Interpersonal Influence' (Info_Infl)	
Definition: the tendency to accept information obtained from another as a guide to appropriate behaviour	
Scale items adapted from: Bearden et al. 1989	
Validated scales (α=0.82)	**Items used in survey** (α=0.79)
To make sure I buy the right product or brand, I often observe what others are buying and using If I have little experience with a product, I often ask my friends about the product I often consult other people to help choose the best alternative available from a product class I frequently gather information from friends or family about a product before I buy	Would you donate blood if your friends did? Would you donate blood if you saw your friend posting about it on Facebook? Your friends have just donated blood and are talking about it on Facebook, does this encourage you to donate?
Susceptibility to 'Normative Interpersonal Influence' (Norm_Infl)	
Definition: the tendency to conform to expectations of others	
Scale items adapted from: Bearden et al. 1989	

(continued)

Table 7.1 (continued)

Validated scales (α=0.88)	**Items used in survey**
I rarely purchase the latest fashion styles until I am sure my friends approve of them It is important that others like the products and brands I buy **When buying products, I generally purchase those brands that I think others will approve of** If other people can see me using a product, I often purchase the brand they expect me to buy	Would you seek approval from your peers before you decided to donate blood?
Intentions to donate blood	
Definition: extent to which participants intend to donate blood in the next 6 months	
Scale items adapted from: Godin et al. 2007	
Validated scales (α=0.83)	**Items used in survey**
During the next 6 months … I intend to give blood again I will give blood again I will try to give blood again	Do you intend to donate blood in the next 6 months?

Table 7.2 Sample characteristics

	All (n=218)	Australia (n=87)	Scotland (n=131)
Age *(see bar charts below)*	Mean=24.22 *min = 18;* *max = 35*	Mean=28.39 *min = 18;* *max = 35*	Mean=21.45 *Min = 18;* *max = 25*
Gender	Male=42.7 % Female=57.3 %	Male=39.1 % Female=60.9 %	Male=45.0 % Female=55.0 %
Uses Facebook	Yes=92.2 % No=7.8 %	Yes=88.5 % No=11.5 %	Yes=94.7 % No=5.3 %
Current blood donor	Yes=67.4 % No=32.6 %	Yes=100 % No=0 %	Yes=45.8 % No=54.2 %
Motivation for donating blood To save people's lives The desire to help To gain personal satisfaction The feeling that you should donate To receive recognition from peers	*Average % =* 50.17 24.82 9.89 10.42 4.70	*Average % =* 45.11 27.54 12.57 11.17 3.61	*Average % =* 53.20 22.76 8.60 10.15 5.29
Use of social media as information source (1–5 scale)	*Mean = 2.33*	*Mean = 2.11*	*Mean = 2.48*
Need for recognition (1–5 scale)	*Mean = 2.24*	*Mean = 1.76*	*Mean = 2.56*

appropriate to infer statistical power of significance. Sample characteristics, as outlined in Table 7.2, indicate the mean age of the sample was 24 (*range = 18–35*), with a higher proportion of women than men.

5.2 *Descriptive Statistics*

Descriptive analysis of the correlation matrices (see Table 7.3) provides preliminary support for hypotheses. Although only subjective norm is correlated with intentions to donate blood for the total sample, in comparing correlational data between Australia and Scotland (see Table 7.4) results indicate the important role of social norms for intentions to donate blood amongst Scottish participants specifically. Australians indicated that social norms are not related to their blood donation intentions. They may be likely to donate blood if they see their friends doing so (high susceptibility to informational interpersonal influence), however, Australians reported low levels of descriptive norms (their friends either don't donate blood or participants are not aware that they donate blood). These results hint at potentially different drivers for influencing donor intentions. Independent sample *t* tests were performed to statistically compare differences between Australian and Scotland construct means. Results can be found in Appendix 1 at the end of this chapter.

5.3 *Hypothesis Testing*

Hierarchical multiple regression analysis (controlling for age, gender and donor status) and moderated multiple regression analysis were used to test the hypothesised relationships summarised in Table 7.5. All independent and moderating variables were mean centred before creating the interaction terms to test for moderating effects. Significant moderation effects for both two-way and three-way interactions were graphed following procedures set forth by Dawson (2014). Table 7.5 summarises the variables used to test each hypothesis, and the analysis outcome.

5.3.1 Hierarchical Multiple Regression Analysis

To test the impact of social norms on intentions to donate blood, hierarchical multiple regression analysis (MRA) was employed controlling for the effect of age, gender and donor status. Hierarchical multiple regression analysis found subjective norm was the only significant social norm predictor of intentions to donate blood ($\beta = 0.222$, $p < 0.01$); supporting Hypothesis 1 (See Table 7.6).

5.3.2 Moderated Multiple Regression Analysis

The main effects of social norms, susceptibility to interpersonal influence and country on intentions are shown in Table 7.7, model 1. To test the moderation effects of susceptibility to interpersonal influence and country on the relationships between social norms and intentions to donate blood, two-way and three-way moderated multiple regression was performed (see Table 7.7, model 3; significant results are bolded).

Table 7.3 Descriptive statistics and correlations ($n=218$)

	Mean	s.d.	1	2	3	4	5	6	7
1. Age	24.22	4.76							
2. Gender (m=1, f=2)	1.57	0.50	0.075						
3. Injunctive norms	4.39	0.91	−0.021	−0.052					
4. Descriptive norms	2.98	1.06	−0.070	−0.035	**0.155***				
5. Subjective norms	3.40	0.93	**−0.160***	−0.022	**0.201****	**0.383****			
6. Normative influence	1.85	1.10	**−0.273****	**−0.149***	0.049	**0.255****	**0.185****		
7. Informational influence	2.92	0.83	−0.008	**−0.142***	**0.233****	**0.154***	**0.311****	**0.268****	
8. Intention to donate blood	3.17	1.46	−0.086	−0.075	0.121	0.108	**0.219****	0.099	**0.414****

Note: *$p<0.05$; **$p<0.01$

Table 7.4 Descriptive statistics and correlations for Australia (a; $n=87$) and Scotland (S; $n=131$)

	A/S	Mean	s.d.	1	2	3	4	5	6	7
1. Age	A	28.39	4.70	6						
	S	21.45	1.94							
2. Gender (m = 1, f = 2)	A	1.61	0.49	0.107						
	S	1.55	0.50	–0.035						
3. Injunctive norms	A	4.39	1.03	–0.006	–0.201^					
	S	4.38	0.33	–0.095	0.066					
4. Descriptive norms	A	2.69	1.03	**0.211***	–0.013	0.194^				
	S	3.17	1.05	0.039	–0.029	0.134				
5. Subjective norms	A	3.34	0.96	**–0.246***	0.042	**0.215***	**0.286****			
	S	3.44	0.92	–0.101	–0.062	**0.191***	**0.447****			
6. Normative influence	A	1.33	0.68	0.076	0.012	–0.089	–0.134	0.089		
	S	2.19	1.19	–0.064	**–0.198***	0.126	**0.315****	**0.225****		
7. Informational influence	A	3.00	0.78	–0.189	–0.044	0.086	0.028	**0.244***	–0.011	
	S	2.86	0.86	0.001	**–0.210***	**0.348****	**0.267****	**0.365****	**0.453****	
8. Intentions to donate blood	A	3.20	1.61	–0.202	–0.035	–0.033	–0.054	0.053	–0.060	**0.259***
	S	3.16	1.35	–0.031	–0.109	**0.270****	**0.243****	**0.359****	**0.200***	**0.533****

Note: ^ = nearing significance ($p<0.075$); * $p<0.05$; ** $p<0.01$

Table 7.5 Summary of hypothesis testing

Variables	Hypotheses		Result
Social norms and donor outcomes	H1	Social norms (descriptive, injunctive and **subjective**) around blood donation will be positively related to intentions to donate blood	Supported
Susceptibility to interpersonal influence	H2	Susceptibility to interpersonal influence (**informational** and normative) will moderate the relationships between social norms (descriptive, **injunctive** and subjective) and intentions to donate blood	Supported
Country differences (Intra-cultural variation)	H3a	The relationships between social norms (descriptive, injunctive and **subjective**) and intentions to donate blood will be stronger for Scottish participants than Australian	Supported
	H3b	The moderation effect of susceptibility to interpersonal influence (**informational** and **normative**) on the relationship between social norms (**descriptive**, **injunctive** and subjective) and intentions to donate blood will be more positive for Scottish participants than Australian	Supported

Note: Bold indicates significant variables in hypothesis

Table 7.6 Results of hierarchical multiple regression models for hypothesis 1a and 1b

	Intentions to donate blood	
Variables	*Model 1*	*Model 2*
Individual control variables		
Age	–0.096	–0.051
Gender	–0.028	–0.035
Donor status	–0.546**	–0.467**
Main effects		
Descriptive norm		–0.036
Injunctive norm		0.131
Subjective norm		**0.222****
F	18.175**	11.805**
R^2	0.300	0.364
Adjusted R^2	0.284	0.333

Note: *$p<0.05$; **$p<0.01$

Hypothesis 2, which suggested that susceptibility to interpersonal influence moderates the relationship between social norms and intentions to donate blood, was supported. The interaction of injunctive norm with susceptibility to informational influence is significant and positive ($\beta=0.181$, $p<0.05$) as illustrated using simple slopes analysis in Fig. 7.2. The relationship between an individual's injunctive norms (belief that people should donate blood) and intentions to donate blood is more positive for those with a higher tendency to accept information obtained from others as a guide to appropriate behaviour (i.e. susceptibility to informational

Table 7.7 Results of moderated multiple regression models for hypothesis 2, 3a and 3b

	Intentions to donate blood		
Variables	*Model 1*	*Model 2*	*Model 3*
Main effects			
Descriptive norm	0.012	−0.011	−0.009
Injunctive norm	0.010	0.047	0.042
Subjective norm	0.096	0.017	0.130
Information influence (Info Infl.)	0.392**	0.406**	0.387**
Normative influence (Norm Infl.)	−0.039	−0.068	−0.081
Country (1=Australia; 0=Scotland)	0.029	0.041	0.032
Two-way interaction terms			
Descriptive norm x info infl.		0.049	0.009
Descriptive norm x norm infl.		−0.071	−0.147
Descriptive norm x country		0.067	0.081
Injunctive norm x info infl.		0.130	**0.181***
Injunctive norm x norm infl.		0.028	0.080
Injunctive norm x country		0.124	0.092
Subjective norm x info infl.		−0.039	−0.056
Subjective norm x norm infl.		0.122	−0.122
Subjective norm x country		0.073	**0.177***
Three-way Interaction Terms			
Descriptive norm x info infl. x country			**0.173***
Descriptive norm x norm infl. x county			0.099
Injunctive norm x info infl. x country			−0.124
Injunctive norm x norm infl. x county			**−0.158***
Subjective norm x info infl. x country			−0.029
Subjective norm x norm infl. x county			0.175^
F	7.810**	3.871**	3.423**
R^2	0.182	0.223	0.268
Adjusted R^2	0.158	0.166	0.190

Country: 1–Australia; 0=Scotland
Note: ^ = nearing significance ($p<0.075$); * $p<0.05$; ** $p<0.01$

influence), as opposed to low. In fact, there appears to be a slightly negative relationship between injunctive norms and intentions to donate blood when susceptibility to informational influence is low.

In examining intra-cultural variation (see Table 7.7), a significant positive interaction of subjective norm and country ($\beta=0.177$, $p<0.05$) was found, as illustrated in Fig. 7.3. This shows that the relationship between an individual's subjective norms (belief that others think they should donate blood) and intentions to donate blood is more positive for those from Scotland as opposed to Australia, in support of H3a.

The significant three-way interaction of descriptive norms, informational influence and country reached significance ($\beta=0.173$, $p<0.05$). Figure 7.4 illustrates

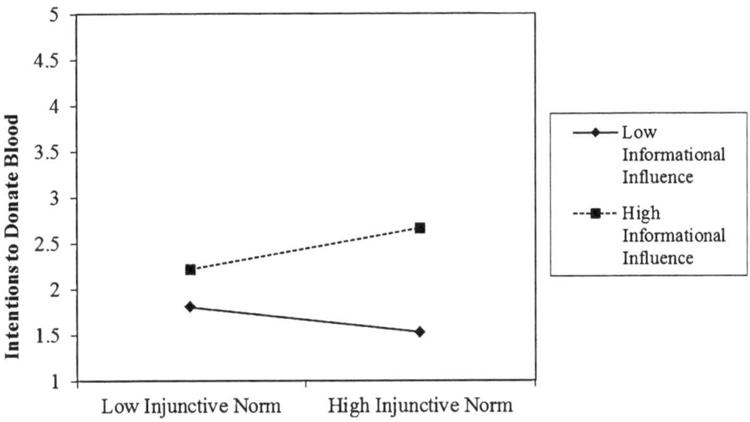

Fig. 7.2 Interaction effect of injunctive norms with susceptibility to informational influence on intentions to donate blood

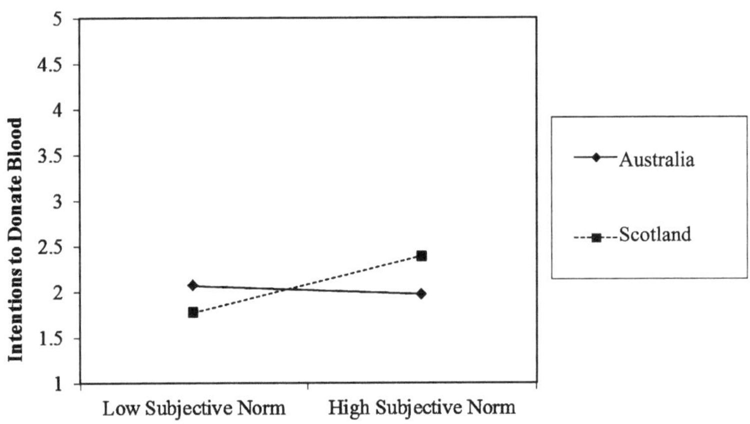

Fig. 7.3 Interaction of subjective norms with country on intentions to donate blood

that the relationship between descriptive norms and intentions to donate blood is most positive when an individual is highly susceptible to informational interpersonal influence and Scottish, as opposed to Australian. In fact, for Australians high in susceptibility to informational influence, there appears to be a negative relationship between descriptive norms and intentions to donate blood. The three-way interaction of injunctive norms, normative influence and country also reached significance, thus, H3b is supported by the findings.

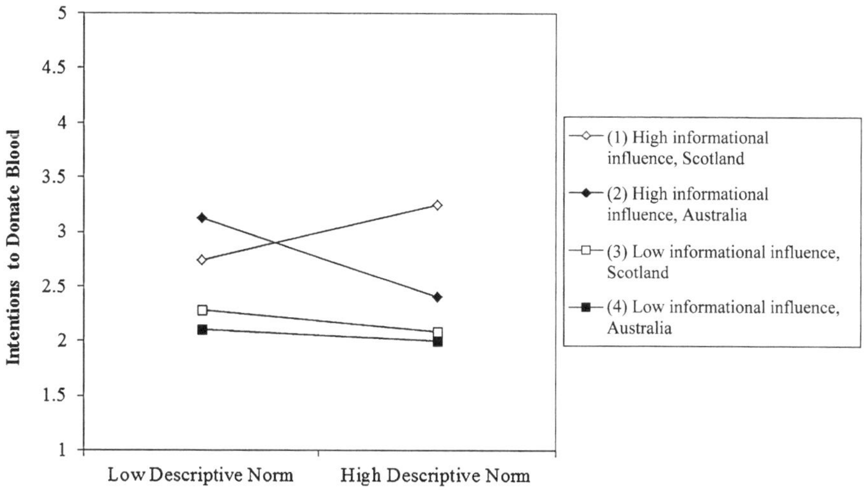

Fig. 7.4 Three-way interaction effect of descriptive norms, informational influence and country on intentions to donate blood

6 Findings and Discussion

The findings reported in this chapter broadly indicate that regardless of country and other influences on decision making processes the majority of people sampled indicate that blood donation in itself is a respected and valued way for them as individuals and people in general to contribute to the improvement of quality of life through altruistic behaviour. This altruistic behaviour is crucial to improve lives through donation of blood for transfusion and manufacturing of related blood products to support a wide variety of essential medical procedures and treatments important to many people across society.

Previous research has focussed on broad influences at a population level that lead people to make the decision to engage in blood donation and make the contribution to enhancing unknown (in most cases) peoples' quality of life. This may overlook more nuanced understandings of how these influences may differ between populations in different countries, even those generally assumed to be culturally similar such as Australia and Scotland. Differences between countries may also be a likely way for marketers to potentially re-examine blanket campaigns currently designed to appeal to an entire population (one size fits all approach). This may be a sufficient approach for more homogeneous societies such as Scotland, but less than optimal in a much more widely multi-cultural society such as Australia. Although the overall desired pro-social destination is the same – persuade enough people to improve the quality of life of others by joining a sufficient and sustainable blood donor population, the decision making journey may be very different in different cultural contexts. Thus it is important for marketers to know where and how along peoples' journeys to behaviour change to deploy campaigns to exert the best and most cost-effective influence.

6.1 Influence of Subjective and Injunctive Social Norms

The first research question was: What is the role of social influence on intentions to donate blood? All participants (both nationalities) indicated that there was a significant influence of what they think their friends think they should do (subjective norms) on intention to donate. That is to say if people believe that those around them believe that they should donate blood then they are more likely to report a positive intention towards donation. Social marketing campaigns need to normalise the discussion of blood donation and ensure that people know that their friends are donating.

Related to this, was the finding that injunctive norms (belief that people should donate blood) were found to positively predict intentions to donate blood but only for those with a higher tendency to base judgements on the actions of others (informational social influence). This finding contrasts with an individual's belief of how what they think their friends think they should do (subjective norms) will influence behaviour regardless of how susceptible they are to social influences. Ensuring that people are aware of the donation behaviour of others is an essential part of the maintenance of a sufficient and sustainable blood supply to support the myriad of medical treatments and products which go a long way to improving the quality of life of large numbers of people in all areas of society.

6.2 Differences Between Australians and Scots

The second research question was: Are there any differences in social influence on donor intentions between Scotland and Australia? A comparison of the data between two culturally similar communities is useful as it challenges the notion that all such similar cultures behave the same way and that therefore social marketing strategies that are effective in one country can be transported to the other. When comparing between Australia and Scotland, the results demonstrated that the Scots were more influenced by others than their Australian counterparts. Australians may be likely to donate blood if they see their friends doing so (high susceptibility to informational interpersonal influence), however, Australians reported low levels of descriptive norms (their friends either don't donate blood or participants are not aware that they donate blood). This is supported by finding that Scottish donors reported significantly higher descriptive norms (know more people who donate blood) and subjective norms (friends think they should donate blood) than the Australians. These indicate that the Scots are more concerned with how they fit in with others than Australians. When Australians and Scots (who report they) are susceptible to the influence of others, there are marked differences in their responses. When Australians know that others are donating blood (descriptive norm), they are less likely to donate themselves whereas the Scots are more likely to donate when they know others are donating. This is an interesting distinction and worthy of further consideration and research as it suggests questions that may be useful in providing evidence for targeted social marketing. If Australians are aware that others donate yet do not do it themselves, is this because they are not influenced by others? Or does it then engender a belief that if others are doing it then I do not have to as it is covered? Other perhaps more pejorative interpretations may also need to be considered – are Australians lazy when it comes to altruistic behaviours and suffer from diffusion of responsibility (Darley and Latane 1968)? The managerial implications of this are that in Australia, marketing campaigns need to focus on the important contribution of each individual whereas in Scotland the message would be to be part of the group. Reflecting cultural tightness (Gelfand et al. 2011), it may be that Scots are unwilling to stand out from the crowd and deviate from norms.

Regardless of susceptibility to interpersonal influence, Scottish participants' intention to donate blood increased the more they thought that society as a whole thinks they should donate blood (injunctive norms). However for Australian donors, tendency to conform to expectations of others *varied* the impact of injunctive norms on intentions to donate blood. Specifically, for those more likely to conform to expectations of others (high normative influence), their intentions increased as injunctive norms increased (similar to the Scots). When Australian donors were less likely to conform to expectations of others (low normative influence) intentions to donate blood decreased the more they thought society thinks they should donate blood (injunctive norms). This again supports the idea that Australians have a tendency to rebel against expectations.

6.3 Social Marketing Implications

This clear distinction by nationality of the influence of social norms on intention to behave indicates the need for a varied tool kit for blood collection agencies in their attempts to influence people to engage in donation behaviour. The research reported in this chapter indicates a strong need to move away from one-size-fits-all campaigns and towards a more nuanced segmented approach. The idea of normalising the issue of blood donation and discussions around the issues involved is one approach that may be successful. The need to re-enforce the message that blood donation is an important and useful thing to do will always be there, but this can be extended by indicating that many people think about it, but not enough do it (aimed at laziness). Marketing experts need to turn their creative talents to ensuring that all aspects of the information are adequately covered, providing all the information to influence each segment of the community in the manner that is most effective for them.

Acknowledgment Australian governments fully fund the Australian Red Cross Blood Service for the provision of blood products and services to the Australian community.

Appendix 1: T-Tests Comparing Construct Means Between Australia and Scotland

Independent sample *t* tests were used to compare variables between participants from Australia ($n=87$) and Scotland ($n=131$) (see Table 7.8). There was a significant difference indicating that Scottish participants reported higher descriptive norms and susceptibility to normative interpersonal influence.

Table 7.8 *T*-test comparison between participants from Australian and Scotland

	Australia		Scotland						
Construct	*Mean*	*s.d.*	*Mean*	*s.d.*	*t*	*df*	Sig.	Mean difference	CI
Injunctive norms	4.39	*1.027*	4.38	*0.833*	0.065	216	0.948	−0.01	−0.241, 0.258
Descriptive norms	2.69	*1.027*	3.17	*1.046*	−3.348	216	**0.001**	0.48	−0.764,−0.198
Subjective norms	3.34	*0.962*	3.44	*0.916*	−0.758	216	0.449	0.10	−0.353, 0.157
Normative influence	1.33	*0.676*	2.19	*1.188*	−6.766	212	**0.000**	0.86	−1.106,−0.607
Informational influence	3.01	*0.783*	2.86	*0.857*	1.272	216	0.205	−0.15	−0.080, 0.371
Intention to donate blood	3.20	*1.613*	3.16	*1.352*	−0.168	162	0.867	−0.04	−0.378, 0.449

T-test analysis also demonstrated significant differences between Scottish blood donors and non-donors; indicating a need to control for the effect of donor status in hypothesis testing. Thus, it was deemed necessary to also test for differences between Australian ($n=87$) and Scottish blood donors ($n=60$) only (excluding Scottish non-donors). All *t*-tests (except injunctive norms) reach significance, with Scottish blood donors scoring higher than Australian blood donors on all constructs (see Table 7.9)

Table 7.9 *T*-test comparison between Australian and Scottish blood donors

	Australia		Scotland						
Construct	*Mean*	*s.d.*	*Mean*	*s.d.*	*t*	*df*	Sig.	Mean difference	CI
Injunctive norms	4.39	*1.027*	4.57	*0.694*	−1.282	145	0.202	0.18	−.463, 0.099
Descriptive norms	2.69	*1.027*	3.57	*0.789*	−5.848	143	**0.000**	0.88	−1.173,−0.581
Subjective norms	3.34	*0.962*	3.70	*0.788*	−2.452	141	**0.015**	0.36	−.642,−0.069
Normative influence	1.33	*0.676*	2.72	*1.403*	−7.089	78	**0.000**	1.39	−1.772,−0.995
Informational influence	3.01	*0.783*	3.31	*0.719*	−2.418	145	**0.017**	0.30	−0559,−0.056
Intention to donate blood	3.20	*1.613*	3.95	*0.852*	−3.682	137	**0.000**	0.75	−1.160,−0.349

References

Ajzen, I. (1991). The theory of planned behavior. *Organizational Behavior and Human Decision Processes, 50*(2), 179–211. doi:10.1016/0749-5978(91)90020-T.

ARCBS. (2014). *1960s medical advances*. Retrieved 19 Sept 2014, from http://www.donateblood.com.au/about-us/history-blood-services/1960s

Armitage, C., & Conner, M. (2001). Social cognitive determinants of blood donation. *Journal of Applied Social Psychology, 31*(7), 1431–1457.

Au, K. (2000). Intra-cultural variation as another construct of international management: A study based on secondary data of 42 countries. *Journal of International Management, 6*(3), 217–238. doi:10.1016/S1075-4253(00)00026-0.

Bearden, W., Netemeyer, R., & Teel, J. (1989). Measurement of consumer susceptibility to interpersonal influence. *Journal of Consumer Research, 15*(4), 473–481.

Bednall, T., Bove, L., Cheetham, A., & Murray, A. (2013). A systematic review and meta-analysis of antecedents of blood donation behavior and intentions. *Social Science and Medicine, 96*(1), 86–94. doi:10.1016/j.socscimed.2013.07.022.

Boldt, E. (1978). Structural tightness and cross-cultural research. *Journal of Cross-Cultural Psychology, 9*(2), 151–165. doi:10.1177/002202217892003.

Burchell, K., Rettie, R., & Patel, K. (2013). Marketing social norms: Social marketing and the 'social norm approach'. *Journal of Consumer Behaviour, 12*(1), 1–9. doi:10.1002/cb.1395.

Burnkrant, R., & Cousineau, A. (1975). Informational and normative social influence in buyer behavior. *Journal of Consumer Research, 2*(3), 206–215.

Chang, C. (2012). Effectiveness of consensus information in advertising: The moderating roles of situational factors and individual differences. *Journal of Business and Psychology, 27*(4), 483–494. doi:10.1007/s10869-012-9258-5.

Charng, H., Piliavin, J., & Callero, P. (1988). Role identity and reasoned action in the prediction of repeated behavior. *Social Psychology Quarterly, 51*(4), 303–317.

Cialdini, R., & Goldstein, N. (2004). Social influence: Compliance and conformity. *Annual Review of Psychology, 55*(1), 591–621.

Cialdini, R., Reno, R., & Kallgren, C. (1990). A focus theory of normative conduct: Recycling the concept of norms to reduce littering in public places. *Journal of Personality and Social Psychology, 58*(6), 1015–1026.

Darley, J., & Latane, B. (1968). Bystander intervention in emergencies: Diffusion of responsibility. *Journal of Personality and Social Psychology, 8*(4), 377–383. doi:10.1037/h0025589.

Dawson, J. F. (2014). Moderation in management research: What, why, when and how. *Journal of Business and Psychology, 29*(1), 1–19. doi:10.1007/s10869-013-9308-7.

Deutsch, M., & Gerard, H. (1955). A study on normative and informational social influences upon individual judgement. *Journal of Abnormal and Social Psychology, 51*(3), 629–636.

France, J. L., France, C. R., & Himawan, L. K. (2007). A path analysis of intention to redonate among experienced blood donors: An extension of the theory of planned behavior. *Transfusion, 47*(6), 1006–1013. doi:10.1111/j.1537-2995.2007.01236.x.

France, J. L., Kowalsky, J. M., France, C. R., McGlone, S. T., Himawan, L. K., Kessler, D. A., & Shaz, B. H. (2014). Development of common metrics for donation attitude, subjective norm, perceived behavioral control, and intention for the blood donation context. *Transfusion, 54*(3 pt2), 839–847. doi:10.1111/trf.12471.

Gelfand, M., & Nishii, L. (2006). On the nature and importance of cultural tightness-looseness. *Journal of Applied Psychology, 91*(6), 1225–1244. doi:10.1037/0021-9010.91.6.1225.

Gelfand, M., Raver, J., Nishii, L., Leslie, L., Lun, J., Lim, B., & Arnadottir, J. (2011). Differences between tight and loose cultures: A 33-Nation study. *Science, 332*(1), 1100–1104.

Germain, M., Glynn, S., Schreiber, G., Gelinas, S., King, M., Jones, M., & Tu, Y. (2007). Determinants of return behavior: A comparison of current and lapsed donors. *Transfusion, 47*(10), 1862–1870. doi:10.1111/j.1537-2995.2007.01409.x.

Godin, G., Conner, M., Sheeran, P., Bélanger-Gravel, A., & Germain, M. (2007). Determinants of repeated blood donation among new and experienced blood donors. *Transfusion, 47*(9), 1607–1615.

Hair, J., Black, W., Babin, B., & Anderson, R. (2010). *Multivariate data analysis*. Englewood Cliffs: Prentice Hall.

Hofstede, G. (1980). *Culture's consequences*. Beverly Hills: SAGE Publications.

Holdershaw, J., Gendall, P., & Wright, M. (2011). Predicting blood donation behaviour: Further application of the theory of planned behaviour. *Journal of Social Marketing, 1*(2), 120–132. doi:10.1108/20426761111141878.

House, R., Javidan, M., Hanges, P., & Dorfman, P. (2002). Understanding cultures and implicit leadership theories across the globe: An introduction to project GLOBE. *Journal of World Business, 37*(1), 3–10. doi:10.1016/S1090-9516(01)00069-4.

Kenny, P., & Hastings, G. (2011). Understanding social norms: Upstream and downstream applications for social marketers. In G. Hastings, K. Angus, & C. Bryant (Eds.), *The SAGE handbook of social marketing* (pp. 61–79). Thousand Oaks, CA: SAGE Publications.

Kongsompong, K., Green, R., & Patterson, P. (2009). Collectivism and social influence in the buying decision: A four-country study of inter- and intra-national differences. *Australasian Marketing Journal, 17*(4), 142–149. doi:10.1016/j.ausmj.2009.05.013.

Kotler, P., & Roberto, E. (1989). The social marketing approach to social change. In P. Kotler & E. Roberto (Eds.), *Social marketing: Strategies for changing public behavior* (pp. 24–47). New York: The Free Press.

Kotler, P., & Zaltman, G. (1971). Social marketing: An approach to planned social change. *Journal of Marketing, 35*(3), 3–12.

Kropp, F., Lavack, A. M., & Silvera, D. H. (2005). Values and collective self-esteem as predictors of consumer susceptibility to interpersonal influence among university students. *International Marketing Review, 22*(1), 7–33.

Kuan, K., Zhong, Y., & Chau, P. (2014). Informational and normative social influence in group-buying: Evidence from self-reported and EEG data. *Journal of Management Information Systems, 30*(4), 151–178.

Lapinski, M., & Rimal, R. (2005). An explication of social norms. *Communication Theory, 15*(2), 127–147.

Lemmens, K., Abraham, C., Hoekstra, T., Ruiter, R., de Kort, W., Brug, J., & Schaalma, H. (2005). Why don't young people volunteer to give blood? An investigation of the correlates of donation intentions among young nondonors. *Transfusion, 45*(6), 945–955. doi:10.1111/j.1537-2995.2005.04379.x.

Masser, B., White, K., Hyde, M., & Terry, D. (2008). The psychology of blood donation: Current research and future directions. *Transfusion Medicine Reviews, 22*(3), 215–233.

Masser, B., White, K., Hyde, M., Terry, D., & Robinson, N. (2009). Predicting blood donation intentions and behavior among Australian blood donors: Testing an extended theory of planned behavior model. *Transfusion, 49*(1), 320–329. doi:10.1111/j.1537-2995.2008.01981.x.

Masser, B., Bednall, T., White, K., & Terry, D. (2012). Predicting the retention of first-time donors using an extended theory of planned behavior. *Transfusion, 52*(6), 1303–1310.

McGuire, W. (1968). Personality and susceptibility to social influence. In E. Borgatta & W. Lambert (Eds.), *Handbook of personality theory and research* (pp. 1130–1187). Chicago: Rand McNally.

McMahon, R., & Byrne, M. (2007). Predicting donation among an Irish sample of donors and nondonors: Extending the theory of planned behavior. *Transfusion, 48*(2), 321–331.

Mourali, M., Laroche, M., & Pons, F. (2005). Individualistic orientation and consumer susceptbility to interpersonal influence. *Journal of Services Marketing, 19*(3), 164–173. doi:10.1108/08876040510596849.

Netemeyer, R., Bearden, W., & Teel, J. (1992). Consumer susceptibility to interpersonal influence and attributional sensitivity. *Psychology and Marketing, 9*(5), 379–394.

Park, W., & Lessig, P. (1977). Students and housewives: Differences in susceptibility to reference group influence. *Journal of Consumer Research, 4*(2), 102–110.

Park, H., & Levine, T. (1999). The theory of reasoned action and self-construal: Evidence from three cultures. *Communication Monographs, 66*(3), 199–218. doi:10.1080/03637759909376474.
Podsakoff, P., & Organ, D. (1986). Self-reports in organizational research: Problems and prospects. *Journal of Management, 12*(4), 531–544.
Podsakoff, P., MacKenzie, S., & Podsakoff, N. (2003). Common method biases in behavioural research: A critical review of the literature and recommended remedies. *Journal of Applied Psychology, 88*(5), 879–903.
Pool, G. J., & Schwegler, A. F. (2007). Differentiating among motives for norm conformity. *Basic and Applied Social Psychology, 29*(1), 47–60. doi:10.1080/01973530701330983.
Prentice, D. (2007). Norms, prescriptive and descriptive. In R. Baumeister & K. Vohs (Eds.), *Encyclopedia of social psychology* (pp. 630–631). Thousand Oaks: SAGE Publications.
Real, K., & Rimal, R. (2007). Friends talk to friends about drinking: Exploring the role of peer communication in the theory of normative social behaviour. *Health Communication, 22*(2), 169–180. doi:10.1080/10410230701454254.
Reich, P., Roberts, P., Laabs, N., Chinn, A., McEvoy, P., Hirschler, N., & Murphy, E. (2006). A randomised trial of blood donor recruitment strategies. *Transfusion, 46*(7), 1090–1096. doi:10.1111/j.1537-2995.2006.00856.x.
Reicher, S., Hopkins, N., & Harrison, K. (2009). Identity matters: On the importance of Scottish identity for Scottish society. In F. Bechhofer & D. McCrone (Eds.), *National identity, nationalism and constitutional change* (pp. 17–40). Hampshire: Palgrave Macmillan.
Richards, E. (2010). Australia and Scotland: The evolution of a long-distance relationship. *Australian Journal of Politics and History, 56*(4), 485–502. doi:10.1111/j.1467-8497.2010.01567.x.
Rimal, R., & Real, K. (2003). Understanding the influence of perceived norms on behaviors. *Communication Theory, 13*(2), 184–203.
Rimal, R., & Real, K. (2005). How behaviours are influenced by perceived norms: A test of the theory of normative social behavior. *Communication Research, 32*(3), 389–414. doi:10.1177/0093650205275385.
Rivis, A., & Sheeran, P. (2003). Descriptive norms as an additional predictor in the theory of planned behaviour: A meta-analysis. *Current Psychology, 22*(3), 218–233. doi:10.1007/s12144-003-1018-2.
Rossiter, J. (2007). Identifying and measuring "Australian values". *Australasian Marketing Journal, 15*(1), 7–13.
Sarason, I., Sarason, B., Pierce, G., Shearin, E., & Sayers, M. (1991). A social learning approach to increasing blood donations. *Journal of Applied Social Psychology, 21*(11), 896–918.
Schultz, P., Nolan, J., Cialdini, R., Goldstein, N., & Griskevicius, V. (2007). The constructive, destructive and reconstructive power of social norms. *Psychological Science, 18*(5), 429–434.
Smith, J., Louis, W., Terry, D., Greenaway, K., Clarke, M., & Cheng, X. (2012). Congruent or conflicted? The impact of injunctive and descriptive norms on environmental intentions. *Journal of Environmental Psychology, 32*(3), 353–361.
Staunton, M., Louis, W. R., Smith, J. R., Terry, D. J., & McDonald, R. I. (2014). How negative descriptive norms for healthy eating undermine the effects of positive injunctive norms. *Journal of Applied Social Psychology, 44*(4), 319–330.
Sue, V., & Ritter, L. (2007). *Conducting online surveys*. Thousand Oaks: SAGE Publications.
Taylor, C. A., & Sorenson, S. B. (2004). Injunctive social norms of adults regarding teen dating violence. *Journal of Adolescent Health, 34*(6), 468–479.
Triandis, H. (1989). The self and social behavior in differing cultural contexts. *Psychological Review, 96*(3), 506–520.
Veldhuizen, I., Ferguson, E., de Kort, W., Donders, R., & Atsma, F. (2011). Exploring the dynamics of the theory of planned behavior in the context of blood donation: Does donation experience make a difference? *Transfusion, 51*(11), 2425–2437.

Chapter 8
On Drenching the Massive, Mature Tourist Destinations in the Sunny and Sandy Social Marketing Innovation

Gonzalo Diáz-Meneses and Ignacio Luri-Rodríguez

1 Introduction

The application of classic management models for sustainability is not enough to ensure quality of life for local inhabitants in a community with a massive tourism industry. In fact, there remain many unsolved problems in these kinds of resort where the development of tourism not only carries important benefits, but also significant counterproductive consequences. For instance, on the side of benefits, the literature has pointed out the creation of employment and the revitalisation of poor or non-industrialised regions. By contrast, on the side of costs, the literature recognises problems related to traffic congestion and waste management WTO/UNWTO (2004). While it is true that the application of classic management models has been positive in optimising these tourism outcomes, it also seems evident that the results might be improved substantially through the application of the social marketing approach (Mathieson and Wall 1982). On this basis, the first objective to be set out by this book chapter is to describe benefits, as well as costs, associated with massive resorts where the development of tourism might be challenged by making the best use of social marketing. To implement this, European, African, Asian and American examples will be given so that real cases and then actual diagnoses are dealt with.

In addition to this residents' perspective and to consider the visitors angle, it seems logical to think that no resort is able to guarantee quality of life without ensuring what is understood by satisfaction with travel and tourism services. In fact,

G. Diáz-Meneses (✉)
Universidad de Las Palmas de Gran Canaria, Las Palmas, Spain
e-mail: gonzalo.diazmeneses@ulpgc.es

I. Luri-Rodríguez
University of Arizona, Tucson, AZ, USA
e-mail: iluri@email.arizona.edu

W. Wymer (ed.), *Innovations in Social Marketing and Public Health Communication*, Applying Quality of Life Research,
DOI 10.1007/978-3-319-19869-9_8

satisfaction with travel and tourism services determines a perception of good experience in the resort and this leads to the feeling of satisfaction with leisure time and life in general (Neal et al. 2007). Consequently, in this book chapter the second objective consisted of posing social marketing as the means of achieving a greater level of visitor's satisfaction with services.

Therefore, in order to accomplish the aim of proposing social marketing as one of the most effective and efficient tools for improving residents, as well as visitors, quality of life, this book chapter is divided into four sections: (1) the theoretical part, where the classic management models for sustainability and the social marketing framework for improving quality of life are contrasted, (2) the social marketing diagnosis for massive tourism industries in order to pose the main problems at the strategic level, (3) the formulation of solutions to overcome the classic starting points and tools, and (4) the conclusions.

2 Classic Management Models for Sustainability Versus Social Marketing for Improving Quality of Life

Tourism and QOL: Not only is tourism by itself not enough to improve people's quality of life, but neither is the application of visitor management models able to create well-being, social support and personal development among resort locals. No doubt, there are beneficial impacts associated with tourism and the classic management models are useful for sustainability, but by considering social marketing, more success might be added regarding quality of life. In fact, and from a theoretical point of view, this is so because the topic of quality of life has not been explored sufficiently in the field of tourism (Andereck and Nyaupane 2011), since hardly any social marketing for tourism has even been put into motion, either theoretically or practically speaking (Dinan and Sargeant 2000; Hall 2014) and because the focus of these classic management frameworks are sustainability, there being slight differences between sustainability and quality of life (Andereck et al. 2007).

Despite the undoubted link between tourism and quality of life, little research has been done to reveal how hospitality services influence a traveller's quality of life. Most of this research effort has focused on the perspective of local residents in the host community (Andereck and Nyaupane 2011), but much remains to be done from the visitor's perspective. From the tourist's point of view, consumer satisfaction has been considered to play a significant role for enhancing specific dimensions of the quality of life construct such as longevity, self-esteem and several other aspects of life. Thus, according to Neal et al. (2007), satisfaction with the service aspects of travel phases (pre-trip, en-route, arrival at destination and return services) determines satisfaction with life in general by means of satisfaction with these travel services. Similarly, these authors point out that trip reflections on perceived freedom from control and work, involvement, arousal, mastery and spontaneity influence quality of life through satisfaction with travel experiences. Likewise, satisfaction with leisure experiences at home causes satisfaction with leisure time and life in general.

The lack of research in this area might be due to the fact that the stress has been put on the community resident structure – the intentions have been prescriptive about what is good for locals and an effort has been made to provide practical management implications to be implemented by the host side. In other words, the bottom line has not been the visitors, as social marketing assumes, but rather the providers, as classic management theory accepts.

In addition to the above reasons, it can be stated that little research has been done along the lines of social marketing for tourism whereby the final aim has been to improve quality of life. To be specific, only a few projects, as well as papers, have been performed under the banner of social marketing in the tourism sector so far. According to Truong and Hall (2013) the lines given limited attention are recreation (Bright 2000), attraction to the desired segment of sustainable tourism (Dinan and Sargeant 2000), change of tourist behaviour regarding gambling, conservation, long-term sociocultural interests and demarketing (Beeton and Benfield 2003), social responsibility in hotels operations to reduce resource use (Shang et al. 2010), poverty alleviation (Truong and Hall 2013) and advertising to dispel negative gender stereotypes (Sirakaya and Sonmez 2000; Chabra et al. 2011). Nevertheless, there are many uncovered lines of research which could consolidate social marketing for tourism. It is imperative that these limitations are overcome since as soon as social marketing is introduced into responsible tourism management, it will create change for improving quality of life, provide better business opportunities and enhance tourist and resident experiences (George and Fry 2010). In Table 8.1, new lines of research are laid out and categorised into six main general fields by considering the notion of impact as systematization criterion.

Table 8.1 Potential lines of research on social marketing for tourism

General field	Line of research	Example
Tourism physical impact	Deterioration of landscape and monuments. Overcrowded cities, overload of public services and infrastructure	Degradation of monumental buildings in Merida, Spain (Ortiz et al. 2013)
Tourism economic impact	Overpricing, seasonal employment and unemployment, standardization in offer of goods and services	Increase of housing prices in Italian touristic cities (Biagi et al. 2014)
Tourism social impact	Effect over language and culture. Satisfaction or dissatisfaction of the locals with tourism	Tourism impact on the quality of life of Virginia state residents (Kim et al. 2013)
Safety and health	Alcohol, binge drinking and drugs. Safe driving. Risk of adventure or sport tourism. Criminality	Tourism increases criminality in Spanish touristic cities (Montolio and Planells-Struse 2013)
Tourist motivators, barriers and satisfaction	Demographic profile of tourists. Reasons to choose a touristic destination. Perceived image of a destination. Satisfaction or dissatisfaction, repeat visitors	Tourists' perception of Guimarães, Portugal (Remoaldo et al. 2014)

2.1 The Classic Management Models for Sustainability

Although it goes beyond the scope of this chapter to explain in detail these models, it is relevant to cite one of these classic management models – the one labelled as 'the recreation opportunity spectrum' – whose contribution has been significant in determining a marked threshold of activity beyond which environmental deterioration would be a reality. Another widely known theoretical model is the carrying capacity framework, according to which a diversity of experiences are identified by considering the limits of a particular resort, its reposition and heritage conservation. Similarly, the visitor activity management model tries to conciliate visitor's needs and resources as a means to resolve conflicts. The visitor impact management model's main objectives are measuring and controlling the impact of threats. Furthermore, the limits of acceptable change model addresses how much change is acceptable in a particular area by considering the conditions of visitors. It is also worth mentioning the tourism optimization management model to empower the stake holders, to go back over the viability of the tourism industry and to recognise the importance of heritage conservation (Hall and McArthur 1998).

Most of these classic management techniques consist of regulating, designing spaces by architectonical and engineering means and putting into practice some marketing operations such as market research, promotions and demarketing. Examples of visitor management techniques include regulating access to certain areas by implementing transport and parking measures. Similarly, regulating visitor numbers and group size, types of visitors permitted and visitor behaviour, as well as equipment which could prohibit activities such as off road-driving. Furthermore, the use of entry fees for conservation purposes and modifications to sites by constructing hardened paths to direct visitors. Finally, some marketing actions such as market research to identify reasons for visiting and to understand how to develop tools to modify behaviour and provision of interpretation programmes by providing guided tours or guides to avoid congestion (Hall and McArthur 1998).

As an example of the classic management model's application for sustainability, the Mediterranean archipelago of Baleares is one of the leading tourist destinations in Europe, with over 10 million visitors annually. Forty per cent of the main islands' (Formentera, Ibiza, Menorca and Mallorca) territory is protected, including a UNESCO Biosphere Reserve (Menorca), a World Heritage Site (city of Ibiza), and the Cabrera National Park and over a hundred other protected natural areas.

From 2000 to 2003, the Centre for Tourism Research and Technologies of the Balearic Islands (CITTIB) researched on sustainability and carrying capacity. By 1998, Baleares already had strict regulation that limited development and land use for tourism purposes. However, the results shown by the CITTIB and other studies forced a moratorium in 2002 that prevented further urbanization without prior approval. A new General Tourism Law and Plan to Organize the Tourism Offer (Plan de Ordenacion de la Oferta Turistica) helped protect the land from uncontrolled use.

2.2 *The Differences Between Management for Sustainability and Social Marketing for Quality of Life*

However, none of these research approaches adopt the precept that the exchange of value is crucial in satisfying consumers' needs; social marketing suggests not only placing emphasis on the exchange of ideas, but also proposes that quality of life be considered. To be specific, social marketing conceives of tourism as a social product with behaviours, rituals, values and symbols related to the participating community's cultural identity, rather than to tangible elements. In other words, culture is central to the exchanges between tourists and residents since it is a system of shared meaning.

Thus, from a tourist's perspective, the product is any activity that could be developed through the visitors' consideration of cultural identity, the environment and other important social issues concerning the resort. From the inhabitant's perspective, the product is any activity developed by natives which takes into account their cultural identity in order to satisfy visitor's needs. Following on from this mixed marketing theory, price in social marketing for tourism would be any effort, sacrifice or perceived time cost for those involved in these kinds of exchanges. For instance, it could stem from any inconvenience related to travel from place of origin to destination, or any bad sensation provoked by saturated physical and affected space, and time. In addition, the place in social marketing for tourism is where cultural exchange take place between inhabitants and visitors. Communication in social marketing for tourism consists of shared meanings and senses which encourage exchanges between locals and visitors.

3 The Social Marketing Diagnosis for Massive Industries: Posing Problems at the Strategic Level for a Social Marketing Approach

Considering the review of the classic literature on sustainability for tourism management, the main environmental impacts and problems related to resort areas are the effect of inappropriate hotel development on the traditional landscape, the absence of planning and development restrictions, the overloading of resort infrastructure in periods of peak usage, the segregation of tourists from local residents, the loss of good quality agricultural land to tourist development, traffic congestion, and the fact that local ecosystems may be polluted by sewage and litter from overdemand in the peak season (Mathieson and Wall 1982).

Providing an example of this, the city of Venice (Italy) is one of the better known and most popular tourist destinations in the world. The city's attractiveness could be a reason to worry, however. More than 20 years ago, Canestrelli and Costa (1991) estimated an optimal level for arrivals in the city, and expressed concern that this level had been surpassed by the 80s. The number of tourists has only increased since then. According to the World Monuments Fund (2014), tourist arrivals have risen by 400 % in the last 5 years.

As a result, the population of Venice is now half that of a decade ago. Inaccessible housing prices, lack of specialized jobs and overloading of public services are creating an exodus that threatens the continuity of one of the most historical cities in Europe.

Some questions might be formulated to measure the major influences on the sociocultural impacts of tourism. According to Mason (2008), these questions should ask who the tourists are, in what type of activities they are engaged, what the scale of tourism is, where tourism is taking place, how able the infrastructure is to deal with demand, what the duration of stay is and what the seasonality of tourism is.

Tourism management requires answers to these questions. As with those in many other popular tourist destinations, authorities in Greece have addressed the topic of seasonality. Since arrivals were not evenly spread throughout the year, how seasonal were the Greek destinations really? Using data from the Greek Tourism Organization and the Greek National Statistical Society, research showed that seasonality was lower in the mainland than in the islands (Donatos and Zairis 1991). While tourism in the small islands was concentrated on the warmer months, Crete was less dependent on these summer visits. Overall, seasonality in Greece is greater than that of competitor countries such as Spain, Italy or Portugal, and could be considered a weakness of the sector (Buhalis 2001).

Problems and questions are often the same but social marketing defines the former in terms of quality of life and the latter in terms of exchanges. Therefore, social marketing for tourism poses a multidimensional approach to problematic issues described by situations such as recycling collaboration and other volunteering responses from visitors, insufficient cultural exchanges between locals and tourists, binge drinking behaviour, saving behaviour related to water and soap by visitors in hotels, overuse of public services, security issues and safety recommendations such as luggage attention and sun protection, safe sexual conduct among young people, respectful reminders for conservation of protected natural areas. Regarding the questions, social marketing wonders who the key exchangers are and suggests that targets for campaigns might be the tourists, the host population, and the tourist industry and government agencies.

Therefore, it is time to bring into focus social marketing as long as this new social science highlights the crucial importance of setting out as an objective the attainment of a better quality of life by encouraging more exchanges between the host community and tourists.

Putting into practice a mixed-marketing approach to assess the massive shortcomings in the tourism product, it might be pointed out that there is frequently an issue regarding a sense of alienation in huge resorts for the host community, in so far as this enormous product offers many elements of foreign identities and too few elements from the local identity, as happens in sun and sand resorts in Spain, Greece, Portugal and Italy for example. Moreover, it might work better on positioning, given that the question being raised at the moment is how to compete with emerging competitors at new resorts in North Africa (such as Marrakesh, Tunisia and Egypt), in Asia (such as Thailand and Malaysia) and in the Caribbean, considering that all of these destinations are committed to improving both infrastructure and quality of service. Maybe the answer comes from the fact that the more identity is related to a product, the more difficult it is for competitors to imitate it. However, despite the need to recover or promote a revival of the traditional cultural identity, it is true that there is a cultural generation gap that cannot be bridged by new technologies without transforming this identity into something derivative and inauthentic.

Following the mixed-marketing diagnosis and from a communication perspective, it might be said that, in countries with extensively developed tourist destinations, image is predominant over identity as long as sunny beaches and excellent infrastructure are highlighted instead of reflecting on who the local people are, what they look like and what they do. In this, mass media is responsible, given that powerful adverting and aggressive promotion campaigns are replacing other personal marketing techniques such as direct marketing, public relations and sales forces. Mass media is useful but it emphasizes quantity and non-personal interaction. In addition, it is clear that the positioning advantage of these established sun and sand destinations is under pressure from increasing globalisation and connectivity, which is leading to a non-different positioning since there are more elements from anywhere, anybody and anytime than from particular places, specific characters and special moments. In this industry, English is the predominant language, which would not necessarily be bad were it not for the fact that it is replacing local languages. Why can a language tourism industry not be developed in these resorts by taking up social marketing technologies?

From a place diagnosis, there is a saturated tourist space where the industry seems to look for quantity alone, which is a deceit, given that success should be measured in terms of visitor's satisfaction and not in the increasing number of visitors or tourists. Moreover, it might be stated that in the emerging custom of all-inclusive packages, convenience works against freedom and satisfaction since the problem stems not only from forcing choice before the tourist is aware of the destination's culture, environment and other social concerns, but also from inhibiting interaction between tourists and locals. Another place problem stems from the historical reality of the very hasty development and cultural discontinuance that occurred between 1960 and 1990 in many of these massive tourist destinations along with the phenomenon of rapid urbanization, which has caused a gap to widen between rural and urban society, and between tradition and modernity.

From the standpoint of price, this kind of massive tourist destination is facing the dilemma of conciliating good prices and high quality, since the emerging competitors are unbeatable in terms of low cost, given that they are in developing countries where the cost of living is cheaper and tourism packages and services are more affordable. Against these new competitors, the tourism industry is working not only on supplying products and on providing services, but also experiences. However, in many cases these experiences are not related to either social responsibility, environmental issues or cultural local identity. The experiences are designed by making good use of some diversification policies based upon new dimensions, such as congress and health, where sun and sand are often associated to these new lines of product. Thus it attempts to provide added value and consequently higher perceived value. Furthermore, these policies try to follow on from the fact that modern marketing highlights the importance of brand rather than price, inviting one to think more in terms of the best or worst rather than in terms of good or bad/expensive or cheap, since value is always positive. Thus, brand equity questions the old considerations and proposes a new framework where knowledge is assimilated into the best operative procedures but is incapable of underlining the importance of value in itself – the value of doing what is right, for example by saving water, recycling and helping others voluntarily. On this basis, the proposed solutions are quite ethically challenging, perhaps because those social causes, humanitarian and environmental concerns are too often avoided.

As a mature tourist destination, the Canary Islands have faced the challenges of a rapidly expanding tourism industry. By 2000, the transformation of the land and problems related to carrying capacity needed to be addressed urgently.

Traditionally, the economy of The Canary Islands had been based on a low-price, sun and sand tourism. However, an overcrowded island loses its appeal to tourists (Santana Jiménez and Hernández 2011). A new model was part of the solution, and more recently the effort has been towards diversifying what's on offer. A tourism consisting of sports, culture or business trips means more added value, higher prices and a sector less dependent on mass- tourism and huge numbers of visitors.

4 Formulating Solutions to Overcome the Classic Starting Points and Tools

In order to formulate solutions, it seems pertinent to start with the optimism of the literature on tourism management by recognising the beneficial impacts of tourism. According to Mathieson and Wall (1982) and considering the traditional massive tourism industry in developed countries, tourism was good for the creation of employment and the revitalisation of poor and non-industrialised regions in the 1960s, and for the promotion of the need to conserve areas of outstanding beauty which have aesthetic and cultural value in the 1980s. However, its ability to engender a rebirth of local arts and crafts, a revival of the social and cultural life of the local inhabitants, or the renewal of local architectural traditions, as well as other dimensions of quality of life, might be called into question.

It is clear that social marketing shares the most important salient principles for sustainability, which according to Mason (2008) are the following: sustainable use of resources, a lessening of environmental impacts, reduction of waste and overconsumption, adoption of internal environmental management, provision of support and involvement with green issues, pursuit of responsible marketing, efficient use of resources, the provision of quality tourist products and experiences, and the safeguarding of local cultures and traditions. Nevertheless, social marketing might be more useful than the methods of classic management for sustainability.

Why social marketing? Marketing is the most advanced social science discipline, management technique and philosophy for social change (Kotler et al. 2002). Why this challenge? If the goal is to satisfy clients holistically so that tourism development can formulate sustainability and quality of life, it will be necessary to use the local identity with its creative industry and consider social equity, environmental protection and economic sustainability. The role of social marketing should guide the whole process by influencing the acceptance of these social ideas between the stakeholders (Jamrozy 2007). In addition and according to Andreasen (1995), social marketing is more effective and efficient than pedagogy, sociology, persuasion, psychology and a mere management approach to induce desired conduct in society, even against a reluctant target. This is so because social marketing is very effective and efficient in terms of making social change in the intimate personal sphere (thanks to a multifactor – or interdisciplinary – treatment which comes from the above-mentioned social sciences) by segmentation and market research, by putting the tourist as the bottom line, and by putting into motion very sophisticated techniques. In fact, even though it may sound politically incorrect, there are contradictions between sustainability and quality of life; saving water and soap, limiting one's driving speed, paying ecological taxes and recycling might make people feel inconvenienced or put upon since it implies effort, demands overpayment for the same product and might be perceived as coming at the expense of leisure time. Therefore, the objectives of satisfying tourists and locals holistically and filling the slight gap existing between sustainability and quality of life might be achieved by putting into motion social marketing strategies and techniques which could overcome these difficult problems.

Strategically speaking, the first step must be taken in looking at local identity; then the question of what the elements of local identity are must be raised and the dimensions related to culturally-sensitive social conduct highlighted. Therefore, information should be gathered in order to determine and name the symbols of these mature massive sun and sand tourist resorts' identities and uncover their customs and codes of behaviour. Consequently, a scale to measure the cultural identity and social responsibility should be developed which could categorise the following dimensions: history and legends, flora and fauna, gastronomy, festivals and sport, art, monuments and music, as well as local customs and codes of conduct.

The second step to be taken should raise the question of how to involve locals with their cultural identity. The answer should be by implementing techniques and designing messages. Thus, there are not only antecedent (prompts, commitment, blockleader and objectives) and consequent (reward, feedback and negative reinforcement) social marketing techniques, but also affective (emotions), cognitive (information) and conative (experiences) approaches. In any case, social marketing should be taken up not only to produce a cultural revival and enhance environmental sustainability in these mass-tourism areas, but also to encourage creativity, enrich experiences, revitalise existing product and valorise assets so that distinction is achieved and competitive advantage is gained.

The third step to be taken might consist of promoting the visitor adoption process, raising the question of how to connect the local with the tourist. The answer is by destroying barriers (against unawareness, it could be useful to provide information with cultural guides, brochures and digital materials and against indifference, emotional campaigns could be designed whereby emotions would serve to connect the tourist with the local inhabitant and both to their social reality) and building facilitators (teaching English to practitioners, as well as offering local languages to visitors). In fact, language is a key feature in any culture; it might be learnt by visitors and language tourism could be developed more extensively. However, the adoption process should be done after performing segmentation studies to connect locals and visitors varying in terms of specificity and objects of cultural, environmental and social interests so that a particular group's experiences might be created (Blamey and Braithwaite 2010). Furthermore, it is not only language that may be shared, but visitors would also be able to learn native cookery, fishing, embroidery, handcrafts, cultivation, among many other such activities, as tourism in these areas became more cultured, knowledge-based and creative. It could be made possible by developing creative spaces, events, relationships and networks in order to enhance visibility, permeability and flexibility. For example, the organisation of workshops, conferences, festivals, interuniversity courses, associations and other potential co-creation opportunities. In addition, a good use of new technologies can be advantageous, for example, by providing the possibility to download an app which would send prompts to make the visitor aware of the surrounding cultural map while wandering around a city, village or particular place. In this way, as far as the visitor drives or walks, information about points of interest in the vicinity such as literary authors' birth places, musical events, historical facts or endemic fauna and flora is updated as they go. The aim is to reach something other than a mere cultural tourism dimension in mass-tourism resorts by consolidating an authentically creative tourism niche in these areas (Richards 2012).

More operationally speaking, social marketers might use social marketing techniques such as the following:

1. The foot-in-the-door technique: This is a method of persuasion that involves getting a person to agree to a large request by first having them agree to a smaller request (Mackenzie-Mohr 2011). For example, trying to encourage a tourist to taste some gastronomical items before they are persuaded to buy it.
2. The face in the door technique: This involves first making an excessive request of the other person which they will most naturally refuse. The trick is to look disappointed but then make a request that is more reasonable. The other person will then be more likely to accept (Mackenzie-Mohr 2011). For example, after having quite a negative emotional reaction to being invited to pay an unaffordable price for a luxury souvenir, they can later be offered a more affordable item such as a CD of folk music.
3. The bait and switch technique (Reilly 1988): This works by adding something additional after getting something perceived as very good value for money. For example, offer tourists something that is very good value (sun & sand); this should be a real bargain, and an offer they cannot possibly refuse, even if they were not initially considering it. Later, enrich the item with something of less value to them and more profit to you (volunteering).
4. The exchange principle (Evans and Hastings 2008): This is based on the principle that if I do something for someone, they must feel obliged to do something for me. For example, offer tourists free transport to a restaurant and in return they will eat there.

5. The contrast principle (Thomas 2007): We notice differences between things, but not absolute measures. Offer tourists the following option: going to the disco or going to a folk music festival which includes modern music.
6. The high ball: This takes advantage of the tendency of people to want more. For example, a travel agent takes tourists to hotels and services that they cannot afford. This, however, raises their desires and the package they eventually buy is more expensive than they had originally planned on.
7. Triggering guilt (Donovan and Henley 2010): Guilt as an emotion is the feeling we get when we believe we have committed an offence by compromising an internal value. Remind your civilised visitors of their environmental values, their belief in fair-play and their good-hearted nature to induce a willingness to participate in recycling at the tourist destination.

In addition to this and following the advice of Kotler et al. (2002), some keys to success from social marketing might be proposed:

1. Take advantage of what is known and has been done before. They watch TV on the plane: what is being shown? Show them not only your sun and sand, but also your history and customs.
2. Start with target markets that are ready for action. Targeting cultural habits in the country of origin.
3. Promoting a single specific behavior. What to say? Know about our culture or buy a bottle of wine, a handmade biscuit or a DVD course of folkloric dance music?
4. Incorporating a tangible object to support the desired behavior. Promoting the tourist destination's literature among tourists. What object to select? Probably the best answer is a book of poetry written by a local author.
5. Understand and address perceived benefits and costs. Tell your visitors about the environmental damage provoked by an excessive use of towels and soap and tell them about how they can save some money by reusing.
6. Convenience. Identify the supply channel as many times as you offer a particular handcraft. For example, indicate the shop or workshop where it can be acquired.
7. Using motivating techniques to induce the desired action. If the target shows interest, antecedent techniques are more effective and efficient; if target does not show interest, it is better to apply consequent techniques; if target is reluctant, sanction is the solution. In other words, be not only effective but also efficient.

5 Conclusions

Attempting to go further into who is thought to demand control under a pure demarketing approach could be the answer to solving the problems associated with mass tourism (Beeton and Benfield 2002). This book chapter highlights concerns about discouraging tourists in general, or a particular profile of visitor, since it might imply a permanent slowdown crisis for a massive tourism industry. Thus, the straightforward classic management approaches are questioned as sustainability might be not competitive in the short term and quality of life might be more so immediately after it is targeted or put in motion as a priority. By contrast, social marketing might bring desired changes to target markets, even in cooperation with original tourist market authorities and companies. In this direction, and although some minor contradictions might be met, social marketing and tourism marketing for sustainable development would be fully compatible. This is so because marketing would be used to change undesired attitudes and behaviour respecting how host members and visitors behave and coexist so that the importance of how members of a community interact with the number and type of visitors and perform leisure activities might be underlined (Batra 2006).

The sun and sand tourism development cycle has reached its mature phase in Europe and this is the reason why a social marketing disruption theory is needed in order to add more value to the impact of massive tourism on not only residents', but also visitors' quality of life (Perdue et al. 1999). Of course the promoted change should be more profitable by means of switching quantities to qualities and by refuting the preconceived idea that the more visitors there are, the more success there will be. Satisfaction is the gate of sustainability and quality of life.

Hopefully, social marketing for creativity might provide intangible competitive advantages in mass tourism resorts by shifting habits and building relational forms of vacation between the visiting and hosting communities. In fact, sun and sand tourism and sustainable tourism should not be considered absolutely opposed if this large-scale tourism is able to induce desired changes in tourists as well as in residents toward a more compatible and integrated framework (Clarke 1997).

The difference between social marketing for tourism in developed countries such as Spain, Greece, Portugal and Italy, and developing countries is substantial since the former aims to optimise quality of life and the latter tries to improve the humanitarian requirements of providing tourism culture service (Alhroot 2012). Nevertheless, the key point is that social marketing for tourism is underdeveloped and it represents an attractive, growing line of research, formulation and implementation.

References

Alhroot, A. (2012). An evaluation of social marketing in humanitarian tourism requirements by using social networking sites. *International Journal of Marketing Studies, 4*, 130–137.

Andereck, K., & Nyaupane, G. (2011). Exploring the nature of tourism and quality of life perceptions among residents. *Journal of Travel Research, 50*(3), 248–260.

Andereck, K., Valentine, K., Vogt, C., & Knopf, R. (2007). A cross-cultural analysis of tourism and quality of life perceptions. *Journal of Sustainable Tourism, 15*(5), 483–502.

Andreasen, A. (1995). *Marketing social change*. San Francisco: Jossey-Bass.

Batra, A. (2006). Tourism marketing for sustainable development. *Assumption University of Bangkok Journal, 26*(1), 59–65.

Beeton, S., & Benfield, R. (2002). Demand control: The case for demarketing as a visitor and environmental management tool. *Journal of Sustainable Tourism, 10*, 497–513.

Biagi, B., Brandano, M. G., & Lambiri, D. (2014). Does tourism affect house prices? Evidence from Italy. *Growth and Change*. In press.

Blamey, R., & Braithwaite, V. (2010). A social values segmentation of the potential ecotourism market. *Journal of Sustainable Tourism, 5*(1), 29–45.

Bright, A. (2000). The role of social marketing in leisure and recreation management. *Journal of Leisure Research, 32*, 12–17.

Buhalis, D. (2001). Tourism in Greece: Strategic analysis and challenges. *Current Issues in Tourism, 4*(5), 440–480.

Canestrelli, E., & Costa, P. (1991). Tourist carrying capacity: A fuzzy approach. *Annals of Tourism Research, 18*(2), 295–311.

Chabra, D., Andereck, K., Yamanoi, K., & Plunkett, D. (2011). Gender equity and social marketing: An analysis of tourism advertisements. *Journal of Travel and Tourism Marketing, 28*, 111–128.

Clarke, J. (1997). A framework of approaches to sustainable tourism. *Journal of Sustainable Tourism, 5*(3), 224–233.

Dinan, C., & Sargeant, A. (2000). Social marketing and sustainable tourism-is there a match? *International Journal of Tourism Research, 2*, 1–14.

Donatos, G., & Zairis, P. (1991). Seasonality of foreign tourism in the Greek island of Crete. *Annals of Tourism Research, 18*(3), 515–519.

Donovan, R., & Henley, N. (2010). *Principles and practice of social marketing* (An international perspective). New York: Cambridge University Press.

Evans, D., & Hastings, G. (2008). *Public health branding: Applying marketing for social change*. New York: Oxford University Press.

George, R., & Fry, N. (2010). Creating change in responsible tourism management through social marketing. *South Africa Journal of Business Management, 41*(1), 11–24.

Hall, M. (2014). *Tourism and social marketing*. Oxford/New York: Roudledge.

Hall, C. M., & McArthur, S. (1998). *Integrated heritage management*. London: Stationery Office. Oxford/NY

Jamrozy, U. (2007). Marketing of tourism: A paradigm shift toward sustainability. *International Journal of Culture, Tourism and Hospitality Research, 1*(2), 117–130.

Kim, K., Uysal, M., & Sirgy, M. J. (2013). How does tourism in a community impact the quality of life of community residents? *Tourism Management, 36*, 527–540.

Kotler, P., Roberto, N., & Lee, N. (2002). *Social marketing: Improving the quality of life*. Thousand Oaks: Sage.

Mackenzie-Mohr, D. (2011). *Fostering sustainable behaviour: An introduction to community based social marketing*. Gabriola Island: New Society Publishers.

Mason, P. (2008). *Tourism impacts, planning and management*. Oxford: Butterworth Heinemann.

Mathieson, A., & Wall, G. (1982). *Tourism, economic, physical and social impacts*. London/New York: Longman Harlow.

Montolio, D., & Planells-Struse, S. (2013). Does tourism boost criminal activity? Evidence from a top touristic country. *Crime and Delinquency*. doi:10.1177/0011128713505489.

Neal, J., Usysal, M., & Sirgy, J. (2007). The effect of tourism services on traveller's quality of life. *Journal of Travel Research, 46*, 154–163.

Ortiz, P., Antunez, V., Martín, J. M., Ortiz, R., Vázquez, M. A., & Galán, E. (2013). Approach to environmental risk analysis for the main monuments in a historical city. *Journal of Cultural Heritage, 15*(4), 432–440.

Perdue, R., Long, P., & Kang, Y. (1999). Boomtown tourism and resident quality of life: The marketing of gaming to host communities' residents. *Journal of Business Research, 44*, 165–177.

Reilly, R. (1988). *Travel and tourism marketing techniques. The travel management library*. Albany: Delmar Publisher.

Remoaldo, P. C., Vareiro, L., Santos, J. F., & Ribeiro, J. C. (2014). Tourists' perceptions of world heritage destinations: The case of Guimarães (Portugal). *Tourism and Hospitality Research, 14*(4), 206–218. doi:10.1177/1467358414541457.

Richards, G. (2012). Tourism, creativity and creative industries. In *Proceeding of creativity and creative industries in challenging times*. Breda: NHTV.

Santana Jiménez, Y., & Hernández, J. M. (2011). Estimating the effect of overcrowding on tourist attraction: The case of Canary Islands. *Tourism Management, 32*, 415–425.

Shang, J., Basil, D., & Wymar, W. (2010). Using social marketing to enhance hotel reuse programs. *Journal of Business Research, 63*, 166–172.

Sirakaya, E., & Sonmez, S. (2000). Gender images in state tourism brochures: An overlooked area in socially responsible tourism marketing. *Journal of Travel Research, 38*, 353–362.

Thomas, M. (2007). Cause related marketing partnership: An application of associative learning theory principle for both short and long success for the brand. *Proquest information and learning company*. Southern Illinois University Cardendale.

Truong, V., & Hall, C. (2013). Social marketing and tourism: What is the evidence? *Social Marketing Quarterly, 19*(2), 110–135.

World Monument Fund. (2014). http://www.wmf.org/sites/default/files/press_releases/2014-Press-Release-ENG.pdf.

WTO/UNWTO (United Nations World Tourism Organisation). (2004). *Indicators of sustainable development for tourism destinations: A guidebook*. Madrid: WTO.

Chapter 9
Innovations in Social Marketing and Public Health Communication: Improving the Quality of Life for Individuals and Communities

Marlize Terblanche-Smit and Nic S. Terblanche

1 Introduction

The purpose of social marketing and public health communication is to influence human behavior for the benefit of societies at large. The HIV/Aids pandemic is a major concern worldwide; more than 36 million people have died from Aids-related causes. Social marketing campaigns play a key role to address this social problem. The education of individuals and communities to alter sexual behavior in order to prevent HIV/Aids is vital to public health and to improve the quality of life of millions of people. Not all social marketing communication campaigns designed to address this social problem seem to be producing the expected results, especially efforts to persuade Generation Y to alter their sexual behavior. Increased social problems and behaviors have forced many practitioners to turn to the use of fear appeals in social advertising, because it appears as if other types of advertising appeals are not having the intended behavioral outcomes. This chapter explores whether the use of fear increases the likelihood of adopting appropriate behavior in order to improve quality of life by preventing individuals from contracting HIV or developing Aids. The tailoring of fear appeal advertising to different segments, specifically Generation Y, when addressing social causes are explored. Moreover, the roles of fear, attitude and behavioral intent are examined to ascertain the influence of fear appeal advertising. Recommendations are made to enhance the effectiveness of HIV/Aids advertising to Generation Y.

M. Terblanche-Smit (✉)
University of Stellenbosch Business School, 610, Bellville 7535, South Africa
e-mail: Marlize.Terblanche-Smit@usb.ac.za

N.S. Terblanche
Department of Business Management, Faculty of Economics and Management Sciences, Stellenbosch University, Matieland 7602, South Africa
e-mail: nst@sun.ac.za

W. Wymer (ed.), *Innovations in Social Marketing and Public Health Communication*, Applying Quality of Life Research,
DOI 10.1007/978-3-319-19869-9_9

2 The Facts About the HIV/AIDS Pandemic

The deaths of over 36 million people in the world due to Aids-related causes could have been prevented. Most of these deaths resulted from unsafe sexual behaviour. Currently there are 35.3 million people living with HIV, including 2.1 million adolescents between 10 and 19 years. Sub-Saharan Africa is affected most severely, with 1 in 20 adults living with HIV, accounting for 69 % of people living with HIV/Aids worldwide (World Health Organisation 2011; Global Aids Review 2014). In South Africa, with the highest prevalence of HIV/Aids in Sub-Saharan, 50 % of HIV infections are transmitted before the age of 20, and an estimated 6.4 million individuals were HIV positive (12.2 % of the population) in 2012 (Shisana et al. 2014). The estimated number of Aids related deaths in South Africa during 2011 was 270,000, with an average life expectancy of 54 years (Avert 2011). Overall HIV prevalence is highest in females, aged 25–49 years and belonging to the Black African race group; furthermore females in the 30–34 year age group and men in the 30–39 age group had the highest levels of HIV prevalence. It is estimated that the prevalence of HIV amongst female adolescents (15–19 years old) are eight times higher compared to men in this age category. This emphasizes concerns regarding adolescents' increased risky behavior such as having multiple sex partners, having sex at a young age and not using condoms. Additionally issues related to attitudes, awareness and knowledge of HIV/Aids further increase the prevalence rates (Shisana et al. 2014; Avert 2011). It is clear to see how important it is to persuade young people that engaging in sexual activity, and practising safe sexual behaviour, can be a matter of life or death. Persuading them to take measures to prevent HIV infection is a vital task of social marketing.

3 Social Marketing Campaigns to Improve Public Health

Ample evidence exists of the influence that marketing initiatives can have on consumer behavior, provided that advertising campaigns are composed and executed effectively (Shimp 2010; Wiles and Danielova 2009; Egan 2007). The purpose of advertisements is to persuade a person to act or behave in a specific manner (O'Guinn et al. 2009). Similarly, social advertising campaigns should ultimately influence the behavioural intent of individuals toward whom prevention campaigns are aimed (Shimp 2010; Govender 2009). Social marketing programmes address various pandemics and anti-social behaviour in order to get people to change destructive behaviors. Examples of social problems addressed include smoking, drug abuse, drunk driving, or unprotected sexual contact and the latter leading to the spread of HIV/Aids – activities where many citizens are not acting in line with accepted healthy social conduct. Social marketing campaigns concerning issues such as safer sexual behavior aim to influence the target market's behavioral patterns and habits. Such campaigns often use emotions to create a behavioral response.

Behavioral theories such as the Theory of Reasoned Action and Theory of Planned behavior are structured around a theoretical sequence of attitude-intention-behavior (Evans et al. 2006). However, in order for an attitude to be formed, and to result in the desired related behavior, certain mediating variables are said to stimulate attitude formation and behavioral action. These mediating variables include prior experience and culture (Schiffman and Kanuk 2007).

The idea of culture (and subculture) as sets of beliefs, values and actions that characterize a certain group of people is well accepted. However, there seem to be clear self-groupings based on race, and such groupings often seem to follow along cultural or subcultural groupings. Marketing communication has to take into account the cultural and economic fabric of society, consisting of different types of people from different racial/culture groups (Lane et al. 2009). Research on race and marketing communication interventions suggest that racial groups differ in responses to communication, advertising effectiveness and attitudes towards messages (Dines and Humez 1995). According to Hawkins et al. (2007), culture directs behavior. As sexual behavior and the acceptance of premarital intercourse stem from a culture's pre-set values, it can be assumed that because different cultural groups have different values; sexual behavior and perceptions related thereto in one cultural group can differ from that of the next. It can be assumed that culture will affect, for example, the age at which individuals become sexually active, as well as with whom and whether protective sexual habits are practiced. In investigating social campaigns and their application in order to result in protective behavior, culture presents itself as a necessary variable to be considered. Since all the marketing mix elements are combined as a strategy to influence a specific target market, Moran (1990) suggested that advertising cannot necessarily address the needs of a multivariate segment and concluded that successful market segmentation should be based on one variable at a time, or two variables at the most. Communication objectives can therefore only be assessed successfully when the number of segmentation variables is limited to one or two.

It is likely that social advertisements using specific emotive elements would attract more attention than a neutral or informative advertisement (Heath et al. 2009). Specific HIV/Aids interventions explored in developing countries include a study by Caldwell and Kleppe (2010), which investigated the roles of early adopters of HIV/Aids public health innovations. These early adopters, who were people living with HIV/Aids, performed the role of public spokes models for HIV/Aids-positive living, but stigmatization, gender roles and poverty, among other factors, made their role difficult to enact. The challenges to social advertising in communicating HIV/Aids messages – in terms of message development and delivery from the perspective of the producer of the messages – were explored by Scott and Williams-Smith (2007). Scott and Williams-Smith (2007) found that successful message development was influenced by stigmatization, conflicting cultural ideals, and resource constraints. When advertising processing takes place, three attentive levels are found: active (high attention), passive (low attention), and implicit (no attention). Emotions processed without attention can still be linked to semantic memory and influence behavior without the respondents' awareness of being influenced. This also implies that the fear emotion could have a similar effect. It is therefore suggested that low attention might be seen as an advantage. A suggestion is that the future of television advertising specifically could be about inserting persuasive emotional ideas into the mind of the consumer (Heath 2011). When this strategizing is linked to a social marketing campaign through creative advertising, effectiveness should increase.

Various international governmental efforts have been employed to reduce the spread of HIV/Aids. Whilst fear has been found to be an important element for social advertising campaigns (UNAIDS 2010; Witte 1998; LaTour and Rotfeld 1997; Tanner et al. 1991; Witte 1992; Beck and Lund 1981), not all social marketing efforts utilize this. When comparing HIV/Aids prevention advertising campaigns of a country like South Africa, which grapple with an extremely high incidence of HIV/Aids, to the fear levels and composition of international campaigns, the South African advertisements seem to have very low levels of fear emotion.

The lack of a fear appeal is evident throughout the NGO loveLife's major multi-million dollar HIV/Aids prevention campaign in South Africa. The loveLife prevention campaign follows an informational appeal approach and is an educational campaign that emphasizes condom use and "positive sexuality" (Peng 2006; Green 2004, cited in Green and Witte 2006). It does not seem that loveLife is producing the expected results, considering the lack of impact on the target audience over a long period of time (Peng 2006). The South African National HIV Prevalence, Incidence and Behaviour Survey, 2012 concludes that HIV prevalence has increased significantly and that the focus of South Africa's response to HIV/Aids has shifted toward medical prevention strategies. The lack of any social marketing campaigns that contribute to the much needed behavioral change to curb the spread of HIV is evident. South Africa is left with an immense challenge, and a comprehensive social marketing campaign that encourages behavioural change in condom usage, monogamy, and sexual behaviour is required. HIV/Aids prevention advertisements must also be tailored to the different cultural needs of South African racial groups. It is critical to influence the behaviour of young people who are beginning to engage in sexual activity. In order to persuade young people that practising safe sexual behaviour can be a matter of life or death, a thorough understanding of this generation's perceptions, attitudes and behavior is required.

4 Understanding Generation Y

A generation is a group of individuals born and living about the same time. Generational marketing addresses the unique needs and behaviors of individuals within a specific generational group and factors in the different characteristics, lifestyles, and attitudes which enhances relationship building (Williams and Page

2011). Generation Y (also referred to as Echo Boomers, Why Generation, Net Generation, Gen Wired, We Generation, DotNet, Ne(x)t Generation, Nexters, First Globals, iPod Generation, and iYGeneration) mostly consists of individuals born between 1978 and 1998 (Williams and Page 2011; Herbison and Boseman 2009) and are currently in the 16–36 age range. From a marketing perspective, Generation Y is one of the largest and most profitable consumer groups. Noble et al. (2009) maintain that Generation Y is regarded as trendsetters, early-adopters and an appreciated market segment due to their size and future disposable income. Social marketers aiming to change the behavior of members of Generation Y should recognize and consider the impact of this group, who grew up in a time of vast and fast-paced change. Generation Y was born into a technological and electronic society where global boundaries became more transparent. This lead to significant respect for ethnic and cultural diversity including heightened social awareness, and a wide array of family types are seen as normal (Williams and Page 2011; Noble et al. 2009).

Generation Y is self-regarding and self-reliant, and have a strong sense of independence, they are results and image-driven, and have a strong need for peer acceptance and connection, fitting in, and social networking. These individuals are open-minded, optimistic, goal oriented, and highly motivated toward what they perceive as success (Binder and Reeves 2010). Traditional mass marketing approaches do not work well for this group, they react positively to real life examples and the truth, uniqueness and information are important to them (Williams 2005). Social marketers must be creative with media and advertising themes to capture Generation Y's attention and deliver messages they can relate to. Social marketing campaigns must identify triggers like appropriate music, language, and images, as well as action verbs that challenge and motivate them to alter their behavior (Luck and Mathews 2010). It is consequently critical to aim HIV/Aids social advertising containing the afore-mentioned features to this sexually active group to alter their attitude and behavior to safe sexual behaviour.

5 The Role of Fear, Attitude and Behavior to Improve Quality of Life

From the previous section it is evident that social marketing campaigns can be better tailored, to fit differing segments like the young-adult or Generation Y target market. This will increase the effectiveness of social marketing campaigns and potentially save many lives. The proliferation of several social problems, especially in developing countries, indicates that not enough change is taking place. Thus, in the quest for crucial change, there has been a review of the effectiveness of fear appeals as a means of influencing behaviour. But how can fear appeals be used effectively? Many marketers have stayed away from using fear appeals because it is difficult to use them effectively (Peng 2006; LaTour and Tanner 2003).

A number of previous fear appeal study models (Arthur and Quester 2004; Witte 1992, 1994) were aimed at clarifying the role of fear in establishing the effectiveness of advertising. These studies also examined the moderating role of coping appraisal (i.e., "How possible is it for me to act this way?") in determining consumer response. These studies furthermore assessed perceptions of severity, susceptibility, response efficacy and self-efficacy as related to the fear appeal. For the purposes of this chapter, however, the influence of different levels of fear-based advertising appeals pertaining to HIV/Aids will be the focus. Ample evidence exists of the influence that marketing initiatives can have on consumer behaviour, provided that advertising campaigns are composed and executed effectively (Shimp 2010; Wiles and Danielova 2009; Egan 2007). The purpose of advertisements is to persuade a person to act or behave in a specific manner (O'Guinn et al. 2009). Similarly, social advertising campaigns should ultimately influence the behavioural intent of individuals toward whom prevention campaigns are aimed (Shimp 2010; Govender 2009).

5.1 Fear Emotion and Appeals

Fear appeal literature indicates that fear can be described by mood adjectives, including feeling frightened, anxious, and/or nauseous, and also by ratings of concern or worry, for instance about a negative health outcome like contracting HIV through unprotected sex (LaTour and Tanner 2003; LaTour and Rotfeld 1997; Henthorne et al. 1993; Rogers 1983). Fear of contracting HIV thus seems to motivate actions, namely changing sexual behaviour, aimed at reducing these unpleasant emotions (Tanner et al. 1991; LaTour et al. 1988). Fear also relates to risk-taking behaviour, as well as to protective sexual behaviour, which is likewise often addressed by social marketing efforts (Tudor 2003). Various other advertising approaches are used, ranging from humour to self-idealization, but which still include the use of fear where an individual is warned that if the current behaviour continues the probability of negative health consequences is high (Belch and Belch 2012).

Research has shown ample evidence in support of incorporating medium to high levels of fear as an emotion in order to facilitate behavioural change among individuals (Terblanche-Smit and Terblanche 2013; Witte 2006; Arthur and Quester 2004; Ruiter et al. 2001; LaTour and Rotfeld 1997; Tanner et al. 1991; Rogers 1975). Bastien (2011) reports on the perception of young people in Tanzania on the role of fear appeals in HIV-prevention messages. The qualitative study used the theoretical principles of the Extended Parallel Process Model. Respondents were shown print media images (posters) and questioned about beliefs on HIV and AIDS, self-efficacy, response-efficacy, perceived susceptibility and the severity of the message. Results indicated that high levels of severity were perceived when confronted with messages that included the discrimination and stigma that HIV infected individuals face, together with pictorial presentations of the physical effects of the illness. Those images that targeted young people induced the highest levels of susceptibility to HIV infection. None of the images could elicit perceptions of self-efficacy to perform protective behaviours. Bastien (2011) argue for the use of local messages (as they showed higher levels of emotion) that find an appropriate level between fear appeals and efficacy.

5.2 *Influence of Fear on Attitude and Behavior*

Different theories and models developed over the past five decades propose two distinctive approaches to studying how fear relates to persuasion. The first approach centres on outcomes related to acceptance of a message's recommendations, namely changing attitudes, intentions and behaviour in line with the recommendations, therefore assuming a linear relationship between fear intensity and persuasion. The second approach centres on outcomes related to rejection of the message, such as defensive avoidance, reactance and denial, thus assuming a curvilinear relationship between the intensity of fear appeal used and effective change (Barth and Bengel 2000; Witte and Allen 2000). Various models to improve the effectiveness of fear appeals in advertising have been proposed over time.

Tay et al. (2000) recommend that the utilization of fear appeals should be segment specific and influence different population segments differently. Segmentation may be based on a variety of variables including age, gender, culture and their involvement in the behaviour under investigation, such as smoking, drunk driving or unprotected sexual contact (Burnett and Oliver 1979 cited in Tay et al 2000; O'Guinn et al. 2009). For example, a HIV/Aids prevention campaign aimed at Generation Y could include higher levels of fear for males versus lower levels of fear for females. Different execution styles, namely, factual information versus 'slice of life,' could also be used for males and females, addressing their specific sexual behaviours (Bakir 2012). Individuals need to be encouraged and supported to change their high-risk behaviour into healthy behaviour in order to prevent the spread of HIV/Aids (Fishbein 2000; Lee and Green 1991). Three variables in particular, namely attitude, norms and self-efficacy, are the function of underlying determinants (Fishbein 2000; Lee and Green 1991). These determinants include beliefs about the outcome of behavior, social and normative prescriptions within that population, and specific barriers to these actions. External influences should be included when evaluating these beliefs: cultural background, perceived vulnerability to infection and personality traits may have a mediating influence on attitudes, norms and self-efficacy beliefs (Fishbein 2000).

Attitude is a mediating variable of behavioral intent considering that marketers often attempt to alter consumers' attitudes in order to evoke a change in their behavioral patterns (Arthur and Quester 2004; Witte 2006). The Protection Motivation Theory (PMT) is a premise that explores the effects that fear appeal will have on attitude change (Arthur and Quester 2004; Rogers 1975). Attitude therefore constitutes an important driver to affect behavioral intent adaptations. Consumer behaviour literature provides evidence of the influence of emotional reactions (i.e. fear of contracting HIV) on attitude (i.e. believing the probability of negative health consequences), as well as the influence that attitude has on behavioral intent (i.e., changing behavior to safe sexual behavior that guarantees protection from contracting HIV) (Hawkins et al. 2007; Bohner and Wänke 2002; Bagozzi et al. 2002).

Growing evidence suggests that well-designed, well-targeted, theory-based behavior change interventions can be effective in reducing the spread of HIV/Aids (Fishbein 2000; Arthur and Quester 2004). Culturally sensitive interventions have been found to more effectively create behavior changes in high-risk populations such as adolescents or Generation Y. This implies that interventions which are based not only on sound theoretical knowledge of behavior change (e.g. social learning theory, the health belief model, and self-efficacy theory), but also take into account cultural beliefs and attitudes, are more likely to succeed to bring about behavior change (Levinson et al. 2004).

6 Concluding Remarks for Social Marketers

Social marketing should influence human behavior for societal benefit. The authors posit that social marketers can, and more importantly should, contribute to the development of (new) social marketing campaigns that will significantly impact on citizen behavior and ultimately the quality of life for individuals and communities. Communicating information about HIV/Aids is a vital intervention to educate the public about prevention and treatment. If individuals and communities are aware of the seriousness of HIV/Aids they will more likely engage in prevention behavior. Knowledge of HIV/Aids remain low, specifically in sub-Saharan Africa (UNAIDS 2013) and there is limited evidence to show that knowledge is adopted and translated into preventative behavior. The stigma towards HIV/Aids and people living with HIV is also still a barrier to effective social marketing and prevention behavior, but evidence-based social marketing communication could influence stigma perceptions. People tend to believe that others, and not themselves, are at risk of contracting HIV/Aids. This creates a false sense of security and impacts negatively on behavior change communication with consequent undesirable risky behavior such as having multiple sexual partnerships, early sexual debut and inconsistent condom use. The various literature sources and research findings reviewed confirm that advertising campaigns evidently can be devised to influence attitude and behavior toward HIV/Aids through the use of different advertising appeals, and more specifically fear appeals.

Support for a segmented approach to HIV/Aids social marketing campaigns were also ascertained, where separate message content will have to be developed and tested for individual segments, to ensure that the message alters their attitude and ultimately their sexual behavior. Generation Y individuals require specialized interventions aimed at raising awareness about the impact of HIV/Aids. Fear appeals can have an impact on their attitude towards HIV/Aids and ultimately increase the likelihood of adopting desired and appropriate behavior. The influence of fear-based advertising appeals and specifically the level of fear appeals pertaining to HIV/Aids social marketing campaigns should be measured in order to inform decision-making and social advertising execution. It is possible that the fear appeals offered in social advertising content are not sufficiently scary or threatening to adapt attitudes in line with recommendations by the advertisements. Additionally, it is also probable that young people believe they cannot implement suggested behaviour based on their circumstances and beliefs about sex. This has specific consequences for non-profit organizations in how they plan and manage social advertising campaigns, as well as for government and corporate businesses that invest in and sponsor social advertising campaigns.

A key issue of this literature and research overview concerns the overall implications for future social advertising development. Future HIV/Aids social advertising campaigns targeted at Generation Y should revisit fear impact levels, and possibly even consider a shock approach, given the reality of HIV/Aids prevalence, especially in Sub-Saharan Africa. Message executions that focus on the severity of the threat of HIV/AIDS (i.e. "HIV/Aids leads to death") and also on the targeted segments' susceptibility to the threat (i.e. "You're at risk of contracting HIV/Aids because you have unprotected sex") could have a stronger impact on behaviour change. Messages that convey how easy it is for young people to become infected with HIV, as well as demonstrating the debilitating effects of HIV/Aids possibly will also have a strong impact. This hopefully will ensure that Generation Y experience a relevant fear that will drive them to change the way they think about HIV/Aids. If this approach is followed, the campaign could ultimately influence them to modify their sexual behaviour to safe sexual behaviour and restrain the debilitating effect of this disease.

References

Arthur, D., & Quester, P. (2004). Who's afraid of that ad? Applying segmentation to the protection motivation model. *Psychology and Marketing, 21*(9), 671–696.

AVERT. (2011). *The South African national HIV survey*. Retrieved August 21, 2013 from http://www.avert.org/safricastats.html

Bagozzi, R. P., Gurhan-Canli, Z., & Priester, J. R. (2002). *The social psychology of consumer behavior*. Great Britain: St Edmundsbury Press.

Bakir, A. (2012). A cross-national analysis of advertisement content. *Journal of International Consumer Marketing, 24*(3), 185–190.

Barth, J., & Bengel, J. (2000). *Prevention through fear? The state of fear appeal research*. Retrieved 22 March 2013 from http://www.juergen-bart.de/en/wp-content/uploads/2007/03/preventionthroughthroughfear.pdf

Bastien, S. (2011). Fear appeals in HIV-prevention messages: young people's perceptions in northern Tanzania. *African Journal of AIDS Research, 10*(4), 435–449.

Beck, K. H., & Lund, A. K. (1981). The effects of health threat seriousness and personal efficacy upon intentions and behavior. *Journal of Applied Social Psychology, 11*(5), 401–415.

Belch, G. E., & Belch, M. A. (2012). *Advertising and promotion: An integrated marketing communications perspective* (9th ed.). New York: McGraw-Hill/Irwin.

Binder, J. L., & Reeves, J. (2010). Bridging the generation gap. *Marketing Health Services, 30*(2), 22.
Bohner, G., & Wänke, M. (2002). *Attitudes and attitude change*. New York: Psychology Press.
Caldwell, M., & Kleppe, I. (2010). Early adopters in the diffusion of an HIV/Aids public health innovation in a developing country. *Advances in Consumer Research, 37*, 1–22.
Dines, G., & Humez, J. M. (1995). *Gender, race and class in media: A text-reader*. London: SAGE Publications.
Egan, J. (2007). *Marketing communications*. London: Thomson Learning.
Evans, M., Jamal, A., & Foxall, G. (2006). *Consumer behavior*. Chichester: Wiley.
Fishbein, M. (2000). The role of theory in HIV prevention. *AIDS Care, 12*(3), 77–278.
Global Aids Review. (2014). Retrieved August 28, 2014 from http://www.aids.gov/federal-resources/around-the-world/global-aids-overview
Govender, S. (2009). *Where half of the new moms have HIV*. http://ww1.aegis.org/news/sun-times/2009/ST091109.html
Green, C., & Witte, K. (2006). Can fear arousal in public health campaigns contribute to the decline of HIV prevalence? *Journal of Health Communication, 11*, 245–259.
Hawkins, D. I., Mothersbaugh, D. L., & Best, R. J. (2007). *Consumer behavior: Building marketing strategy* (10th ed.). New York: McGraw-Hill/Irwin.
Heath, R. G. (2011). The secret of television's success: Emotional content or rational information? After fifty years the debate continues. *Journal of Advertising Research, 51*(1), 112–123.
Heath, G. H., Nairn, A. C., & Bottomley, P. A. (2009). How effective is creativity? Emotive content in TV advertising does not increase attention. *Journal of Advertising Research, 49*(4), 450–463.
Henthorne, T. L., LaTour, M. S., & Nataraajan, R. (1993). Fear appeals in print advertising: An analysis of arousal and ad response. *Journal of Advertising, 22*(2), 59–68.
Herbison, G., & Boseman, G. (2009). Here they come – Generation Y. Are you ready? *Journal of Financial Service Professionals, 63*(3), 33–34.
Lane, W. R., King, K. W., & Russell, J. T. (2009). *Kleppner's advertising procedure* (17th ed.). Englewood Cliffs: Pearson Prentice Hall.
LaTour, M. S., & Rotfeld, H. J. (1997). There are threats and (maybe) fear-caused arousal: Theory and confusions of appeals to fear and fear arousal itself. *Journal of Advertising, 26*(3), 45–59.
LaTour, M. S., & Tanner, J. F. (2003). Radon: Appealing to our fears. *Psychology and Marketing, 20*(5), 377–394.
LaTour, M., Zahra, S., & Shaker, A. (1988). Fear appeals as advertising strategy: Should they be used? *Journal of Services Marketing, 2*(4), 5–14.
Lee, C., & Green, R. T. (1991). Cross-cultural examination of the Fishbein behavioral intentions model. *Journal of International Business Studies, 22*(2), 289–305.
Levinson, R. A., Sadigursky, C., & Erchak, G. M. (2004). The impact of cultural context on Brazilian adolescents sexual practices. *Adolescence, 39*(154), 203–227.
Luck, E., & Mathews, S. (2010). What advertisers need to know about the iYGeneration: An Australian perspective. *Journal of Promotion Management, 16*(1/2), 134.
Moran, W. T. (1990). Brand presence and the perceptual frame. *Journal of Advertising Research, 10*, 9–16.
Noble, S. M., Haytko, D. L., & Phillips, J. (2009). What drives college-age Generation Y consumers? *Journal of Business Research, 62*, 617–628.
O'Guinn, T. C., Allen, C. T., & Semenik, R. J. (2009). *Advertising & integrated brand promotion* (5th ed.). Mason: South-Western Cengage Learning.
Peng, T. (2006). *South Africa: LoveLife faces up to funding cuts and critics*. http://allafrica.com/stories/html
Rogers, R. W. (1975). A protection motivation theory of fear appeals and attitude change. *Journal of Psychology, 91*, 93–114.
Rogers, R. W. (1983). Cognitive and physiological processes in fear appeals and attitude change: A revised theory of protection motivation. In R. Petty & J. Cacioppo (Eds.), *Social psychophysiology*. New York: Guilford.

Ruiter, R. A. C., Abraham, C., & Kok, G. (2001). Scary warnings and rational precautions: A review of the psychology of fear appeals. *Psychology and Health, 16*, 613–630.
Schiffman, L. G., & Kanuk, L. L. (2007). *Consumer behavior* (9th ed.). Upper Saddle River: Pearson Prentice Hall.
Scott, A. D., & Williams-Smith, S. A. (2007). The director's cut: Exploring cultural implications in HIV/Aids communication from the producer's perspective. *Advances in Consumer Research, 34*, 475–480.
Shimp, T. A. (2010). *Integrated marketing communication in advertising and promotion* (8th ed.). South-Western: Cengage Learning.
Shisana, O., Rehle, T., Simbayi, L., Zuma, K., Jooste, S., Zungu, N., Labadarios, D., & Onoya, D. (2014). *South African national HIV prevalence, incidence and behaviour survey, 2012*. Cape Town: HSRC Press.
Tanner, J. F., Hunt, J. B., & Eppright, D. R. (1991). The protection motivation model: A normative model of fear appeals. *Journal of Marketing, 55*(3), 36–45.
Tay, R., Ozanne, L., & Santiono, J. (2000). Advertising and road safety: A segmentation approach. In *Proceedings of ANZMAC 2000, visionary marketing for the 21st century: Facing the challenges* (1248–1251). Nathan: Griffith University School of Marketing and Management.
Terblanche-Smit, M., & Terblanche, N. S. (2013). HIV/AIDS fear appeal advertisement directed at different marketing segments: Some considerations for corporate sponsors and NPO's. *South African Journal of Business Management, 44*(4), 65–76.
Tudor, A. (2003). A (macro) sociology of fear? *The Sociological Review, 51*, 238–256.
UNAIDS. (2010). *Country progress report on the declaration of commitment on HIV/Aids, 2010*. Republic of South Africa. South Africa. Retrieved July 5, 2013 from http://data.unaids.org/pub/report/2010/southafrica_2010_country_progress_report_en.pdf
UNAIDS. (2013). *UNAIDS Report on the global AIDS epidemic 2013*. Geneva: UNAIDS. Retrieved August 12, 2014 from http://www.unaids.org/en/media/unaids/contentassets/documents/epidemiology/2013/gr2013/UNAIDS_Global_Report_2013_en.pdf
Wiles, M. A., & Danielova, A. (2009). The worth of product placement in successful films: An event study analysis. *Journal of Marketing, 73*, 44–63.
Williams, G. (2005). Using multi-generational marketing to target donors. *Nonprofit World, 23*(5), 8–13.
Williams, K. C., & Page, R. A. (2011). Marketing to the generations. *Journal of Behavioral Studies in Business, 3*, 1–17.
Witte, K. (1992). Putting fear back into fear appeals: The extended parallel process model. *Communication monographs, 59*, 329–349.
Witte, K. (1994). Fear control and danger control: A test of the extended parallel process model (EPPM). *Communication Monographs, 61*, 113–134.
Witte, K. (1998). Theory based interventions and evaluations of outreach efforts. Seattle: National Network of Libraries of Medicine.
Witte, K. (2006). *Theory-based interventions and evaluations of outreach efforts*. Department of Communication, Michigan: National Network of Libraries of Medicine.
Witte, K., & Allen, M. (2000). A meta-analysis of fear appeals: Implications for effective public health campaigns. *Health Education and Behavior, 27*(5), 591–615.
World Health Organisation. (2011). *Global Health Observatory*. Retrieved March 5, 2013 from www.who.int/gho/hiv/en.html. National Network of Libraries of Medicine.

Chapter 10
Behavioural Factors Determining Fruit Consumption in Adolescents and Characteristics of Advertising Campaigns Towards Possible Increased Consumption

Joana Rita Silvestre Godinho and Helena Alves

1 Introduction

The World Health Organization (WHO) has considered obesity as one of the ten risk factors for health, and prevention of this epidemic as a priority challenge for public health in the twenty-first century.[1] According to the data, 30–45 million children and adolescents between 5 and 17 years old are obese, corresponding to 3 % of the world's population in this age group. Garcia-Marco et al. (2011) state that the prevalence of obesity and adjacent co-morbidity, above all in the youngest age groups, has increased drastically in the last decades. For the authors, nutrition and physical activity are very important in fighting obesity, as they allow growth, healthy development and continuous improvement of emotional well-being in children and adolescents.

In recent years, various national and international initiatives have emerged to promote healthy lifestyles and identify the importance of young people's choices. However, these initiatives have had a limited impact (British Medical Association 2003), due to insufficient understanding of the factors associated with young people's choices (Story et al. 2002). Altering eating behaviour requires not only basic knowledge about nutrition, but also about factors of motivation and volitional in order to guide self-regulation processes (Lange et al. 2013).

Increasing fruit consumption is one way of contributing to reducing obesity (Rolls et al. 2004) given its low energetic density, high fibre content and increased effect of satisfaction (Tetens and Alinia 2009). Epidemiological evidence indicates that the nutrients present in fruit have a crucial role in preventing cardiovascular disease and forms of cancer (Boeing et al. 2012).

[1] www.who.int. "Health Topics, obesity".

J.R.S. Godinho (✉) • H. Alves
Department of Business and Economics, University of Beira Interior, Covilhã, Portugal
e-mail: godinho_joana@hotmail.com; halves@ubi.pt

W. Wymer (ed.), *Innovations in Social Marketing and Public Health Communication*, Applying Quality of Life Research,
DOI 10.1007/978-3-319-19869-9_10

This work intends, therefore, to contribute to studying the determinant behavioural factors that can be important in fruit consumption in adolescents and obtain answers as to how social marketing can help towards a possible increase in consumption, so contributing to diminishing these phenomena.

2 Social Marketing

According to Fertman and Allensworth (2010), social marketing promotes changes in behaviour, encouraging individuals to accept a new behaviour and reject the potential one, modify the present one or abandon a previous one. Social marketing possesses an adaptable structure in which its principles can be used in a great variety of ways in health campaigns (Corcoran 2013). According to the National Social Marketing Centre (NSMC 2011), there is increasing evidence to suggest that social marketing can improve the impact and efficiency of campaigns. Most social marketing campaigns drawn up in the field of obesity are centred on persuading the individual, leading him to adopt healthy behaviour (downstream), while recognizing that to maximize their effectiveness social marketing needs a change in the social determinants of health and safety (upstream). For Evans (2008), social marketing can give children and adolescents reasons and opportunities to get involved in healthy alternatives, in tune with their desires and needs.

For the members of WHO, messages must be consistent, coherent, simple and clear, but above all must allow communication through various means and be appropriate to the cultural and social context of the target public. To help reduce the appearance of chronic diseases, the WHO and the Food and Agriculture Organization (FAO) (WHO 2003) suggested implementation of target-campaigns, aimed at increasing fruit and vegetable intake, and stated that effective health communications are able to develop individuals' awareness, increase knowledge levels and induce long-term changes.

The use of social marketing in promoting healthy eating habits has been studied in countries such as the United States of America, Canada, Australia and New Zealand, the United Kingdom, Italy, Belgium, the Netherlands, Norway, Switzerland, France and Germany (Kapetanaki et al. 2014). The choice of food is a complex behaviour that can be influenced by various factors and situations, such as culture, politics, psychological and biological factors, environmental costs and social elements (Stead et al. 2007). According to Shive and Morris (2006), social marketing has been applied to a variety of behaviours in the field of health, and has shown itself to be effective in improving nutrition, especially in situations marked by nutritional deficiency. According to Wymer (2011), a typical approach of social marketing is the development of a short advertising campaign whose primary objective is to encourage people to eat more healthily or take more physical exercise.

Nevertheless, obesity rates continue to rise, proving that social marketing campaigns have been ineffective. For Wymer (2011), among the possible options for improving social marketing strategies we find consumers' sensitivity to the negative influence of food industry marketing, the development of a social consumer movement against the type of marketing used by food production companies, so as to warn governments of the need to regulate the food industry.

Evans et al. (2010) and Foltz et al. (2012) mention that social marketing should act on different fronts, and within the family, this type of marketing can encourage parents to adopt protective behaviour as they are seen as models for their children. Therefore, if parents participate in physical activity and follow a healthy diet, their children will do likewise at home, at school and in the community. For the same authors, mobilizing the community has been an important component of social marketing, acting in promoting physical activity and improved eating habits among parents and children. At school, the same authors say that social marketing can act through changing eating behaviour and physical activity, as well as in relation to school tuck-shops and food vending machines. According to Baranowski et al. (2003), research into behavioural and biological influences on obesity behaviour seems promising.

3 Theories of Health Behaviour

Young people's nutritional behaviour is influenced by multiple environmental, personal and social factors (Story et al. 2002). Behavioural theories are useful in explaining these various influences (Sumonja and Novakovic 2013). According to Godinho et al. (2013a), the effectiveness of health communication also depends on how it is theoretically stimulated. The authors add that the determinants of health behaviour, established by socio-cognitive models, are essential targets in developing messages to promote healthy behaviour, such as fruit consumption. The most prominent theories and models in changing health behaviour are: *Theory of Planned Behavior* (TPB), *Social Cognitive Theory* (SCT), *Transtheoretical Model* (TTM), *Health Belief Model* (HBM) and *Health Action Process Approach* (HAPA), which include a variety of cognitions, influencing health behaviours directly or indirectly (Schwarzer and Luszczynska 2006).

Changing health behaviour refers to processes of motivation and action, allowing the abandonment of behaviour harmful to health in favour of adopting and maintaining behaviour which improves this (Schwarzer and Luszczynska 2008). For the authors, this process includes a variety of social, emotional and cognitive factors. So it is essential to identify the best set of factors that allow the forecast or suitable explanation of the change in health behaviour.

The HAPA model was developed to overcome some of the limitations of other models (Schwarzer 2008a). According to Luszczynska and Schwarger (2003), the HAPA model describes the mechanisms in action when individuals become motivated to alter their habits, when they adopt them and how they maintain those new habits when they try to resist temptation, and if they manage to get over setbacks. The HAPA model is divided in two phases in the behaviour-changing process: a motivational phase that includes the formation of behaviour intentions, and a phase of volitional that begins once the intention has been defined, including the translation of that intention into behaviour (Scholz et al. 2009). At the initial stage of motivation, the individual develops an intention towards action, considering that within this first stage, the risk perception is seen as the first step towards altering health behaviour (Renner and Schwarzer 2005). In the same way, according to Schwarzer (2008a), the expectations of positive results are recognized as important factors in the motivation phase, when someone ponders the pros and cons of certain behavioural results. For Schwarzer (2008a), action self-efficacy is the first phase of the process, when an individual has not yet acted but has already formed the motivation to do so. When the individual has formed an inclination to adopt a particular health behaviour, this good intention has to be transformed in detailed instructions, about how to carry out the desired action (Schwarzer and Luszczynska 2008). Once the action has been initiated, it must be maintained. This is not managed through a single act of will, but involves skills and strategies of self-regulation. According to Luszczynska and Schwarzer (2003), maintenance self-efficacy represents optimistic beliefs about an individual's capacity, so as to cope with barriers that can arise during the period of maintenance. According to Gollwitzer (1999), planning of actions (or implementation of intentions), translates intentions into particular actions, which according to Luszczynska et al. (2007), specifies the when, where and how of a desired action, i.e., planning serves as a bridge between intentions and behaviour (Schwarzer et al. 2007). Increased action planning should lead to a greater rate of adoption of a behaviour, since it is a facilitator of the transition between intention and action (Reuter et al. 2010). The HAPA model is a hybrid model that has been defined as a good predictor of a wide range of healthy behaviours (Schwarzer et al. 2007), including fruit consumption, and can be conceptualized as a staged model, principally for intervention purposes (Schwarzer 2008b). This model has already been used in some studies to analyze fruit and vegetable consumption, but it is mostly used in studies with adults, and it is a challenge to apply it to adolescents. In addition, the results of the model sequence are not always consistent.

Therefore, for example, concerning the influence of the perceived risk, Renner and Schwarzer (2005) state that this forms the first step towards the change in behaviour. However, Schwarzer et al. (2007) found that the risk perception appears as a not particularly important factor in the prevention of health behaviours and is considered negligible in the case of fruit consumption. Therefore, and in this study of fruit consumption behaviour in adolescents, the following hypothesis can be formulated:

Hypothesis 1 (H_1): The risk perception does not have a significant influence on fruit consumption in adolescents.

Following the same line of reasoning, if the risk perception does not contribute much to the intention towards a behaviour (Schwarzer and Renner 2000), Renner et al. (2007) concluding there is no significant relationship between risk perception and intention, the following hypothesis can be formulated:

Hypothesis 2 (H_2): The risk perception does not have a significant influence on adolescents' intention to consume fruit.

Regarding the expectations of a positive result, Renner et al. (2008) state these contribute substantially to forming an intention. The study by Godinho et al. (2013b) concluded that the expectations of a positive result are significantly and positively associated with the intention to consume fruit. From this information, the following hypothesis is formulated:

Hypothesis 3 (H_3): Expectation of the result has a positive influence on adolescents' intention to consume fruit.

According to Luszczynska and Schwarzer (2003), individuals with high action self-efficacy imagine success, anticipate potential results of various strategies and are more likely to begin a new behaviour. According to studies by Anderson-Bill et al. (2000) and (Luszczynska et al. 2004), action self-efficacy is associated with healthy eating patterns, and particularly with fruit (Brug et al. 1995; De Bourdeaudhuij and Van Oost 2000; Young et al. 2004; Bere and Klepp 2004, 2005; Luszczynska et al. 2007). In the study made by Anderson-Bill et al. (Anderson-Bill et al. 2007), participants with greater confidence in their ability to make healthy choices presented lower fat consumption and higher values of fruit, fibre and vegetable consumption. Opposing this, Resnicow et al. (1997) and Neumark-Sztainer et al. (2003) said there was no such relationship. Based on this information, the following hypothesis is formulated:

Hypothesis 4 (H_4): Action self-efficacy has a positive influence on adolescents' fruit consumption.

The perception of self-efficacy together with expectations of a positive result contribute considerably to forming an intention (Renner et al. 2008). In a study by Renner and Schwarzer (2005), action self-efficacy emerges as a significant predictor of intentions. Also in the study by Godinho et al. (2013b), perception of self-efficacy is associated significantly and positively with the intention to consume fruit in adults. The aim is therefore to check the following hypothesis:

Hypothesis 5 (H_5): Action self-efficacy has a positive influence on adolescents' intention to consume fruit.

Action self-efficacy has a strong influence on behaviour, through maintenance self-efficacy (Schwarzer and Renner 2000). From this information, the following hypothesis is formed:

Hypothesis 6 (H_6): Action self-efficacy has a positive influence on maintenance self-efficacy in adolescents' fruit consumption.

According to (Sheeran et al. 2005), the effects of planning intervention can be moderated by individuals' intention. Based on this information, the following hypothesis is formulated:

Hypothesis 7 (H_7): Intention has a positive influence on action planning in adolescents' fruit consumption.

In the study by Schwarzer and Renner (2000), intention has an influence on behaviour to follow a diet rich in vitamins and low in fat. For De Bourdeaudhuij and Van Oost (2000); (Lien et al. 2002) and Godinho et al. (2013b), there is an association between intention and fruit consumption. According to a study pertaining to participation in physical exercise by Renner et al. (2007), this was found not to be associated with intention. Then again, Bere and Klepp (2004, 2005) claimed there was no association between intention and fruit consumption. From this information, the following hypothesis is formulated:

Hypothesis 8 (H_8): Intention has a positive influence on adolescents' fruit consumption.

In the study by Renner and Schwarzer (2005), maintenance self-efficacy contributes to forecasting consumption of a diet low in fat and rich in vitamins. So the intention is to check the following hypothesis:

Hypothesis 9 (H_9): Maintenance self-efficacy has a positive influence on adolescents' fruit consumption.

Action planning is a pre-requisite to beginning new behaviour (Lange et al. 2013). Increased action planning should lead to a higher rate of behaviour adoption (Reuter et al. 2010). Random clinical trials have proved that planning interventions help in the adoption and maintenance of healthy behaviour (Luszczynska et al. 2007). According to Guillaumie et al. (2012), action planning promotes increased fruit consumption significantly. In the studies by Norman and Conner (2005, Study 1) and Schwarzer et al. (2007, Study 4), it was not possible to prove the mediating effect of planning between intention and behaviour, as opposed to the one by Norman and Conner (2005, Study 2) which confirmed that effect. Therefore, the following hypothesis is formulated:

Hypothesis 10 (H_{10}): Action planning has a positive influence on adolescents' fruit consumption.

For (Ford et al. 2000), Steptoe et al.(2004), Schwarzer and Knoll (2007), Anderson-Bill et al. (2007, 2011), and Poddar et al. (2012) family and friends' support for healthy eating habits is associated with better eating behaviour, as by receiving more support, individuals are more likely to increase belief in self-efficacy. Pérez-Rodrigo and Aranceta (2003) add that in adolescence there is more autonomy in eating choices, and at this age, friends have a great influence in the development of eating habits and lifestyles.

According to De Bourdeaudhuij and Van Oost (2000), Neumark-Sztainer et al. (2003), and Young et al. (2004), there is an association between parental support for healthy eating habits and fruit consumption. Fruit consumption among their friends also has an influence on adolescents' greater consumption (Woodward et al. 1996; De Bourdeaudhuij and Van Oost 2000).

The HAPA model does not include the variable of social support, but given the evidence of some studies about the relationship between this variable and adolescents' fruit consumption, it is added to try to explain their fruit consumption. Therefore, the following hypothesis is formulated:

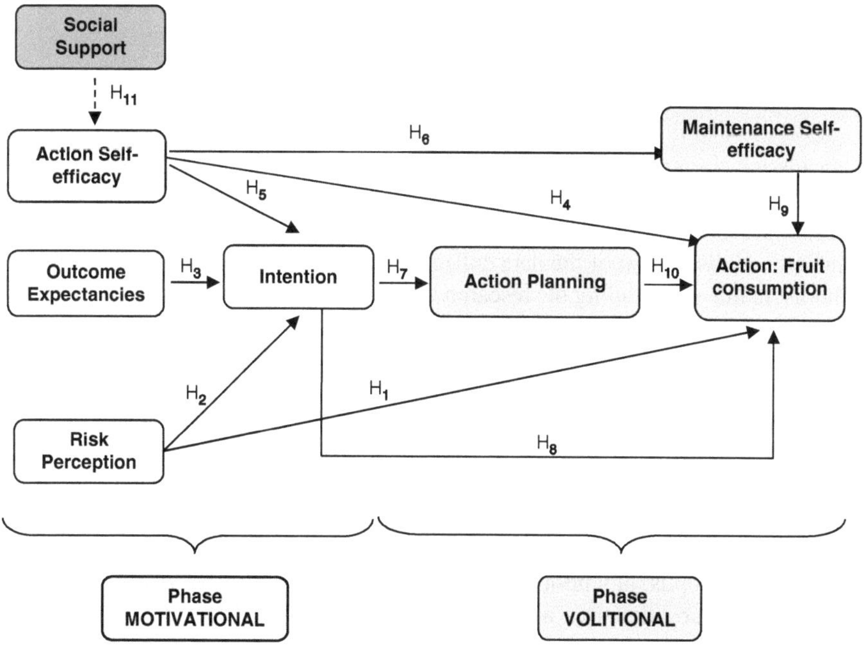

Fig. 10.1 Model of research analysis

Hypothesis 11 (H_{11}): Social support has a positive influence on action self-efficacy towards adolescents' fruit consumption.

Figure 10.1 shows the proposed relationships and respective research hypotheses. The model includes three predictors of the intention to consume fruit, in the motivational or pre-intentional phase (action self-efficacy, outcome expectancies and risk perception), and three predictors referring to behaviour towards fruit consumption in the volitional or post-intentional phase (intention, maintenance self-efficacy and action planning). Added to the original model proposed by the HAPA theory was social support as a variable influencing action self-efficacy. With this model, the aim was to find out which constructs are determinant for improved behaviour in adolescents' fruit consumption.

The objectives of this study, as mentioned before, also concern relating this model to advertising campaigns about food. According to a study made by Proctor et al. (2003), children who are more exposed to advertising seem to be less likely to consume fruit daily, but high exposure to healthy food can increase consumption of this type of food (Klepp et al. 2007). So the intention is also to analyze the following hypothesis:

Hypothesis 12 (H_{12}): The model manages to give a better explanation of the response behaviour of adolescents to advertising campaigns encouraging fruit consumption.

4 Methodology

4.1 Research Design and Sample

Considering the nature of the subject studied and the non-existence of sufficient relevant information, a qualitative analysis based on three focus groups was chosen in this transversal study. At a second stage, a quantitative approach was selected in analysis and discussion of the data collected through questionnaires applied in two schools, in this way guiding the research to a result that could be generalized. Given the nature of the study in question, it became necessary to record the data-collecting instruments through the Platform for Monitoring Surveys in Schools (MIME),[2] requesting authorization from the schools and the adolescents' parents.

The population studied is formed of young people of both sexes aged between 15 and 21. The sample of convenience covers pupils at two Portuguese schools, designated here as A and B, with school A (n= 191) being urban and B (n= 75) more rural, making it possible to carry out research into the perceptions and opinions of the school population in both settings in relation to the proposed topic. The final sample is 266 pupils, of whom 42.1 % are boys and 57.9 % girls, who at the time of applying the questionnaires attended the 10th (47.7 %), 11th (31.2 %) or 12th (21.1 %) years at school.

4.2 Instruments and Data-Collection Procedures

The focus groups were dealt with on two different days. The first focus group was on 12 November 2013 and concerned a female team in the Basketball Club belonging to the same district as the schools surveyed and was made up of 11 adolescents. The second and third focus groups were at a third secondary school (C), one group of adolescents following professional education and another in regular education, both formed of nine adolescents, on 13 December 2013. After gathering data from the focus groups, these were transcribed and content analysis was subsequently carried out.

To confirm the questions dealt with in the focus groups and to test the proposed model, a questionnaire survey was drawn up. Each question in the survey was based on scales already validated in other studies, in order to test the proposed model and analyze the variables included therein. Table 10.1 presents each author used, as well as the degree of reliability of each scale.

After drawing up the questionnaire survey, it was pre-tested on 10 adolescents with the same characteristics as the population studied.

---

[2] The questionnaire surveys and focus groups were recorded on the MIME platform (http://mime.gepe.min-edu.pt/) under the number 0399300001.

Table 10.1 Validated scales used in the questionnaire survey applied to adolescents in schools (**A**) and (**B**)

Variable	Example of item[a]	Item[b]	Response scale	Alpha
Risk perception: vulnerability (Perloff and Fetzer 1986) Seriousness (Rosenstock 1974)	What is the probability of you developing an illness related to obesity? In your opinion, how serious is obesity?	2	Extremely improbable (1) to extremely probable (7) ------------------------ Not at all serious (1) to very serious (7)	.79 --------- n.a.[c]
Consumption (Luszczynska et al. 2007)	In the last two weeks, how often did you eat a piece of fruit?	1 ------ 2[d]	Never. Once a week, a few times a week, once a day. Twice a day. Three times a day and more than three times a day.	n.a.
Outcome expectancies (Godinho et al. 2013a)	In your opinion, what are or would be the benefits/ consequences of eating fruit daily?	16	Completely disagree (1) to completely agree (7)	.76
Action planning (Schwarzer et al. 2007)	Some people would like to improve their eating habits consuming fruit daily, while others would not. And you?	3	Completely disagree (1) to completely agree (7)	.79
Coping planning – barriers (Godinho et al. 2013a)	How much does each of the following aspects make it difficult or would make it difficult to consume fruit daily?	11	It does not make it difficult at all (1) it makes it a lot more difficult (7)	.86
Coping planning – Strategies (Godinho et al. 2013a)	In your opinion, what strategies do you consider most effective to improve fruit consumption?	10	Not at all important (1) to very important (7)	.86
Social support (Sallis et al. 1987)	Regarding your family and friends, in the last three months, how have they influenced your habit of eating fruit daily?	9	Completely disagree (1) to completely agree (7)	Friends (.80 to .87) Family (.83 to .87)
Action self-efficacy (Godinho et al. 2013b)	Some people feel it is difficult to eat fruit every day, while others think it is easier. And you?	4	Completely disagree (1) to completely agree (7)	.87
Self-efficacy of maintenance (Luszczynska and Schwarzer 2003)	After beginning to eat fruit every day it is important to keep this habit over time. Do you feel able to keep up this habit?	4	Completely disagree (1) to completely agree (7)	.77

(continued)

Table 10.1 (continued)

Variable	Example of item[a]	Item[b]	Response scale	Alpha
Intention (Godinho et al. 2013b)	Next week, what is your intention to eat fruit every day?	3	Completely disagree (1) to completely agree (7)	.95
Advertising campaigns				

Note: All the items in this section were drawn up by us supported by the data obtained through the focus groups

[a]All the items were translated from English to Portuguese and adapted to the population and the matter studied

[b]The number of items used was adapted to the population and the matter studied

[c]n.a. – not available

[d]Two questions referring to consumption on the survey questionnaire were elaborated by us, supported by the data obtained through the focus groups

4.3 Data Treatment

The questionnaire surveys were analyzed using *IBM SPSS Statistics®– Statistical Package for the Social Sciences*, version 21.0.0 and *SmartPLS®* version 2.0 M3 software. The questions with a negative sense placed in the questionnaire, were inverted in the database, in order to be treated in the same way statistically, also making for easier interpretation. Regarding the focus groups and the open response questions, these were treated through content analysis using the *QSR NVIVO®* version 8.0 software.

5 Presentation and Discussion of the Results

5.1 Analysis of the Proposed Model

Analysis of the proposed model was through a two-stage process involving separate assessment of the measuring and structural models (Hair et al. 2011). First, the reliability and validity of the measurement model was analyzed and the structural model was assessed at a second stage.

Initially, in order to assess the measuring models, it was necessary to check which constructs were measured through the formative and reflective indicators. This distinction is necessary, because these two types of indicators will have different treatment in future analyses. According to Brei and Neto (2006), in a model presenting formative characteristics, variations in the indicators are expected to cause or originate alterations in the construct with which they are linked. These authors say that in the case of a model with reflective characteristics, the direction of the causality goes from the construct to its indicators, i.e., in this model, changes in the construct cause changes in the indicators.

Regarding the reflective indicators, according to (Hair et al. 2011), the suitability of the measurement model is assessed through: (i) individual reliability of the indicators, (ii) internal consistency and (iii) validity. Concerning the individual reliability of the indicators, this can be analyzed by examining the loadings for each reflective indicator. Hair et al. (2011) indicate that for the indicators to be accepted, they can present loadings of 0.6–0.7. Table 10.2 shows there are 11 indicators presenting loadings below the desired values, and so they were eliminated.

As for internal consistency and composite reliability, these can be examined using the *Cronbach* alpha coefficient (**α**) and composite reliability (***ρc***) and according to Hair et al. (2011), the values of both should be above 0.70. Table 10.2 shows the *Cronbach* **α** and ***ρc*** values for each construct with reflective indicators, after taking out the indicators with loadings under 0.6, all indicators presenting acceptable values. Concerning assessment of discriminant validity, the aim was to evaluate the degree of differentiation of the various constructs of the proposed model through

Table 10.2 Result of analysis of the measurement model – reflective constructs

Variable	Indicator	Type of indicator	*Loadings* (λ)	α	ρ_c	AVE
Risk perception	Question E1	R	0.714068			
	Question E2	R	*0.102066*			
	Question F	R	*−0.659681*			
Intention	Question P1	R	0.912254	0.875881	0.924355	0.803432
	Question P2	R	0.948750			
	Question P3	R	0.823384			
Maintenance self-efficacy	Question O1	R	0.891025	0.910830	0.937074	0.788454
	Question O2	R	0.903202			
	Question O3	R	0.917156			
	Question O4	R	0.838419			
Social support	Question M1a	R	*0.120902*	0.871854	0.895559	0.518748
	Question M1b	R	*−0.066986*			
	Question M2a	R	0.761041			
	Question M2b	R	0.651297			
	Question M3a	R	0.768380			
	Question M3b	R	0.660181			
	Question M4a	R	0.752711			
	Question M4b	R	0.684457			
	Question M5a	R	0.735057			
	Question M5b	R	0.629158			
	Question M6a	R	*0.092096*			
	Question M6b	R	*−0.060110*			
	Question M7a	R	*0.063168*			
	Question M7b	R	*−0.115904*			
	Question M8a	R	*0.182558*			
	Question M9a	R	*0.072869*			
	Question M9b	R	*0.102134*			

a measure of variance between one construct and its indicators. Hair et al. (2011) suggest that Average Variance Extracted (AVE) should have a value over 0.50 and Table 10.2 reveals that all the constructs present acceptable values.

According to Hair et al. (2011), analysis of formative indicators involves three processes: (i) observation of the indicator weights, so as to assess the relative contribution of each indicator; (ii) analysis of possible multi-collinearity; and (iii) statistical significance of the weights using the bootstrapping technique. For analysis of multi-collinearity, the tolerance value was determined for each formative indicator, as well as the Variance Inflation Factor (VIF), measures that for Hair et al. (2011) indicate the degree to which each independent variable is explained by other independent variables. To analyze multi-collinearity, Hair et al. (2011) recommend elimination of problematic indicators with values equal to or above 5, and it can be seen that all the indicators present values under 5, i.e., there are no problems of multi-collinearity between the formative indicators used in the model. According to Hair et al. (2011), if all weights are significant, the indicators should be kept. Analysis of the weights of each indicator lets us understand the composition of each variable and find out the information about how each indicator contributes to the respective construct. As can be observed in Table 10.3, only some indicators are statistically significant for a confidence level of 99 % and 95 %, so these results suggest the indicators that do not meet that requirement should be eliminated.

After analyzing the measurement model, it is necessary to assess the structural model in which the various dependent relationships between constructs are specified. According to Hair et al. (2011), to evaluate a structural model two criteria should be analyzed: (i) assessment of the model's explanatory capacity (R_2) and (ii) the value and statistical significance of the structural coefficients. According to the same authors, in marketing research studies, an R_2 with a value of 0.75, 0.5 or 0.25 for latent endogenous variables in the structural model can be described as substantial, moderate or weak, respectively. This being so, the greater the R_2 value associated with each dependent construct, the better the model proposed. The results obtained demonstrate that the R_2 value is weak for action self-efficacy (0.170868), i.e., 17 % of the variance of this construct is explained by social support. Concerning intention, the R_2 value is moderate (0.553172), with 55 % of its variance being explained by action self-efficacy, risk perception and outcome expectancies. Action planning (0.230526) has a weak level of explanation with 23 % of its significance being explained by intention. The R_2 value is weak for maintenance self-efficacy(0.298741), i.e., 30 % of the variance of this construct is explained by action self-efficacy. Fruit consumption with 47 % of its significance, i.e., a weak, almost moderate, level (0.465762) being explained by action self-efficacy, risk perception, intention, maintenance self-efficacy and action planning.

After evaluation of the model's explanatory capacity, it is necessary to assess the values of the various structural coefficients, i.e., direct effects. Besides these analyses, the statistical significance of the various relationships should also be observed, through the t statistic. It also becomes necessary to explain to what extent the predictive variables contribute to the explained variance of the endogenous variables. The variance of an endogenous construct explained by another latent variable is

Table 10.3 Result of analysis of the measurement model – formative constructs

Variable	Indicator	Type of indicator	Weights (γ)	t statistic
Action self-efficacy	Question N1	F	0.596589	8.502964***
	Question N2	F	−0.018085	_0.185933_
	Question N3	F	0.384648	5.370155***
	Question N4	F	0.175127	_1.929692*_
Outcome expectancies	Question I1	F	−0.038174	_0.233249_
	Question I2	F	0.107771	_0.657506_
	Question I3	F	−0.072010	_0.525004_
	Question I4	F	0.351409	2.164431**
	Question I5	F	0.073918	_0.504768_
	Question I6	F	0.120258	_0.781301_
	Question I7	F	0.076546	_0.491464_
	Question I8	F	0.078715	_0.499348_
	Question I9	F	0.201918	_1.542274_
	Question I10	F	0.122532	_0.938286_
	Question I11	F	0.098247	_0.72947_
	Question I12	F	−0.203296	_1.800642*_
	Question I13	F	−0.005742	_0.051820_
	Question I14	F	0.123700	_1.156971_
	Question I15	F	0.255726	_1.770657*_
	Question I16	F	0.352190	2.309798**
Action planning	Question J1	F	0.683237	3.487514***
	Question J2	F	0.085100	_0.467491_
	Question J3	F	0.312886	_1.437122_

*significance level of 10 % (critical value of the t statistic above 1.65)
**significance level of 5 %it (critical value of the t statistic above 1.96)
***significance level of 1 % (critical value of the t statistic above 2.58)

obtained by the absolute value of the result of multiplying the coefficient (β) by its corresponding coefficient of relationship between both variables. Finally, once the model's explanatory power is assessed, it is necessary to clarify to what extent the predictive variables contribute to the explained variance in the endogenous variables, which is represented by the coefficient β. This represents the path coefficients through the bootstrapping procedure of SmartPLS®, with the values corresponding to direct effects (Table 10.4). Next, the statistical significance of the various structural coefficients (direct effects) was tested, to analyze the significance of the relationships between the constructs representing the research hypotheses. Through the bootstrapping technique in SmartPLS® the t statistics referring to each relationship or path were obtained (Table 10.4). To apply the technique, we selected as the number of cases, the value equal to the number of observations in the original sample (266) and in the number of samples, the figure of 1000 was chosen. According to Hair et al. (2011), for a significance level of 10 %(*), the critical value of the t

Table 10.4 Results of the structural model

Hypotheses	Path coefficient (β)	t statistic	Hypothesis supported
H_1: risk perception→ Fruit consumption	0.068718$^{n.s.}$	1.457196	Yes
H_2: risk perception→ Intention	0.007358$^{n.s.}$	0.157543	Yes
H_3: outcome expectancies→ Intention	0.172586***	2.938195	Yes
H_4: action self-efficacy→ Fruit consumption	0.198546**	2.550701	Yes
H_5: action self-efficacy→ Intention	0.649997***	13.340207	Yes
H_6: action self-efficacy→ Maintenance self-efficacy	0.546572***	10.442913	Yes
H_7: intention→ Action planning	0.480131***	8.889700	Yes
H_8: intention → Fruit consumption	0.550670***	8.076596	Yes
H_9: maintenance self-efficacy→ Fruit consumption	−0.111347**	2.296202	No
H_{10}: action planning→ Fruit consumption	0.082547$^{n.s.}$	1.333575	No
H_{11}: social support→ Action self-efficacy	0.413362***	8.039108	Yes

n.s. = not significant
*significance level of 10 % (critical value of the t statistic above 1.65)
**significance level of 5 %it (critical value of the t statistic above 1.96)
***significance level of 1 % (critical value of the t statistic above 2.58)

statistic should be above 1.65, in the case of a significance level of 5 %(**), it should be 1.96 and for a level of 1 %(***), the value should be 2.58. According to Table 10.4, hypotheses H_9 and H_{10}, are not supported by the results of this study.

Figure 10.2 illustrates graphically a summarized assessment of the proposed model, concerning both the measuring and the structural models.

Concerning the variables explored, the proposed model is seen to be able to explain 46.6 % of the explained variance of the variables in question, and this value suggests there are other determinant factors of adolescents' fruit consumption which need to be studied.

From the empirical results obtained, action self-efficacy is shown to influence fruit consumption (H_4). The relationship between these two constructs has a β value of 0.199, i.e., a robust relationship, since it is close to 0.2, as referred to by Chin (1998), and is also significant in the bootstrapping test with a significance level of 0.05. These results are consistent with those found by Brug et al. (1995), De Bourdeaudhuij and Van Oost (2000), Young et al. (2004), Bere and Klepp (2004, 2005), Luszczynska et al. (2007), and Anderson-Bill et al. (2007).

As for the analysis of the influence of action self-efficacy on intention (H_5), this finds empirical support in this study, agreeing with the results obtained in other

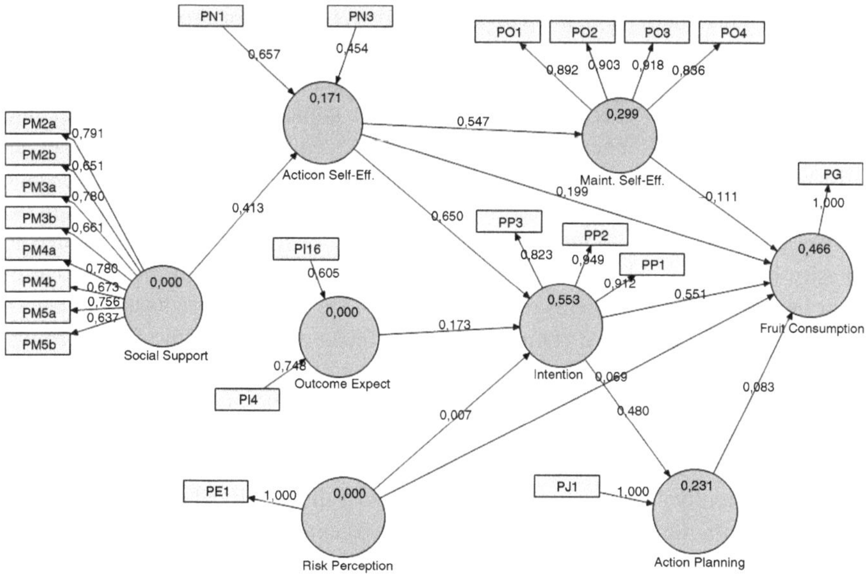

Fig. 10.2 Summarized assessment of the proposed model

research (Renner et al. 2008; Renner and Schwarzer 2005; Godinho et al. 2013b). The relationship has a β value of 0.649, i.e., a robust relationship, since it is above 0.2, and is also significant in the bootstrapping test with a significance level of 0.01. The effect of the explained variance of action self-efficacy on intention shows the highest value, and therefore has a very significant role in adolescents' intention to consume fruit. This value of action self-efficacy is also influenced by the indirect effect of social support.

Regarding the influence of action self-efficacy on maintenance self-efficacy (H_6), the empirical data are able to support the hypothesis which is in line with what is stated in the literature, especially by Schwarzer and Renner (2000). The relationship has a β value of 0.547, i.e., a robust relationship, since it is above 0.2, and is also significant in the bootstrapping test with a significance level of 0.01. The effect of the explained variance of action self-efficacy on maintenance self-efficacy shows a weak, but significant, value (29.9 %), with action self-efficacy also being influenced by the indirect effect of social support. Concerning action self-efficacy for daily fruit consumption, the young people surveyed stated they managed to consume fruit every day ($\bar{x}=5.66$), even if: they have to establish an eating plan so as not to forget to consume it ($\bar{x}=4.94$), have to get over the habit of non-consumption ($\bar{x}=4.92$), are tired and do not feel like eating this type of food ($\bar{x}=4.76$).

The possible influence of risk perception on fruit consumption (H_1) is not recognized, and so the hypothesis is confirmed and has empirical support in the research results, in agreement with the previous study by Schwarzer et al. (2007). These authors do not value this construct as an important factor in prevention of health behaviour. This relationship has a β value of 0.069, i.e., it is not a robust relationship, since it is not close to 0.2, and nor is it significant in the bootstrapping test with an explained variance effect of -0.9 %. In addition, the influence of risk perception on intention (H_2) is not recognized, agreeing with authors such as Schwarzer and Renner (2000) and Renner et al. (2007). Risk perception was found not to be an effective predictor of intention, since it presents a variance of –0.2 %, with a β value of 0.007, being neither a robust nor significant relationship. In risk perception, in the survey the adolescents' opinion on the probability of having an illness related to obesity is very low ($\overline{x} = 2.52$). When asked about the probability of someone of their own age having problems related to obesity, the answer presents an average of $\overline{x} = 4.50$. These results are complemented by those obtained in the focus groups, where 11 of the 29 adolescents asked stated there was a very high probability. As for perception of the seriousness of the illness, the adolescence said it was a very serious illness, with a response average of $\overline{x} = 6.12$.

Concerning the influence of outcome expectancies on intention (H_3), this presents a statistically significant value in the light of the empirical data of this study and agrees with the results of Renner et al. (2008) and Godinho et al. (2013b). This relationship has a β value of 0.172, being close to 0.2, and also significant in the bootstrapping test with a significance level of 0.01. In the survey, when asked about outcome expectancies in relation to fruit consumption, 16 questions were asked aiming to obtain adolescents' opinion on the positive or negative expectations they had regarding daily fruit consumption. As for positive expectations, most pupils mentioned that fruit would improve their health ($\overline{x} = 5.95$), that it would prevent cardiovascular diseases ($\overline{x} = 5.56$) and that they would eat a smaller amount of other unhealthy food ($\overline{x} = 4.85$). Regarding negative expectations, the adolescents agreed that most people would not make fun of them due to eating that food ($\overline{x} = 6.38$), it would not be a sacrifice to eat fruit every day ($\overline{x} = 5.97$), eating habits would become healthier because of these changes ($\overline{x} = 5.00$) and that fruit would make them feel full after meals ($\overline{x} = 4.45$). Similarly, in the focus groups, the adolescents highlighted that the benefits inherent to fruit consumption would be: a healthier choice, in that it prevents illnesses, contains vitamins, contributes to longevity, promotes a feeling of being full, avoids consumption of other types of food harmful to health and the fact of it being a more accessible choice. On the other hand, other young people stated that fruit does not make them feel full, in excess it is harmful and that it is necessary to be careful with the pesticides fruit may contain. The result obtained for this question agrees with those previously found by Krolner et al. (2011).

As for the influence of social support on action self-efficacy (H_{11}), this is shown to be statistically significant in this research, the results being consistent with those obtained by Ford et al. (2000), Pérez-Rodrigo and Aranceta (2003), Steptoe et al. (2004), Anderson-Bill et al. (2007, 2011), and Schwarzer and Knoll (2007) who argue that social support is important for adolescents to create and maintain healthy eating habits. The relationship between these two constructs presents a β value of 0.413, which is a robust relationship and one that is also significant in the bootstrapping test with a significance level of 0.01. This relationship had already been found by De Bourdeaudhuij and Van Oost (2000), Neumark-Sztainer et al. (2003), and Young et al. (2004), who concluded on a correlation between parental support and fruit consumption. The effect of the explained variance of social support on action self-efficacy gives a value of 17.1 %. Despite this being an age-group subject to major transformations in terms of personality, the opinion of friends and family has some impact on young people. Questions related to the family have a higher weighting than those related to friends, i.e., adolescents put the family's opinions first. In the theoretical model of the original HAPA, social support is not considered as a construct, but it is considered interesting to include it so as to determine whether family and friends have an influence on adolescents' fruit consumption. In the survey, in most questions, the adolescents stated that friends do not influence them either positively or negatively concerning daily fruit consumption. But family members encourage them positively, reminding them to eat fruit every day ($\bar{x}=5.05$) and comment when they are not doing so ($\bar{x}=4.55$), by speaking to them about improving their eating habits ($\bar{x}=4.55$), and congratulating them on improving them ($\bar{x}=4.38$). Regarding the focus groups, the interviewees stated that the opinion of others has some importance, with that of their parents being most important, principally in relation to healthy habits, pointing out that their parents' opinion is positive while that of their friends is not always. When asked about the type of influence received from school, participants in the focus groups mentioned as positive influences, the fact there was cut fruit in the tuck shop, that fizzy drinks and chocolate had been withdrawn and that the canteen provided healthy meals. As negative influences, they mentioned the lack of more initiatives to improve healthy habits, the existence of vending machines selling less healthy food and such items being sold directly.

The influence of intention on action planning (H_7) is statistically significant, this result being consistent with the study by Sheeran et al. (2005). This relationship has a β value of 0.480, and as such is considered robust, and also significant in the bootstrapping test with a significance level of 0.01. The results demonstrate that the effect of the explained variance of intention on action planning is 23.1 %, which is a weak value, i.e., many more factors can influence this construct. Therefore, action planning is indirectly influenced by social support, action self-efficacy, outcome expectancies and risk perception.

In the light of the empirical results obtained, the influence of intention on fruit consumption (H_8) is confirmed, these results being consistent with those obtained by Schwarzer and Renner (2000) referring to consumption of healthy food, and those obtained by De Bourdeaudhuij and Van Oost (2000), Lien et al. (2002), and Godinho et al. (2013b) in relation to fruit consumption. This relationship has a β value of 0.550, i.e., a robust relationship, and it is also significant in the bootstrapping test with a significance level of 0.01. These results show that intention is the construct with greatest influence on adolescents' fruit consumption. Concerning adolescents' intention to consume fruit every day, those in the survey admitted that on the day the survey was applied they would eat fruit ($\bar{x}=5.27$), and that they would eat fruit from that day onwards ($\bar{x}=5.20$). However, to the last question, most of them indicated value 2 on the scale, with an average of $\bar{x}=3.88$, mentioning that they intended to consume a minimum of three portions of fruit per day. Following the reasoning of Schwarzer (2008a), the individual intention to change a given habit is the best path towards behaviour change, which proves, in terms of the results obtained, that adolescents have an individual intention to consume fruit every day, presenting a lower intention in relation to the quantity (three items) of fruit daily.

The relationship between maintenance self-efficacy and consumption (H_9), was not supported, unlike what was found in the study by Renner and Schwarzer (2005). The relationship between the two constructs has a β value of (−0.111), i.e., not a robust relationship, since it is not close to 0.2, but it is significant in the bootstrapping test with a t level above 1.96. It was not possible to prove this relationship, having an effect of explained variance of −3.2 %. Probably, this effect is due to the fact that despite the existence of some tools regarding motivations, which are essential for keeping the fruit-consumption habit, when passing from the motivational to the practical part there may be other factors that influence that maintenance, interfering negatively in the consumption construct. The greatest percentage of the young people surveyed agreed they felt able to maintain the habit even if they were worried about other aspects of their life ($\bar{x}$ =4.74), and needed more time to develop daily routines towards fruit consumption ($\bar{x}$ =4.71), even if family/friends did not alter their eating habits ($\bar{x}$ =4.58) and even if they had to restart several times until they could keep the habit ($\bar{x}$ =4.47). As for the focus groups, 27 of the 29 adolescents stated they consider it easy to keep the habit, after having started to consume fruit every day.

The influence of action planning on fruit consumption (H_{10}), despite finding support in the studies by Luszczynska et al. (2007), Reuter et al. (2010), and Lange et al. (2013), regarding its influence on health behaviours and Guillaumie et al. (2012) relating to the influence on fruit consumption, does not find empirical support in this research. This relationship has a β value of 0.083, not a robust relationship, and nor is it statistically significant in the bootstrapping test. These results agree with the studies by Norman and Conner (2005, Study 1) and Schwarzer et al. (2007, Study 4), which also did not manage to prove the mediating effect of planning between intention and behaviour. The effect of the explained variance between these two constructs is 3.2 %. The reasons for these results are possibly similar to the previous hypothesis. Although adolescents have a good motivational formation, when moving into practice, some factors interfere with achievement of the main objective, i.e., fruit consumption. For young people, there are obviously difficulties in planning and maintaining strategies, in order to transform fruit consumption into regular practice. Concerning action planning, the adolescents were asked in the survey if they would or would not like to improve their eating habits by eating more fruit, making concrete plans as to when, where and how they could increase that consumption. For the three questions asked, there was greater incidence of answers at 4 on the scale, in relation to planning to improve eating habits.

As for the barriers to fruit consumption, the adolescents stated with greater incidence of answers at 4 on the scale, that their hectic life makes consumption of this type of food difficult and that it is difficult to find options that include fruit when they eat out. In the focus groups, regarding difficulties that can prevent adolescents from consuming daily portions of fruit, the peeling of fruit was mentioned, that the rush of everyday life stops them having an appetite for this food, that the fruit in the canteen is sometimes of poor quality, of little variety and rather inaccessible, and they pointed out laziness to eat this food explaining the time it takes to prepare it.

As the best strategies, the adolescents named the fact of having fruit at home, with an average of $\bar{x}=5.91$, eating a variety of fruit so as not to get tired of it ($\bar{x}=5.74$), getting into the habit of eating fruit at the end of meals ($\bar{x}=5.73$), having a good eating plan ($\bar{x}=5.47$) and making healthier choices including fruit when eating out ($\bar{x}=5.30$). The focus groups mentioned as strategies for fruit consumption, willpower and understanding the seriousness of not eating this type of food. The adolescents in this study stated, with an average of $\bar{x}=5.28$, that they have a notion there are practical ways to prepare fruit, which seems to indicate it would be a good strategy to place ready-to-eat fruit in school vending machines.

Concerning the frequency of fruit consumption, the adolescents present a greater incidence of answers on eating one item of fruit twice a day (29.7 %), the least significant response being never eating fruit (2.6 %).

5.2 *The HAPA Model and Advertising Campaigns*

To understand whether adolescents' reaction to certain advertising campaigns could be related to the variables inherent to the HAPA model (H_{12}), a multi-group analysis of the model was carried out as a function of their preference between two such campaigns related to products that could be consumed as alternatives: one for fruit consumption and the other for chocolate. So the sample was divided in two groups, those who said they felt like consuming the product advertised in campaign A, for fruit and campaign B, for chocolate. The structural models referring to the different campaigns follow below Figs. 10.3 and 10.4.

By comparing the two campaigns, the intention was to determine the differences in the behaviour of an adolescent who chooses a campaign directed more towards fruit consumption with another for a less healthy choice.

The two products were chosen as able to be carried and consumed at the same times of day, i.e., competing with each other. We can conclude that of the eleven paths analyzed, between the two campaigns, eight are statistically significant. Regarding hypothesis H_{12} of the study, this is confirmed, showing that the adolescents who chose campaign A present behaviour tending more towards fruit consumption. According to Proctor et al. (2003), children more exposed to advertising seem less likely to consume fruit every day, but high exposure to healthy food can increase the consumption of this type of food (Klepp et al. 2007).

Most differences between the two campaigns are highlighted in the adolescents who chose campaign A, i.e., they present behaviour tending more towards fruit consumption.

The young people who chose campaign A present a significant path of action self-efficacy towards maintenance self-efficacy, i.e., they manage to have the necessary tools to maintain their habits of fruit consumption more effectively.

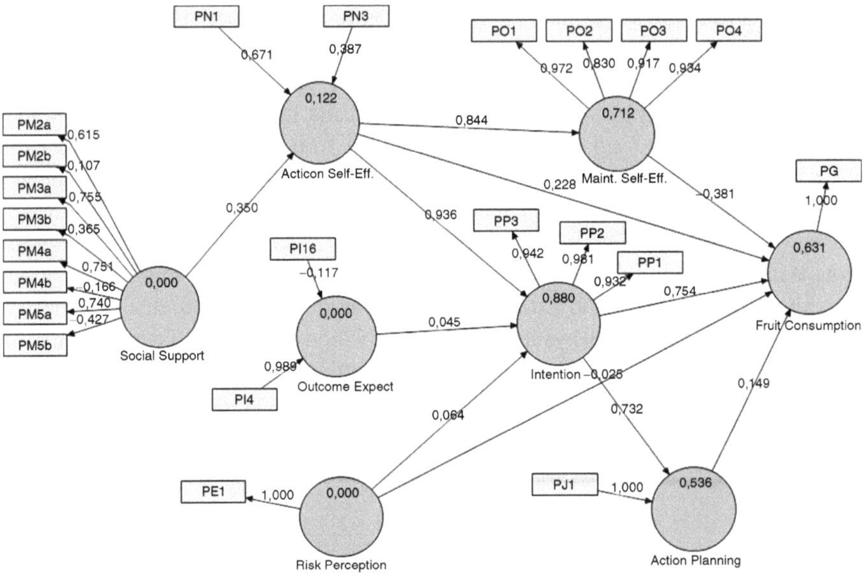

Fig. 10.3 Structural model referring to preference for campaign A

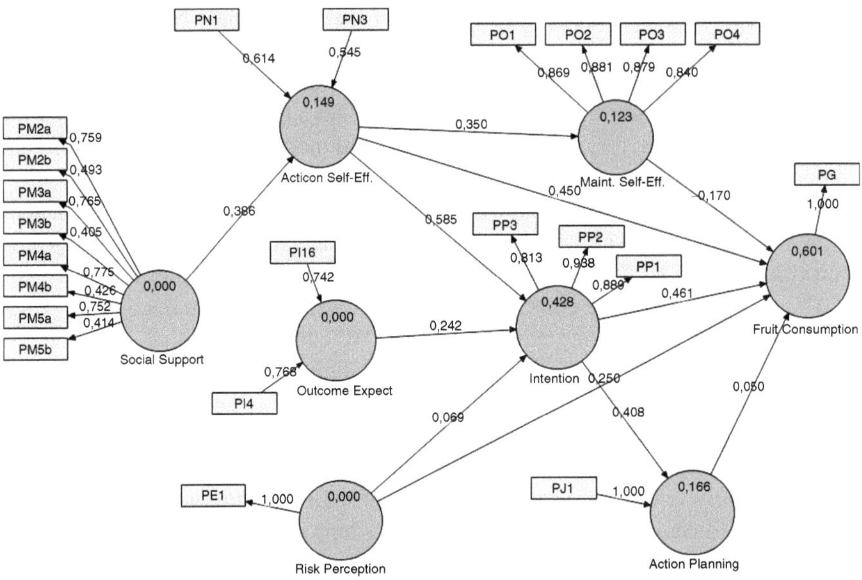

Fig. 10.4 Structural model referring to preference for campaign B

However, the connection between maintenance self-efficacy and fruit consumption has a negative effect, i.e., young people have the bases necessary to manage to maintain fruit consumption, but this does not transfer to final consumption. These adolescents also present a high value of action self-efficacy towards the intention to consume fruit, as well as better planning for consumption of this food, it being explicit for these young people, when, where and how they will eat this food. The adolescents who chose campaign A also present a high value of intention to actually consume fruit. The adolescents who chose campaign B have greater expectations of the result of the intention, being less concerned about other people making fun of them for eating fruit, contrary to campaign A ($\gamma = -0.117$). This aspect may be due to the fact of adolescents who tend to prefer fruit being more worried about being criticized by other adolescents because of that preference. The young people who chose campaign B present a higher value of action self-efficacy towards fruit consumption, and are therefore more self-efficacious in that choice and reveal a greater risk perception with regard to the consequences of not eating this food. Nevertheless, as a whole, the adolescents who preferred campaign A have a set of characteristics that allow them to consume this type of food more regularly, and possibly, for those reasons chose the campaign for fruit.

Summarizing, assessment of the proposed model responds to the objectives intended, and we can state that the HAPA models concentrating on analysis of health behaviours, more specifically in the field of healthy food consumption, are interesting to study due to the possibility of developing effective strategies for social marketing. The value of the explained variance of the construct referring to fruit consumption, although weak, is almost moderate (46.6 %), finding a similar or even higher value than in other studies, such as those by Schwarzer and Renner (2000), Renner and Schwarzer (2005), Renner et al. (2008), Schwarzer and Luszczynska (2008), and Scholz et al. (2009) made with the HAPA model. The result obtained in this study reveals the need for more research to determine what factors affect the remaining amount still to be explained in adolescents' fruit consumption.

6 Conclusions and Final Reflections

Obesity has become a major public health problem leading to great expenditure in this sector, considering that in terms of strategy more emphasis has been given to treatment rather than prevention. Recent years have seen a slight increase in national prevention campaigns, but unfortunately they are scarce or short-lived and cannot therefore reach the defined objectives. Although this generation of young people have access to all types of information, ironically this has been found to be neither sufficient, nor effective to remedy the damage obesity has been causing. The importance of better knowledge in fighting this disease is unquestionable, through greater research into young people's eating behaviour, providing tools so that institutions or organizations can regulate and support their practices. The approach to this problem is proposed specifically from the social marketing viewpoint, since this is a very interesting and pertinent strategy that can bring beneficial solutions to the issue. As coverage of the fight against obesity is vast, this study opted to analyze adolescents' fruit consumption behaviour, since this type of food should be prominent in a balanced diet, as opposed to other less healthy food.

The incentive to create solutions in response to this challenge, i.e., determine the behavioural factors that are decisive in adolescents' fruit consumption was one of the objectives of this research. Initially, to respond to this aim it was necessary to review the literature available so far on the subject in question. This review demonstrated that obesity has been studied in this country but research has rarely connected with social market campaign initiatives regarding this phenomenon, as has happened in other countries for many years. This finding demonstrates the obvious need to study social marketing, to stimulate strategies and solutions to prevent obesity.

To attain the general objective of this work, we analyzed the determinant factors of adolescents' behaviour regarding fruit consumption through the HAPA behavioural theory model, adding social support to it. It was also analyzed how the model would be able to better explain fruit consumption behaviour in adolescents, considering the choice of different advertising campaigns.

The proposed model is able to explain 46.6 % of the variance in adolescents' fruit consumption, demonstrating the need for further study on the subject.

The main antecedent of adolescents' fruit consumption is intention, which gathers the indirect impact of action self-efficacy and outcome expectancies, the relationship between risk perception and intention being non-significant.

The relationship between maintenance self-efficacy and fruit consumption, although significant, presents a negative value.

Social support was included in the proposed model and makes a direct contribution to action self-efficacy, demonstrating that this variable influences adolescents' food choices.

The last multi-group analysis attempted to identify the differences that could exist regarding the proposed model, in an adolescent who chose a campaign more directed to fruit consumption or another for less healthy food. The results obtained indicate that the model gives a better explanation for adolescents who chose a campaign more directed to fruit, presenting behaviour more open to consumption of this food. These young people have greater action self-efficacy towards maintenance self-efficacy, greater action self-efficacy towards intention and greater intention to consume fruit. The adolescents who chose the campaign for the less healthy food have greater outcome expectancies for the intention and are less concerned if other people make fun of them for eating fruit, compared to the other young people who preferred the campaign for fruit, revealing greater action self-efficacy towards fruit consumption and greater risk perception for consuming this item.

Concerning the viability of strategies for adolescents to consume a greater quantity of fruit, they themselves mentioned the fact of having fruit at home, consumption of a variety of fruit, acquiring the habit of eating fruit after meals and following a good diet, meaning healthier choices that include fruit when they eat out.

As for the barriers to fruit consumption, the adolescents surveyed mentioned the difficulty in finding options that include this item when they eat out, lack of time through having a busy life, and when they are very hungry they do not feel like eating fruit, the need to peel it and the poor quality, variety and accessibility of this food in the canteen.

Inclusion of social support, not much used in the HAPA model, aimed to determine more explanatory variables of fruit consumption in adolescents, since this is an age-group that can be influenced by family and friends. This construct showed itself to be significant in explaining adolescents' fruit consumption.

These results demonstrate that social support is important for adolescents to create and maintain the habit of eating this food. Despite being a time of major transformations in terms of personality, the opinion of family and friends has some impact on young people. So part of the effort to encourage fruit consumption could include making parents aware of the need to form that social support. Then again, advertising campaigns could use peer groups as groups of reference, as it is also seen that they too can serve as a reference for fruit consumption. Schools should also encourage fruit consumption, making it available in a practical and accessible way. Fruit should be fresh, varied, of a high quality and be available in both the tuck shop and the canteen, preferably already prepared so as to overcome some of the barriers to fruit consumption expressed by the adolescents. The government should provide appropriate guidelines so that in the scope of their autonomy schools can offer a better catering service and distribute fresh fruit. In this connection, limited access to highly calorific foodstuffs with low levels of nutrients, particularly those available in vending machines, would also be beneficial.

Concerning the influence of outcome expectancies on intention, this shows the need for adolescents to have more and more information about the health benefits of eating fruit, thereby increasing the intention to consume it. Bearing this aspect in mind and according to Pollard et al. (2008), campaigns focused on fruit consumption should permit increased knowledge about the recommended daily fruit intake, improving perception of the need to consume this type of food and simultaneously lowering the barriers to its consumption.

In terms of advertising campaigns, the government should turn increasingly to social marketing activities aiming to increase adolescents' fruit consumption, implementing legislation that limits advertising of less healthy food, making them more expensive and less accessible (Hoek 2005), as young people are found to be conscious of the varying costs of options. It should also regulate the need for health professionals in the field of food in schools, local authorities and all institutions linked to feeding children and young people, as these could create awareness in adolescents.

While it is certain there is still a long road to travel in fighting obesity, social marketing strategies constitute a competitive advantage in relation to advertising of rather unhealthy food, and can therefore attain better levels of health in adolescents and allow in the long-term better economic and social returns for the health sector, which would mean improved quality of life for both adolescents and society in general.

Similarly to others, this study has some limitations. First of all, it is a transversal study limited to only two schools. It would therefore be interesting to carry out a longitudinal study to assess adolescents in two different periods, as well as a study with a regional or national sample. In a future study, application of individual interviews, instead of focus groups, could avoid opinion bias. It would be important to analyze other factors influencing adolescents' fruit consumption which were not considered here, such as body mass index, action control and self-efficacy of recovery. Use of strategies to assess different forms of applying social marketing could be interesting, in a second period, in order to determine their effectiveness in altering behaviour. Regarding advertising campaigns, it would be challenging to determine more characteristics that form a good campaign for fruit consumption, as well as other social marketing strategies that manage to attain that objective.

To summarize, it is hoped that the results of this research, together with similar studies already made, can contribute to filling existing gaps in the literature and simultaneously help to implement viable strategies in terms of social marketing to combat obesity, involving political, family, social and school entities that can contribute to improving the quality of life of individuals and society in general.

References

Anderson-Bill, E., Winett, R., & Wojcik, J. (2000). Social cognitive determinants of nutrition behavior among supermarket shoppers: A structural equation analysis. *Health Psychology, 19*(5), 479–486.

Anderson-Bill, E., Winett, R., & Wojcik, J. (2007). Self-regulation, self-efficacy, outcome expectations, and social support: Social cognitive theory and nutrition behavior. *Annals of Behavioral Medicine, 34*(3), 304–312.

Anderson-Bill, E., Winett, R., & Wojcik, J. (2011). Social cognitive determinants of nutrition and physical activity among web-health users enrolling in an online intervention: The influence of social support, self-efficacy, outcome expectations, and self-regulation. *Journal of Medical Internet Research, 13*(1), e28. doi:10.2196/jmir.1551.

Baranowski, T., Cullen, K., Nicklas, T., Thompson, D., & Baranowski, J. (2003). Are current health behavioral change models helpful in guiding prevention of weight gain efforts? *Obesity Research, 11*, 23S–43S.

Bere, E., & Klepp, K. (2004). Correlates of fruit and vegetable intake among Norwegian schoolchildren: Parental and self-reports. *Public Health Nutrition, 7*(8), 991–998.

Bere, E., & Klepp, K. (2005). *Changes in accessibility and preferences predict children's future fruit and vegetable intake*. Resource document. International Journal of Behavioral Nutrition and Physical Activity. http://www.ncbi.nlm.nih.gov/pmc/articles/PMC1262749/. Accessed 25 Mar 2014.

Boeing, H., Bechthold, A., Bub, A., Ellinger, S., Haller, D., Kroke, A., Leschik-Bonnet, E., Müller, M., Oberritter, H., Schulze, M., Stehle, P., & Watzl, B. (2012). Critical review: Vegetables and fruit in the prevention of chronic diseases. *European Journal of Nutrition, 51*(6), 637–663. doi:10.1007/s00394-012-0380-y.

Brei, V., & Neto, G. (2006). O uso da técnica de modelagem em equações estruturais na área de marketing: um estudo comparativo entre publicações no Brasil e exterior. *Revista de Administração Contemporânea, 10*(4), 131–151.

British Medical Association. (2003). *Adolescent health.* http://image.guardian.co.uk/sys-files/Society/documents/2003/12/08/BMA_AdolescentHealth.pdf. Accessed 15 May 2013.

Brug, J., Lechener, L., & De Vries, H. (1995). Psychosocial determinants of fruit and vegetable consumption. *Appetite, 25*(3), 285–296.

Chin, W. (1998). The partial least squares approach to structural equation modelling. In G. Marcoulides (Ed.), *Modern methods for business research* (pp. 295–336). Mahwah: Laurence Erlbaum Associates.

Corcoran, N. (2013). *Communicating health: Strategies for health promotion.* London: Sage.

De Bourdeaudhuij, I., & Van Oost, P. (2000). Personal and family determinants of dietary behaviour in adolescents and their parents. *Psychology and Health, 15*(6), 751–770. doi:10.1080/08870440008405579.

Evans, W. (2008). Social marketing campaigns and children's media use. *The Future of Children, 18*(1), 181–203.

Evans, W., Christoffel, K., Necheles, J., & Becken, A. (2010). Social marketing as a childhood obesity prevention strategy. *Obesity, 18*(1), S23S–S26S. doi:10.1038/oby.2009.428.

Fertman, C., & Allesnsworth, D. (2010). *Health promotion programs – From theory to practice.* San Francisco: Jossey-Bass.

Foltz, J., May, A., Belay, B., Nihiser, A., Dooywma, C., & Blanck, H. (2012). Population-level intervention strategies and examples for obesity prevention in children. *Annual Review of Nutrition, 32*, 391–415. doi:10.1146/annurev-nutr-071811-150646.

Ford, E., Ahluwalia, I., & Galuska, D. (2000). Social relationships and cardiovascular disease risk factors: Findings from the third national health and nutrition examination survey. *Preventive Medicine, 30*(2), 83–92.

Garcia-Marco, L., Vicente-Rodríguez, G., Borys, J., Le Bodo, Y., Pettigrew, S., & Moreno, L. (2011). Contribution of social marketing strategies to community-based obesity prevention programmes in children. *International Journal of Obesity, 35*(4), 472–479. doi:10.1038/ijo.2010.221.

Godinho, C., Alvarez, M., & Lima, M. (2013a). Formative research on HAPA model determinants for fruit and vegetable intake: Target beliefs for audiences at different stages of change. *Health Education Research, 28*(6), 1014–1028. doi:10.1093/her/cyt076.

Godinho, C., Alvarez, M., Lima, M., & Schwarzer, R. (2013b). Will is not enough: Coping planning and action control as mediators in the prediction of fruit and vegetable intake. *British Journal of Health Psychology*. doi:10.1111/bjhp.12084.

Gollwitzer, P. (1999). Implementation intentions: Strong effects of simple plans. *American Psychologist, 54*(7), 493–503. doi:10.1037/0003-066X.54.7.493.

Guillaumie, L., Godin, G., Manderscheid, J., Spitz, E., & Muller, L. (2012). The impact of self-efficacy and implementation intentions-based interventions on fruit and vegetables intake among adults. *Psychology and Health, 27*(1), 30–50. doi:10.1080/08870446.2010.541910.

Hair, J., Ringle, C., & Sarstedt, M. (2011). PLS-SEM: Indeed a silver bullet. *Journal of Marketing Theory and Practice, 19*(2), 139–151.

Hoek, J. (2005). Marketing communications and obesity: A view from the dark side. Resource document. *Journal of the New Zealand Medical Association.* http://journal.nzma.org.nz/journal/118-1220/1608/. Accessed 1 Mar 2014.

Kapetanaki, A., Brennan, D., & Caraher, M. (2014). Social marketing and healthy eating: Findings from young people in Greece. Resource document. *International Review on Public and Nonprofit Marketing.* Online first at: http://link.springer.com/article/10.1007/s12208-013-0112-x. Accessed 1 Apr 2014.

Klepp, K.-I., Wind, M., De Bourdeaudhuij, I., Pérez-Rodrigo, C., Due, P., Bjelland, M., & Brug, J. (2007). Television viewing and exposure to food-related commercials among European school children, associations with fruit and vegetable intake: A cross sectional study. *International Journal of Behavioral Nutrition and Physical Activity, 4*(46). doi:10.1186/1479-5868-4-46.

Krolner, R., Rasmussen, M., Brug, J., Klepp, K., Wind, M., & Due, P. (2011). Determinants of fruit and vegetable consumption among children and adolescents: A review of the literature. Part II: Qualitative studies. *International Journal of Behavioral Nutrition and Physical Activity, 8*(112). doi:10.1186/1479-5868-8-112.

Lange, D., Richert, J., Koring, M., Knoll, N., Schwarzer, R., & Lippke, S. (2013). Self-regulation prompts can increase fruit consumption: A one-hour randomized controlled online trial. *Psychology and Health, 28*(5), 533–545. doi:10.1080/08870446.2012.751107.

Lien, N., Lytle, A., & Komro, K. (2002). Applying theory of planned behavior to fruit and vegetable consumption of young adolescents. *American Journal of Health Promotion, 16*(4), 189–197.

Luszczynska, A., & Schwarzer, R. (2003). Planning and self-efficacy in the adoption and maintenance of breast self-examination: A longitudinal study on self-regulatory cognitions. *Psychology and Health, 18*(1), 93–108. doi:10.1080/0887044021000019358.

Luszczynska, A., Gibbons, X., & Piko, B. (2004). Self-regulatory cognitions, social comparison and perceived peers' behaviors as predictors of nutrition and physical activity: A comparison among adolescents in Hungary, Poland, Turkey and USA. *Psychology and Health, 19*(5), 577–593. doi:10.1080/0887044042000205844.

Luszczynska, A., Tryburcy, M., & Schwarzer, R. (2007). Improving fruit and vegetable consumption: A self-efficacy intervention compared with a combined self-efficacy and planning intervention. *Health Education Research, 22*(5), 630–638. doi:10.1093/her/cyl133.

Neumark-Sztainer, D., Wall, M., Perry, C., & Story, M. (2003). Correlates of fruit and vegetables intake among adolescents: Findings from project EAT. *Preventive Medicine, 37*(3), 198–208.

Norman, P., & Conner, M. (2005). The theory of planned behavior and exercise: Evidence for the mediating and moderating roles of planning on intention-behavior relationships. *Journal of Sport and Exercise Psychology, 27*(4), 488–504.

NSMC. (2011). *Big pocket guide: To using social marketing for behavior change*. http://www.thensmc.com/sites/default/files/Big_pocket_guide_2011.pdf. Accessed 17 Feb 2014.

Pérez-Rodrigo, C., & Aranceta, J. (2003). Nutrition education in schools: Experiences and challenges. *European Journal of Clinical Nutrition, 47*(S.1), S82–S85. doi:10.1038/sj.ejcn.1601824.

Perloff, L., & Fetzer, B. (1986). Self-other judgments and perceived vulnerability to victimization. *Journal of Personality and Social Psychology, 50*(3), 502–510.

Poddar, K., Hosig, K., Anderson-Bill, E., Nicklos-Richardson, S., & Ducan, S. (2012). Dairy intake and related self-regulation improved in college students using online nutrition education. *Journal of the Academy of Nutrition and Dietetics, 12*(112), 1976–1986. doi:10.1016/j.jand.2012.07.026.

Pollard, C., Miller, M., Daly, A., Crouchley, K., O'Donoghue, K., Lang, A., & Binns, C. (2008). Increasing fruit and vegetable consumption: Success of the Western Australian go for 2&5 campaign. *Public Health Nutrition, 11*(3), 314–320.

Proctor, M., Moore, L., Gao, D., Cupples, L., Bradlee, M., Hood, M., & Ellison, R. (2003). Television viewing and change in body fat from preschool to early adolescence: The Framingham Children's Study. *International Journal of Obesity and Related Metabolic Disorders, 27*(7), 827–833.

Renner, B., & Schwarzer, R. (2005). The motivation to eat a healthy diet: How intender and non-intenders differ in terms of risk perception, outcomes expectancies, self-efficacy, and nutrition behavior. *Polish Psychological Bulletin, 36*(1), 7–15.

Renner, B., Spivak, Y., Kwon, S., & Schwarzer, R. (2007). Does age make a difference? Predicting physical activity of South Koreans. *Psychology and Aging, 22*(3), 482–493.

Renner, B., Kwon, S., Yang, B.-H., Paik, K.-C., Kim, S., Roh, S., Song, J., & Schwarzer, R. (2008). Social-cognitive predictors of dietary behaviors in South Korean men and women. *International Journal of Behavioral Medicine, 15*(1), 4–13. doi:10.1080/10705500701783785.

Resnicow, K., Davis-Hearn, M., Smith, M., Baranowski, T., Lin, L., Baranowski, J., Doyle, C., & Wang, D. (1997). Social-cognitive predictors of fruit and vegetable intake in children. *Health Psychology, 16*(3), 272–276.

Reuter, T., Ziegelmann, J., Wiedemann, A., Geiser, C., Lippke, S., & Schwarzer, R. (2010). Changes intentions, planning, and self-efficacy predict changes in behaviors. *Journal of Health Psychology, 15*(6), 935–947. doi:10.1177/1359105309360071.

Rolls, B., Ello-Martin, J., & Tohill, B. (2004). What can intervention studies tell us about the relationship between fruit and vegetable consumption and weight management? *Nutrition Reviews, 62*(1), 1–17.

Rosenstock, I. (1974). Historical origins of the health belief model. In M. Becker (Ed.), *The health belief model and personal health behavior* (pp. 1–8). Thorofare: Charles, B. Slack, Inc.

Sallis, J., Grossman, R., Pinski, R., Patterson, T., & Nader, P. (1987). The development of scales to measure social support for diet and exercise behaviors. *Preventive Medicine, 16*(6), 825–836.

Scholz, U., Nagy, G., Gohner, W., Luszczynska, A., & Kliegel, M. (2009). Changes in self-regulatory cognitions as predictors of changes in smoking and nutrition behavior. *Psychology and Health, 24*(5), 545–561. doi:10.1080/08870440801902519.

Schwarzer, R. (2008a). Modeling health behavior change: How to predict and modify the adoption and maintenance of health behaviors. *Applied Psychology: An International Review, 57*(1), 1–29. doi:10.1111/j.1464-0597.2007.00325.x.

Schwarzer, R. (2008b). Some burning issues in research on health behavior change. *Applied Psychology: An International Review, 57*(1), 84–93. doi:10.1111/j.1464-0597.2007.00324.x.

Schwarzer, R., & Knoll, N. (2007). Functional roles of social support within the stress and coping process: A theoretical and empirical overview. *International Journal of Psychology, 42*(4), 243–252. doi:10.1080/00207590701396641.

Schwarzer, R., & Luszczynska, A. (2006). Self-efficacy, adolescents' risk-taking behaviors, and health. In F. Pajares & T. Urdan (Eds.), *Self-efficacy beliefs of adolescents: A volume in the series adolescent and education* (Vol. 5, pp. 139–159). Greenwich: Information Age Publishing.

Schwarzer, R., & Luszczynska, A. (2008). How to overcome health-compromising behaviors: The health action process approach. *European Psychologist, 13*(2), 141–151. doi:10.1027/1016-9040.13.2.141.

Schwarzer, R., & Renner, B. (2000). Social-cognitive predictors of health behavior: Action self-efficacy and coping self-efficacy. *Health Psychology, 19*(5), 487–495.

Schwarzer, R., Schuz, B., Ziegelmann, J., Lippke, S., Luszczynska, A., & Scholz, U. (2007). Adoption and maintenance of four health behaviors: Theory-guided longitudinal studies on dental flossing, seat belt Use, dietary behavior, and physical activity. *Annals of Behavioral Medicine, 33*(2), 156–166.

Sheeran, P., Webb, T., & Gollwitzer, P. (2005). The interplay between goal intentions and implementations intentions. *Personality and Social Psychology Bulletin, 31*(1), 87–98.

Shive, S., & Morris, M. (2006). Evaluation of the energize your life! social marketing campaign pilot study to increase fruit intake among community college students. *Journal of American College Health, 55*(1), 33–39.

Stead, M., Gordon, R., Angus, K., & McDermott, L. (2007). A systematic review of social marketing effectiveness. *Health Education, 107*(2), 126–191. doi:10.1108/09654280710731548.

Steptoe, A., Peekins-Porras, L., Rink, E., Hilton, S., & Cappuccio, F. (2004). Psychological and social predictors of changes in fruit and vegetable consumption over 12 months following behavioral and nutrition education counseling. *Health Psychology, 23*(6), 574–581.

Story, M., Neumark-Sztainer, D., & French, S. (2002). Individual and environmental influences on adolescent eating behaviors. *Journal of the American Dietetic Association, 102*(3S), S40–S51.

Sumonja, S., & Novakovic, B. (2013). Determinants of fruit, vegetable, and dairy consumption in a sample of schoolchildren, northern Serbia, 2012. *Preventing Chronic Disease, 10*. doi:10.5888/pcd10.130072.

Tetens, I., & Alinia, S. (2009). The role of fruit consumption in the prevention of obesity. Resource document. *Journal of Horticultural Science and Biotechnology*. http://www.jhortscib.com/isafruit/isa_pp047_051.pdf. Accessed 22 Jan 2014.

Woodward, D., Boon, J., Cumming, F., Ball, P., Williams, H., & Hornsby, H. (1996). Adolescents' reported usage of selected foods in relation to their perceptions and social norms for those foods. *Appetite, 27*(2), 109–117.

World Health Organization. (2003). Diet, nutrition, and the prevention of chronic disease: Report of a joint WHO/FAO expert consultation, Series No. 916, Geneva. Document resource. http://whqlibdoc.who.int/trs/who_trs_916.pdf. Accessed 18 Feb 2014.

Wymer, W. (2011). Developing more effective social marketing strategies. *Journal of Social Marketing, 1*(1), 17–31. doi:10.1108/20426761111104400.

Young, E., Fors, S., Fasha, E., & Hayes, D. (2004). Associations between perceived parent behaviors and middle school student fruit and vegetable consumption. *Journal of Nutrition Education and Behavior, 36*(1), 2–8.

Joana Rita Silvestre Godinho is a dietician and consults on nutrition and dietetics in private medical clinics and gymnasiums. She has worked in a local authority, in continuous care in an old people's home and in a dialysis clinic. She was involved in the Mun-Si project, a study about child obesity and was co-author of two scientific studies about nutrition in patients receiving dialysis presented at EDTNA. This study was elaborated in the scope of a master dissertation on Health Unit Management at the University of Beira Interior, Portugal.

Helena Alves is Assistant Professor of Marketing at the Business and Economics Department and researcher at NECE, University of Beira Interior, Portugal. Her areas of expertise include Customer Satisfaction, Services marketing, Tourism marketing and public and nonprofit marketing, having authored and co-authored several articles and book chapters on these themes. Her teaching experience includes degree, master and Ph.D. levels in Portugal and Spain (University of Extremadura, University of León and University of Valencia). Currently, she is the editor of the ***International Review of Public and Nonprofit Marketing***, and is also on the editorial board of several journals such as The Service Industries Journal, The Management Decision Journal, The Service Business Journal, The Portuguese Marketing Review, among others.

Part II
Applied Research

Chapter 11
Promoting Mental Health and Wellbeing in Individuals and Communities: The 'Act-Belong-Commit' Campaign

Robert J. Donovan and Julia Anwar-McHenry

1 Introduction

Mental Health has been defined by the World Health Organization (WHO) as: '*…a state of wellbeing in which the individual realises his or her own abilities, can cope with the normal stresses of life, can work productively and fruitfully, and is able to make a contribution to his or her community*' (Herrman et al. 2005). Lay people in Australia and elsewhere have similar views. 'Mentally healthy' individuals are described as: being content with who they are and what they have; being in control of their lives; being socially and mentally competent; emotionally stable; generally happy, enthusiastic and energetic most of the time; able to cope with problems and crises in life; and being alert, interested and involved in things in their lives (Donovan et al. 2003). A key point in both the WHO and lay perspectives is that mental health is far more than simply the absence of a mental illness (Friedli 2009).

Mental health *promotion* can be defined as interventions designed to maximise mental health and wellbeing by increasing the coping capacity of communities and individuals and by improving environments that affect mental health. Mental health promotion aims to improve the wellbeing of all people regardless of whether or not they have a mental illness. This perspective acknowledges that people with a mental illness also have periods of mental wellness. Mental illness p*revention* refers to interventions that prevent the development of a disorder by targeting known risk factors, while e*arly intervention* involves actions that specifically target people

For information on how an organisation can become involved with the Act-Belong-Commit campaign, contact the first author (r.donovan@curtin.edu.au) or the campaign manager Amberlee Laws (a.laws@curtin.edu.au). For more information on the campaign, visit www.actbelongcommit.org.au

R.J. Donovan (✉) • J. Anwar-McHenry
Curtin University, Perth, Australia
e-mail: r.donovan@curtin.edu.au; julia.anwarmchenry@curtin.edu.au

W. Wymer (ed.), *Innovations in Social Marketing and Public Health Communication*, Applying Quality of Life Research,
DOI 10.1007/978-3-319-19869-9_11

displaying the early signs and symptoms of a mental disorder. As for health in general, such interventions need to occur not only at the individual level but also at the policy and structural level (e.g., housing, education, employment, physical environment, discrimination, etc.) (Herrman et al. 2005).

While it is true that mental health promotion (usually followed by 'prevention and early intervention') is talked about more than a few decades ago, and there have been many commendable documents setting out 'frameworks' for mental health promotion (for example Herrman et al. 2005; Patterson 2009; Barry et al. 2005; Saxena and Garrison 2004; Department of Health 2012), Act-Belong-Commit is the world's first and only population-wide mental health promotion program, as distinct from mental illness prevention or early intervention initiatives. While there are a number of school and worksite interventions aimed at building positive mental health, most community wide campaigns have aimed at increasing awareness of specific mental illnesses, education about stress reduction and coping strategies, encouraging help-seeking, early detection and treatment of mental problems, and the de-stigmatisation of mental illness (Patterson 2009; Barry et al. 2005; Saxena and Garrison 2004). Current examples include the 'Time to Change' campaign in England (www.time-to-change.org.uk), 'Beyond Blue' in Australia (www.beyondblue.org.au) and 'It's Up to Us' in San Diego, California (www.up2sd.org).

In line with the principles of the Ottawa Charter for Health Promotion (WHO 1986) and the seventh principle of the Perth Charter for the Promotion of Mental Health and Wellbeing (Anwar McHenry and Donovan 2013) (i.e., 'mental health promotion must take place at the individual and societal levels'), Act-Belong-Commit utilises social marketing, with a community development approach through social franchising, to influence individual behaviour and to create supportive environments for fostering and maintaining mental health and wellbeing. That is, the campaign targets individuals to engage in mentally healthy activities while at the same time supporting and encouraging organizations that offer mentally healthy activities to promote, and increase participation in, their activities.

2 Development of the Act-Belong-Commit Framework for the Promotion of Mental Health

In 2002 the Health Promotion Foundation of Western Australia ('Healthway') commissioned research to inform the development of a mental health promotion campaign in Western Australia (WA). Adopting a grounded theory approach, this research first examined people's perceptions of mental health and the behaviours thought to protect and promote good mental health. The subsequently developed grounded theory was followed by an extensive review of the scientific literature on factors influencing mental health and wellbeing. As noted above, while terminology and depth of understanding differed, there was much commonality between lay people's and behavioural scientists' views on what factors build resilience and good mental health and wellbeing. Various implementation strategies were developed on the basis of the research findings. Healthway then appointed the researchers to conduct a 2-year pilot of the campaign in six regional towns throughout the state in 2005–2007. On the basis of the pilot study results, the campaign was launched state-wide in 2008 with further funding from the Mental Health Commission of Western Australia (WA).

The ongoing development and implementation of the Act-Belong-Commit campaign is coordinated by 'Mentally Healthy WA' (MHWA), based at Curtin University in the state's capital. Mentally Healthy WA (the "franchisor") partners with a diverse range of community groups, local governments, and state-wide government and non-government organisations. MHWA provides franchises with initial and ongoing training, overall strategic direction, scientific resources, merchandising, mass media advertising, publicity, and event sponsorship. MHWA also conducts population impact surveys and surveys of partners/franchisees. The social franchise model enables the Act-Belong-Commit campaign to grow and expand its impact and geographical reach without necessarily increasing the size of the franchiser "hub" (Beckmann and Zeyen 2014). The origins and rationale of the campaign are described in detail in Donovan et al. (2003, 2006, 2007a, b).

2.1 *Overall Campaign Message: The Act-Belong-Commit Brand*

In the tradition of Aristotle's 'virtue is cultivated by practice', Act-Belong-Commit is focused on getting people to engage in behaviors known to improve and maintain good mental health. According to Aristotle "*we become just by doing just acts, temperate by doing temperate acts, brave by doing brave acts*" (cited in (Sandel 2012)). The Act-Belong-Commit 'philosophy' similarly states that "*we become mentally healthy by engaging in mentally healthy activities*". The *Act-Belong-Commit* brand is therefore a simple message to act on (see Fig. 11.1). The three verbs 'act', 'belong', and 'commit' were chosen as they not only provide a colloquial 'ABC', but also represent the three major domains of factors that both the literature and people in general consider contribute to good mental health (Donovan et al. 2003, 2007a). They are articulated as follows:

Act:	Keep alert and engaged by keeping mentally, socially, spiritually and physically active
Belong:	Develop a strong sense of identity and belonging by keeping up family relationships, friendships, joining groups, and participating in community activities
Commit:	Do things that provide meaning and purpose in life, such as taking up challenges, supporting causes and helping others

Overall, the Act-Belong-Commit message encourages people to be physically, spiritually, socially, and mentally **act**ive, in ways that increase their sense of

belonging to the communities in which they live, work, play, and recover, and that involve **commit**ments to causes or challenges that provide meaning and purpose in their lives. There is substantial scientific evidence that these three behavioral domains contribute to increasing levels of positive mental health and wellbeing (and in fact, to physical health) (Patterson 2009; Barry et al. 2005; Saxena and Garrison 2004; Donovan et al. 2006; Donovan and Anwar McHenry 2014). Furthermore, although different groups may articulate the domains differently and place different emphases on each, these three domains appear universal across different cultures. The three domains also provide a hierarchy for increasing levels of involvement, and thus a deeper contribution to wellbeing. For example, an individual may choose to be physically active by going for a run, increase their sense of belonging by joining a running group, and derive a sense of challenge and meaning by setting goals for participation in a fun run to raise funds for a charitable cause. Similarly, one can read a book, join a book club, and books can be selected that are challenging to read and require concentration and new learnings.

The Act-Belong-Commit framework also has implications for suicide prevention in that according to Joiner (Joiner 2005), the desire or motivation to suicide is driven by two factors: low or 'thwarted' belongingness and perceived burdensomeness. Given that *Belong* is about building and maintaining connections with others, including community and civic organisations and institutions, and that *Commit* involves doing things that provide meaning and purpose in life, including taking up causes and volunteering that helps society and other individuals, the Act-Belong-Commit campaign can be viewed as strengthening two major protective factors for suicide.

Fig. 11.1 Act-Belong-Commit branding

By encouraging participation in public events by people with different demographic and ethnic backgrounds, the campaign also contributes to greater understanding between groups and to what Aristotle called 'civic virtue'; that is, greater feelings of obligation and responsibilities towards communities to which people have a greater sense of belonging (Beckmann and Zeyen 2014).

3 Campaign Implementation: A Social Franchising Model

The campaign targets individuals to engage in activities that enhance their mental health while encouraging community partners/franchises to promote their activities under the banner of the *Act-Belong-Commit* message (Donovan et al. 2007b; Jalleh et al. 2007). That is, the Act-Belong-Commit campaign makes extensive use of social franchising to facilitate participation in mentally healthy activities and for the delivery and implementation of the campaign at a local community level. Social franchising emulates the successful commercial franchise model to achieve social goals (Richardson and Turnbull 2008). The main advantages of franchising include efficient and low risk expansion with a recognised brand despite resource scarcity, and the ability to mobilise decentralised social capital and ensure local ownership (Beckmann and Zeyen 2014; Montagu 2002; Volvery and Hackl 2010). The social franchise model differs from the commercial model in that an assurance of moral consensus or enthusiastic embrace of the social cause needs to be present with similar understandings about how objectives should be attained to enable franchisees to actively contribute and take ownership over the initiative (Volvery and Hackl 2010). Franchises sign a Memorandum of Understanding (MOU) to ensure message integrity and consistency with evidence, branding consistency with permitted variations, sharing of activities and learnings between partners, and regular submission of process evaluation data.

These collaborative community partnerships/social franchises involve local people in implementation, thus ensuring both local commitment and relevance, which are considered essential for the success of health promoting campaigns (Barnett and Kendall 2011; Annor and Allen 2008). Partnerships with sectors other than health (i.e., sport, recreation, the arts, education, charities, etc.) not only make mental health 'everybody's business', but also are necessary to more effectively address the social determinants of mental health and wellbeing (Quinn and Biggs 2010).

The development and implementation of the Act-Belong-Commit campaign is coordinated by Mentally Healthy WA, based at Curtin University in Perth, the state's capital. Mentally Healthy WA (the "franchisor") partners with a diverse range of community groups (e.g., theatre groups; women's health groups; sporting groups; recreational and hobby groups, see under 'Partners' at actbelongcommit.org.au), local governments, and state-wide organisations. MHWA provides franchises with initial and ongoing training, overall strategic direction, scientific resources, merchandising, mass media advertising, publicity, and event sponsorship. MHWA also conducts population impact surveys and surveys of partners/

Fig. 11.2 Act-Belong-Commit self-help guide

franchisees (Patterson 2009; Barry et al. 2005; Saxena and Garrison 2004). Importantly in an area where funding is not readily available, the social franchise model enables the Act-Belong-Commit campaign to grow and expand its impact and geographical reach without necessarily increasing the size of the franchiser "hub" (Beckmann and Zeyen 2014).

The campaign has a number of resources, including a self-help guide ("A Great Way to Live Life: the Act-Belong-Commit Guide to Keeping Mentally Healthy"; Fig. 11.2), which not only provides individuals with a tool for enhancing their mental health, but also provides the clinician with a helpful tool in the clinical setting. The Guide is downloadable from the website or can be completed online. Other resources include a mobile phone app, a search tool to find clubs and organisations in one's areas of interest, various fact sheets, curriculum materials for schools and worksites, and print and video advertisements (visit actbelongcommit.org.au).

4 Campaign Evolution

The campaign began as a community-wide population approach with a primary prevention focus. As the first mental health promotion campaign, an initial primary objective was simply to put mental health (in a positive sense) 'on people's agenda'. Another objective was to broaden the context of mental health to include community activities and organisations, not just a 'health department' context. The latter objective has been overwhelmingly successful. No doubt due to the initial television commercial's broad appeal and direct on-the-ground approaches to a variety of community organisations, the vast majority of organisations asking to partner with the campaign have been non-health related.

As the campaign achieved greater awareness in the community, a number of organisations began asking for the campaign to be incorporated in their activities. This resulted in several targeted activities and materials, such as a peer educator led seminar for keeping mentally healthy in retirement, primary and secondary schools curriculum components, incorporation of the message in pain clinics, and materials for new mothers (to assist with post natal depression). More recently, given numerous contacts from individuals with a mental illness who reported being helped by responding to the campaign messages, we are conducting a trial assisting patients in recovery on discharge from hospital. This trial is based on patients working through the self-help guide with the assistance of mental health professionals. In addition, we are conducting workshops in positive mental health promotion and training in the use of the guide to the mental health workforce in Western Australia.

5 Campaign Evaluation

Process and impact evaluations of the campaign are conducted annually amongst the general population (e.g. Anwar McHenry et al. 2012) and organisations that partner with the campaign (e.g. Jalleh et al. 2013). The general population questionnaire measures exposure to the campaign and the impact of the campaign in terms of individual behaviour change, changes in beliefs about mental health and mental illness, and perceived effectiveness of the campaign in increasing openness towards mental health issues and reducing stigma surrounding mental illness. The partner questionnaire measures the extent to which organisations have benefited from the partnership in terms of staff capacity, organisation awareness, promotion of events, and obtaining funds for specific activities.

In 2012 the campaign reach in the 18+ general population was 70 %. Among those reached by the campaign, 29 % reported a change in the way they thought about mental health and mental illness, with responses consistent with the communication objectives of the campaign. With respect to the campaign influencing their behaviour, 14 % of those reached by the campaign reported they had done or tried to do something for their mental health. When these respondents were prompted with reasons for doing something, 37 % nominated "I was generally happy but wanted to enjoy life more", 20 % that "I wanted more meaning and purpose in my life", and 34 % that "I was somewhat unhappy and wanted to lift my mood". That is, the campaign appears to attract involvement by those already mentally healthy as well as those who may be depressed or at risk of becoming depressed.

With respect to perceived societal impact, just over three in four (78 %) believed the campaign would make people more open about mental health issues (less than 1 % stated 'less'). When asked about perceived willingness to talk about mental health issues compared to the previous year, a greater proportion of respondents reached by the campaign reported that people were "more willing", than those not reached by the campaign (54 % vs. 41 %). Approximately two in three (71 %) considered that the campaign would reduce stigma associated with mental illness. Mindful of unintended negative effects, importantly, only 1 % considered the campaign would increase stigma.

Finally, when asked whether they 'approved, disapproved, or had no opinion either way of campaigns like *Act-Belong-Commit* that promote what people can do to improve their mental health', almost all respondents (93 %) stated that they approved of such campaigns; less than 1 % disapproved.

The partner questionnaires conducted in 2006 and 2008 revealed a positive impact on organisations that collaborated with the campaign. The model of partnership exchange, which offers practical assistance for delivery of the campaign message, was fundamental to gaining community collaboration through mutually beneficial exchanges. Substantial media publicity of partner organisation's events was indicative of the strength of these partnerships and partner organisations believed the campaign offered significant benefits, including assistance securing funding and sponsorship.

6 Campaign Diffusion

The campaign is diffusing throughout Australia and internationally. In Western Australia where the statewide campaign began in 2008, approximately 140 organisations across the state have signed MOUs to partner with the campaign. Via conference presentations, word-of-mouth, and internet searches, nearly 40 organisations in four of the other Australian states have been stimulated to join the campaign. However, only one other state (Tasmania) has a state hub that funds a statewide campaign. Internationally, a London Osteopath centre is a partner and a group at Waseda University in Japan have adapted the campaign to target children affected by the 2011 Tsunami (Takenaka et al. 2012) (see Fig. 11.3; note that in Japanese the meaning of 'commit' is better translated in the word 'challenge'). Most recently, the National Institute for Public Health at the University of Southern Denmark has received funding from the Danish Ministry of Health to conduct a nationwide campaign in Denmark – the first international hub.

7 Comment on Campaign Success

The success of the *Act-Belong-Commit* campaign stems from a number of factors related to the fundamental principles of marketing. First, it was based on extensive formative research with members of the general population as well as key stakeholders in the mental health area. The resulting messages were designed to reinforce

Fig. 11.3 Japanese adaptation

and increase the salience of factors that most people intuitively believed (and the scientific evidence showed) were good for their mental health, but which they rarely thought about, particularly in a proactive, preventative manner. Second, the campaign not only targeted individuals to change their thinking and do something proactive for their mental health, but simultaneously targeted community organisations that provide opportunities for individuals to act on their intentions. These organisations were treated as 'franchises' and were offered and received considerable benefits for promoting the campaign message – not the least of which was that the campaign facilitated these organisations achieving their own goals. The campaign also permitted considerable autonomy and flexibility in the way the franchises delivered the campaign messages.

The original advertising communications positioned mental health in the same preventative context as physical health. This not only facilitated an increase in mental health literacy, but also decreased stigma and provided a positive context in which to talk more openly about mental health and mental illness. Finally, the campaign is marked by its use of mass communication strategies enabling broader campaign awareness and population-wide engagement (O'Hara et al. 2011), along with community development strategies to achieve targeted mental health promotion delivery at a local level.

The success of this campaign model is further evident in the number and types of organisations that have signed on since the state-wide expansion began in 2008. The campaign has attracted interest from community groups across a broad variety of institutions (e.g., schools, workplaces, hospitals, etc.), various areas of interest such as sport and recreation, hobbies, the arts, animal protection, walking groups, welfare, and so on, as well as state-wide non-health government departments and NGOs. These cover a diversity of demographic groups varying in ethnicity, gender, age, and socioeconomic status. These partnerships prompted the development of new initiatives and different modes of partnerships and campaign delivery tailored to specific target groups and settings. Furthermore, despite limited campaign support outside of the state of Western Australia, organisations in all but two states and territories in Australia have signed agreements with MHWA and the campaign is now spreading internationally.

8 Concluding Comment

The major role for mental health promotion is to strengthen the positive aspects of mental health at a population level. This not only increases resilience to mental health problems, but is a key element for community resilience, individual wellbeing, and quality of life via a flourishing, rather than languishing population (Keyes 2007).

The *Act-Belong-Commit* campaign is an effective model for mental health promotion on a population-based scale. The key features of the campaign are embodied in its clear consumer orientation and its community-based social franchising approach within an overall social marketing framework.

Acknowledgements The Mentally Healthy WA Act-Belong-Commit Campaign is funded by Healthway (the Western Australian Health Promotion Foundation) and the Mental Health Commission of Western Australia, and supported by WA Country Health Services, several Local Governments, and Curtin University.

References

Annor, S., & Allen, P. (2008). Why is it difficult to promote public mental health? A study of policy implementation at local level. *Journal of Public Mental Health, 7*(4), 17–29.

Anwar McHenry, J., & Donovan, R. J. (2013). The development of the Perth charter for the promotion of mental health and wellbeing. *International Journal of Mental Health Promotion*. doi:10.1080/14623730.2013.810402.

Anwar McHenry, J., Donovan, R. J., Jalleh, G., & Laws, A. (2012). Impact evaluation of the Act-Belong-Commit mental health promotion campaign. *Journal of Public Mental Health, 11*(4), 186–195.

Barnett, L., & Kendall, E. (2011). Culturally appropriate methods for enhancing the participation of Aboriginal Australians in health-promoting programs. *Health Promotion Journal of Australia, 22*, 27–32.

Barry, M. M., Domitrovich, C., & Lara, M. A. (2005). The implementation of mental health promotion programmes. *IUHPE: Promotion and Education* (Suppl 2), 30–35.

Beckmann, M., & Zeyen, A. (2014). Franchising as a strategy for combining small and large group advantages (logics) in social entrepreneurship: A Hayekian perspective. *Nonprofit and Voluntary Sector Quarterly, 43*, 502–522 (online).

Department of Health. (2012). *No health without mental health. Mental health strategy implementation framework.* London: Centre for Mental Health, Department of Health, Mind, NHS Confederation Mental Health Network, Rethink Mental Illness, Turning Point.

Donovan, R. J., & Anwar McHenry, J. (2014). Act-Belong-Commit: Lifestyle medicine for keeping mentally healthy. *American Journal of Lifestyle Medicine, 8*(1), 33–42.

Donovan, R. J., Watson, N., Henley, N., Williams, A., Silburn, S., Zubrick, S., James, R., Cross, D., Hamilton, G., & Roberts, C. (2003). *Mental health promotion scoping project.* Report to Healthway. Perth: Centre for Behavioural Research in Cancer Control, Curtin University.

Donovan, R. J., James, R., Jalleh, G., & Sidebottom, C. (2006). Implementing mental health promotion: The Act-Belong-Commit mentally healthy WA campaign in Western Australia. *International Journal of Mental Health Promotion, 8*(1), 33–42.

Donovan, R. J., Henley, N., Jalleh, G., Silburn, S. R., Zubrick, S. R., & Williams, A. (2007a). People's beliefs about factors contributing to mental health: Implications for mental health promotion. *Health Promotion Journal of Australia, 18*(1), 50–56.

Donovan, R. J., James, R., & Jalleh, G. (2007b). Community-based social marketing to promote positive mental health: The Act-Belong-Commit campaign in rural Western Australia. In G. Hastings (Ed.), *Social marketing: Why should the devil have all the best tunes?* (pp. 336–343). London: Butterworth Heinemann.

Friedli, L. (2009). *Mental health, resilience and inequalities.* Copenhagen: World Health Organisation.

Herrman, H., Saxena, S., & Moodie, R. (Eds.). (2005). *Promoting mental health: Concepts, emerging evidence, practice.* Geneva: World Health Organization.

Jalleh, G., Donovan, R. J., James, R., & Ambridge, J. (2007). Process evaluation of the Act-Belong-Commit mentally health WA campaign: First 12 months data. *Health Promotion Journal of Australia, 18*(3), 217–220.

Jalleh, G., Anwar McHenry, J., Donovan, R., & Laws, A. (2013). Impact on community organisations that partnered with the Act-Belong-Commit mental health promotion campaign. *Health Promotion Journal of Australia, 24*(1), 44–48.

Joiner, T. E. (2005). *Why people die by suicide.* Cambridge: Harvard University Press.

Keyes, C. L. M. (2007). Promoting and protecting mental health as flourishing: A complementary strategy for improving national mental health. *American Psychologist, 62*(2), 95–108.

Montagu, D. (2002). Franchising of health services in low-income countries. *Health Policy and Planning, 17*(2), 121–130.

O'Hara, B. J., Bauman, A. E., King, E. L., & Phongsavan, P. (2011). Process evaluation of the advertising campaign for the NSW Get Healthy Information and Coaching Service®. *Health Promotion Journal of Australia, 22*, 68–71.

Patterson, A. (2009). *Building the foundations for mental health and wellbeing: Review of Australian and international mental health promotion, prevention and early intervention policy.* Hobart: Department of Health and Human Services.

Quinn, N., & Biggs, H. (2010). Creating partnerships to improve community mental health and well-being in an area of high deprivation: Lessons from a study with high-rise flat residents in east Glasgow. *Journal of Public Mental Health, 9*(4), 16–21.

Richardson, K., & Turnbull, G. (2008). *Opposites attract: How social franchising can speed up the growth of social enterprise*. Surrey: INSPIRE Development Partnership.
Sandel, M. J. (2012). *What money can't buy: The moral limits of markets*. New York: Farrar, Straus, and Giroux.
Saxena, S., & Garrison, P. J. (2004). *Mental health promotion: Case studies from countries*. Geneva: World Health Organisation and World Federation for Mental Health.
Takenaka, K., Bao, H., Shimazaki, T., Lee, Y. H., & Konuma, K. (2012) Mental health promotion contributing to resilience for children after Tsunami disaster in Japan. Poster Presentation. In *The seventh world conference on the promotion of mental health and the prevention of mental and behavioural disorders*. Perth, pp. 5–6. http://www.papersearch.net/view/detail.asp?detail_key=20212446
Volvery, T., & Hackl, V. (2010). The promise of social franchising as a model to achieve social goals. In A. Fayolle & H. Matley (Eds.), *Handbook of research on social entrepreneurship*. Cheltenham: Edward Elgar.
WHO. (1986). *Ottawa charter for health promotion*. Geneva: WHO.

Chapter 12
Preparation Without Panic: A Comprehensive Social Marketing Approach to Planning for a Potential Pandemic

Sandra C. Jones, Don Iverson, Max Sutherland, Chris Puplick, Julian Gold, Louise Waters, and Lynda Berends

1 Introduction

1.1 Avian Influenza

The first outbreak of human disease from Avian influenza A (H_5N_1) was reported in 1997 in Hong Kong (Yuen et al. 1998). In late 2003 human cases began to be confirmed across Asia and Africa, and the virus increasingly captured the world's

S.C. Jones (✉) • L. Berends
Centre for Health and Social Research (CHaSR), Australian Catholic University, Melbourne, VIC, Australia
e-mail: Sandra.Jones@acu.edu.au; Lynda.Berends@acu.edu.au

D. Iverson
Faculty of Health, Arts and Design, Swinburne University of Technology, Hawthorn, VIC, Australia
e-mail: diverson@swin.edu.au

M. Sutherland
Independent Consultant, Melbourne, VIC, Australia
e-mail: max.sutherland@me.com

C. Puplick
ISSUS SOLUTIONS P/L, Sydney, NSW, Australia
e-mail: puplick@ozemail.com.au

J. Gold
The Albion Centre, Surry Hills, NSW, Australia
e-mail: Julian.Gold@sesiahs.health.nsw.gov.au

L. Waters
NSW Ministry of Health, Sydney, NSW, Australia
e-mail: lwate@doh.health.nsw.gov.au

W. Wymer (ed.), *Innovations in Social Marketing and Public Health Communication*, Applying Quality of Life Research,
DOI 10.1007/978-3-319-19869-9_12

attention – largely because influenza A is the only strain that has ever been shown to have the capacity to cause a pandemic (Sellwood et al. 2007).

H_5N_1 can be spread by migratory birds and mechanical means (e.g., from one farm to another on the soil captured by tractor tyres), it can be transmitted from birds to mammals (including pigs, seals, whales, mink, ferrets, tigers, leopards, stone marten and domestic cats), and it can be transmitted from birds to humans (Alexander 2000; Hien et al. 2004). However, in May 2006, the discovery of H_5N_1 infection within an extended family in north Sumatra presented the possibility of the first human-to-human transmission of the virus (Butler 2006).

With more incident reports of the virus infecting humans, H_5N_1 began to be categorised as a global public health threat. Concern about a possible pandemic was based on a number of factors. First, given the wide-ranging flight paths of migratory birds, the virus had the potential to be spread to domestic poultry in a number of countries. Second, there was concern that the H_5N_1 virus could mutate rapidly when it existed within a large contained domestic flock. Third, the close contact that occurs in many Asian countries between humans and domestic poultry provided numerous opportunities for the virus to infect humans through direct contact with infected poultry or surfaces that had been contaminated by infected birds. Fourth, the lack of a vaccine combined with the lack of natural immunity to H_5N_1 amongst the world's population created the opportunity for a pandemic to occur . Fifth, the avian influenza outbreak in north Sumatra raised significant concerns about whether countries were prepared to respond to an avian influenza outbreak and capable of doing so in a manner that results in the control of local outbreaks (Butler 2006).

1.2 A Challenge for Social Marketing?

While it is clear that the outcomes needed to address a potential bird flu pandemic can be achieved by effective social marketing (i.e., the outcomes involve voluntary behaviour change), the disease itself is fundamentally different to the majority of conditions to which social marketing has been applied. For example, Kotler's list of 50 major issues that social marketing can benefit includes 22 issues for improved health, 20 of which relate to chronic conditions such as tobacco use, physical inactivity, and dietary intake), but only two relate to communicable diseases and both of these have simple and proven preventive strategies (i.e., immunisation and the use of condoms) (Kotler et al. 2002). We argue, however, that social marketing is central to efforts to control a potential bird flu pandemic for the reasons noted below.

- *We are selling a behaviour*: The most effective tools currently available for reducing mortality and morbidity from a pandemic are basic hygiene and self-protection behaviours. In the case of bird flu an additional set of behaviours could relate to domestic poultry farmers and industries; in the event of an outbreak, there would need to be an immediate identification and culling of infected birds.
- *The behaviour change is voluntary*: The nature of these behaviours is such that the decision to engage, or not engage, in the behaviour is entirely voluntary.

While there are some measures that could require policy changes or legal sanctions (such as closure of schools or increased quarantine procedures), most of the effective measures currently available are those for which it would not be possible to impose, or apply, the force of law – such as hand washing and the use of disposable tissues.

- *The beneficiary is the individual, group, or society*: In the case of a bird flu pandemic, the beneficiaries of an individual's behaviour change include the individuals themselves (engaging in personal protection reduces their risk of contracting the disease), their families and social groups, and the population as a whole (by reducing potential sources of transmission).
- *Exchange with the consumer is essential*: In order to persuade individuals to engage in this voluntary behaviour change – particularly as many of the behaviours are effortful or are socially or psychologically challenging – we need to persuade consumers that the personal benefits of engaging in these behaviours exceed the perceived personal costs.
- *A consumer orientation is needed:* As with any social marketing program, the application of a consumer orientation is fundamental to the success of the behaviour change effort. In order to develop appropriate communication strategies, we need to fully understand the target audiences' knowledge, beliefs, attitudes, concerns and current behaviours. This can only be achieved by extensive and appropriate market research with the different target audiences.
- *There is a need to select and influence the target audience*: Market segmentation is a key component of effective social marketing, as we know that different market segments and different needs and will respond to different appeals. In the case of a potential pandemic such as bird flu, it is obviously important to target the entire population; however, some segments will be seen to be of higher priority (e.g., health care workers, international travellers, persons in low income housing units, domestic poultry farmers) and different strategies will need to be used to ensure we reach, and persuade, all groups within the population.
- *There is a need to incorporate all 4Ps of the marketing mix:* An effective strategy to engage the population in the appropriate responses to reduce the impact of a pandemic requires a careful consideration of the 4Ps. In brief:

  - Product – What we are "selling" is a set of behaviours that individuals can engage in to reduce their risk of contracting, and transmitting, bird flu;
  - Price – In order to persuade people to engage in these behaviours, we need to reduce the perceived personal costs of engaging in them (financial, social, psychological etc.) and increase the perceived benefits (increased protection from the disease);
  - Place – Given the need to provide information, services and products to the entire population, we need to use a range of channels to disseminate information and facilitate the behaviour change; and
  - Promotion – Given the potential for the disease to spread rapidly once it achieves effective human-to-human transmission, we need to develop effective messages and a clear and comprehensive plan for the media channels for their dissemination.

1.3 The 'Preparation Without Panic' Project

It was in this context that the research team was awarded funding from Australia's National Health and Medical Research Council to undertake a comprehensive study to inform government policy and practice in the event of an avian influenza pandemic – specifically how to prepare (but not panic) the general public.

The research phases included: a media analysis of coverage of a potential pandemic; extensive qualitative formative research; two population CATI surveys; two airport intercept surveys; message development; and message testing.

2 Phase 1: Analysis of News Media Coverage of a Potential Pandemic

This study used Protection Motivation Theory (PMT) components as a conceptual framework to explore how the Australian media portrayed the health risk of avian influenza by reviewing newspaper stories published during 2006.[1]

2.1 Method

All major Australian national and metropolitan daily broadsheet and tabloid newspapers available through Factiva.com were searched for the period 1 January 2006 to 31 December 2006. Documents were analysed using a coding framework developed from a variety of sources. The coding scheme by Washer (2004) was examined and literature on media analysis of other health issues was reviewed to assist in the construction of appropriate themes.

2.2 Results

A total of 850 articles were identified and analysed. The frequency of reporting was higher in the first 5 months, coinciding with reports of the first human cases in Turkey, Iraq, Egypt and Cambodia, new cases and fatalities in Indonesia and China, and the increasing incidence in animals across Europe and Africa.

Using a Protection Motivation Theory framework (Rogers 1975), the identified articles were examined for references to themes depicting (1) "vulnerability", or the likelihood of avian influenza occurring, (2) "severity" or seriousness of the avian influenza threat, and (3) adaptive response or actions taken to avoid infection.

[1] For full details of this study, contact the first author.

Vulnerability The focus was on reporting the incidence of both human and animal cases around the world. Coverage of scientific concerns on the potential for the virus to mutate (which is necessary for human-to-human transmission) accounted for 13 % of stories. Avian influenza was reported as a potential threat to Australia in 24 % of the articles.

Severity Over 50 % of the articles reported that avian influenza was "deadly", and 35 % mentioned an avian influenza pandemic.

Adaptive Responses Nearly 30 % of the articles addressed some sort of treatment or prevention, with 19 % specifically mentioning a drug or vaccine for human cases. The impact of avian influenza on the world or local economies was addressed in 14 % of articles, and methods of self-protection such as hand washing were mentioned in just over 10 % of articles.

2.3 Discussion

Avian influenza received considerable coverage in the Australian media in 2006. The intensity of media coverage reduced over time, both in terms of total print news coverage and the nature of the coverage. The potential impacts of this pattern of coverage are twofold. First, the use of high-fear language (such as "panic" and "death") had the potential to cause elevated levels of concern among members of the general public at a time when the risk to the Australian population was extremely low. Second, the initial emphasis on avian influenza followed by the apparent reduction in coverage had the potential to artificially reassure the general public that avian influenza no longer posed a threat to Australia. In both instances, the meaning people derived from the situation, a primary determinant of their quality of life (Skevington 2002) was likely to be at odds with the reality of the situation.

It is particularly concerning that there was limited media coverage that focused on protective or preventative issues. The media coverage of avian influenza provided numerous, ongoing opportunities for journalists and health writers to discuss, or even emphasise, the value of preventative behaviours such as hand washing, use of disposable tissues, and other hygiene practices known to reduce the likelihood of transmission of influenza and other infectious diseases. There was no discussion of actions that domestic poultry farmers or the poultry industry could take. Further, much of the media coverage stated, or at least implied, that Australia would be well prepared to handle a potential pandemic. Finally, a high proportion of articles suggested that appropriate treatments were currently available or would become available in time, thereby implying that Australia had the ability to ameliorate the effects of an avian pandemic. Thus, by inference, members of the general public may have felt that it was unnecessary for them to undertake simple preventative actions (such as increased hygiene) when a pharmacological treatment or a vaccine would be available to avert a pandemic.

3 Phase 2: Qualitative Formative Research with Consumers

The purpose of this research phase was to gather preliminary information on the Australian public's knowledge of, and concerns about, avian influenza (H5N1); with the primary aim being to inform the development of future communication strategies.[2]

3.1 Method

Four focus groups were conducted in April 2006 (total n = 32), and eight in July 2006 (total n = 64). The groups were conducted by two commercial research companies, using a discussion guide developed in consultation with the research team, with specific inclusion criteria and quotas to ensure representation of participants from a range of potential at-risk groups.

3.2 Results

Key themes arising from the focus groups were that bird flu[3] is a disease associated with poor people in Asian countries, that Australians are 'safe' from such outbreaks, and that the disease could be 'caught' rather than spread. Even when *forced* to think of bird flu, by virtue of direct questioning by the focus group moderator, this still was not seen as an issue of concern for Australia. Importantly, it was not simply that Australia was far from mind when thinking of bird flu, but that participants also saw Australia as a haven protected from bird flu.

Emotionally, participants expressed a strong belief that bird flu was merely media scare mongering. Participants' past experiences with similar scares (especially SARS) had given them a perception that the media exaggerates potential health scares *("It's another example of media hype over scares that never eventuate here. Its just like SARS, the Y2K bug...")*. This view was supported by participants' perceptions that the media coverage had died down *("More concerned a year ago, but now hear less about it")*, reflecting that this was just another media "beat-up" and that the unnecessary overreaction of the media was dying down.

It is important to note that the participants described bird flu as a disease that can be *caught*, rather than a disease that can be *spread*. The general consensus in the

---

[2] For full details of this study: Jones, S. C., Iverson, D., & Waters, L. (2010). "Just don't eat chicken": The challenge of engaging Australian adults in appropriate preventive behaviours for bird flu. *International Journal of Nonprofit & Voluntary Sector Marketing, 15*(1), 78–90.

[3] Note that the focus group participants used the term 'bird flu' and rejected 'avian influenza' as a term that sounded too scientific and not consistent with their perceptions and conversations about the topic (thus the term 'bird flu' is used throughout the results and discussion).

April focus groups was that bird flu is transmitted directly from bird to human (i.e., by physical contact) and the single most common belief as to how one catches bird flu directly related to the consumption of a diseased bird. Of interest is the finding that many believed that this mode of infection could be prevented by thorough cooking of the infected bird.

In the second round of focus groups (July), there was an increase in the use of words such as 'contagious' and 'epidemic', suggesting an increased awareness of the fact that the disease could be caught – possibly associated with media coverage of human-to-human transmission in Indonesia – although the perception that it was a problem 'over there' remained strong across all groups.

The participants had difficulty engaging in a discussion of what could be done to help prevent the spread of bird flu. A hypothetical scenario had to be introduced to engage the participants in the concept of bird flu *in Australia*, and thereby contextualise the question of what could be done. The responses, however, still highlighted the fact that this was considered a far-fetched scenario with preventative measures almost exclusively focused on travel restrictions and border control and quarantine protection (and not eating chicken). No spontaneous mention was made of mask wearing or bunkering down – the key solution was to restrict the consumption of chicken and eggs.

Participants expressed confidence in the Government and "people in the know" to let them know "when they should panic", which means that they can relax until they are informed otherwise. However, the process of the research – which for many involved processing bird flu issues for the first time – raised areas of confusion and areas of information they would want addressed in the advent of bird flu in Australia. These included: "*How is it spread,*" "*Access to vaccines,*" "*What are steps we should take,*" "*Mortality rate if get bird flu,*" and "*Symptoms – what to look for*".

3.3 Discussion

Contrary to our expectation that the media coverage may have resulted in a high degree of concern among the general public about a potential bird flu pandemic, it was evident that the participants had very little knowledge of, or interest in, bird flu. They required considerable prompting to enter into a discussion of bird flu, and few of them spontaneously mentioned it when thinking of diseases that they were concerned about.

The differentiation between *caught* and *spread* is an important one, as it highlights the lack of urgency or panic associated with bird flu. If bird flu is *caught*, then it can be prevented by avoiding direct contact with the contagion. In contrast, to have a disease *spread*, suggests mass contamination, indiscriminately affecting large numbers of people. It was also clear from the focus groups that many participants perceived bird flu to be "yet another" media beat-up, rather than a genuine health risk. The perceived reduction in media coverage over the last few months of 2006 supported the belief that this was just another example of the media exaggerating a disease risk.

4 Phase 3: CATI Survey of Australian Adults (May 2006)

The purpose of this research phase was to determine the Australian public's knowledge of avian influenza, their willingness to engage in preventive behaviours, and their acceptance of potential messages and spokespeople for communication campaigns in the event of a bird flu pandemic.[4]

4.1 Method

A computer-assisted telephone survey (CATI) was conducted between 16th and 20th May 2006. The sampling frame was the Desktop Marketing System (DTMS), which is a form of the electronic White Pages. Of the 2816 telephone numbers called, 1185 eligible households[5] were identified and 203 interviews were completed with persons from the eligible households (response rate of 17.1 %). The interview length averaged 11.27 min.

4.2 Results

Of the 203 respondents 51.7 % (105) were female, and 75.9 % were born in Australia. Respondents were spread across all age groups, with 12.4 % aged between 18 and 34 years; 19.7 % aged 35–44 years; 19.2 % aged 45–54 years; 24.6 % aged 55–64 years; and 23.6 % aged over 65 years.

Respondents were first asked a general open-ended question about infectious diseases: "Living in Australia in 2006, what *infectious* diseases come to mind?" The most commonly first-mentioned (i.e., top of mind) diseases were HIV/AIDS (22.2 %), influenza/flu (18.2 %) and avian/bird flu (14.3 %). Respondents were asked which disease was of *greatest* concern to them. Not surprisingly, this list was similar; the diseases of greatest concern to respondents were HIV/AIDS (18 %) and influenza/flu (15 %).

Respondents were then asked a series of specific questions about bird flu. Over half the respondents stated that it was either very likely (21.7 %) or somewhat likely (37.4 %) that bird flu would spread from human to human; although there was a far lower level of agreement that this would be the case in Australia. Importantly, less than one quarter of respondents were very concerned (10.8 %) or somewhat concerned (12.8 %) that they themselves or someone in their immediate family might catch bird flu.

[4]For full details of this study: Jones, S. C., & Iverson, D. (2008). What Australians know and believe about bird flu: Results of a population telephone survey. *Health Promotion Practice, 9*(4 Supplement), 73S–82S.

[5]That is, they were active telephone numbers of residential addresses.

Respondents were fairly evenly divided in their level of confidence in the Federal government's ability to handle an outbreak of bird flu. However, the majority were in favour of the government quarantining persons who had been exposed to bird flu (96.1 %), closing the borders to visitors from countries with outbreaks (81.8 %), and encouraging people to work from home when possible (74.9 %). There was less support for the closing of schools (65.5 %) or offering people experimental vaccines or drugs (54.2 %).

The actions respondents were themselves most willing to take were increasing their hand washing (83.3 %) and cleaning items they share with other people (71.4 %). There were, however, several actions that a large proportion of the respondents stated they would not be prepared to take – including avoiding physical contact with people (50.7 %), purchasing face masks (39.9 %), asking their doctor for a prescription for a flu vaccine or antiviral drugs (34.0 %), making plans to keep their children at home from school (32.0 %), and cleaning items they share with other people (26.1 %).

There was a marked increase in the respondents' willingness to engage in these protective behaviors in the event that the Federal government issued a warning that there was an increased risk of bird flu. However, there were some actions which a significant minority stated they would still not engage in, including avoiding physical contact with people (27.1 %) and asking their doctor for flu vaccines or antiviral drugs (17.2 %). Surprisingly, 10.8 % of respondents indicated they would not keep their children at home from school even if advised to do so by the Federal government.

4.3 *Discussion*

Awareness and concern about bird flu as an infectious disease was low with only 20 % of respondents spontaneously identifying it in an open ended question (14 % as the top-of-mind disease), and only 11 % identifying it as being an infectious disease of great concern to them. This is noticeably lower than the 62 % of US residents who indicated in January 2006 that they were concerned about the possibility of a bird flu pandemic (Blendon et al. 2006). While over half of Australians believed that bird flu would spread from human to human, only a quarter believed this would occur in Australia.

In both Australia and the US there appeared to be widespread support for bird flu control measures initiated by the Federal government. The Australian public was willing to take preventive measures if they were advised to do so by the government. The level of support for control measures in the event of an anticipated bird flu outbreak is generally consistent with the actual support reported by Hong Kong residents for complying with the recommended SARS-related precautionary measures (Leung et al. 2003). However, in that survey less than half the respondents reported actually practicing five of the seven recommended precautionary measures. If the Australian public complied with only those Commonwealth-recommended actions with which they agreed, the ability to control an actual bird flu outbreak would likely be significantly compromised.

5 Phase 4: CATI 2 (September 2006)

This phase of the study was designed to (a) collect data from a larger sample than the previous CATI; and (b) to determine whether there had been any changes in the Australian public's knowledge, beliefs, attitudes, or willingness to engage in preventive behaviours since the initial survey was conducted in May 2006.[6]

5.1 *Method*

A computer-assisted telephone survey (CATI) was conducted 28th August and 14th September 2006. The sampling frame was again the Desktop Marketing System (DTMS). Of the 9,159 telephone numbers called, 5,565 eligible households were identified and 805 interviews were completed with persons from the eligible households (response rate of 14.5 %). The interview length averaged 12.36 min.

5.2 *Results*

Of the 805 respondents 55.0 % (443) were female, and 78.8 % were born in Australia. Respondents were again spread across all age groups, with 18.5 % aged between 18 and 34 years; 17.5 % aged 35–44 years; 23.3 % aged 45–54 years; 18.9 % aged 55–64 years; and 21.5 % aged 65 years and over.

The three most commonly mentioned top-of-mind diseases were HIV/AIDS (23.4 %), meningococcal disease (10.6 %), and influenza/flu (10.4 %). Importantly, bird flu fell from the third to fifth most-frequently mentioned disease (including first and subsequent mentions), with only 10.8 % of respondents spontaneously mentioning bird flu, compared to 20.3 % in survey one.

Consistent with this, the disease of greatest concern was meningococcal disease (14.8 %), compared to only 4.4 % in survey one. Among the other most concerning diseases were HIV/AIDS and influenza/flu. The drop in spontaneous mentions of bird flu was reflected in a drop in the proportion of respondents identifying this is the disease of most concern (from 10.8 % to 5.6 % in survey two).

[6]For full details of this study: Jones, S. C., Iverson, D., Waters, L., Sutherland, M., Gold, J., & Puplick, C. (2012). How quickly did bird flu go off the public radar? Results of a follow-up CATI survey of Australian adults. In K. M. Taylor & B. O'Connor (Eds.), *Avian Influenza: Molecular Evolution, Outbreaks and Prevention/Control*. Nova Publishers.

Just over one quarter (27.3 %) of respondents agreed that bird flu *had ever* been spread[7] from human to human. Less than quarter of respondents believed that this would occur in Australia, or reported that they were very concerned or somewhat concerned that they or a member of their family may catch bird flu (there was a sizeable increase in the proportion reporting that they are not at all concerned between survey one and survey two).

As with the previous survey, the majority of respondents were in favour of the government quarantining those who had been exposed to bird flu, closing the borders to visitors from countries where people have bird flu, and requiring people to work from home when possible. They were less in favour of the government closing schools and offering people experimental vaccines or drugs although the proportion in favour had increased considerably since survey one.

When asked what actions they thought would be *their* highest priority to protect themselves and their families if we had bird flu in Australia, the most commonly mentioned actions were to enquire about or have a vaccine, avoid people or places who might be infected, and to isolate or quarantine themselves (although even these were mentioned by less than one quarter of respondents). An even smaller proportion of respondents spontaneously mentioned the actions which are actually most likely to reduce the spread of bird flu; washing hands more frequently (3.5 %), wearing face masks (5.5 %), and using disposable tissues rather than handkerchiefs (none).

5.3 *Discussion*

The first, and perhaps most important, finding from this second CATI survey was that – only 4 months later – bird flu was increasingly "off the radar" for the majority of the Australian population. The findings in relation to meningococcal disease were surprising, and add considerable support to the often-stated view that the media serves an agenda setting function in relation to health and medical issues. All mentions of meningococcal disease increased from 5.9 % in May to 19.9 % in September; top of mind mentions increased from 4.9 % to 10.6 %; and mentions of meningococcal disease as the disease of most concern increased from 4.4 % to 14.8 % (surpassing even HIV/AIDS). A retrospective search of Australian and New Zealand newsprint coverage for the periods 01 April to 31 May and 01 August to 30 September 2006 found that in the former period there were 68 articles relating to meningococcal disease and in the latter period 238. It is reasonable to assume that the increase in awareness and concern for meningococcal disease was a result of this high level of media coverage of the condition.

A second important finding was that the general public appeared willing to engage in the appropriate preventive and protective behaviours, but were lacking

[7] Note that in the previous survey we asked whether they believed it would ever spread human-to-human, but by the time of survey two human-to-human transmission had been confirmed.

awareness of what these behaviours are. That is, respondents' spontaneous mentions of high priority actions to protect themselves and their families were vaccination (although there was at the time no vaccine available for bird flu) and avoiding infected others and quarantining themselves. Only a very small proportion of respondents spontaneously mentioned hand washing or wearing face masks, and none mentioned use of disposable tissues. However, when asked about their willingness to engage in these behaviours were they advised to do so, almost 90 % responded that they would be willing to engage in more frequent hand washing and change to the exclusive use of disposable tissues, and almost 70 % that they would be willing to wear face masks.

6 Phase 5: Airport Intercept Surveys (Oct–Nov 2006)

The purpose of this phase was to determine the likely and preferred sources of information about bird flu among residents and visitors in the event of an outbreak or pandemic within the country of destination.[8]

6.1 *Method*

Two airport intercept surveys were conducted in late 2006. The target group was business & economy travellers across six major airlines, departing for Asia and Europe from Sydney International Airport. The first survey was conducted on the weekend of 28th and 29th October 2006, and the second on the weekend of 25th and 26th November 2006.

6.2 *Results*

A total of 310 departing travellers completed the survey. Half (50.3 %) were female and 61.3 % were born in Australia. The age distribution was: 14.5 % aged between 18 and 24 years; 22.6 % aged 25–34 years; 20.6 % aged 35–44 years; 19.1 % aged 45–54 years; 17.1 % aged 55–64 years; and 6.1 % aged 65 years and over.

Respondents were asked "where would you go for information about bird flu?" The overwhelming majority said they would seek information from the Internet (40.3 %); this response was given by almost four times as many respondents as any

[8] For full details of this study: Waters, L., Jones, S. C. (2007). Where would Australian travellers seek information about bird flu? Results of two airport intercept surveys. Proceedings of the Australian and New Zealand Marketing Academy (ANZMAC) Conference, 2976–2982.

other source of information. This was followed by doctors/GPs (11.3 %), the Department of Health (7.4 %), and 'the government' (non-specific) and Department of Foreign Affairs and Trade (DFAT) (both 6.1 %).

In regards to seeking information from doctors/GPs, there were no significant differences associated with respondent gender, age or education. However, in regards to seeking information from the internet, this was more common among male respondents, those aged 18–44, and those with a university education.

6.3 Discussion

The respondents' preferred and likely sources of information have serious implications for communication strategies in the event of a bird flu outbreak. The electronic revolution provides new opportunities and challenges for effective transfer of health information (Freimuth et al. 2000), and the internet in particular poses significant challenges to risk communication efforts. The internet as an entity contains an enormous body of information about health issues, for example at the time of the survey 7,020,000 results were found when 'bird flu' was typed into the search engine *Google*. However, many websites are of questionable credibility and quality, and many sites are not easily accessible or understood (Cline and Haynes 2001; Benigeri and Pluye 2003; Dolan et al. 2004). Thus, it would be easy for the public to unknowingly source incorrect, misleading or confusing information, which they could then pass on to other members of the public. This information could then lead the public to respond to health issues in a way that is not conducive to management of the health issue, in this case a bird flu pandemic. In other words, their quality of life could be compromised by misperceptions regarding the level of risk involved and the appropriateness and effectiveness of strategies for prevention; with negative health consequences.

7 Phase 6: Message Testing

The qualitative and quantitative studies (phases one through five) consistently found that people were generally unconcerned about bird flu and did not see the problem as an issue for Australia.[9] Thus, this research phase was undertaken to pre-test, modify, and re-test the 'ready-to-use' campaign materials for a pandemic preparedness campaign.

[9] For full details of this study: Jones, S. C., Waters, L., Holland, O., Bevins, J., & Iverson, D. (2010). Developing pandemic communication strategies: Preparation without panic. *Journal of Business Research, 63*, 126–132.

7.1 Method

A leading Australian advertising agency was contracted to prepare campaign concepts for testing. The agency undertook the campaign development as two independent teams, each developing an alternative approach. This dual approach resulted in two very different campaigns for testing: a presenter approach (Spokes People), and a non-presenter approach (Paper People). Each campaign consisted of two phases: Phase 1 for pre-pandemic communications, and Phase 2 for communications in the event of detection of bird flu cases in Australia.

The advertising concepts (story boards and print ads) were first tested in a series of eight focus groups (July 2006), four in Victoria and four in New South Wales. Four distinct groups were purposively recruited: Young Adults/Travelers; Mothers with children aged 0–16 years; Adults Aged 50+; and Regional Community.

The results were used to make modifications to the campaign materials, and develop one coherent campaign to address both pandemic phases. The modified materials were then tested in a second series of focus groups (October 2006) in the same two states, with the same four distinct consumer segments.

7.2 Results

The 'Paper People' concept used cut-out paper people (which most people would remember making as children) as its visual theme, providing a very flexible and immediately recognizable vehicle for the campaign. It was intended to communicate that a virus is transmitted most easily when people are all together; thus our closeness is what makes us vulnerable; and that individuals and organizations need to work together to minimize the potential dangers of bird flu. Further, the paper people concept was seen as a way to represent *all* people in Australia. The Paper People concept tested as effective in Phase 1, with this more gentle approach inherently less likely to raise anxieties and more likely to increase confidence that the government was on top of the problem and knew what to do. However, when used in Phase 2, the concept didn't seem to reflect the (newly perceived) gravity of the situation.

The Spokes People campaign utilized a team of trusted medical/scientific professionals, each eminently qualified to speak to a specific phase of any pandemic – impending, happening or ending. The agency designed the campaign to be flexible and to balance empathy with gravitas; the campaign used a team approach to reduce reliance on any one spokesperson, an important consideration in a pandemic crisis. The Spokes People concept when used in Phase 1 tended to raise anxieties, to the extent that it appeared it may even produce panic in-and-of-itself so was clearly too heavy for the awareness-raising phase. Conversely, when used in Phase 2 the Spokes People concept increased confidence that we're on top of the problem and are able to deal with it. The concept was credible and the inclusion of a human face was well received and perceived as treating people as intelligent.

Other key factors that were incorporated into the strategic thinking behind the modification of the ad concepts and development of the final ads for testing were that bird flu was not really on the public radar; and that the three actions which are actually most likely to reduce the spread of bird flu hardly gained entry onto the population's *high priority actions* unprompted, but once reminded of them, they generally embraced each action as do-able.

The Phase One *Paper People* was an effective communication device as it symbolized the everyman, emphasised connection and co-operation, and was a simple visual device that everyone could understand. Similarly, the use of the colour red to indicate germs was an immediately noticed and easily understood device. The Wash, Wipe, Wear[10] message was simple, easily remembered, and was often played back by focus group participants. The suggested actions were accepted as appropriate behaviour in the event of a pandemic (although a misunderstanding existed around the hand washing concept and some participants baulked at the idea of wearing a face mask). The revised Phase One was much more effective than the initial execution. The campaign still resulted in people taking the issue more seriously and becoming considerably more anxious about the threat. However, the big difference from the testing of the original concept was that people now asked fewer questions, and were left feeling personally less scared and more prepared and more confident about the government's response.

The revisions to the Phase Two Spokes People campaign eliminated the criticisms raised in the initial concept testing. Participants still felt scared but did not raise questions this time about the futility of the required actions; participants were much more accepting of the '*wash, wipe, wear*' message now that the message had been explained and communicated in Phase One. The transition from Paper People in Phase One to the use of the real people and a more serious tone in Phase Two worked well and was perceived as consistent by participants – that is, a different messenger but the same message. Participants reported that having a real person at this stage was very reassuring, and made them feel that someone was taking charge. Both the Chief Medical Officer (CMO) role and the man himself had credibility and gravitas and his measured, calm tone was perceived as reassuring; the inclusion of Fiona Stanley (an eminent Australian epidemiologist and physician) was endorsed as demonstrating to the public that a team is in place and working on the problem. The accompanying print ads were seen to be very clear, informative, and easy to read.

7.3 Discussion

Inoculation theory (Anderson and McGuire 1965; McGuire 1970) suggests that if people are given the worst-case scenario when only a hypothetical risk of catastrophe exists, they will process the risk less dangerously, come to terms with it, and be

[10] Wash (your hands), Wipe (your nose with a disposable tissue), Wear (a face mask).

less likely to panic should a pandemic occur, than if they were to remain in an uninformed state. That is, to learn what a bird flu pandemic really is going to do at the same time as you learn that a pandemic has begun, would seem most conducive to eliciting a panic response.

This phase of the research suggested that in the early stages of a pandemic (i.e., prior to the identification of cases within a given country), communications should focus on increasing awareness of the disease and communicating important, but simple, protective behaviours to reduce the risk of transmission. Such a Phase I Campaign would be strategically important – both in addressing the public's current level of complacency and in enabling the government to be seen to have acted – but a need exists to clearly communicate both the wash message and the need to take preventative actions *prior* to the confirmation of cases in local population. In later stages of a pandemic (i.e., where cases have been confirmed within a country or a region), communication campaigns need to effectively communicate the key messages for each stage of pandemic and motivate the public to engage in the correct preventive actions without creating unnecessary panic in the community. As such, these measures shift across both preventative and tertiary paradigms. They support a positive (and well-informed) perception of quality of life (Skevington 2002), by strengthening people's confidence and capacity for action to reduce the risk of infection. Similarly, support for broader mechanisms that enable personal and social well-being, such as financial security, supportive relationships, and reduced discrimination maintain the potential for a healthy quality of life to be maintained at community level when the risk of infection is high and compounded by other challenges such as HIV/AIDS (Basavaraj et al. 2010; Horwood et al. 2015).

8 Conclusions and Recommendations

The findings from the media analysis study suggested that media coverage regarding avian influenza had likely raised the 'fear' level amongst the Australian public, while providing them with little or no information about what to do in the event of an avian influenza outbreak. Thus, in the event of a potential pandemic, a national communication strategy needs to be developed in advance of an outbreak, including the development and pre-testing of specific media messages. If this isn't done, the most likely responses in the event of an outbreak will be fear and panic, both of which undermine public health efforts to control the outbreak.

The findings from the two CATI and two airport surveys suggest the Australian government and relevant NOGs and professional organisations would encounter a number of significant communication challenges in the event of a bird flu outbreak. First, the public must be aware of bird flu, have a reasonable understanding of its seriousness and perceive that they and their family are susceptible. Second, the government must have clearly identified control measures that the public can take prior to and during a bird flu outbreak, and have a strategy for communicating these measures in an effective manner to the public. Third, the government will need to convince persons that they need to comply with all of the recommended control measures, not just those that they personally believe are important. Fourth, the government must have an effective communication strategy directed at medical personnel who are likely to encounter persons concerned about bird flu. This is important as in the SARS outbreak medical personnel were found to have critical gaps in their knowledge (Deng et al. 2006). Fifth, the communication strategy should try to create a sense of social responsibility and empathy amongst the population as this may increase the likelihood that they will comply with all the recommended control measures (Nickell et al. 2004) and support others facing multiple challenges. Sixth, the government must carefully select the persons and/or organizations that will have responsibility for being the 'public face' of any media campaign. Our results indicate medical personnel and medical organizations are likely to be perceived by the public as being the most credible sources for delivering bird flu messages. And, finally, there should be at least two components of any communication strategy – one that prepares persons in the event of a bird flu outbreak, and one that directs persons to take specific actions during the actual outbreak.

On this latter point it is encouraging to note that when the public actually encounters an infectious disease outbreak they are much more likely comply with recommended control measures (Blendon et al. 2004). However, it is equally important that this awareness-raising does not happen too far in advance of cases occurring in Australia as our results suggest that communicating risk in advance of its emergence, at least via the mass media, results in the public discounting the reality of the risk.

In relation to specific communication channels, we recommend that in the event of a potential pandemic, the government develops a comprehensive, credible and useful website about bird flu (given the frequency with which the Internet was mentioned as a source of information, especially by travellers). This site would need to be promoted widely to ensure reach to all national and international travellers, and to maximise the likelihood that people will access the site without effort. Ideally the public would not have to know what the site is and/or have to search for the site; it would be designed so that the site surfaces when "bird flu" is typed into a search engine. One such way of ensuring this is for the government to purchase those keywords relating to bird flu in each of the major search engines (such as Google, Yahoo, MSN) to ensure this website is at the top of any list of retrieved sites.

8.1 *Implications for Social Marketing*

Potential pandemics pose a major challenge for global social marketing. In the event that a pandemic does occur, social marketers throughout the world (along with governments, health services, and businesses) will face a task on a scale which has not previously been experienced – in terms of both the potential for widespread mortality and the speed with which high-quality comprehensive social marketing campaigns will need to be mounted. This would perhaps provide the ultimate test of the efficacy of social marketing as a tool for bringing about behaviour change for the benefit of the individual, group and society. Additionally, in the case of a pandemic, a need exists to go beyond education/marketing. Social marketing or educational interventions are unlikely to work in isolation (see Rothschild 1999), and will need to be combined with policy and legislative actions such as closures of schools and workplaces and restrictions on air travel. However, such marketing campaigns will be an essential *first step* in raising awareness and knowledge.

Developers of social marketing campaigns will face a number of challenges, including: the need to raise awareness and concern about a bird flu outbreak to a level that motivates consumers to respond but not to a level that causes public panic; the need to ensure that control measures are clearly identified to the public prior to and during a bird flu outbreak, and that a strategy exists for communicating these measures in an effective manner to the public; and the need to convince persons that they need to comply with all of the recommended control measures, not just those that they personally feel are important. Further, they will need to have an associated strategy for their social marketing campaigns' targeting intermediaries – such as general practitioners and other medical personnel, schools, business owners, and commercial and public organisations which could be utilised to disseminate information and resources. In this way, both individual and community perceptions regarding a healthy quality of life are likely to be supported even when the risks of infection are considerable.

Perhaps the most significant challenge for social marketing is apathy – both from consumers and from those who could potentially communicate with them. At the time the study was conducted, a general consensus existed within the scientific community that a bird flu pandemic would occur. The estimates regarding how widespread or virulent the pandemic would be varied significantly but even the most conservative estimates involved millions of deaths. In future cases of potential pandemics, given such uncertainties, social marketers (like consumers) may be tempted to take a wait and see approach, reasoning that no one should not waste financial and academic resources on researching and developing campaigns for a problem that may not eventuate. Taking such an approach is socially irresponsible given the consequences of an actual outbreak – presumptive planning and action is the only socially responsible approach.

8.2 Fast Forward to October 2014

In March 2014 the first cases of Ebola were reported in West Africa. The Ebola virus initially involves transmission of the virus from animals to humans via human contact with animal body fluids; once in the human population Ebola spreads from human-to-human through direct contact with the bodily fluids of infected persons or via materials (e.g., clothing) or surfaces (e.g., bathroom counters) on which the bodily fluids are present. While the average case fatality rate is estimated at 50 % it can be much higher (i.e., >80 %) (WHO Ebola virus disease Fact sheet; updated

September 2014). As of October 12, 2014 more than 4490 deaths have been attributed to Ebola in West Africa, with the largest number of cases occurring in Liberia.

When the outbreak was first reported there was little sense of concern, and certainly not panic, in Western countries as the epidemic was in a specific area of Africa. The WHO raised concerns early but these concerns did not appear to capture the attention of the international press or Western leaders. That all changed when Nina Pham, a nurse at a large Dallas, Texas hospital was diagnosed with an Ebola infection in October 2014 after treating a patient who died of Ebola on October 8. Within a week a second nurse who was involved in treating the patient became infected. Panic and blame attribution quickly occurred in the US.

A story in the Wall Street Journal (Armour and Hughes 2014) included a quote from US Representative Fred Upton from Michigan at a Congressional Hearing: "We need to protect the American people, first and foremost. People's lives are at stake, and the response so far has been unacceptable". The hospital in which the Ebola patient was treated admitted making mistakes and issued a public apology; the Director of the US Centres for Disease Control and Prevention (CDC) indicated that infection control protocol was broken in managing the patient but which aspects of the protocol were broken has not been determined. The second nurse who was infected travelled on a plane to Cleveland, Ohio and the passengers on the plane are being tracked down to determine their health status and who they came in contact with. Two schools in Cleveland were closed down because one of the teachers was on the plane with the infected nurse. The reactive nature of this 'intervention' on the risk for Ebola transmission illustrates the potential for the general community's quality of life to be considerably undermined. The information is unplanned, inadequately monitored, and lack's messages that enhance the community's capacity to respond to the actual risk for infection.

Ebola cases have been confirmed in France and Spain, while a suspected case in Denmark was not confirmed, The international media's attention is now on the Ebola situation but the stories and editorials imply that there is no plan in place that can control an Ebola outbreak should it occur. For example, an editorial in the New York Times (Osterholm 2014) stated that "What is not getting said publicly, despite briefings and discussions in the inner circles of the world's public health agencies, is that we are in totally unchartered waters and that Mother Nature is the only force in charge of the crisis at this time". He goes on to state that "If we wait for vaccines and new drugs to arrive to end the Ebola epidemic, instead of taking major action now, we risk the disease's reaching from West Africa to our own backyards". This editorial was written a few weeks before the first Ebola case occurred in the US.

The insights gained from our research with the bird flu situation clearly apply to the 2014 Ebola situation. There is no discernible plan to increase awareness amongst the target populations – in this case the general public, and front-line public health and health care workers. There appears to be little confidence in statements made by government, hospital and public health officials that 'an outbreak can be contained'. As of this date there is no social marketing initiative in the US and most certainly there is not one in Australia. The general response seems to be 'don't worry, we have a world class health care system that can manage an outbreak'. It appears to us that the lessons we learned from studying the bird flu pandemic have not been applied in the current Ebola situation.

The lesson is clear – countries have to anticipate problems (the Ebola outbreak could have been anticipated given the extent of international travel alone), and be prepared by having a comprehensive public health education program, based on social marketing principles, ready to be implemented prior to the outbreak landing on a country's soil. A social marketing initiative combined with effective public health and health care control measures will have the greatest likelihood of reducing panic, maintaining a healthy quality of life, and resulting in the best possible outcome.

Acknowledgements This research was funded by an Urgent Research Grant from the National Health and Medical Research Council.

References

Alexander, D. J. (2000). A review of avian influenza in different bird species. *Veterinary Microbiology, 74*(1–2), 3–13.

Anderson, L. R., & McGuire, W. J. (1965). Prior reassurance of group consensus as a factor in producing resistance to persuasion. *Sociometry, 28*(1), 44–56.

Armour, S., & Hughes, S. (2014). U.S. Ebola Response Called 'Unacceptable' Amid Growing Fears. *Wall Street Journal.*

Basavaraj, K. H., Navya, M. A., & Rashmi, R. (2010). Quality of life in HIV/AIDS. *Indian Journal of Sexually Transmitted Disease, 31*, 75–80.

Benigeri, M., & Pluye, P. (2003). Shortcomings of health information on the internet. *Health Promotion International, 18*(4), 381–386.

Blendon, R. J., Benson, J. M., DesRoches, C. M., Raleigh, E., & Taylor-Clark, K. T. (2004). The public's response to severe acute respiratory syndrome in Toronto and the United States. *Clinical Infectious Diseases, 38*, 925–931.

Blendon, R. J., Benson, J. M., Fleischfresser, C., Weldon, K. J., & Herrmann, M. J. (2006). Avian flu survey; 17–25 Jan 2006. from http://www.hsph.harvard.edu/disasters/articles/Loree-Blendon.pdf

Butler, D. (2006). Pandemic 'dry run' is cause for concern. *Nature, 441*(7093), 554–555.

Cline, R. J. W., & Haynes, K. M. (2001). Consumer health information seeking on the internet: The state of the art. *Health Education Research, 16*(6), 671–692.

Deng, J.-F., Olowokure, B., Kaydos-Daniels, S. C., Chang, H. J., Barwick, R. S., & Lee, M. L. (2006). Severe acute respiratory syndrome (SARS): Knowledge, attitudes, practices and sources of information among physicians answering a SARS fever hotline service. *Public Health, 120*, 15–19.

Dolan, G., Iredale, R., Williams, R., & Ameen, J. (2004). Consumer use of the internet for health information: A survey of primary care patients. *International Journal of Consumer Studies, 28*(2), 147–153.

Freimuth, V., Linnan, H. W., & Potter, P. (2000). Communicating the threat of emerging infections to the public. *Emerging Infectious Diseases, 6*(4), 337–347.

Hien, T. T., de Jong, M., & Farrar, J. (2004). Avian influenza: A challenge to global health care structures. *New England Journal of Medicine, 351*(23), 2363–2365.

Horwood, C. M., Youngleson, M. S., Moses, E., Stern, A., & Barker, P. (2015). Using adapted quality-improvement approaches to strengthen community-based health systems and improve care in high HIV-burden sub-Saharan African countries. *AIDS, 29*, S155–S164. doi:10.1097/QAD.0000000000000716.

Kotler, P., Roberto, N., & Lee, N. (2002). *Social marketing: Improving the quality of life* (2nd ed.). Thousand Oaks: Sage.

Leung, G. M., Lam, T. H., Ho, L. M., Ho, S. Y., Chan, B. H., Wong, I. O., & Hedley, A. J. (2003). The impact of community psychological responses on outbreak control for severe acute respiratory syndrome in Hong Kong. *Journal of Epidemiology and Community Health, 57*, 857–863.

McGuire, W. J. (1970). A vaccine for brainwash. *Psychology Today, 3*(9), 36–39.

Nickell, L. A., Crighton, E. J., Tracy, C. S., Al-Enazy, H., Bolaju, Y., Hanjrah, S., Hussain, A., Makhlouf, S., & Upshur, R. E. (2004). Psychosocial effects of SARS on hospital staff: Survey of a large tertiary care institution. *Canadian Medical Association Journal, 170*(5), 793–798.

Osterholm, M. (2014). What we're afraid to say about Ebola. *New York Times*.

Rogers, R. W. (1975). A protection motivation theory of fear appeals and attitude change. *Journal of Psychology, 91*(1), 93–114.

Rothschild, M. L. (1999). Carrots, sticks, and promises: A conceptual framework for the management of public health and social issue behaviors. *Journal of Marketing, 63*(4), 24–37.

Sellwood, C., Asgari-Jirhandeh, N., & Salimee, S. (2007). Bird flu: If or when?: Planning for the next pandemic. *Postgraduate Medicine Journal, 83*(981), 445–450.

Skevington, S. M. (2002). Advancing cross-cultural research on quality of life: Observations drawn from the WHOQOL development. *Quality of Life Research, 11*, 135–144.

Washer, P. (2004). Representations of SARS in the British newspapers. *Social Science & Medicine, 59*(12), 2561–2571.

Yuen, K. Y., Chan, P. K., Peiris, M., Tsang, D. N., Que, T. L., Shortridge, K. F., Cheung, P. T., To, W. K., Ho, E. T., Sung, R., & Cheng, A. F. (1998). Clinical features and rapid viral diagnosis of human disease associated with avian influenza A H5N1 virus. *Lancet, 351*(9101), 467–471.

Chapter 13
FASD Prevention Interventions Valued by Australian and Canadian Women

Sharyn Rundle-Thiele, Robin Thurmeier, Sameer Deshpande, Magdalena Cismaru, Anne Lavack, Noreen Agrey, and Renata Anibaldi

1 Introduction

Fetal Alcohol Spectrum Disorders (FASD) describes a set of debilitating conditions caused by fetal exposure to alcohol, including alterations to the developing brain, low birth weight, distinctive facial features, heart defects, behavioural problems and intellectual disability (Henderson et al. 2007; Mattson et al. 2011; Payne et al. 2011; Testa et al. 2003; Treit et al. 2014) and these may last for life (Rangmar et al. 2015). FASD has negative health, social, and cultural consequences for affected children, their families, and society, as well as substantial economic costs (Popova et al. 2011). Children with FASD are more likely to go into formal care and/or experience

S. Rundle-Thiele (✉) • R. Anibaldi
Social Marketing @ Griffith, Department of Marketing and Menzies Health Institute Queensland, Griffith University, Brisbane, QLD, Australia
e-mail: s.rundle-thiele@griffith.edu.au; r.anibaldi@griffith.edu.au

R. Thurmeier
College of Nursing, University of Saskatchewan, Saskatoon, SK, Canada
e-mail: robin.thurmeier@usask.ca

S. Deshpande
Faculty of Management, University of Lethbridge, Lethbridge, AB, Canada
e-mail: Sameer.deshpande@uleth.ca

M. Cismaru
Faculty of Business Administration, University of Regina, Regina, SK, Canada
e-mail: Magdalena.Cismaru@uregina.ca

A. Lavack
School of Business & Economics, Thompson Rivers University, Kamloops, BC, Canada
e-mail: alavack@tru.ca

N. Agrey
Saskatchewan Prevention Institute, Saskatoon, SK, Canada

W. Wymer (ed.), *Innovations in Social Marketing and Public Health Communication*, Applying Quality of Life Research,
DOI 10.1007/978-3-319-19869-9_13

behavioural/learning problems in school. In addition, there may be social stigma associated with families having children with FASD (Public Health Agency of Canada 2005), and the prevalent disabilities common in FASD, combined with the very poor outcomes of these children, undoubtedly have an effect on the family of the affected individual (Rasmussen et al. 2008). Of further concern, clinical reports indicate that a poor quality of life is a grim reality for most adults with FASD because their broad spectrum neurobehavioral deficits continue to impair functioning across the lifespan (Grant et al. 2005). In the Canadian context, a study by Stade et al. (2006) on health and quality of life outcomes of children with FASD provided direct evidence for significantly poorer health-related quality of life scores compared with the norm sample, particularly for cognitive and emotional variables. Children with FASD had lower mean health-related quality of life scores than children with significant disabilities (i.e., blindness, cerebral palsy, deafness and cognitive impairment) and those who were survivors of childhood cancers.

There is some evidence that the prevalence of FASD in high income countries may be as high as 2–5 % (May et al. 2009). However, there is great variation in estimates for populations as different diagnostic guidelines are applied across and within countries and there is evidence of under-reporting and/or under-detection (see Watkins et al. 2013, for a full discussion on prevalence). The estimation of FASD population prevalence rates remains challenged. Internationally, there are multiple sets of diagnostic criteria for FASD (Watkins et al. 2013) and superior validity of any one set has yet to be established or agreed. While some countries, such as Canada, have adopted specific diagnostic criteria, other countries, such as Australia, were in the process of developing agreed national diagnostic guidelines at the time of writing. In Canada, where a national set of diagnostic guidelines is available, it has been estimated that 9 in 1000 born babies are affected by FASD (Public Health Agency of Canada 2005). In Australia, national prevalence rates have not been estimated (Australian National Preventive Health Agency 2012).

Although the establishment of diagnostic criteria is a necessary step for estimating population incidence of FASD, the reliability of estimates requires effective and consistent screening and reporting. In Australia, the evidence for screening tests is poor and according to Payne et al. (2011), in 2007 only 22 % of paediatricians and 46 % of health professionals (including aboriginal health workers, allied health professionals, community nurses, general practitioners and obstetricians) routinely asked pregnant women about alcohol consumption in the state of Western Australia. The Payne et al. (2010, 2011) studies also reported reluctance of some health professionals to diagnose a child with FASD due to the social stigma that may be attached to the affected child and family. Furthermore, attempts to ask women about their alcohol consumption during pregnancy rely on self-reported behaviour, which has previously been shown to be inaccurate due to significant under reporting of alcohol consumption (Rundle-Thiele 2009).

The economic costs of FASD include direct costs such as specialist medical care and indirect costs such as productivity losses. In Canada, the annual economic cost of FASD for individuals aged 0–53 years old in 2007 was estimated to be CAD$5.3 billion (Stade et al. 2009). People with a FASD diagnosis are more likely to have received special education, be unemployed and receive a disability pension than members of the general population (Rangmar et al. 2015).

Canadian data suggests women may drink during pregnancy because they are unaware of the pregnancy, unaware of the dangers of alcohol use, feel social pressures to drink, or may have addiction issues (Saskatchewan Prevention Institute 2006; Floyd et al. 1999). One of the groups most at risk of having a child with FASD is "women who are over 30 and have 'successful careers'" (Best Start 2003, p. 2). This group tends to be a frequent drinker during the periconception period (Floyd et al. 1999; Muhajarine et al. 1997). While pregnancy seems like a motivator to abstain, researchers found 9–14 % of women in this group continue drinking during pregnancy (Alberta Alcohol and Drug Abuse Commission [AADAC] 2004) leading to higher FASD risk levels that in turn have significant quality of life implications.

1.1 Prevention of FASD

FASD is the only non-genetic cause of intellectual disabilities in children (O'Leary 2004) and is entirely preventable. Research has not confirmed whether there is any safe amount or time to drink alcohol during pregnancy. When compared to men, women's physiology is slower to process alcohol placing them at higher levels of risk for acute and chronic effects of alcohol misuse (National Health and Medical Research Council [NHMRC] 2009).

Primary prevention focusing on alcohol abstinence during pregnancy seeks to avert the initial occurrence of a health problem through education, environmental improvements, and strategies requiring the audience to self-initiate behaviour changes (Deshpande et al. 2005; WHO 1998). North American studies indicate that educational, legal, and community-based prevention interventions have focussed on targeting the individual with the aim of raising awareness of the consequences of FASD (see Deshpande et al. 2005 and Cismaru et al. 2010 for reviews). In developed nations such as Canada and Australia, health guidelines advise that refraining from alcohol consumption is the safest choice to make while pregnant (Health Canada 1996; The Centre for Addiction and Mental Health 2011; NHMRC 2009).

The effectiveness of prevention programs is not clearly established as many did not include an evaluation component (Saskatchewan Prevention Institute 2007). The reviews on interventions by Deshpande et al. (2005) and Cismaru et al. (2010) indicated that while knowledge increased over time, campaigns had no measurable influence on behaviour change. However, there is a need for such interventions to continue as knowledge of the consequences of alcohol consumption in pregnancy is not widespread, especially outside of North America. For example, in a study by Peadon et al. (2010) that targeted Australian women aged between 18 and 45 years, only 61.5 % of women reported they had heard about the effects of alcohol on the fetus and 55.3 % reported they had heard of FASD. While many respondents reported they had knowledge of the effects of alcohol on pregnancy or the unborn child, when questioned further most were not able to identify the exact effects. For example, only 17 % were able to identify low birth weight, 10 % were able to identify brain damage and 7 % were able to identify birth defects/deformities as effects of FASD. Without specific knowledge, individuals making decisions about whether to drink alcohol (or not) are not able to successfully weigh the costs and benefits of their behaviours.

The potential for social marketing to change behaviour (i.e., reduce alcohol consumption in pregnant women by offering alternative solutions) has received limited attention (Deshpande et al. 2005; Hanson et al. 2012; Mengel et al. 2005), with no published study to date seeking to undertake formative research into social marketing interventions. Social marketing is defined as a tool used to influence individual behaviour by reducing barriers and offering benefits that are superior to those offered by current behaviours (Kotler and Lee 2008) and has been implemented to reduce alcohol consumption in several different target populations (see Stead et al. 2007; Kubacki et al. 2015).

Social marketers need to ensure interventions are driven by customer insight, together with empirical evidence based on past experience about what works (French 2011). While there is evidence for effectiveness of communication-based campaigns, including fear messages, there is a need for social marketers to avoid over-reliance on this strategy and employ a wider suite of tactics to bring about positive behaviour change. Social marketers would do well to look beyond 'promotion' and consider adjusting the other three marketing P's – place, price and product. Additional research is required to gain insights into the target group's attitudes, particularly the perceived benefits and barriers for alcohol consumption during pregnancy, and into the types of interventions that would be valued by the at-risk group.

2 Our Research

Against this background, the current study aimed to:

1. Explore attitudes about alcohol use during pregnancy, specifically the perceived barriers and benefits associated with alcohol consumption and abstinence during pregnancy or while contemplating pregnancy.
2. Determine an appropriate community-based social marketing strategy to promote alcohol abstinence during pregnancy or while contemplating pregnancy.

This study is important because women who are planning to get pregnant, or who are in their first pregnancy – are experiencing a major life stage change and consequently they are more likely to be receptive to alcohol abstinence strategies.

2.1 Methods

Qualitative research allows for deep exploration of issues and it favours the emergence of novel insights which may not result from quantitative research. Focus groups and in-depth interviews have been used effectively in the past for in-depth investigations of attitudes towards alcohol (for example Fry 2010; Kubacki et al. 2011). The group context and the unstructured format of focus groups serve to facilitate, rather than inhibit, the disclosure of information, particularly for sensitive topics such as alcohol (Barrie et al. 2011).

Focus groups and interviews were conducted with members of the target audience in Canada and in Australia. Researchers based at Griffith University, in Brisbane, Australia and at the University of Regina in Canada independently recruited participants for this research and conducted data collection in accordance with their respective institutions' ethics requirements.

The focus groups and interviews lasted 60–90 min, and were audio-recorded and transcribed. The researchers conducted thematic analysis informed by a critical interpretation approach to identify salient themes through iterative readings of the transcripts (van Manen 1997). The results of the analyses from the Australian and Canadian settings were compared for similarities and differences and are presented in this article.

2.2 *Canadian Setting*

Recruitment information was distributed through the Saskatoon Health Region, the Saskatchewan FASD Coordinating Committee, and Saskatoon newspapers. A snowball recruitment technique was also employed. Participants had to meet the following criteria: (1) between 25 and 45 years old, (2) over 2 years of post-secondary education, (3) employed in a professional field, and (4) contemplating pregnancy or already pregnant. Researchers conducted four focus groups with the target group in the provinces of Saskatchewan and Alberta between July 2008 and April 2009. The participants were informed about conditions of confidentiality and anonymity at the beginning of each discussion.

Twenty women participated in the focus group interviews. The age range for participants was 29–44 years (mean 32.75) and ten women were pregnant at the time. With regards to education, two held a diploma, nine held an undergraduate degree, seven held a graduate degree, and two held a post-graduate degree. Seven women listed education as their field of employment, five worked in the business sector, four worked in non-governmental organizations, two worked in health, one worked in policing, and one worked in the government.

2.3 *Australian Setting*

Four focus groups and three individual depth interviews were conducted in early 2012 with women who were planning to get pregnant, were currently pregnant or had a child under the age of 6 months. Women were recruited from an Australian electronic mailing list of women who had previously assisted university research who had previously indicated they were willing to be contacted to assist university research. An email was sent in late 2011 to the list of 528 women who had previously reported they were planning to get pregnant or were pregnant at the time and who were available to participate in a group discussion (for those who lived in the local area) or an individual depth interview (for those living in a remote region).

A total of 24 respondents from South Australia, New South Wales, Victoria, Queensland and Western Australia participated in this research. Women were aged between 25 and 39, and worked in a variety of fields including film, law, psychology, public relations, education and human resource management. The majority of women participating in this study were university-educated, holding degrees or post-graduate degrees in a wide range of disciplines. Participants included women who were planning pregnancy, women who were pregnant, or women who had recently had a first child.

2.3.1 Focus Group Protocols

For the Canadian focus groups, two protocols were developed. Protocol 1 focused on alcohol use before and during pregnancy, and community interventions. Protocol 2 focused on questions to encourage "brainstorming" of preferred social marketing interventions. A single protocol was developed for use in the Australian focus groups which had the same focus as the two Canadian protocols. See Table 13.1 for sample questions from each protocol.

2.4 Results and Discussion

Two major themes emerged from the examination of perceived benefits and barriers for alcohol use while pregnant: (1) there is conflicting information about alcohol use during pregnancy; and (2) alcohol use is influenced by peer groups. The analysis of focus group discussions on current and potential FASD preventive interventions indicated that the current prevention messages are too simplistic. These focus groups engendered a range of ideas that could inform future social marketing campaigns that focus on the individual and their social, physical and institutional environments.

Overall, women found more barriers than benefits to alcohol abstinence and found it difficult to articulate the benefits of abstaining from drinking alcohol if they were not pregnant or breastfeeding. The health of the child and becoming pregnant acted as barriers to alcohol use prior to and during pregnancy. The benefits perceived to derive from avoiding alcohol during pregnancy included having a healthier life for self and child and continuation of fun and emotional release from choosing socializing activities without alcohol.

Table 13.1 Sample of interview questions

Protocol #1: Attitudes about alcohol consumption during or prior to pregnancy	
Alcohol use	What are some of the factors that contribute to alcohol consumption? Are there benefits women receive from consuming alcohol during pregnancy?
Alcohol abstinence	Are there benefits that women receive from abstaining from consuming alcohol during pregnancy? What are some important factors that help promote alcohol abstinence while trying to become pregnant or during pregnancy?
Prevention methods	Are there key circumstances in which women are more likely to pay attention to recommendations to maintain alcohol abstinence when trying to get pregnant or during pregnancy? When are those circumstances?
Protocol #2: Social marketing and program development[a]	
Program questions	What if women were given the opportunity and encouraged to socialize in a way that did not involve alcohol? Would there be any barriers/disadvantages to using this program? If yes, what are they?
Logistics	At what physical location should these activities be conducted? How long should the activities last during each interaction?
Incentives	What kind of incentives would be necessary to get your attention? Does there need to be an incentive to get women to abstain from alcohol or is the socializing aspect enough to encourage them?
Building a program	Let's try to put the stuff we just talked about together and build a program. Who do you think should put this program together? Are there any groups that you would be uncomfortable taking this service from?
Cost	Would women be willing to pay money to get involved in these activities? What would that participation be worth?

[a]This question was asked for each of the program alternatives (see Table 13.2). Once the women picked the most popular program idea, the questions following were asked addressing their favourite program idea

2.4.1 Conflicting Information About Alcohol Use During Pregnancy

Although health guidelines in both Australia and Canada recommend total abstinence from alcohol during pregnancy, women in both countries felt there was conflicting and contradictory information about drinking alcohol during pregnancy. As one Canadian participant stated, "The social stigma is based on very little facts and conflicting studies."

Participants reported conducting their own research to understand whether they should (or should not) drink alcohol while pregnant by asking doctors, friends and family members, or by searching the internet. Participants were hearing incompatible messages from different sources, such as the necessity for abstinence for the whole pregnancy, abstinence for the first trimester only, or that a glass of wine a day will not harm a fetus. The women considered conflicting information to be a barrier to creating a positive behaviour change.

Participants also noted that the information surrounding alcohol was not as clear as that on drugs and smoking. Consistent with evidence presented in Peadon et al.

(2010), the Australian women in this study were unable to express or identify the effects of alcohol on pregnancy or on the unborn child. When probed, some participants felt alcohol might lead to intellectual problems and deafness, while most were largely unaware of the potential consequences of consuming alcohol during pregnancy.

Women who are pregnant for the first time are motivated to do the right thing that gives their baby the best chance. Respondents reported relaxing self-imposed rules over time during their pregnancy, and that abstinence was less likely in second and subsequent pregnancies.

2.4.2 Alcohol Use Is Influenced by Peer Groups

Particularly for women prior to conception or in the first trimester, participation in social activities was a key reason for alcohol use within the target audience in both Australia and Canada. Women referred to social exclusion and the avoidance strategies that they employed to avoid drinking alcohol, including holding a drink of wine all night and ordering drinks that appeared to be alcoholic beverages to avoid questioning. Meeting with friends, families, and co-workers usually involved alcoholic drinks. There seemed to be perceived societal expectations that alcohol would be consumed and often non-alcoholic alternatives were not offered. Participants reported pressure to drink alcohol from partners who purchased drinks for them, as well as parents and peers, and some reported avoiding social occasions to avoid the social pressure to drink.

The Canadian women suggested that if fun, easy, inexpensive alcohol alternatives were available, they would select them. For example, non-alcoholic drinks in restaurants are typically the same price as the alcohol versions. The participants felt that non-alcoholic drink options should be priced lower; the current practice of pricing these two options similarly was considered a barrier to selecting the non-alcoholic drink option. The avoidance of social situation and the absence of alcohol alternatives resulted in feelings of exclusion on celebratory occasions with many respondents commenting on their inability to celebrate at key events including anniversaries, birthdays, parties and weddings. One Canadian woman shared, "I was in a pretty stressed job for nearly 10 years and the only way that we all bonded was to go for drinks after a really brutal day....But we also had staff members who were pregnant and it's been a challenge for them because they feel… they are not part of the team as much."

The stress of these work-related situations was often magnified by the fact that women who are pregnant may not want to reveal their pregnancy to co-workers during the first trimester. The frequent questioning about pregnancy when one turns down alcohol in social settings was perceived as a barrier to abstinence while pregnant. As one Australian woman shared, "People always want to know why you're not drinking." This can be considered problematic and intrusive if a woman is having trouble conceiving or has not yet revealed her pregnancy.

2.5 Preferred Interventions

The Canadian focus groups were shown current FASD prevention materials and they had the view that the campaigns were overly simplistic and were inappropriate to reach their target group. The participants felt current campaigns did not convey the seriousness of FASD to their demographic group and needed to have more sophisticated language. Current messaging did not seem to be reaching the target group, as these women were surprised to learn they were considered at risk of having a child with FASD because of light to moderate alcohol consumption during pregnancy. The participants agreed FASD is a serious health issue and developing prevention messaging that included abstinence strategies was important. Linking the FASD prevention message with community programs was important as well. Knowing about opportunities for education, networking, and where to find assistance in abstaining from alcohol were key elements raised during the discussion. Canadian women were asked to select the intervention they would be most likely to use. See Table 13.2.

While the telephone helpline was unpopular, and activity classes were viewed as already being available, the most popular intervention was perceived to be a combination of in-person education classes with an online networking website. Networking at the education classes themselves was not of interest, but combining the classes with the online website could provide the networking and further discussion opportunities some women were interested in. The website could also provide a platform for developing the education classes, with moderators creating topics based on online discussions. The participants felt this opportunity could be a positive form of group peer support they may not find within their normal social circle. It was also

Table 13.2 Community intervention strategies

Community intervention	Details
1. Activity classes	Socializing events for women who are pregnant (or trying to become pregnant). Could include activities such as cooking classes, book clubs, prenatal yoga, etc. Information would be provided to the women about health pregnancy, including alcohol use and pregnancy
2. Education classes	Similar to prenatal classes, but could be attended by women who are trying to become pregnant as well. Would include information about alcohol use and pregnancy
3. Non-alcohol socializing events	Dry events in the community where women could meet with peers. Could include providing information about already available community activities, and/or linking women with others who are interested in socializing without alcohol
4. Toll-free pregnancy helpline	Women would be able to speak with a health professional about any concerns they may have specific to pregnancy, including alcohol use
5. Online networking website	Would include evidence-based information, a forum, and live chats with health professionals and networking with other women who are pregnant or trying to become pregnant

revealed that some women are reluctant to ask their doctors questions about alcohol consumption so an online confidential question forum would be ideal. The website moderator should be a health professional specializing in pregnancy who can provide evidence-based information without sounding "preachy". Canadian women were also interested in being informed about updated lists of prenatal services. These services could include prenatal activity classes, educational opportunities, birthing options, and a list of health providers available to provide information about alcohol use during pregnancy.

The Australian focus group respondents articulated a wide range of initiatives that they would value, and these were consistent with initiatives reported by Canadian women. There was general consensus among participants that information on FASD prevention from credible, trusted sources (including government, universities and/or health practitioners) involving consistent, clear messaging and an engaging format both in online and offline formats is needed. The overall preference was for a non-commercial (e.g., government or university) entity to offer information on pregnancy along with general health and nutrition advice following formats employed by commercial marketers (e.g., www.huggies.com.au).

3 Implications for Social Marketing

The results suggest that an education focus should continue given that knowledge and awareness about FASD is not uniform. Negative appeals may be best to create fear and guilt; however, social marketers must also employ heuristics. Messaging that involves healthy, happy babies that love their parents, or children succeeding academically and socially in school offer positive means to support a decision to avoid alcohol during pregnancy. Furthermore, information must be delivered in a way that engages the target audience. Attention needs to be directed towards complexity, level of language, and tone. Consistency, clarity, and accessibility are necessary to weigh up risks and assist women to make their own choices. For the Canadian target group, a greater understanding of the research behind the development of the Canadian guidelines would be beneficial in making the right decision.

Information targeting women needs to be supported by alternatives that are valued by the market, enabling social interaction, support and an avenue to reinforce online and offline messages. The timing of interventions is also crucial, with the results suggesting that the ideal time to target women is before and during their first pregnancy with repeated messaging (perhaps evolving) over time to reinforce benefits of not drinking alcohol.

Consistent with the findings reported by Floyd et al. (1999), the factors that influence consumption of alcohol involve social norms within the peer group. Women encounter significant social pressure to drink alcohol during pregnancy. The target group could be assisted in abstaining from alcohol if friends and families were willing to participate in social activities that did not involve alcohol. Consideration needs to be directed towards the significant others who surround pregnant women.

For example, interventions such as community message campaigns and partner information may assist to reduce the social pressure reported by participants in this study. Pregnant women should not be encouraged to drink in cases where they are willing to avoid alcohol. Alcohol-free beverages need to be available offering pregnant women an alternative to alcohol for celebratory occasions. Moreover, attractive pricing can be used to further stimulate demand for non-alcohol alternatives to assist pregnant women to abstain from alcohol. Providing information in combination with a community intervention strategy could create social norms and empower women to demand alcohol-free alternatives.

Creating tailored campaigns, websites, and in-person educational sessions based on insights presented in the current study along with alcohol-free alternatives to facilitate continuation of socialization with peers will likely increase feelings of vulnerability and susceptibility towards having a child with FASD, as well as create self-efficacy and response efficacy towards alcohol abstinence. Efforts directed towards the prevention of FASD are needed given that FASD lowers quality of life.

4 Limitations and Future Research Directions

While focus groups are useful for initiating inquiries into unexplored topics and for generating insight into social complexities surrounding alcohol use prior to and during pregnancy, they do not provide generalizable results (Krueger and Casey 2009). This study was dominated by women residing in metropolitan areas in five Australian states and in two provinces of Canada; additional research across the two countries is recommended.

Further insights could be gained from undertaking formative research to extend our understanding. Additional research would assist to yield insight into how social marketing interventions can be implemented to reduce the growing prevalence of FASD in the broader communities. Specifically, we recommend that formative research be undertaken to identify the barriers and benefits for the partners, parents and employers of pregnant and breastfeeding women.

Further opportunities exist to develop and test interventions targeting educated women in Australia and Canada. A social marketing campaign utilising one or more of the initiatives identified in this formative research study can be assessed using a control group and an intervention group and a repeated measures design to test program effectiveness.

References

Alberta Alcohol & Drug Abuse Commission. (2004). *Windows of opportunity: A statistical profile of substance use among women in their childbearing years in Alberta*. Edmonton: AADAC.

Australian National Preventive Health Agency. (2012). Australian National Preventive Health Agency (ANPHA) submission: The house of representatives standing committee on social policy and legal affairs, inquiry into Foetal Alcohol Spectrum Disorder (FASD). Canberra, ACT, Australia.

Barrie, L. R., Jones, S. C., & Wiesen, E. (2011). "At least I'm not drink-driving": Formative research for a social marketing campaign to reduce drug-driving among young drivers. *Australasian Marketing Journal, 19*(1), 71–75. doi:10.1016/j.ausmj.2010.11.010.

Best Start. (2003). *Keys to a successful alcohol and pregnancy communication campaign*. Toronto: Ontario's Maternal, Newborn and Early Child Development Resource Centre. www.beststart.org/resources/alc_reduction/pdf/keys.pdf

Cismaru, M., Deshpande, S., Thurmeier, R., Lavack, A., & Agrey, N. (2010). Preventing fetal *alcohol* spectrum disorder: The role of protection motivation theory. *Health Marketing Quarterly, 27*(1), 66–85. doi:10.1080/07359680903519776.

Deshpande, S., Basil, M., Basford, L., Thorpe, K., Piquette-Tomei, N., Droessler, J., et al. (2005). Promoting alcohol abstinence among pregnant women: Potential social change strategies. *Health Marketing Quarterly, 23*(2), 45–67. doi:10.1300/J026v23n02_04.

Floyd, L. R., Decoufle, P., & Hungerford, D. W. (1999). Alcohol use prior to pregnancy recognition. *American Journal of Preventative Medicine, 17*(2), 101–107.

French, J. (2011). Why nudging is not enough. *Journal of Social Marketing, 11*(2), 154–162.

Fry, M.-L. (2010). Countering consumption in a culture of intoxication. *Journal of Marketing Management, 26*(13), 1279–1294.

Grant, T., Huggins, J., Connor, P., & Streissguth, A. (2005). Quality of life and psychosocial profile among young women with fetal alcohol spectrum disorders. *Mental Health Aspects of Developmental Disabilities, 8*(2), 33–39.

Hanson, J. D., Winberg, H., & Elliott, A. (2012). Development of a media campaign on fetal alcohol spectrum disorders for Northern Plains American Indian communities. *Health Promotion Practice, 13*(6), 842–847. http://hpp.sagepub.com/content/early/2011/12/12/1524839911404232.full.pdf+html. Accessed 27 Jan 2012.

Health Canada. (1996). *Joint statement: Prevention of fetal alcohol syndrome (FASD) and fetal alcohol effects (FAE) in Canada*. Ottawa: Health Canada.

Henderson, J., Kesmodel, U., & Gray, R. (2007). Systematic review of the fetal effects of prenatal binge drinking. *Journal of Epidemiological & Community Health, 61*, 1069–1073.

Kotler, P., & Lee, N. (2008). *Social marketing: Influencing behaviors for good*. Thousand Oaks: Sage.

Krueger, R. A., & Casey, M. A. (2009). *Focus groups: A practical approach for applied research* (4th ed.). Washington, DC: Sage.

Kubacki, K., Siemieniako, D., & Rundle-Thiele, S. R. (2011). College binge drinking: A new approach. *Journal of Consumer Marketing, 28*(3), 225–233. doi:10.1108/07363761111127644.

Kubacki, K., Rundle-Thiele, S. R., Pang, B., & Buyucek, N. (2015). Minimizing alcohol harm: A systematic social marketing review (2000–2014). *Journal of Business Research* (in press).

Mattson, S. N., Crocker, N., & Nguyen, T. T. (2011). Fetal alcohol spectrum disorders: Neuropsychological and behavioural features. *Neuropsychological Review, 21*, 81–101. doi:10.1007/s11065-011-9167-9.

May, P. A., Gossage, J. P., Kalberg, W. O., Robinson, L. K., Buckley, D., Manning, M., & Hoyme, H. E. (2009). Prevalence and epidemiologic characteristics of FASD from various research methods with an emphasis on recent in-school studies. *Developmental Disabilities Research Reviews, 15*(3), 176–192.

Mengel, M. B., Ulione, M., Wedding, D., Jones, E. T., & Shurn, D. (2005). Increasing FASD knowledge by a targeted media campaign: Outcome determined by message frequency. *International Journal of FASD, 3*, 1–13.

Muhajarine, N., D'Arcy, C., & Edouard, L. (1997). Prevalence and predictors of health risk behaviours during early pregnancy: Saskatoon pregnancy and health study. *Canadian Journal of Public Health, 88*(6), 375–79.

National Health and Medical Research Council. (2009). *Australian guidelines to reduce health risks from drinking alcohol*. Retrieved from http://www.nhmrc.gov.au/_files_nhmrc/publications/attachments/ds10-alcohol.pdf

O'Leary, C. M. (2004). Fetal alcohol syndrome: Diagnosis, epidemiology, and developmental outcomes. *Journal of Paediatric and Child Health, 40*, 2–7. doi:10.1111/j.1440-1754.2004.00280.x.
Payne, J. M., France, K. E., Henley, N., D'Antoine, H. A., Bartu, A. E., O'Leary, C. M., et al. (2010). RE-AIM evaluation of the alcohol and pregnancy project: Educational resources to inform health professionals about prenatal alcohol exposure and fetal alcohol spectrum disorder. *Evaluation and the Health Professions, 34*(1), 57–80. doi:10.1177/0163278710381261.
Payne, J. M., France, K. E., Henley, N., D'Antoine, H. A., Bartu, A. E., Raewyn, C., et al. (2011). Paediatricians' knowledge, attitudes and practice following provision of educational resources about prevention of prenatal alcohol exposure and fetal alcohol spectrum disorder. *Journal of Paediatrics and Child Health, 47*(10), 704–710. doi:10.1111/j.1440-1754.2011.02037.x.
Peadon, E., Payne, J., Henley, N., D'Antoine, H., Bartu, A., O'Leary, C., et al. (2010). Women's knowledge and attitudes regarding alcohol consumption in pregnancy: A national survey. *BMC Public Health, 10*, 510.
Popova, S., Stade, B., Bekmuradov, D., Lange, S., & Rehm, J. (2011). What do we know about the economic impact of fetal alcohol spectrum disorder? A systematic literature review. *Alcohol and Alcoholism, 46*(4), 490–497.
Public Health Agency of Canada. (2005). *Fetal alcohol spectrum disorder (FASD): A framework for action*. Ottawa: Public Health Agency of Canada.
Rangmar, J., Hjern, A., Vinnerljung, B., Stromland, K., & Aronson, M. (2015). Psychosocial outcomes of fetal alcohol syndrome in adulthood. *Pediatrics, 135*(1), e52. doi:10.1542/peds.2014-1915.
Rasmussen, C., Andrew, G., Zwaigenbaum, L., & Tough, S. (2008). Neurobehavioural outcomes of children with fetal alcohol spectrum disorders: A Canadian perspective. *Paediatrics & Child Health, 13*(3), 185–191.
Rundle-Thiele, S. R. (2009). Social gain: Is corporate social responsibility enough? *Australasian Marketing Journal, 17*(4), 204–210. doi:10.1016/j.ausmj.2009.06.006.
Saskatchewan Prevention Institute. (2006). *Saskatchewan Prevention Institute: FASD prevention – Post-campaign survey*. Saskatoon: Saskatchewan Prevention Institute.
Saskatchewan Prevention Institute. (2007). *Creating effective primary prevention FASD resources: Evaluation processes in health promotion*. Saskatoon: Canada Northwest FASD Research Network.
Stade, B. C., Stevens, B., Ungar, W. J., Beyene, J., & Koren, G. (2006). Health-related quality of life of Canadian children and youth prenatally exposed to alcohol. *Health and Quality of Life Outcomes, 4*, 81. doi:10.1186/1477-7525-4-81.
Stade, B., Ali, A., Bennett, D., Campbell, D., Johnson, M., Lens, C., et al. (2009). The burden of prenatal exposure to alcohol: Revised measurement of cost, 2007. *The Canadian Journal of Clinical Pharmacology, 16*(1), 91–102.
Stead, M., Gordon, R., Angus, K., & McDermott, L. (2007). A systematic review of social marketing effectiveness. *Health Education, 107*(2), 126–191. doi:10.1108/09654280710731548.
Testa, M., Quigley, B., & Das Eiden, R. (2003). The effects of prenatal alcohol exposure on infant mental development: A meta-analytic review. *Alcohol and Alcoholism, 38*(4), 295–304. doi:10.1093/alcalc/agg087.
The Centre for Addiction and Mental Health. (2011). *Low-risk drinking guidelines*. http://www.lrdg.net/guidelines.html. Accessed 30 Jan 2011.
Treit, S., Zhou, D., Lebel, C., Rasmussen, C., Andrew, G., & Beaulieu, C. (2014). Longitudinal MRI reveals impaired cortical thinning in children and adolescents prenatally exposed to alcohol. *Human Brain Mapping, 35*, 4892–4903. doi:10.1002/hbm.22520.
Van Manen, M. (1997). *Researching lived experience: Human science for an action sensitive pedagogy*. London: The Althouse Press.
Watkins, R. E., Elliott, E. J., Wilkins, A., Mutch, R. C., Fitzpatrick, J. P., Payne, J. M., et al. (2013). Recommendations from a consensus development workshop on the diagnosis of fetal alcohol spectrum disorders in Australia. *BMC Pediatrics, 13*, 156. doi:10.1186/1471-2431-13-156.
World Health Organisation (WHO). Health Promotion Glossary. Geneva, Switzerland: WHO Division of Health Promotion, Education and Communications, 1998.

Chapter 14
Does Social Marketing Have a Role in Skin Cancer Education and Prevention?

Tim Crowley and Maurice Murphy

1 Introduction

The skin is the body's largest organ. Its job is to protect internal organs against damage, heat and infection. The skin is also the most exposed organ to sunlight and other forms of harmful ultraviolet rays (Cancer Research UK 2011). Most skin cancers are caused by too much ultraviolet (UV) radiation – the kind found in sunlight and sunbeds. The sun produces two types of ultraviolet radiation, which reach the earth's surface – Ultraviolet A rays (UVA) and Ultraviolet B rays (UVB). It is estimated that 80–85 % of UV rays pass through the clouds (Irish Cancer Society 2009). UVB rays cause sunburn and skin cancer and UVA rays cause premature aging of the skin as well as skin cancer (Stanford Medicine 2011). It is estimated that 80–90 % of all cases of skin cancer are caused by the UV rays of the sun and therefore these cancers could be prevented if people protected themselves from overexposure to these rays. The ultraviolet rays are strongest from 11 am to 3 pm. This is not related to the hottest part of the day, which is usually later in the afternoon (Irish Cancer Society 2010).

Sunrays on tanned skin or on pale skin are never without danger. Suntan is the answer of the skin to wounds caused by ultraviolet rays (Canadian Cancer Society 2009). It is estimated that 90 % of all skin cancers are preventable, with virtually all the risk coming from the sun and the use of sunbeds/sunlamps (Irish Cancer Society 2009). Damage to the skin, by the sun, is permanent. This damage also builds up; that means damage to the skin in 1 year is added to damage done in previous years (Irish Cancer Society 2009). Most skin cancers develop on parts of the body that are the most exposed to the sun: the head, face, neck, hands and arms. Tanning is not an effective way of protecting the body; tanning is actually a sign that the skin has been

T. Crowley • M. Murphy (✉)
Cork Institute of Technology, Cork, Ireland
e-mail: maurice.murphy@cit.ie

W. Wymer (ed.), *Innovations in Social Marketing and Public Health Communication*, Applying Quality of Life Research,
DOI 10.1007/978-3-319-19869-9_14

damaged by the sun (Canadian Cancer Society 2009). In later life this can lead to skin cancer. Skin cancer can take 20–30 years to develop, so the rates of skin cancer today reflect the trends of the 1970s and 1980s (Canadian Cancer Society 2009).

There are two types of skin cancer – malignant melanoma (the serious type) and non- melanoma skin cancer (the less serious type). Melanoma skin cancer develops in cells in the outer layers of the skin and can grow from a mole, freckle or a normal part of the skin (Irish Cancer Society 2009). Melanoma is considered the most dangerous and difficult to treat of the two types of skin cancer (Irish Cancer Society 2009). Estimates suggest that the incidence of non-melanoma skin cancers increased by an average of 3–8 % per year in Europe, the USA, Canada and Australia from the 1960s to the 1990s (Diepgen and Mahler 2002). Worldwide, almost 200,000 people were diagnosed with malignant melanoma in 2008 and around 46,000 people died as a result. The highest rates of malignant melanoma are in Australia and New Zealand (Cancer Research UK 2011).

Skin cancer is the most common type of cancer in Ireland (Irish Cancer Society 2010). In Ireland, one in every eight men (12.5 %) and one in every ten women (10 %) will develop skin cancer by the age of 74 years (Irish Cancer Society 2009). Two thirds of Irish people have a higher risk of developing skin cancer because of their fair skin type (Irish Cancer Society 2009). Three in four Irish people believe that a sunny day in the Mediterranean poses a strong risk for the development of skin cancer, but only one in four Irish people feel that a sunny day in Ireland poses the same risk (Condon 2003). Recent research shows that 40 % of Irish people believe that a temperature of 25 °C in Spain is stronger and more damaging than the equivalent in Ireland and are therefore significantly more likely to use sun protection when away on holidays than in Ireland (Irish Cancer Society 2009).

Irish Central Statistics Office data show there were 144 deaths in Ireland from melanoma in 2008 (Irish Cancer Society 2010). Cases of skin cancer diagnosed in Ireland each year increased by 36 % in the 10 years between 1997 and 2007 (Baxter 2009). There were 5,687 new cases of skin cancer in 1997, but in 2007, 7,743 new cases were diagnosed – including malignant and non-melanoma skin cancer (Baxter 2009). Of those new cases detected in 2007, 667 were malignant melanomas and of those, 313 were found in males and 354 were found in females. Non-melanoma skin cancer accounted for 7,076 of the new cases detected in 2007 (Baxter 2009).

The Irish Cancer Society argued there had been an 84 % increase in the number of melanoma skin cancers detected in males, and a 48 % increase in melanoma skin cancers detected in females, over the 10 years from 1997 to 2007 (Irish Cancer Society 2010). There had also been a 75 % increase in Irish women under 50 presenting with malignant melanoma in the same time period (Baxter 2009). Cases of non-melanoma cancers in Ireland increased by 32 % in males and 36 % in females between 1997 and 2007 (Baxter 2009). With 80–85 % of UV rays passing through the clouds, the Irish Cancer Society (2010) has major concerns for children, with 46 % of children getting burned in the summer months in Ireland. Children who get severely sunburned are twice as likely to get skin cancer as adults (Canadian Cancer Society 2009). This is a very worrying statistic as research has shown that skin cancer builds up over time (Canadian Cancer Society 2009). It is estimated that

50–80 % of a person's lifetime sun exposure occurs before the age of 18 years (Canadian Cancer Society 2009). This has huge implications for the quality of life in adulthood.

2 Motivations for Tanning

The most intense form of intermittent sun exposure is intentional sun exposure that is essentially motivated by the acquisition of a tan or by the possibility to go uncovered in the sun (Autier 2004). Sunbathing and sunbed use are the most typical intentional sun exposure behaviours, and people attracted to sunbathing activities are also more attracted to indoor tanning (Irish Cancer Society 2010). The following detail the main motivations for sun exposure.

2.1 *Socio-cultural Appearance Based Motives Influencing Tanning*

It has been suggested that appearance-related motivations are strong factors for tanning (Danoff-Burg and Mosher 2006). Research has shown that perceived attractiveness is one of the strongest predictors of behaviours associated with getting a tan, such as spending more time sunbathing and using tanning beds (Murray and Turner 2004). Many people who tan maintain that their motivation for tanning relates to their aesthetic preference for a tanned appearance (Knight et al. 2002). The desire to tan for appearance reasons is a major motive for going out in the sun or under a sunbed (Mathys et al. 2002). Studies have shown that attractive people generate a greater positive social response, which may help to explain why many people invest large amounts of time, energy, and money into achieving and maintaining a look that they feel is attractive (Knight et al. 2002). The social norm of what is deemed to be attractive has changed over time but "the look" that has prevailed throughout the last few decades is that of a lean, conditioned, tanned individual (Danoff-Burg and Mosher 2006).

2.2 *Belief that Tanning Is Safe/Healthy: The Vitamin D Debate*

Among the most frequent reasons suggested for the prevalence of tanning and the increased use of commercial in-door tanning facilities, is the public's perception that tanning and especially artificial tanning is safe or even healthy (Autier 2004). The popularity of indoor tanning facilities is due to the common belief that indoor tanning produces a safer tan than one caused by natural sun exposure (Sayre and

Dowdy 2003). The good health effects attributed by the tanning industry to UV radiation are numerous, from the healing of Seasonal Affective Disorder (SAD), to the prevention of breast, colon and prostate cancers (Autier 2004). The tanning industry strives to convince the public that indoor tanning is healthy (Kemp and Tapp 2008). It does this by emphasising that tanning produces a psychological sense of well-being and induces Vitamin D production, which lowers one's overall cancer risk as well as the risk of osteoporosis, hypertension, diabetes, depression and multiple sclerosis (Levine et al. 2005). While there is considerable debate in the academic literature regarding positives (Gillie 2006) and negatives (Diffey 2004) of sun exposure, little balanced debate filters through to consumer media. The issue is further complicated by the lack of a readily comprehendible guide to optimal quantities of Vitamin D across different population groups (Irish Cancer Society 2010).

2.3 Media Influences on the Motivation to Tan

Media influence has been found to be a causal risk factor for body dissatisfaction (Groesz et al. 2002). The impact of media image on body satisfaction and self-esteem has been the subject of a large body of research across areas such as eating disorders, sexualisation, smoking initiation and gender stereotyping (Jones and Rossiter 2008; Sargent 2005). In an experimental study, participants who viewed magazine advertisements with tanned models, had higher ratings (than controls who viewed neutral stimuli), on the importance of tanning to overall attractiveness, suggesting that this form of media influence causes greater positive evaluation of a tanned appearance (Cafri et al. 2006). A previous study also found a significant association between media influences and a measure of tanned appearance attitudes (Jackson and Aiken 2000). It has also been found that as long as the psychological association between having a tan and appearance continues to be reinforced in the promotional materials used by tanning salons, the use of sunbeds is likely to continue to increase, especially among teenagers and young adults (Dixon et al. 2007). It has been indicated that pre-adolescent girls use media images as a basis for deciding on ideal physical attractiveness, even though the images portrayed are unrealistic or represent poor role models and unwise behaviours (Kemp and Tapp 2008).

2.4 Peer Group Pressure and Sensation Seeking as Motivators for Tanning

Adolescents who suffer from peer group pressure and have weak parental role models have been found to be more susceptible to tanning bed use (Kemp and Tapp 2008). Sensation seeking is a personality trait that regulates the tendency to seek varied, novel and intense sensations and experiences (Donohew and Hoyle 1999).

Sensation seeking has been shown to relate to interaction with deviant peers (Greene and Banerjee 2009), and association with deviant peers has been linked to using a sunbed (Donohew and Hoyle 1999). In the context of tanning bed use, the pathway of influence for sensation seekers to engage in higher tanning bed use includes association with others who tan (Bancrjcc et al. 2009). It is believed, sensation seeking may contribute to tanning bed use indirectly, through interacting with friends and/or acquaintances that use tanning beds (Autier et al. 1999).

Prinstein et al. (2001) documented that adolescent health risk behaviours such as, cigarette smoking, alcohol consumption and drug use are related to their friends' engagement in these health- risk behaviours. By applying the same principle to tanning bed use, it has been suggested that tanning bed use is a behaviour that high sensation seekers in the same peer group perform (together or separately), either because they find the act of using a tanning bed exciting, or they underestimate the risk associated with tanning bed use. In terms of practical implications, the design and implementation of campaigns to reduce tanning bed use must be targeted differently to low and high sensation seekers, because sensation seeking is a strong predictor of tanning bed use (Bränström et al. 2001). This should ensure that the population's quality of life will be improved.

3 Research Objectives

The aim of this study is to show how social marketing can create awareness and educate people on the dangers of skin cancer and ultimately aid in the prevention of this disease by changing poor sun protective behaviours and improving quality of life. The research objectives are as follows:

1. How can the social norm of a tan being desirable/healthy/sexy be challenged?
2. How can the media be used to change this social norm?
3. Who are the key segments that need to be targeted to ensure better sun protection behaviour and a better quality of life?
4. To what extent is the Vitamin D issue affecting sun protection behaviour?

Ten semi-structured interviews were conducted for the purposes of this research between March and July 2012. The interviews were held with leading personnel from the fields of skin cancer prevention, health education and social marketing both in Ireland as well as abroad. These people were sourced using a judgement sample from developing contacts over the course of the study by making initial contact with key personnel in the Irish Cancer Society, as well as personal academic contacts developed with social marketers abroad. The Irish Cancer Society was asked to recommend people who were relevant to the study and these individuals were then sent an email requesting an interview. The interview questions were developed from the four research objectives listed above and were consistent with the overall theme of the research. All interviewees were interviewed over the telephone and a digital voice recorder recorded the interview. Transcripts of interviews were analysed for key themes.

4 Discussion of Results

4.1 The Need to Change the Social Norm of a Tanned-Look Being Considered Healthy, Through Peer Modelling and Role Modelling

There is a clear need to change the social norm of a tan being desirable, attractive and sexy. The media is a key vehicle for the delivery of successful campaigns that lead to behaviour change and the resulting change in social norms. It is a key platform for changing the belief that a tanned look equates to a sexy, desirable look which is a vital element for successfully changing the prevailing social norm of a tan being desirable, among some segments of the population.

The use of both peer and role modelling is extremely important in changing social norms and improving quality of life. Peer modelling is an extremely important method for altering social norms. Targeting individuals that can sway their peers is extremely important. This is very relevant to adolescents who want to copy their friends and for whom peer acceptance and peer bonding is important in terms of carving out their identity. The great thing about this strategy is that the participants do not even need to know they are practising the sun safe method. For example, the social marketer needs to look outside the box and instead of advocating that adolescents wear a hat in the sun for protection reasons, they should instead try to make the wearing of a hat the "cool", trendy or fun option to adopt.

The individual does not even need to know they are practising the sun safe method – a simple example is offering a shaded play area for children during peak UV exposure time. This can be coupled with a shaded adult area where parents can supervise their children. These individuals do not necessarily need to know they are being protected from the sun during the peak times (12 noon – 2 pm) as they are gaining a benefit anyway from being indoors or in the shade having fun. It is important that social marketers can offer a greater benefit to people who practise the sun safe option compared to those who do not.

Good segmentation is vital as not everyone will want the same benefit from staying out of the sun, so knowing the audience is important to ensure an appropriate incentive for each group. It is also vital that the messages are framed positively and state what can be gained from staying out of the sun rather than the dangers of staying in the sun. People should not be discouraged from going out in the sun, but rather they should be encouraged to go out, be active and have fun in the sun *but* to do it in a safe manner and wear sun screen or protective clothing. Negative messaging may not have the desired effect as too many people will disregard the message. Messages, where appropriate, should also be framed in a positive manner as it is a fact that people actually feel better in the sun and that being in the sun is good for one's quality of life.

Changing social norms may also be done through the use of a famous role model wearing a hat or making the wearing of hats a trendy option through peer modelling. Consequently, adolescents will start wearing a hat because it is the "cool thing to do". Through the use of peer modelling these good sun protection behaviours will spread as children do not want to be "the odd one out". The social marketer will have achieved their goal where adolescents are wearing hats to protect themselves from the sun, however the adolescents may not know the reason but are simply wearing the hats because they are "cool" and all their friends are wearing them.

Peer modelling is not just relevant to adolescents. The use of peer-influence can be used for people from all age groups. For example, if we can develop a norm of applying sun screen on a building site or on a farmyard, those who do not conform to this workplace norm will be put under pressure until they perform the behaviour of applying sun screen. The idea is to get a few individuals (who are often looked up to) openly practising sun safe methods of protection and through the use of peer modelling, their behaviour should spread thus creating a norm of applying sun screen or using some form of sun protection.

The use of role models is therefore important and the most important role model for an adolescent whilst growing up is their parents. Parents have a massive influence on behaviour, beliefs, norms, habits and so forth and the creation of these values are based on parental influence. This is why the targeting of parents to ensure they act as suitable role models is vitally important. The targeting of parents regarding the creation of a sun safe norm, habit or attitude in adolescents is also important. With the use of peer modelling this behaviour can then spread even further throughout large groups of friends and into the school yard.

Non-parental role models also have huge power over impressionable youths and what they say or do is often imitated. This is why the creation of positive role models by the media in terms of skin protection is very important. Simply put, positive role models need to be fully utilised in the battle against skin cancer. There is of course a danger of negative role models disseminating negative messages such as the glorification of sunbeds. This is another reason why positive role models need to be worked with to counter the negative messages.

However, it is extremely important that social marketers realise the importance and role of segmentation regarding role models as no one role model will appeal to the entire adolescent market – a famous female pop star, although popular with young females, will more than likely not hold much appeal for a young male. This is why using multiple role models for each segment is vital. Social marketers have to identify each segment and find out what they value and then find a credible celebrity or role model that appeals to this specific segment. Once the role model is identified they can then be used to promote the sun safe message. The role model must act and be seen to actively promote the sun safe behaviour such as applying sun screen or wearing protective clothing.

The media again plays a huge role in terms of changing social norms through the use of role modelling. The media has often been criticised in the past for the creation of negative role models that glamorise the use of sunbeds along with the desirability of the tanned look. Creating partnerships with the media can limit the effect of these negative role models simply by not allowing anything that promotes unsafe skin protection. It is vital that the media not only limit the glorification of sunbed use from certain negative role models but also promote positive role models that are practising sun safe behaviour. This includes portraying celebrities and other role models who promote the natural pale look as being more acceptable to society. The media has often in the past not positively portrayed celebrities that have promoted their natural pale look, however, thankfully, this is not the case anymore as the pale look begins its re-emergence. Working with the media and building a good relationship with them is imperative to improving overall quality of life.

The use of role models with social media is another vitally important element in the communications mix that must be fully utilised by skin cancer specialists. Using role models who are active on social networking sites such as Twitter and Facebook is an added bonus. These role models must be encouraged to use their personal accounts to educate their followers on the dangers of skin cancer and help inform them of the importance of being sun-safe. The use of their personal accounts will carry much more weight with a young target audience.

The promotion of sun-safe behaviour is not the only option or strategy available to the social marketer; the full range of de-marketing activities should be utilised. The social marketer needs to target what people care most about and if that is looking attractive, then they can use this to de-market tanning by explaining that excess exposure to the sun leads to wrinkly, damaged and leathery skin and poorer quality of life. The image of tanning is thus altered in people's minds. If people see tanning as sexy, then the social marketer must show that tanning, is in fact, not sexy and consequently show the damage it causes. This can be done through the media or through community initiatives where people are shown the damage that has already been caused to their own skin and the damage that will occur if they do not stop as well as a poorer quality of life.

4.2 The Need for Good Skin Cancer Message Segmentation

As there are multiple segments that must be successfully targeted in relation to skin cancer campaigns, the use of segmentation is vitally important. Segments such as those who play sport outdoors, sun seekers, sunbed users and even the "tanorexic" or addicted segment must all have messages tailored specifically for them. All these groups have different motivations for being outdoors in the sun and will therefore need different messages and slogans to effectively reach them and gain their attention. As a result social marketers must be aware that a "one size fits all" mind-set is not suitable regarding skin cancer education and prevention.

Segmentation is important and there must be multiple messages developed for multiple segments. Smaller sub-campaigns with different text, slogans and so forth highlighting the different methods of protection are vital. Numerous messages combined with highlighting the different methods of protection is the way forward – not everyone will wear a hat but they might apply sunscreen while another segment may not apply sunscreen but may seek shade when out in the sun. This is why multiple messaging is vital. People must be made aware of all the different means of sun protection as no one segment has the same characteristics. It is therefore clear that having just one message is not sufficient in terms of sun protection. There has to be different messaging, slogans, pictures and so forth for each segment.

A vital group that must also be worked with is the fashion industry including the cosmetics industry. The use of less tanned models is imperative in the overall goal of changing the social norm where a tan is seen as sexy and attractive. Working with the fashion industry can help make the transition between using models that are tanned to using models that portray their natural skin type. This transition is achievable much like the transition from super skinny size-zero models to models that portray a more realistic and healthy body size. However, this is unlikely to happen naturally so it is vital that the fashion industry is worked with. This also applies to cosmetics firms – at the moment a small few cosmetics firms provide a limited range of creams, lipsticks and moisturisers that have built in sun protection factor that protect people from the sun's harmful UV rays. Creating a mutually beneficial partnership with these cosmetics firms is an achievable aim in improving people's quality of life.

The key to the success of working with the fashion/cosmetics industries is the mutually beneficial aspect. Both parties will gain from this as the cosmetics firms can incorporate the sun-safe logo or Irish Cancer Society/Cancer Research UK approval in their advertising materials which will give them a competitive advantage over their rivals. The skin cancer groups will have their message incorporated in massive advertising campaigns that will be seen throughout the world meaning the sun-safe message will reach a far wider audience than they could ever have hoped for based on their limited budgets. It will also help establish a social norm of good sun protective behaviour.

With regard to the fashion industry, another group that must be targeted are beauticians. Educating beauticians is a viable strategy so they inform their clients of the dangers of skin cancer due to excess UV rays or from the use of sunbeds. Having beauticians advocate good sun-safe practices would be a major plus as they could not only make their clientele more aware of the dangers of sun exposure but they can also advise them that the natural look is the best option. Beauticians will be listened to due to their expertise and should be targeted while in training college. Having the dangers of skin cancer incorporated into a subject taught in training college so as to fully inform beauticians is a tactic that is worth following up. This will again help establish a social norm of good sun protective behaviour and ensure an improved quality of life.

There is a major difficulty regarding skin cancer where the consequences are usually years down the line. The health community needs to make these dangers a current problem. The use of beauticians is also vital here, thus highlighting the importance and relevance of the earlier recommendations regarding beauticians. Techniques such as the use of UV camera lenses and photo booths that show current damage to a person's skin as well as over their lifetime are excellent tactics for making people more sun safe, as they can see the damage they have already done to their skin and further damage if they do not change their behaviour. Not only will this make the danger of skin cancer a real current worry, but it will also make people more aware of the damage they continue to do in the sun. This makes skin cancer a current issue and should help change the norm regarding sun protective behaviour. It is vital that social marketers offer sun-safe alternatives that are of greater benefit to the individual now and not in the distant future, thus giving them a real incentive to undertake the sun safe activity and improve their quality of life.

Social marketers must ascertain what each segment values, and then create a message around that knowledge. It is imperative that the social marketer is always led by the audience; they must put themselves in the shoes of the customer and see life from their perspective. Consequently, messages are tailored for each audience or segment. These messages must then be disseminated effectively through a communication medium that will reach the target audience but in a way that the messages are easily understandable and easy to take on board. It is imperative that the language used is suitable for each segment or audience. This means that health professionals must not be allowed create the message. Their input must be limited to providing the relevant information to the social marketer who can then frame the facts to create an easily understandable message for each specific audience.

The use of technology is also extremely relevant and important for effective segmentation. Social media, namely Twitter and Facebook have become hugely popular in recent times among younger adults and this must be taken advantage of. However, there is a danger that social media may be perceived as a panacea where all messages and slogans are delivered; this is not an effective strategy. Social media is extremely effective for certain segments, namely the adolescent market that place a high value on technology and use social media sites daily. This, however, is not the case for audiences of a more mature nature who do not value nor use such social media sites.

It is important that communication avenues are found that appeal to each audience. For example, older Irish farmers and fishermen were cited as notoriously hard groups to target as they often do not value wearing sun protection – many believing it as a non-manly thing to do. This mind-set is extremely hard to change as it has been instilled over a lifetime. However, an ideal way to target these groups is through official publications relating to their professions or past times e.g. magazines that appeal to fishermen or newspapers like *The Irish Farmers' Journal* are ideal avenues to utilise in order to reach each audience. It is important that each segment is reached through a means they value. Other segments may be reached with sun protection messages through magazines or newspapers that they read regularly. Social marketers must be led by an insight into the customer and their habits.

Social marketers should also go one step further and target the government and lobby for legislation banning sunbeds completely. This would remove the temptation that some people cannot resist regarding sunbed use as they would no longer be available. A ban on sunbeds as in the state of Victoria, Australia and in Brazil, is the future. This will however take time but in the short term, pressure should be put on government agencies to implement a complete ban on under 18s using sunbeds and on the coin operated unsupervised sunbeds. This will help create a social norm where using sunbeds is not the popular thing to do and is frowned upon by society.

Social marketers should also target law makers to introduce a tax on the use of sunbeds. This would result in tanning prices increasing thus making it expensive for people especially adolescents. The revenue generated through taxation can be put back into either campaign budgets or into healthcare facilities. Governments must be targeted in terms of what is important to them – each audience is different and the government is no exception. The key to gaining the government's attention may be through highlighting the healthcare costs or health implications associated with skin cancer and a poorer quality of life.

4.3 Health-Based Clarification on the Vitamin D Debate

Groups that are not utilised to their full potential are doctors and the health community. This group has a lot more to offer on many levels ranging from early diagnosis to educating their patients on skin cancer, Vitamin D and so forth. General practitioners have to take a more active role regarding the Vitamin D debate. Doctors are a very powerful force and must be utilised to ensure people realise skin cancer is a current problem and as a result are regularly checking their moles and more importantly are aware of the dangers of skin cancer. Proper education is important as scare mongering can lead to people being too frightened to seek professional help meaning their condition only worsens. Doctors need to make their patients aware of the importance of early diagnosis and seeking help immediately if they feel there is an abnormality on their skin.

With regards to skin cancer campaigns or health campaigns in general, it is vital that mixed messages do not exist in the public domain. There is a huge danger that even one mixed message will compromise an entire campaign, therefore, the Vitamin D issue must be resolved immediately. The Vitamin D debate has been dividing health experts for years with no one recommended level of sunshine being agreed on. Health experts have to agree on one message to disseminate to the public on the recommended time in the sun to ensure adequate levels of Vitamin D. At the moment there are too many mixed messages on what is the correct level of Vitamin D, therefore all interested parties, including GPs must work together and coordinate their activities to come up with one clear, easily understandable message that can be transmitted by all interested parties thus eliminating mixed messaging and doubt on the issue.

The recommendation regarding exposure in the sun for adequate levels of Vitamin D is to use the World Health Organisation's message where they recommend 5–15 min general exposure on the hands and face 3 times per week. The public should also be made aware of other methods of gaining Vitamin D such as vitamin supplementation and through eating certain foods. This will counteract the doubt that the sunbed industry peddle to the general public regarding Vitamin D levels. Doctors also need to take a more active role in relation to the Vitamin D debate in educating their patients on the safe ways to increase their Vitamin D levels. Sunbeds, although advertised as the answer (by the sunbed industry), are not in any way an appropriate alternative to increase Vitamin D.

The media must also be fully utilised in getting the correct Vitamin D message out to the general public. The media should be given the facts relating to Vitamin D and encouraged to end the debate on the issue and the doubt that has been generated by the sunbed industry. Once again, having a good relationship between social marketers and the media is vital. Being able to supply accurate information to the media and having them report positively regarding the Vitamin D debate is hugely important.

There is a real problem with mixed messaging in relation to skin cancer campaigns in general as there are multiple organisations that independently run health awareness initiatives. This shows the urgent need for coordination of all health promotion activities which would eliminate the situation where different government agencies give conflicting advice. For instance, the skin cancer message is to try and stay indoors between 12 noon and 2 pm as these are the hottest parts of the day and then there are the anti-obesity and other health campaigns that encourage people to "get out and be active". It is imperative that not only do all skin cancer groups work together but that there is also coordination between all government agencies so that contradicting messages like this do not happen. For example, an anti-obesity campaign can encourage people to be active but with the added information to use sunscreen whilst outside. Having coordination between different health promotion agencies is vitally important as each group's message will reach far wider audiences thus increasing the likelihood of the messages being taken on board.

4.4 The Need for "Nudge Theory" in Social Marketing

The social marketer can also manipulate a person's behaviour, unknown to the individual, through limiting their options. If the social marketer wants people to only wear sun cream of Sun Protection Factor (SPF) 15 or higher they can try and limit the amount of outlets selling sun creams under SPF 15. Social marketers should investigate the possibility of chemists and supermarkets restricting the sale of sun creams under SPF 15. If this is successful, people will be forced to purchase higher sun creams thus taking the safer option. However, they may not realise this as they do not have the option to purchase a lower protection sun cream. This once again illustrates that the individual does not always need to be aware they are practising the sun safe method – the key being that they have been nudged to adopt the correct behaviour.

This nudge strategy can also be used regarding sunbed use. An option for the social marketer is to work with gyms, health clubs or any other outlet where an individual can use a sunbed and educate them of the dangers. The social marketer must attempt to show that sunbeds are dangerous and as a result are bad for business, as each company is ultimately showing a complete lack of care for their clientele by supplying the sunbed service. If the social marketer can get even one gym or health club to abolish their sunbed service, this may put other companies in their industry under pressure to follow suit, as they will not want to appear irresponsible. This strategy may even lead to a new social norm where sunbeds are not a service provided by gyms and health clubs. This strategy, if successful will change people's behaviour as they no longer have the choice of using sunbeds and therefore improve their quality of life. The decision has been made for them as the dangerous sunbed activity is removed from their reach.

The work on skin cancer prevention carried out in Australia must also be studied and used as a template where appropriate. The media in Australia has been successfully working with health professionals and social marketers for years leading to notable behavioural change. Domestic television shows in Australia such as *Home & Away* have been successfully communicating sun-safe messages in recent times such as the application of sun cream, wearing protective clothing and also seeking shade. This TV show has reinforced the messages that the *Slip, Slop, Slap* campaign first introduced. It is vital that these Australian initiatives are copied in Ireland where possible as it is a very good template to work from.

The key to success for any health communication message is to have a long term approach – the same way that the *Slip, Slop, Slap* campaign has been run in a continuous manner. Having the media reinforce campaign messages is also vitally important. Social marketers should work with weather forecasters to ensure that people are aware of how strong the sun (UV index) is for their particular area or region on any given day. This will make sure people do not underestimate the power of the sun, especially in Ireland on cloudy days.

Australia has also been very successful in targeting school children, sports coaches and the school system itself. This is an excellent strategy and must be analysed in Ireland. Both schools and sporting clubs must develop a policy on sun protection and refuse children (who do not have adequate sun protection) access to outdoor activities for that day. With this strategy in place, children will learn extremely fast not to forget their sun screen or protective clothing as they will not want to miss out on the fun outside with all their friends and classmates. They may forget it one day but they will remember their sun protective gear the next day. This will also help create a social norm through the use of peer modelling where everyone is doing it so it becomes the norm; the use of sunscreen becomes the default setting for each child. This will also help instil good habits for later in life. It is also vital that a policy is created to enable teachers to apply sun screen to children. This may be that another teacher or school principal is in attendance to act in a supervisory role but it is important that there is someone in the school who is authorised to apply sunscreen.

The targeting of adolescents with sun protection messages is vital; childhood is an especially important time for children as they are creating habits and norms that will follow them through life. Changing these habits after they develop can be an arduous task thus highlighting the importance of targeting adolescents at an early age so as to ensure the development of sun safe habits such as applying sunscreen or wearing hats. The media is especially important in relating to young adolescents. Creating a positive sun protection habit when one is an adolescent is extremely important because once the adolescent becomes older, they may have already got into habits (often negative sun protection habits) and at this stage the behaviour is much harder to change. Targeting these adolescents at an early age and instilling positive sun protection habits is therefore vital to ensuring a good quality of life.

5 Conclusion

Changing people's behaviour towards the sun can be done in a variety of ways. The promotion of the ideal sun protection behaviour is not always the best strategy. Changing the social norm and making good sun protection strategies the norm is the key. This can be achieved through the use of nudge tactics to adopt the desired behaviour. These strategies can gain significant results and must be investigated. Lobbying the government can also be a worthwhile activity as laws and regulations can restrict the individual's choice of behaviour and ultimately lead to a better quality of life.

References

Autier, P. (2004). Perspectives in melanoma prevention: The case of sunbeds. *European Journal of Cancer, 40*(16), 2367–2376.

Autier, P., Dore, J., Negrier, S., Lienard, D., Panizzon, R., Lejeune, F. J., Guggisberg, D., & Eggermont, A. (1999). Sunscreen use and duration of sun exposure: A double-blind, randomized trial. *Journal of the National Cancer Institute, 91*(15), 1304–1309.

Banerjee, S., Green, K., Bagdasarov, Z., & Campo, S. (2009). My friends love to tan: Examining sensation seeking and the mediating role of association with friends who use tanning beds on tanning bed use intentions. *Health Education Research, 24*(6), 989–998.

Baxter, G. (2009). Skin cancer on the rise in Ireland. *Irish Medical Times*, Retrieved 11 May 2011, from http://www.imt.ie/news/public-health/2009/05/skin-cancer-on-the-rise- in-Ireland

Bränström, R., Brandberg, Y., Holm, L., Sjoberg, L., & Ullen, H. (2001). Beliefs, knowledge and attitudes as predictors of sunbathing habits and use of sun protection among Swedish adolescents. *European Journal of Cancer Prevention: The Official Journal of the European Cancer Prevention Organisation (ECP), 10*(4), 337–345.

Cafri, G., Thompson, J., Roehrig, M., Van Den Berg, P., Jacobson, P., & Stark, S. (2006). An investigation of appearance motives for tanning: The development and evaluation of the Physical Appearance Reasons for Tanning Scale (PARTS) and its relation to sunbathing and indoor tanning intentions. *Body Image, 3*(3), 199–209.

Canadian Cancer Society. (2009). *Skin cancer – The most common cancer in Canada.* Retrieved June 16, 2011, from http://www.cancer.ca/quebec/about%20us/media%20centre/qc-media%20 releases/qc- quebec%20media%20releases/qc_escouades_o_soleil.aspx

Cancer Research UK. (2011). *Skin cancer statistics – Key facts: Cancer research UK.* Retrieved June 30, 2011, from http://info.cancerresearchuk.org/cancerstats/types/skin/cancerstats-key-facts-on-skin-cancer

Condon, D. (2003). *Irish awareness of skin cancer alarmingly low*. Retrieved February 23, 2011, from http://www.irishhealth.com/article.html?id=4931

Danoff-Burg, S., & Mosher, C. (2006). Predictors of tanning salon use. *Journal of Health Psychology, 11*(3), 511–518.

Diepgen, T., & Mahler, V. (2002). The epidemiology of skin cancer. *The British Journal of Dermatology, 146*(61), 1–6.

Diffey, B. (2004). The future incidence of cutaneous melanoma within the U.K. *British Journal of Dermatology, 151*(4), 868–872.

Dixon, H., Dobbinson, S., Wakefield, M., Jamsen, K., & McLeod, K. (2007). Portrayal of tanning, clothing fashion and shade use in Australian women's magazines, 1987–2005. *Health Education Research, 23*(5), 791–802.

Donohew, R., & Hoyle, R. (1999). Sensation seeking and drug use by adolescents and their friends: Models for marijuana and alcohol. *Journal of Studies on Alcohol and Drugs, 60*(5), 622–631.

Gillie, O. (2006). A new government policy is needed for sunlight and vitamin D. *British Journal of Dermatology, 154*(6), 1052–1061.

Greene, K., & Banerjee, S. (2009). Examining unsupervised time with peers and the role of association with delinquent peers on adolescent smoking. *Nicotine & Tobacco Research, 11*(4), 371–380.

Groesz, L., Levine, M., & Murnen, S. (2002). The effect of experimental presentation of thin media images on body satisfaction: A meta-analytic review. *International Journal of Eating Disorders, 31*(1), 1–16.

Irish Cancer Society. (2009). *Have fun and be sunsmart*. Retrieved February 22, 2011, from http://www.cancer.ie/search/site_search_results.php?cx=010506766483967972395%3A9occ

Irish Cancer Society. (2010). *What is the skin? Preventing cancer, saving lives from cancer, supporting patients*. Retrieved February 22, 2011, from http://www.cancer.ie/cancerInfo/melanoma_skin_whatis.php#common

Jackson, K., & Aiken, L. (2000). A psychosocial model of sun protection and sunbathing in young women: The impact of health beliefs, attitudes, norms, and self-efficacy for sun protection. *Health Psychology, 19*(5), 469–478.

Jones, S., & Rossiter, J. (2008). Young adults' perceptions of smoking actors. *Health Education, 108*(6), 450–462.

Kemp, G., & Tapp, A. (2008). *Social marketing-based strategy for sun protection interventions*. Available at http://eprints.uwe.ac.uk/20/. Accessed 7 July 2010.

Knight, J., Kirincich, A., Farmer, E., & Hood, A. (2002). Awareness of the risks of tanning lamps does not influence behavior among college students. *Archives of Dermatology, 138*(10), 1311–1315.

Levine, J., Sorace, M., Spencer, J., & Siegal, D. (2005). The indoor UV tanning industry: A review of skin cancer risk, health benefit claims, and regulation. *Journal of the American Academy of Dermatology, 53*(6), 1038–1044.

Mathys, P., Moser, M., Bressoud, D., Gerber, B., & Braun-Fahrlander, C. (2002). Benützungsverhalten von solarienbesucherinnen und besuchern in der Schweiz. *Social and Preventive Medicine, 47*(5), 318–329.

Murray, C., & Turner, E. (2004). Health, risk and sunbed use: A qualitative study. *Health, Risk & Society, 6*(1), 67–80.

Prinstein, M., Boergers, J., & Spirito, A. (2001). Adolescents' and their friends' health-risk behavior: Factors that alter or add to peer influence. *Journal of Pediatric Psychology, 26*(5), 287–298.

Sargent, J. (2005). Smoking in movies: Impact on adolescent smoking. *Adolescent Medicine Clinics, 16*(2), 345–370.

Sayre, R., & Dowdy, J. (2003). Sunbathing vs. indoor tanning: A realistic perspective. *Photodermatology, Photoimmunology and Photomedicine, 19*(2), 105–107.

Stanford Medicine. (2011). *Ultraviolet radiation – Causes of skin cancer*. Stanford Cancer Center. California, USA. Retrieved May 11, 2011, from http://cancer.stanford.edu/skincancer/skin/causes/uvrad.html

Chapter 15
Tomorrow's World: Collaborations, Consultations and Conversations for Change

Sinead Duane, Christine Domegan, Patricia McHugh, Michelle Devaney, and Aoife Callan

1 A Quality of Life Problem: Antibiotic Resistance (ABR)

Since their discovery in the 1940s, antibiotics have been heralded as a miracle drug saving millions of lives. Antibiotics have made the treatment of illnesses such as ear infections, pneumonia and pelvic inflammatory disease possible and when used correctly are an important part of our health system. Without effective antibiotics quality of life for individuals and communities will significantly change, making for example, the treatment of cancer or major surgery less safe (Tomson and Vlad 2014). Connected to antibiotics is Antibiotic Resistance (ABR), a phenomenon that causes bacteria to become resistant to antibiotics, making them less effective. ABR is not new and occurs naturally however, the intensity of the ABR spread and its impact on the effectiveness of treatments is of increasing concern (Levy and Marshall 2004).

S. Duane (✉)
J.E. Cairnes School of Business and Economics, National University of Ireland, Galway, Ireland

Discipline of General Practice, National University of Ireland, Galway, Ireland
e-mail: sinead.duane@nuigalway.ie

C. Domegan • P. McHugh • M. Devaney
J.E. Cairnes School of Business and Economics, National University of Ireland, Galway, Ireland
e-mail: christine.domegan@nuigalway.ie; patricia.mchugh@nuigalway.ie; michelle.devaney@nuigalway.ie

A. Callan
Discipline of General Practice, National University of Ireland, Galway, Ireland
e-mail: aoife.callan@nuigalway.ie

W. Wymer (ed.), *Innovations in Social Marketing and Public Health Communication*, Applying Quality of Life Research,
DOI 10.1007/978-3-319-19869-9_15

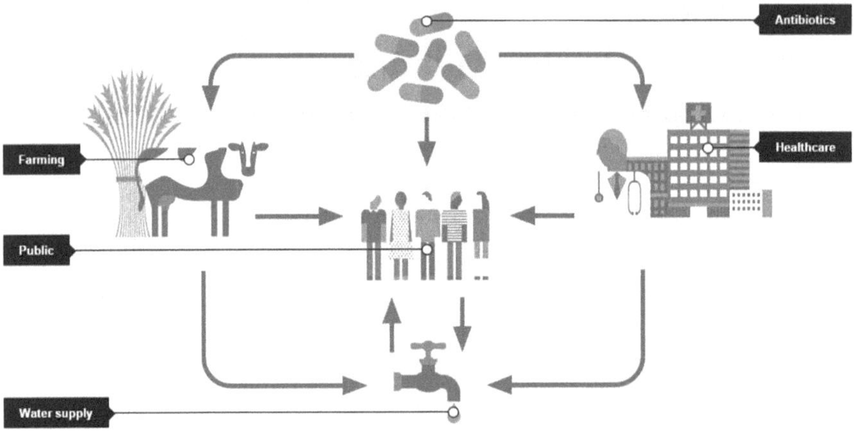

Fig. 15.1 Broad factors contributing to ABR (Source: BBC 2014)

Our continued overuse and misuse of antibiotics has us moving into a post antibiotic era where ABR is one of the world's most pressing public health problems threatening the quality of life for all mankind (Department of Health 2013).

Many factors contribute to the development of ABR at a population and global scale, from the inappropriate and overuse of antibiotics within human and animal health systems to medical tourism and the agricultural use of antibiotics for intensive farming. Figure 15.1 illustrates some of the interrelated factors contributing to the spread of ABR, visually demonstrating that while the individual or the public are central to the issue of ABR, sectors, such as agriculture and healthcare, with their associated infrastructures, institutions and policies, are equally important.

Figure 15.1 also suggests improvements in quality of life associated with ABR will not take place overnight, and the threat of ABR cannot be eradicated. However, the threat to quality of life from ABR can be fully understood and the responsibility for implementing change strategies, shared through effective cooperation and complex problem solving (Department of Health 2013). ABR should be addressed through scientific discovery and changes in behaviour at individual, community and population levels (Amyes 2000). ABR causes a collective action problem whereby the more we use antibiotics the greater the consequences (Anomaly 2013; Edgar et al. 2009). Strategies tackling ABR must do so from multiple levels, ranging from the individual, the community to health facilities and the entire health sector (Tomson and Vlad 2014). This approach goes beyond awareness raising, incorporating a 'broadened' perspective to simultaneously facilitate both behaviour and social change and presents an emerging opportunity for "rethinking the boundaries of social marketing" (Wymer 2011, p. 99).

2 Social Marketing; A Broadened Change Agenda for Antibiotic Resistance

To improve quality of life, many, if not all social marketing problems, including ABR, could be considered in terms of a broadened change agenda. This requires communities and individuals collaborating for change, sometimes simultaneously. This simultaneous movement is away from short term campaigns, towards "*holistic and multi-layered interventions*" (Dibb 2014, p. 1168) integrating a more strategic approach. As Brennan and Parker (2014, p. 3) note, the consideration of the "*behavioural ecological environment in which behaviours occur and managing the environment in addition to the individual*" is necessary to expand and challenge the way we frame quality of life issues.

However, coordinating change around complex problems, such as ABR, remains difficult. Short term once-off interventions remain easier to design and implement; fewer stakeholders are involved and those participating tend to come from similar backgrounds and expertise. The integrative strategies called for in the broadening social marketing literature (Beall et al. 2012; Carvalho and Mazzon 2013; Dibb 2014; Rundle-Thiele et al. 2013; Brennan and Parker 2014), require nurturing of partnerships between different stakeholders, influencers and individuals from different levels in society. Stakeholders, influencers and individuals working towards quality of life change must also exhibit other attributes such as shared definition and understanding of the complex problem, barriers and solutions as well as active engagement and effective communications (Brennan and Parker 2014; Lefebvre 2013). In this manner, change agents go beyond micro or sector levels. Each subsector is interrelated, meaning social marketers must understand the extent of the problem from a holistic society based level, before action can be taken at localised levels. This macro perspective broadens the issue beyond behavioural change targeted at the individual to social change for society.

In accepting the need for a multi-stakeholder integrative approach to ABR and a broadened change agenda, how can these more complex aspects of change be investigated? We believe that consulting with individuals and a diverse range of community stakeholders together in the design of ABR measures and policy's is fundamental to behavioural and social change progress. The case presented within this chapter illustrates, potentially, that all quality of life problems facing social marketers in the twenty-first century are complex. Stakeholders are often diverse and solutions fragmented. As the complexity accelerates, so does the need for a longer term strategic approach to facilitate social change. This case study details how Collective Intelligence (CI) (Warfield 1974, 1994, 2006) is applied by university wide stakeholders (researchers, staff, doctors, pharmacists, management and students) who are directly and indirectly involved with ABR on one university campus. Through collaborative problem solving and group methodologies supported by software and a collective 'space' for conversations, the stakeholders generated 21 barriers to change and 15 resolutions. As part of CI, stakeholders – individuals and community members – also developed a structural ABR barrier map to visualize ABR barriers that significantly aggravate other ABR barriers, thereby building consensus about multi-factor interdependency and potential change strategies.

These ABR barriers, options and graphical findings illustrate a systems methodology to develop broader resolutions to complex quality of life issues. This case study demonstrates that domains rich in the traditions of participation, consensus building, collaboration and group methodologies can assist in improving the quality of life for individuals and communities. The case study concludes with a conceptual and empirical discussion of the implications for social marketers who might wish to move beyond individual behaviour change to scaling up collaborations, consultations,conversations and change at mid and upstream levels for tomorrow's world. Social marketers can use these findings to develop strategies to improve quality of life in the future by assisting in the preservation of antibiotics for future generations.

3 Methodology

Collective Intelligence (CI) is used to facilitate discussion and consensus building. Participants reach a consensus on how best to address a complex issue and the design of resolutions through reflective negotiations and voting for a broadened change strategy. In a typical CI session, participants, with expertise and insight into a problem engage in: (a) developing an understanding of the situation, (b) establishing an integrative basis for thinking about the way forward and (c) producing a strategic framework for effective change (Hogan et al. 2014). The design of CI takes into account the contextual factors that may impact on group work by integrating the influence of culture into the discussion. It also benefits the researcher, as the sessions provide deeper insights into how attitudes are influenced by group work itself (Broome and Fulbright 1995).

'Antibiotics on Campus – Be part of the Conversation' were consensus building consultations organised on one university campus in Ireland. Two consultations were held, the first with campus community stakeholders, the second with student stakeholders only. The aim of the consultations was to contextualise the ABR issue in the campus community, by identifying and mapping the perceived barriers to change from a multi-stakeholder perspective. The CI consensus methodologies and computer software aspects of CI centred around four stages, used to collect data. The same stages were used in both consultations:

1. **Idea Generation:** At the beginning of each session the researchers defined what they meant by ABR. Participants in both sessions were asked the guidance question: '*What are the barriers to reducing antibiotic resistance on campus*? Each participant was given the opportunity to clarify their idea before it was placed on a board for discussion later. Once each participant had nominated an idea, the participants subsequently rank ordered each other's ideas based on the importance they attached to them, using nominal group technique.

2. **Idea Categorisation:** To help facilitate the conversation, four idea categories were identified based upon the ABR literature. The idea categories for ABR were (i) community, (ii) hospitals, (iii) environment and (iv) other. A voting process took place on the most important barriers within each category for inclusion in structuring.
3. **Structuring Barriers:** The 15 barriers that received the highest votes were entered into the interpretative structural modelling (ISM) software, where a series of relational questions, "*Does Barrier A significantly aggravate Barrier B?*" were asked to the participants. A yes/no vote was taken and entered in the ISM software. Structuring continued until all relational barriers were voted upon and a structural barrier map was generated (Figs. 15.3 and 15.4).
4. **Generating Resolutions:** To conclude the CI events, participants were divided into four sub-groups, to work with two categories from stage 2. Participants were provided with the facilitation question: "*What are the options for overcoming the barriers in the [category title]?*" and asked to explain their resolutions with the entire group. All participants then discussed the proposed resolutions they perceived to be the most feasible, impactful and timely in each category. Figure 15.2 shows the participants engaging in the consultations.

Fig. 15.2 Illustration of participants engaging in idea generation, structuring of barriers and generation of resolutions

Both CI consultations incorporated university campus stakeholders, the first CI consultation invited stakeholders from across the campus community, the second CI consultation was restricted to the student population across the 6 Colleges and Schools within the university. In both consultations the participants were defined from a holistic community perspective and not just the health sector view of ABR. Participants were first classified as primary (p), secondary (s) or influencers (i). **Primary stakeholders** were those groups whose economic and societal welfare is dependent on prescribing or consuming antibiotics e.g. general practitioners, microbiologists, pharmacists and/or medical students. **Secondary stakeholders** refer to those that were not directly involved in the prescription or consumption of antibiotics but are involved in the preservation of welfare on the university campus e.g. the department of health or nurses and/or health promotion students. **Influencers** are those groups who influence the prescribing or consumption of antibiotics on campus and beyond, but are not dependent on them for their economic and societal welfare e.g. campus media, student union initiatives and/or arts students.

Prospective participants were recruited through a judgemental sampling strategy. A sample frame was compiled and agreed by a multidisciplinary, expert four person panel drawing upon secondary sources e.g. campus directory and discussions with campus groups. Two methods were used during recruitment. In the first method, community stakeholders in all three categories were contacted via letter accompanied by an information leaflet about the event including the context and the time required, one uninterrupted day of their time for informed consent (N = 30; (5p; 5s and 5i) × 2). Potential participants were followed up with a telephone call within 5 days of receiving the letter. In the second recruitment method, social media and other internal communications such as the University's student newsletter and announcements within lectures were used to recruit students from across all Schools and Colleges as well as all three categories. Once contact was established, potential student participants were sent an information leaflet.

Before each consultation formally began, a lay person's description of ABR was presented to the group. The structure for the day was clarified, and each participant was asked to introduce themselves and their background. Three facilitators were present in the room, one who moderated the consultation, the other two to assist. The participants were free to ask questions at any stage during the consultation. The analysis of the consultations consisted of interpreting the barrier maps and the solutions discussed. The consultations were video and audio recorded to ensure that the interactions between participants were observed and for reference if any clarification needed sought.

4 Results

The two consultations (community and student) generated 21 barriers in total; the community consultations produced 8 barriers while the student consultations generated 13 barriers placed into the 4 pre-determined literature informed categories

(Tables 15.1 and 15.2; Figs. 15.3 and 15.4). Overall, 15 solutions emerged, 9 from the community stakeholders and 6 from the student stakeholders. The most voted community barrier (Table 15.1) was the 'Overuse of antibiotics' (30 votes). The next most important barriers were 'Lack of knowledge of ABR', 'Lack of personal responsibility' and 'A reluctance of patients to accept the advice of prescribers'. The lowest voted community barrier was 'A reluctance by prescribers to refuse patients antibiotics when demanded' (four votes). The low vote suggested although this barrier was important, it was less important to the group than the others. Community stakeholders also discussed possible resolutions (Table 15.1). Examples

Table 15.1 Community stakeholder barriers and resolutions

Barriers	Resolutions
Overuse of antibiotics (30 votes)	Hosting a 'think tank' (like this event) of stakeholders to discuss the issue on campus
Lack of knowledge of AMR (29 votes)	Develop a strategy document with recommendations to present to the management team which could be implemented on campus
Lack of personal responsibility (17 votes)	Implement public reporting by the GPs on how much antibiotics GPs prescribe
A reluctance of patients to accept the advice of prescribers (16 votes)	

Table 15.2 Student barriers and resolutions

Barriers	Resolutions
Refusal to different between virus and bacteria (17 votes)	GPs inform patients more about the difference between bacteria and virus
No new antibiotics' (14 votes)	More campus awareness
Reluctance to consider alternatives to antibiotics (13 votes)	More promotions within the health centre

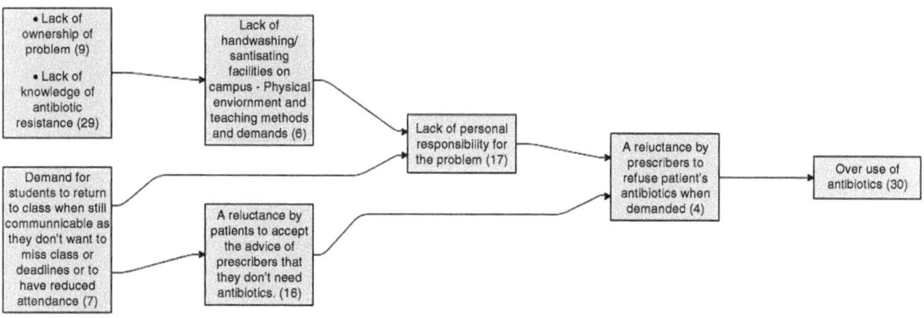

Fig. 15.3 A structural barrier map for community stakeholders

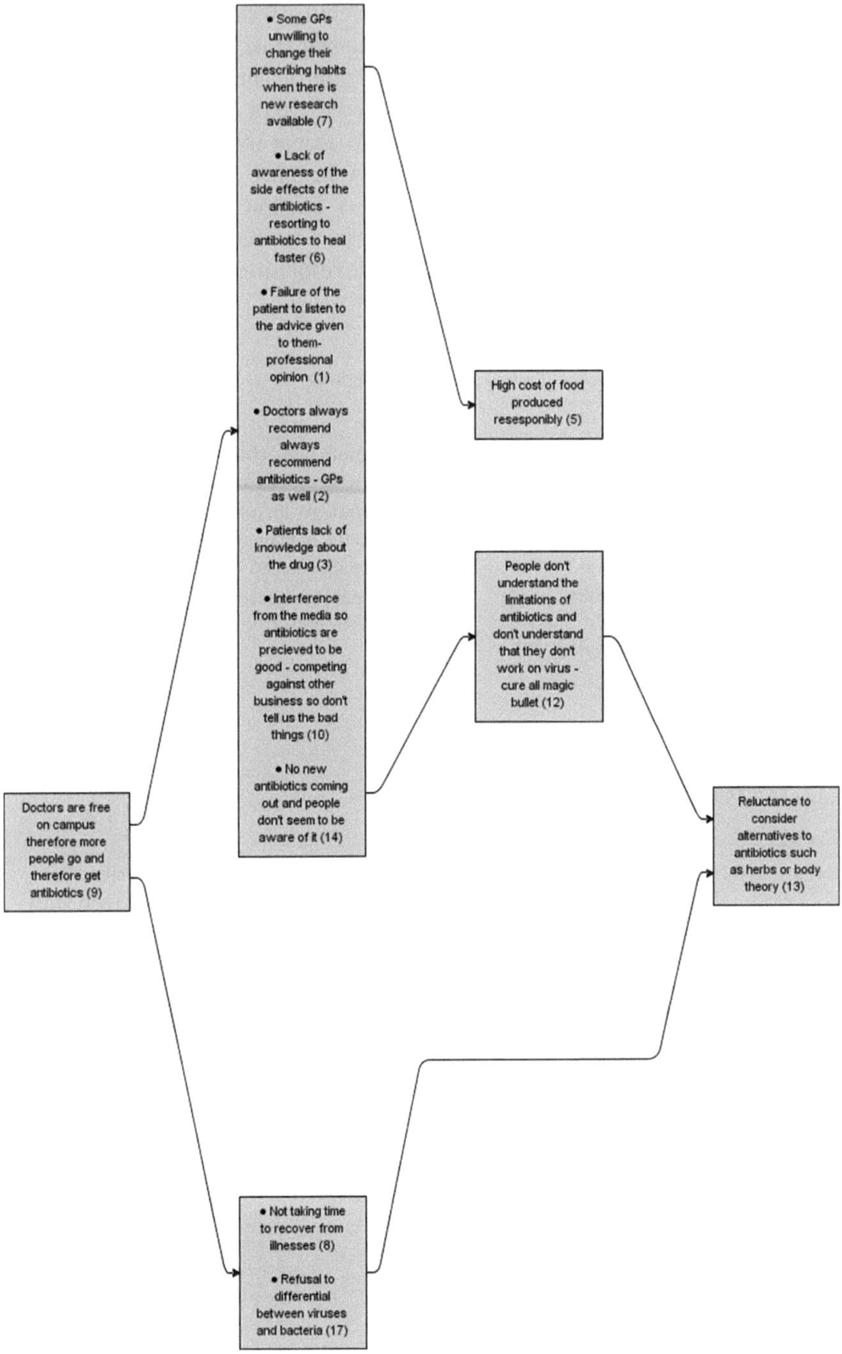

Fig. 15.4 A structural barrier map for students

of resolutions included hosting 'think tanks' and developing campus wide strategies recommendations.

The Community Stakeholder Structural Barrier Map (Fig. 15.3), generated in Step 3 of the CI process, is read from left to right. The barriers to the left significantly aggravate the barriers to the right. For example, 'Lack of ownership of the problem' significantly aggravates 'Lack of hand washing/sanitizing facilities on campus'. Barriers grouped together in the same box, such as 'Lack of ownership of the problem' and 'Lack of knowledge of AMR' are reciprocally inter-related and they significantly aggravate one another. Three different barrier aggravation pathways are evident in Fig. 15.3, with directional arrows indicating aggravating barriers.

The highest voted Student barrier (Table 15.2) was 'Refusal to differentiate between virus and bacteria' (17 votes). 'No new antibiotics' and 'Reluctance to consider alternatives to antibiotics' were the next two most important barriers. The Student barrier that received the lowest vote, 'Failure of the patient to listen to the advice given to them' designating it as the least important barrier to the group. Student resolutions (Table 15.2) included 'More campus awareness' and 'More promotions within the health centre' and 'Consult and Agree with All Relevant Stakeholders'.

The Student Structural Barrier Map (Fig. 15.4) displays one barrier significantly aggravating each other (furthest left box). This barrier concerns 'Doctors being free on campus'. It creates 3 aggravation pathways and significantly aggravates 12 other barriers to the right of it.

5 Discussion

5.1 Social Marketing's Broadened Change Agenda

The graphical representation of community and student consultation barrier maps of ABR on campus is the most tangible outcome of this CI application. Importantly, the findings reveal a potential broadened change agenda along with possible tensions and conflict points. The community stakeholders took a 'behavioural ecological environment' perspective discussing the infrastructural blockages to change on campus, e.g. 'lack of hand washing facilities' as well as clashing behavioural issues e.g. the reluctance by academic staff to overlook or account for short term illnesses such as colds and flues. Their resolutions focused on a long term, multidisciplinary and strategic view of developing a campus wide policy.

> Today's think tank was the start of the solution, it was a great think tank of people from multidisciplines to come together to discuss the issue… the first solution is to address the fact that there is an issue…and not just people from the immediate health care environment (Community Stakeholder Consultation)

The student stakeholders valued the free GP-patient interactions and recognised the over eagerness and/or pressure on students to get back to health given the immediacy of sitting exams. They displayed a shorter term, more individualised understanding of the problem and a knowledge-action gap, not as evident to the same extent in the community stakeholder conversations.

> If they informed their patients more about the differences between viruses and bacteria, then the patient will be aware that the antibiotic won't solve a simple flu (Student Stakeholder Consultation)

Both community and student stakeholders' consultations reveal barriers to ABR and how stakeholders perceive these barriers to be interrelated and connected. These CI consultations also connected the views, experiences and knowledge of different stakeholders to facilitate the development of co-authored actions for change. The conversation suggests that macro and meso interventions go beyond individual campaigns to a collective, scaled-up ABR campus movement.

'Antibiotics on Campus – Be part of the Conversation' engagement with community and student stakeholders provides a rich understanding of what to mobilise on and how to mobilise – how best to move forward. Comparing the two maps (Figs. 15.3 and 15.4), it becomes apparent that the free health centre on campus is central to student views on ABR, as a lot of their views focused on the prescription and consumption of antibiotics. Conversely, the community stakeholders, who do not have access to free health care focused more on the lack of ownership of the problem. This rich understanding derives from the synergies of intelligence, expertise and lived experiences of community stakeholders and students. Richness derives from working together to develop a holistic understanding of the problem, addressing problem complexity and formulating a set of options matched to the complexity of the problem.

If social marketing is to move to a broadened change agenda, i.e. beyond behavioural change to social change, the adoption of a collaborative approach such as the one exemplified within this case is essential. Integrating interventions for ABR on campus translates into infrastructural modification, complimenting knowledge-action gaps for individuals (Figs. 15.3 and 15.4). The barrier maps generated within this case, present a road map for integrated holistic change which can be used to develop long term strategies, therefore improving and/or maintaining quality of life for all.

5.2 *Stakeholders Becoming Transformative Partnerships for Quality of Life and Broadened Change*

The rich insights generated within the barrier maps also illustrate the benefits of adopting a multi-stakeholder – primary, secondary, influencers – approach to solving ABR as a complex problem. As Dibb (2014) describes, different interests and agendas when faced with problem solving can lead to conflict and tension if not managed. CI is a conflict management strategy which encourages the stakeholders involved to span boundaries and seek collective, joint solutions, encouraging multi-stakeholders to invest in strategically planned solutions from a societal community wide perspective. By adopting a multi-stakeholder ethos, quality of life and in this case ABR, becomes the business of all.

For multi-stakeholder based approaches to be successful in improving quality of life, all stakeholders need to move beyond their own short term objectives to building longer term strategic partnerships with diverse individuals and organisations. As once off transactions between stakeholders mature into longer term relationships, transformative partnerships can be formed. By investing in a common goal, whilst maintaining personal objectives but sharing similar values and nurturing trust and commitment from all those involved, quality of life can be maintained and/or improved from the short into the long term.

These consultations were the first time that multidisciplinary stakeholders from different backgrounds and sectors of the campus community were brought together to discuss the issue of ABR on campus. These consultations created a mutual awareness of the role of other parties in the problem, as well as identifying commonalities between stakeholders which could be built upon. Although the stakeholders in the room may have adopted sector specific objectives, their participation allowed them to become aware of the common mission between stakeholders – to address the spread of ABR.

> Get a group of people together, a task force and write a strategy and implementation plan, for the University management team, that sets out a number of actions and recommendations to deal with the issue of antibiotic on campus and how to solve it… (Community Stakeholder Consultation)

These consultations also benefited from the multidisciplinary nature of the consultations – this allowed participants the freedom to 'think outside the box' and to discuss shared goals and values. At the beginning of the consultations not every member saw themselves as a key stakeholder. If there were too many 'experts' in the room, the secondary stakeholders or influencers may have felt less inclined to participate openly, or may not have recognised their role or fit within any strategy. These unconventional stakeholders brought a new and fresh perspective on both barrier and resolutions. It, as Brennan and Parker note (2014, p. 194) lifts "the social marketer's perspective from the micro to meso and macro level factors that exist in social change". Once the shared goals and values between stakeholders are nurtured overtime, through open conversation, the long term relationship between participants and stakeholders could foster into transformative partnerships fuelled by trust and commitment (Duane 2012; Morgan and Hunt 1994). Trust and commitment will be maintained if the partners work openly to develop a strategic goal to address the issue on campus within the consultation.

6 Conclusion

Quality of life issues can be about complex problem solving for the social marketer. Resolutions to complex problems for tomorrow's world, as seen in this case study on ABR, demands change, spanning different sectors and diverse stakeholders. Change of this nature tasks the social marketer to undertake rich collaborations, consultations and conversations through group methodologies such as collective intelligence, with a view towards a broadened behaviour and social change agenda.

Acknowledgements The 'Antibiotics on Campus – Be part of the Conversation' event was funded as part of the Explore initiative, lead by researchers in the Department of General Practice, Marketing and Economics in conjunction with the HRB ICE SIMPle study.

References

Amyes, S. (2000). The rise in bacterial resistance: Is partly because there have been no new classes of antibiotics since the 1960s. *BMJ, 320*, 199.

Anomaly, J. (2013). Collective action and individual choice: Rethinking how we regulate narcotics and antibiotics. *Journal of Medical Ethics, 39*, 752–756.

BBC. (2014). *Human vs superbug: Too late to turn the tide?*http://www.bbc.co.uk/guides/z8kccdm. Accessed 20 Oct 2014.

Beall, T., Wayman, J., D'Agostino, H., Liang, A., & Perellis, C. (2012). Social marketing at a critical turning point. *Journal of Social Marketing, 2*, 103–117.

Brennan, L., & Parker, L. (2014). Beyond behaviour change: Social marketing and social change. *Journal of Social Marketing, 4*, 194–197.

Broome, B. J., & Fulbright, L. (1995). A multistage influence model of barriers to group problem solving a participant-generated agenda for small group research. *Small Group Research, 26*, 25–55.

Carvalho, H. C., & Mazzon, J. A. (2013). Homo economicus and social marketing: Questioning traditional models of behavior. *Journal of Social Marketing, 3*, 162–175.

Department of Health. (2013). *UK five year antimicrobial resistance strategy 2013 to 2018*. London: Department of Health.

Dibb, S. (2014). Up, up and away: Social marketing breaks free. *Journal of Marketing Management, 30*(11–12), 1159–1185. doi:10.1080/0267257X.2014.943264.

Duane, S. (2012). *A social marketing partnership framework: An extension of Morgan and Hunt's (1994) commitment – Trust key mediating variable model*. Galway: National University of Ireland.

Edgar, T., Boyd, S. D., & Palamé, M. J. (2009). Sustainability for behaviour change in the fight against antibiotic resistance: A social marketing framework. *Journal of Antimicrobial Chemotherapy, 63*, 230–237.

Hogan, M. J., Johnston, H., Broome, B., Mcmoreland, C., Walsh, J., Smale, B., Duggan, J., Andriessen, J., Leyden, K. M., Domegan, C., Mchugh, P., Hogan, V., Harney, O., Groarke, J., Noone, C., & Groarke, A. M. (2014). Consulting with citizens in the design of wellbeing measures and policies: Lessons from a systems science application. Social Indicator Research, 1–21.

Lefebvre, R. C. (2013). *Social marketing and social change: Strategies and tools for improving health, well-being, and the environment*. San Francisco: Wiley.

Levy, S. B., & Marshall, B. (2004). Antibacterial resistance worldwide: Causes, challenges and responses. *Nature Medicine, 10*, S122–S129.

Morgan, R. M., & Hunt, S. D. (1994). The commitment-trust theory of relationship marketing. *The Journal of Marketing, 58*(3), 20–38.

Rundle-Thiele, S., Kubacki, K., Leo, C., Arli, D., Cairns, J., Dietrich, T., Palmer, J., & Szablewska, N. (2013). Social marketing: Current issues and future challenges. In K. Kubacki & S. Rundle-Thiele (Eds.), *Contemporary issues in social marketing*. Newcastle: Cambridge Scholars Publishing. ISBN 9781443850247.

Tomson, G., & Vlad, I. (2014). The need to look at antibiotic resistance from a health systems perspective. *Upsala Journal of Medical Sciences, 119*, 117–124.

Warfield, J. N. (1974). *Structuring complex systems*. Columbus: Battelle Memorial Institute.

Warfield, J. N. (1994). *A science of generic design: Managing complexity through systems design*. Salinas: Intersystems.

Warfield, J. N. (2006). *An introduction to systems science*. Singapore: World Scientific.

Wymer, W. (2011). Developing more effective social marketing strategies. *Journal of Social Marketing, 1*, 17–31.

Chapter 16
'Working Without Occupational Health and Safety Is a Thing of the Past': The Effectiveness of a Workplace Health and Safety Campaign in Andalusia (Spain)

Mª José Montero-Simó, Rafael Araque-Padilla, and Juan M. Rey-Pino

1 The Social Marketing Field and Occupational Health and Safety

The key aim of social marketing is to effect positive and sustainable behavioral change for the greater social good (Hastings and Domegan 2007). Within this field we find social communication – often the most visible dimension of social marketing in action (Montero et al. 2009).

Social marketing is applied across a range of issues of concern to citizens, such as addictions, diet, or physical exercise (Stead et al. 2007). The present work offers a practical example of the application of social marketing – or, more specifically, social communication – to the issue of Occupational Health and Safety (from now OHS).

2 An OHS Awareness-Raising Campaign: 'Working Without Occupational Health and Safety Is a Thing of the Past'

The Occupational Health and Safety Law 31/1995 of 8th November sets out a series of requirements designed to foster a culture of OHS in Spanish society. In response to this legislation, at regional level (specifically, in the autonomous community of

This work is part of a research project with reference number: N°14883 funded by the Regional Ministry of Employment of the Regional Government of Andalusia (Spain).

M.J. Montero-Simó (✉) • R. Araque-Padilla
Universidad Loyola Andalucía, Córdoba, Spain
e-mail: jmontero@uloyola.es; raraque@uloyola.es

J.M. Rey-Pino
University of Granada, Granada, Spain
e-mail: jrey@ugr.es

W. Wymer (ed.), *Innovations in Social Marketing and Public Health Communication*, Applying Quality of Life Research,
DOI 10.1007/978-3-319-19869-9_16

Andalusia in southern Spain), the overarching OHS Plan for Andalusia 2003–2008 established a series of objectives for implementing this culture, including the development of sector-specific and cross-cutting risk prevention programs (Junta de Andalucía).

Within the framework of this plan, a series of measures were established, including: awareness-raising campaigns aimed at the Andalusian public; the implementation of educational initiatives for primary, secondary, and high school students on the basics of how to create a culture of risk prevention; raising the level of knowledge on health and safety issues among businesses and employees; interventions in sectors requiring special attention; and specific support programs designed to help firms by facilitating the process of implementing health and safety mechanisms.

This chapter will focus on one such initiative, namely an awareness-raising campaign implemented across Andalusia, entitled 'Working Without Occupational Health and Safety is a Thing of the Past' (*Trabajar Sin Prevención es Cosa del Pasado*). The campaign included television advertising, radio slots, billboard and press advertising, workplace education and training activities, posters, and leaflets aimed at businesses. Launched in the autumn of 2009 by the Andalusian Health and Safety Institute, part of the Andalusian government, its key aim was to raise awareness among the Andalusian population of the need to apply appropriate occupational health and safety measures.

Figure 16.1 shows the campaign poster in which the slogan appears beneath an image of Charles Chaplin, from the film City Lights.

By way of example of the other formats used in the campaign, the audiovisual advertising can be found via the following link: www.juntadeandalucia.es/empleo/webiaprl/iaprl/node/756.

3 Analyzing Campaign Effectiveness

The present work studied the recall and impact of the communication campaign, focusing on its impact at the cognitive, affective, and conative (behavioral) level (Bretón and Buela 2006). This approach makes it possible to both test the effectiveness of the media promotion and also analyze recall of the campaign.

3.1 The Data

To obtain information on campaign recall and effectiveness a telephone survey was undertaken among families in Andalusia, using computer assisted telephone interviewing (CATI) (Abreu 2006).

Fig. 16.1 Campaign poster

3.1.1 The Sample

The sample used in the study comprised 1,600 families. This corresponds to an overall confidence level of 95 % in the results for the entire autonomous community of Andalusia, with a margin of error in the estimated proportions of 2.5 %, on the assumption of a maximum uncertainty of $p=0.5$. The sample was distributed across the eight provinces of Andalusia and took into account issues of both representativeness and proportionality. The selection of the sample units was based on the standard procedures of CATI, which provide virtually random results in samples of a certain volume, such as in the present case.

In terms of composition, 90 % of the sample comprised individuals who lived with other family members, with households of 3 or 4 people being the most common (50.1 %). In the case of approximately 3 out of 10 interviewees, the household included adults aged 65 years or over. In some 33 % of the households in the survey there were minors, the majority of whom were in the 6–14-year age range.

Some 83.4 % of those surveyed had work experience. Over three quarters of those who were in work were employed in the service sector, reflecting the nature of the business base in Andalusia. Next, in descending order by sector, came jobs in industry (12.4 %), construction (7.9 %), and the primary sector (2.5 %). In terms of gender balance, some 89.4 % of the male respondents and 77.6 % of the females were in work or had worked in the past.

3.1.2 The Measurement Scales

The household questionnaire was divided into two sets of questions, one covering health and safety culture and the other looking at socio-demographic issues.

In terms of measuring the impact of communication and dissemination activities, the aim of the study was twofold:

(a) **To ascertain the penetration of the advertising campaign implemented in the autumn of 2009 entitled 'Working Without Occupational Health and Safety is a Thing of the Past'**. Here the survey started by assessing the type of activities that had made an impact on the interviewee, and went on to examine their spontaneous recall of mass media advertising of OHS issues and, more specifically, of the advertising campaign under study.

(b) **To establish the impact of the advertising campaign in terms of its effect on the interviewees at the cognitive, affective, and behavioral level**.

The socio-demographic questions, such as gender, age, and household composition provided details on the profile of respondents, which could point to recommendations for future targeted actions and priority locations in the planning undertaken by the body responsible for such campaigns.

The main statistical techniques employed in the study were measures of central tendency (descriptive, such as the mean, median, and mode), measures of dispersion (descriptive, such as standard and asymmetric deviation), frequency analysis, and contingency tables.

3.2 Effectiveness of Campaign Visibility: Analysis of Recall

A distinction was made between spontaneous and prompted recall of the campaign.

Some 18.6 % of the sample reported having seen information leaflets on OHS. In other media, 12.8 % had seen television adverts: 3.0 % had seen billboard advertising; 2.4 % had seen press advertising; and 1.1 % had heard radio advertising (Fig. 16.2).

Some 16.8 % of interviewees had seen advertising in some conventional media or other (Fig. 16.3).

In terms of recall, of the 269 individuals who registered having experienced OHS advertising in conventional mass communication media, 53.5 % were not able to precisely recall what they had seen or heard. In other words, the recall level was just

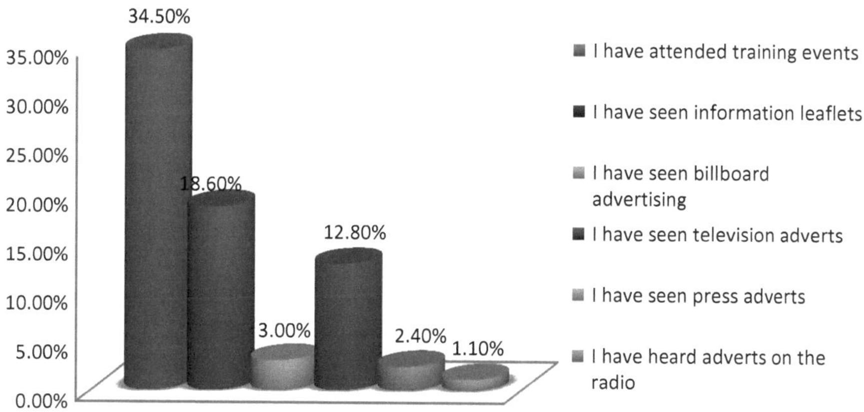

Fig. 16.2 Health and safety awareness-raising activities experienced by interviewees (multiple choice)

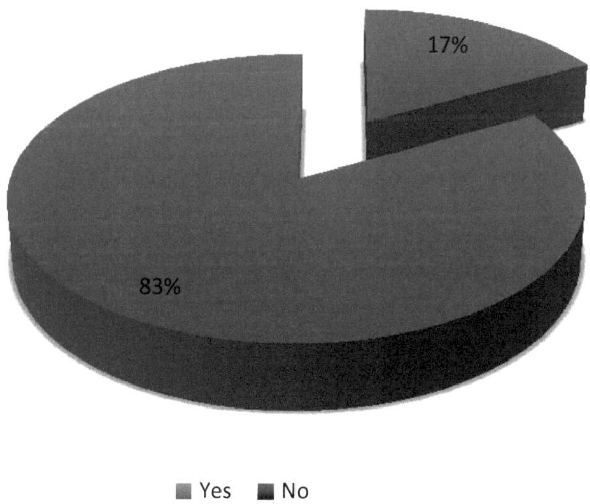

Fig. 16.3 Percentage of interviewees who had experienced OHS advertising in conventional media

9 % of the survey population. Figure 16.4 shows the spontaneous recall rate for the 125 individuals who reported having seen or heard messages about health and safety during the campaign.

Just two people spontaneously recalled the Andalusian government's Charles Chaplin advert. Without access to the media plan and its impact indices it was impossible to calculate spontaneous recall of the ad relative to the exact number of people exposed to it. Therefore we estimated the percentage based on the total number of interviewees, arriving at a spontaneous recall rate of 0.125 % for the advert.

Those who did not spontaneously mention the campaign were asked the following question: *Do you recall having seen or heard an advert by the Andalusian government based on a silent Charles Chaplin film, with the slogan 'Working Without Occupational Health and Safety is a Thing of the Past'?*

Three individuals in the sample remembered having seen an advert from the Andalusian government but could not specify the topic: 0.18 % of the population therefore recalled the regional government as advertiser, but could not provide any further detail. The advert was associated with the topic of construction by 47 individuals (3 % of the population), while 36 individuals recalled other specific organizational health and safety-related topics (2.30 % of the population). Meanwhile, 37 respondents associated the advert with health and safety outside the organizational context, such as the home, traffic accidents, smoking and health, and fire prevention (2.34 % of the total).

The level of recall was similar for employed and unemployed respondents. There were no significant differences in recall relative to the level of concern expressed by participants in the survey for issues associated with workplace health and safety. In socio-demographic terms, nor were there significant differences in recall among men and women, or among different age ranges.

Prompted recall stood at 29.4 % of those who had seen or heard some form of OHS advertising in the mass media (Fig. 16.5). No differences were observed for gender or age.

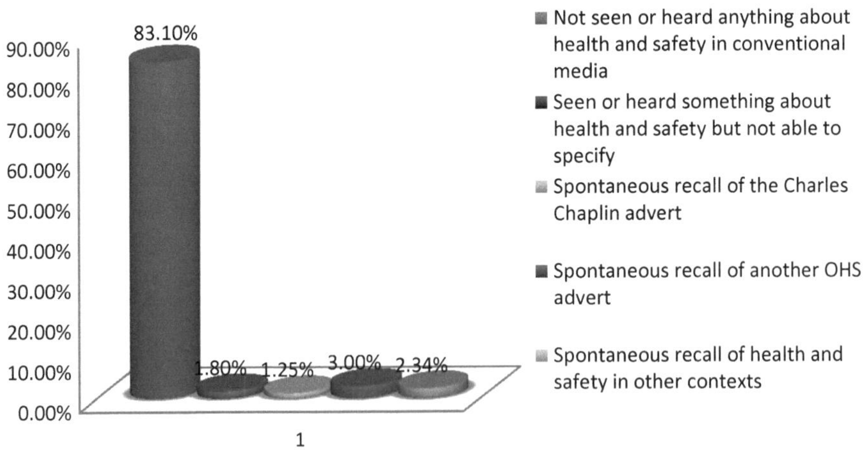

Fig. 16.4 Recall of health and safety advertising in conventional media

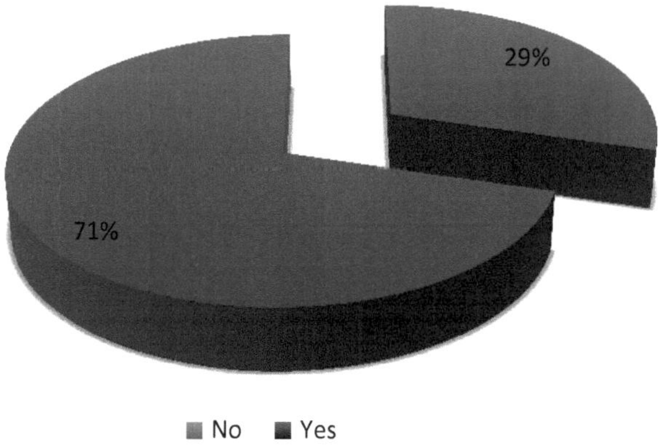

Fig. 16.5 Prompted recall of the Andalusian government's health and safety advert

These results demonstrate that spontaneous recall was virtually inexistent, only improving when the name of the campaign was suggested.

3.3 Evaluation of the Impact of the Advertising Campaign

Impact analysis of the campaign at the affective level revealed that 82.2 % of the 79 individuals who recalled the advert liked it (Fig. 16.6), while 1.3 % disliked it and 16.5 % were indifferent toward it. At the affective level there were no statistically significant differences in impact among men and women or between different age groups.

Figure 16.7 shows the impressions of the advert expressed by the three groups (like, dislike, and indifferent).

The only respondent who did not like the advert found it unpleasant, while the majority of those who did like it thought it interesting and striking.

With regard to the visual advert's capacity to make people think about health and safety, 58.6 % of those who recalled it when prompted reported that it had made them aware of the importance of OHS. This percentage is significant to the extent that the advert, acting on the cognitive level, successfully primes the individual to continue in the right direction in terms of health and safety.

Some 22.9 % reported that the advert had reaffirmed their existing awareness that health and safety is an important topic, while for 18.6 % the advert had made no impact in terms of making them think about the importance of health and safety, hence this can be considered a nil effect at the cognitive level. No significant variations were found when classifying the individuals according to socio-demographic variables (employment status, gender, age, or size or composition of the family unit).

In terms of behavioral impact, of those interviewees who recalled having seen the advert and reflected on its message, 33.3 % had thought about – to a certain or significant degree – changing their approach in terms of the possible risks in their

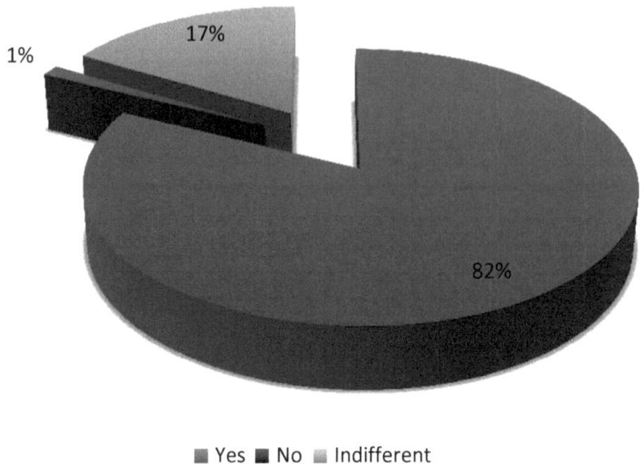

Fig. 16.6 Respondents liked the advert

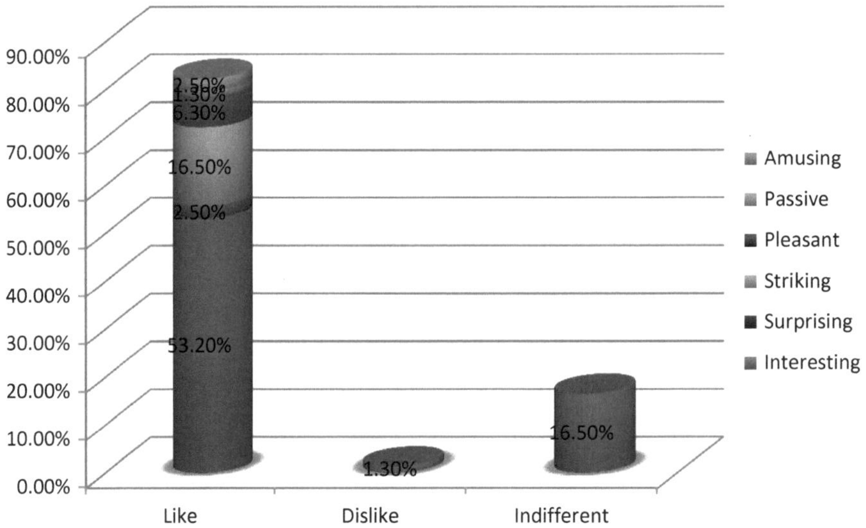

Fig. 16.7 Impact of the advert at the affective level

home or working lives. This contrasts with the 31.9 % who felt the advert had had no such effect on their behavior. The employment status of the interviewees was found to have no effect on their behavioral responses.

Given the limited number of observations, significant conclusions cannot be drawn regarding the relationship between the impact of the advert and the phase of the transtheoretical model in which the individual was to be found. It would appear that even the more aware do not present a higher level of recall.

4 Conclusions: Implications for Future Campaigns

It was found that 57.4 % of citizens had, at some point in their lives, experienced some kind of activity related to creating a health and safety culture. This percentage is not very high, considering the range of activities concerned (advertising campaigns, training, and incentivization).

Of all the types of awareness-raising activity recalled by the citizens of Andalusia, training stands out in particular. In this regard, just over a third of Andalusians report having received some kind of health and safety training. This figure rises to 40.5 % in the case of workplace health and safety. It can be deduced that, despite the efforts of regional government, there is a lack of motivation to achieve an OHS culture within the Andalusian business base, at both employer and employee level.

With regard to campaigns in mass communication media, the level of recall relating to health and safety information is low and imprecise, with just 16.8 % recalling having seen or heard something. When asked to specify, this percentage drops to 7.8 % of the Andalusian population. We regard this to be excessively low, given the use of mass media.

Focusing our attention specifically on the campaign under study, the following results are particularly worth highlighting:

- Spontaneous recall of the campaign among Andalusians stands at 0.125 %. We can conclude that the campaign went largely unnoticed.
- The findings suggest that, of those individuals who recalled having seen or heard something about health and safety from a mass media campaign (269 respondents), 79 recalled that of the Andalusian government when prompted.
- Analysis of the advert's impact across the three dimensions (affective, cognitive and behavioral) reveals that it had a major emotional impact among those who recalled it when prompted, with over 80 % having liked it. The campaign was also more effective on a cognitive level (awareness of OHS issues) than on the behavioral level (awareness translated into action) (Table 16.1).

Table 16.1 Summary of the results analysis for the advertising campaign

Recall	Spontaneous	Nil (2/1600)
	Prompted	Low (79/269)
Impact	Affective	Like (82.2 %) Positive descriptions (81 %)
	Cognitive	Recognize importance of workplace H&S (58.6 %) Reaffirmed importance of workplace H&S (22.9 %) Nil effect (18.6 %)
	Behavioral	Major effect (33.3 %) Nil effect (31.9 %)

5 Recommendations

In light of these results it is evident that the campaign failed on the level of dissemination – that is, in terms of media planning, not in the creative dimension, as it seems – according to the results of the prompted recall – that the advert was well received on the affective and cognitive level.

On the behavioral level, the literature (particularly that of social marketing) typically finds that it is necessary to implement complementary activities alongside social communication initiatives so as to foster better results in terms of sustainable behavioral change (Hastings and Domegan 2007). To achieve this, training activities are recommended. In the present study such activities attracted scores that would need to be improved in the future if better results are to be achieved in behavioral terms.

References

Abreu, I. (2006). El pre test y el post test publicitario: un caso de aplicación a una campaña universitaria de prevención. *UNIrevista, 1*(3), 11–21.

Bretón, J., & Buela, G. (2006). Cuestionario para la evaluación del impacto de campañas publicitarias sobre prevención del VIH/SIDA. *Psicothema, 18*(3), 557–564.

Hastings, G., & Domegan, C. (2007). *Social marketing. From tunes to symphonies*. London: Routledge.

Junta de Andalucía. (s.f.). *Consejería de Economía, innovación, Ciencia y Empleo*. Recuperado el 14 de 09 de 2014, de Seguridad y Salud Laboral: http://www.juntadeandalucia.es/organismos/economiainnovacioncienciayempleo/areas/seguridad-salud.html

Montero, M. J., Araque, R. A., & Rey, J. M. (2009). Occupational health and safety in the framework of corporate social responsibility. *Safety Science, 47*, 1440–1445.

Stead, M., Gordon, R., Angus, K., & McDermott, L. (2007). A systematic review of social marketing effectiveness. *Health Education, 107*(2), 126–191.

Chapter 17
Improving Quality of Life by Preventing Obesity

Tatiana Levit, Lisa Watson, and Anne M. Lavack

1 Introduction

Obesity has become a serious health issue world-wide (WHO 2014). Numerous studies connect obesity to significant impairments in quality of life, including physical, psychological, and social distress (Kolotkin et al. 2001). With linkages between obesity and a variety of serious health issues such as diabetes, cancer, heart disease, and shortened life expectancy, countries are grappling with the issue of how to persuade citizens to maintain a healthy weight, in order to improve quality of life (Popkin et al. 2012).

Public health agencies around the world have turned to social marketing campaigns as a means to educate citizens and persuade them to adopt healthier habits with regard to diet, exercise, and weight management (Grier and Bryant 2005; Lefebvre and Flora 1988). Social marketing involves using marketing concepts to persuade people to adopt behaviors that are better for themselves and society (Andreasen 1994). In the public health sector, social marketing campaigns have been primarily focused on motivating and supporting individual behavior change (Andreasen 2002), but it is recognized that other structural and social changes are often needed to support those initiatives (Donovan 2011; Hoek and Jones 2011; McKenzie-Mohr 2000; Rothschild 1999).

T. Levit (✉) • L. Watson
Paul J. Hill School of Business, University of Regina,
3737 Wascana Parkway, S4S 0A2 Regina, SK, Canada
e-mail: Tatiana.Levit@uregina.ca; Lisa.Watson@uregina.ca

A.M. Lavack
School of Business and Economics, Thompson Rivers University,
900 McGill Road, V2C 0C8 Kamloops, BC, Canada
e-mail: alavack@tru.ca

W. Wymer (ed.), *Innovations in Social Marketing and Public Health Communication*, Applying Quality of Life Research,
DOI 10.1007/978-3-319-19869-9_17

Unfortunately, many social marketing campaigns targeted toward reducing obesity have not been as successful as campaign developers had hoped. This chapter will review the literature to analyze ways in which traditional social marketing techniques may be counter-productive in the context of obesity. More specifically, this paper considers how the issue of obesity may differ from other social marketing target issues, as well as the ways in which those differences impact campaign design. Among the social marketing issues to be examined are the impact of using fear and shame appeals, how target audiences respond to those appeals, how best to offer solutions or advice for losing weight, and the need to integrate structural social changes into the campaign which go beyond individual behavior. We conclude with an analysis of several anti-obesity campaigns that adopt various approaches and discuss how these approaches make the campaigns more or less effective.

2 Social Marketing Principles

To understand how social marketing might play a role in reducing obesity, it is important to understand what social marketing is all about. Social marketing is defined as using marketing principles to increase the acceptability of a social idea (Kotler and Zaltman 1971) or to foster social change or improvement (Lefebvre 2011). Social marketing is usually associated with eliciting voluntary individual behavior change. Social marketing interventions are most commonly used when it becomes important to change personal behavior which has a negative personal or social impact (Andreasen 2002). However, as with any marketing campaign, the decision about whether or not to change one's behavior ultimately lies in the hands of the individual (Andreasen 2002). Therefore, motivating the individual's desire to change is a critical step in the social marketing process.

Rothschild (1999) has argued that social marketers should use the full array of tools available to them, which may include a combination of education, marketing, and law as incentives for behavior change. Hoek and Jones (2011) have discussed education, policy, and regulation in the context of 'downstream' and 'upstream' social marketing. 'Downstream' social marketing focuses on individual behavior change among members of the primary campaign audience. In the case of anti-obesity campaigns, 'downstream' activities would focus on making people understand the connection between body weight and quality of life, and encouraging them to lose excessive weight and to maintain healthy body weight. This may involve educating people about healthy eating, or suggesting ways to introduce more exercise into one's day. 'Upstream' social marketing, on the other hand, uses education, policy, and regulation as a means of altering the social landscape to be consistent with, and supportive of, the behavior that is being sought. In an obesity context, 'upstream' initiatives might include challenging the acceptability of obesity as a social norm, creating municipal commuter bike lanes, supporting community programs that make healthy foods accessible in inner city food deserts, or incenting restaurants and food manufacturers to reduce portion sizes. From this perspective, both education and law are important components of the social marketing toolkit (Donovan 2011).

3 Behavioral Models and Principles of Behavior Change

Social marketing campaigns can only be effective when they are built upon a fundamental understanding about how to create behavior change. Two types of models of health-related behavior change are generally used as a foundation for social marketing campaigns.

The first category of models focuses on the underlying motivators of change, and usually suggests that people can be motivated by fear appeals to change their behavior in order to protect themselves from negative consequences. This category of motivational models includes Protection Motivation Theory (PMT; Rogers 1975; Maddux and Rogers 1983) and the Extended Parallel Processing Model (EPPM; Witte 1992).

The second category of models for health-related behavior change places much more emphasis on the change process, rather than emphasizing the underlying motivators. The most prominent of these models is the Trans-Theoretical Model (TTM; Prochaska and DiClemente 1982; DiClemente and Prochaska 1998). TTM identifies the stages and processes that people go through while moving towards a long term change in habitual behavior, including pre-contemplation, contemplation, preparation, action, and maintenance or relapse.

In order to be successful in motivating and achieving long term behavioral change, it is usually necessary to understand and apply a combination of behavioral motivations and processes for behavior change. The Integrated Model for Social Marketers (IMSM; Cismaru et al. 2008) recommends combining both a motivational model (PMT) and a process model (TTM), in order to increase the effectiveness of social marketing campaigns.

To return to the first category of models which examine the motivators of behavior change, it is important to note that these models involve fundamentally common elements. These models are all targeted toward individuals and are rooted in fear appeals. A requirement of these models is that individuals must process the message in such a way that fear will incite them to change their behavior.

This first category of behavioral change models is commonly used in social marketing campaign messages which identify a health threat and recommend ways in which individuals in the target audience can change their behavior to lessen their likelihood of being impacted by that health threat. According to these models, after members of the target audience are exposed to such a message, they appraise its content to determine whether they perceive the threat being communicated in the message to be substantive enough to act upon, and they also consider a set of possible action responses (Armitage and Conner 2000). Fear arousal involves an assessment of the perceived *severity* of the threat and one's perceived personal *vulnerability* to that threat. If the threat is perceived to be substantive, *fear* is aroused. If fear is not aroused, the target will not be motivated to act. Because fear is central to change motivation, there must be strong message content outlining the severity of the threat as well as the individual vulnerability to the threat (Witte and Allen 2000). When fear is aroused, targets also appraise their own ability to *cope* by averting the threat. This ability is assessed through a determination of whether they perceive that some action would be effective in averting the threat (called *response efficacy*) and whether they believe they would be capable of carrying out that action (called *self-efficacy*). In order to facilitate this assessment, social marketing messages should recommend specific actions that the target audience can take, reinforce the effectiveness of these actions, and provide supports to make these actions as easy as possible.

The major models of behavior change also recognize that motivation to act is affected by weighing the perceived *rewards* associated with taking action against the *costs* of such action. If response costs are too high relative to perceived benefits, motivation to respond decreases. Therefore, it is important for social marketing campaigns to emphasize benefits, provide added incentives, and offer ways to reduce costs in order to increase the probability of behavior change. When developing a coping response, if the associated benefits are perceived to outweigh the costs, members of the target audience will be intrinsically motivated to *act adaptively* to control the threat. Controlling the threat is achieved through carrying out recommended actions for eliminating or reducing the threat, such as changing personal habits. If the costs outweigh the benefits, members of the target audience may be motivated to act *maladaptively* to control fear. Controlling fear is often achieved through responses such as issue avoidance, denial, and counterargument (Witte 1992). Understanding how to apply motivational models of behavior change to social marketing campaigns increases the likelihood of the target audience responding adaptively to the campaign's message. Fear is a great motivator of change as long as individuals believe they are able to protect themselves (Witte and Allen 2000).

While motivating members of the target audience to initially change their behavior is important, such initial motivation is usually not enough by itself. Actual long term behavior change is necessary in order for social marketing campaigns to be deemed successful. This is where the second category of models for health-related behavior change becomes important, by focusing on the change process itself. As mentioned earlier, the Trans-Theoretical Model (TTM) is the best known of this category of models, and TTM's change process is integral to the design of many social marketing campaigns.

It should be noted that the first category of models we discussed, which focus on the underlying motivators of change, are also closely associated with the early stages of TTM. These motivational models provide insight into the internal processes that help move *pre-contemplators* (who do not even recognize a need to change) and *contemplators* (who are motivated to explore the possibility of change) into *preparation* and *action* phases. Research suggests that the majority of people who are found in the first two stages of pre-contemplation and contemplation may stay there for a long time unless something makes them realize that a change is sorely needed and actually possible (Velicer et al. 1995). Once that motivation to act is present, social marketing campaigns should be structured around the remaining phases of the TTM by providing the target audience with the tools to *prepare* to change, helping them to *act* on that behavioral change, and continuing to help them *maintain* that behavior over the long term in order to achieve *termination* of unhealthy behavior and to avoid *relapse*.

4 Obesity-Specific Issues that May Affect Social Marketing Campaign Design

4.1 Denormalization of Obesity

In the 1950s and 1960s, smoking was a dominant social norm and smokers comprised nearly half of the population in Western countries (Garfinkel 1997). This social norm has changed dramatically in the ensuing decades, as the level of smoking prevalence has been substantially reduced. Public health advocates were able to reduce tobacco consumption and gradually change how the public perceived smoking through a variety of strategies, among which denormalization and marginalization were particularly important (Wiley 2013). Some have suggested that it may be possible to denormalize obesity in the same way, by gradually changing public norms about the social acceptability of obesity (Callahan 2013).

With obesity on the rise and reaching the status of an epidemic, being obese has gradually become so widespread that it has turned into a social norm. Motivating individual change in an environment where obesity has been normalized becomes an extremely difficult task (Callahan 2013; Lupton 2014). Individuals who are obese and are thinking about trying to change their diet and exercise behavior are likely to experience a decrease in perceived self-efficacy when they see obesity all around them (Brennan and Binney 2010). Just as the social effects of smoking encourage people to light up when they are around other smokers and motivate teenagers to start smoking to "fit in" with their peers, there is evidence that one's likelihood of being obese is influenced by the weight of those in one's social network. Longitudinal evidence shows that chances of becoming obese are 37–57 % higher if there is an obese spouse, adult sibling or friend (Christakis and Fowler 2007).

However, unlike smoking, many obese people do not seem to be aware of the fact that they are obese. Evidence suggests that personal level of obesity is significantly under-estimated and under-reported because people use those around them as a benchmark for what is normal (Callahan 2013). Those who are obese simply see themselves as being like everybody else, and thus don't perceive their personal level of obesity to be a problem. Within this contest, motivating behavioral change becomes very difficult.

On the other hand, current celebrity culture idealizes the very slim, which suggests that there should be a strong existing motivation to be slim (Strahan et al. 2006). Yet if this were the case, then obesity campaigns should have had an easier time motivating behavior change. Given the conflicting messages of what people see as the norm around them in real life combined with the seemingly unattainable ideal that they see in popular media, many people may feel confused or overwhelmed and thus respond through inaction (Gander 2014).

To return to the smoking comparison, although smoking was also once a social norm, when the scientific evidence that smoking was linked to cancer became overwhelming, public attitudes and culture slowly shifted (Garfinkel 1997). Widespread information about the health dangers of smoking became available in the mid-1950s, and smoking prevalence in Western societies gradually declined over the decades since that time. Governments began to use all of the available tools in an attempt to change public opinion and reduce smoking prevalence (Callahan 2013). Such tools included educating the public about the dangers of smoking, providing quit-lines and other support services to help smokers quit, implementing clean indoor air laws to create an environment conducive to quitting, raising tobacco prices through increased taxes, and using public policy and legislative means to limit the ways in which tobacco companies could market their products (such as labeling regulations and restrictions on advertising).

To review the comparable case for obesity, over the last few decades there has also been mounting evidence demonstrating that obesity is associated with a wide range of health problems. A parallel can be made that if governments commit to introducing legislation and other structural social interventions that support healthier lifestyles at a societal level, they may see the same sort of steady progress toward healthier weight within the population, similar to the situation with the gradual reduction in smoking prevalence.

4.2 Complex Problems Require Complex Solutions

Tackling the issue of obesity is more complex than many other social marketing issues. With smoking, drunk driving, and AIDS prevention, for example, solution choices are reasonably straightforward: find ways to avoid smoking; find alternative means of transport when drinking alcohol; choose an appropriate method of avoiding transfer of body fluids. Obesity is a more complex problem involving many contributing factors on both the individual and structural levels. Individual lifestyle based on poor diet and inactivity is an obvious contributor, but this is just part of a complex set of biological, psychological, cultural, and economic factors that play a role. The full obesity system map contains over 100 different variables, such as dietary norms, biologically "hardwired" and culturally acquired tastes, genetics, illness, medication, stress, employment, time limitations, socioeconomic factors, restricted access to healthful choices, omnipresent unhealthful food and drinks and their advertising, reliance on labor-saving devices and dominance of motorized transportation, and obesogenic built environments that reduce walkability or activity (UK Department of Health 2007). This complexity makes the obesity issue extremely challenging from a social marketing point of view.

Because the most direct causes of obesity are known to be poor diet and lack of exercise, the most popular social marketing model for obesity campaigns puts the responsibility for change directly on the target audience. But even the issues of diet and exercise are complex. In the case of a healthy diet, scientific evidence about the causes of, and dietary solutions to, weight loss are often contradictory. Message content regarding what constitutes healthy eating has changed over time and the public seems well aware of the changing landscape when it comes to so-called expert advice (Freedman 2011; Lupton 2014). These contradictions and the sense that no food is entirely healthy can leave one feeling paralyzed and unable to act. Thus, when it comes to healthy eating, there are systemic reasons for societal evaluations of response efficacy and self-efficacy to be low. Navigating healthy eating requires a considerable amount of education and skill (Drichoutis et al. 2006). Even those who are motivated to do so may struggle to read food labels and understand what nutritional information means (Cowburn and Stockley 2005; Wills et al. 2009). In addition, a key systemic barrier is that healthy food is more expensive and less readily accessible, particularly in low income areas, making it more difficult for some target groups to take action, even when motivated (Drichoutis et al. 2005). Therefore, it is important to carefully research the unique barriers to change faced by the target audience, and design campaigns that meet their needs by choosing appropriately from the wide array of educational tools and interventions. By so doing, perceived self-efficacy should increase and result in higher levels of motivation to take action within the campaign target audience.

In the case of exercise, people's pre-existing issues and ability levels mean that there is no "one size fits all" solution. Some of the underlying causes preventing exercise, such as fear or embarrassment (Andersen 1999; Wouters et al. 2009), can be identified and used to select appropriate campaign messages that will make the target audience feel safe in responding. From a motivational perspective, it is important to make increasing physical activity seem manageable, in order to ensure that response efficacy and self-efficacy are activated. People often have a difficult time changing both diet and exercise at the same time (UK Department of Health 2008). A recent study showed that when someone spends more time in any given week focusing on eating more healthily, they devote less time to exercise, and vice versa (Caldwell 2013). As such, campaigns that recommend incremental changes to lifestyle by adding in small, new changes to either diet or exercise over time may be more successful. While diet plus exercise is ideal, if a target is only able to focus on one thing at a time, studies show that, in isolation, dietary changes have a greater impact on long term weight loss than exercise alone (Miller et al. 1997), thus a stronger focus on dietary changes may be appropriate in social marketing campaigns.

When a social marketing obesity campaign puts the responsibility for change on the target audience, it ignores the systemic problems that lead to poor eating habits and sedentary lifestyles, such as the relatively high price of healthy food and the ready availability of modern conveniences (Rayner 2007). Without government interventions to address these sorts of environmental inhibitors, the effectiveness of social marketing campaigns to reduce obesity will be limited (McCormick and

Stone 2007; Emery et al. 2007). Governments currently seem afraid to intervene actively with the food industry, claiming that the food industry has no incentive to change, and would be unwilling to change, in order to benefit the greater good (Shill et al. 2012). Legislative and public policy changes are needed in order to create the kind of socio-cultural environment that would provide incentives for, and ease of adoption of, physical activity and healthy eating (Walls et al. 2011). This further suggests that interventions that go beyond individual behavior change are critical for ensuring that governmental social marketing campaigns succeed.

5 Tailoring Social Marketing Approaches to Obese Audiences

Given the numerous differences between obesity and other behaviorally focused issues that make use of social marketing campaigns, it is also important to consider the structural elements of traditional social marketing campaigns that may not be well suited to addressing some issues that are unique to the obesity issue.

5.1 Types of Appeals: Health Fear, Social Shame, or Positive Lifestyle Changes?

Behavior change models and their associated social marketing campaigns are usually grounded in fear appeals. While there are many negative health consequences associated with obesity, there is also a significant amount of social discrimination related to obesity. Obesity campaigns can elicit health-related fear of physical consequences, as well as fear of social consequences in the form of shaming. Thus, it is worth examining the relative effectiveness of these two approaches in an obesity context.

Despite ethical controversy, strong fear appeals combined with high efficacy action messages have been proven most effective at eliciting behavior change at a meta-analytic level (Witte and Allen 2000). Health threats are the foundation for most social marketing campaigns that focus on negative health outcomes (for example, anti-smoking campaigns focus on cancer and safe sex campaigns focus on HIV and AIDS). While these outcomes have been accepted by society as truisms, the same cannot be said for society's views of obesity. Research shows that many obese people do not recognize themselves as such, nor do they necessarily recognize it as a problem (Callahan 2013). Thomas et al. (2010) found that obese audience members may counter-argue against negative health threat claims made about obesity, which leads to low perceived campaign response efficacy. According to motivational theories of behavior change, such counter-argument would, in turn, lead to inaction and failure to change.

While social denormalization of unhealthy behaviors through social fear and shaming has seen some evidence of success with young adult and teen audiences in the example of smoking (Wiley 2013), it should be noted that smoking differs from obesity because it is entirely preventable and its associated actions are fewer and less complex. With regard to AIDS prevention campaigns, on the other hand, those with HIV had been subjected to victim blaming for having contracted the virus, so AIDS prevention campaigns had to actively de-stigmatize HIV in order to encourage those who were infected with HIV to become engaged in intervention programs (Wiley 2013). Like the HIV example, the stigmatization of obesity has been shown to reduce the effectiveness of social marketing campaigns (Puhl et al. 2013).

Research overwhelmingly demonstrates that the use of shaming does not work in obesity campaigns, even though shaming may work for other social marketing issues. Arousing weight stigma through victim blaming can actually lead to increased caloric intake among the target audience (Schvey et al. 2011; Tomiyama 2014), which decreases one's perceived ability to control one's eating (Major et al. 2014). Weight stigma also reduces motivation to exercise among obese people, particularly when they internalize societal ideals about weight (Vartanian and Novak 2011). Such negative impacts on self-efficacy serve to reduce motivation to change as negative appeals invoke maladaptive emotion-focused coping responses (Bennett 1998; Brennan and Binney 2010; Puhl et al. 2013). Campaigns that overtly target obese people and focus only on their weight are interpreted by obese people as being 'victim blaming' (Thomas et al. 2010) and are seen as an over-simplification of a complex problem (Piggin 2012; Thomas et al. 2010). From this evidence, it seems clear that obesity campaigns that focus on obesity and weight loss may induce shame and thus be ineffective or counterproductive to achieving their behavior change goals. Several studies have found that obese individuals respond better to non-stigmatizing interventions that do not mention obesity or focus on weight loss, but that instead use positive messages and focus on adopting a healthier lifestyle (Lewis et al. 2010; Puhl et al. 2012; Thomas et al. 2010, 2014).

There is conflicting evidence regarding whether or not diet and exercise should be addressed within the same campaign as a means to achieve a healthier lifestyle. While the UK Department of Health (2008) found that the target market would typically focus on diet over exercise when both were presented together, campaigns that offer multiple health behaviors as ways to reduce obesity have been shown to be more successful overall (Puhl et al. 2012). In today's society, the phrase "diet and exercise" is used ubiquitously in relation to weight loss. As such, it is reasonable that study respondents would want, and expect to see, both kinds of behavior change options presented in a single campaign. This desire for more complex and action-oriented message content contradicts traditional marketing theory which usually suggests that simpler messages are better, but this more complex approach for obesity campaigns may reap better results than highly focused and simple motivational campaigns. This suggests that placing less emphasis on the motivation to change and more emphasis on improving self-efficacy through thoughtful selection of recommended actions and supports would result in a more effective campaign. These conclusions may further imply that campaigns that are targeted to specific audience segments may be less effective in an obesity context.

5.2 Segmenting the Audience and Targeting

Social marketers must often choose between targeting the easiest converts and targeting the populations that are most at-risk for the behavior in question. In terms of the TTM, targeting contemplators and preparers will get faster results than focusing on the much larger pre-contemplator segment that is less likely to respond. Unfortunately, those who are most at risk are often more likely to be pre-contemplators because perceived and/or real barriers to change are deemed too high (Lupton 2014). Obesity research conducted by GFK Bluemoon (2007) uncovered six attitudinal segments that offer similarities with the TTM's phases of change (Lupton 2014). Two of these attitudinal segments, Endeavourers and Balance Attainers, included those who already engaged in healthy behavior. In terms of social marketing, those who have started the change process have already identified the benefits of change and are not appropriate as primary targets for motivational campaigns. Two other attitudinal segments, Defiant Resisters and Quiet Fatalists, were more likely to include at-risk individuals facing structural barriers to behavior change. The remaining attitudinal segments, Apathetic Postponers and Help Seekers, show consistency with those in the contemplation and preparation phases of the TTM who are seen as having higher potential to be motivated to begin the change process. Despite the fact that the pre-contemplation segment includes the most at-risk population, those in the contemplation and preparation stages of change are more likely to achieve higher rates of change. This often results in campaigns choosing to target the population in these two stages. Because social marketing campaigns rely on change rates as benchmarks for success, those in the contemplation and preparation stages of change are more attractive targets than their at-risk pre-contemplator counterparts who may be more in need of intervention.

Obesity is an issue that is affecting a range of different groups in a range of different ways for a range of different reasons. As such, targeting is more complex than in other social marketing contexts. Childhood obesity is one of today's most pressing health issues, with U.S. rates having tripled in the last three decades (Lytle 2012). Several reviews have concluded that intervention programs to reduce the risk of unhealthy weight gain in children have been unsuccessful (Summerbell et al. 2005; Kamath et al. 2008). Consistent with general marketing principles, one issue to consider is how social marketing campaigns should be targeted to have the highest impact. While many children's products rely on "pester power" and are targeted directly to the children (Marshall et al. 2007; Lawlor and Prothero 2011), some products that are designed for children are targeted towards parents (Cross 2002). Social marketing campaigns should be no different. There is ample evidence showing that children's food choices are substantially impacted by their parents (Seiders and Petty 2007), as are their advertising consumption and responses (Grier et al. 2007). However, pre-campaign research has shown that parents are often unaware, or refuse to recognize, that their children are obese (Piggin and Lee 2011; Teegardin 2012). As such, family-based approaches that target parents and children with appropriately tailored and complementary messages and structural supports are being advocated (Lytle 2012; Richards et al. 2009). Schools have also been identified as an important physical and social environment for children to learn normative behavior, and providing healthy foods in schools has become a major government priority (Lytle 2012).

6 Analysis of Various Obesity Campaign Approaches and Their Impacts

This section looks at a select set of obesity campaigns that have adopted a range of social marketing approaches to motivate behavior change. They are analyzed with respect to expectations of success based on obesity's differences relative to other public health issues as noted earlier. The public response to, and success of, these campaigns are also considered.

6.1 *Cut Your Portions. Cut Your Risk: Health-Related Fear*

The New York City Department of Health and Mental Hygiene (NYC DOHMH) campaign, "*Cut Your Portions. Cut Your Risk*," used health fear appeals to raise awareness about increasing portion sizes and their severe health consequences (Craig and Waldhorn 2012). This campaign was extremely graphic, showing pictures of Type 2 Diabetes sufferers who had undergone amputations. This campaign was designed to focus on the severity of the health threat and elicit a strong sense of fear in its audience. While initial reaction to these types of strongly shocking health-focused fear appeals does tend to be negative, they also tend to garner response and elicit more motivation to change than any other type of individually directed appeal (Witte and Allen 2000). NYC DOHMH also ran complementary campaigns that raised awareness about counting calories, making smart choices while dining out, and the negative effects of sugary drinks. The graphic images in the "*Pouring on the Pounds*" campaign depicted a sugary drink pouring into human fat. New York City Council supported these denormalization campaigns with structural requirements such as limiting maximum portions sizes for sugary drinks (Wiley 2013) and requiring restaurants to post calorie counts on their menus (Craig and Waldhorn 2012). While controversial, the coordinated and attention-getting health-related fear appeals in the NYC DOHMH campaign are achieving their desired denormalization results.

6.2 *Strong4Life: Social Fear Through Shaming*

Despite existing research arguing that weight stigmatization reduces the effectiveness of obesity interventions, Children's Healthcare of Atlanta's Strong4Life "*Stop Sugarcoating It, Georgia*" campaign opted to use a fear appeal approach which focused much more strongly on shaming than health. The campaign used black and white pictures of obese children alongside taglines such as "It's hard to be a little girl when you're not" and "Fat prevention begins at home. And the buffet line." The decision to use this campaign approach was based on the results of a survey showing that 50 % of respondents didn't see childhood obesity as an issue and that 75 % of parents with overweight or obese children didn't see their children as having weight problems (Teegardin 2012). However, the campaign resulted in a public outcry strongly opposing the stigmatization of obesity through the use of uncomfortable social messages. Motivational behavior change theories recommend that fear-driven messages should also offer content to help increase perceived response efficacy and self-efficacy. While the Strong4Life ads included a website address that offered such advice, the ads themselves garnered a backlash for not using a problem-solution format (Teegardin 2012). A subsequent study by Barry et al. (2014) found that exposure to these controversial ads had no effect on attitudes toward the seriousness of childhood obesity or support for obesity prevention policies.

6.3 *Change4Life: Shaming Society, Not the Individual*

The UK "Change4Life: Eat well, move more, live longer" campaign (2007–2009) was developed to reduce the number of children classified as overweight or obese. However, it was carefully crafted to use a positive tone and avoid shaming (Piggin 2012). The campaign claimed to target not just the obese, but "everyone." The campaign materials did not use the words 'obesity' or 'obese,' nor did they include images of obese people (Piggin 2012). The campaign used animated humanoid characters and thus was family-friendly, but while it was targeted primarily towards parents, it carefully avoided placing responsibility on them (Piggin 2012). Instead, it turned to modern lifestyles as the cause and offered proactive solutions to prevent serious health problems arising from build up of excessive fat by improving diet and increasing exercise. This included parents showing love by offering healthy snacks rather than trying to win children's affection with unhealthy options (Evans et al. 2011). Consistent with theories of motivation, each ad demonstrates fear-arousing consequences of a sedentary lifestyle and poor eating habits that result in harm to internal organs and a reduced length of life. However, each ad also ends with affirmation of self-efficacy, as the animated family becomes happy upon finding out that there are positive changes they can make. While this approach goes against the social marketing premise of carefully segmenting audiences, it fits with research findings that obese people reject campaign messages which focus on weight rather than health and lifestyle.

The UK Change4Life campaign was strongly criticized for failing to specifically target at-risk groups and for losing valuable opportunities to engage and educate by avoiding the word 'obesity,' given that reducing childhood obesity was its primary objective (Evans et al. 2011; Piggin and Lee 2011). Thus, the UK Change4Life campaign was criticized for taking too 'soft' an approach by focusing on lifestyle, while the Atlanta Strong4Life campaign had been criticized for taking too 'hard' an approach by addressing obesity head-on. Both of these campaigns may have alienated some of their intended target audiences, but for completely opposite reasons.

Social marketing benchmarks are generally meant to be behavioral, so a campaign designed around lifestyle change is actually an appropriate fit with social marketing theory. Because the UK campaign's recommended lifestyle changes do ultimately lead to weight loss and reduced obesity levels, the campaign did still address its benchmarks. However, some argued that a focus on both diet and exercise contradicted the single message recommendation made by the UK Department of Health and thus left the campaign unfocused (Piggin and Lee 2011). Another argument was that the campaign was unfocused and caused confusion because it solicited and attracted involvement from thousands of local partners and hundreds of national partners, from community groups to schools to private firms, that each created their own sub-campaigns. While the main campaign was based on carefully segmented and tailored materials, these materials were not always followed by the partners (Piggin 2012). Additional controversy occurred because partners included firms that made products contributing to obesity (e.g., PepsiCo, Kellogg's, Mars). While allowing these partners to participate may seem hypocritical, community-based buy-in is critical for creating an environment that supports change. As such, sub-campaigns that occur across one's entire environment can work together to create a structural and cultural impact. Despite the varied complaints the Change4Life campaign received, it did show clear signs of success.

6.4 *Measure Up and Swap It: Separating Fear from Action*

The Australian Department of Health and Ageing presented an initial fear-based 2008 campaign called "*Measure Up*," followed by a solution-driven (and much lighter in tone) 2011 campaign called "*Swap It, Don't Stop It*".

The Phase 1 "*Measure Up*" campaign encouraged people to take their waist mea surement and was designed to educate adults about the dangers of intra-abdominal fat (Lupton 2014). The campaign argued that, "the more you gain, the more you have to lose," and attempted to evoke fear of losing one's appearance, health, the length of one's life, and one's relationship with loved ones. However, it left all of the blame and impetus on the victim, and offered no solutions to the threat being raised (Lupton 2014). The campaign targeted Apathetic Postponers and Help Seekers with individual behavior change messages, but did not target the most at-risk pre-contemplation segments because of their "enormous barriers to change" (GFK Bluemoon 2007, p. 7). Despite the fact that the target audience found the messaging to be realistic, some found measuring one's waist to be disempowering and argued that the campaign promoted a panic mentality (Thomas et al. 2014). In other words, while the threat was accepted as legitimate, the target audience responded maladaptively because no viable coping mechanisms were presented. While this campaign garnered high awareness, the lack of solutions did little to garner public support (Lupton 2014;

King et al. 2013). For this reason, experts were recommending that the campaign integrate the type of community and government-based structural interventions that are generally key to campaign success (King et al. 2013; Lupton 2014).

Phase 2, "*Swap It, Don't Stop It*", was launched several months after the "*Measure Up*" campaign. This campaign was designed to show the target audience how easy it is to make small lifestyle changes that can make you healthier (Lupton 2014). The Phase 2 campaign did not use fear, but instead used friendly balloon characters and focused only on positive action-oriented messaging. While the general concept of the campaign seemed to be reasonably well received in terms of response efficacy (Thomas et al. 2014), some of the target audience reported having doubts about self-efficacy, as they felt that the "simple" swaps being proposed to change diet and increase activity were not quite as simple as implied. In many cases, environmental barriers inhibited action. For example, biking to work instead of taking one's car may sound simple unless one lives an hour's ride away and there are no showers at your workplace for when you arrive (Lupton 2014). As a result, only minor increases in attitudes and lifestyle changes were seen (Lupton 2014; Myers 2012). Campaign research also indicated that having too much time between the initial fear campaign and the second action-oriented campaign may have reduced their combined effectiveness (Lupton 2014; Thomas et al. 2014).

6.5 Let's Move: Total Focus on the Positive

First Lady Michele Obama's *"Let's Move"* campaign was launched in 2010 with the goal of solving the challenge of childhood obesity within a generation (Obama 2010). While the overall goal of the campaign is weight loss, primarily in children, the campaign does not use threats or fear to motivate action. It uses entirely positive messaging and is designed exclusively around on-going behavioral changes through components like "three veggie Thursday" and "small plate Saturday" (Puhl et al. 2012, 2013), as well as other structural and community-based changes like an improved National School Lunch Program and creation of the "Let's Move City/Town" designation (Cappellano 2011). It focuses on both nutrition and exercise in one campaign. It employs social marketing's entire range of tools including all 4 P's, education, and law; and it includes campaign content for audience segments ranging from parents to health professionals and community leaders (Cappellano 2011). The campaign was designed to incorporate not just 'downstream' individual behavior change, but also 'upstream' partnerships with public health and community organizations including such things as changes to front-of-package food labeling and increasing access to, and affordability of, healthy foods (Obama 2010). Most importantly, the elements of the campaign designed to achieve individual behavior change do not make use of stigmatization or fear messaging (Puhl et al. 2013). Instead, the campaign uses a wide array of positive messages that focus on several small ways to eat healthier and exercise more (Puhl et al. 2012, 2013). While it is too early to see if national obesity rates are falling in the United States, participation rates have been high both upstream and downstream. As with Change4Life, this should create an environment that is more supportive of healthy lifestyle changes, particularly for at-risk groups. Based on previous obesity campaign research and social marketing theory, this approach should be more successful for encouraging healthier lifestyles, thereby reducing obesity rates.

7 Conclusion

In this chapter we have explained how social marketing principles can be used, with modifications, in the development of obesity campaigns. Motivational behavior change theories play a key role in many social marketing campaigns, since arousing fear is often an important part of driving behavior change. However, as seen from our discussion in this chapter, fear (if used without affirming self-efficacy) and shaming can result in maladaptive behaviors in the context of obesity campaigns, resulting in a campaign that is largely ineffective. Over-targeting obese individuals might potentially (and ineffectively) put substantial blame on them, thereby creating resistance, while at the same time alienating the rest of the population who are also at risk of becoming obese in the future. Campaigns that are more inclusive and use positive language will generally have a better chance of being successful.

Sometimes social marketing interventions require more than motivating changes to individual behavior in order to be effective. Complex problems often call for complex interventions that require broader structural change or community mobilization (McKenzie-Mohr 2000). Such changes typically involve government interventions to incent or mandate change at a level that is beyond the individual's control.

Social marketing campaign creators often think that social marketing is just about changing personal behavior through personal motivation. However, a comprehensive social marketing campaign should recognize that there are many other activities that should be initiated to help individuals in their efforts to change. Creating an environment which makes it easier to engage in healthy eating or more exercise can be a major part of the social marketing effort. Such 'downstream' and 'upstream' activities are not external to social marketing but, in fact, are integral to effective social marketing efforts. Promoting change in a stealth manner means giving consumers a gentle 'nudge' by creating an enabling social context (Thaler and Sunstein 2008). This helps to make behavior change almost effortless, or at least easier, and reduces the amount of conscious or active decision-making that is required of individuals. Such an approach can help to contribute substantially toward improving the quality of life for those with obesity issues.

References

Andersen, R. E. (1999). Exercise, an active lifestyle, and obesity: Making the exercise prescription work. *The Physician and Sports Medicine, 27*(10), 41–50.

Andreasen, A. R. (1994). Social marketing: Its definition and domain. *Journal of Public Policy and Marketing, 13*(1), 108–114.

Andreasen, A. R. (2002). Marketing social marketing in the social change marketplace. *Journal of Public Policy and Marketing, 21*(1), 3–13.
Armitage, C. J., & Conner, M. (2000). Social cognition models and health behaviour: A structured review. *Psychology and Health, 15*(2), 173–189.
Barry, C. L., Gollust, S. E., McGinty, E. E., & Niederdeppe, J. (2014). Effects of messages from a media campaign to increase public awareness of childhood obesity. *Obesity, 22*(2), 466–473.
Bennett, R. (1998). Shame, guilt and responses to non-profit and public sector ads. *International Journal of Advertising, 17*(4), 483–499.
Brennan, L., & Binney, W. (2010). Fear, guilt, and shame appeals in social marketing. *Journal of Business Research, 63*(2), 140–146.
Caldwell, E. (2013). *Exercise or make dinner? Study finds adults trade one healthy act for another.* Ohio State University Research News. https://cph.osu.edu/research/news?page=3. Accessed 23 July 2014.
Callahan, D. (2013). Obesity: Chasing an elusive epidemic. *Hastings Center Report, 43*(1), 34–40.
Cappellano, K. L. (2011). Let's move-tools to fuel a healthier population. *Nutrition Today, 46*(3), 149–154.
Christakis, N. A., & Fowler, J. H. (2007). The spread of obesity in a large social network over 32 years. *New England Journal of Medicine, 357*(4), 370–379.
Cismaru, M., Lavack, A. M., Hadjistavropoulos, H., & Dorsch, K. D. (2008). Understanding health behavior: An integrated model for social marketers. *Social Marketing Quarterly, 14*(2), 2–32.
Cowburn, G., & Stockley, L. (2005). Consumer understanding and use of nutritional labeling: A systematic review. *Public Health Nutrition, 8*(1), 21–28.
Craig, S., & Waldhorn, A. (2012). *Health department launches new ad campaign spotlighting increasing portion sizes and their devastating consequences.* New York: Department of Health and Mental Hygiene, Press Release # 001–12. http://www.nyc.gov/html/doh/html/pr2012/pr001-12.shtml. Accessed 24 June 2014.
Cross, G. (2002). Valves of desire: A historian's perspective on parents, children, and marketing. *Journal of Consumer Research, 29*(3), 441–447.
DiClemente, C. C., & Prochaska, J. O. (1998). Toward a comprehensive, transtheoretical model of change: Stages of change and addictive behaviors. In W. R. Miller & N. Heather (Eds.), *Treating addictive behaviors* (2nd ed., pp. 3–24). New York: Plenum Press.
Donovan, R. (2011). Social marketing's mythunderstandings. *Journal of Social Marketing, 1*(1), 8–16.
Drichoutis, A., Lazaridis, P., & Nayga, R. M., Jr. (2005). Nutrition knowledge and consumer use of nutritional food labels. *European Review of Agricultural Economics, 32*(1), 93–118.
Drichoutis, A., Lazaridis, P., & Nayga, R. M., Jr. (2006). Consumers' use of nutritional labels: A review of research studies and issues. *Academy of Marketing Science Review, 10*(9), 1.
Emery, S. L., Szczypka, G., Powell, L. M., & Chaloupka, F. J. (2007). Public health obesity-related TV advertising: Lessons learned from tobacco. *American Journal of Preventive Medicine, 33*(4 S), S257–S263.
Evans, B., Colls, R., & Horschelmann, K. (2011). 'Change4Life for your kids': Embodied collectives and public health pedagogy. *Sport, Education and Society, 16*(3), 323–341.
Freedman, D. H. (2011). How to fix the obesity crisis. *Scientific American, 304*(2), 40–47.
Gander, K. (2014). Obesity now seen as normal by society, warns Chief Medical Officer. *The independent.* http://www.independent.co.uk/news/uk/home-news/obesity-now-seen-as-normal-by-society-warns-chief-medical-officer-9219466.html. Accessed 21 July 2014.
Garfinkel, L. (1997). Trends in cigarette smoking in the United States. *Preventive Medicine, 26*(4), 447–450.
GFK Bluemoon. (2007). *Australian Better Health Initiative diet, exercise and weight. Developmental communications research report.* Sydney: GFK Bluemoon.
Grier, S., & Bryant, C. A. (2005). Social marketing in public health. *Annual Review of Public Health, 26*, 319–339.

Grier, S. A., Mensinger, J., Huang, S. H., Kumanyika, S. K., & Stettler, N. (2007). Fast-food marketing and children's fast-food consumption: Exploring parents' influences in an ethnically diverse sample. *Journal of Public Policy and Marketing, 26*(2), 221–235.

Hoek, J., & Jones, S. C. (2011). Regulation, public health and social marketing: A behaviour change trinity. *Journal of Social Marketing, 1*(1), 32–44.

Kamath, C. C., Vickers, K. S., Ehrlich, A., McGovern, L., Johnson, J., Singhal, V., Paulo, R., Hettinger, A., Erwin, P., & Montori, V. M. (2008). Behavioral interventions to prevent childhood obesity: A systematic review and metaanalyses of randomized trials. *The Journal of Clinical Endocrinology and Metabolism, 93*(12), 4606–4615.

King, E. L., Grunseit, A. C., O'Hara, B. J., & Bauman, A. E. (2013). Evaluating the effectiveness of an Australian obesity mass-media campaign: How did the 'Measure-Up' campaign measure up in New South Wales? *Health Education Research, 28*(6), 1029–1039.

Kolotkin, R. L., Meter, K., & Williams, G. R. (2001). Quality of life and obesity. *Obesity Reviews, 2*(4), 219–229.

Kotler, P., & Zaltman, G. (1971). Social marketing: An approach to planned social change. *Journal of Marketing, 35*(3), 3–12.

Lawlor, M. A., & Prothero, A. (2011). Pester power–a battle of wills between children and their parents. *Journal of Marketing Management, 27*(5–6), 561–581.

Lefebvre, R. C. (2011). An integrative model for social marketing. *Journal of Social Marketing, 1*(1), 54–72.

Lefebvre, R. C., & Flora, J. A. (1988). Social marketing and public health intervention. *Health Education Quarterly, 15*(3), 299–315.

Lewis, S., Thomas, S. L., Hyde, J., Castle, D., Blood, R. W., & Komesaroff, P. A. (2010). 'I don't eat a hamburger and large chips every day!' A qualitative study of the impact of public health messages about obesity on obese adults. *BMC Public Health, 10*(1), 309–317.

Lupton, D. (2014). "How do you measure up?" Assumptions about "obesity" and health-related behaviors and beliefs in two Australian "obesity" prevention campaigns. *Fat Studies: An Interdisciplinary Journal of Body Weight and Society, 3*(1), 32–44.

Lytle, L. A. (2012). Dealing with the childhood obesity epidemic: A public health approach. *Abdominal Imaging, 37*(5), 719–724.

Maddux, J. E., & Rogers, R. W. (1983). Protection motivation and self-efficacy: A revised theory of fear appeals and attitude change. *Journal of Experimental Social Psychology, 19*(5), 469–479.

Major, B., Hunger, J. M., Bunyan, D. P., & Miller, C. T. (2014). The ironic effects of weight stigma. *Journal of Experimental Social Psychology, 51*, 74–80.

Marshall, D., O'Donohoe, S., & Kline, S. (2007). Families, food, and pester power: Beyond the blame game? *Journal of Consumer Behaviour, 6*(4), 164–181.

McCormick, B., & Stone, I. (2007). Economic costs of obesity and the case for government intervention. *Obesity Reviews, 8*(s1), 161–164.

McKenzie-Mohr, D. (2000). Fostering sustainable behavior through community-based social marketing. *American Psychologist, 55*(5), 531–537.

Miller, W. C., Koceja, D. M., & Hamilton, E. J. (1997). A meta-analysis of the past 25 years of weight loss research using diet, exercise or diet plus exercise intervention. *International Journal of Obesity, 21*(10), 941–947.

Myers, P. (2012). *Evaluation of the "swap it, don't stop it" social marketing campaigns*. Sydney: The Social Research Centre.

Obama, M. (2010, February 9). First Lady Michelle Obama launches Let's Move: America's move to raise a healthier generation of kids. The White House Press Release. The White House).https://www.whitehouse.gov/the-press-office/first-lady-michelle-obama-launches-letsmove-americas-move-raise-a-healthier-genera. Accessed 23 July 2014

Piggin, J. (2012). Turning health research into health promotion: A study of causality and 'critical insights' in a United Kingdom health campaign. *Health Policy, 107*(2), 296–303.

Piggin, J., & Lee, J. (2011). 'Don't mention obesity': Contradictions and tensions in the UK Change4Life health promotion campaign. *Journal of Health Psychology, 16*(8), 1151–1164.
Popkin, B. M., Adair, L. S., & Ng, S. W. (2012). Global nutrition transition and the pandemic of obesity in developing countries. *Nutrition Reviews, 70*(1), 3–21.
Prochaska, J. O., & DiClemente, C. C. (1982). Transtheoretical therapy: Toward a more integrative model of change. *Psychotherapy: Theory, Research and Practice, 19*(3), 276–288.
Puhl, R., Peterson, J. L., & Luedicke, J. (2012). Fighting obesity or obese persons? Public perceptions of obesity-related health messages. *International Journal of Obesity, 37*(6), 774–782.
Puhl, R., Luedicke, J., & Peterson, J. L. (2013). Public reactions to obesity-related health campaigns: A randomized controlled trial. *American Journal of Preventive Medicine, 45*(1), 36–48.
Rayner, M. (2007). Social marketing: How might this contribute to tackling obesity? *Obesity Reviews, 8*(Suppl 1), 195–199.
Richards, J., Hackett, A., Duggan, B., Ellis, T., Forrest, D., & Grey, P. (2009). An evaluation of an attempt to change the snacking habits of pre-school children using social marketing. *Public Health, 123*, e31–e37.
Rogers, R. W. (1975). A protection motivation theory of fear appeals and attitude change. *Journal of Psychology, 91*(1), 93–114.
Rothschild, M. L. (1999). Carrots, sticks, and promises: A conceptual framework for the management of public health and social issue behaviors. *Journal of Marketing, 63*(4), 24–37.
Schvey, N. A., Puhl, R. M., & Brownell, K. D. (2011). The impact of weight stigma on caloric consumption. *Obesity, 19*(10), 1957–1962.
Seiders, K., & Petty, R. D. (2007). Taming the obesity beast: Children, marketing, and public policy considerations. *Journal of Public Policy and Marketing, 26*(2), 236–242.
Shill, J., Mavoa, H., Allender, S., Lawrence, M., Sacks, G., Peeters, A., Crammond, B., & Swinburn, B. (2012). Government regulation to promote healthy food environments–a view from inside state governments. *Obesity Reviews, 13*(2), 162–173.
Strahan, E. J., Wilson, A. E., Cressman, K. E., & Buote, V. M. (2006). Comparing to perfection: How cultural norms for appearance affect social comparisons and self-image. *Body Image, 3*(3), 211–227.
Summerbell, C. D., Waters, E., Edmunds, L., Kelly, S. A. M., Brown, T., & Campbell, K. J. (2005). Interventions for preventing obesity in children. *Cochrane Database of Systematic Reviews, 3*(3), 1–70.
Teegardin, C. (2012). *Grim childhood obesity ads stir critics*. The Atlanta Journal-Constitution. http://www.ajc.com/news/news/local/grim-childhood-obesity-ads-stir-critics/nQPtQ/. Accessed 6 Sept 2014.
Thaler, R. H., & Sunstein, C. R. (2008). *Nudge: Improving decisions about health, wealth, and happiness*. New Haven: Yale University Press.
Thomas, S. L., Lewis, S., Hyde, J., Castle, D., & Komesaroff, P. (2010). 'The solution needs to be complex'. Obese adults' attitudes about the effectiveness of individual and population based interventions for obesity. *BMC Public Health, 10*(420), 1–9.
Thomas, S. L., Olds, T., Pettigrew, S., Yeatman, H., Hyde, J., & Dragovic, C. (2014). Parent and child interactions with two contrasting anti-obesity advertising campaigns: A qualitative analysis. *BMC Public Health, 14*, 151.
Tomiyama, A. J. (2014). Weight stigma is stressful: A review of evidence for the cyclic obesity/weight-based stigma model. *Appetite, 82*, 8–15.
UK Department of Health. (2007). *Tackling obesities: Future choice – Obesity system atlas*. London: UK Department of Health.
UK Department of Health. (2008). *Healthy weight, healthy lives: Consumer insight summary*. London: UK Department of Health.
Vartanian, L. R., & Novak, S. A. (2011). Internalized societal attitudes moderate the impact of weight stigma on avoidance of exercise. *Obesity, 19*(4), 757–762.
Velicer, W. F., Fava, J. L., Prochaska, J. O., Abrams, D. B., Emmons, K. M., & Pierce, J. P. (1995). Distribution of smokers by stage in three representative samples. *Preventive Medicine, 24*(4), 401–411.

Walls, H. L., Peeters, A., Proietto, J., & McNeil, J. J. (2011). Public health campaigns and obesity-a critique. *BMC Public Health, 11*(1), 136–142.
WHO. (2014). *Obesity and overweight-fact sheet no. 311*. World Health Organization (WHO). http://www.who.int/mediacentre/factsheets/fs311/en/. Accessed 22 July 2014.
Wiley, L. F. (2013). Shame, blame, and the emerging law of obesity control. *U.C. Davis Law Review, 47*(1), 121–188.
Wills, J. M., Schmidt, D. B., Pillo-Blocka, F., & Cairns, G. (2009). Exploring global consumer attitudes toward nutrition information on food labels. *Nutrition Reviews, 67*(s1), S102–S106.
Witte, K. (1992). Putting the fear back into fear appeals: The extended parallel process model. *Communications Monographs, 59*(4), 329–349.
Witte, K., & Allen, M. (2000). A meta-analysis of fear appeals: Implications for effective public health campaigns. *Health Education and Behavior, 27*(5), 591–615.
Wouters, E. J., van Nunen, A. M., Vingerhoets, A. J., & Geenen, R. (2009). Setting overweight adults in motion: The role of health beliefs. *Obesity Facts, 2*(6), 362–369.

Chapter 18
The *One for One Movement*: The New Social Business Model

M. Isabel Sánchez-Hernández

1 Introduction

This chapter explores a new business model, the *one for one movement*, not very well known at the moment, but considered a new trend with high possibilities to expand, a model which focus is eminent social and which specific components are social justice, customer understanding and actors' benefits. Build on for-profit enterprises, the *one for one* movement could be considered a model specially created for social innovation.

Social innovation is in the academy agenda today. On the ground it is not new because people have always tried to find new solutions for pressing social needs According to the *Open Book of Social Innovation* (Murray et al. 2010), social innovations are new ideas (products, services and also models) that simultaneously meet social needs and create new social relationships or collaborations and, that is the *one for one movement* explained in this chapter.

The *Guide for Social Innovation* published by the European Commission in 2013 describes the process by which new responses to social needs are being developed in order to deliver better social outcomes. This process is basically composed of four main elements (COM 2013). First, the process starts by the identification of new, unmet or inadequately met social needs. Second, social innovation fosters the development of new solutions in response to these social needs. Third, it is important to evaluate of the effectiveness of new solutions in meeting social needs and, finally the process look for the scaling up of effective social innovations. The *one for one movement* was born to met social needs and has developed a new creative solution to meet them, the solution *one for one* seems to be effective and is growing up in the market as it is shown as follows.

M.I. Sánchez-Hernández (✉)
University of Extremadura, Badajoz, Spain
e-mail: isanchez@unex.es

W. Wymer (ed.), *Innovations in Social Marketing and Public Health Communication*, Applying Quality of Life Research,
DOI 10.1007/978-3-319-19869-9_18

2 The Social Trend in Business

Today's businesses face challenges from new community expectations concerning the role they play in society. According to Cresti (2010) the key word in the debate is Corporate Social Responsibility (CSR). On the basis of CSR is the key idea that any business has the duty of value creation for all stakeholders, going beyond the imperative of shareholder's satisfaction. Consequently, companies are confronting new competitive challenges related to their CSR actions addressed to their different stakeholders and one of these challenges is the attention to a new more responsible and critical consumer very well informed in real time, with opinion about disparities around the world. In this new context, a widespread opinion is that a company's social undertaking combined with profit-oriented behaviors may create added value for the company. The social trend in business consists of reconciling economic and social aspects because the common welfare must not compromise the company's survival and quite the opposite, could be a source of competitive advantages.

Marketing is also involved in this social trend in business. The origins of the social marketing concept can be found in the well known article written by Philip Kotler and Gerald Zaltman, titled *Social Marketing: An Approach to Planned Social Change* (Kotler and Zaltman 1971). Alan Andreasen, in the article titled *Social Marketing: its definition and domain* and arguing that social marketing had been defined improperly in much of the literature, defined social marketing as "the adaptation of commercial marketing technologies to programs designed to influence the voluntary behavior of target audiences to improve their personal welfare and that of the society of which they are a part" (Andreasen 1994, p. 110).

In practice, the majority of social marketing campaigns focus on changing behavior to increase the well-being of individuals or society (Hasting 2007). In this line, Kotler et al. (2002, p. 394), in the book *Social marketing: Improving the quality of life*, defined social marketing as "the use of marketing principles and techniques to influence a target audience to voluntarily accept, reject, modify, or abandon a behavior for the benefit of individuals, groups, or society as a whole". Authors like Peattie and Peattie (2009) consider the difficulties of applying the classical discipline of marketing to the social marketing perspective. Conventional marketing pursuits of more sustainable consumption but the logic of social marketing promotes more sustainable lifestyles and, associated to this aim, social marketing promotes reductions in consumption. As it will be shown later, the *one for one movement* is not avoiding consumption, rather the opposite, it invite to consume twice as the consumer pay for one unit for own consumption and one other unit for someone in need.

From a conceptual point of view, the discipline of marketing is rooted in exchange theory (Bagozzi 1975). In marketing history, the exchange process was viewed narrowly as a strictly economic exchange of some payment for some tangible product. However, marketing is essentially considered a means of meeting and satisfying certain needs of people and, nowadays it is important to remark the existence of a huge variety of consumer needs. At this respect, altruism is a human need, sentiment or behavior whereby we seek to benefit another person even at an absolute cost to ourselves (Gintis et al. 2003). Contemporary research in social marketing (Kotler et al. 2002; Donovan and Henley 2003) seems to be supporting Meeker's (1971) contention that altruistic motives share a place beside other exchange rules (Batson 1995). According to Hormuth (1999), acts have symbolic functions and meanings for a person. Creating meaningful progress towards improving quality of life of people in need requires more radical solutions than just simple donations. In fact, new solutions are appearing in the market to attend the altruism of consumers in developed countries. Additionally, the acquisition of certain products labeled "social" may be done to acquire an identity for the self or create an impression upon others. In this context, the *one for one* purchase behavior could be considered a special kind of altruistic act that carries symbolic social functions and could be used for self-identity formation or self-presentation to others who one is (Hopper and Nielsen 1991).

3 What's the *One for One* Movement?

The social marketing field needs to further its developmental progress by increasing its use of concepts from new fields like social movements (Wymer 2011). The *one for one* brands, held by socially responsible companies, focus a great deal of their efforts and resources to make a positive difference in the world. Companies in the movement are among a unique and growing group of triple bottom line companies who understand that profit is not the only way to measure business success because people and planet also matter (Elkington 1998).

Although **business models** have received limited attention from researchers (Linder and Cantrel 2000) and no consensus exists regarding the definition, nature, structure, and evolution of business models, (Morris et al. 2005) bring order to the various perspectives. Following the authors, most perspectives include the **business's offerings**, considering the **firm's value proposition** and activities undertaken to produce them. Bearing in mind that a firm's ability to earn a rate of profit in excess of its costs of capital depends on some degree upon the establishment of competitive advantage over rivals, any business model builds upon the value chain concept and the **strategic positioning** of the firm in the market (Porter and Kramer 2006). Further, the model involves choices about firm boundaries and relates to transaction cost economics and, fundamental for the choices between cost and differentiation advantage and between broad or narrow market scope (in strategic terms), any business model draws on resource-base theory (Penrose 1959; Barney 1991) emphasizing the **role of resources and capabilities** in forming the basis of competitive advantage. A resource is considered any physical or financial asset that the firm posses, as well as employees' skills and organizational processes. Instead, a capability is something a firm is able to perform, which stems from resources and also from routines upon which the firm can draw (Winter 2003).

Narrowly, the *one for one* movement is a revolutionary business model based on creating for-profit companies with a non-profit mission. Companies involved in the movement are part business and part charity, involving consumers in the process. Customers love the fact that they are changing the quality of life of people in need with their every day choices. Consumers who purchase *one for one* have the opportunity to feel well, look good and do good, and all at the same time. And it is so simple for customers to do good, just buying a product from one of these companies because the support of customers allows the *one to one* movement to fight childhood hunger and basic needs both domestically and globally.

According to Saul (2010) characterization of social business, the movement can be considered a new kind of social innovation. Social ventures operate under a for-profit business model in which success is measured by the positive impact a company makes in addressing a specific social issue. The primary purpose of a for-profit social business is to generate a "social profit" by harnessing the power of commerce. The nature of this kind of business models allows companies to react swiftly to market opportunities, thereby leveraging the maximum social profit through the wonders of capitalism.

To understand the *one for one* movement it is necessary to imagine what the world would look like if every one of us took a portion of what we know, what we like and what use to consume, and gave it to someone else in need. The result will be that we would collectively change the world. It is that vision which inspires the movement *one for one*. The movement is based on a plain and simple idea: "one sold, one given". In the next sections we will show different companies into the movement trying to discover the main characteristics of this creative new business model.

3.1 Origins: TOMS

The buy-a-pair, give-a-pair mission has been popularized around the word by the company TOMS. It is very illustrative of what TOMS is and what TOMS wants the message you will find when opening the TOMS Shoes web page (Fig. 18.1). TOMS, as the company starting the *one for one movement* wants to use business to improve lives.

Blake Mycoskie is the soul of TOMS. He first founded the company TOMS Shoes in 2006 wanting to help children in a village in Argentina without adequate shoes to protect their feet. The company would match every pair of shoes purchased with a pair of new shoes for a child in need. In 2011 Mycoskie expanded the business and TOMS Eyewear was launched.

What began as a simple idea has evolved into a powerful business model helping address need, and also advance health, education and economic opportunity for children and their communities around the world. In 2014 Mycoskie is thrilled to launch TOMS Roasting Co. and, with every bag of coffee purchased, TOMS will provide 1 week of clean water to a person in need.

Fig. 18.1 The first message opening the TOMS Shoes web page (Source: www.toms.com [Accessed 15/11/14])

3.2 *Other Companies into the Movement*

At the moment, probably we can find around 20 companies that could be included into the *one for one* movement. Next paragraphs show a selection of them with the aim to learn more about the movement, to know what they do and how they do it.

3.2.1 141 Eyewear

"You buy, we give" is the slogan used in 141 Eyewear to identify the company with the *one for one* movement. The company is part business and part charity. They are conscious that people do not believe in portions of proceeds or percentages for people in need. 141 Eyewear offer to their clients, by buying one pair of glasses, immediately change someone's life. For every purchase, the company gives a new pair of prescription glasses to a person in need. The company's name is a play on its "*one-for-one*" business model: the company donates a pair of frames to a needy child for each pair purchased in one of the 65 boutiques that carry the brand throughout USA and Canada.

This company was born in Portland with a social mission that is to change the way of doing business in the optical sector. In summer 2009, while discussing eyewear and the possibility of starting their own company, the founders decided that they would change the optical industry by the way they will do business. They were on the mission to share their passion for eyewear and giving by creating a for-profit company with a non-profit soul.

3.2.2 Proof Eyewear

Proof Eyewear is headquartered in Boise, Idaho (USA) and is sold in more than 20 countries worldwide. Proof say to be pioneers in sustainable eyewear. The idea to start Proof surfaced in 2010, when their founders were trying to create a bamboo ski pole in a garage. The idea was a failure, but in the following year, while building up the idea of a bamboo or wood consumer product, the first prototypes for Proof were created. The company was founded in 2011, but its roots are in the 1960s in a family sawmill in southern Utah. The Proof's founders spent their early years working in the family business and still have direct ties today. Their experience taught them love for entrepreneurship and nature.

Proof Eyewear is also a great *one for one* brand. Their *one for one* eyewear model is versatile, folds up for easy storage and transport and is both stylish and affordable. As part of Proof's buy one give one initiative, they pledge to send a pair of *one for one* glasses to a recent surgery recipient in India for every pair purchased. In addition, the company also pledge to give a significant portion of their sales to worthy causes that they believe in. To date they've helped fund an eye clinic in India, organized sunglass recycling initiatives and participated in critical replanting efforts in Haiti.

3.2.3 Twins for Peace

For Twins for Peace being cool is about being good- kind, human and generous. In 2009, the French twins Alexandre and Maxime created the concept of Twins for peace. The brand aims to promote humanitarian values through shoes, clothes and accessories. Every pair of shoe purchased, they donate a locally and sustainably produced shoe in a country we have chosen for a "Shoe Project". In addition, a percentage of our sales in clothing help fund accessibility to healthcare and part of the proceeds from accessories help in the development of education programs. As they take being good very seriously, they hand deliver their given items in conjunction with humanitarian organizations with deep working knowledge of the country.

3.2.4 Two Degrees

Two Degrees is a food producer. The brand has a powerful meaning, two degrees means the separation between the client and a hungry child. "Buy a bar, feed a hungry child" is the slogan used. The company produces a line of all-natural, gluten-free, low sodium, vegan, kosher and genetically modified organism-free nutrition bars in several flavors and distributes bars to health food, specialty, grocery, college and food service channels across the USA. The meals are locally sourced, and the company partners with global nonprofits and NGOs in order to fulfill this mission: "help feed 200 million hungry children".

3.2.5 SoapBox Soaps

"Soap = hope" is the short and striking phrase used in advertising. SoapBox Soaps, a company from USA, wants to change the world through everyday soap purchases. Starting in 2012, in just 2 years they have donated soap internationally to ten countries at the moment in four continents. They also provide soap in USA to struggling families at homeless shelters, women shelters and nursing homes.

Donations depend on the product chosen by the customer. For instance, when a customer buys a bottle of liquid hand soap, whether in a store or online, SoapBox donates a month of clean drinking water development though their charity partner, RainCatcher, through the ONEHOPE Foundation. It makes up the 10 % of SoapBox's profit margins on this product. RainCatcher works in various countries in the world with a concentration towards Sub-Saharan Africa. The company has chosen to work with this organization because of two major reasons. First, their community-driven approach of listening before building what that community needs and, second over 95 % of their installations are still working 5 years after installment.

3.2.6 Better World Books

Better World Books loves books and believes deeply in the power of the written word to change quality of lives and transform the world. The founders, college friends in South Bend, Indiana (USA), envisioned in 2003 a different kind of company with a built-in social benefit by generating revenue to fund literacy.

For the company, the triple bottom line comes in different forms. Doing good is written into their business model, it is not just a part of Better World Books' business, they say that "it is the business". The founders imagined sharing equity among employees, offering good perks and benefits. They have created an open, fearless and fair place to work, where the culture is marked by diversity, equal opportunities, and a shared love of books—a place where employees and customers alike would be part of a groundbreaking community changing the world, book by book. In this context, one of the ways they make a difference is the *one for one* movement. Every time someone purchases a book from BetterWorldBooks.com, they donate a book to someone in need. The books they donate go through hundreds of non-profit organizations. In particular, Books for Africa and Feed the Children partner with the company to take large numbers of donated books and get them to people who need them.

When this company acquires books, it takes ownership of them and then resells them to the public or donates them to charitable organizations. When it resells the books or donates them, ownership passes from Better World Books to the buyer or the recipient. As a for profit social enterprise the company does make money on the books collected and sold. The company not only finds new homes for millions of used books, it also donates a significant portion of profits to support the work of literacy partners, and dozens of other nonprofit organizations around the globe.

As the company say into the web page, to date, every dollar of profit has been re-invested and there has never been an economic distribution of any kind to any of the owners or employees of Better World Books. This creative social model proves that it is possible to do good and do well at the same time.

3.2.7 No More Bedless Pets

No directly related to human quality of live, but taking care about the best friends of humans, No More Bedless Pets is a buy one-give one pet supply company that donates a pet bed to an animal in need with every bed you purchase. The network is comprised of around 500 public charity rescue groups, spay/neuter organizations and shelters actively saving lives and reducing shelter deaths in USA.

4 Characterizing the *One for One* Business Model

Kaplan (2012) announced the need to business model innovation across sectors in order to promote economic prosperity and to find solutions for the contemporary big social system challenges. After to have review the scarce available information about *one for one* movement and to have deep into some of the most famous and successful examples in real business today, we are in position to delimitate the general characteristics of this new business model. Figure 18.2 shows the main drivers of the *one for one* business model to be commented as follows.

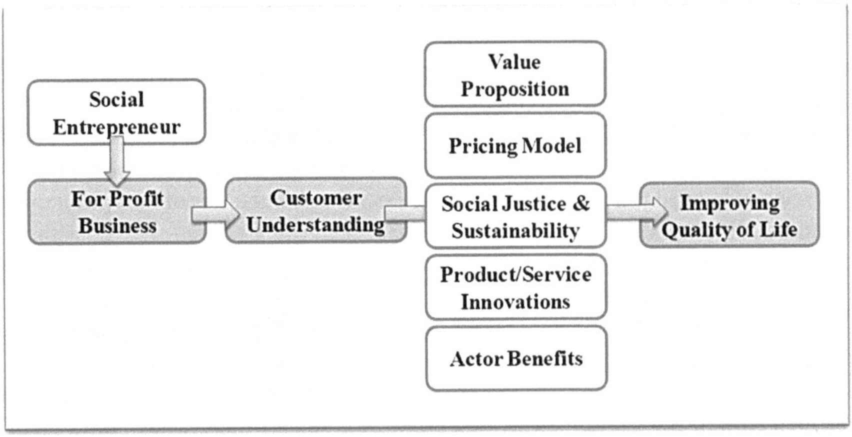

Fig. 18.2 Drivers of the *one for one* business model (Source: Own)

Let's go to start by delimitating the specific components of the model focusing the attention on the *one for one* entrepreneur. Without doubt we are facing **a special kind of social entrepreneurship**. According to Zahra et al. (2009, p. 519), social entrepreneurship "encompasses the activities and processes undertaken to discover, define, and exploit opportunities in order to enhance social wealth by creating new ventures or managing existing organizations in an innovative manner". When an entrepreneur decide starting with a new venture based on the *one for one* movement he or she is **enhancing quality of life** for someone in need. In terms of profits, it is a classical business. The model has to generate revenue because it is a **for-profit business** (Saul 2010).

Consumer understanding is a specific component to difference this model from others. The desire to buy good products or services, sometimes costly, joins with the possibility to create social wealth and quality of life for someone with no opportunities to consume. Companies into the movement are selling more than **new products and services**. They are also "selling" **social justice** and **sustainability**. In this new business model, balancing the motives to create social wealth with the need for profits and economic efficiency are not tricky at all. Moving to the **pricing model**, the *one for one* movement is not in conflict with the logic of marketing. A key contribution of the movement is the harmony between key ethical concerns and economic thinking. The movement fosters responsible consumerism, but consumerism any way. The **value proposition** of any business into the movement is high and this fact increases customers' willingness to pay. The **actors' benefits** are so clear, high consumer satisfaction and improvements in the **quality of life** of people in need. All this elements have been previously considered in academic literature in the field of business models but is the first time that the *one for one* movement has been described as a new business model at the best of our knowledge.

Table 18.1 offers a review of academic literature supporting each driver of the new model described here.

Table 18.1 Business models literature supporting the *one for one* business model

Specific components	Source
Social entrepreneur	Seelos and Mair (2005)
For-profit business	Saul (2010)
Customer understanding	Markides (1999)
Value proposition	Weill and Vitale (2013)
Pricing model	Linder and Cantrell (2001)
Social justice and sustainability	Afuah and Tucci (2001)
Product/service innovation	Dubosson-Torbay et al. (2001)
Actor benefits	Timmers (1998)
Quality of life	Darby and Jenkins (2006)

Source: Own

5 How the Movement Is Impacting People's Quality of Life

In order to show the impact of the selected companies in the people's quality of life, Table 18.2 informs about what the companies explain in their respective web sites and, what they have not disclosed.

Not all companies into the movement have the same communication policy and not all of them have the same levels of transparency. If normal business has the social and "voluntary duty" of disclosure, with more reasons will do it companies that are half business and half charity. Companies into the *one for one* movement are somehow obliged to do it. At this respect, the best analyzed practice is the *Giving Report* published by TOMS in the business site. The company understands that giving back to the community is an important part of any Corporate Social Responsibility program. For instance, in TOMS are proud to be probably the only company in the world with a *Chief Giving Officer*.

Table 18.2 The *one for one* business model impact

Brand	Impact in improving people's quality of life
TOMS	TOMS has given more than 35 million pairs of new shoes to children in need and helped restore sight to over 250,000 people
Two degrees	One million meals donated
141 Eyewear	The company sold more than 1,400 frames per year and each purchase is matched with a donation
Proof Eyewear	Proof Eyewear has different programs upheld with the standards of 1 % of the Planet, a worldwide network of that give at least 1 % of their annual revenue to environmental causes. In general, inside the product package is a return envelope for customers to donate their unwanted glasses to OneSight, the charity organization
Twins for Peace	The profits of the sales are supporting different projects like 'Projeto Alavanca' (deprived children of the São Remo favela in São Paulo, Brazil) or 'Cruzada por los Niños' (children in Mozambique supported also by the Spanish charity)
Better World Books	More than $13 million for over 80 literacy and education non-profit organizations, sending over a million books to their partner programs & saving over 63,000 t of books from landfills
No More Bedless Pets	In 2013 alone, more than $1.1 million dollars was raised for the network partners around USA. They're using that money to end the pets killing
SoapBox Soaps	No clear information available

Source: Own from the websites of each company

6 Some Conclusions and Reflections About the Future of the Movement

The *one for one* movement is starting to be well known as companies in the movement are starting to explain their business models better. At the beginning there has been some confusion about the role of social business but now they are trying to do a better job explaining themselves. The movement is a contemporary radical solution to improve quality of life of people in need and, more than just the development of new products. According to Peattie and Peattie (2009), sustainability is related to the creation of new social products and product substitutions amongst consumers, including the promotion and acceptance of concepts such as responsible consumption, voluntary simplicity and sustainable lifestyles and consumption reduction. *One for one* movement is quite the opposite, inviting consumers to consume twice, for them and for someone in need. The old anti-consumption challenge is change by the new double-consumption proposal probably better accepted by consumers and by marketing discipline. Why to feel guilty when living in the first world, having the opportunity to consume good products? Is consumption reduction directly related with the improvement of quality of life of people in need? The answer is not. Instead, spending our money in any product knowing that someone will receive the same product will be a social and responsible experience and consumers seem to be willing to pay for.

The movement could be considered a new business model working to create purchasing with meaning that support worthy causes such as helping save and restore sight. Thanks to this movement thousands of basic articles for assuring human dignity are being donated. Things to improve life conditions, such shoes or glasses, are starting to be provided by companies committed to the movement because their clients are willing to contribute for a fairer world. This chapter has analyzed the movement as a new business model in the market and the most reputed cases have been described. USA is clearly the country leader at the moment but, reflecting about the future of the movement we can say the movement will expand. The commitment of new companies to improve quality of life of people in need around the world could be a fact in the near future. In addition, some efforts have to be done in order to improve communication with principal stakeholders, their customers. More transparency and a bigger effort to demonstrate how these companies are really improving quality of life of people in need will help the movement to grow up.

References

Afuah, A., & Tucci, C. L. (2001). *Internet business models*. New York: McGraw-Hill/Irwin.

Andreasen, A. R. (1994). Social marketing: Its definition and domain. *Journal of public policy & marketing, 13*(1), 108–114.

Bagozzi, R. P. (1975). Marketing as exchange. *The Journal of Marketing, 39*(4), 32–39.

Barney, J. B. (1991). Firm resources and sustained competitive advantage. *Journal of Management, 17*, 99–120.
Batson, C. D. (1995). Pro-social motivation: Why do we help others? In A. T. Tesser (Ed.), *Advanced social psychology* (pp. 332–381). New York: McGraw-Hill.
COM. (2013). *The guide for social innovation*. Regional and Urban Policy (February). http://ec.europa.eu. Accessed 12 Oct 2014.
Cresti, E. (2010). Sustainability management control systems. Toward a socially responsible planning and control framework. In M. G. Baldarelli (Ed.), *Civil economy, democracy, transparency and social and environmental accounting research role* (pp. 103–123). Milano: McGraw-Hill.
Darby, L., & Jenkins, H. (2006). Applying sustainability indicators to the social enterprise business model: The development and application of an indicator set for Newport Wastesavers, Wales. *International Journal of Social Economics, 33*(5/6), 411–431.
Donovan, R., & Henley, N. (2003). *Social marketing: Principles and practice*. Melbourne: IP Communications.
Dubosson-Torbay, M., Osterwalder, A., & Pigneur, Y. (2001). E-business model design, classification and measurements. *Thunderbird International Business Review, 44*(1), 5–23.
Elkington, J. (1998). *Cannibals with forks: The triple bottom line of 21st century business* (2nd ed.). Oxford: Capstone Publishing.
Gintis, H., Bowles, S., Boyd, R., & Fehr, E. (2003). Explaining altruistic behavior in humans. *Evolution and Human Behavior, 24*(3), 153–172.
Hastings, G. (2007). *Social marketing: Why should the devil have all the best tunes?* Amsterdam: Butterworth-Heinemann.
Hopper, J. R., & Nielsen, J. M. (1991). Recycling as altruistic behavior: Normative and behavioural strategies to expand participation in a community recycling program. *Environment and Behavior, 23*(2), 195–200.
Hormuth, S. E. (1999). Social meaning and social context of environmentally-relevant behavior: Shopping, wrapping, and disposing. *Journal of Environmental Psychology, 19*(3), 277–86.
Kaplan, S. (2012). *The business model innovation factory: How to stay relevant when the world is changing*. Hoboken: Wiley.
Kotler, P., & Zaltman, G. (1971). Social marketing: An approach to planned social change. *The Journal of Marketing, 35*, 3–12.
Kotler, P., Roberto, N., & Lee, N. (2002). *Social marketing: Improving the quality of life*. Thousand Oaks: Sage.
Linder, J. C., & Cantrell, S. (2000). *Changing business models*. Chicago: Institute for Strategic Change, Accenture.
Linder, J. C., & Cantrell, S. (2001). Five business-model myths that hold companies back. *Strategy & Leadership, 29*(6), 13–18.
Markides, C. (1999). A dynamic view of strategy. *Sloan Management Review, 40*(3), 55–63.
Meeker, B. F. (1971). Decisions and exchange. *American Sociological Review, 36*, 485–495.
Morris, M., Schindehutte, M., & Allen, J. (2005). The entrepreneur's business model: Toward a unified perspective. *Journal of Business Research, 58*(6), 726–735.
Murray, R., Caulier-Grice, J., & Mulgan, G. (2010). *The open book of social innovation*. London: Nesta.
Peattie, K., & Peattie, S. (2009). Social marketing: A pathway to consumption reduction? *Journal of Business Research, 62*(2), 260–268.
Penrose, E. T. (1959). *The theory of the growth of the firm*. New York: Wiley.
Porter, M. E., & Kramer, M. R. (2006). Strategy and society: The link between competitive advantage and corporate social responsibility. *Harvard Business Review, 84*(12), 76–92.
Saul, J. (2010). *Social innovation, inc.: 5 strategies for driving business growth through social change*. San Francisco: Jossey-Bass.
Seelos, C., & Mair, J. (2005). Social entrepreneurship: Creating new business models to serve the poor. *Business Horizons, 48*(3), 241–246.

Timmers, P. (1998). Business models for electronic markets. *Electron Commer Europe, 8*(April), 1–6.

Weill, P., & Vitale, M. (2013). *Place to space: Migrating to eBusiness models*. Boston: Harvard Business Press.

Winter, S. G. (2003). Understanding dynamic capabilities. *Strategic Management Journal, 24*, 991–995.

Wymer, W. (2011). Developing more effective social marketing strategies. *Journal of Social Marketing, 1*(1), 17–31.

Zahra, S. A., Gedajlovic, E., Neubaum, D. O., & Shulman, J. M. (2009). A typology of social entrepreneurs: Motives, search processes and ethical challenges. *Journal of Business Venturing, 24*(5), 519–532.

Chapter 19
The Nature of Family Decision Making at the Bottom of the Pyramid (BoP): Social and Managerial Implications

Shruti Gupta and Christina Sesa

1 Introduction

Sita is a 21 year old married woman who lives with her husband and his brother (unmarried) in the same household in Mumbai, India. Sita and her husband have completed 8 years of education, both work as a janitor and earn approximately $2 per day. In her household, all basic and discretionary products are decided and purchased by Sita's husband. At times, Sita suggests certain products for purchase to her husband but most of the times her husband is the decider. On the other hand, Seema, 36 years old is an unmarried woman who lives in the same household with both her parents, a younger unmarried sister (22 years old), a married sister (32 years) who co-inhabits with her husband and two children. All adult members in Seema's household are employed and earn approximately $2 per day. Contrary to Sita's household, all basic and discretionary products in Seema's household are purchased by Seema's younger sister who is 22 years old and is the only family member who has completed high school. All other members of the household submit their wish list to Seema's sister who is the buyer.

The above contrasting cases present a unique and different nature of the family unit and decision making that doesn't quite fit the stereotype of a typical family characterized by a married couple and their biological children. Though research in the area of consumer behavior has identified the significant influence of family members on purchase behavior of the household, most of this research has been contained to western societies (Brown 1979; Cotte and Wood 2004; Hamilton 2009; O'Malley and Prothero 2007). This research stream has identified the structure of family and the roles played by its members along with shopping role stereotypes by matching certain product categories with specific family members.

S. Gupta (✉) • C. Sesa
The Pennsylvania State University, Abington, PA, USA
e-mail: Sxg37@psu.edu

W. Wymer (ed.), *Innovations in Social Marketing and Public Health Communication*, Applying Quality of Life Research,
DOI 10.1007/978-3-319-19869-9_19

The above cases also describe prototypical profiles of consumers at the bottom of the pyramid. A growing stream of research under the labels of bottom of pyramid (BoP) and subsistence consumers has increasingly pointed out the market attractiveness of this segment to multinational companies. These poor consumers are individuals who earn approximately $2 per day. The largest BoP market in the world by size of population is in India where according to a 2011 World Bank estimate, 69 % of the country's total population (approximately 1.2 billion) earns $2 per day. Much has been written about the market attractiveness of the BoP to the multinationals who have shown an increased interest in marketing products to this low income segment (Prahalad 2004; Prahalad and Hammond 2002; Prahalad and Hart 2002). This market segment is viewed as a growth opportunity for consumer product multinationals that face saturated markets in middle and high income economies. These consumer groups at the same time are also considered to be highly vulnerable as a result of their low levels of literacy, income, opportunity, market access and social and political power (Santos and Laczniak 2009).

In this paper, we begin with the description of BoP consumers followed by a brief literature review of family decision making as it has been explained mostly within the western context. Next, we provide details of a qualitative study followed by a discussion of the nature of family decision making in BoP households and the different roles of its members. Finally, we offer explanations for how and why the nature of decision making at the bottom of the pyramid tends to be different from the western households along with from a qualitative study conducted with 58 urban poor consumers in India who provide detailed accounts of their family purchase behavior.

2 Conceptual Background

2.1 Bottom of the Pyramid Consumer and Marketplace

The bottom of the pyramid or base of pyramid marketplace is also commonly referred to as subsistence markets in literature (Elaydi and Harrison 2010; Viswanathan 2007; Viswanathan and Rosa 2010; Viswanathan et al. 2010a; Weidner et al. 2010). Viswanathan and Rosa (2010) define the term subsistence as "barely having sufficient resources for day-to-day living, yet allowing for the possibility of abundance in other life dimensions – such as familial and community networks of relationships" (p. 535). According to the Merriam-Webster dictionary, subsistence means "a: the minimum (as of food and shelter) necessary to support life, and; b: a source or means of obtaining the necessities of life." These definitions suggest that existence at the subsistence level seeks to support life by meeting the most basic and essential needs.

Viswanathan and Rosa (2010) justify the use of the term "subsistence marketplaces" to be descriptive and not patronizing, to draw the need and attention of researchers and practitioners to understand the dynamics of these marketplaces in their own right. The authors stress that these markets comprise of individual consumers and their families, entrepreneurs, communities and markets that makes them different any other type of marketplace. The importance of the subsistence marketplaces draws from its size – aggregated purchasing power in excess of $5 trillion; and an additional one billion customers from developing economies are expected to enter the global market for discretionary spending by 2020 (Hammond et al. 2007). The size of the BOP population is estimated at approximately four billion people (about two-thirds of the worldwide population), with the projection to grow to six billion over the next 40 years, presenting a compelling case for companies to target this consumer segment (Prahalad and Hammond 2002; Prahalad and Hart 2002). The prospective reward for companies who choose to target this segment include "...growth, profits, and incalculable contributions to the humankind" by providing a better life to the poor (Prahalad and Hart 2002, p. 2). The overarching implication of this paradigm is that when companies target the BOP segment, it reduces the cost to the consumers to use goods and services and in turn helps improve their standard of living (Prahalad and Hammond 2002). The literature is full of suggestions that stress on the growth of consumption in subsistence marketplaces and the expansion of products and services being successfully marketed that contradict the common viewpoint that the poor are not interested in sophisticated products and/or cannot afford to purchase them.

People who live in subsistence conditions have been identified as individuals who earn less than $2 per day, lack access to food, education and healthcare (all basic necessities), live under conditions of extreme deprivation, live in substandard housing, have limited or no education and lack access to reliable transportation, potable water and sanitation (Sridharan and Viswanathan 2008; Viswanathan and Rosa 2010; Viswanathan et al. 2010a; Weidner et al. 2010). Some researchers have proposed that these subsistence marketplaces are an intertwined system of consumers and micro entrepreneurs (Sridharan and Viswanathan 2008; Viswanathan et al. 2010), where, one is inseparable from the other. This symbiotic buyer-seller relationship provides them with skills (i.e., bargaining, price, quantity, weight of the product) that they use interchangeably between both roles. Because of the extreme conditions under which subsistence consumers survive, basic needs are often unmet and companies that have been successful in these marketplaces are the ones that have "...displayed the vision to identify and address some of the critical needs that face subsistence consumers" (p. 563, Weidner et al. 2010). In addition, the low level of literacy that characterizes subsistence consumers translates into poor marketplace skills, too. The poor struggle with reading product labels, store signs or product use instructions and subtracting purchase price from cash on hand, all that restricts their ability to best utilize their limited funds (Viswanathan et al. 2010b). Another ramification of low literacy and numerical skills is the short-term planning horizons (1–2 days) for these consumers. These short term horizons become a bigger problem because of the uncertainty in the external environment along with the absence of any law enforcement or protection (Viswanathan 2007).

Resource Constraints BoP markets are characterized by several resource constraints including a paucity of information, education and infrastructure along with financial restraints (Viswanathan et al. 2009). The primary marketplace exchange for a subsistence consumer is limited to the neighborhood store despite the fact that the latter often charges a price premium. This stems from several reasons: uncertainty about financial income ties them to the neighborhood store that extends credit, travel to other stores due to transportation costs associated with long distances. The poor also choose to not purchase in larger quantities in order conserve limited funds for an unforeseen emergency in the future.

Resource Abundance Despite severe physical and financial resource constraints, the poor also have an abundance of assets that include labor, human capital (health that determines the ability to work and skills and education that determine the return on labor), housing (or productive asset), household relations (that allows the poor to pool resources and share consumption) and social capital (the relationship ties between members of the household and communities) (Moser 1998). Therefore, the poor manage complex asset portfolios and it's this asset management that may influence their vulnerability in the marketplace. According to the 1990 World Development Report, a poverty reduction strategy takes into consideration the above assets in the following three pronged approach: first, economic growth, that uses the poor's labor as their most valuable asset; second, investments in basic health and education (human capital) that would allow the poor to leverage their labor; and, third, provide social safety nets in terms of protective measures and policy to protect vulnerable populations.

2.2 Family Purchase Behavior

In a seminal paper, Harry L. Davis (1976) argued that the family unit as a whole is the critical decision maker within a household. Research mostly conducted within the context of western markets has identified the significant influence that family members have on consumer decision making (Brown 1979; Cotte and Wood 2004; Hamilton 2009; O'Malley and Prothero 2007). The model for family decision making identifies various purchase related roles adopted by the same or different family members (Sheth 1974). The five roles prototypical in a family are initiator or gatekeeper, influencer, decider, buyer and user (Engel et al. 1973).

Spousal roles have been shown to play a significant role in family decision making with categories such as wife dominant, husband dominant or joint and autonomic decisions (Herbst 1952). In the western societies, this structure has been influenced with shifting spousal roles in the family with women in the workforce and as more husbands assume greater household roles (Xia et al. 2006). Despite this, spousal roles have also been correlated with certain purchase categories where husbands are mostly responsible for purchase of technical products and repeat purchase of nondurables tend to be more wife dominant (Sproles and Kendall 1986). Wife dominant purchase relates mostly to products are consumed by the entire family where her product and brand decision is driven by orders or requests from family members and on her judgment of what they like or dislike and what is 'good for them' p. 241 (Davis 1976). The concept of joint decision making established in western markets (Foster and Olshavsky 1988; Shepherd and Woodruff 1988) has been mostly studied in relation to high involvement products as opposed to low involvement products which tend to be more habitual in nature and therefore, don't require a joint decision.

Another stream of research in the area of family influence in decision making in western societies has also identified the role of children (Caruana and Vassallo 2003; Williams and Burns 2000). This research suggests that children influence purchase of products that directly impact them and therefore is most applicable to certain product categories, i.e., toys, snacks and other food items, family holidays (Foxman et al. 1989; Kim and Lee 1997).

The above literature review assumes three key patterns in family decision making in western markets. First, joint decisions are more applicable to high involvement products. Second, husband and wife dominant purchase categories drive family purchase behavior and third and lastly, children influence product and brand choice. While these patterns have been studied and established in western markets, it is important to establish if the above findings are generalizable to BoP households, thereby, creating a gap in research that justifies additional investigation in this area.

3 Methodology

We used a long interview based approach of qualitative research for this study that allow the researcher to capture consumers' beliefs, feelings and motivations in their own words and to obtain a 'thick' description of phenomenon under investigation (McCracken 1988). This method also enables a closer examination of the data to extract rich explanations of observations and relationships, and offers considerable flexibility in understanding the complexities of consumer behavior (Carson et al. 2001). The choice of methodology was especially suitable to research in the BoP area. This area is a newer and emerging stream of research with a paucity of scholarly studies. As a result, qualitative research can be useful in the early stages of theory building. Additionally, the BOP consumers are often illiterate or less educated and subsequently unable to indicate their thoughts and opinions on a more quantitative measurement scale. Additionally, the choice of the method is also consistent with other studies in the BOP area (Viswanathan et al. 2009, 2010).

The research was conducted in India for two reasons. First, the country has occupied center stage in BoP literature with a large numbers of success stories (Prahalad 2004; Prahalad and Hammond 2002). Second, India has a BoP population (those with annual incomes below US$3,000 in local purchasing power) of nearly 925 million, the largest in the world (Hammond et al. 2007). Therefore, with the large size of the BoP population, India carries the potential to become one of the most profitable BoP markets in the world thereby, making a compelling case for companies interested in tapping the market potential.

For the study, interviews were conducted in the city of Mumbai and Kolkata. This geographical location was selected for three specific reasons. First, both cities attract a significant portion of rural consumers from the country in search of employment, thereby providing access to both types of BOP consumers – urban and rural. Second, both cities are one of the largest in its state and the country and therefore, it is not uncommon to find people living in poverty but at the same time exposed to modern media, newer technologies, urban lifestyles and consumption trends. Third, both authors are proficient in Hindi (the national language in India) which is widely spoken and understood in both cities. Since BoP consumers typically have low literacy levels, proficiency in the language understood by them was essential for data collection.

Informants were recruited through the housekeeping staff at an academic organization in Mumbai and at a non-governmental organization (NGO) in Kolkata. In addition, a snowball sampling method also allowed the researchers to recruit additional participants for the study by asking the previous informants to recommend others who met the eligibility criterion – personal income of approximately US$2–4 day (which converted to approximately Rupees 3000–6000 per month). This sampling method allowed one study participant to recommend others from her social network who met the sample selection criterion. One of the co-authors and a trained research assistant (also fluent in Hindi) conducted the interviews. The co-author responsible for data collection personally trained the research assistant in the interviewing process and data collection. In addition, both authors reviewed the translation and back translation of the interview guide for the study. Finally, both authors who are proficient in Hindi heard the audio recordings of all interviews and reviewed the English transcriptions to ensure accuracy and attention to detail.

3.1 Sample

Out of the 58 study participants, 26 were men and 32 were women. The female participants were between the ages of 23–58 years, mostly employed in housekeeping work, most of them married and with a personal income that ranged between Rupees 2800–4500 per month. Most of them indicated that were responsible for their household purchases. The male participants were between the ages of 25–56 years, mostly employed in housekeeping work, married and with a personal income between Rupees 3500–5000 per month. Almost all informants had a minimum of 1–5 years of education though there were five informants who were completely illiterate.

3.2 Procedure

An interview guide was used to explore and understand the nature of family decision making at the bottom of the pyramid. During the interview, initial conversation starters were often followed with several "how" and "why" questions to probe the answers further. Both interviewers agreed that after a brief warm-up, all informants were comfortable in the interview and proactively shared their thoughts and responses to the probe questions. The interviews began with a conversation to elicit general and background information on the informant, such as age, marital and family status, educational level, employment status and household composition. All responses pertaining to the socio-demographic profile of the informant was manually recorded by the researchers. The in-depth investigations involved an unstructured approach of asking questions in a conversational style. These interviews lasted about 30–50 min and were recorded. Each participant was compensated with a monetary award of Rupees 300 (approximately $5).

4 Findings

4.1 Family Composition

BoP families exhibited a structure similar to the western markets with a husband, wife and children. However, different from western markets, the BoP family also included members of the extended family (i.e., brother in law, aunt etc.) who cohabited in the same household. Unlike the research conducted amongst BoP households in Zimbabwe by Chikweche et al. (2012), where, the husband resided in the urban area for employment and the family resided in the rural areas, our research revealed a different structure. BoP families in our study lived together in the urban area with most members of the family gainfully employed. It was also common for two or three generations in the family to live together where the older generation, mostly women had either retired from the workforce and were full time home makers. This phenomenon may be attributed to the social structure of India where it is a common norm for adult children to live with parents even after marriage. In addition to the social factor, the economics of multiple members cohabiting in the same household signals a cost saving that might be considered a necessity in a BoP household.

4.2 High Involvement Decision Making

Our findings show that the concept of low involvement purchase didn't exist in BoP families. Each purchase decisions regardless of price or nature of product (food or personal hygiene) was very important to the buyer. Given the limited income, each interviewee stressed on the importance of making the "right" purchase decision whether it was a staple food item, like rice and oil or a personal hygiene product such as bar soap or shampoo. Clearly, the concept of routine or habitual purchase behavior is non-existent in BoP households. Several reasons might explain the above trend. First, some study participants reported that they are paid on a daily basis and were employed in occupations where daily employment was not guaranteed. Overwhelmingly, all study participants were employed in low or no skill occupations and voiced their concern regarding the permanency of their employment. Several study participants revealed that they had frequently been either laid off or fired from their previous jobs and had experienced frequent periods of unemployment. This automatically implied that the disposable fund to purchase products was unpredictable and not guaranteed. In this case, the unpredictable availability of disposable funds in combination with unpredictable employment translated into a high involvement decision for all purchase. Second, an unpredictable supply of dependable quality products mostly in the perishable and staple food category meant that the BoP buyer would evaluate the purchase and a purposeful decision with time and cognitive effort spent on investigating and observing the quality of the product before making the decision to purchase. The buyer or decider in our study elaborated on how she would observe, touch and examine the food item before making the decision to purchase it and despite the pressure by the store owner or surrounding buyers to make a speedy decision. Third and last, frequent changes in price of products purchased on a daily basis meant that the buyer would have to request and confirm the product price for each item on her shopping list before the purchase. Such changes in the product price might be attributed to fluctuating product supply or a promotional offer in the case of packaged non-durables.

The above three conditions give rise to three dominant patterns of purchase behavior in BoP households – first, purchase on "as needed" basis; second, purchase when the products are available and lastly, purchase when disposable funds are available (Chikweche et al. 2012). BoP households purchase products in small quantities sometimes on a daily basis. For example, food products are purchased on a daily basis for the following reasons – perception of freshness, limited funds and lack of appropriate space in the home for stocking up that would prevent product spoilage.

4.3 Shopping Roles in BoP Households

Though some prior research suggests that in BoP households' husbands and wives are assumed to perform similar roles in purchase decisions for non-durables such as food and personal hygiene (Sridharan and Viswanthan 2008), our study didn't find to be case. Our research showed that one female member of the household, not necessarily the wife and/or employed, predominantly performed the role of initiator, decider and buyer (Engel et al. 1973) though all members of the household were users. This was particularly true for the case of staple food/cooking items such as rice, grains, vegetables etc. There was also a minor incidence in our study where we found that an employed male member would be the decider for the family. This spousal role was rare and not as common in our sample. The main reasons identified for the justification of the choice of family member to serve in the role of the decider were trust and marketplace literacy. Usually but not universally, the buyer was an individual who demonstrated some level of marketplace literacy in terms of reading brand names, checking product price printed on product labels and product expiration date, an important product attribute in India where lack of climate controlled warehouses imply a high incidence of product spoilage.

The role of initiator and influencer of the purchase varied and depended on the age and gender of the family member. For example, shampoo, bar soap and other cosmetic product purchase (such as a fairness cream) were mostly suggested and influenced by the young female adult member of the family. At the same time, purchase of packaged instant foods and candy were mostly influenced by young children. Therefore, the age of the family member played a significant role in influencing the choice of products that impacted them the most. This is similar to the research that examines the influence of children in family decision making (Foxman et al. 1989; Kim and Lee 1997). Interestingly, the retail store owner is also an influencer in BoP family purchase. Several study informants revealed that both product and brand choice were often influenced by the information provided by the retailer. This product or brand information included but was not limited to product attributes, benefit, promotional offer and the choice of the social network. In addition to the store owner, the social network and media (outdoor advertisements, television and celebrity endorsements in the case of personal hygiene products) were also identified as key sources of information that influenced product and brand choice.

4.4 *Lack of Price Sensitivity and Retail Store Loyalty*

The decider in the BoP family showed an overwhelming lack of price sensitivity for most household purchases. All study informants stated that they didn't engage in comparison shopping to determine the lowest price point for the product, even in the case of staple food items. Overwhelmingly, each BoP family exhibited a deep rooted loyalty to the neighborhood store where all study participants shopped at the local neighborhood independent retailer for all non-durable products for both personal and household needs. These retailers are frequently referred to as "kirana" in Mumbai and "modi" in Kolkata. For consistency, this paper will refer to these independent retailers as "kirana" in the remainder of the paper. The "kirana" retail sector in India is quite fragmented and estimated at US$437 billion in retail value in 2011 (Boston Consulting Group 2012). "Kirana" stores are characterized by a low cost structure, presence in residential areas, consumer familiarity and are family owned and operated (Pratibandla 2012). These stores are built on a relatively small area and offer a limited range of products that include packaged unbranded commodities like rice, flour, salt, spices etc. along with branded and packaged fast moving consumer goods (Pratibandla 2012; The Economic Times 2012). This store format thrives on the socio- economic model of repeated interactions with customers in a close geographical proximity – this resulting in trust arising through repeated interactions (Pratibandla 2012). In our study we found that the neighborhood or slum where the participant lived would have several "kirana" stores within a small area. Despite this, each participant was loyal to only one and didn't engage in any comparison shopping or variety seeking behavior.

The first reason for this loyalty the decision to be price sensitive may be attributed to a sense of belongingness. Almost all female study participants mentioned that the "kirana" store owner would address them as "bhabhi" (sister in law) or "didi" (elder sister). These salutations are common part of a conversation with a female member in the Indian society and also the norm. In addition, each informant expressed that when addressed by the store owner as "bhabhi" or "didi", it made them feel important and respected. It is quite likely that this feeling might influence the store loyalty in two different ways: first, by being loyal the buyer engages in reciprocal behavior and responds to the respect that she receives from the store owner. Second, the loyalty response is an outcome of the sense of belongingness wherein, she is now viewed as a member of his social network. One explanation for this behavioral outcome lies in the concept of social capital (Woolcock and Narayan 2000) that refers to networks of family, friends and associates that allow people to act collectively and draw from during times of a crisis. The importance of building social capital might explain why BoP consumers prefer to patronize local retailers who charge higher prices but the capital accrued from the ongoing, long term relationship might also allow for credit to the consumer in times of financial hardship (Sridharan and Viswanathan 2008). A second reason may be explained in terms of a sense of lineage. Almost all study participants explained their loyalty to the "kirana" store as one that was grounded in the purchase behavior of the family and members of the social network in the past. Several of them recounted that their family and friends had shopped at that particular "kirana" store for years and it wouldn't be appropriate to change that where, defecting or changing to a different "kirana" store would be perceived as a deceitful act. This form of loyalty that is tied to the family influence or lineage has been studied in the context of brand loyalty (Olsen 1993). The role of family influence in consumer decision making lies in the concept of consumer socialization which explains how young individuals develop consumer related skills, knowledge and attitudes (Moschis and Churchill 1978; Ward 1974). However, though consumer socialization has the biggest impact in the child hood years, the process does continue during the adult life cycle (Brim 1968; Moschis 1987) and into the elderly years (Smith and Moschis 1984) as grown-ups adults make changes to current consumption preferences and behaviors and adopt new ones in the marketplace. The same is the case for BoP consumers who might be migrants from the rural areas to the city and learn consumer related skills and attitudes akin to a child. Although our finding supports the research led by Chikweche and his colleagues (2012) but differs in the rationale for the above phenomenon. The above researchers attributed to the lack of price sensitivity to product shortages common in Zimbabwe to explain why BoP households might not have the option to be price sensitive.

5 Discussion and Contribution

This research has raised several interesting observations that contrast the nature of family decision making in BoP households with the research conducted in western markets. The structure of family in BoP households doesn't mimic the nuclear family prevalent in western economies at all income levels and characterized by a husband, wife and children. Instead, BoP families are composed of extended members of the family and different generations either cohabiting together or the employed member of the family living in an urban area with the family in the rural region. The concept of routine or habitual decisions prevalent in the case of consumer non-durables such as food and personal hygiene products in western markets is non-existent in BoP markets where regardless of the price and nature of product, BoP consumers go through a deliberation and effortful process to integrate product information from multiple sources (such as store owner, social network, family members, media etc.) in the decision to purchase. The concept of joint decision making, where husbands and wives collaborate on household purchase was an unknown phenomenon in BoP household. Almost all decisions regardless of the nature of product or price were autonomic decisions albeit significantly influenced by other members of the household. A single designated decider or buyer was responsible for almost all purchases for the entire family. The buyer was mostly a female, not necessarily employed and with some level of marketplace literacy.

The one area where the family decision making mimicked its western counterpart was in the role of children. All study participants revealed that children influenced product and/or brand purchase for products that was either meant for their sole consumption or directly impacted them. For example, purchase of instant packaged food like Maggi noodles, cookies, candy, carbonated beverage etc. were influenced by the choice of the minor child. On the other hand, young adult children initiated and influenced the purchase of personal hygiene products meant for their personal consumption such as fairness cream, hair shampoo, soap etc. However, in contrast to the role of children in family decisions studied in western markets, school age children in BoP households also influenced and validated the purchase decision for products that didn't relate or impact them directly. This mostly was the case where the buyer would ask the school age child to validate the purchase by checking the product price and the expiration date as printed on the label. This was an important role universally relatable to most BoP households in the event when the buyer was illiterate and due to unexpected situation had to make the purchase for the family.

This research raises the need for marketers to recognize the heterogeneity of BoP households when compared to western counterparts and the different nature of decision making and shopping roles. The findings here suggest that marketers of consumer non-durable products, mostly large multinational companies need to customize marketing strategies to acknowledge the different shopping roles performed by family members and the impact of resource constraints and abundance common to BoP households. One area in which marketers can benefit from this research is marketing communication. Given that the social network and kirana owner influence product purchase, companies might want to deliver product knowledge in a way that uses the above channels to disseminate information instead of media channels to reach the BoP consumer. The distribution strategy of consumer marketers might also benefit from this research. Given the reliance on the social networks of BoP consumers' market information, companies might choose to introduce a direct distribution system where consumers purchase products from a member of their community who also serves as the distributor for the company instead of purchasing through the kirana store. This member of the social network would then be more sensitive to the economic constraints of BoP households and would strive to make the product available at the lowest price possible. Companies can also revise the product strategy to ensure that product quality is a dependable attribute for BoP consumers. This may be achieved by executing marketplace literacy education program to empower the BoP consumer with a better understanding of marketplace exchanges and allow them to gain control over their role as a consumer by becoming more informed of the marketplace environment. Research by Viswanathan et al. (2009) reveals that the benefit of providing information and education to the poor lies in their empowerment and not in protection from exploitation or harm.

Finally, this research makes a contribution to the call for research using the transformative consumer research (TCR) perspective which seeks to enhance "life in relation to the myriad conditions, demands, potentialities, and effects of consumption" p. 6 (Mick 2006). The purpose of the TCR agenda is to generate insights into poverty alleviation by understanding consumption by the poor. In the area of consumer decision making, the TCR approach advocates to help the poor become better decision makers by customizing market information to fit their cognitive and emotional abilities (Blocker et al. 2011). This is important since though the poor are subject to the same set of factors in decision making as their affluent counterparts, the impact of a bad decision carries are far greater impact for the former thus, exacerbating their vulnerability in the marketplace. We hope that the findings of this study and suggested implications for marketing practice will have help improve the well-being of the poor, reduce their vulnerability through innovative marketplace interventions which in turn will empower the poor consumers.

References

Blocker, C., Ruth, J., Sridharan, S., Beckwith, C., & Ekici, A. (2011). Applying a transformative consumer research lens to understanding and alleviating poverty. *Journal of Research for Consumers, 19*, 1–9.

Brim, O. G. (1968). Adult socialization. In J. A. Clausen (Ed.), *Socialization and society*. Boston: Little, Brown.

Brown, W. (1979). The family and consumer decision making: A cultural view. *Academy of Marketing Science Journal, 7*(4), 335–345.

Carson, D., Gilmore, A., Perry, C., & Gronhaug, K. (2001). *Qualitative marketing research*. London: Sage.

Caruana, A., & Vassallo, R. (2003). Children's perception of their influence over purchases: The role of parental communications patterns. *Journal of Consumer Marketing, 20*(1), 55–66.

Chikweche, T., Stanton, J., & Fletcher, R. (2012). Family purchase decision making at the bottom of the pyramid. *Journal of Consumer Marketing, 29*(3), 202–213.

Cotte, J., & Wood, S. (2004). Families and innovative consumer behavior: A triadic study of siblings and parents. *Journal of Consumer Research, 31*(1), 78–86.

Davis, H. (1976). Decision making within the household. *Journal of Consumer Research, 2*(4), 241–260.
Elaydi, R., & Harrison, C. (2010). Strategic motivations and choice in subsistence markets. *Journal of Business Research, 63*(6), 651–655.
Engel, J., Kollat Kollat, D. B., & Blackwell, R. (1973). *Consumer behavior* (2nd ed.). New York: Holt.
Foster, I. R., & Olshavsky, R. W. (1988). *Extending information processing theory to family purchase decision making.* In Proceedings of the Society for Consumer Psychology, pp. 87–90.
Foxman, E. R., Tansuhaj, P. S., & Ekstrom, K. M. (1989). Family members' perceptions of adolescents' influence in family decision making. *Journal of Consumer Research, 4*, 482–491.
Hamilton, K. (2009). Consumer decision making in low-income families: The case of conflict avoidance. *Journal of Consumer Behaviour, 8*(5), 252–267.
Hammond, A., Kramer, W., Katz, R., Tran, J., & Walker, C. (2007). The next 4 billion. *Innovations: Technology, Governance, Globalization, 2*(1–2), 147–158.
Herbst, P. G. (1952). The measurement of family relationships. *Human Relations, 5*, 3–35.
Kim, C., & Lee, H. (1997). Development of family triadic measures for children's purchase influence. *Journal of Marketing Research, 34*(3), 307–321.
McCracken, G. (1988). *The long interview*. Newbury Park: Sage.
Mick, D. G. (2006). Meaning and mattering through transformative consumer research. In C. Pechmann & L. L. Price (Eds.), *Advances in consumer research* (Vol. 33). Provo: Association for Consumer Research.
Moschis, G. P. (1987). *Consumer socialization*. Lexington: Lexington Books.
Moschis, G. P., & Churchill, G. A., Jr. (1978). Consumer socialization: A theoretical and empirical analysis. *Journal of Marketing Research, 15*(4), 599–609.
Moser, C. (1998). The asset vulnerability framework: Reassessing urban poverty reduction strategies. *World Development, 26*(1), 1–19.
O'Malley, L., & Prothero, A. (2007). Contemporary families and consumption. *Journal of Consumer Behaviour, 6*(4), 159–163.
Prahalad, C. K. (2004). *The fortune at the bottom of the pyramid: Eradicating poverty through profits* (4th ed.). Upper Saddle River: Wharton School.
Prahalad, C. K., & Hammond, A. (2002). Serving the world's poor, profitably. *Harvard Business Review, 80*(9), 48–57.
Prahalad, C. K., & Hart, S. L. (2002). The fortune at the bottom of the pyramid. *Strategy + Business, 26*(1), 2–14.
Pratibandla, M. (2012). Foreign direct investment in India's retail sector: Some issues. In *Working paper no. 366*. Bangalore: Indian Institute of Management.
Santos, N. J. C., & Laczniak, G. R. (2009). Marketing to the poor: An integrative justice model for engaging impoverished market segments. *Journal of Public Policy and Marketing, 28*(1), 3–15.
Shepherd, C. D., & Woodruff, R. B. (1988). A muddling through model of family purchase conflict management. *Proceedings of the Society for Consumer Psychology, 9*, 73–86.
Sheth, J. (1974). *Models in buyer behavior*. New York: Harper and Row.
Smith, R. B., & Moschis, G. P. (1984). Consumer socialization of the elderly: An exploratory study. *Advances in Consumer Research, 11*(1), 548–552.
Sproles, G. B., & Kendall, E. I. (1986). A methodology for profiling consumers' decision making styles. *Journal of Consumer Affairs, 20*(2), 267–279.
Sridharan, S., & Viswanathan, M. (2008). Marketing in subsistence marketplaces: Consumption and entrepreneurship in a South Indian context. *The Journal of Consumer Marketing, 25*(7), 455–462.
Viswanathan, M. (2007). Understanding product and market interactions in subsistence marketplaces: A study in South India. In J. A. Rosa & M. Viswanathan (Eds.), *Advances in international management – Product and market development for subsistence marketplaces* (1st ed., Vol. 20). San Diego: Elsevier.

Viswanathan, M., & Rosa, J. A. (2010). Understanding subsistence marketplaces: Toward sustainable consumption and commerce for a better world. *Journal of Business Research, 63*(6), 535–537.

Viswanathan, M., Srinivas, S., Gau, R., & Ritchie, R. (2009). Designing marketplace literacy education in resource-constrained contexts: Implications for public policy and marketing. *Journal of Public Policy and Marketing, 28*(1), 85–94.

Viswanathan, M., Rosa, J. A., & Ruth, J. A. (2010a). Exchanges in marketing systems: The case of subsistence consumer-merchants in Chennai, India. *Journal of Marketing, 74*(May), 1–17.

Viswanathan, M., Rosa, J. A., & Ruth, J. (2010b). Relationships and commitment as cornerstones in marketing systems: Subsistence consumer merchants in Chennai, India. *Journal of Marketing, 74*(May), 1–17.

Ward, S. (1974). Consumer socialization. *Journal of Consumer Research, 1*(2), 1–14.

Weidner, K. L., Rosa, J. A., & Viswanathan, M. (2010). Marketing to subsistence consumers: Lessons from practice. *Journal of Business Research, 63*(6), 559–569.

Williams, L. A., & Burns, A. C. (2000). Exploring the dimensionality of children's direct influence attempts. *Advances in Consumer Research, 27*, 64–71.

Woolcock, M., & Narayan, D. (2000). Social capital: Implications for development theory, practice and policy. *The World Bank Research Observer, 15*(2), 225–249.

Xia, Y., Ahmed, Z. U., Ghingold, M., Hwa, N. K., Li, T. W., & Ying, T. C. (2006). Spousal influence in Singaporean family purchase decision making process. *Asia Pacific Journal of Marketing and Logistics, 18*(3), 201–222.

Chapter 20
Designing Social Marketing Activities to Impact the Shaping of Expectations of Migrants in Health Service Encounters: The Case of African Migrant Blood Donation in Australia

Ahmed Shahriar Ferdous, Michael Polonsky, Bianca Brijnath, and Andre M.N. Renzaho

1 Introduction

An individual's expectations of future health encounters, like all service encounters, are shaped by that individual's past experiences (Burnett and Peel 2001; Karmi 1992). In the case of migrants and refugees moving from low and middle income countries (frequently referred to as developing countries) to high income countries (frequently referred to as developed countries), these past experiences occur in home countries that often have significantly resulted in lower quality health systems (Kinnon 1999). As such, these individuals' expectations of and encounters with the health services in their host country might be shaped by potentially negative past home country experiences. Their expectations will also be influenced by the

A.S. Ferdous (✉)
Department of Marketing, Deakin University,
Waterfront Campus Locked Bag 200001, Geelong, VIC 3220, Australia
e-mail: ahmed.ferdous@deakin.edu.au

M. Polonsky
Department of Marketing, Deakin University,
Melbourne Burwood Campus, 221 Burwood Highway, Burwood, VIC 3125, Australia
e-mail: michael.polonsky@deakin.edu.au

B. Brijnath
Department of General Practice, Monash University,
Ferntree Gully Road, Notting Hill, VIC 3125, Australia
e-mail: Bianca.Brijnath@monash.edu

A.M.N. Renzaho
School of Social Sciences and Psychology, University of Western Sydney,
Locked Bag 1797, Penrith, NSW 2751, Australia
e-mail: andre.renzaho@uws.edu.au

W. Wymer (ed.), *Innovations in Social Marketing and Public Health Communication*, Applying Quality of Life Research,
DOI 10.1007/978-3-319-19869-9_20

perceived differences in culture, language, and infrastructure between the two countries. This is often broadly referred to as psychic difference, which is "the subjectively perceived distance to a given foreign country" (Håkanson and Ambos 2010, p. 196). The more similar the home and host country are, the less the psychic distance (Burnett and Peel 2001; Kinnon 1999; Sousa and Bradley 2006). High levels of psychic distance will be especially problematic for host country health providers when trying to communicate with migrants about local health services, such as blood donation. In addition, these host country services may be new to migrants and refugees, and as potentially novice consumers of these services, they may have more difficulty in evaluating host service experiences (Dagger and Sweeney 2007).

Given that consumer expectations can be shaped or influenced by social marketing, countries accepting migrants or refugees can use up-stream social marketing (i.e., promoting behavioral change through changes in policy and the broader environment) and downstream social marketing (i.e., focusing on changes in behavior at the individual level) to assist migrants and refugees in forming more realistic positive expectations of host country health systems and services (Wymer 2011). Furthermore, effective social marketing programs can assist in improving aspects of quality of life within migrant and refugee communities through the better health outcomes associated with participating in health services, as well as facilitating social inclusion and the wider social participation of migrants within their host countries.

This chapter examines how the experiences of African migrants and refugees in their home and adopted host countries shape their expectations of health service encounters, focusing on blood donation in Australia. The data are sourced from nine focus group discussions (FGDs) involving 88 African migrants and refugees living in Australia. The focus groups explored a variety of factors associated with blood donation, which form the basis of their blood donation expectations in both their home country and Australia. Building on the insights provided, the chapter then proposes a conceptual model that highlights the connection between migrants' past experience and how this shapes their future expectations of health service encounters, based partly on the psychic distance (Håkanson 2014) between migrants' home and host countries. All these factors need to be considered when implementing social marketing activities to shape the health service expectations of migrants and refugees (Boenigk et al. 2014). We conclude with suggestions concerning how this model can be used when targeting migrant consumers in health and other contexts.

2 Blood Donation in Australia

In Australia only one in 30 people donate blood while one in three will require a blood donation in their lifetime (ARCBS 2010). These rates are lower than in the US at 5 % (Gillespie and Hillyer 2002) and the UK at 6 % (McVittie et al. 2006). Among migrant groups in Australia, the donation rates are purported to be even lower than the average Australian donation rate at 3 % (Flood et al. 2006; Reid and

Wood 2008). The increase in migrant populations could raise issues in terms of Australia's ability to be self-sufficient (Flood et al. 2006) in sourcing blood products in the future if it does not have adequate supplies to meet all the communities' needs. This concern has also been identified as an issue in other developed countries with high numbers of migrants, such as the UK (Lattimore et al. 2014), Germany (Boenigk et al. 2014), and France (Grassineau et al. 2007). To ensure the successful functioning of the Australian and other developed countries' health systems it is critical that blood donation rates increase and that this increase is also reflected in diverse migrant communities (Boenigk et al. 2014), of which sub-Saharan African migrants are one of the fastest growing groups (Hugo 2009). Some African migrants also have certain unique blood characteristics, meaning that supplies cannot be met from within a predominantly Caucasian blood donor population (Grassineau et al. 2007), thus making growth in the pool of donors even more important.

3 Blood Donation Among African Communities in Africa and Host Countries

In Africa blood has familial, religious, and economic properties. Blood is believed to be a conduit for personality traits, defines kinship, and connects donor and recipient long after it has left the donor's body (Geissler 2005; Grassineau et al. 2007; Ottong et al. 1997; Weiss 1998). Research suggests that Africans sometimes prefer that their donations go to family members rather than strangers (Olaiya et al. 2004). Superstition is also important as in some instances there is a fear that if a relative or friend receives blood donated by a thief or witch, they too could become a thief or witch through the transfer of such negative traits via the donor's blood (Ottong et al. 1997). There may also be religious reasons why blood donation is perceived negatively. For example, Jehovah's Witnesses are prohibited from giving blood, and this religion is practiced widely in sub-Saharan Africa (Umeora et al. 2005).

Blood is also imbued with economic and political values and can be exchanged for cash or medical services in some countries. Sometimes blood may even be perceived to be stolen, an accusation made not just in Africa but also in Papua New Guinea (Street 2009) and India (Minocha 1996). Perceptions of the "stealing" of blood for the medical benefit of Western nations or for occult practices has obstructed a number of clinical trials in Africa (Fairhead et al. 2006). There are also misconceptions with regard to the negative health impacts of blood donation. For example, research from Ghana, Gambia and Zambia has shown that some believe even extracting small amounts of blood may be harmful to the donor's health and virility (Nchito et al. 2004; Newton et al. 2009). Other researchers have found that some people in Africa believe they could catch HIV though blood donation (Olaiya et al. 2004). Anxieties about the negative consequences associated with blood may have travelled with African migrants to their adopted host countries (Grassineau et al. 2007), although other researchers have not found these views to be widespread in the African migrant community in Australia (Polonsky et al. 2011b).

There is only limited research on African migrants' views of blood donation within their host countries. This work is important as it explains African migrants' host country experiences, which influence their host country participation vis-à-vis blood donation. Work in Canada has found that some African communities have explicitly been excluded from blood donation because of a negative perception concerning their blood safety, and this has translated into lower levels of future blood donation behavior (Tran et al. 2013). At one point in Israel, African migrants' donations that were taken were simply not used because of underlying blood safety issues, resulting in a negative backlash from within the African Israeli community (Merav and Lena 2011). Other research has found that there is a perception within migrant African communities that African blood will not be wanted in their Caucasian host community (Grassineau et al. 2007; Polonsky et al. 2011a), although such negative views on the part of migrants have arisen from a general perception of discrimination in the community rather than any policies related specifically to blood donation (Polonsky et al. 2011a). Differences between the home and host countries in relation to blood donation may make the local process more confusing for migrant donors and also impede donation. For example, in many African countries direct replacement donation (i.e., people donating to help a person who is known to them) and paid donation are more popular than anonymous voluntary donation (Tagny et al. 2010). Thus, relying solely on voluntary anonymous donation, as occurs in Australia, may seem "foreign" (i.e., represent higher cultural or physic distance) to many African migrants.

The multiple meanings associated with blood donation amongst African migrant communities illustrate that considerable information and misinformation related to home and host country experiences circulates about blood and blood donation encounters. These complex factors influence how migrants perceive blood donation services in their home and host countries, and this in turn impacts migrants' future expectations of blood service encounters in their host countries (in this case Australia). In the next subsection, we describe the research method used to explore the factors that influence home and host country expectations and experiences of blood donation amongst African migrants in Australia.

4 Method

To identify the various factors impacting blood donation experiences and the perceptions of African migrants leading to the formation of expectations in Australia, in-depth qualitative methods were employed. This comprised focus group discussions (FGDs), which were facilitated by bilingual members of the African community to ensure the process was inclusive irrespective of migrants' preferred language, with the majority of participants being from sub-Saharan African countries. FGDs also encourage group interaction, allow consensus or divergence on particular issues, and facilitate responses from those averse to being interviewed individually or considering they have nothing to say (Kitzinger 1995).

This flexible and iterative research design meant that the sample size was determined by data saturation. That is, when no new themes, categories or explanations emerged, data collection ceased (Marshall 1996; Mays and Pope 2000). From March to April 2010, nine FGDs comprising 88 participants from a cross-section of African countries were conducted in the state of Victoria, Australia. Three FGDs were conducted in regional Victoria and six in urban Melbourne. Two FGDs were with young people, 16–24 years old, four were single gender FGDs with individuals aged 25 years and over, and the remaining three were mixed gender discussions with individuals 25 years and over.

Participants were purposively sampled from a range of African community groups, recruited from women's groups, sports clubs, and health, community and religious organisations (Renzaho et al. 2010). We also engaged an African Review Panel, which is a lay steering committee, to help facilitate community mobilisation and recruitment (Renzaho 2009; Wilson et al. 2010). Participation in the focus groups required that participants had to have been born in Africa and be at least 16 years of age (which is the minimum age for donation). Each discussion took 60–90 min, was recorded, and was then professionally transcribed. Respondents were offered a $15 gift voucher to participate in the study. The study protocol was approved by Deakin University and the Australian Red Cross Blood Service Ethics committees.

Data analysis was completed using an iterative comparative thematic analysis approach (Ryan and Bernard 2003). Two of the authors independently read through the transcripts and identified themes. They then compared results, resolved differences, and achieved a consensus on themes, with further refinements and comparisons undertaken as required. Final themes identified were incorporated in NVivo for analysis, which were related back to the peer-reviewed literature. Such an approach follows standard techniques for qualitative data analysis (Pope et al. 2000; Thorne 2000). All data have been de-identified to ensure participants' anonymity.

5 Findings

The responses obtained from the FGD participants were categorized under three underlying themes, each with several associated sub-themes. These related to how past experiences and perceptions influenced expectations of Australian blood donation service encounters: (1) past experiences attached to home country blood donation; (2) knowledge and experience of blood donation in the host country, Australia; (3) strategies or programs that could be implemented to encourage African migrants to donate blood in Australia. Each of these and the associated sub-themes are discussed below.

5.1 Past Experiences Attached to Home Country Blood Donation

Four sub-themes emerged that impacted African migrants' past experiences of blood donation in their respective home countries: (a) individual perceptions of blood service encounters, (b) services delivered by blood/health centers, (c) supernatural and religious influences, and (d) health consequences associated with blood donation.

Participants described the overall blood donation experience as an act of sacrifice and heroism, and consequently there was overwhelming support for blood donation. Donation was viewed as "saving someone's life," "helping the needy," "an act of rescue," "a gift," and something voluntarily undertaken regardless of race, culture, ethnicity, or creed. As one respondent said, "*I feel like donating blood is an action of love 'cause it helps to revive those who are in need of blood*" (Female, 25+, refugee from Burundi). Another added: "*Even if it's a stranger but you know that he or she needs blood, you can help*" (Female, 25+, urban, refugee background from Sudan).

The importance of the sacrifice, voluntarism and heroism invested in donating blood was linked to the multiple meanings associated with blood and the risks of donation. African migrants linked blood to health, strength, vitality, and kinship, and in this respect blood was seen as a precious commodity. Participants noted that blood is "precious," "it's your life" and something to be treasured: "*We Africans take treasure in our blood, we are very protective. So by God's grace if I am ok with my blood why would I waste it?*" (Female, 25+, urban, migrant background from Ghana). There was a socioeconomic connection with those who were poorer. People from refugee backgrounds were seen to have weaker blood or not enough blood: "*Many of us have come from under-developed countries. Our blood is not enough for ourselves, it is better to keep it*" (Female, 25+, urban, refugee background from the Horn of Africa).

There was some wariness of the blood service centers in Australia based on past experiences of donating to blood banks or blood centers in Africa. Participants reported that they believed that blood centers in Africa often shipped blood overseas or sold blood for profit, thus denying those who were poor and in need: "*If I was in Africa I wouldn't give my blood [to the blood center] because I don't know where it's going*" (16–24, rural, refugee background from Sudan). Several respondents indicated that they thought in Africa there was corruption in terms of who would get the blood, or that it was sold.

Disapproval of the blood service in home country centers was also communicated to children and younger members of African communities, including those who had migrated to Australia, and thus past negative issues appear to influence current perceptions: "*My mum says that her uncle used to give blood all the time and he got like an infection because the needle wasn't clean. The same with my dad. My dad gave blood and he has this massive scar on his arm because the needle wasn't clean while he gave blood in Africa*" (16–24, urban, refugee background from Uganda). These negative experiences may have related to the re-use of equipment in Africa, a problem that is eliminated with the adoption of sterile single use equipment in many countries, but past negative issues still influence current perceptions.

The FGDs also revealed that negative experiences of the blood service centers in Africa resulted in many people donating in response to immediate appeals from family and community members, referred to as "replacement donation" in the literature, rather than to meet the needs of anonymous donors (Farrugia et al. 2010). In African contexts donors tend to know the recipient:

> I remember in Africa I went to some of my friends and said "Oh my sister's son is sick in the hospital and we need to donate blood." I was able to get about five different people to say "Yeah, I'll volunteer to donate." It was impromptu information and they were really ready. (Male, 25+, urban, migrant background from Nigeria)

It was also found through the FGD data that religious and supernatural beliefs influence the blood donation experience in home countries, although none of the FGD respondents suggested that these factors influence African migrants in Australia. Participants described how in Africa such beliefs prevailed:

> ...if you talk about the Jehovah Witness, they have a high number of followers in Africa and they have their own ideas and they don't donate blood. (Male, 25+, urban, migrant background from Ghana)
>
> Some people drink blood and that's witchcraft and so they are scared that if they give blood that maybe someone will drink it or something bad might happen to them. (Male, 25+, urban, migrant background from Nigeria)

In terms of health consequences, participants indicated that giving blood could lead to "*dizziness*," "*oedema in the feet*," "*fainting*," "*pain and soreness from needles*," and "*feeling unwell*," which is consistent with the global literature on why people do not donate blood (Kowalsky et al. 2014). However, a few participants also considered that positive health effects are associated with donating blood, such as "*reduced blood pressure*" and "*fresh blood being circulated in the body*."

The negative health effects of donation in combination with the perceived inherent risks of donation (e.g., blood donation could lead to weakness, the fear of potential witchcraft, and possible religious censure) has led to blood donation being viewed as an act of sacrifice and love. Participants were, however, concerned that their gift should go to the "*right person*," whom they defined as "*suffering*" and in need of the blood. Many worried that their blood might simply be stored in a blood "bank" or fridge until it expired and was then thrown away. Participants were more inclined to donate directly to people than to blood donation centers or blood "banks" as they called them:

> If someone needs blood, then I'm ready to do it, but only if someone needs it, then I'll give it. I'll not give it to be put in a fridge or a bank. (Female, 25+, urban, refugee background from the Horn of Africa)
>
> If I know this blood will just go to someone who seriously needs blood, I would just donate my blood to that person. But if I give my blood to the blood bank, I don't know where it is going. (Female, 25+, urban, refugee background from Sudan)

These responses seem to be related to the different approach to blood donation within Africa, where direct replacement is the norm (Tagny et al. 2010).

5.2 Experience and Knowledge of the Blood Donation Process in Australia

Few FGD participants had actually given or attempted to give blood in Australia, a fact which was related to their knowledge of the blood donation process and service experience among African migrants in Australia. Specifically, the deterrents to donation reported by these migrants were: (a) community disapproval, (b) a low level of knowledge concerning blood donation in Australia, and (c) age and length of stay in the host country.

It was suggested that there could be *community disapproval* from elders and parents associated with blood donation, including those who remained in Africa, which would limit blood donation in Australia. There was a perception that there was a general disapproval of women donating and this may have contributed to none of the women in the sample ever having given blood or having attempted to give blood. It should, however, be recognized that in women iron deficiencies can result in increased blood donation deferrals.

There was also a general *lack of knowledge* about the donation process in Australia. Participants did not know how much blood constituted a donation in Australia, where they could donate, the criteria for being eligible to donate, reasons for deferral, how the blood was stored and used, and what kinds of people (e.g., trauma patients, cancer patients, surgery patients) would benefit from their donation. For many African migrants, the FGDs were the first time they had discussed blood donation. It seems that misinformation and confusion about the blood donation process in Australia is highly prevalent, but this confusion or lack of information may also have existed with regard to the blood donation process in their home country:

> You go for a blood test and then they take maybe say four bottles and then if they didn't find any disease in it or anything, they just keep it and then the next person will go and then they all combine it together. (Male, 16–24, rural, refugee background from Sudan)
>
> If they take your blood are they going to put it in a different compound or different sort of a [place], this is the Muslim drawer and Christian store? Do they do that? (Male, 25+, rural, refugee background from Sudan)
>
> When somebody is going to give blood, you actually pay for the service here if blood is given to you right? So why is that when people go to donate blood, that they don't get given that reward? (Male, 25+, urban, migrant background from Ghana)

This latter view may reflect the fact that in many countries donors are paid (Farrugia et al. 2010), whereas in Australia blood donation is voluntary and non-remunerated.

In addition, respondents wondered what *kinds of tests* would be performed on their blood, if their blood would be "cleansed" prior to donation, and if it were not accepted as a donation, how it would be disposed of or whether it would be used in other ways. Unsurprisingly, not knowing about the donation process in Australia deterred many from trying to donate. As one respondent succinctly put it, "*If they [African migrants] don't get enough information about how to donate, they will not give*" (Female, 25+, urban, refugee background from Sudan). It should be noted that a lack of information and understanding of the process is not unique to African migrants, but affects large segments of potential donors globally, especially those from developing countries (Lownik et al. 2012).

The decision to donate blood in the host country (Australia) also seems to be affected by *age* and *length* of stay. Respondents widely agreed that young African migrants as well as second generation Africans in Australia would be better acculturated to Australian society and therefore more likely to give blood, and would have a stronger knowledge of the processes and a better sense of their entitlements. However, as African migration to Australia only started in earnest in the 1990s (Hugo 2009), there are few second generation African Australians who would yet be eligible to donate. There was a general sense that the "*younger ones are doing better than the older ones*" in adjusting to life in Australia, as they have higher levels of education and have had greater exposure to multicultural lifestyles compared to their elders. As respondents suggested:

> I think the younger generation are more open minded than the older ones. The older ones stick to their beliefs and all that, but the younger ones have a much more open minded thing, and so they will be more willing to ignore traditional values and some religious things to donate blood, but the older ones are not. (Female, 25+, urban, migrant from Zimbabwe)
>
> I think among the youth there is the potential for educating them and getting different outcomes from them because they are young and hopefully they will integrate. The integration process is smoother as well. (Male, 25+, urban, migrant background from Nigeria)

However, young people said that if they donated without prior parental or elder consent (even if they were over 18 years old), there was the potential for cultural conflict. A few were prepared to give even if their communities did not approve if they thought that donating blood would save a life:

> If someone's life is in danger and I know that I can help them, then yeah I would do it. I don't care if they [parents] would be angry later. I would still do it. (Female, 16–24, urban, refugee background from Sierra Leone
>
> Okay, like, say a situation, like you knew the person, like they are really sick and the blood was going to save their life and your parents say "No," which probably wouldn't happen, but if they say "No," you just ignore them and do it... The only reason why they would say no, it's not because they don't want to save the person's life, it's because of the safety or something like that. (Female, 16–24, urban, refugee background from Sierra Leone)

However, many young people also did not know about the blood donation process and were confused about how to donate. One young person thought that they could die from giving blood and another half-jokingly said "*If you went and checked after 24 hours, if your blood is not going forward, can you like get it back off them?*" (Female, 16–24, rural, refugee background from Sudan). Far from being open-minded, as one young respondent pointed out, "*Some of the young people don't really want to donate their blood, they want to keep it*" (Male, 16–24, rural, refugee background from Sudan).

5.3 Strategies and Programs to Encourage African Migrants to Donate Blood in Australia

There was universal consensus that the blood service should communicate more frequently and clearly with African communities about the need for donation, the process of donation, and the potential side-effects of donating. Specifically, participants wanted to know about donor selection criteria and reasons for deferral, how much they could donate, where their closest blood center was, at what age they could start donating and until what age they could continue, and even about other kinds of donation, such as organ donation.

Suggestions on how to improve African communities' access to donation centers ranged from media campaigns on the need for blood donation to targeting community centers with mobile blood donation vans. One woman said:

> Blood banks target work places and big services. Why not target communities? Bring a donor van and ask people. Huge numbers will give blood. (Female, 25+, urban, refugee background from the Horn of Africa)

Building on existing African cultural beliefs about blood, participants also said that the blood service should offer something that "strengthened" or "restored" people after they had donated, suggesting that the issue of knowledge about the effects of donation is important:

> If you give blood you're losing something and you need this replaced for you to survive. And if there is anything that they can provide after one has donated blood that would be very encouraging. (Male, 25+, urban, refugee background from Burundi)

Participants believed that their blood could be strengthened through diet, tonics, vitamins, and exercise. Also, while they did not want money or financial compensation to donate blood, most wanted to be acknowledged for their donation via things such as donation cards, certificates, acknowledgment via the media, and in some cases individualised "thank you" cards from potential recipients. Being acknowledged and appreciated was very important to participants:

> I'm living in this community, I'd like to donate blood but if I give this blood is it appreciated? Am I considered as a person in this polity you know? That's key. (Male, 25+, urban, migrant background from Nigeria)
>
> If they just contacted your parents or family or church or something and just say thank you, words that are coming from the heart. (Female, 16–24 years, urban, refugee background from Sierra Leone)

6 Discussion

Generally, past studies focusing on migrants' and refugees' health encounters have argued that past home country experiences shape their expectations of health service encounters in their host countries (Karmi 1992). For example, Burnett and Peel

(2001) found that migrants from developing (i.e., low and middle income) countries may expect hospital referrals for medical conditions that are treated in primary care within developed countries, and this can lead to disappointment amongst migrants when they are treated differently to the way in which they would have been in their home country, even though the "different" host country health care might address the underlying health issue.

The extant literature on how past experiences shape future expectations suggests that any gaps will result in dissatisfaction or confusion on the part of these consumers. This is also supported by respondents in our study. Previous studies suggest that in most cases migrants carry over their past home experiences and beliefs to their new host country (Bhattacharya 2008; Burnett and Peel 2001). Therefore, it can be argued that for the migrants referred to above, their past experiences and beliefs about the blood donation process in their home and host countries influence their expectations of blood donation encounters in Australia (i.e., the host country).

To take into consideration how social marketers can address these issues, we put forward a conceptual model (see Fig. 20.1 Part B) that integrates the premise that migrants' past experiences in both home and host countries will shape their expectations of host country health service encounters, including blood donation. In fact, we believe that the proposed model could apply to most health and other service encounters where such gaps exist.

Drawing on the findings from the FGDs, the proposed conceptual model identifies a number of underlying factors that are attached to migrants' experience of health services. Factors such as *individual perception of blood service encounters, services delivered by blood centers, supernatural* and *religious influences,* and *perceived health consequences* are found to impact the blood donation experience of African migrants in their home countries, which is consistent with factors identified with regard to influences on migrants and blood donation in Germany (Boenigk et al. 2014) as well as in other contexts. Factors such as *community disapproval, level of knowledge, age* and *length of stay* are found to impact African migrants' experience in their host country (i.e., Australia).

The model proposes that individual migrants' expectations of health service encounters in their new environment (i.e., the host country) will also be influenced by the psychic differences/similarities between the home and host countries (see Fig. 20.1 Part A), which will need to be tested in future research. The concept of "psychic distance" is viewed as "the subjectively perceived distance to a given foreign country" (Håkanson and Ambos 2010, p. 196) and is operationalised through sub-dimensions, such as perceived difference between culture, language, industrial development, education, and political level in home and host countries (Dow and Karunaratna 2006). Studies also suggest that individual perceptions of differences and similarities are asymmetric, and are dependent on the psychic distant/similarities between countries (Håkanson 2014; Sousa and Bradley 2006). These factors have not previously been tested within health or social marketing contexts.

We suggest in the proposed model (Fig. 20.1 Part A) that psychic distance between home and host countries will influence how migrants experience health service encounters and in turn form expectations in their host country. For example,

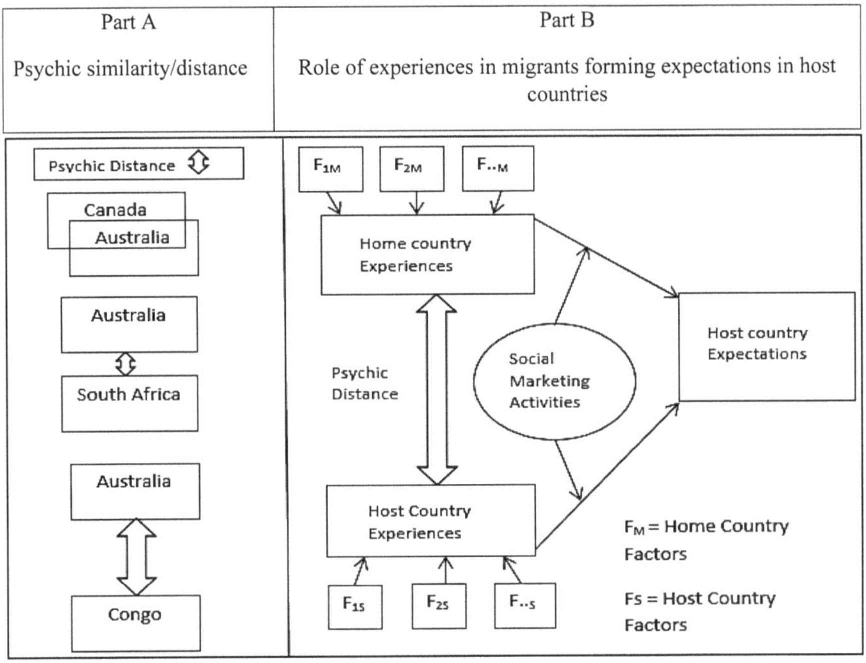

Fig. 20.1 Conceptual framework

as illustrated in the conceptual model, the psychic distance between Canada and Australia will be less compared to that between Australia and Congo. Thus, migrants to Australia from Canada are assumed to have experienced similar health service encounters in their home country and hence form expectations similar to people in the host country. In contrast, migrants from Congo to Australia are expected to experience high psychic distance and be more likely to have different experiences of health service encounters in their home country, thus being novice consumers in their host country, which results in them forming different expectations of Australian health services. The implication of considering psychic distance is that social marketing initiatives will need to be designed differently depending on which groups of migrants are being targeted. If the psychic difference is high, social marketing may need to focus on explaining how services are delivered within the host market, as well as addressing underlying expectations which would not be applicable in a host market. However, such differences could occur even if the home and host environments have many similarities. For example, the US and Australia may be similar in many ways, but in Australia it is illegal to pay for blood donation, whereas in the US there are multiple blood collection channels with some channels paying for blood donation and others relying on voluntary, non-remunerated donations.

As highlighted in the third major theme within the findings – *strategies and programs encouraging African migrants to donate blood in Australia* – African migrants are found to have limited knowledge about the blood donation process in

Australia, which may be due to the effects of socioeconomic variables impacting African communities' knowledge of the blood donation process in Australia. Our conceptual model also proposes that health policy makers, planners and social marketers can take these important findings into consideration when designing upstream and downstream social marketing intervention campaigns targeting African migrants or refugees (see Fig. 20.1 Part B). For example, if migrants do not trust health services in their home countries, it will be important for any social marketing initiatives at least to seek to address this issue. However, such initiatives would potentially be expensive as they require a culturally relevant, sustained and multi-pronged approach. Simply telling people to "trust" a system with which they are unfamiliar will not necessarily work.

7 Lessons Learned and Social Marketing Recommendations

A better understanding and shaping of health service expectations through the delivery of effective social marketing strategies and programs are likely to assist in improving migrants' quality of life within the migrant and refugee community, facilitating more informed decision making, as well as improved social inclusion within the host country. Studies suggest that social marketing might include a combination of "upstream" interventions, i.e., interventions that focus on policy and regulation, thereby changing the broader environment to support and promote behavioral change, and "downstream" interventions, i.e., focusing on individual-level behavioral change (Hoek and Jones 2011; Wymer 2011).

Participants in our study advocated interventions that include targeted information with regard to issues such as the blood donation processes, reasons for deferral, the side effects of donation, the potential recipients of donation, and donations beyond just blood (e.g., eyes and organs). From an upstream social marketing perspective, information could be disseminated by the blood service in collaboration with local health and community centers where African migrants might already have established connections and trust in staff members to shape future expectations of blood service encounters. Together with this information, alternative collection processes could potentially make access easier. For example, mobile blood donation could occur in the community. These upstream interventions would also ensure that the process was inclusive of all those in the community, especially sub-groups who may be more excluded, such as those not in the work force or with varying levels of literacy.

From a downstream social marketing perspective, overcoming the perceived side effects attached to blood donation could be addressed through the provision of restoratives reflecting cultural values that view blood as connected to strength and vitality. It may also be useful to build on the sense of community through group donations. Group donations already occur within Australia and could be expanded to target wider communities. An additional benefit of group donations is that as community "events," such activities would not just include those donating but also others in the community who make up support networks, and thus group donation may change the wider communities' views on blood donation. While this could mean there are larger crowds in donation centers, it would demystify the donation process within the wider migrant non-donor population. This would make donating blood a social norm that spreads throughout the community, increasing knowledge of the process and addressing any negative perceptions of health services more widely.

Undertaking upstream and downstream activities that communicate in a way that engages migrant communities and also create trust within communities is something that has been proposed by other research focusing on migrant blood donation (Boenigk et al. 2014). The specific actions would need to consider the issues illustrated in Fig. 20.1 to ensure that these target each specific community appropriately. There is always a trade-off with regard to cost and return, with organisations such as blood services having limited marketing budgets. Developing programs that can be adapted to multiple cultural groups may be one approach that could be applied, thus spreading any internal investments across donor groups and increasing the efficiency of investments in social marketing initiatives.

Acknowledgements The authors would like to acknowledge the Australian Red Cross Blood Service (the Blood Service) and the Australian Government that fund the Blood Service for the provision of blood, blood products and services to the Australian community. The authors would also like to thank the members of the African community who assisted them with this research. Professor Andre Renzaho is supported by an ARC Future Fellowship (FT110100345) and Dr. Bianca Brijnath is supported by an NHMRC fellowship.

References

Australian Red Cross Blood Service. (2010). *All about blood*. Retrieved from http://www.donateblood.com.au/all-about-blood

Bhattacharya, G. (2008). The Indian diaspora in transnational context: Social relations and cultural identities of immigrants to New York City. *Journal of Intercultural Studies, 29*(1), 65–80.

Boenigk, S., Mews, M., & de Kort, W. (2014). Missing minorities: Explaining low migrant blood donation participation and developing recruitment tactics. *International Journal of Voluntary and Nonprofit Organizations*, 1–21. doi:10.1007/s11266-014-9477-7.

Burnett, A., & Peel, M. (2001). Asylum seekers and refugees in Britain: Health needs of asylum seekers and refugees. *British Medical Journal, 322*, 544–547.

Dagger, T. S., & Sweeney, J. C. (2007). Service quality attribute weights how do novice and longer-term customers construct service quality perceptions? *Journal of Service Research, 10*(1), 22–42.

Dow, D., & Karunaratna, A. (2006). Developing a multidimensional instrument to measure psychic distance stimuli. *Journal of International Business Studies, 37*(5), 578–602.

Fairhead, J., Leach, M., & Small, M. (2006). Where techno-science meets poverty: Medical research and the economy of blood in the Gambia, West Africa. *Social Science and Medicine, 63*(4), 1109–1120.

Farrugia, A., Penrod, J., & Bult, J. (2010). Payment, compensation and replacement – The ethics and motivation of blood and plasma donation. *Vox Sanguinis, 99*(3), 202–211.

Flood, P., Wills, P., Lawler, P., Ryan, G., & Rickard, K. A. (2006). *Review of Australia's plasma fractionation arrangements*. Canberra. Retrieved from http://www.health.gov.au/plasmafractionationreview

Geissler, P. W. (2005). "Kachinja are coming!" Encounters around medical research work in a Kenyan village. *Africa: Journal of the International African Institute, 75*(2), 173–202.

Gillespie, T. W., & Hillyer, C. D. (2002). Blood donors and factors impacting the blood donation decision. *Transfusion Medicine Reviews, 16*(2), 115–130.

Grassineau, D., Papa, K., Ducourneau, A., Duboz, P., Boëtsch, G., & Chiaroni, J. (2007). Improving minority blood donation: Anthropologic approach in a migrant community. *Transfusion, 47*(3), 402–409.

Håkanson, L. (2014). The role of psychic distance in international trade: A longitudinal analysis. *International Marketing Review, 31*(3), 210–236.

Håkanson, L., & Ambos, B. (2010). The antecedents of psychic distance. *Journal of International Management, 16*(3), 195–210.

Hoek, J., & Jones, S. C. (2011). Regulation, public health and social marketing: A behaviour change trinity. *Journal of Social Marketing, 1*(1), 32–44.

Hugo, G. (2009). Migration between Africa and Australia: A demographic perspective. In Australian Human Rights Commission (Ed.), *African Australians: A review of human rights and social inclusion issues*. Sydney: Australian Human Rights Commission.

Karmi, G. (1992). Refugee health. *British Medical Journal, 305*(6), 205–206.

Kinnon, D. (1999). *Canadian research on immigration and health: An overview*. Ottawa: Health Canada.

Kitzinger, J. (1995). Qualitative research: Introducing focus groups. *British Medical Journal, 311*, 299–302.

Kowalsky, J. M., France, C. R., France, J. L., Whitehouse, E. A., & Himawan, L. K. (2014). Blood donation fears inventory: Development and validation of a measure of fear specific to the blood donation setting. *Transfusion and Apheresis Science*. doi:10.1016/j.transci.2014.07.007.

Lattimore, S., Wickenden, C., & Brailsford, S. R. (2014). Blood donors in England and North Wales: Demography and patterns of donation. *Transfusion*. doi:10.1111/trf.12835.

Lownik, E., Riley, E., Konstenius, T., Riley, W., & McCullough, J. (2012). Knowledge, attitudes and practices surveys of blood donation in developing countries. *Vox Sanguinis, 103*(1), 64–74.

Marshall, M. N. (1996). Sampling for qualitative research. *Family Practice, 13*(6), 522–525.

Mays, N., & Pope, C. (2000). Qualitative research in health care. Assessing quality in qualitative research. *British Medical Journal, 320*, 50–52.

McVittie, C., Harris, L., & Tiliopoulos, N. (2006). "I intend to donate but..." Non-donors' views of blood donation in the UK. *Psychology, Health and Medicine, 11*(1), 1–6.

Merav, B. N., & Lena, G. (2011). Investigating the factors affecting blood donation among Israelis. *International Emergency Nursing, 19*(1), 37–43.

Minocha, A. A. (1996). *Perceptions and interactions in a medical setting: A sociological study of a women's hospital*. New Delhi: Hindustan Publishing Corporation.

Nchito, M., Wenzel Geissler, P., Mubila, L., Friis, H., & Olsen, A. (2004). Effects of iron and multimicronutrient supplementation on geophagy: A two-by-two factorial study among Zambian schoolchildren in Lusaka. *Transactions of the Royal Society of Tropical Medicine and Hygiene, 98*(4), 218–227.

Newton, S., Doku, V., Geissler, W., Asante, K. P., & Cousens, S. (2009). Drawing blood from young children: Lessons learned from a trial in Ghana. *Transactions of the Royal Society of Tropical Medicine and Hygiene, 103*(5), 497–499.

Olaiya, M. A., Alakija, W., Ajala, A., & Olatunji, R. O. (2004). Knowledge, attitudes, beliefs and motivations towards blood donations among blood donors in Lagos, Nigeria. *Transfusion Medicine, 14*(1), 13–17.

Ottong, J. G., Asuquo, E. E. J., Olaniran, N. S., Duke, F. D., & Abia, R. P. (1997). Community mobilization for blood donation, Cross River State, Nigeria. *International Journal of Gynaecology and Obstetrics, 59*(2), S119–S125.

Polonsky, M. J., Brijnath, B., & Renzaho, A. (2011a). "They don't want our blood": Social inclusion and blood donation among African migrants in Australia. *Social Science and Medicine, 73*(2), 336–342.
Polonsky, M. J., Renzaho, A., & Brijnath, B. (2011b). Barriers to blood donation in African communities in Australia: The role of home and host country culture and experience. *Transfusion, 51*(8), 1809–1819.
Pope, C., Ziebland, S., & Mays, N. (2000). Qualitative research in health care. Analysing qualitative data. *British Medical Journal, 320*(7227), 114–116.
Reid, M., & Wood, A. (2008). An investigation into blood donation intentions among non-donors. *International Journal of Nonprofit and Voluntary Sector Marketing, 13*(1), 31–43.
Renzaho, A. M. (2009). Challenges of negotiating obesity-related findings with African migrants in Australia: Lessons learnt from the African migrant capacity building and performance appraisal project. *Nutrition and Dietetics, 66*, 145–150.
Renzaho, A. M. N., Green, J., Mellor, D., & Swinburn, B. (2010). Parenting, family functioning and lifestyle in a new culture: The case of African migrants in Melbourne, Victoria, Australia. *Child and Family Social Work, 16*(2), 228–240.
Ryan, G. W., & Bernard, H. R. (2003). Techniques to identify themes. *Field Methods, 15*(1), 85–109.
Sousa, C. M., & Bradley, F. (2006). Cultural distance and psychic distance: Two peas in a pod? *Journal of International Marketing, 14*(1), 49–70.
Street, A. (2009). Failed recipients: Extracting blood in a Papua New Guinean hospital. *Body and Society, 15*(2), 193–215.
Tagny, C. T., Owusu-Ofori, S., Mbanya, D., & Deneys, V. (2010). The blood donor in sub-Saharan Africa: A review. *Transfusion Medicine, 20*(1), 1–10.
Thorne, S. (2000). Data analysis in qualitative research. *Evidence Based Nursing, 3*(3), 68–70.
Tran, N. Y., Charbonneau, J., & Valderrama-Benitez, V. (2013). Blood donation practices, motivations and beliefs in Montreal's Black communities: The modern gift under a new light. *Ethnicity and Health, 18*(6), 508–529.
Umeora, O. U., Onuh, S. O., & Umeora, M. C. (2005). Socio-cultural barriers to voluntary blood donation for obstetric use in a rural Nigerian village. *African Journal of Reproductive Health, 9*(3), 72–76.
Weiss, B. (1998). Electric vampires: Haya rumours of the commodified body. In M. Lambeck & A. Strathern (Eds.), *Bodies and person: Comparative perspectives from Africa and Melanesia* (pp. 172–194). Cambridge: Cambridge University Press.
Wilson, A., Renzaho, A. M., McCabe, M., & Swinburn, B. (2010). Towards understanding the new food environment for refugees from the Horn of Africa in Australia. *Health & Place, 16*(5), 969–976.
Wymer, W. (2011). Developing more effective social marketing strategies. *Journal of Social Marketing, 1*(1), 17–31.

Chapter 21
Sustainability Marketing: Reconfiguring the Boundaries of Social Marketing

Ken Peattie

1 Introduction: The Mutation of Marketing

It is clear from Bartels' (1988) "*History of Marketing*" that marketing's story is one of continual evolution. Much of this evolution reflects changes in the emphasis, scope and sophistication of marketing theory and practice. What began with the practical steps and informal decision processes that had supported the selling of goods and services since pre-industrial times, developed during the early twentieth century into a formalised discipline then largely concerned with the creation, distribution and selling of products. The emerging fields of psychology and social research gradually allowed the needs of consumers to be first better understood, and then to become the focus of the discipline as *'modern managerial marketing'* emerged mid-century. Since then much of the evolution has been a question of sub-division and specialisation, with the application of marketing to particular spheres, from politics and public services, to charities and the arts. The most important sub-division, the emergence of services marketing as a distinct sub-discipline, also contributed to a further evolution of focus and philosophy as relationship marketing emerged. This moved marketing away from an emphasis on products and transactions, towards a focus on intangibles and the nurturing of long-term relationships with customers (Vargo and Lusch 2004). Technology has also acted as an evolutionary force. Initially this was through product and production system innovation, but in more recent decades the emphasis has been on the role of information and communication technologies in informing marketing decisions, and in facilitating the emergence of online and interactive marketing.

K. Peattie (✉)
Sustainable Places Research Institute, Cardiff University,
33 Park Place, Cardiff CF10 3BA, UK
e-mail: Peattie@cardiff.ac.uk

W. Wymer (ed.), *Innovations in Social Marketing and Public Health Communication*, Applying Quality of Life Research,
DOI 10.1007/978-3-319-19869-9_21

This chapter seeks to consider the implications for social marketing and marketers of one of the more recent evolutionary changes in marketing thought and practice: the emergence of sustainability oriented marketing. In doing so, it looks back at the role that other marketing '*types*' have played as antecedents to sustainability marketing, and looks forward to a world in which the increasing interconnections between the social and commercial spheres could largely erase the boundaries that currently are thought to exist between social and commercial marketing theory and practice.

The evolutionary '*mutation*' that led to the creation of social marketing represented one of the leaps of marketing into a new sphere of society. This is perhaps most easily envisioned through Pearce's "*Three Systems of the Economy*" model (Pearce 2003). As the name suggests, it divides economic activity into three systems, the first being the commercial sector comprised of for-profit enterprises ranging in scope from small businesses serving a single community to global corporations.[1] It is from this sector that marketing emerged. The second system is the public sector, including arms of government ranging from local community councils through to international institutions such as the United Nations or European Union. The third system (also referred to as the "*Third Sector*") is something of a catch-all for other activities and organisations, and includes charities, voluntary organisations, trade unions and social enterprises (trading organisations that primarily apply the methods of business in the pursuit of primarily social goals (Peattie and Morley 2008)), again varying from the local to the global.

The philosophies and techniques derived from commercial marketing have, over time, become increasingly influential in other sectors. Therefore we now see particular causes and candidates being marketed to us as voters or donors via sophisticated charities or political marketing campaigns, or as citizens public services are marketed to us. For social enterprises, it has more been a question of professionalising an area in which they have tended to be weak (Shaw 2004), and blending understanding from conventional commercial marketing and charities and non-profit sector marketing to reflect their nature as '*hybrid organisations*' (Defourny and Nyssens 2006).

Social marketing's emergence as a new sub-discipline in the early 1970s was formalized with Kotler and Zaltman's (1971) seminal *Journal of Marketing* paper. This built on the question posed by the sociologist Wiebe (1951), "*Can we sell brotherhood like soap?*" Instead of marketing products, politicians, worthy causes or public services to us, marketing theory and practice began to be applied to influence our behaviour in order to achieve social goals. All the power of marketing accrued from decades of research both of and within marketing, and the practical experience that informed it, was now being applied to change, not just our behaviour as consumers, but how we lived our lives and behaved as citizens. A point worth noting at this stage is that the very foundation of social marketing implicitly rested on the notion of society being comprised of distinct sectors, and the translation

[1] Pearce's first system also includes the 'black economy' of organisations that operate outside the law.

of commercially derived marketing theory and practice from the commercial system to inform the social marketing efforts that public, non-profit and voluntary bodies engage in.

The evolution and fragmentation of a discipline creates both opportunities and risks. This is true in relation to marketing and marketers, and perhaps is true for social marketers in particular. Opportunities come from the possibilities that understanding derived from one branch of marketing can enrich others, or perhaps the discipline as a whole. Such is the case with services marketers generating a rich understanding of relationship marketing that others have benefitted from. Risks come from the potential that social marketing might become an *'off-shoot'* discipline that then becomes somewhat isolated from the continuing evolution of the mainstream. Peattie and Peattie (2003) use the analogy of ethnic populations of emigrants whose culture stops evolving once they become established in a new land. They remain as an outpost of traditional values that becomes increasingly different to the culture of their homeland as it continues to evolve. Something of this phenomenon was observed by Hastings (2003) when describing how a decade's worth of development in commercial relationship marketing had been overlooked by social marketers, despite the potential value of a relational perspective for their work. It is important for the future development of social marketing for the field to avoid becoming inward looking and disconnected from ongoing advances in the wider world of marketing scholarship and commercial practice.

2 The Social-Commercial Marketing Relationship

The relationship between marketing in the commercial sector and in the public and third sectors is an intriguing one. The simplest and most commonly shared element is that commercial marketing provides a source of learning for marketers in the other sectors. This would include both social marketers and marketers of public services, and third sector organisations including charities, social enterprises and voluntary organisations. Beyond this, Dibb and Carrigan (2013) characterise the relationship between commercial and social marketing as challenging, uneasy and complex. Commercial marketers may be a source of inspiration and learning for social marketers, but they can also represent '*the competition*'. This can be the case for marketers of public services for which a commercial equivalent exists. At its simplest, marketers for a leisure centre owned by local government would compete with commercial sports and leisure centres. Similarly private and public schools and colleges will both engage in marketing and will compete to attract students. For social marketers, there may also be an element of direct competition that goes beyond normal commercial parallels of rivalry (trying to meet the same consumer need in different ways), to represent a more fundamentally adversarial relationship. The most obvious and best known example of such '*combative*' social marketing is the enduring battle between the tobacco companies whose marketers constantly seek out new ways to entice people to smoke, and the social marketers seeking to promote smoking cessation as a public health goal (Hastings and Saren 2003).

The relationship between social and commercial marketers can also be complementary, particularly when the commercial product is perceived as being one part of a solution to a particular social problem. Therefore the overall marketing mix for a social marketing campaign might involve a tangible product from commercial companies such as condoms for sexual health or nicotine patches to aid smoking cessation. Similarly social marketers trying to promote travel mode behavioural change away from the use of the private car may well end up trying to promote the services of commercial bus and train companies as part of the overall solution. The social marketer seeking to promote dental hygiene and the commercial marketer promoting toothpaste both have an interest in more children brushing their teeth.

In the past there has perhaps been a tendency to view the relationship between social and commercial marketers as naturally drawn towards the antipathetic. This is not surprising given that some of the highest profile arenas for social marketing efforts have been smoking cessation, responsible alcohol consumption and combatting '*junk food*' marketing to promote healthier eating behaviours, particularly amongst the young. This may simply reflect Hunt's (1994) observation that research into relationships within marketing seems to be drawn towards the dysfunctional. However, there is nothing to say that relations between social and mainstream commercial marketing need to be hostile, even when there is a potential conflict of interest. In an age when demonstrating corporate social responsibility (CSR) is widely acknowledged as a priority for businesses, they are often keen to reduce any perceived harm linked to production or consumption of their products. This makes them potentially willing to support social marketing campaigns linked to harm reduction, with the proviso that it doesn't overly impact their core business. Hastings and Saren (2003) see social marketing as having a role in '*bridging the gap*' between commercial marketing and public health (or other policy spheres), because they understand both the potential applications and power of marketing (and its limits) as well as the social issues to which it might be applied. This makes social marketers well placed to conceive of novel and marketing-orientated solutions that can bring commerce and public policy together. So although a tobacco firm-social marketing alliance would be somewhat unrealistic, in fields such as food and alcohol consumption, partnerships are becoming increasingly common. Road Crew, one of social marketing's most iconic success stories, involved an intervention to reduce drink driving deaths by encouraging young males (the campaign's target) to take advantage of a subsidised local '*limo*' service to, from and between bars. The success of the campaign depended on support from the local community, but it also benefitted from financial support from the drinks industry and from local bartenders promoting the service to their customer base (Rothschild et al. 2006).

The growing popularity of commercial/social marketing partnerships was underlined by the 10th "*Innovations in Social Marketing*" conference in 2005 adopting "*Stretching the Limits of Partnerships*" as the conference theme. One obvious advantage of collaborative partnerships for social marketers is that they can help to overcome the resource limitations that they face, particularly when it comes to reaching their target audience. For example Health Canada has a sophisticated programme of partnerships with commercial organisations going back to the late 1980s involving a range of social marketing campaigns. One of them, the "*Back to Sleep*" campaign from 2000 sought to encourage new parents to lay their infants to sleep on their backs, since this reduces the risk of sudden infant death syndrome (SIDS). The campaign used conventional mass media through a print ad published in various magazines, and a 30 s public service announcement on TV. However, by partnering with Proctor & Gamble and their Pampers diaper/nappy brand, the campaign could complement these efforts with cost-effective communication delivered direct to the target audience. This came courtesy of the campaign's "*Back to Sleep*" message being printed on the two smallest sizes of Pampers in English, French, and Spanish. P&G also added it to their existing educational pamphlets distributed to new mothers through the majority of hospitals in Canada, and the company promoted SIDS awareness through their own commercial advertising campaigns. The results of this campaign were an increase in awareness from 44 % (in 1999) to 66 % (in 2001), that the proper position to place a baby during sleep is on his/her back, and among parents or caregivers that had taken action to reduce the risk of SIDS, 69 % said that they laid their babies on their backs to sleep, up from 41 % in 1999.

The "*Back to Sleep*" campaign represents a traditional social/commercial marketing partnership in which social and commercial marketing combined to influence the behaviour of parents in a classic '*downstream*' campaign. Although it was not a commercial strategy in the sense of changing what consumers purchased, it did fit very strongly with the Pampers' vision of "C*aring for children's health and development*".

3 Commercial Marketing: An Evolution Towards the Social?

As the growing tendency towards partnerships between social marketers and companies to address social issues implies, commercial companies and marketers are being increasing drawn towards engaging in social issues. This is not a new phenomenon, as the activities of Quaker businesses in previous centuries clearly demonstrate. However, addressing social issues as an element of thought and practice within the marketing discipline is a product of recent decades. It was at around the same time that social marketing was establishing itself as a sub-discipline in the early 1970s that societal marketing also emerged as an alternative perspective on commercial marketing. In doing so the similarities of terminology ensured a future of confusion between the two amongst students, practitioners and sometime scholars, a confusion nicely supplemented in recent years by the addition of social media marketing into the marketing lexicon. As with social marketing, it was Philip Kotler's (1972) reassessment of marketing's scope and potential implications that largely sparked the interest in societal marketing. Societal marketing challenged principles derived from neo-classical economics that society's collective best interests lay in satisfying the individual desires of consumers in an effective and profitable way. Kotler proposed that marketing also needed to consider '*long-run consumer welfare*' and cited marketing related problems such as individual car use creating congestion and pollution, the nutritional issues posed by the rise in '*junk food*' consumption, the waste generated by packaging, and the health problems caused by smoking and alcohol. The argument was not that marketing and marketers were inherently '*anti-social*' since there were many examples of companies that had sought to develop products that did provide long-term benefits for consumers (such as Kellogg's emphasis on marketing nutritious foods). However, the notion that the long-run welfare of consumers should be a responsibility of marketers, was a novel one within mainstream marketing thought.

The fact that the societal marketing concept came from Kotler and was enshrined in his text-book writing from 1967 onwards meant that it was quickly established as a core marketing concept (Crane and Desmond 2002). It did however evolve over time, and by 2000 the Millennium edition of Kotler's "*Marketing Management*" (Kotler 2000) defined societal marketing in terms of pursuing '*society's wellbeing*'. This enshrining of a responsibility to pursue societal wellbeing provides an obvious line of common interest between commercial and social marketers, and helps to explain the commercial motivations behind some of the partnership activities already mentioned. Another point worth mentioning is that some of the societal impacts of commercial marketing activities that inspired Kotler's thinking in 1972 to argue for changes in what companies market are key areas that social marketers have sought to tackle through behavioural change amongst consumers including healthier food choices (Pettigrew and Pescud 2012), reduced car use (Haq et al. 2008), responsible drinking (Jones 2011) or smoking cessation (Hastings and Saren 2003).

Another thread of marketing thought that has similarities to societal marketing is ethical marketing. They are not quite synonymous because Kotler's vision of societal marketing was ultimately a self-interested rather than an altruistic one from the perspective of companies, or as he put it "*The enlightened marketer attempts to satisfy the consumer and enhance his total wellbeing on the theory that what is good in the long run for consumer is good for business*" (p. 57). The ethical dimensions of commercial marketing were brought into focus during the 1960s by the likes of Patterson (1966) and Bartels (1967). Since then exactly what constitutes ethical marketing practices has been the subject of considerable debate, and a number of key dimensions of ethical marketing are explored by Laczniak and Murphy (2006). Amongst the perspectives they discuss are the notions that ethical marketing '*puts people first*' to ensure that marketing creates a perceived and real social benefit, and that it goes beyond both legal requirements and a consumer perspective to consider a range of stakeholders and their wellbeing in relation to marketing decisions, activities and consequences.

A corollary to the concept of ethical marketing, is that of ethical consumption. There is an acknowledged growth in the influence that ethical issues relating to the working conditions, freedom and pay of workers in poorer countries, the use of child labour or perceived environmental damage on the concerns, decision making processes and purchasing of consumers (O'Rourke 2012). However, understanding ethical consumption is complicated by challenges in defining and delineating ethical consumer behaviour and in the extent to which there is often a gap between consumers' expressed ethical concerns and actual consumption behaviour (Bray et al. 2011). For our purposes the most interesting aspect of ethical consumption is that it removes the consumer from the neo-classical straitjacket of individual personal self-interest to consider the welfare of others involved in the production of goods, or impacted by their consumption or production. In doing so it creates a concept of consumer social responsibility as a parallel to conventional CSR, which cuts across the conventional mainstream marketing vision of the consumer as a sovereign who has rights and wields power, but without any wider sense of responsibility (Brinkmann and Peattie 2009).

Ethical consumption introduces the figure of the citizen-consumer which Gabriel and Lang (1995) define as '*a responsible consumer, a socially-aware consumer, a consumer who thinks ahead and tempers his or her desires by social awareness, a consumer whose actions must be morally defensible and who must occasionally be prepared to sacrifice...*'. The existence of such a consumer, and of the notion of consumer social responsibility, is relevant to social marketers since they may need to promote a sense of responsibility amongst consumers either in relation to their own wellbeing (as is the case with responsible drinking) or that of future generations or people in other places (for example when trying to reduce greenhouse gas emissions). This combining of the roles of citizen and consumer, in which our desires and actions as consumers are tempered by our concerns and values as citizens, provides another important intersection of the worlds of the social and commercial marketer.

Conventionally, research into pro-environmental behaviour (PEB) separates out the two roles. Research into consumers examines our willingness to change what we buy, and how we use (and sometimes dispose of) it. Research into our behaviour as citizens has a focus on our willingness to contribute to the public good through political action, charitable donations and voluntary contributions to improving the environmental quality of the communities within which we live (Turaga et al. 2010). With the growth in interest in the concept of the '*citizen consumer*' and in sustainability motivated consumer activism (Kozinets and Handelman 2004), there is a growing recognition that peoples' motivations for engaging in the two types of PEB may share more similarities than researchers have previously realised (Turaga et al. 2010). This potentially opens up opportunities for mutual learning, and fruitful partnerships, between social and commercial marketers if they realise they have a shared interest in promoting PEBs.

4 Sustainability Marketing: Moving Towards Reintegration?

Concern about the environmental impact of our consumption and production activities drives another thread of unconventional marketing thinking that first emerged in the 1970s. Growing concern about resource consumption and pollution, combined with the oil and energy crises of the early-to-mid 1970s, focused attention on sectors like oil, cars and chemicals and on the search for technical solutions to resource and pollution challenges. This concern was reflected in the emergence of '*ecological marketing*' suggesting that marketers as well as technicians had a role in combatting environmental problems (Henion and Kinnear 1976). New product introductions such as smaller-engine cars, or products positioned on the basis of '*naturalness*' were both symptomatic of this early ecological concern in marketing. From a perspective of consumer behaviour, some of the earliest research on marketing and the environment in the 1970s focused on issues such as energy conservation behaviours and involvement in recycling (Kilbourne and Beckmann 1998). These represented two areas that social marketers became increasingly interested in as the use of social marketing extended beyond the health oriented applications which dominated its early development and into other spheres such as environmental protection (Maibach 1993).

The '*ecological marketing*' of the 1970s evolved into '*green marketing*' during the 1980s with an increased emphasis on environmental concern as an opportunity for commercial marketers to create profitable products and services whose unique selling proposition was an improved environmental (and sometimes social) performance. Further media coverage of environmental causes, and the popularity of green consumer guides as a genre, ensured that environmental issues began to impact a wider range of industries, companies and consumer decisions than ever before. The mainstreaming of sustainable development as a concept following the publication of the Brundtland report (WCED 1987) saw businesses and policy makers agreeing that we needed to pursue a form of economic development that "*meets the needs of the present without compromising the ability of future generations to meet their own needs*" (WCED 1987, p. 43). Although the concept of sustainable development has been criticised for vagueness, being subject to multiple-interpretations and having a vulnerability to being '*hijacked*' it provided a valuable common goal that businesses and policy-makers could agree upon, and it stressed the interdependence of our environmental, social and economic systems.

Moving into the 1990s and beyond, attempts to integrate the principles of sustainability with marketing have emerged as "*Sustainable Marketing*" (Fuller 1999; Martin and Schouten 2011) or "*Sustainability Marketing*" (Belz and Peattie 2010). A core element of these new visions of more sustainable marketing is the need for a physical cradle-to-grave view of the lifecycle of a product. This in turn requires a more holistic production and consumption systems view of the process by which our wants and needs as consumers are met (Lebel and Lorek 2008). This can be done through life-cycle analysis that considers all the socio-environmental impacts that occur back down the supply chain that underpins production, and through all stages of the consumption process encompassing the use and disposal of products. This perspective has significant implications for commercial marketers as it expands their focus far beyond the interface and interaction between a company and its customers. It also extends the timescale and scope of consumer behaviour from a marketing perspective. Although in theory marketing should consider consumer behaviour as a multi-faceted and multi-stage process, in practice the thinking of marketing practitioners and scholars seems to be magnetically drawn to purchase as a specific action on the part of consumers. Economically this makes perfect sense. Getting people to purchase is the point at which money changes hands, generating the market share and sales revenue by which the success of marketing and marketers is ultimately likely to be judged. The purchase also (generally) represents the moment when, for tangible goods, ownership passes from the producer to the consumer, and in doing so making a product the consumer's responsibility. To understand consumption from a sustainability perspective, what happens post-purchase is very important. For food products, the sustainability impacts do not only reflect how the food was grown, processed, packaged, transported and sold. They also reflect how the consumer went on to store and cook the food, whether they stored and reused any leftovers, and what they ultimately did with any waste. For some durable products such as cars or washing machines, the overwhelming majority of sustainability impacts occur within the product use stage of the consumption life-cycle.

The total product life-cycle approach adopted for sustainability marketing tends to promote another element of reintegration within marketing theory, particularly between goods and services marketing. In particular one solution to the promotion of more sustainable production-consumption systems is through product-service substitutions and the creation of product-service systems (Lebel and Lorek 2008). These involve an emphasis on the use of tangible products accessed as part of a service instead of conventional purchase and use models of consumption. One of the best known examples is the use of car sharing services as an alternative to a car ownership model to provide individuals with mobility. From the marketer's perspective moving customers towards PSS provides a dual challenge in terms of persuading consumers to adopt a significantly different mode of consumption, and transforming their own business models, marketing perspective and capabilities away from product-based towards service-based marketing (Baines et al. 2007). Switching from a product purchase to a service and use model also requires an emphasis on customer service and customer relationship management.

A further point of reconnection between product marketing and services/relationship marketing driven by environmental issues in some key market sectors including cars, electronics, batteries and packaging is the concept of extended producer responsibility (EPR) embedded in product take-back laws. The best known of these are the European *End of Life Vehicles (ELV)* and the *Waste Electronic and Electrical Equipment (WEEE) Directives* both requiring manufacturers to resume responsibility for old product when it reaches the end of its useful life. Although this can just involve taking financial responsibility to fund appropriate disposal and recycling arrangements, for manufacturers in markets from cars to canned beer there can be strategic value in taking physical responsibility for old product in order to recycle/remanufacture it. Developing and operating reverse logistics systems to address this opportunity also creates a long-term relationship management challenge in maintaining links with customers and motivating them to return old product appropriately into reverse logistics system for their retrieval (Seitz and Peattie 2004).

One interesting aspect of the emerging visions of sustainability oriented marketing is that they appear to embody an attempt to reintegrate some of the threads of marketing theory that became separated out from the 1970 onwards. The sustainability agenda involves businesses considering in an integrated way both issues of social equity and justice, and environmental quality and protection (Belz and Peattie 2010). Therefore contemporary sustainability marketing represents an integration of societal marketing (as a marketing approach that encompasses wider long-term social wellbeing), green/environmental marketing that seeks to appeal to customers on the basis of superior ecological performance, and ethical marketing that appeals to customers on the basis of a superior contribution to social justice and equity (Belz and Peattie 2010). Sustainability also provides both theoretical and practical justification for taking a more services and relationship based view of the marketing of tangible products. If companies are seeking to move consumption of tangible products from a purchase and ownership model towards a pay for use model, or if EPR regulations are forcing them to assume responsibility for a product long after the consumer has purchased it, marketers have little choice but to think less about products and transactions, and more about service and relationship building.

5 Sustainability Marketing Meets Social Marketing

The final element of marketing '*reintegration*' that a sustainability marketing perspective promotes is between commercial marketing and social marketing. It is not the case that all sustainability marketing activity presents opportunities for the application of social marketing. Many sustainability marketing initiatives will involve technical improvements to production processes, or design improvements to products, that can improve the overall socio-environmental impact of the production-consumption system without any need for behaviour change along the way. However, a clue to the potential importance of social marketing approaches in making such systems more sustainable comes from an analysis of exactly which of our activities as consumers have the most impact on the planet. The "*European Environmental Impact of Products*" (EIPRO) project rigorously analyzed the research base on the environmental impacts of consumer products (Tukker and Jansen 2006). It assessed 255 domestic product types (including services) against a range of impacts including pollution, human and environmental health risks, and greenhouse gas emissions. It concluded that 70–80 % of our total impacts from domestic consumption relate to:

- What we eat and drink, how it is produced, stored, prepared and disposed of;
- Our homes, including their construction and maintenance, and how we run them in terms of energy use; and
- How we travel for work, shopping, leisure and holidays.

The remaining impacts are mostly from water use, domestic equipment (appliances, computers, and home entertainment), furniture, clothing, and shoes. Similar results were produced by Spangenberg and Lorek's (2002) study of German consumption which concluded that construction and housing, food and nutrition, and transport and mobility were the most crucial '*consumption clusters*', accounting for 70 % of associated material extraction and energy use and more than 90 % of land use. These are all sectors in which behavioural change beyond simple product choice is crucial in the pursuit of sustainability, or as Tim Jackson (2005) framed it in his comprehensive study of research relevant to motivating sustainable consumption, achieving behavioural change is "*Fast becoming the 'Holy Grail' of sustainable development policy*" (p. 105). What is also striking is the extent to which social marketing has a track record of application to behaviours in these key sectors involving food and drink choices, modes of transport and household management particularly relating to waste and energy. So those consumption sectors in which sustainability marketing is most needed, and where changes in consumer behaviour are required, represent significant opportunities for the application of social marketing principles, practices and experience.

Examples of commercial consumer marketers becoming active in behavioural change campaigns in these spheres are becoming increasingly visible. One example of a very conventional product marketing company moving into this territory comes from the "*Mobility Plan*" of the Ford Motor Company unveiled in early 2015. This included a number of strategies explicitly aimed at easing socio-environmental problems linked to car use including traffic congestion and air pollution. The solutions proposed included technology changes, '*smarter*' use of vehicles and encouraging behavioural changes amongst vehicle users. Amongst the company's pilot experiments is a London based car-sharing scheme, called "*City Driving On-Demand*". This seeks to move drivers away from car ownership, to using shared vehicles that can be reserved through a smartphone app or call centre. The cars are available 24/7 and can be unlocked via the app or a membership card, and use is priced per minute, with fuel, insurance and the London Congestion Charge all included. A second experiment called "*Share-car*" working with ZoomCar in Bangalore aims to improve mobility opportunities for small groups such as co-workers or families from a particular neighbourhood through sharing a vehicle amongst multiple drivers. One aim being to develop an effective shared ownership and use model. The marketing challenges involved in these experiments are not the same as persuading Ford customers to upgrade to a new model, or to persuade customers of other firms to change alliegance. These were challenges of changing people's transport behaviours, and as such have to address the conventional social marketing challenges of making such a change easy, affordable and attractive.

The centrality of life-cycle thinking, when considering the socio-environmental implications of our consumption, is another fact that nudges commercial marketers embracing sustainability towards the social marketer's territory. Instead of being focused on purchase as an activity within the overall consumption process, sustainability outcomes depend to a large extent on product use and disposal stages. Therefore instead of being fixated on outcomes at the supermarket checkout, the sustainability oriented marketer is becoming increasingly interested in what happens within the home, or in the case of disposal, at the recycling centre or the kerbside. This is territory within which the social marketer has more experience. Commercial marketers seeking to reduce the socio-environmental impacts linked to how food is consumed within the home to avoid waste, or seeking to change how domestic appliances are used to reduce energy consumption and CO_2 emissions, are effectively also working towards public policy goals which social marketers have been pursuing through interventions for decades. Therefore when Proctor & Gamble began lifecycle analysis of their product lines, it revealed the extent to which impacts for some key brands (particularly for energy and water use) were linked to consumption activities rather than their production systems. This prompted the company to develop its "*Future Friendly*" multi-brand campaign aiming to promote more sustainable consumption practices in the home and a supporting product line aimed at reducing impacts.

Perhaps the most successful example of companies promoting a pro-sustainability consumer behaviour change (PSCB) that related to the use rather than to the purchasing of their products, are the campaigns to wash clothes at lower temperatures. Improvements in the technical quality of washing detergents allowed for effective washing at lower temperatures, reducing the energy and carbon emissions burden associated with their consumption. However, the potential for these improvements could only be realised if consumers changed how they used their washing machines. This was tackled through campaigns such as Proctor & Gamble's "*Turn to 30*" campaign, and "*Think Climate*" from Marks & Spencer which encouraged consumers to wash clothes at lower temperatures (and in doing so reducing the environmental burden associated with both the detergents and the clothes). These campaigns were highly influential and largely responsible for an increase in the proportion of UK households washing at a reduced temperature of 30° from 2 % in 2002, to 17 % in 2007 (following the P&G campaign) and then to 38 % by 2011 following the M&S campaign (Carbon Trust 2011).

Much of the attention in sustainability marketing is on the environmental impacts of products, but sustainability also has important ethical dimensions linked to the social implications of production and consumption. An enduring sustainability marketing success story that integrates the ethical and the environmental in appealing to consumers is Fairtrade marketing. The roots of Fairtrade lie in the selling of relatively poor quality coffee through unconventional channels (such as churches) to a relatively small minority of highly ethically motivated consumers. It is only relatively recently that Fairtrade companies have fully embraced marketing principles as part of a '*mainstreaming*' process that has led to Fairtrade product offerings appearing from major branded companies such as Cadburys, Nestle, Starbucks and Marks & Spencer. From a social marketing perspective, what is interesting about Fairtrade marketing is the extent to which it resembles social marketing practice rather than conventional commercial marketing. Witkowski (2005) noted that Fairtrade marketing campaigns could justifiably be viewed as social marketing as well as commercial marketing initiatives. Golding and Peattie (2006) further explore this idea of treating Fairtrade marketing as social marketing because in essence what it being marketed, is not a better tasting coffee, but a social proposition that workers in poorer countries deserve a fair level of pay for their efforts allowing them to live, and their community, region and/or country to develop. This was written at a time when Fairtrade was engaged in an effort to break out of its existing market niche to become more mainstream and more widely available and therefore able to do more good. The challenges Fairtrade marketers faced at this time were similar to those often faced by social marketers: a David-versus-Goliath marketing budget mismatch with entrenched commercial players, a need to overcome ingrained consumer habits relating to coffee consumption, and a proposition that stressed benefits to others more than for the consumer. Golding and Peattie argue that, although marketing literature has tended to treat the marketing of products and the marketing of social ideas as two very different things, in Fairtrade the two have come together. Instead of commercial and social marketing being considered as two separate types of marketing, they are perhaps better envisaged as existing on a continuum that emphasises commercial attributes at one end and social attributes at the other. An activity such as Fairtrade, undertaken by social enterprises (rather than players from the conventional commercial sector) who utilise business methods in pursuit of primarily social goals exist somewhere in the middle of such a continuum and are able to draw on both social and commercial marketing wisdom to guide their efforts. Such a '*blended*' approach to combining the two is evident in the success of Café Direct whose marketing campaign combines an emphasis on both product quality and taste, and the social mission of the company.

6 A Sustainable Lifestyles Perspective

One of the implications of commercial marketers becoming interested in the socio-environmental dimensions of their products and services is that evaluating them is difficult without gaining an understanding of the consumer's overall lifestyle. Commercial marketing has traditionally focused on the satisfaction of individual wants and needs through the marketing and consumption of specific goods or services. It also tends to judge elements of consumption in relation to sustainability issues on the basis of the motives that underpin a particular behaviour, rather than the ultimate consequences of that behaviour. At its simplest, an energy saving product might be marketed to a consumer as both better for the environment, and good in terms of saving you money as a '*good for you, good for the planet*' type of '*win-win*' scenario. The complicating factor is what the consumer spends the saved money on, the so-called '*rebound effect*' (Azevedo 2014). If this is on something even more energy intensive, the planetary benefit is not accrued. Similarly consumers may be very environmentally aware, and translate that awareness into a range of PSCBs, yet retain certain behaviours that they view as '*non-negotiable*' such as private car use, foreign holidays and regular meat consumption, despite being aware of their relative non-sustainability. Such consumers, which McDonald et al. (2012) describe as "*Exceptors*" may engage in many positive behaviours, but with their benefits being outweighed by the reluctance to abandon the 2 week holiday involving a long-haul flight to somewhere sunny. Therefore the ecologically and ethically concerned person who registers as a '*green consumer*' because they purchase organic food, ethical coffee, low energy lightbulbs, a low emissions vehicle and travel as an eco-tourist may have a higher environmental footprint than the stay-at-home climate sceptic with little interest in environmental issues.

For the commercial marketer seeking to encourage consumers to integrate sustainability principles into their purchase choices, and use and disposal of products, promoting consistency of behaviour becomes a key goal. This is perhaps another area where social marketers have relevant experience. Although some social marketing campaigns focus on '*one shot*' behaviours such as immunizations for children, it is more common for social marketing campaigns to focus on a pattern of consistent behaviour linked to healthy eating, responsible drinking, safe sex or an active lifestyle. In the case of safety-orientated behaviours such as wearing seatbelts or cycle helmets or the avoidance of speeding, consistency is central to the proposition being put to the target market, since a single lapse could prove fatal. Of course it would be unrealistic to assume that social marketers have the answer to encouraging citizens who are concerned about their environmental impacts to abandon sunshine holidays abroad. It would also be untrue to say that commercial marketers do not understand consistency in behaviour, since developing brand loyalty and repeat purchasing are at the root of many commercial marketing practices. What may be fair to say is that social marketers tend to focus more on persuading their targets not to indulge in exceptions to key behaviours, and that they do have, for example, experience of encouraging people to reduce some of those key '*exceptor*' behaviours. Taking private car use as an example, reduced usage through car sharing schemes has been a successful focus of community-based social marketing campaigns (McKenzie-Mohr 2000).

In trying to grapple with emerging concepts like "*Lifestyles of Health and Sustainability*" (Kotler 2011) sustainability oriented commercial marketers are again entering territory which is more familiar to social marketers (Barr et al. 2006). Health interventions, which form the heartland of the social marketing discipline, frequently require a very multi-dimensional understanding of a person's overall lifestyle and particular health risks. A simple example being obesity campaigns that integrate the very different behavioural spheres of diet and exercise. The realities of promoting PCSBs are that they tend to require an understanding of overall consumer lifestyles, and are frequently more related to the use and disposal of a product rather than its purchase. Promoting PCSBs also often require a demarketing of some form of existing behaviour in favour of another, and with notable exceptions in fields such as tourism (Medway et al. 2010), demarketing is an approach rarely applied in commerce. It is however a mainstay of key social marketing battlegrounds such as smoking cessation or responsible drinking.

One of the most sophisticated attempts to develop a commercial marketing perspective to promote sustainable lifestyles is the Unilever sustainability strategy framed as their "*Sustainable Living Plan*". It is one of a number of '*Big Brand*' sustainability strategies developed by major companies within consumer goods markets that also includes Marks and Spencer's "*Plan A*", P&G's "*Sustainability Vision*", PepsiCo's "*Performance with Purpose*" or Walmart's "*Sustainability Commitment*" (Dauvergne and Lister 2012). Unilever's plan was introduced in 2010 with strategies for improving customers' health, hygiene and nutrition; enhancing livelihoods back down the supply chains and reducing environmental impacts related to its products. It included the goal of 'halving' its environmental footprint including the impacts associated with the consumer use phase (e.g. energy and water used for clothes washing or showering). Analysis revealed that the use phase was responsible for 65 % of the company's greenhouse gas emissions and over 80 % of its water footprint (Unilever 2014). In commenting on progress the company noted that '*We are making good progress in the areas of the value chain which we control, such as manufacturing. But we are finding the consumer use phase harder to address. It is dependent on a wide range of external factors, such as the energy used in consumer appliances (e.g. washing machines, hot water heaters, showers) and the carbon intensity of the energy supplied to people's homes, as well as consumer behaviour*' (Unilever 2014).

The response to this challenge is described by B V Pradeep, Vice President, Consumer & Market Insight, Unilever as follows: "*Several years ago, I was part of a team that had a clear mission: to develop a best practice toolkit for behaviour change. We drew on skills from inside and outside Unilever – psychologists and academics from leading universities; hygiene experts; and colleagues from our research laboratories, marketing departments and those out meeting with people who cook, clean and wash with our products across the world. We developed the 'Five Levers for Change' – a set of principles brought together in a new approach, which, if applied to behaviour change interventions, will increase the likelihood of having a lasting impact.*" (Unilever 2012). The resulting '*Five Levers for Change*' model sought to address PSBs relevant to Unilever products in terms of five 'levers' that contribute to shifting behaviour and which should be considered, designed and applied in relation to potential barriers, triggers and motivators that might exist for any target consumer group:

1. **Make the new behaviour understood**: make people aware of the behaviour and its relevance to them;
2. **Make it easy**: give people confidence in their ability to chance, and make the change as convenient as possible;
3. **Make it desirable:** so that it fits with peoples' actual or aspiration self-image and is seen as socially normal and acceptable;
4. **Make it rewarding**: ensure that people know when they're doing the behaviour 'right' and experience some form of psychological or practical pay-off;
5. **Make it a habit**: remind consumers and reinforce behaviours to keep people going;

What will strike any social marketer is the familiarity of such an approach, and the extent to which this model effectively rediscovers the essence of social marketing and reapplies it in a commercial context. Another notable facet is the emphasis that Unilever has placed within its applications of the 5-Levers model on an underpinning of sound behavioural change theory, and detailed insights into consumer behaviour derived from research. This means that its interventions appear to embody the key components of social marketing (Lefevbre and Flora 1988) or the benchmark criteria from the UK's National Social Marketing Centre (Blair-Stevens and

French 2007) better than many of those explicitly positioned as social marketing interventions and discussed in journals and conferences dedicated to the topic. It is perhaps in the scale of resources available for understanding and influencing behaviour that Unilever's sustainable living initiatives go beyond what social marketers might be familiar with. Returning to the example of encouraging teeth cleaning as a health behaviour, Unilever were able to measure the effects of an advertisement to encourage parents to act as a role model to specifically encourage evening teeth brushing by embedding motion sensors in the children's tooth brushes. This revealed an impact on actual behaviour change that follow up survey data on habits amongst the trial group and a control group had failed to find (Unilever 2012).

In implementing their plan Unilever also frequently cross presumed boundaries between the social and commercial. When Kotler and Lee (2008) sought to illustrate the different, and often more difficult, behaviour change challenges that social marketers face to contrast with their commercial peers, an example they used was persuading people to take shorter showers (and thereby reducing their pleasure). However, this is exactly one of the elements of the Sustainable Living Plan, particularly in water stressed regions such as Australia. There is an irony in a company including in its marketing of shower gel products an attempt to encourage consumers to use less water as a pro-social environmental behaviour, since they are effectively selling soap like brotherhood.

The emphasis on consumer lifestyle change in the sustainability strategies of companies like Unilever, P&G and Marks & Spencer has been something of a ground-breaking development in recent years. However, there is evidence suggesting that it may become much more the norm amongst major consumer brand companies in the near future. A survey published by BSR/Futerra (2013) explored the current and future predicted emphasis on lifestyle change amongst leading global companies. The survey involved marketers working for 54 of the world's leading brands in global sectors including fast moving consumer goods, retailing, financial services and entertainment. The results showed that 39 % of the companies were already actively seeking to encourage more sustainable lifestyles amongst consumers, but that their motivations were relatively reactive with an emphasis on risk, regulation and reputation as drivers. By 2018 however, companies anticipated a different situation with significant growth in consumer interest in sustainable lifestyles, and increasing business opportunities in terms of innovation, profit and increasing market share. A further 40 % of the companies surveyed were planning new actions on promoting sustainable lifestyles in a 3–5 year time horizon. Perhaps not surprisingly the sectors where the most change was occurring were those linked to food and drink, cars and energy – amongst the key components of the consumers' ecological footprint.

One notable thing about the array of commercial initiatives seeking to promote behaviour change amongst consumers to create more sustainable lifestyles is the extent to which the logic of social marketing is being applied without the vocabulary or the explicit involvement of social marketers. This is a puzzle and also a missed opportunity for both. One answer to the puzzle might be the word '*social*'. A recurring social marketing witticism is that the phrase '*social marketing*' pleases no-one, since those who are pro-social tend to dislike '*marketing*' and vice versa.

However, in an age where companies are becoming so publicly exercised about their social responsibilities, this seems unlikely. Alternatively a fear of confusion with social media marketing may prompt companies to want to talk '*behaviour change*' and not '*social marketing*'. Perhaps more likely is that commercial marketers are unaware of a body of expertise and experience that exists under a heading of social marketing, which even when discovered might seem on a casual perusal to be dedicated to public sector health campaigns, with little relevance to companies' attempts to influence their consumers' lifestyles.

7 Social or Commercial Motives: Does It Matter?

The move of commercial companies into the promotion of sustainable lifestyles is clearly something to be welcomed. However, as with any deliberate or unplanned shift of responsibilities from the public to the commercial sector, there is the potential for risk and unintended consequences. There is no doubt that major companies have the resources and the experience needed to develop effective campaigns to influence their consumers' behaviour in order to meet their strategic objectives. If those objectives are aligned with those of society in tackling socio-environmental problems, is there any reason to be concerned? There are obvious arguments that have been rehearsed within the corporate social responsibility (CSR) literature, that commercial strategies change with pressures and priorities in the business environment. Therefore allowing campaigns for social change to become dependent on commercial partnerships and contributions may risk a change in business fortunes realigning company priorities in a way that '*strands*' the campaign. A campaign that has made the switch from public support and resources, to at least partial commercial support and resources, may find it difficult to make the return journey.

More subtly perhaps is the notion that the resources behind a campaign, and a commercial company's involvement in it, can make a crucial difference in the nature and consequences of that campaign. One famous (or some might say infamous) campaign that demonstrated this dates from the time that social marketing itself was emerging at the beginning of the 1970s. The *Keep America Beautiful* anti-litter public service advertising campaign was first aired on the second Earth Day in 1971, and was later named number 50 in the 100 most influential campaigns of the twentieth century by *Ad Age Magazine*. It featured the iconic images of '*Iron Eye Cody*' a Native American warrior moved to tears by the careless despoiling of the landscape through littering. This industry funded campaign sought to persuade individual citizens not to drop litter and to spoil the environment for everyone, but to take it home or dispose of it responsibly instead. As an attempt at socially beneficial behaviour change with the strapline "*People start pollution; people can stop it*", the campaign appeared to be beyond criticism. However, like the image of Iron Eye, who proved to be originally of Italian descent, not all was as it seemed. The sponsors of the campaign included firms such as the American Can Company, the Owens-Illinois Glass Company and the Dixie Cup Company who all produced and marketed single use cans and bottles. For them, a key strategic threat was the proposed introduction of legislation designed to reduce litter through container refund-deposit schemes intended to promote bottle and can recycling. A campaign that promoted the importance of individual behaviour rather than industry action, and that could be shown to be effective in reducing littering (in 300 communities where it was aired, reported littering rates went down by as much as 88 %), was an important part of their efforts to defuse pressure in favour of regulation (Rogers 2005).

Social marketing as a discipline has consistently faced a line of criticism along the lines of '*who gets to decide how others should behave?*' (Hastings et al. 2000; Brenkert 2002). This question is knotty enough to tackle when the people doing the deciding are the elected representatives within a democracy, who at least have a mandate through election victory to decide upon society's best interests. Once commercial companies move beyond selling us products, and begin to market us lifestyles and patterns of behaviour, those knots start to become a little tighter. Listening to the words of the managers behind the campaigns such as those of Unilever, P&G and Marks & Spencer leaves little doubt that these are laudable campaigns, promoted by management teams with a genuine interest in social welfare and their customers' wellbeing, and that align closely with policy-maker priorities and efforts. However, how should the social marketing community react, for example, to a campaign launched by a tobacco company to shift the behaviour of their customers from smoking cigarettes to using their new line of e-cigarettes, on the basis that it should improve their health outcomes and the environmental impacts linked to tobacco production and consumption?

8 Social Marketing Within Companies?

The need for firms engaged in sustainability marketing to consider the production and consumption system they exist within holistically, and to tackle the social and environmental impacts of those involved within that whole system is well established. This draws the focus of the sustainability marketer beyond the company to consider the role of the consumer and any post-use systems involving products (e.g. waste, reuse or recycling) and also back up the firm's supply chain. In terms of whose behaviours might need to change to facilitate more sustainable production and consumption, in addition to those of the consumer, companies may well be faced with an internal marketing challenge of promoting the adoption of more sustainability-orientated practices amongst their own employees, and amongst suppliers through sustainable supply chain management.

The adoption of sustainability orientated business practices within companies can create significant internal behaviour change challenges for companies (Esty and Winston 2009). Papakosmas et al. (2012), writing, it is worth noting, in *Social Marketing Quarterly*, propose an approach to promoting sustainability oriented behaviour changes amongst an organizations' employees that they label '*Organization-Based Social Marketing*'. As such it represents a set of ideas drawn from social marketing, community-based social marketing and (from commercial marketing theory) internal marketing. Although they stress that this approach could be used by organizations regardless of their profit orientation, it is clear that the types of pressures to adopt more sustainable business practices that they see driving the process are common amongst businesses. The implication is that businesses increasingly accept that they need to operate more sustainability, but at the level of learning how to do that, it is social marketers with their experience of promoting behaviour change, and pro-sustainability behaviours in particular, that may well hold crucial knowledge.

9 Conclusion: Time to Join Up and Join the Party?

The scope and boundaries of social marketing theory and practice has been a subject of discussion for some time, and the increasingly blurred and permeable boundary between social marketing and commercial (societal) marketing is only one facet of this. Polonsky (quoted in Dibb and Carrigan 2013, p. 11) suggests that "*…in reality commercial and social marketing are the same, but the distinction is in the emphasis, as applies in almost all marketing situations. Thus, we might think of commercial marketers focusing on the benefits to the self, and social marketers focusing on the benefits to society. However, in reality, both social and commercial marketers are focusing increasingly on both types of benefits.*" Others have argued for a need to make social marketing more distinctive from mainstream commercial marketing. Hastings and Saren (2003) argue that social marketing can go beyond exploiting the potential of marketing to promote social good, to become also a form of critical marketing that seeks to address the social consequences of (commercial) marketing. Similarly Wymer (2010) argues that the discipline's focus on the individual and changing their behaviour by emphasising persuasive communication has limited what it can achieve. Instead he argues for a wider remit for social marketers to focus more on changing the environment within which individuals exist and behave, and on working against those forces (including commercial marketing activities) that drive individual behaviour in unhelpful and unhealthy directions. In doing so social marketers would become more akin to activists and less like advertisers (and by extension perhaps less like their commercial peers).

It is also worth noting that it is not only the boundary between social and commercial marketing that has become increasingly impermeable and difficult to define. The other approaches to tackling social issues that social marketing was meant to represent progress from have also themselves continued to evolve (Hastings 2003). Health education for example has evolved into health promotion, and in doing so moved away from the old expert-led paradigm to become increasingly consumer focused and (social) marketing-like (Hastings 2003). Although one can identify differences between core concepts within social and commercial marketing, or between social marketing and other approaches to social change (such as social persuasion or social learning), trying to draw boundaries between social marketing, commercial marketing and other social change approaches seems increasingly difficult to do with clarity and consistency. An illustration of this comes from a paper published in Social Marketing Quarterly which asked "*Is the Greening of Firms Helping Consumers to Go Green?*" (Raska and Shaw 2012). This considers the implications for social marketing of the interplay between a commercial firms' own pro-environmental energy saving initiatives, their stated motivations for such initiatives, the consumer's loyalty to that company's brand and their perception about its motives for energy saving, and the consumer's own attitudes and intentions towards energy saving behaviours. Within such papers the boundary lines between CSR, commercial marketing and social marketing are becoming ever more indistinct, and theory and practice linked to the pursuit of sustainability seem to be acting as the principle eraser.

In his *Journal of Marketing 75th Anniversary Issue* contribution, Kotler (2011) chose to focus on the environmental imperative as the key challenge now facing the marketing discipline. In the near future he predicted the "*ramping up of two marketing perspectives*" as a consequence: demarketing, and social marketing. However in the past health, rather than the environment, represents the dominant set of themes in social marketing practice and scholarship. This can be illustrated by Truong's (2014) systematic review of the social marketing literature in which 76.5 % of all published articles concern, health, safety and addiction issues compared to 6.6 % dedicated to environmental protection, poverty alleviation and community engagement combined. It is perhaps for this reason, that social marketers who have read this far may be tempted to consider the ideas presented here as (hopefully) interesting, but irrelevant to them because their interests lie in health promotion rather than in '*sustainability*'. That would represent another mistaken drawing of a boundary line that in practice does not exist. The mistake is often rooted in the common assumption that the sustainability agenda is primarily an environmental one. This is not the case, the sustainability agenda is a holistic and integrated one that takes into account a range of elements of wellbeing, with health a very important component within it. In reality environmental and social issues are frequently intertwined, particularly within relatively poor countries where poverty can be a driver of environmental destruction, but also exacerbated by it. There is also an increasingly evident connection between human health and environmental quality in term of air and water quality and climate change, meaning that our ability to promote health outcomes will partly depend on encouraging behaviours that protect the health of the planet and the ecosystems on which we all depend (Aron and Patz 2001). Environmental welfare often leads sustainability discussions because of the simple fact that social wellbeing and economic prosperity both ultimately depend on environmental systems and the ecological resources and services they provide for us. However, although an issue like climate change is frequently spoken of as if it were a specifically environmental one, its implications mean that it is also very much a social, health, wellbeing, economic and development issue.

The intertwining of the health agenda with other elements of sustainability is clearly visible when considering the humble bicycle. In an era when inactivity is perceived as one of the major threats to health and wellbeing in industrialised nations, and when traffic congestion represents both a major quality-of-life irritant and a threat to human and environmental health, promoting bicycle use would seem to be a prime candidate for campaigns for social marketers whether they're interested in promoting exercise, cutting pollution or making our cities safer and more pleasant to live in. Similarly reducing red meat consumption can be interpreted as an environmental protection agenda due to the relative energy and greenhouse gas intensity of red meat as a form of protein, or as a health agenda due to the negative health implications of excess meat consumption. The opportunities for more '*joined up*' social marketing agendas for sustainability seem apparent, as do the potential for partnerships with commercial companies with a vested interest (such as manufacturers of bikes and vegetarian food). However, whilst policy makers persist in viewing health and environment as existing within distinct silos, progress in developing such integrated campaigns will be limited.

Partnerships between social marketers and commercial marketers represent only one way in which companies can engage with social issues, and is by no means the most common. There are a range of types of initiatives including cause-related marketing campaigns, social partnerships with NGOs, corporate philanthropy and employee volunteering. A growing phenomenon is that of multi-sector partnerships (also known also as social alliances or cross-sector partnerships) between companies and organisations from the public or third sectors (Seitanidi and Crane 2009). Such partnerships are seen as potentially important when tackling complex contemporary social challenges that single organisations will be unlikely to make progress with unaided. Berger et al. (2004, p. 44) for example suggest that it is "*difficult to imagine successfully addressing global problems, such as the AIDS pandemic or terrorism, and domestic concerns, such as the educational achievement gap between income classes and races, without some sort of cross-sector understanding, agreement, and collaboration*". Sustainability issues present exactly the types of complex challenges that such partnerships seem well-suited to tackle, and there is a growing interest in their potential and their application (see for example Steger et al. 2009). However, one notable facet of the use (and study) of multi-sector partnerships to tackle sustainability challenges is the extent to which the focus remains on relationships between businesses and NGOs. The potential for partnerships between businesses and public sector organisations, and in particular for partnerships with a behavioural change focus within which social marketers could play an important part, remains under-discussed by comparison. Dauvergne and Lister's (2012, p. 41) exploration of '*Big Brand*' sustainability examined such '*partnerships for power*', but they were almost entirely in the context of company-NGO tie ups (with an emphasis on NGO cause promotion, not consumer/citizen behaviour change). They also discuss the growing realisation amongst governments that they can harness the power and growing legitimacy of these brand-based thought leaders to tackle governance issues relating to sustainability challenges. This includes highlighting the work of Walmart working with the US Conference of Mayors to help American cities to reduce energy consumption and tackle carbon emissions or with the Chinese government to improve the quality and efficiency within factories and promote concepts such as product safety and sustainable forest management certification. Such partnerships can address the '*upstream*' components of a consumption and production system in ways that can complement any '*downstream*' social marketing interventions aiming to directly influence consumption behaviours.

Returning to the notion of there being three distinct systems within our economy, Phillis et al. (2008), writing on the topic of social innovation, make a number of interesting observations about the drivers, consequences and potential benefits of the blurring of the boundaries between the conventional sectors: "*A host of factors have eroded the boundaries between the non-profit, government and business sectors. In the absence of these boundaries, ideas, values, roles, relationships and capital now flow more freely between sectors. This cross-sector fertilization underlies three critical mechanisms of social innovation: exchanges of ideas and values, shifts in roles and relationships, and the integration of private capital with public and philanthropic support*" (p. 40). This cross-pollination of ideas, roles and efforts, they argue, makes the intersection where the sectors meet a key source of social innovation and the creation of novel forms of social value. They also observe that the most difficult and important social problems that face us (and which social marketers should at least aspire to play a part in tackling), cannot be understood, let alone solved, without a combined effort across all three sectors. However, a third observation they make is that although most stakeholders recognise the principle of the boundaries between the sectors dissolving, in practice most tend to "*continue to toil in silos*" (p. 42). This raises the question of who can make the necessary connections between the different sectors and how to translate the promise of integrated efforts to resolve social problems into a practical reality. It is here that social marketers have a natural role to play, as they are used to the priorities of policy makers and the language and methods of business (Hastings and Saren 2003). They are also well versed in trying to create effective marketing campaigns to tackle issues where resources are scarce because they are not directly related to increasing profit and sales for someone.

Faced with a growing environmental crisis "*Companies need to make drastic changes in their research-and-development, production, financial, and marketing practices if sustainability is to be achieved*" (Kotler 2011, p. 132). It is also difficult to escape the conclusion that companies will need to market to us lifestyles in which we live and consume differently, and in material terms consume less, and this will be a hard sell. This chapter has outlined a variety of ways in which sustainability oriented marketing challenges require commercial marketers to tackle problems and understand issues that are more familiar to their colleagues from social marketing. One logical consequence of this is that the conventional flow of marketing learning, from commercial practitioners and scholars to those in social marketing, may need to be reversed. Both Andreasen (2003) and Hastings and Saren (2003) consider that the further development of social marketing requires a shift in the relationship with mainstream commercial marketing from parent–child to adult-to-adult. The sustainability agenda perhaps creates a similar need for a shift in the relationship between the two fields from teacher-pupil to mutual learners. The big brand companies are increasingly on a mission to help move our economies and societies towards sustainability by influencing consumer behaviour and promoting more sustainable lifestyles. This means that it is the commercial marketers who are moving into new spheres and, as the details of Unilever's search for insights with which to develop their 5-Levers model shows, they are eager to benefit from existing expertise. With decades of experience in behaviour and lifestyle change, social marketers have a great deal to bring to this particular party – but the party invitations do not yet seem to have been issued. Commercial and social marketers do not just share a mindset and a toolbox, they increasingly share a pro-sustainability agenda. As this becomes more widely recognized, the opportunities to combine efforts, skills and knowledge to the benefit of all, will surely increase in the near future. It could be quite a party, and social marketers should be ready for it.

References

Andreasen, A. R. (2003). The life trajectory of social marketing: Some implications. *Marketing Theory, 3*(3), 293–303.

Aron, J. L., & Patz, J. A. (2001). *Ecosystem change and public health: A global perspective*. Baltimore: John Hopkins Press.

Azevedo, I. L. (2014). Consumer end-use energy efficiency and rebound effects. *Annual Review of Environment and Resources, 39*, 393–418.

Baines, T. S., Lightfoot, H. W., Evans, S., et al. (2007). State-of-the-art in product-service systems. Proceedings of the Institute of Mechanical Engineers. *Part B: Journal of Engineering Manufacture, 221*, 1543–1552.

Barr, S., Gilg, A., & Shaw, G. (2006). *Promoting sustainable lifestyles: A social marketing approach, department for environment*. London: Food and Rural Affairs.

Bartels, R. (1967). A model for ethics in marketing. *Journal of Marketing, 31*(1), 20–26.

Bartels, R. (1988). *The history of marketing thought* (3rd ed.). Homewood: Richard D. Irwin.

Berger, I., Cunningham, P., & Drumwright, M. (2004). Social alliances: Company/nonprofit collaboration. *California Management Review, 47*(1), 58–90.

Belz, F. M., & Peattie, K. (2010). *Sustainability marketing: A global perspective*. Chichester: Wiley.

Blair-Stevens, C., & French, J. (2007). *Social marketing: Big pocket guide* (2nd ed.). National Social Marketing Centre: London.

Bray, J., Johns, N., & Kilburn, D. (2011). An exploratory study into the factors impeding ethical consumption. *Journal of Business Ethics, 98*(4), 597–608.

Brenkert, G. C. (2002). Ethical challenges of social marketing. *Journal of Public Policy and Marketing, 21*(1), 14–25.

Brinkmann, J., & Peattie, K. (2009). Consumer ethics research: Reframing the debate about consumption for good. *EJBO Electronic Journal of Business Ethics and Organization Studies, 13*(1), 22–31.

BSR/Futerra. (2013). *Value-gap: The business value of changing consumer behaviors*. London: Survey Report from the Sustainable Lifestyles Frontier Group, Business for Social Responsibility and Futerra.

Carbon Trust. (2011). *International carbon flows: Clothing*. London: The Carbon Trust.

Crane, A., & Desmond, J. (2002). Societal marketing and morality. *European Journal of Marketing, 36*(5/6), 548–569.

Dauvergne, P., & Lister, J. (2012). Big brand sustainability: Governance prospects and environmental limits. *Global Environmental Change, 22*, 36–45.

Defourny, J., & Nyssens, M. (2006). Defining social enterprise. In M. Nyssens (Ed.), *Social enterprise – At the crossroads of market, public and civil society*. London: Routledge.

Dibb, S., & Carrigan, M. (2013). Social marketing transformed: Kotler, Polonsky and Hastings reflect on social marketing in a period of social change. *European Journal of Marketing, 47*(9), 1376–1398.
Esty, D. C., & Winston, A. S. (2009). *Green to gold* (2nd ed.). Hoboken: Wiley.
Fuller, D. A. (1999). *Sustainable marketing: Managerial-ecological issues*. Thousand Oaks: Sage.
Gabriel, Y., & Lang, T. (1995). *The unmanageable consumer*. Sage: Thousand Oakes.
Golding, K., & Peattie, K. (2005). In search of a golden blend: Perspectives on the marketing of fair trade coffee. *Sustainable Development, 13*(3), 154–165.
Haq, G., Whitelegg, J., Cinderby, S., & Owen, A. (2008). The use of personalised social marketing to foster voluntary behavioural change for sustainable travel and lifestyles. *Local Environment, 13*(7), 549–569.
Hastings, G. (2003). Relational paradigms in social marketing. *Journal of Macromarketing, 23*(1), 6–15.
Hastings, G., & Saren, M. (2003). The critical contribution of social marketing: Theory and application. *Marketing Theory, 3*(3), 305–322.
Hastings, G. B., MacFadyen, L., & Anderson, S. (2000). Whose behaviour is it anyway? The broader potential of social marketing. *Social Marketing Quarterly, 5*(2), 46–58.
Henion, K. E., & Kinnear, T. C. (1976). *Ecological marketing*. Chicago: American Marketing Association.
Hunt, S. D. (1994). On rethinking marketing: Our discipline, our practice, our methods. *European Journal of Marketing, 28*(3), 13–25.
Jackson, T. (2005). *Motivating sustainable consumption: A review of evidence on consumer behaviour and behavioural change*. London: Policy Studies Institute.
Jones, S. C. (2011). Social marketing's response to the alcohol problem: Who's conducting the orchestra. In G. Hastings, K. Angus, & C. Bryant (Eds.), *The sage handbook of social marketing* (pp. 253–270). London: Sage.
Kilbourne, W. E., & Beckmann, S. C. (1998). Review and critical assessment of research on marketing and the environment. *Journal of Marketing Management, 14*(6), 513–532.
Kotler, P. (1972). What consumerism means for marketers. *Harvard Business Review, 50*, 48–57.
Kotler, P. (2000). *Marketing management: The millennium edition* (10th ed.). Prentice-Hall: London (International).
Kotler, P. (2011). Reinventing marketing to manage the environmental imperative. *Journal of Marketing, 75*(4), 132–135.
Kotler, P., & Lee, N. R. (2008). *Social marketing: Influencing behaviors for good*. Thousand Oaks: Sage.
Kotler, P., & Zaltman, G. (1971). Social marketing: An approach to planned social change. *Journal of Marketing, 35*, 3–12.
Kozinets, R. V., & Handelman, J. M. (2004). Adversaries of consumption: Consumer movements, activism, and ideology. *Journal of Consumer Research, 31*, 691–704.
Laczniak, G. R., & Murphy, P. E. (2006). Normative perspectives for ethical and socially responsible marketing. *Journal of Macromarketing, 26*(2), 154–177.
Lebel, L., & Lorek, S. (2008). Enabling sustainable production-consumption systems. *Annual Review of Environment and Resources, 33*, 241–275.
Lefevbre, R. C., & Flora, J. A. (1988). Social marketing and public health intervention. *Health Education Quarterly, 15*(3), 299–315.
Maibach, E. (1993). Social marketing for the environment: Using information campaigns to promote environmental awareness and behavior change. *Health Promotion International, 8*(3), 209–224.
Martin, D., & Schouten, J. (2011). *Sustainable marketing*. Upper Saddle River: Prentice-Hall/Pearson.
McDonald, S., Oates, C. J., Alevizou, P. J., Young, C. W., & Hwang, K. (2012). Individual strategies for sustainable consumption. *Journal of Marketing Management, 28*(3/4), 445–468.
McKenzie-Mohr, D. (2000). Promoting sustainable behavior: An introduction to community-based social Marketing. *Journal of Social Issues, 56*, 543–554.

Medway, D., Warnaby, G., & Dharni, S. (2010). Demarketing places: Rationales and strategies. *Journal of Marketing Management, 27*(1–2), 124–142.
O'Rourke, D. (2012). *Shopping for good*. Boston: MIT Press.
Papakosmas, M. F., Noble, G., & Glynn, J. (2012). Organization-based social marketing: An alternative approach for organizations adopting sustainable business practices. *Social Marketing Quarterly, 18*(2), 87–97.
Patterson, J. M. (1966). What are the social and ethical responsibilities of marketing executives? *Journal of Marketing, 30*(3), 12–15.
Pearce, J. (2003). *Social enterprise in anytown*. London: Calouste Gulkenkian Foundation.
Peattie, K., & Morley, A. (2008). Eight paradoxes of the social enterprise research agenda. *Social Enterprise Journal, 4*(2), 91–107.
Peattie, S., & Peattie, K. (2003). Ready to fly solo? Reducing social marketing's dependence on commercial marketing theory. *Marketing Theory, 3*(3), 365–385.
Pettigrew, S., & Pescud, M. (2012). Improving parents' child-feeding practices: A social marketing challenge. *Journal of Social Marketing, 2*(1), 8–22.
Phillis, R., Deiglmeier, K., & Miller, D. T. (2008). Rediscovering social innovation. *Stanford Social Innovation Review, 6*(4), 34–43.
Raska, D., & Shaw, D. (2012). Is the greening of firms helping consumers to go green? *Social Marketing Quarterly, 18*(1), 50–54.
Rogers, H. (2005). *Gone tomorrow: The hidden life of garbage*. New York: The New Press.
Rothschild, M. L., Mastin, B., & Miller, T. W. (2006). Reducing alcohol-impaired driving crashes through the use of social marketing. *Accident Analysis and Prevention, 38*(6), 1218–1230.
Seitanidi, M. M., & Crane, A. (2009). Implementing CSR through partnerships: Understanding the selection, design and institutionalisation of nonprofit-business partnerships. *Journal of Business Ethics, 85*, 413–429.
Seitz, M. A., & Peattie, K. (2004). Meeting the closed-loop challenge: The case of remanufacturing. *California Management Review, 43*(3), 16–25.
Shaw, E. (2004). Marketing in the social enterprise context: Is it entrepreneurial? *Qualitative Market Research: An International Journal, 7*(3), 94–205.
Spangenberg, J., & Lorek, S. (2002). Environmentally sustainable household consumption: From aggregate environmental pressures to priority fields of action. *Ecological Economics, 43*, 127–140.
Steger, V., Somers, A. L., Salzmann, O., & Moursourian, S. (2009). *Sustainability partnerships*. London: Palgrave MacMillian.
Truong, V. D. (2014). Social marketing: A systematic review of research 1998–2012. *Social Marketing Quarterly, 20*(1), 15–34.
Tukker, A., & Jansen, B. (2006). Environmental impacts of products: A detailed review of studies. *Journal of Industrial Ecology, 10*, 159–182.
Turaga, R. M. R., Howarth, R. B., & Borsuki, M. E. (2010). Pro-environmental behaviour: Rational choice meets moral motivation. *Annals of the New York Academy of Sciences, 1185*, 211–224 (1 Ecological Economics Reviews).
Unilever PLC. (2012). *Inspiring sustainable living, expert insight into consumer behaviour & Unilever's Five Levers for change*. London: Unilever PLC and Futerra Communications.
Unilever PLC. (2014). *Unilever sustainable living plan 2013: Making progress driving change*. Retrieved from http://www.unilever.com/sustainable-living-2014/
Vargo, S. L., & Lusch, R. F. (2004). Evolving to a new dominant logic for marketing. *Journal of Marketing, 68*(1), 1–17.
WCED. (1987). *Our common future (The Brundtland Report), world commission on environment and development*. Oxford: Oxford University Press.
Wiebe, G. D. (1951). Merchandising commodities and citizenship on television. *Public Opinion Quarterly, 15*(Winter), 679–691.
Witkowski, T. H. (2005). Fair trade marketing: An alternative system for globalization and development. *Journal of Marketing Theory and Practice, 13*(4), 22–33.
Wymer, W. (2010). Rethinking the boundaries of social marketing: Activism or advertising? *Journal of Business Research, 63*(2), 99–103.

MIX
Papier aus verantwortungsvollen Quellen
Paper from responsible sources
FSC® C105338

If you have any concerns about our products,
you can contact us on
ProductSafety@springernature.com

In case Publisher is established outside the EU,
the EU authorized representative is:
Springer Nature Customer Service Center GmbH
Europaplatz 3, 69115 Heidelberg, Germany

Printed by Libri Plureos GmbH
in Hamburg, Germany